MACROPOLITICAL THEORY

HANDBOOK OF POLITICAL SCIENCE

Volume 3

MACROPOLITICAL THEORY

Edited by
FRED I. GREENSTEIN Princeton University
NELSON W. POLSBY University of California, Berkeley

 ADDISON-WESLEY PUBLISHING COMPANY

Reading, Massachusetts
Menlo Park, California · London · Amsterdam · Don Mills, Ontario · Sydney

This book is in the
ADDISON-WESLEY SERIES IN POLITICAL SCIENCE

ISBN 0-201-02603-1
ABCDEFGHIJ-HA-798765

PREFACE

Early in his career, the fledgling political scientist learns that his discipline is ill-defined, amorphous, and heterogeneous. This perception will in no way be rebutted by the appearance of a presumably encyclopedic eight-volume work entitled *The Handbook of Political Science.* Indeed, the persistent amorphousness of our discipline has constituted a central challenge to the editors of the *Handbook* and has brought to its creation both hazards and opportunities. The opportunities were apparent enough to us when we took on the editorial duties of the *Handbook;* the hazards became clearer later on.

At the outset, it seemed to us a rare occasion when a publisher opens quite so large a canvas and invites a pair of editors to paint on it as they will—or can. We immediately saw that in order to do the job at all we would have to cajole a goodly number of our colleagues into the belief that our canvas was in reality Tom Sawyer's fence. We did not set out at the beginning, however, with a precise vision of the final product—i.e., a work that would be composed of these particular eight volumes, dealing with the present array and number of contributions and enlisting all the present contributors. Rather, the *Handbook* is the product of a long and in some ways accidental process. An account of this process is in order if only because, by describing the necessarily adventitious character of the "decisions" that produced this work, we can help the reader to see that the *Handbook* is not an attempt to make a collective pronouncement of Truth chiseled in stone, but rather an assembly of contributions, each an individual scholarly effort, whose overall purpose is to give a warts-and-all portrait of a discipline that is still in a process of becoming.

We first became involved in discussions about the project in 1965. Addison-Wesley had already discussed the possibility of a handbook with a number of other political scientists, encouraged by their happy experience with a two-volume compendium of highly respected review essays in social psychology (Lindzey, 1954), which has since been revised and expanded into a five-volume work (Lindzey and Aronson, 1968–69).

Of the various people to whom Addison-Wesley aired the handbook idea, we evidently were among the most persistent in encouraging such a project. No doubt the reason was that we were still close to our own graduate work in a department where a careful reading of many of the chapters in *The Handbook of Social Psychology* was in some ways more fundamental to learning our trade than a comparable exposure to many of the more conspicuous intellectual edifices of the political science of the time. Gardner Lindzey, in writing his introductory statement to the first edition of *The Handbook of Social Psychology* (reprinted in the second edition), described *our* needs as well as those of budding social psychologists in saying that

> the accelerating expansion of social psychology in the past two decades has led to an acute need for a source book more advanced than the ordinary textbook in the field but yet more focused than scattered periodical literature. . . . It was this state of affairs that led us to assemble a book that would represent the major areas of social psychology at a level of difficulty appropriate for graduate students. In addition to serving the needs of graduate instruction, we anticipate that the volumes will be useful in advanced undergraduate courses and as a reference book for professional psychologists.

With the substitution of "political science" in the appropriate places, Lindzey's description of his own purposes and audiences reflects precisely what we thought Addison-Wesley might most usefully seek to accomplish with a political science handbook.

In choosing a pair of editors, the publisher might well have followed a balancing strategy, looking for two political scientists who were poles apart in their background, training, and views of the discipline. The publisher might then have sought divine intervention, praying for the miracle that would bring the editors into sufficient agreement to make the planning of the *Handbook*—or *any* handbook—possible at all. Instead they found a pair of editors with complementary but basically similar and congenial perspectives. We were then both teaching at Wesleyan University and had been to graduate school together at Yale, at a time when the political science department there was making its widely recognized contribution to the modernization of the discipline. Each had recently spent a year in the interdisciplinary ambience of the Center for Advanced Study in the Behavioral Sciences. Moreover, we were both specialists in American politics, the "field" which in 1973 still accounted for three-quarters of the contributions to *The American Political Science Review*. There were also complementary divergencies. Within political science, Polsby's work and interests had been in national politics and policy-making, whereas Greenstein's were more in mass, extragovernmental aspects of political behavior. Outside political science, Polsby's interests were directed more toward sociology and law, and Greenstein's tended toward psychiatry and clinical and social psychology.

To begin with, neither we nor the publisher could be sure without first gathering evidence that the discipline of political science was "ready" for a handbook comparable to the Lindzey work. We were sure that, if it was at all possible for us to bring such a handbook into being, we would have to employ the Aristotelian tack of working within and building upon existing categories of endeavor, rather than the Platonic (or Procrustean) mode of inventing a coherent set of master categories and persuading contributors to use them. First, at our request the publisher inquired of a number of distinguished political scientists whether they felt a need would be served by a handbook of political science similar to *The Handbook of Social Psychology*. This inquiry went to political scientists who had themselves been involved in extensive editorial activities or who were especially known for their attention to political science as a discipline. The responses were quite uniform in favoring such a handbook. The particular suggestions about how such a handbook might be *organized,* however, were exceptionally varied. But fortunately we had asked one further question: What half-dozen or so individuals were so authoritative or original in their contributions on some topic as to make them prime candidates for inclusion in any political science handbook, no matter what its final overall shape? Here agreement reemerged; the consultants were remarkably unanimous in the individuals named.

Seizing the advantage provided by that consensus, we reached the following agreement with the publisher. We would write the individuals who constituted what we now saw as a prime list of candidates for inclusion as authors and ask whether they would be willing to contribute to a handbook of political science, given a long lead time and freedom to choose the topic of their essay. (We did suggest possible topics to each.) It was agreed that unless we were able to enlist most of those with whom we were corresponding as a core group of contributors, we would not proceed with a handbook. Since all but one of that group indicated willingness to contribute, we signed a publishing agreement (in September 1967) and proceeded to expand our core group to a full set of contributors to what we then envisaged as a three-volume handbook, drawing on our core contributors for advice. Our queries to the core contributors were a search not so much for structural and organizational suggestions as for concrete topics and specific contributors to add to the initial list.

The well-worn term "incremental" suggests itself as a summary of how the table of contents of *The Handbook of Political Science* then took shape. As the number of contributors increased, and as contributors themselves continued to make suggestions about possible rearrangements in the division of labor and to remark on gaps, the planned three volumes expanded to eight, most of which, however, were shorter than the originally intended three. Throughout, Addison-Wesley left it to us and the contributors, within the very broadest of boundaries, to define the overall length of the project and of the individual contributions. And throughout, we urged the contributors not to seek intellectual anonymity in the guise of being "merely" summarizers—or embalmers—of their fields but rather to endeavor to place a distinctive intellectual stamp on their contributions.

A necessary condition of enlisting the initial group of contributors was a production deadline so far in the future as to dissolve the concern of rational individuals about adding to their intellectual encumbrances. As it turned out, our "safely remote" initial deadline (1970) was in fact a drastic underestimation of the number of postponements and delays.* Along with delays there have been occasional withdrawals, as individual contributors recognized that even with a long fuse the task of preparing a handbook article would be a major one and would inevitably preempt time from other projects and interests. Departing contributors were often helpful in suggesting alternatives. Both through the late enlistment of such substitutes and through the addition of collaborators taken on by invited contributors, we feel we have been spared a table of contents that anachronistically represents only the cohort of those individuals who were responsible for the shape of political science circa 1967.

Whether one builds a handbook table of contents a priori or ex post facto, *some* basis of organization emerges. We might have organized a handbook around:

1. *"political things"* (e.g., the French bureaucracy, the U.S. Constitution, political parties);

2. *nodes or clusters in the literature* (community power, group theory, issue voting);

3. *subdisciplines* (public administration, public law, comparative government, political theory, international relations);

4. *functions* (planning, law-making, adjudication);

5. *geography* (the American Congress, the British Cabinet, the politicoeconomic institutions of the U.S.S.R.);

6. or any combination of the above and further possibilities.

Any of our colleagues who have tried to construct a curriculum in political science will sympathize with our dilemma. There is, quite simply, no

---

* For the comparable experience of *Handbook of Social Psychology* editors with delays, see Lindzey, 1954, p. vii, Lindzey and Aronson, 1968–69, p. ix.

sovereign way to organize our discipline. Although much of our knowledge is cumulative, there is no set beginning or end to political science. Apart from certain quite restricted subdisciplinary areas (notably the mathematical and statistical), political scientists do not have to learn a particular bit of information or master a particular technique at a particular stage as a prerequisite to further study. And the discipline lacks a single widely accepted frame of reference or principle of organization. Consequently, we evolved a table of contents that to some extent adopted nearly *all* the approaches above. (None of our chapter titles contains a geographical reference, but many of the chapters employ one or more explicitly specified political systems as data sources.)

The protean classifications of subspecialization within political science and the ups and downs in subspecialty interests over the years are extensively reviewed by Dwight Waldo in his essay in Volume 1 on political science as discipline and profession. A further way to recognize the diversity and change in our discipline—as well as the persisting elements—is to note the divisions of disciplinary interests used by the directories of the American Political Science Association, the membership of which constitutes the great bulk of all political scientists. A glance at the three successive directories which have been current during our editorial activities is instructive.

The 1961 *Biographical Directory of the American Political Science Association* (APSA, 1961) represents a last glimpse at a parsimonious, staid set of subdisciplinary categories that would have been readily recognizable at the 1930 Annual Meeting of the Association.

1. American National Government
2. Comparative Government
3. International Law and Relations
4. Political Parties
5. Political Theory
6. Public Administration
7. Public Law
8. State and Local Government

In the next *Biographical Directory* (APSA, 1968), there appeared a categorization that was at once pared down and much expanded from the 1961 classification. A mere three "general fields" were listed. The first was "Contemporary Political Systems." Members electing this general field were asked to specify the country or countries in which they were interested, and those countries were listed parenthetically after the members' names in the subdisciplinary listing, presumably out of a desire to play down the importance of "area studies" as an intellectual focus and to accentuate the importance of functional or analytic bases of intellectual endeavor. "International Law, Organization, and Politics" was the second general field, and "Political Theory and Philosophy" was the third. But the 26 categories in Table 1 were provided for the listing of "specialized fields." They included some venerable subdivisions, perhaps in slightly more fashionable phrasing, and other distinctly nonvenerable subdivisions, at least one of which (political socialization) did not even exist in the general vocabulary of political scientists ten years earlier. In this *Handbook*, the 1968 categories have many parallels, including the general principle of organization that excludes geography as a specialized field criterion while at the same time recognizing that political scientists can and should study and compare diverse political settings. Diplomatically avoiding the presentation of a structured classification, the editors of the 1968 *Directory* relied on the alphabet for their sequence of specialized fields.

TABLE 1 Subdisciplinary categories used in *Biographical Directory* of the American Political Science Association, 1968

1. Administrative law
2. Administration: organization, processes, behavior
3. Budget and fiscal management
4. Constitutional law
5. Executive: organization, processes, behavior
6. Foreign policy
7. Government regulation of business
8. International law
9. International organization and administration
10. International politics
11. Judiciary: organization, processes, behavior
12. Legislature: organization, processes, behavior
13. Methodology
14. Metropolitan and urban government and politics
15. National security policy
16. Personnel administration
17. Political and constitutional history
18. Political parties and elections: organizations and processes
19. Political psychology
20. Political socialization
21. Political theory and philosophy (empirical)
22. Political theory and philosophy (historical)
23. Political theory and philosophy (normative)
24. Public opinion
25. Revolutions and political violence
26. State and local government and politics
27. Voting behavior

Even with this burgeoning of options, many members of the discipline evidently felt that their interests were not adequately covered. Goodly numbers took advantage of an opportunity provided in the questionnaire to the APSA membership to list "other" specialties, referring, for example, to "political sociology," "political behavior," "political development," "policy studies," "communication," "federalism," and "interest groups."

The 1973 *Biographical Directory* (APSA, 1973) attempted still another basis of classification, a revised version of the classification used in the 1970 *National Science Foundation Register of Scientific and Technical Personnel.* Braving a structured rather than alphabetic classification, the authors of this taxonomy divided the discipline into nine major classes and a total of 60 specialized classifications, with a return to the antique dichotomy of foreign versus U.S. politics. The specifics of the 1973 listing are given in Table 2.

TABLE 2 Subdisciplinary categories used in *Biographical Directory* of the American Political Science Association, 1973

I	Foreign and Cross-National Political Institutions and Behavior
1.	Analyses of particular systems or subsystems
2.	Decision-making processes
3.	Elites and their oppositions
4.	Mass participation and communications
5.	Parties, mass movements, secondary associations
6.	Political development and modernization
7.	Politics of planning
8.	Values, ideologies, belief systems, political culture
II	International Law, Organization, and Politics
9.	International law
10.	International organization and administration
11.	International politics
III	Methodology
12.	Computer techniques
13.	Content analysis
14.	Epistemology and philosophy of science
15.	Experimental design
16.	Field data collection
17.	Measurement and index construction
18.	Model building
19.	Statistical analysis
20.	Survey design and analysis
IV	Political Stability, Instability, and Change
21.	Cultural modification and diffusion
22.	Personality and motivation
23.	Political leadership and recruitment
24.	Political socialization
25.	Revolution and violence
26.	Schools and political education
27.	Social and economic stratification

(continued)

As will be evident, the present *Handbook* contains articles on topics that appear on neither of the two recent differentiated lists and omits topics on each. Some "omissions" were inadvertent. Others were deliberate, resulting from our conclusion either that the work on a particular topic did not appear ripe for review at this time or that the topic overlapped sufficiently with others already commissioned so that we might leave it out in the interests of preventing our rapidly expanding project from becoming hopelessly large. There also were instances in which we failed to find (or

keep) authors on topics that we might otherwise have included. Hence readers should be forewarned about a feature of the *Handbook* that they should
know without forewarning is bound to exist: incompleteness. Each reviewer
will note "strange omissions." For us it is more extraordinary that so many
able people were willing to invest so much effort in this enterprise.

It should be evident from our history of the project that we consider the
rubrics under which scholarly work is classified to be less important than the
caliber of the scholarship and that we recognize the incorrigible tendency of
inquiry to overflow the pigeonholes to which it has been assigned, as well as
the desirability that scholars rather than editors (or other administrators)
define the boundaries of their endeavors. Therefore we have used rather
simple principles for aggregating essays into their respective volumes and
given them straightforward titles.

The essays in Volume 1 on the nature of political theory which follow
Waldo's extensive discussion of the scope of political science are far from
innocent of reference to empirical matters. This comports with the common
observation that matters of theoretical interest are by no means removed
from the concerns of the real world. And although we have used the titles
Micropolitical Theory and *Macropolitical Theory* for Volumes 2 and 3, we have
meant no more thereby than to identify the scale and mode of conceptualization typical of the topics in these volumes. Here again the reader will find
selections that extensively review empirical findings.

Similarly, although the titles of Volumes 4, 5, and 6 on extragovernmental, governmental, and policy-output aspects of government and politics
may appear to imply mere data compilations, the contents of these volumes
are far from atheoretical. This is also emphatically true of Volume 8, which
carries the title *International Politics*, a field that in recent decades has continuously raised difficult theoretical issues, including issues about the proper
nature of theory. Volume 7 carries the title *Strategies of Inquiry* rather than
Methodology to call attention to the fact that contributors to that volume have
emphasized linking techniques of inquiry to substantive issues. In short, contributions to the eight volumes connect in many ways that can be only
imperfectly suggested by the editors' table of contents or even by the comprehensive index at the end of Volume 8.

It can scarcely surprise readers of a multiple-authored work to learn
that what is before them is a collective effort. It gives us pleasure to acknowledge obligations to five groups of people who helped to lighten our part of
the load. First of all, to our contributors we owe a debt of gratitude for their
patience, cooperation, and willingness to find the time in their exceedingly
busy schedules to produce the essays that make up this *Handbook*. Second, we
thank the many helpful Addison-Wesley staff members with whom we have
worked for their good cheer toward us and for their optimism about this
project. Third, the senior scholars who initially advised Addison-Wesley to

undertake the project, and who may even have pointed the publishers in our direction, know who they are. We believe it would add still another burden to the things they must answer for in our profession if we named them publicly, but we want to record our rueful, belated appreciation to them. Fourth, Kathleen Peters and Barbara Kelly in Berkeley and Lee L. Messina, Catherine Smith, and Frances C. Root in Middletown kept the paper flowing back and forth across the country and helped us immeasurably in getting the job done. Finally, our love and gratitude to Barbara Greenstein and Linda Polsby. And we are happy to report to Michael, Amy, and Jessica Greenstein, and to Lisa, Emily, and Daniel Polsby that at long last their fathers are off the long-distance telephone.

Princeton, New Jersey   F.I.G.
Berkeley, California   N.W.P.

REFERENCES

American Political Science Association (1961). *Biographical Directory of The American Political Science Association,* fourth edition. (Franklin L. Burdette, ed.) Washington, D.C.

American Political Science Association (1968). *Biographical Directory,* fifth edition. Washington, D.C.

American Political Science Association (1973). *Biographical Directory,* sixth edition. Washington, D.C.

Lindzey, Gardner, ed. (1954). *Handbook of Social Psychology,* 2 volumes. Cambridge, Mass.: Addison-Wesley.

Lindzey, Gardner, and Elliot Aronson, eds. (1968–69). *The Handbook of Social Psychology,* second edition, 5 volumes. Reading, Mass.: Addison-Wesley.

CONTENTS

CONTENTS OF OTHER VOLUMES IN THIS SERIES

POLITICAL DEVELOPMENT

SAMUEL P. HUNTINGTON AND JORGE I. DOMÍNGUEZ

I. POLITICAL DEVELOPMENT IN POLITICAL SCIENCE

In the early 1970s the term *political development* was still a newcomer to the vocabulary and the conceptual warehouse of political science. If this *Handbook* had been prepared a decade earlier, it would still have contained disquisitions on political parties, constitutionalism, policy-making, group theory, political power, political participation, federalism, international organization, judicial behavior, organizational decision-making, and a host of other intriguing topics. Unless its editors were endowed with uncommon prescience, however, it would not have included a paper on political development. The study of political development had its roots in the 1950s, but the conscious conceptualizing and systematizing of this study took place only in the 1960s. That decade, indeed, saw a mammoth outpouring of articles and books on the meanings, uses, sequences, crises, causes, consequences, patterns, dimensions, components, and theories of political development.[1]

   This outpouring was largely a product of the joining together of two streams of scholarly activity. One was the expansion of area studies in the late 1940s and 1950s. Before World War II scholars of comparative politics, reflecting the political conditions of the day, limited their attention almost exclusively to Western Europe and North America. After World War II scholarship followed the flag into the Cold War against the Soviet Union and then into the expansion of the American presence in Asia, the Middle East, Latin America, and Africa. At major universities area study programs sprang into being, devoted to the expansion of American knowledge and understanding of these countries and continents. With the active encouragement and support of the major foundations, professors and students sallied forth to previously exotic lands and produced what quickly became an immense library on the politics and institutions of particular countries and regions. Except for the Soviet Union and the People's Republic of China, these areas were part of what was defined as the Third World (because it was not one of the two protagonists in the Cold War) or the underdeveloped or less-developed or developing countries (because they were generally poorer and less industrialized than First World countries).

The second stream contributing to the study of political development stemmed from what has come to be called the "behavioral revolution" in political science. This involved an effort to combine theoretical rigor and empirical research and to test generalizations through systematic cross-national comparisons. The desire for theoretical rigor led political scientists to take over and to adapt from the leading contemporary school of sociological analysis such concepts as structure, function, input, output, feedback, and system. These concepts gave political scientists a systematic framework to use in the analysis and comparison of politics in different countries. Not surprisingly, one of the first major works to do this was *The Politics of the Developing Areas* by Gabriel Almond, James S. Coleman, and their associates, published in 1960. The behavioral revolution also involved a major effort to make more precise and quantitative measurements of political phenomena than had been made before. The improvement in the statistical services of governments and international agencies made it possible to amass large quantities of data on the social, demographic, economic, and, at times, political characteristics of societies.[2] The development of survey research in the United States, followed by its export abroad, created substantial data files on the background characteristics, attitudes, values, and behavior patterns of individuals. The refinement of more sophisticated means of mathematical analysis (factor analysis, regression, path analysis) plus the emergence of the high-speed computer as a standard tool of social science research made it feasible to analyze the relationships among a variety of variables in ways that had been totally impossible previously. The potentialities of survey research for the study of political development were first exploited significantly by Daniel Lerner in his analysis of *The Passing of Traditional Society,* published in 1958.[3] The ways in which aggregate cross-national data could be used were dramatically suggested by Karl Deutsch in his 1961 path-breaking article on "Social Mobilization and Political Development."

In the early 1960s the streams, from area studies on the one hand and from the behavioral revolution on the other, came together to produce a conscious focus on the problem of political development. The merger could often be seen quite explicitly in the careers of political scientists who became specialists in political development. Not infrequently they would start as specialists in one country or region among the developing areas, write their dissertation and first book on some aspect of the politics of "their" country, and then move on to broader, more comparative studies of political development in general, employing the concepts and methods derived from the behavioral revolution and, quite naturally, often attempting to generalize the relationships that they found in their first study of one country into relationships more or less relevant to most countries.

The study of political development in the 1960s was nothing if not eclectic. At least three major schools of political development analysis existed. The system-function approach combined elements of systems theory and structural functionalism, was derived from the work and heavily influenced by the analyses of Talcott Parsons, and was reflected in the work of such scholars as Marion Levy (1966), David Easton (1953, 1965a, 1965b), Gabriel Almond and G. Bingham Powell (1966), Almond (1970), David Apter (1965, 1971), Leonard Binder (1962), and Fred Riggs (1964). The social-process approach attempted to relate political behavior and processes to social processes such as urbanization, industrialization, and increasing media consumption through comparative quantitative analyses of national societies. It is reflected in the work of Lerner (1958), Deutsch (1961), Raymond Tanter (1967), Martin Needler (1968), Phillips Cutright (1963), Hayward Alker, Jr. (1966), Michael Hudson (1968), and a host of others. The comparative history approach represented, in some sense, a combination of a more traditional approach with intense efforts at systematic rigor. It was reflected in the work of Cyril Black (1966), S. N. Eisenstadt (1966), Seymour Martin Lipset (1963), Barrington Moore, Jr. (1966), Dankwart Rustow (1967), Reinhard Bendix (1964), Samuel P. Huntington (1968), and, in some measure, Lucian Pye and the Social Science Research Council Committee on Comparative Politics. Each of these approaches had its advantages and limitations; in combination they shed substantial new light on the processes of political development.

This concern with a "thing" called political development also quite naturally led scholars to attempt to define what that thing is. The definitions proliferated at an alarming rate, in part because the term "political development" had positive connotations and hence political scientists tended to apply it to things that they thought important and/or desirable. Logically, this usage served no necessary or useful function, and hence in one sense political development was a superfluous concept. For political scientists it performed a legitimating function rather than an analytical function (Huntington, 1971a). There was, nonetheless, a large and often impressive body of literature that could only be classified as political development studies. However defined, the field was booming, and however illogical it might be, it was called political development. In this literature the term was generally used in four different general ways.

1. *Geographical.* This was, in effect, a shorthand way of referring to the politics of the developing countries, that is, the poor or less-industrialized countries of Asia, Africa, and Latin America. In this sense almost any study of some aspect of the politics of these countries could be termed a study in political development even though the subject, concepts, and methods employed might be vir-

tually identical with those that would be used to study the politics of a "developed" country. Thus, a survey study of the attitudes of citizens toward their government in Tanzania would often be called a study in political development while the same questionnaire applied in Great Britain would not be.

2. *Derivative.* In this instance political development was held to refer to the political aspects and consequences of the broader process of modernization. Modernization presumably involved industrialization, urbanization, increasing literacy and mass media consumption, economic growth, greater social and occupational mobility, and related processes. In many studies political development was identified with political modernization. In this respect the study of political development was simply one branch of the broader concern of social science, dating back to the sociological classics of Maine, Weber, Toennies, and Durkheim, with the transition from a traditional, agrarian society to a modern, industrial one. As much research indicated, however, the political consequences of modernization often involved higher levels of conflict, violence, and disruption, which seemed somewhat incongruous subjects for a "positive" sounding label like political development.

3. *Teleological.* Political development would, in this case, be defined as movement toward one or more goals or states of being for the political system. In some instances political development would be said to involve movement toward several different goals, the attainment of any one of which might be possible only at the cost of some compromise in the attainment of others. This made political development a concept involving some inherent contradictions. Or, if political development was identified with movement toward one particular goal, that movement (e.g., democratization) usually already had a perfectly good name and hence political development became a superfluous label. Among the various goals, movement toward which was identified as political development, were democracy, stability, legitimacy, participation, mobilization, institutionalization, equality, capability, differentiation, identity, penetration, distribution, integration, rationalization, bureaucratization, security, welfare, justice, liberty. In many cases movement toward these goals was implicitly or explicitly assumed to be part of a more general process of modernization. In other cases a sharp distinction was made between modernization and political development; the latter, conceived as the institutionalization of political organizations and procedures, could occur in either modern or traditional societies and was often undermined by the socioeconomic change associated with modernization, leading to "political decay" (Huntington, 1965).

4. *Functional.* Political development was here thought of as a movement toward the politics characteristic of a modern, industrial society. Presumably one could argue that such a society requires certain types of political processes, values, leadership, and institutions or, at least, that it functions more effectively

if it has certain types of politics that are more appropriate than other types. Most nonindustrial societies, for instance, do not have political parties, while most industrialized societies do have some type of political party system. Hence one might conclude that political parties are, in some sense, a functional necessity in an industrialized society and hence that the development of political parties is one aspect of political development. This is, it should be noted, a way of defining political development that is distinctly different from the view of it as a derivative of the process of modernization. For it is quite conceivable that political parties may be functionally desirable in a modern society but that the process of modernization may in fact move in ways that hamper the development of political parties. Political development, in this sense, is not the political consequences of modernization but the political requisites for an effectively functioning modern society.

Political development has thus been variously defined as a pattern of change which occurs in a particular type of society, which is produced by a particular cause, which is directed toward particular goals, or which is functionally required by particular social and economic conditions. These approaches are logically distinct but, in practice, overlap a great deal. In this essay we shall be concerned largely with what goes on in the area of overlap. Insofar as any one definitional approach has priority, it will be political development conceived as the political consequences of modernization. Discussions of political development often focus more on development *toward* what than on development *of* what. Two "whats," development toward which has been the subject of extensive analysis, are political democracy and political stability. Both these topics are, at least in part, covered by other essays in this *Handbook* as well as by our analysis in sections IV and V of this essay. At this point, consequently, we shall only briefly call attention to the issues that have been raised concerning the relationship of each of these goals to socioeconomic modernization.

Political Democracy

Early analysts of political development often tended to define the process of political development as progress toward political democracy. The development of democracy, in turn, was related to the process of economic development. In his 1959 essay on the social requisites of democracy, Lipset presented data that showed a high correlation between the existence of democratic institutions and high levels of economic development. Subsequent studies have produced additional evidence underwriting this relationship (Russett, 1964; Dahl, 1971). In attempting to explain why democracy and economic development should go hand in hand, scholars have placed particular stress on the role of communications (Cutright, 1963a; McCrone and Cnudde, 1967; Dahl, 1971, pp. 74–76). The issue has also been raised whether the relation of political democracy to economic development is of a linear or curvilinear character. The evidence would appear to suggest that, at the very least, there are thresholds in economic development beyond which the probability of a society having a democratic regime is extremely high and also beyond which that probability does not increase significantly with further economic development (Neubauer, 1967; Dahl, 1971; Jackman, 1973). It has, however, also been suggested that while democracy may tend to appear when societies pass through a transition zone (or over a threshold) of per capita income in U.S. 1960 dollars of $300 to $600, this relationship has in fact only been established for countries in western and northern Europe during the course of the century from 1830 to 1930 (Sunshine, 1972).

One particularly useful result of this type of analysis relating levels of economic development and political democracy comes from focusing attention on the "deviant cases," in which the hypothesized and generally valid relationship does not hold. Cutright's analysis (1963), for instance, shows that during the period from 1940 to 1960 Chile, the Philippines, Ireland, and India were significantly more democratic than they "ought" to have been according to the level of their communications development, while Spain, Portugal, the Eastern European countries, Germany, and Japan were less democratic than they "ought" to have been. Both types of deviants pose the question of the causes (external intervention, colonial legacy, idiosyncratic leadership) for their variation from the normal pattern. In the former group of countries, presumably the continued stability of democracy would require significant increases in the level of communications development; in the latter countries, presumably social pressures were likely to move the political system in a more democratic direction or the government would have to engage in increased repression to contain and reduce the level of communications and development. In the early 1970s the rising levels of economic development among many less-developed countries in southern Europe, Asia, and Latin America made these hypotheses and generalizations by political scientists of increasing political relevance. Countries such as Spain, Greece, Brazil, South Korea, Taiwan appeared to confront increasing strains between their economic and political systems, strains that were recognized by at least some leaders of these countries, who struggled to find the means for "liberalization" and "political decompression" in their societies. (See Huntington and Nelson, 1976.)

Political Stability

Political stability, like political democracy, has often been viewed as the goal of political development, although with rare exceptions the articulation of this goal has been more implicit than explicit. Perhaps one reason is that in contrast to political democracy, political stability is extraordinarily hard to define. Political democracy can be relatively easily measured in terms of electoral competition, suffrage requirements, voting participation, turnover in office, and freedom of press and speech. Political stability is not so readily pinned down. Indeed, one scholar could still observe in the early 1970s that the concept of political stability "remains as elusive as other abstract concepts in political science research" (Hurwitz, 1973). In his review of the literature Hurwitz found five different approaches to political stability. By and large, however, two elements predominate in concepts of political stability: order and continuity. The first involves the relative absence of violence, force, coercion, and disruption from the political system. The second identifies stability with a relative absence of change in the critical components of the political system, a lack of discontinuity in political evolution, the absence from the society of significant social forces and political movements that wish to bring about fundamental changes in the political system. Stability is somewhat like legitimacy in that it is much easier to know when it is missing than when it is present. Empirical studies of stability have generally measured stability by indicators of instability. Low levels of deaths from political violence, coups d'état, assassinations, insurrections, riots, repressive forces, and intergroup violence are taken as evidence of stability; so also are infrequent changes in political institutions and political actors.

Stability, it should be noted, does not necessarily mean the absence of change in all components of a political system. It involves relative continuity and absence of change in the more fundamental underlying components of the political system, such as the basic political values, the culture, and the fundamental institutional (or constitutional) structure of politics. Continuity in the culture and the constitution, in the broad sense of both words, is clearly involved in any meaningful concept of political stability. On the other hand, such a concept of stability is quite compatible with gradual changes in group participation in politics, political leadership, and governmental policies (Huntington, 1971a). Indeed, if the socioeconomic environment of the political system is changing, changes in participation, leadership, and policy may well be essential to maintain continuity in culture and institutions. As Burke observed, "A state without the means of some change is without the means of its conservation," and to be stable a political system has to provide regularized and accepted means for changing its participants, leaders, and policies in an orderly (i.e., relatively peaceful) manner. Stability thus involves the institutionalization of political organizations and procedures, and the degree of stability reflects the extent to which political institutions provide channels for political participation by those groups and individuals attempting to participate in politics (Huntington, 1968).

How is socioeconomic modernization related to political stability? Early explorations of this subject often called attention to the extent to which modern societies also seemed to be relatively stable politically, while more traditional or less developed societies often seemed to lack continuity and order in their political systems. Consequently it was assumed that socioeconomic modernization would increase political stability. In fact, of course, this does not happen, at least in the short run. Closer to the truth is the proposition that "modernity breeds stability but modernization breeds instability" (Huntington, 1968). Political instability and particularly political violence occur when men become dissatisfied, and they become dissatisfied when their achievements and capabilities fall below their aspirations. This gives rise to a sense of "relative deprivation," which in the absence of other means of reducing the gap between aspiration and capability predisposes men to violence. A "relative deprivation" framework for the analysis of the causes of civil violence and political instability was utilized by Davies (1962, 1969), Feierabend and Feierabend (1966), Huntington (1968), Feierabend, Feierabend, and Nesvold (1969), and, most comprehensively, by Gurr (1970, 1973). Although the case was also made that "diffuse support for the structure of political authority" and beliefs in the past efficacy of violence in obtaining goals were more significant than relative deprivation in explaining the resort to political violence (Muller, 1972; also Grofman and Muller, 1972), the relative deprivation theory still dominated scholarly work on political instability in the early 1970s.

The most common circumstances in which a gap develops between a group's aspirations for social, economic, and political goods and its capabilities of obtaining those goods are those in which the group's (a) aspirations increase and its capabilities remain constant; (b) aspirations and capabilities increase, but the latter at a slower rate than the former; (c) aspirations remain constant and its capabilities decrease; (d) aspirations increase and its capabilities increase at first and then decline.[4] Under these conditions the group will be predisposed to civil violence. If, on the other hand, the capabilities of the group increase faster than its aspirations, or if they decline more slowly than its aspirations, or if both aspirations and capabilities remain constant (even though a gap may exist between them), the predisposition of the group to engage in civil violence will be low.

Civil violence is thus likely when aspirations and capabilities are changing and when the gap between them is increasing. This is, of course, precisely what takes place during the process of socioeconomic modernization. Changes then occur in the aspirations and capabilities of most groups in society with respect to their economic wealth and income, social status, and political power. Increases in literacy, education, and mass media consumption and exposure to modern values, ideas, and styles of life increase the desires of the affected social groups. The capabilities of these groups may in some cases remain constant (case a). More generally the capabilities also increase but at a slower rate than the aspirations (case b); education outruns employment, mass media exposure grows more rapidly than per capita gross national product. In some cases, as in the early phases of modernization in the countryside, some groups may suffer an absolute decline in material well-being (case c). In other instances economic development may proceed at a good pace for a few years but then be followed by a downturn, which may have particularly drastic effects on certain groups (case d)—the classic *J*-curve phenomenon.

More specifically, the relation between socioeconomic modernization and political stability can be analyzed in terms of the impact on the latter of *levels* of modernization, *rates* of modernization, and *ratios* between modernization variables. Evidence concerning these relationships is often noncomparable or contradictory, but in general the following propositions emerged in the early 1970s.

1. Although there is some data to suggest a linear relationship between levels of economic development and political stability (Flanigan and Fogelman, 1970), no relationship (Schneider and Schneider, 1971), and even a negative relationship with respect to military intervention (Putnam, 1967), the bulk of the evidence reveals a curvilinear relationship between these two variables, with countries at intermediate levels of economic development most prone to political disorder and civil violence (Russett, 1964; Huntington, 1968; Feiera-bend, Feierabend, and Nesvold, 1969; Hibbs, 1973). Thus, the relations of political democracy and political stability to socioeconomic modernization follow rather different courses. With the shift from low to medium to high levels of socioeconomic modernization, the probability of democracy increases and then levels off, while the probability of political stability initially declines and then increases substantially.

2. High rates of economic development contribute to political stability (Alker and Russett, 1964; Bwy, 1971; Flanigan and Fogelman, 1970; Hibbs, 1973) and, conversely, deteriorating economic conditions enhance social con-flict and military intervention (Fossum, 1967; Needler, 1972; Welch and Smith, 1974).

3. High rates of urban migration also tend to reduce political instability and collective violence (Huntington, 1968; Tilly, 1969, 1973; Flanigan and Fogel-man, 1970).

4. High rates of change in social mobilization more generally may (Feiera-bend, Feierabend, and Nesvold, 1969) or may not (Schneider and Schneider, 1971) have a significant association with political violence.

5. A high ratio of social mobilization to economic development tends to pro-duce political instability (Needler, 1968; Schneider and Schneider, 1971), or, as one study concluded, "The most detrimental combination of factors appears to be a rapid increase in proportion of the population receiving primary edu-cation, but a slow rate of percentage change in GDP [gross domestic product] per capita. This set of circumstances is most conducive to political unrest among the transitional group of countries." (Feierabend, Feierabend, and Nesvold, 1969)

6. A high ratio of social mobilization and/or political participation to politi-cal institutionalization tends to be associated either directly (Huntington,

1968; Schneider and Schneider, 1971) or indirectly (Hibbs, 1973) with political instability, and institutionalization itself has a strong negative relationship to political instability (Putnam, 1967; Needler, 1968; Schneider and Schneider, 1971; Hibbs, 1973).

Socioeconomic modernization also has effects on the forms of political violence and instability. In traditional societies such violence is likely to involve a limited number of actors with limited goals. As modernization proceeds, however, more groups become socially mobilized and participant in politics. As a result the forms of violence and instability diversify and also become broader in scope. In the early phases of modernization, when politics is elitist and conspiratorial, the military coup d'état is likely to be a prevalent form of political instability. It is, however, a technique that can succeed only so long as political participation remains limited. As societies modernize and participation broadens, the coup becomes a less effective and a less frequent form of political action. On a global basis coups are much more prevalent in countries at lower rather than higher levels of economic development. As societies become more modern without becoming more stable, riots and other forms of mass violence displace coups and other forms of conspiratorial violence. And the coups that do occur in more highly developed societies usually involve greater amounts of violence than those that occur in less-developed countries.

The remainder of this essay will be concerned largely with the effects of socioeconomic modernization on four other selected aspects of the political system:

1. political culture, that is, the values, attitudes, orientations, myths, and beliefs that people have about politics and government and particularly about the legitimacy of government and their relation to government

2. political participation, that is, the nature and scope of people's activities that are designed to affect governmental decision-making

3. political institutions, that is, the nature of the formal organizations through which society makes authoritative decisions and, particularly, the extent to which such institutions are democratic or authoritarian and the relative importance of partisan and bureaucratic institutions

4. political integration, that is, the extent to which politics is not characterized by sharp cleavages along ethnic, racial, religious, class, cultural, or territorial lines.

Before considering the specific relationships between socioeconomic modernization and these four political variables, however, the next section will first identify the principal independent variables associated with modernization which various theories and analyses have pointed to as exercising a substantial influence on political development.

II. WHAT INFLUENCES POLITICAL DEVELOPMENT

The political systems of relatively primitive, traditional, agrarian societies clearly differ significantly from those of highly complex, modern, industrial societies. There are also major differences among the processes by which modern political systems have evolved out of traditional ones as well as among different types of modern political systems. Why is political development in some societies characterized by sharp cleavages and great violence while in other societies it is relatively harmonious and peaceful? Why have some societies developed into pluralistic, democratic political systems while others have endured dictatorial or totalitarian regimes? Why do some societies seem to stagnate politically while others gradually adapt to changing circumstances? What causes some societies to develop relatively high levels of social cohesion and public trust while others seemingly flounder in a normless "praetorian" state? Why is the legitimacy of some governments virtually unquestioned while that of others is virtually unacknowledged? Why in some societies have large masses of the population become participants in politics while in others this remains the privilege of only a small elite?

The answers to these questions are multiple and diverse. Cases can and have been made for the preeminence of almost every conceivable explanatory variable. Our purpose here is not to weigh the relative importance of these variables but rather to present the most important of them in a systematic manner and to suggest those aspects of political development to which each may be particularly relevant. All in all the principal explanatory variables of political development can be analyzed in terms of five major categories.

1. Phases

Societies evolve from traditional through transitional into modern phases. Conceivably the process and product of political development may be shaped much more by what happens in one of these phases than by what happens in the others. The process of political development in the transitional and modern phases and the nature of the political system in those phases could be decisively influenced by the nature of the traditional society and political system. Or political development and the political system in the transitional and modern phases could be decisively influenced by the nature of the transitional phase. Or politics in the modern phases might reflect primarily the level of modernity which the society had achieved in that phase.

Consider, for instance, the relative influence of the different phases on the extent to which a society has democratic or nondemocratic political institutions in the modern phase. One theory, as we have noted, argues that the degree of political democracy in a system reflects the level of economic development of the society. Consequently, societies that are more modern and developed should have more democratic politics. A second theory relates the democratic or non-democratic character of the modern political system to the nature of the transitional process and particularly to the extent to which this process was violent or peaceful and the extent to which socioeconomic change was rapid or gradual. A third theory argues, however, that the degree of democracy in a transitional or modern society will be decisively shaped by the nature of the previously existing traditional society. Societies that were governed by centralized bureaucratic empires in their traditional phase are likely to be governed by centralized totalitarian or authoritarian regimes in their modern phase. Conversely, societies in which feudalism prevailed in the traditional phase are likely to have democratic and pluralistic political systems in their modern phase (Apter, 1965, pp. 81–123; Huntington, 1968, pp. 140–91). Thus according to this approach, the extent to which political development takes a democratic or autocratic direction is shaped not by how far the society has gone in its modern phase but where it started in its traditional phase. The "level of modernity" theory implies that communist societies will "converge" toward the Western democratic model as they become more economically developed; the "nature of tradition" theory implies that they were, in effect, predestined from the very beginning of their development to be nondemocratic polities for all time.

2. Factors

Political development may also be explained by reference to the relative influence of cultural, social, economic, and political factors in shaping the processes and products of political change. A Marxist approach would, of course, place primary emphasis on the economic factors, particularly the extent to which and manner in which capitalism developed and the scope and independence of the bourgeois class. "No bourgeois, no democracy" is the way one leading Marxist scholar sums up the relation between class formation and political development (Moore, 1966, p. 418; see also Kautsky, 1972; Horowitz, 1966). Some non-Marxist approaches emphasize other aspects of economic development as being determinative, such as the rate of economic development, the relationship between social mobilization and economic development, the balance or unevenness of economic development among regions, patterns of land ownership and tenure, the methods and timing of the commercialization of agriculture, the relative importance of extractive (and particularly enclave) industries vis-a-vis manufacturing and import substitution industries, and a variety of other factors.

Alternatively, political development can be explained primarily by reference to social factors, such as the nature and evolution of the status system in the society, the opportunities for social mobility, the nature of communal (racial, national, linguistic, religious) differences in the society. It has, for instance, been argued that the development of stable democratic institutions is impossible in a society in which there are deep communal cleavages (Melson and Wolpe, 1971; Rabushka and Shepsle, 1972). Cultural factors may also play a major role in influencing political development at all phases in the process of modernization. It has been suggested, for instance, that whether a traditional society has a consummatory or instrumental culture decisively affects the extent to which it is able to adapt gradually to modernization or must make a total and often politically revolutionary break with its past (Apter, 1965, pp. 81–122 and *passim*).

Finally, political development may also be influenced by political factors. The nature of the traditional political system, the sequences and ways in which new groups enter politics, the values of the political elites, the skills of political leaders, the relation between the expansion of political participation and the development of political institutions all presumably have some impact on the pattern of political change.

One key issue in analyzing the roles of economic, social, cultural, and political factors in development is the extent to which the relative importance of these factors may vary with the different phases of modernization. Economic and social factors, for instance, may be of greater importance in the earlier phases of political development while political factors may be of greater influence in later phases (Adelman and Morris, 1967).

3. *Environments*

The political evolution of a society is influenced by its external as well as its domestic environment. The relative influence of the two differs drastically in different societies and at different times in the same society. The evolution of any society clearly will reflect its situational environment in terms of geography and previous history. Beyond this, external influences on political development may take the form of (a) importation by individuals and groups within the society of ideas, models, techniques, resources, and institutions from other societies; where importation is extensive and unavoidable, except at high costs, the result is a state of *dependence* by the one society on another; (b) intervention by individuals and groups from other societies through political, military, economic, or cultural means to affect directly or indirectly the political development of the society; (c) government by individuals and groups from other societies (colonialism); and (d) reaction by individuals and groups within the society against the threat of foreign intervention or rule (defensive modernization). The impact of external environments appears to be considerably greater on later-modernizing societies than on the earlier modernizers.[5]

4. Timing

Timing refers to whether a society entered the process of modernization earlier or later than other societies. By and large it is possible to rank societies in these terms and to draw broad distinctions between early and late developers. Many of these differences have a profound impact on political development. For instance, in late developers as compared with early developers: (a) the state normally plays a more important and more coercive role in the process of industrialization; (b) the bourgeoisie is likely to be weaker and hence, according to some theories, democracy is less likely to emerge; (c) exogenous influences on political development are likely to be more important; (d) rates of social mobilization are likely to be high compared with rates of industrialization; (e) overall rates of socioeconomic change are likely to be higher and hence social tensions sharper; (f) in part as a result of these earlier factors, mass participation in politics is broader and popular demands on the political system more intense in comparison with the level of economic development and political institutionalization; and (g) in part as a consequence, violence and instability are more likely to be prevalent (Black, 1966, pp. 67–71, 96–98; Benjamin, 1972, pp. 19–20; Collier, 1972).

5. Sequences

The sequence in which various political, social, and economic processes occur in the modernization may drastically affect political development. It has, for instance, been argued that "the probabilities of a political system's developing in a nonviolent, nonauthoritarian, and eventually democratically stable manner are maximized when a national identity emerges first, followed by the institutionalization of the central government, and then by the emergence of mass parties and a mass electorate" (Nordlinger, 1968). In this case the probabilities for the maximization of certain political variables are said to depend on the sequence in which other political variables emerge. In a somewhat similar vein it has been posited that "the most effective sequence" of political development is to establish national unity first, then governmental authority, and then political equality (Rustow, 1967, pp. 120–32, 276). And along the same lines it has been suggested that a lower level of coercion will appear in the process of modernization if the political system develops institutionalized capacities for identity, legitimacy, penetration, participation, and distribution, in that order (Binder *et al.*, 1971, pp. 310–13). Another sequential analysis argues that the expansion of political participation in a society before the development of political institutions through which that participation can take place leads to political instability and violence (Huntington, 1968). It has also been suggested that the probability of agrarian revolution is decisively influenced by the sequence in which commercialization of agriculture, the politicization of the peasantry, and the growth of urban centers occurs in a society. A sequence of politicization, commercialization, and urbanization leads to rural revolution, while a commercialization-politicization-urbanization sequence tends to produce agrarian reform. Other sequences of these three independent variables have little, no, or uncertain effect on the probability of agrarian reform or revolution (Powell, 1971, pp. 212–17).

The extent to which various aspects and steps in development occur sequentially or simultaneously is also of paramount importance. The appearance of problems or crises sequentially is likely to promote peaceful change, stable government, and more democratic institutions; the simultaneous appearance of problems or crises is likely to "overload" the political system, producing sharp cleavages, violence, and repression.

6. Rates

The rates of change in the social, economic, cultural, and political components of modernization clearly have important implications for political institutions, processes, and participation. Differences in rates of change in the components of modernization shade into and may produce differences in sequences of change. In addition, however, the overall rates of change within one society may differ from those in another. Rapid rates of socioeconomic change are more likely than slower rates to lead to social conflict and political disruption. Substantial changes in political values and institutions normally require substantial periods of time, and hence adaptation of the political system may lag behind broader changes in society. In general, the rates of socioeconomic change among late-developing countries are much higher than they were among the earlier developers. Consequently the tendencies toward instability, violence, and autocratic rule are also greater among the later developers. Dyssynchronous or unbalanced change, such as rapid urbanization coupled with slow industrialization, also can create crises and stresses for the political system.

The principal variables affecting the political development of societies can thus be analyzed in terms of the influence of (a) the traditional, transitional, and modern phases of development; (b) cultural, social, economic, and political factors; (c) domestic and foreign environments; (d) the early or late timing of modernization; (e) the degree of simultaneous or sequential change, and if the latter, the nature of the sequence; and (f) the rates of change in the components of modernization.

III. POLITICAL CULTURE

The political culture of a society consists of the empirical beliefs about expressive political symbols and values and other orientations of the members of the society toward political objects.[6] It is the product of the collective history of a political system and the life histories of the individuals who currently make up the system. It is rooted both in public events and private experiences and embodies a society's central political values. Although central political values can change through time, they change very slowly. For example, according to S. M. Lipset, a reading of the American historical record "suggests that there is more continuity than change with respect to the main elements in the national value system." Under the impact of economic growth and social change, institutional arrangements make adjustments to new conditions *within* the framework of a dominant value system. But the central values themselves change slowly "or not at all" (Lipset, 1963, pp. 117–18; see also Almond and Verba, 1965, pp. 5–13; Pye and Verba, 1965, pp. 7–10, 513).

In their study of *The Civic Culture*, Almond and Verba argue that there are three broad types of political culture: parochial, subject, and participant. In a parochial political culture the individual has at most a very dim awareness of the existence of a larger political system beyond the village or tribal group. There are no specialized political roles. There are few expectations of change in the political system. Therefore, the individual's cognitive, affective, and evaluative orientations toward the political system—the inputs and outputs— and toward the self as a political actor approach zero. In a subject political culture there is a high frequency of orientations toward a differentiated political system beyond one's local world and toward the output objects, or administrative structures, of that system. But orientations toward specifically input objects and toward the self as a political participant continue to approach zero. In the participant political culture members of the society are positively oriented not only toward the system as a whole and toward the output, or administrative structures, but also toward the input, or political structures, and toward the self as an active participant (Almond and Verba, 1965, pp. 14–18). These are, of course, ideal types; empirical studies generally show various "mixes" of these types existing in actuality.

The relationship between political culture and political change is also affected by the specific content of political culture. Different traditional or parochial societies have responded differently to similar external stimuli, such as the same European colonial power pursuing similar policies. Though the concepts "parochial" or "traditional" point to cross-cultural similarities in political orientation among peoples at a given point in history, they tell us little about the relationship between a society's central political values and likely future processes of large-scale political change. One needs hypotheses that deal with the congruence between political culture and political structures and with the consequences of the content of given political cultures for political change.

Political Culture and Political Structures

Political culture and political structures are congruent when there is a high degree of compatibility between political roles and structures on the one hand, and the central political values of the system on the other (Inkeles and Levinson, 1969, pp. 480–88; Almond and Verba, 1965, pp. 20–22; Eckstein, 1961, 1966). The individual can use the available political opportunities with adequate gratification and can accept demands with minimal pain and anxiety. When demands exist they are kept from becoming disruptive by control mechanisms that individuals have internalized and by external control mechanisms (government, civic organizations, churches, etc.) that the individual perceives as legitimate. Political cognition must be accurate, and affect to and evaluation of political roles and structures must be positive.

A parochial political culture that is congruent with its structures would have high and positive cognitive, affective, and evaluative orientations toward the diffuse structures of village, tribe, and religion and would be without likelihood of change (Banfield, 1958). A subject political culture congruent with its structures would have these orientations toward the political system as a whole and toward its output, or administrative, aspects. A participant political culture that is congruent with its structures would have high cognitive, and positive affective, and evaluative orientations toward the political system as a whole, its inputs and outputs, and toward the self as a participant.

Political change is not likely under conditions of congruence between political culture and political structures. The motivations for change, which arise out of discontent, are likely to be low or to be kept under internalized or external controls that are perceived as legitimate. Political change occurs when congruence between political culture and structures erodes or breaks down.

One major source of change is international contact. A frequent result of such contact is that persons from a separate and distinct political culture are introduced into the established system even though they may not be compatible with it. These new members of the system may not only affect the recipient political culture but also change themselves away from the cultural patterns of the system from which they came. International contact may also introduce into an established system alien institutions such as churches, business corporations, armies, and political parties. This importation of alien institutions also may change the recipient political culture drastically while changing the imported institutions themselves away from the patterns of their system of origin.

Partly because of contact with the outside world, partly because of internal processes of modernization, strains may develop in the relationship between culture and structures, leading to political change. As a result some domestic leaders and institutions may seek to impose further drastic change on the society. These changes may be so marked that the previous stability between culture and structures is thoroughly disrupted. Alternatively, elites may seek to freeze the social system in some idealized form to prevent change. But this freeze, in turn, creates new tensions of its own.

In short, external agents may lead to cultural or other change, or they may affect internal processes of modernization and institutions, which may, in turn, lead to cultural change. Not all change, internally or externally induced, is cultural change. But when such cultural change does occur, major instabilities appear in the political system, and political change toward reestablishing congruence between culture and structure is probable.

Political Cultures and Political Acculturation

Political cultures rarely give way completely to the new, no matter how ruthless the impact of innovation. However, the coming of Europe to the southern hemisphere took place with such force, persistence, and thoroughness that a great number of changes took place. Colonial powers imposed new political structures that created new lines of authority, new sources of legitimacy, new types of demands on the citizenry, and new capabilities to penetrate the society, which in many instances had been weak theretofore. To administer these new structures—and in the Americas and Australia to settle these continents—colonial powers sent individuals who brought with them the central political values that were prevalent in the colonial power. In Africa and Asia these individuals, both as role models of how a governor should govern and through the impact of their policies on the society, induced noncongruence between the previously existing political culture and the new or drastically modified political structures.

Even where formal colonial control was avoided, the political-military-economic threat of European states and the United States forced countries to provide some sort of response. There were two fundamental responses: a country could become more like the West through acculturation or could attempt cultural resistance. In cases of culture borrowing, indigenous institutions broke down preexisting convergence between culture and structure in order to bring about a certain amount of change, while preventing the importation of people and institutions from the West, which might have caused less-controlled change.

The Recipient Political Culture

The response of the political cultures that existed prior to European entry to the breakdown of congruence can be analyzed in terms of syncretism. Syncretism occurs when an overt form of one culture is not perceived in the same fashion by members of another but is perceived in such a way that it can be reinterpreted to conform to the borrowing culture's own patterns of meaning and yet retain essentially its original function. Syncretism, therefore, is a process of reinterpretation with retention of the original function. The probability of acceptance of new political cultural forms is increased to the extent that innovations are susceptible to reinterpretation in the conceptual framework of the recipient group (Foster, 1962).

Political cultures can be classified as consummatory or instrumental according to their response to cultural change, including but not limited to acculturation. Consummatory cultures link most social relationships with the religious sphere and ascribe religious meanings or value to most behavior patterns. Instrumental cultures do not evaluate social conduct in terms of wider, transcendental meanings but only in terms of more narrow and particular ones. Gratification in consummatory cultures follows from the transcendental values associated with an act; gratification in instrumental cultures follows from the immediate practical ends achieved by the act. In an instrumental culture there are tendencies toward differentiation among the religious, cultural, political, economic, and scientific spheres; in consummatory cultures there is little if any differentiation among these spheres.

Acculturation through syncretism is likely to proceed in a gradual and orderly fashion in instrumental cultures that are confronted with European culture; consummatory cultures, on the other hand, will either resist all change (a change in one sphere is very threatening because it affects everything else) or, when they change, change totally and rapidly. They may reappear, therefore, in revolutionary form. Instrumental cultures can perceive localized similarities with other cultures and can reinterpret and adopt them; consummatory cultures are much less capable of following the syncretic route (Apter, 1965, pp. 83–94; Eisenstadt, 1966, pp. 2–5, 156–57).

Consummatory and instrumental classifications are ideal types. Political cultures *tend* in one direction or another. More importantly, they may be only partly consummatory (and therefore partly instrumental) when only certain types of activity are undifferentiated from the religious and the mystical. For example, when political but not economic activities are endowed with religious/mystical significance, as we shall see among the Ganda, then change may take place in the economic sphere but less so in the political. When economic but not political activities are endowed with sacred significance, as we shall see in India, the polity but less so the economy will tend to change. Consequently, syncretism operates only in those parts of the culture that are instrumental. There are also, therefore, mixed cultures—partly instrumental, partly consummatory.

The Fon of Dahomey had a consummatory value system pervading both the economy and the polity. Hierarchical authority, based on kingship, was closely intertwined with the religious beliefs of the society and provided a justification for other activities. After resisting bitterly the coming of the French, Dahomey—the smallest territory of former French West Africa, the last to come under French control, and the poorest in natural resources—proved the most receptive to political and economic change because it sought to acquire a new, total, modern culture. The Fon flocked to French schools; no other territory in French Africa had so high a percentage of children in school. The elite migrated throughout French Africa, became successful imperial civil servants, and adapted to Christianity.

The Ganda of Uganda, in contrast, had an instrumental value system except for the political sphere. It was a mixed culture. The Ganda were able to make considerable changes in economic activity; they were even able to adapt to Christianity. But the mystical role of the king—the *kabaka*—was intimately linked to the nature and very identity of the people. Nonpolitical change could be received. Political change was accepted very slowly and only when it did not threaten the position of the *kabaka*. The Ganda's inability to cope with political change has remained a major problem for themselves and for Uganda. Their failure to accept limitations on the power of the *kabaka* led Ugandan authorities to depose the *kabaka*. The long-range effects of this on the Ganda are not yet clear. In contrast to the Fon and Ganda, the Ibo of Nigeria had generalized instrumental values. They had individualized responses to innovation; they adapted to commercial life; and they pursued practical and nonideological politics (Apter, 1965, pp. 95–96, 99–106, 111–21).

Larger societies can also be analyzed in terms of the consummatory-instrumental continuum. Comparing China and Japan, Fairbank, Reischauer, and Craig argue that "it was the overall cohesion and structural stability of Chinese civilization that basically inhibited its rapid response to the Western menace." The Chinese were "in the grip of their past," with their religion, politics, and economics looking backwards and being intimately interconnected with each other. In the face of the Western thrust in the nineteenth century, many Chinese responded by playing traditional roles. The Japanese, in contrast, tended to react by seeking specific objectives. Fairbank, Reischauer, and Craig call the Meiji leaders "pragmatists and utilitarians, ready to adopt whatever techniques, institutions, or ideas seemed useful" (Fairbank, Reischauer, and Craig, 1965, pp. 404–5, 266; see also pp. 181–83, 262–66, 320–28, 495, 642). Japan's change, though rapid, was controlled. The more extravagant excesses of cultural borrowing were already being curtailed by the 1890s. The rate of political and economic change strengthened rather than weakened positive orientations toward the polity. Though there were strains, the basic instrumental characteristics of the political culture allowed sufficient political cultural borrowing at a rapid pace so that new political forces could be incorporated into the political system. The changing instrumental political culture remained largely congruent with the changing political structures.

China had an essentially consummatory culture. It linked political, economic, social, ideological, and mystical elements. Its basic response was to resist the impact of change. It sought to reaffirm or restore the old Confucian system rather than to modernize it. The Chinese Restoration's ideal society was one of static harmony among all closely integrated values, not of dynamic, segmented growth. After its failure and the deposition of the emperor, the political system decayed into praetorianism. Lacking the traditional ideological and ceremonial sanctions of the Son of Heaven and not having developed modern sanctions, the successors of the Chinese empire had to rely increasingly on military force. China differed from other consummatory value societies in that there was no replacement of political culture provided through colonial domination.

This may have been caused by the greater strength of traditional consumma-tory culture in China compared with Dahomey; it is more likely that China's greater economic, political and military resources, relative to Dahomey, ac-count for more of the difference in the ability to defend its traditional culture.

The inability to engage in instrumental, syncretic change leads to resis-tance and often to breakdown. It can also lead to radical, drastic change, as it did in China and Vietnam, and to the establishment of a revolutionary con-summatory culture. McAlister and Mus stress the paradoxical nature of re-sponse to change characteristic of consummatory cultures, in their analysis of Vietnam. They argue that "for the Vietnamese everything is religion down to the simplest acts. . . . Within Vietnam's former traditional society this whole system of beliefs was embodied in the Emperor, whose ritual acts symbolized the spiritual feelings of the Vietnamese. . . . Government in traditional Vietnam was thus inseparable from religion . . . the Emperor sanctified all action." (McAlister and Mus, 1970, p. 78; see also pp. 58–63, 78–79, 80, 94–100, 114–19; FitzGerald, 1972). Therefore, the elimination of imperial authority during French colonial rule threatened the core of Vietnam's social order. The impact of France destroyed the system, and the Vietnamese elite—like the Fon—rapidly shifted its values. The landowners of the Mekong Delta sent their sons to the Sorbonne, the Ecole Polytechnique, to law and medical schools in Paris and Marseilles; they had cellars of French wine; and they became closely inte-grated in the French economic and political system in Vietnam. Vietnamese intellectuals were trained in European institutions, which dislodged them from Vietnamese culture. Their cultural references were French.

The peasants in the villages, however, remained true to the resistance pat-tern of consummatory political values. They came to see the French-protected emperor and the elite as their enemy. In their consummatory value system there was either identification or antagonism with the political structures: there was no room for compromise. With the rise of communism a new recipe for total change was provided. A new sacred consummatory collectivity was available in which all values would be integrated. The communist revolution, in their view, was authentic because it provided a complete replacement of the political structures with which their political culture was incongruent. A new consummatorily oriented set of political structures would become compatible with their consummatory political culture. From resistance and breakdown to revolution—this is the pattern of consummatory value systems. The threat of ac-culturation was met by a new sacred collectivity that had a new, though differ-ent, congruence between culture and structure.

Indian culture has stressed consummatory values in areas other than poli-tics. According to Lloyd and Suzanne Rudolph, the *jati*, or local subcaste in traditional India, "established by ascription the group within which a person might marry and, more broadly, the social, economic and moral circumstances of his life." The political sphere was rather separate. No single state developed in India with which the survival of the cultural tradition was identified. The last Hindi rulers of large sections of India preceded the British conquest by several centuries. The Moghul empire ruled politically but outside the "Great Tradition" of the caste system. By the time of the coming of the British, even Moghul rule had been weakening and disintegrating. The *jati* system at the local level was regulated by the norms of the tradition and enforced by the locally dominant subcaste. But if the political system was outside the consummatory system of values, it was nevertheless a source of mobility within the tradition because of its contribution to the legitimation of the process of "sanskritization," as we shall see (Rudolph and Rudolph, 1967, p. 29; see also pp. 20–21, 29–30).

The Donor Political Culture

Political change resulting from noncongruence in processes of acculturation depends not only on the recipient political culture but also on the response of the traveling political culture to those whom it finds at the end of its voyage from Europe. There are two main patterns of response: agglomerative and assimilative. The agglomerative political culture is corporative and hierarchical; when it encounters a different culture, it proceeds to establish superordinate and subordinate relationships within a new single hierarchical context. Everyone's basic humanity is asserted in various degrees; groups within the new hierarchy have independently defined privileges and jurisdictions, which are protected by the general system, no matter how lowly the groups may be. The assimilative political culture is egalitarian; consequently, when it encounters persons of a different culture it must either accept or reject their humanity. There are few gradations of rank and privilege in the new context: one either is a member of the society, with full rights and privileges, or is denied membership altogether. In the cases of denial of membership, one may either undergo harsh slavery or be placed in "reservations" or "bantustans" outside the core of the society. As in the earlier discussion, these are ideal types, too. Political cultures *tend* in one direction or another. Moreover, they may be agglomerative only in some respects, demanding assimilation in some spheres of life but not in others.

The explanation for the different pattern of response comes from cultural fragment theory. A political cultural fragment is a part of a given culture which is detached from the whole and migrates to new soil. There the cultural fragment reproduces many of the beliefs and institutions that the country from which it came had at the time of fragmentation. Thus the Spanish fragments reproduced many of the corporate characteristics of Spanish political culture, and Anglo-Dutch-Liberian fragments reproduced the bourgeois ethos from which they came.

Once the cultural fragment is detached, however, it proceeds along its own historical path, different from the history of its place of origin. Thus an egalitarian or liberal group in Europe would continue to be buffeted and modified by other European political and cultural strains, from conservatism to socialism, in a familiar setting with long-standing historical roots. The detached liberal cultural fragment, on the other hand, is not exposed to these continual modifications in its own new soil and thus proceeds along a historical path that is less "tainted" than Europe's by the interplay of various ideas and social forces. Liberal fragments tend to have assimilative responses, feudal fragments agglomerative ones (Hartz, 1964, pp. 3–19, 49–62).

In a narrower sense, colonial *policies* may also exhibit agglomerative and assimilative tendencies. Rupert Emerson has noted that the French found "the true inspiration for their colonial activities in the doctrine of assimilation." A revolutionary decree of 1792 declared that all men living in the French colonies, without distinction of color, were French citizens with all the rights assured by the Constitution. On the other hand the tendency of the British had been "to assume that peoples are properly distinct and separate." The British were more likely to believe in different breeds of people, some who ruled and some who were ruled; the French were more ideologically committed to the oneness of humanity. Actual differences in the consequences of policies are more debatable. But the fact remains that these two tendencies did inspire different specific policies, with different rationales, enthusiasms, and objectives (Emerson, 1960, p. 69; see also pp. 69–82; Hodgkin, 1957, pp. 33–47).

One outstanding case of an agglomerative cultural response was the coming of Spain to the Americas. From the very beginning the Spanish "Great Tradition" sought to define clearly the superordinate and subordinate relations between Spaniards and Indians and to protect to some degree the rights of the latter while doing so. An *encomienda* was a distribution and entrusting of a community of Indians to a Spanish colonist. The colonist could exact various forms of tribute but was also obliged to protect the Indians and to induce their conversion to Christianity. A vast legal and ecclesiastical framework attempted to enforce those norms. Indians remained under the formal tutelage of the state. Many lived in their own towns, governed themselves locally, and preserved in many cases their customs and languages. Spaniards were legally forbidden from infringing upon the rights of the Indian towns and communities; even the Inquisition had no formal authority over them.

Free mulattoes and zambos (Negro-Indian mixture) also had defined rights and prohibitions. They were accepted into the militia, but they were not admitted into craft guilds. They could not appear in the streets after dark, carry arms of their own, or have Indian servants, and their women were forbidden by law to possess or wear luxurious clothes. They could not be forced to work in the mines provided they worked for recognized employers. Finally, the status of slaves in Latin America was far "milder" than in the United States, including better conditions of food, shelter, clothing, labor, and discipline, marriage of one's choice, stability of family life, appeal to the courts under certain circumstances, and manumission.

Although this was a fundamentally agglomerative response by the colonists, it was not a "pure" one. For example, there were considerable and persistent efforts to convert everyone to Christianity. Although allowances were made for religious syncretism with Indian and African beliefs, the thrust of religious policy and behavior was assimilative. Moreover, although legal efforts were made to slow down the rate of miscegenation, formal endogamy (the prevailing norm) was never totally successful because the legitimation of Christian marriages, regardless of ethnic source, was also valued and concubinage was widespread (Morse, 1964, pp. 132, 134, 136–37, 142–44, 147–49; Haring, 1963, pp. 38–68, 194–208; Elkins, 1963, pp. 52–80; Martinez-Alier, 1974).

The assimilative response, with its radical egalitarianism and its radical rejections, was the characteristic response of settlers from Great Britain and the Netherlands. Louis Hartz has discussed at length their ambivalent behavior toward Indians and Negroes in the United States: from segregation through slavery or reservations to the attempt to achieve full assimilation into the political community with speed and without variations. Australian settlers undertook punitive expeditions against the natives and sought to isolate them in order to prevent them from disturbing a homogeneous, egalitarian society. The "White Australia" policy was instituted toward Asian immigrants. In South Africa, where the excesses of apartheid highlight the situation, there is in fact a long history of sharp distinctions between members and nonmembers of the political system (Hartz, 1964, pp. 94–103, 205–15, 298–303).

The assimilative response was not limited to white peoples of northwestern Europe. J. Gus Liebenow has found another example of this pattern in Liberia. The standards of Southern American Negroes who settled in Liberia were those of the antebellum American South. These black freedmen sought to reproduce that culture in Liberia, including the institutions, values, dress, and speech, of the society that had rejected them. Black Americo-Liberians rejected only the situation that denied them full participation in American society. The cultural stress was on their being transplanted Americans. Their views of Africa and Africans were, in the main, those of nineteenth-century whites in the United States. As Liebenow has written, "The bonds of culture were stronger than the bonds of race, and the settlers clung tenaciously to the subtle differences that set them apart from the tribal 'savages' in their midst."

The Americo-Liberian community seized the land of the tribal African peoples and paid little or nothing for it. Wage differences were large; Americo-Liberian farmers had an unregulated power to "fine" their tribal employees; and the apprenticeship system under which young natives were assigned to Americo-Liberian families until they came of age almost reproduced the slavery bonds of the American South. The indigenous African was expected to work without pay in road construction and to pay taxes. Neither initial legislation nor the Constitution of 1847 recognized the tribal native as a citizen. Citizenship was only extended in 1904 to lay claim to the countryside in the face of European incursions. Some assimilation did take place—on Americo-Liberian terms: a tribal native had to speak English, convert to Protestant Christianity, give up polygamy, and accept the institutions and myths of the dominant community (Liebenow, 1969, pp. 15, 25–27).

Political Change within Agglomerative Political Culture

Agglomerative patterns can be generalized beyond cases of acculturation. In traditional agglomerative cultures, change is slow, but continuous, and proceeds according to the norms of sanskritization. Sanskritization in India is the process by which a low Hindu caste or tribal or other group changes its customs, ritual, ideology, and way of life in the direction of a higher and, frequently, "twice-born" caste. A claim to a higher rank order position is made. Then the political system came into play: the state is used as a legitimator of the newly sought and acquired caste rank within the traditional structure. After recognition is won from the state it is sought from the macrosociety and, last and most slowly, from the microsociety of the village. Under British rule the state performed many of these functions through the official ranking of castes in the census. In short, as the political sphere was differentiated from the others, it served as a channel of mobility within the traditional structure. Because the state was relatively autonomous from other value spheres, more rapid change in the political system was possible than in other spheres. Thus, while castes—through their associations—have taken to many typical forms of modern interest group behavior in the political system, traditional values still persist in other areas of social life, especially at the village level. A modern central state could arise in India even if consummatory values in other aspects of life still resisted it (Srinivas, 1966, pp. 5–7, 10–17, 23, 32–35; Rudolph and Rudolph, 1967, pp. 31–32, 63–64; Hardgrave, 1969, pp. 160–61, 264–65; Eisenstadt, 1966, pp. 125–26).

Although sanskritization has been stated by scholars of India as a culture-specific process, its characteristics are more broadly shared by other agglomerative cultures with hierarchical, or vertical, traditions of social organization. As a general process, sanskritization has eight major characteristics (Domínguez, 1972b, 35–38, pp. 212–21).

1. Groups and strata have well-defined traditional rights and prohibitions, at least at the local level, which encompass most or all aspects of social life.

2. Mobility that results from sanskritization is in no sense a "new" pattern of behavior dependent on modernization.

3. The political system makes the process possible and plays a crucial legitimating role.

4. The upwardly mobile take on the traditional perquisites of high-status groups in the system. The structure of the system remains unaffected. Change is positional, not structural.

5. Mobility occurs in response to local conditions, challenges, and opportunities. It is a local, not a national or systemwide, group or stratum that is positionally mobile. The positional change process is fragmented.

6. It has mixed goals. The claim to higher status relies on a restored recognition of alleged ancestral high status; as such it looks to the past. But in terms of actual social relations it seeks to adjust real relations with other groups; as such it looks to the present and the future.

7. The process is essentially an exchange of one kind of status for another. Though it may lead to more wealth and there may be some bribery, the process does not depend on the legal public purchase of higher status.

8. The behavior depends on organization. It is a group, not an individual, process; the society has established procedures that can be seized on to press the claims.

Colonial Latin America shares with India the first four characteristics with respect to mobility for Indians and blacks. Colonial Latin America also exhibits a good deal of the fragmentation of the process in the fifth characteristic, the adjustive goals of the sixth, and the procedural features of the eighth. Moreover, the fifth, sixth, and seventh apply virtually in full to processes that affected Indians only. The eighth factor—the legitimacy of organized caste or ethnic group behavior—remains a decisive difference between the two cultures. Since independence, social mobility through sanskritization faded away in Latin America. But mobility continued through miscegenation, and social stratification depended on a wider variety of factors than is normally the case elsewhere.

Charles Wagley has argued that social stratification in Latin America depends on ancestry, physical appearance, and sociocultural status. Change in income, occupation, customs, social status, and language can make it possible for an Indian to be considered a Ladino, or mestizo, and even for whole Indian communities to shift through time to being considered mestizo communities, provided they have changed their sociocultural status. The higher-ranked groups in Latin America are, in many ways, more modern than lower-ranked groups. Therefore, sanskritization and modernization in Latin America—but not necessarily in India—are closely related. But even in Latin America the primary motivation seems to be the emulation of the higher-ranked groups in the traditional system in order to obtain for oneself and one's community a higher rank in that system—not necessarily to change or to overthrow the system (Wagley, 1963, pp. 132–47, 1965, pp. 536–43; Adams, 1960, pp. 238–42, 253–56, 261–62).

Modernization within Political Cultures

Change within a political culture may also occur as a result of social mobilization. Social mobilization is the process by which major clusters of old social, economic, and psychological commitments are eroded or broken and people become available for new patterns of socialization and behavior. Social mobilization makes a people far more aware of government and politics. Therefore more aspects of the culture tend to become politicized (Deutsch, 1961, p. 494).

Within social mobilization, education seems to be the single most important factor. Almond and Verba have found nine instances of cross-national uniformity in their comparison of the political attitudes of the more educated with those of the less educated: the former are more aware of the impact of government than the latter; they also are more likely to follow politics and election campaigns, have more political information, have opinions on a wider range of political subjects, engage in more political discussions, feel free to discuss politics with a wider range of people, consider themselves more capable of influencing the government, join organizations and be active in them, and believe that other people are trustworthy and helpful. In short, social mobilization—and education in particular—is likely to be an important source of change in political cultures over time. Parochial and subject traits are likely to be eroded and more cognitive and positive affective and evaluative orientations toward the political system as a whole, inputs, outputs, and the self as a participant are likely to appear as social mobilization accelerates (Almond and Verba, 1965, pp. 315–21; Inkeles, 1969b, pp. 1131–41). Social mobilization is likely to be a major factor in creating a condition of unstable congruence between political culture and political structures. The central political values are likely to change, though slowly.

If processes of modernization continue for a very long time, the expected result is the emergence of a new cultural type: modern man. Alex Inkeles has defined nine traits, based on a survey of 6,000 young males in six countries (1966, pp. 141–44; 1969a, p. 210; 1969b, pp. 1122–23).

1. Modern man is ready for new political experiences and is more open to political innovation and change than his traditional ancestor.

2. He has a disposition to form or hold political opinions over a large number of problems and issues that arise not only in his immediate environment but also outside of it. He is also more politically tolerant. He is more aware of the diversity of attitudes and opinions around him. He can acknowledge those differences without fear and need not approach them autocratically or hierarchically. He neither automatically accepts the opinions of those above him nor automatically rejects the opinions of those below him in the power hierarchy.

3. He is oriented toward the present or the future, rather than the past. Time is a resource not to be wasted.

4. He is oriented toward and involved in political planning and organizing and believes in them as a way of handling life (see also Banfield, 1958, pp. 7–12).

5. He believes that man can learn to dominate his environment in order to advance his purposes and goals rather than being dominated by it.

6. He has more confidence that his world is calculable and that other people and political institutions around him can be expected to fulfill their obligations and responsibilities. Fate or whim do not dictate conduct.

7. He is more aware of the dignity of others and more disposed to show respect for others.

8. He has more faith in science and technology.

9. He believes in distributive justice, that is, that rewards should be made according to contribution, not according to whim or special properties of the person.

In sum, modern political man, according to Inkeles, is identified with and allegiant to leaders and organizations that transcend the parochial and primordial. He is interested in and informed about public affairs. He participates in politics. He is positively oriented and knowledgeable about recognizable political and governmental processes, and he accepts a rational structure of rules and regulations as desirable. Modern political man is politically active, involved, and rational.

There is, however, some question as to whether all of these traits identified by Inkeles have been observed empirically. Our discussion of political participation indicates that political parties and other modern political organizations continue to play a very important role, which may not be expected from Inkeles' second point. We have also suggested that political conflict does not seem to fade away with modernization. Inkeles' comments about political tolerance and respect for the dignity of others are not easily reconciled with much of the evidence we review in this essay. The discussion on political integration suggests that ascriptive criteria—the "special properties of the person"—continue to have a very important political function. Rewards are often sought not according to contribution but for one's ethnic, cultural, or religious group. Rather than having faith in science and technology, or being open to political innovation, people are often opposed to them.

Modern individuals do seem more aware of the impact of politics, more politically informed, more likely to try to influence politics, or more likely to join political organizations than their traditional ancestors. But the *direction* of this increased political sensitivity and activity is another matter. Modern individuals may be more likely to trust in and cooperate with other members of their cultural group—but in order to resist political participation by other groups and government-induced science and technology!

Strains of Change

Change in political culture arises out of instability between central values and structures. These macrochanges have important microimplications and roots, at the level of both the personality and the local community. Lucian Pye has hypothesized that the demands of acculturation in Burma produced a wide range of deep and disturbing reactions, which may have reduced political effectiveness. These demands are threats to the individual's sense of identity. They can impede the individual's competence in human and political relations, and the resulting fears of inadequacy produce anxieties that further paralyze action. Acculturation places serious strains on the personal identity of political leaders and, consequently, on their ability to forge and strengthen national identity. A corollary is a widespread ambivalence toward the traditional and the modern, a frequent shifting between available alternatives, and an unreliability and anxious unsteadiness in the conduct of national affairs (Pye, 1962, pp. 255–66, 287).

The broad outlines of these feelings of ambivalence have been confirmed by psychological research in other areas. Leonard Doob's research among the Luo, the Ganda, and the Zulu in Africa and among Jamaicans shows a similar pattern of ambivalence toward modernizing outsiders, of antagonism toward unchanging traditional leaders, but of continuity and syncretism in relating the old and the new. Nevertheless Doob hypothesizes that people whose core values are changing from old to new ways are likely to remain in a state of conflict concerning the advantages and disadvantages of both old and new beliefs and values (Doob, 1960, pp. 117–24, 150–57). Mannoni's (1964) research in Madagascar (see, however, Fanon's 1967 critique) reveals further the complex relation between personal and national identity. Mannoni found (as did Pye, 1962, in Burma) a sequence of first finding satisfaction in the warm dependency relationship with the colonizers, then experiencing the anxieties of acculturation and discrimination, and finally coming to resentment as a result of sensing a threat of abandonment by the colonizers. Therefore it is probable that the demands of acculturation will bring about crises of identity in the community and in the individuals, which will tend to reinforce each other. The resulting political change, then, will be primarily concerned with the need to establish or reestablish personal and national identity.

There is a second disruptive impact of acculturation on the individual and the community. The impact of the West disturbed the traditional social and moral order. Traditional methods of conflict resolution began to break down. The introduction of a Western court system provided an alternative to traditional means, especially for those who wished to circumvent the traditional administration of justice because they foresaw that it would render an unfavorable outcome. The result was an increase in the rate of litigation. The increase of litigation in Bengal and Java was of such magnitude that it cannot be explained simply as a result of improved statistical reporting. Litigation eroded traditional methods of conflict resolution based on arbitration and compromise. This erosion had a serious effect on patterns of land tenure, leading to a partial breakdown of communal landholding in favor of private property as Western legal concepts of ownership were introduced. The new legal methods, consequently, reduced predictability and increased disorder (Rudolph and Rudolph, 1967, pp. 258, 261–62; Pye, 1966, pp. 117–21).

The introduction of Western law, moreover, followed the syncretic pattern. In Asia colonial authorities stressed the majesty of the law and the need for everything to be followed in the proper, prescribed fashion. Therefore many came to believe that the power of the law lay in its ritual. The magical potency of the European's law lay entirely in carrying out the right incantations. The need to perform the ritual became associated with resisting all novel and unprecedented decisions. In Latin America, in contrast, there has been a tradition of more casual attitude toward human-made law. At its best the law provides a goal for which one strives. During colonial times local officials often failed or refused to apply royal decrees, without penalty. With the coming of independence the gap between hortatory constitutions and political reality continued to grow. Even in cases of "revolutionary constitutions," such as the Mexican Constitution of 1917, a considerable gap exists between the written word as a goal worth striving for and its implementation (Pye, 1966, pp. 123–24; Morse, 1964, pp. 175–76; Haring, 1963, pp. 57, 60–61, 64, 66, 100–8; Scott, 1964, pp. 17, 46, 263, 300). Therefore, even when modern legal concepts have been or are being borrowed, syncretic processes may cushion the impact of legal reform on the society.

A third strain is the uneven impact of the diffusion of Western cultural patterns. A gap tends to develop between the more Westernized sectors of the population and those that preserve the main elements of the traditional culture. "Westernization" is used consciously here: it means the syncretic adoption of Western central political values. In contrast, modernization (literacy, industrialization, etc.) could be adopted or promoted without surrendering central, traditional, non-Western values, as in Meiji Japan. The gap often coincides with the elite-mass gap. In open competitive systems, such as India, the syncretic fusion of tradition and modernity in the mass political culture, stressing primordial affiliations as a basis for political action, is likely to modify and perhaps displace the more rationalistic elite political culture. In single-party noncompetitive systems the elite will seek to introduce planned changes in the mass political culture (Weiner, 1971, pp. 241–44; Pye, 1966, pp. 17–18). Until either method of narrowing the elite-mass political cultural gap works, the uneven pattern of diffusion of Westernization is likely to add yet another burden to the processes of political change.

Political Planning, Change, and Culture

Many states, old and new, try to plan change in their country's political culture. The most dramatically successful case of planned political cultural change is probably the Soviet Union. The result of such change, according to Frederick Barghoorn, is a participatory subject culture: citizens must be obedient to their rulers' demands but they must also display enthusiasm and initiative in complying with their leaders' instructions. The method is well known. People are enrolled in "voluntary" organizations wherein they are mobilized for active and continuous participation in political activity. The citizenry is swept up in successive campaigns to achieve whatever goals have been given priority. A consummatory value pattern, linking all spheres of life, is thus established in a modernizing polity. This is what David Apter has called a mobilization system.

A mobilization system has a future-oriented ideology.[7] It stresses direct planning, the urgency of action, and the drastic restratification of society. "The atmosphere of mobilization," Apter has written, "is one of crisis and attack. Normalcy or passivity can even be regarded as dangerous. Individuals are called upon to declare themselves even in the most humble activities. There is no legitimate sphere of personal privacy, nor is privacy a recognized value. All social life becomes politicized" (Barghoorn, 1966, pp. 14–17; see also Apter, 1965, p. 360).

The mobilization system may have brought about some changes in the political culture of Cuba. Richard Fagen argues that important constants in the emerging revolutionary behavior pattern are cooperation, egalitarianism, sacrifice, service, hard work, self-improvement, obedience, and incorruptibility. Good citizens engage in preordained activities, struggle to raise production, and study in their spare time. Good citizens are also "responsive to calls from the authorities." The primary mechanism for effecting individual and cultural transformation is directed participation in revolutionary organizations and in revolutionary campaigns (such as campaigns against illiteracy and for the ten-million-ton sugar harvest in 1970). Although Fagen makes clear that there is still present "substantial fragility in new Cuban patterns of belief and behavior," his central hypothesis is that central political values are being transformed (Fagen, 1969, pp. 14, 157; see also pp. 10, 16, 153). The correspondence between the Soviet and Cuban cases suggests that successful planned change in political culture, indeed, aims at and leads to a participatory subject culture.

But planned political cultural change has more often failed. The explosion of one-party ideology in Africa appears to have served more as a relief for the elite from the strains of political reality than as an effective guide to planned political change. Aristide Zolberg has argued that ideological formulations have resembled a "religious ritual" in which political ideology "becomes an incantation which genuinely transforms reality, even if nothing else happens, by changing men's view of it." At one time or another such countries as Ghana,

Mali, and Indonesia were perceived to be mobilization systems as described here (Zolberg, 1966, p. 65; Apter, 1963, p. 93). The record of the late 1960s suggests a far more modest view of the accomplishments of mobilization systems. To date, other than in communist systems, planned political cultural change through mobilization has been rare and has fared poorly. Political culture tends to resist change and, when it changes, it does so more slowly than ideologues may desire.

Political Cultural Requisites for Modernizing Political Change

The most crucial political belief for political modernization is political identity: the extent to which individuals consider themselves unambiguous members of a given nation. The importance of having a political culture that provides a keen sense of national identity is one of the most pervasive themes of the literature (Verba, 1965, pp. 529–34; Deutsch, 1966, pp. 164–67; Rustow, 1967, p. 35).

A second requisite is the ability to trust one's fellow citizens and to work with them. The capacity to trust has been described in many forms. Daniel Lerner, for example, focused on *empathy* as the capacity to see oneself in the other fellow's situation. Beyond trust, the associational capabilities of a people are decisive. It is not enough to trust each other. They must be able to work together. As Banfield put it, "Successful self-government depends . . . upon the possibility of concerting the behavior of a large number of people in matters of public concern" (Banfield, 1958, pp. 7–8; Dahl, 1975; Lerner, 1958, pp. 49–50; Huntington, 1968, pp. 28–32). A political culture that has low associational capabilities is likely to have considerable difficulty in building a modern, complex, and adaptable political system.

Thirdly, individuals must believe that they can have an impact on politics and government, that they can and should participate actively to do so, and that the output of government—as a result of their and other people's inputs—has relevance for their own lives. A modern political system requires the active legitimation of its acts by its citizens and the ability to reach them authoritatively and with significant impact. Simply put, modern governments require a political culture that, in fact, allows them to govern (Verba, 1965, pp. 537–43; Almond and Verba, 1965, pp. 337–43).

There can be considerable political change in political cultures that do not meet these requisites. However, it is unlikely that one could call that kind of change "modernization" or "development." Not all political change is "forward looking," not all political cultures welcome change, and certainly not all of them welcome modernizing political change. The hypotheses that have been explored here concerning the relationship between political change and political culture should suggest, in fact, that modernizing political change is a difficult business and, moreover, rare.

IV. POLITICAL PARTICIPATION

Nature of Political Participation

Political participation may be defined in various ways.[8] The term is here used to refer to the activity of private citizens designed to influence government decision-making. On the one hand this definition limits attention to activity rather than attitudes and to the behavior of private citizens rather than of those who are professionally and continuously involved in public affairs. On the other hand it also includes all efforts to influence government decision-making, legal or illegal, violent or peaceful, successful or unsuccessful. Moreover it also includes not only activity designed by the actor him or herself to influence governmental decision-making but also activity designed by someone other than the actor to influence governmental decision-making. The former may be termed *autonomous* participation, the latter *mobilized* participation. The forms that political participation may take vary from one society to another, but typically they include voting and other electoral activity, collective lobbying efforts to affect governmental decisions, organizational activity, particularized contacting, and anomic or violent action. Most political participation is a group activity and typically is organized on the basis of social class, interest group, communal group, neighborhood, face-to-face patron-client group or faction, and political party. The overall levels of political participation obviously vary greatly from one society to another and change over time within a particular society.

Why Socioeconomic Modernization Increases Participation

"Traditional society," declared Daniel Lerner in 1958, "is non-participant. . . . Modern society is participant." In the years since, it has become commonly accepted that the principal political difference between traditional and modern societies concerns the scope and intensity of political participation. In wealthier and more industrialized, urbanized, complex societies, more people become involved in politics in more ways than they do in less developed, agricultural, rural, more primitive economic and social systems. "It comes as no surprise," commented one set of authors a decade after Lerner, "to learn that a nation's level of political participation co-varies with its level of economic development" (Nie, Powell, and Prewitt, 1969). The cross-national and longitudinal evidence to support this proposition is overwhelming; it ranges from the demonstration of apparently global relationships between the distribution of employment in the primary, secondary, and tertiary sectors and the levels of political mobilization to the discovery that levels of voting participation among the fifty states "are a function of levels of economic development" (Milbrath, 1965; Dye, 1966). Increases in socioeconomic modernity and the expansion of political participation seemingly march hand in hand through history. The higher the level of socioeconomic development in a society, the higher the level of its political participation and, presumably, the higher the ratio of autonomous participation to mobilized participation.

Why should there be this relationship between socioeconomic development and political participation? At a broad level several links are apparent.

1. Within a society levels of political participation tend to vary with socioeconomic status. Those who have more education and income and are in high-status occupations usually are more participant than those who are poor, uneducated, and in low-status occupations. Economic development expands the proportion of higher-status roles in a society: more people become literate, educated, better off financially, and engaged in middle-class occupations. These factors obviously correlate very strongly with each other. But studies indicate that each also tends to have an independent effect of varying strength in different societies on political participation. Income appears to be strongly related to political participation and education perhaps even more so. In his six-nation study, for instance, Inkeles found education to have a consistently high relation to active citizenship when other variables, such as factory experience, rural or urban origin, media consumption, and length of urban residence, were held constant. Length of factory experience also had a consistent, if less strong, relation to active citizenship in all six countries. On the average each additional year of education added about 2.5 points to an individual's active participation score (rated from 0 to 100), while each additional year of factory work added about 1.25 points. Similarly, Almond and Verba concluded that "among the demographic variables usually investigated—sex, place of residence, occupation, income, age, and so on—none compares with the educational variable in the extent to which it seems to determine political attitudes." Education and other status variables are, however, more clearly related to some forms of political participation than to others. In the Verba-Nie five-nation study, for instance, education had a strong relation with both campaign activity and communal activity, a weak relation with voting, and virtually no relation with particularized contacting (Inkeles, 1969b, Almond and Verba, 1965; Verba, Nie, and Kim, 1971).

Why do status variables tend to produce greater political participation? The overwhelming evidence from a variety of studies indicates that high status is associated with feelings of political efficacy and competence and that those who feel politically efficacious are much more likely to participate in politics than those who do not. The status variables, in short, are related to participation through attitudinal variables. Indeed, high-status individuals who do not feel politically efficacious do not participate significantly more in politics than similarly inefficacious low-status individuals. In addition, higher-status people, particularly more highly educated individuals, are more likely than lower-status people to feel that it is the duty of a citizen to participate in politics, and people who have this sense of duty do, in fact, participate more (Dahl, 1961; Milbrath, 1965).

2. Socioeconomic development also promotes political participation because it leads to a multiplication of organizations and associations and the involvement of larger numbers of people in such groups. Business organizations, farmer associations, labor unions, community organizations as well as cultural, recreational, and even religious organizations are more characteristic of more highly developed societies. Individuals who belong to and participate actively in such organizations are much more likely also to participate in politics than individuals who do not belong to such organizations. Indeed, an increasing amount of evidence has suggested that organizational involvement may be a more important factor than socioeconomic status in explaining differences in political participation. A careful reanalysis of the Almond-Verba data for the United States, Great Britain, Germany, Italy, and Mexico showed that while socioeconomic status explained roughly 10 percent of the variance in participation, organizational involvement explained roughly 25 percent of that variance. Other studies have suggested similar conclusions (Nie, Powell, Prewitt, 1969; Erbe, 1964; Lipset, 1960).

The increased participation of individuals in organized groups is, by and large, a function of economic development. How does economic development increase organizational involvement? There would appear to be two distinct routes: one via socioeconomic participation and one more directly via group consciousness.

In most countries people with higher education, income, and occupational status tend to be more involved in organizations than people less well endowed with these attributes. In some countries, however, this relationship is much more striking than it is in others. This is particularly the case in the United States. In 1955, 82 percent of those Americans in the highest of five socioeconomic classes belonged to organizations as compared with only 8 percent of those in the lowest class. Erbe's study of three Iowa communities found social status and organizational involvement to be more closely related to each other than either was to political participation (Lipset, 1960; Erbe, 1964; Orum, 1966). Organizational activity varies directly with education in the United States but not in Norway. More generally, Nie and his associates found the following product-moment correlation coefficients between social status and organizational involvement in their five countries (Rokkan, 1970; Nie, Powell, and Prewitt, 1969).

United States	.435
United Kingdom	.313
Italy	.304
Mexico	.227
Germany	.213

Substantial differences thus exist among societies in the degree of association between social status and organizational involvement. A close relationship between organizational involvement and social status tends to reinforce class distinctions in participation. In societies in which another factor may be responsible for organizational involvement, that variable may tend to counterbalance the effects of social status on political participation. Class or group consciousness may produce high levels of organizational involvement and of political participation. Thus, the less rigid the class structure of a society, the more important are class and status variables in explaining differences in participation. The more rigid the class structure of a society and hence the greater the class or group consciousness of the lower-status population, the less the extent to which political participation tends to be related to socioeconomic status, provided that low-status group participation is not held down by either political repression or a "negative" self-image by the group that it "should not" participate in politics. Class rigidity thus promotes group consciousness and political participation only in societies in which other conditions permit political activity by low-status groups.

Organizational involvement leads to political participation in ways rather different from the ways in which socioeconomic status does. Social status, as we have indicated, promotes participation primarily through changes in attitudes about politics. Organizational involvement, on the other hand, tends to produce increased participation without any significant change in attitudes. The reanalysis of the Almond-Verba data showed that 60 percent of the political participation resulting from social status was by way of changes in attitudes: increased sense of duty to participate, more political information, greater perceived impact of government on individual interests, greater political efficacy, more political attentiveness. In contrast, 60 percent of the political participation resulting from organizational involvement was the product of a direct relationship without intervention of the attitude variables (Nie, Powell, and Prewitt, 1969). In somewhat similar fashion, the mobilization of Venezuelan peasants into unions and political parties occurred before the peasants had developed feelings of political efficacy. This mobilization produced high rates of political participation, which in turn led the peasants to develop feelings of political efficacy (Mathiason and Powell, 1972). Similarly, migrants to Mexico City were much more involved in "community-based political activity" and voted more often than native-born residents, although the latter scored much higher on cognitive involvement in the political process. The behavioral participation of the migrants in politics was "largely independent of high levels of political information, supportive psychological orientations or other kinds of traits or resources commonly assumed to be requisites for sustained political participation" (Cornelius, 1972). The involvement of low-status people in organizations is thus likely to be the product of the development of a distinct sense of group consciousness. The group may be a class, a communal group, or a neighborhood. The more intense the identification of the individual with the group, the more likely he or she is to be organizationally involved and politically participant.

3. Economic and social modernization produces tensions and strains among social groups, new groups emerge, established groups are threatened, low-status groups seize opportunities to improve their lot. As a result conflicts multiply between social classes, regions, and communal groups. Social conflict intensifies and, in some cases, virtually creates group consciousness, which in turn leads to collective action by the group to develop and protect its claims vis-a-vis other groups. The group, in short, is forced to turn to politics.

Experiences involving intense or sustained conflict or challenges to the group's existence thus may intensify group identification and give rise to sustained patterns of political participation. Recent high voting rates in West Virginia, for instance, have been explained by the extent to which, from the 1890s through the 1920s, "the state was an open battleground in the effort to unionize its miners. Contrary to what was taking place in other border and southern states, in West Virginia that group which was least likely to participate in politics—the lower socioeconomic status group, the 'working man'—was being motivated and 'organized' to participate" (Johnson, 1971). Similarly, the disposition of urban migrants in Mexico City to work collectively "is largely a product of urban socialization experiences, particularly collective politicizing experiences such as land invasions, confrontation with the police, government agencies, landowners, or other authority figures, and other types of experiences culminating in 'negative sanctions' " (Cornelius, 1972). Such collective experiences that generate group consciousness may stimulate a political culture or style favorable to participation, which will continue beyond the generation that underwent the experience.

In other circumstances, sustained high-level group identification and political participation may also require sustained external conflict. Squatters in new urban settlements, for instance, often find that they have to engage in collective political action to seize land, to defend their settlement against eviction, or to secure elementary city services. Once the community has been securely established, however, the need for and salience of collective political action declines, and both the squatters and their children may instead pursue goals, such as improvement of their residences or higher-paying jobs, which require individual efforts at socioeconomic mobility. Thus, Mexico City migrants from rural areas were more politically active than both natives generally and their own sons specifically, despite the fact that the two latter groups had more of the attitudinal and psychological orientations normally associated with political participation (Cornelius, 1972). Among the migrants, however, "continued perceptions of external threat ('out-group hostility')" to the survival of the community or the security of individual land tenure produced high levels of community identification and participation. Similarly, in American cities the greater the conflict among ethnic groups, the higher the rates of political participation by the members of those groups (Lane, 1959).

4. Economic development in part requires and in part produces a notable expansion of the functions of government. While the scope of governmental activity clearly is influenced by the political values and ideologies dominant in the society, it is even more highly influenced by the level of economic development of the society. Highly industrialized societies run by governments devoted to free-enterprise capitalism typically have more highly socialized economies than agrarian societies run by committed socialists. The former simply require more governmental promotional, regulatory, and redistributional activity. The more that governmental actions affect groups within society, however, the more those groups see the relevance of government to their own ends and the more active they become in their efforts to influence governmental decision-making. Groups often become politically active in order to stop government from making increasing demands on them in the form of taxes, services, and regulations.

5. Socioeconomic modernization normally takes place in the context of national development. The nation-state is the vehicle of socioeconomic modernization. Consequently, the relationship between the individual and the nation-state becomes critical for him and his identity with the state tends to override his other loyalties. That identity is theoretically expressed in the concept of citizenship, which presumably overrides distinctions of social class and communal group and which furnishes the basis for mass political participation. All citizens are equal before the state; all have certain minimal equal rights and responsibilities to participate in the state. Socioeconomic modernization thus implies a political culture and outlook that, in some measure, legitimizes and hence facilitates political participation. And this is the case in both democratic and communist societies.

Limits to the Development-Participation Relationship

Given the pronouncements of social scientists, the weight of the statistical evidence, and these seemingly persuasive causal relationships, one might well expect a more or less one-to-one relationship between the level of socioeconomic modernity in a society and its level of political participation. In fact, however, this is far from the case. While there is a general tendency for many forms of national political participation to increase with economic development, this is by no means a universal phenomenon. Other things being equal, economic development tends to enhance political participation. But other things are rarely equal, and many factors that are not necessarily shaped by economic development in themselves shape political participation. Judgments as to the overall level of political participation in societies are virtually impossible to make. When one does look, however, at particular forms of participation, especially voting participation, one can see variations in levels which have no discernible positive relationships to socioeconomic development.

1. Socioeconomic modernization normally increases irreversibly, if irregularly, with time. In many societies, however, levels of political participation fluctuate quite widely over brief periods of time. There may be sudden expansions ("participation explosions") and equally well marked declines in participation. For almost forty years, for instance, beginning in the 1890s, voting participation rates in the United States declined markedly, although this was also a period of significant economic and particularly industrial development. In Turkey and Colombia in the years after World War II there were periods of substantial decrease in voting participation. In Kenya, Uganda, and other African states political participation levels apparently peaked in the years immediately before and after independence, which were then followed by years of significant "departicipation" (Bienen, 1974; Kasfir, 1972). Similarly, the participation levels of particular groups in the society may vary over time with apparently little relation to levels of socioeconomic modernization. Changes at both the group and the society levels are sufficiently sustained so as not to be written off as simply temporary aberrations from the socioeconomic modernization model.

2. Substantial differences in political participation exist among societies which do not correspond with differences in their levels of socioeconomic development. The poor communist societies in Asia (particularly China and North Vietnam) clearly have had extraordinarily high levels of mobilized participation. Many societies that are much less economically developed than the United States have substantially higher rates of voting participation.

3. Differences in participation rates among areas within societies do not necessarily correspond with differences in socioeconomic modernization. In Turkey, India, and elsewhere voting participation is significantly higher in less developed parts of the country than in the more developed parts. Even in the United States, where there is a strong correlation among the states between voting turnout and economic development, a state like West Virginia may deviate significantly from this pattern and have a high level of turnout despite its relatively low level of economic development.

What are the reasons for these variations from the otherwise prevailing relationship between modernity and participation?

First, many of those factors related to socioeconomic modernization or affected by it which in turn promote political participation may themselves have other causes in addition to the process of socioeconomic modernization. Group conflict and consciousness, organizational involvement, and the expansion of governmental activities tend to be promoted by the processes of economic development. But they may also result from migration, exploitation, war, aggression, political leadership, ideological and religious differences, which in turn can occur quite independently of economic development. The one factor promoting political participation which appears unlikely to vary independently of socioeconomic modernization is the status structure in society. As societies become more developed, however, variations in political participation may be shaped less by status structure than by political and organizational factors that are not necessarily determined by the level of economic development.

Second, some aspects of socioeconomic modernization may have little direct impact themselves on political participation. This is most notably the case with respect to urbanization. Interestingly enough, Lerner, in his work in the late 1950s, assigned a primary role to urbanization. He hypothesized and his data seemed to support the proposition that urbanization led to literacy, which led to media consumption, which in turn was related to political participation. Subsequently other scholars analyzed these presumed causal relationships and came up with somewhat different patterns, but they still attributed a major primary role to urbanization. (Alker, 1966, for instance, tended to downgrade the role of media consumption and instead stressed a more direct line from urbanization to literacy to participation. Tanter, 1967, argued that the causal path was from urbanization to literacy to media consumption and then from both literacy and media consumption to participation.) In fact, however, there does not appear to be any consistent global difference in the levels of rural and urban political participation. In some societies voting rates are higher in the rural areas; in other societies in the urban areas. Thirty-five years ago Herbert Tingsten made this point quite explicitly in his pioneering work on political behavior. He noted that urban voting rates seemed to be higher than rural rates in Sweden, Norway, Iceland, Finland, Austria, and Germany but that rural rates were higher than urban rates in Bulgaria and Switzerland, while in France, Denmark, and Poland the results were mixed or showed no differences. He thus concluded that while in several countries the urban population was "politically the more active," it was, nonetheless, a fact that "no general 'rule' can be formulated for electoral participation in town and country" (Tingsten, 1963).

Later studies have validated this proposition. In many countries there is no real difference between urban and rural voting participation rates; in some countries, such as France and Japan, rural voting rates are higher than urban ones (Tarrow, 1971; Milbrath, 1965). In those countries in which urban rates are higher, the apparent direct relationship is spurious, a result of differences in education and occupation. When these factors are held constant, locality size and length of urban residence appear to have no significant independent effect on political participation. In his comparative analysis of the factors responsible for "active citizenship" in six countries, Inkeles found a mild relationship between length of urban residence and active citizenship in Argentina, Chile, and Nigeria but much weaker relationships in India and East Pakistan. Once education and factory experience were controlled for, however, these relationships disappeared and, indeed, in Argentina and Chile became mildly negative (Inkeles, 1969b). Urbanism thus had no independent effect on active citizenship. In another study of India it was again found that, when education was controlled for, "those who live in cities vote *slightly* less frequently than those who live in rural areas" (Goel, 1970). In their reanalysis of the Almond-Verba data for the United States, United Kingdom, Germany, Italy, and Mexico, Nie and his associates came to a similar conclusion. Urbanization, in terms of size of place of residence, had no independent impact on overall political participation and in only one marginal instance (the United States) on national political participation. On the other hand, there were consistent weak negative correlations between size of locality and efforts to influence local governmental decisions. In no instance, however, did urbanization explain more than 2 percent of the variance in participation (Nie, Powell, and Prewitt, 1969). In short, cases in which urban political participation is higher than rural political participation are caused by differences in social status, education, and occupation.

In terms of aggregate voting rates, much of the difference between urban and rural residence has been due to the difference between the voting rates of women. Over time, as occurred historically in Europe and is occurring at the present time in India, the difference between rural and urban voting turnout tends to decline as the voting rates of rural women begin to approximate those of urban women (Tingsten, 1963; Field, 1971).

The third reason for variations from the prevailing relationship between modernity and participation is that there are some ways in which socioeconomic modernization may tend to reduce political participation. The expansion of the scope of governmental activity, for instance, may have negative as well as positive consequences for the levels of political participation. People are likely to perceive government as more relevant to their own concerns, but this need not be accompanied by increases in their feelings of political efficacy. The increasing concentration of governmental activities at the national level and away from the local level may well have just the reverse effect. So also may increased specialization in governmental activities, the professionalization of governmental personnel, and the increase in the proportion of complex and technical programs and policies within the total assortment of government activities. In traditional society governmental decisions are more likely to deal with individual benefits or particularistic issues. Socioeconomic modernization is likely to promote a relative decline of particularistic decision-making, a marked expansion of more generalized decision-making dealing with collective benefits, and the development of more routinized procedures for handling individual needs. The incentives for personal contacting and small-group lobbying, particularly by low-status individuals and groups, may consequently be reduced. Modernization may also increase the social distance between governmental officials and low-status citizens. The peasant who could appeal to and even negotiate with the village chief or local landlord may be totally incapable of dealing with the urban-trained agrarian reform official sent out from the capital city.

The purpose of political participation is to affect governmental decision-making. Consequently such activity has to be directed at and have an impact on the loci where decisions are made. In a traditional society most decisions affecting villagers' lives presumably were made by the village chief and council, who were therefore the targets of whatever political participation the villagers engaged in. As society becomes more modern, however, an increasing proportion of the governmental decision-making that affects the villagers takes place not at the village level but at the national level. This shift in the locus of decision-making is likely to occur much more rapidly than the shift in the locus of political action by the villagers. Thus, in a traditional society perhaps 90 percent of the governmental decisions affecting a villager are made at the village level and 10 percent at the national level. As the society modernizes this distribution may rapidly approach 50–50. In all likelihood, however, the bulk of the political participation of the villager, say 80 percent, still is focused at the village level. The amount of national governmental decision-making affecting society increases at a faster rate than the amount of political participation affecting national government. The ratio of political activity by individuals to governmental decisions affecting them actually goes down. In addition, of course, the inhabitants of any one village can expect to have only marginal influence on decisions that affect many villages. Hence, while the total amount of political participation may increase in society, so also may the feelings of alienation and political inefficacy.

Socioeconomic modernization also tends to increase the functional specificity of relationships and organizations, including those related to politics. In a traditional agrarian society the elite and mass are presumably related to each other through diffuse ties, which encompass economic, social, religious, and political relationships. This multifunctionality of relationships makes it easier for the landlord or village chief to mobilize his followers for political purposes. In a modern society political organizers attempt to create "parties of integration," designed to provide comparable diffuse multifunctional relationships and also high levels of political participation. In fact, in elections in Turkey, India, Thailand, and elsewhere the highest voting turnouts are precisely in those traditional rural areas where the local leaders can capitalize on their social prestige and cultural superiority and on economic incentives and implicit or explicit coercion to mobilize their supporters to the polls. Similarly, modern parties of integration, combining social, cultural, and welfare functions with purely political ones, tend to be very successful in producing substantial voting turnouts. Political organizations and leaders that are only political, in contrast, are not likely to produce comparable rates of participation. In short, organizational multifunctionality correlates positively with political participation. The overall tendency in modernizing societies, however, is toward more specific functional relationships. To the extent that this occurs in politics, that is, to the extent that organs of political participation become distinct and specialized purely in political participation, they will become less successful at it. The expansion of political participation leads, paradoxically, to the development of a professional political class, which, by segregating off political relationships from other relationships, tends to reduce or to limit political participation.

Economic development also tends to multiply the opportunities for individual social and economic mobility, both horizontal and vertical. In the short run individual social mobility is likely to decrease political participation. If individuals can achieve their goals by moving to the city, shifting to higher-status employment, or improving their economic well-being, these may in some measure be a substitute for political participation. More generally, in Hirschman's terms, the multiplication of the opportunities for and incentives to "exit" reduces the probability that people will resort to "voice" (Hirschman, 1970). Confronted with increasing economic uncertainty and declining standard of living, a peasant is more likely to move to the city than to engage in corrective political action, provided the costs of migration are bearable. Economic development—communications networks, roads, bus lines, urban job opportunities—reduces the uncertainties and costs of migration and hence keeps down the level of rural political participation. Where migration is impossible or difficult, peasants are more likely to resort to politics, despite its uncertainties and risks. In a similar fashion, confronted with a neighborhood problem in a central city, whites, who have a choice between migration and political action, are likely to choose the former while blacks, for whom migration is presumably a much less real option, are more likely to resort to politics (Orbell and Uno, 1972).

The fact that urban political participation rates are not, by and large, higher than rural rates, once education and occupation are controlled for, would suggest that there may be compensating features in the urban environment which act to keep participation down despite the presumably more intense stimuli from mass media and interpersonal contacts. The broader opportunities for social and economic mobility will increase political participation in the long run but may tend to reduce it in the short run. Economic development thus may produce greater pressures and stimuli to participate in politics but may also, other things being equal, lessen the incentive to do so by opening up more appealing opportunities to participate in other things.

The Forms and Bases of Participation

As societies modernize, changes presumably take place not only in the levels of participation but also in its forms and bases. In a traditional society electoral, lobbying, and organizational activity at the national level are presumably rather limited. Governmental decisions at all levels tend to deal with individual benefits and particularistic issues. Contacting activities are, consequently, of critical importance for both higher and lower status individuals. The development of a more complex society tends to involve the creation of a bureaucracy and routinized procedures for handling many of these issues and hence the creation of obstacles to contacting by lower-status individuals. At the same time decision-making tends to become more generalized, dealing with collective benefits and costs, which facilitates action by those higher-status individuals and highly conscious groups capable of engaging in concerted lobbying efforts to achieve their objectives.

A simple theory of political modernization would also suggest a shift in relative importance from more traditional bases of participation (patron-client and communal group) to more modern ones (class, interest group, party). In fact, however, modernization does not necessarily decrease the role of patron-client relationships and communal groups. Instead it is more likely to supplement these with other bases. In a more modern society, in short, the bases of participation will be more complex and diverse than they are in traditional society.

Patron-client relations provide a means for the vertical mobilization of lower-status individuals by the established elites in traditional societies.[9] In purely traditional societies patron-client relations may exist with little overt political content. The introduction of competitive elections gives the client one additional resource—the vote—which he can exchange with his patron for other benefits. Patron-client politics frequently can lead to high levels of voting participation in rural areas. It is a continuingly important feature of politics in India, the Philippines, Turkey, and Colombia. In these countries patron-client groups often form the basic local unit of party politics, with one leading local figure lining up with one party and mobilizing his or her followers for that purpose while rival local leaders work through other parties.

Migration to the cities removes potential clients from the patron-client system. However, it may also reinforce the stability of that system in the countryside by draining off surplus population, which might otherwise lead to class and revolutionary politics, and it can also lead to the introduction of patron-client patterns into the urban environment. This is especially likely to be the case where rural elites also move into the city, as has been noted in Brazil (Reis, 1974). Beyond that, the relation between the urban migrant and urban *cacique*, or ward boss, often resembles that of the rural patron-client. There are, however, two differences: (1) the urban *cacique*-client relationship is more explicitly and primarily political in character and (2) the status differences between *cacique* and client are likely to be less than between rural patron and client.

In the urban areas patron-client relations may gradually lose their predominantly personalistic character and evolve into more institutionalized machine politics. Even in societies at high levels of development, however, the under-lying cliental patterns may remain. The Liberal Democratic party in Japan, for instance, has maintained its voting strength, despite the migration of its rural constituents into the cities, by developing local associations (*koenkai*) around individual leaders which essentially involve complex patron-client ex-changes. Some of these associations have twenty to thirty thousand members, and the entire system is appropriately called one of "organizational clientelism" (Watanuki, 1974).

In a traditional society political participation at the national level is limited to members of the upper class, and consequently the units of participation are primarily intraclass cliques supplemented in some measure by patron-client groupings. As the scope of participation broadens, however, the opportunities for class and interest-group participation multiply in both the rural and urban areas. In some circumstances peasants may be mobilized on a horizontal or class basis for electoral or lobbying purposes. Rural class-based politics, how-ever, is often likely to involve violence and to take revolutionary forms. In urban areas class-based politics is more typical of industrial workers and white-collar middle-class groups than of the poorest urban dwellers, who, if organized at all, are likely to be organized on a neighborhood basis. In general, class con-sciousness is rare among all low-income groups.

Neighborhood participation can be based on either the rural village or the urban ward or barrio. In cities the neighborhood is probably more important for political organization than any other base. This is particularly true for new settlements within the city. Many of the most important services that city gov-ernment provides are distributed on a geographical basis: water supply, sewage disposal, police and fire protection. Neighborhoods organize to demand these services. New settlements may also have to establish their collective or individual rights to land and to legal recognition. In rural areas the village may be a base for political organization, but, except in some circumstances (such as central Italy), the competition among villages is less intense than that among urban barrios. By and large a higher percentage of urban barrios than of rural vil-lagers is organized for political demand-making.

Socioeconomic change more often increases than reduces communal group consciousness, political activity, and intergroup violence. The extent to which communal groups become the base for political participation depends, in large part, on the relations among the groups. These, in turn, reflect the number, size, location, and power of the groups. Different patterns of communal par-ticipation reflect the extent to which:

1. there is a large number of small communal groups in the society or a small number of larger ones;

2. different groups have different sources of power (education, wealth, coer-cion, external affiliations, organization);

3. the government is controlled by a majority, plurality, or minority communal group;

4. communal groups are geographically segregated in different regions or between rural and urban areas or are intermixed in close proximity;

5. some groups that have been viewed as "backward" or "traditional" improve their socioeconomic status and threaten to produce a "status reversal" vis-à-vis traditionally dominant groups. (See below, Section VI, "Political Integration.")

In general it would appear that the structuring of politics on communal bases and the mobilization of people through communal appeals tend to produce higher levels of political participation than the structuring of politics in terms of patron-client relations, class, or neighborhood. Structuring politics on communal bases, of course, can also lead to a breakdown of cooperative relations among communal groups, increased communal hostility and antagonism, communal violence, and potentially serious threats to national integration. Hence governments may attempt to reduce both political participation and communal group hostility because of the close relationship between the two.

Modernization presumably does lead to increased socioeconomic differentiation within a communal group (Rudolph and Rudolph, 1967). But these tendencies have often been exaggerated. The members of a communal group who significantly improve their socioeconomic status above the average levels of the group may cease to identify primarily with the group and decrease their interactions with group members. To the extent that they do divorce themselves from the group, they also deprive the group of more sophisticated and probably more moderate leadership and intensify the homogeneity of those who continue to identify with the group. In this instance individual socioeconomic mobility by some may reinforce tendencies toward collective political action by others.

The political party is the distinctive organization of modern, participant politics (Huntington, 1968). It is unknown in societies with low levels of political participation, and it first emerged as a continuing feature of politics with the broadening of political participation in the United States in the late eighteenth and early nineteenth centuries. In some instances, as with the Leninist party of professional revolutionaries, the political party is a primary base of political identification and action. More frequently the party is a supplementary overlay that serves as a vehicle of political expression for some other type of group or as a way of coordinating and integrating the political activities of two or more groups. Other bases of political organization typically reflect more specialized motives and interests on the part of their members. The party, in some measure, is often different because it attempts to unite together for particular political objectives mobilized and autonomous participants with a variety of different motives. In general the greater the extent to which parties are tied in closely with traditional patron-client groupings, communal groups, or occupation-class groups like peasant syndicates and labor unions, the more important role they tend to play in fostering political participation. The level of participation and to some extent its forms will be set by the extent to which the cleavages between two or more bases of participation coincide and thus appeals to one base are reinforced by appeals to other bases.

V. POLITICAL INSTITUTIONS

Political Institutions and Socioeconomic Modernization

Politics—that is, deciding who gets what, when, and how for a society—often, but not always, takes place through formal organizations and procedures. To the extent that these organizations and procedures become stable, recurring, and valued patterns of behavior, they become political institutions. The development and decay of its political institutions are clearly central themes in the evolution of any society. It was, indeed, once argued that political development itself should be defined as political institutionalization. On subsequent reflection, however, there did not seem to be much to be gained by trying to identify one rather diffuse, controversial, and value-laden concept (like political development) with a somewhat more specific, analytical, and value-free concept (like institutionalization). (See Huntington, 1965, 1971a.)

In analyzing the relations between political institutions and socioeconomic modernization, three dimensions of the former are of critical importance.

1. The level of institutionalization of the organizations and procedures. This can be measured in terms of their adaptability, autonomy, complexity, and coherence (Huntington, 1968). Levels of institutionalization obviously vary from one organization or procedure to another and from one political system to another. They also vary from time to time for any one organization, procedure, or political system; institutional development can occur and so can institutional decay.

2. The degree of modernity or tradition of the organization, procedure, or political system. Modern political systems differ from traditional ones in their (a) bases of legitimacy and nature of governing authority, (b) scope and nature of arrangements for political participation (input institutions), and (c) scope and complexity of bureaucracy (output institutions).

3. The extent to which the institutions provide for concentration or pluralism in the distribution of power. Traditional political systems differ from modern systems in the amount of power in the system; in each, however, the power that exists can be concentrated or dispersed. A democratic political system is one in which there is a large amount of power (broad participation in politics) and in which power is also dispersed rather than concentrated.

The processes of socioeconomic modernization presumably have some impact on each of these three dimensions of political institutions. The anti-institutional behavioral stress in political science plus the widespread implicit acceptance in social science of Marxist assumptions about the primacy of economics have, indeed, combined to focus extensive scholarly attention on how socioeconomic modernization affects political institutions. Conversely, however, political institutions themselves also limit and channel subsequent political change and the patterns of socioeconomic development. In a small effort to redress the balance between political institutions as a dependent and independent variable, the next section will deal in somewhat summary fashion with the implications of socioeconomic modernization for political institutions, while the following two sections will attempt to highlight the ways in which political institutions may affect subsequent political change and economic development.

The Implication of Modernization for Political Institutions

In Part I of this essay a distinction was made between the derivative and functional approaches to political development. The former views political development as the political component of the overall process of societal change called modernization. The functional approach, in contrast, views political development as the emergence of those political institutions and practices that best meet the needs of modern society. As was argued at that point, however, the derivative approach often involves a somewhat paradoxical and perhaps misleading use of the term "political development." For in actual practice the only assertion that can conclusively be made about the political effects of modernization is that it will ultimately either destroy the traditional political institutions in the society or induce drastic changes in them so as to adapt them to the broader and more diversified demands of modern society. In fact, modernization often expands political participation more rapidly than it leads to the development of modern participatory political institutions. This produces a praetorian condition of disorder, violence, and the lack of legitimate political procedures for resolving political issues. Political instability is the likely political fruit of socioeconomic modernization. (See Huntington, 1968.)

In some instances, however, modernization can lead to the creation of modern political institutions by the adaptation of traditional ones or the generation of new institutions out of a revolutionary process. In general the emergence of a modern society functionally requires the rationalization of authority, the expansion of political participation, and the differentiation of structures. In institutional terms this means the development of (a) governing institutions that embody new sources of legitimacy, (b) participatory institutions that provide channels for relating the newly participant groups to the governing institutions, and (c) bureaucratic institutions that provide structures for the discharge of those administrative functions that modern society requires of its political system.

Governing Institutions and Bases of Legitimacy

The governing institutions of traditional societies typically involve an emperor or king assisted by one or more councils composed of bureaucrats or aristocrats. The legitimacy of such institutions is based on prescription, religion, and heredity. As will be noted below, conciliar institutions in traditional systems can evolve into modern representative parliaments. Those monarchies that survive the evolution from traditional to modern society do so only by surrendering their power to other institutions whose authority is compatible with modern concepts of legitimacy.

The disestablishment of traditional governing institutions is not necessarily followed by the emergence of modern governing institutions. It may instead lead to a period in which modern concepts of legitimacy (electoral, revolutionary, nationalist) are accepted in theory but are seldom adhered to in practice. After they secured their independence from Spain, for instance, the countries of Central and South America almost uniformly adopted constitutions based on those of the United States or republican France. For most of the rest of the century for most of these countries, these constitutions had only a vague relation to political reality. In actual fact, politics evolved from the phase of the caudillos to that of the centralizing dictator, who was able to establish his authority because he was able to create a strong military force. In the twentieth century, similarly, no society identifies the coup d'état as a legitimate source of political authority, yet clearly in many less developed countries it is, in practice, the means to power in the central government.

The commonly accepted sources of legitimacy in modern societies are electoral, revolutionary, and nationalist. According to the first, governments are to be obeyed because they have been selected by popular vote through a reasonably open and competitive electoral process. According to the second, governments are to be obeyed because they are the instrument of history for the creation of a new and more perfect social order. According to the third, governments are to be obeyed because they embody the will of one community (usually ethnic and linguistic) of people to assert their separate identity and establish their independence from control by the agents of other communities of people. Each of these three sources of legitimacy implies distinctive types of governing institutions. Electoral legitimacy requires an electoral system and, usually, competitive political parties. Revolutionary legitimacy usually requires a well-developed ideology, the carrier of which is the dominant political party in the system. The institutions for nationalist legitimacy are less distinct, and this legitimacy is often combined with electoral or revolutionary legitimacy. Where foreign rule is a reality, legitimacy inheres in the nationalist movement.

Where a formally independent government has been established, legitimacy often has to be periodically renewed by the assertion of the independence of the government against real or presumed foreign threats to that independence.

Participatory Institutions

In traditional societies political participation is limited, and participatory institutions are usually few and weak. A bureaucratic empire may have no formal participatory institutions. A more dispersed or feudal system may include councils or assemblies of noblemen, prelates, and their retainers; in some instances there may even be systems of representation developed for particular social classes and towns and other corporate bodies. The emergence of more fully developed participatory institutions usually comes, however, with the rise of the middle class and its accompanying demands for representation in government through one or more legislative assemblies chosen through an electoral process based on geographical constituencies.

The expansion of participation inevitably involves competition and in large part may be the result of competition among elite cliques seeking to maximize their power. This process of competition leads those cliques to attempt to mobilize new supporters, hence to broaden the political arena and the politically participant groups, and then to organize these supporters so as to enhance their political effectiveness. As a result, politics gradually evolves from the politics of personality, status, and patron-client relations to more continuing factional and group alignments, which leads eventually to the emergence of political parties. In some sense a political party is simply an institutionalized faction, a contestant in the struggle for power whose existence has become relatively independent of the leadership and presence of particular individuals. Parties may originate in the assembly as legislative factions, which then attempt to extend their roots into the society at large. Or they may grow out of other cliques, usually recruited from the elite of the society, who organize outside the existing political institutions and in opposition to the existing political system. They then attempt to mobilize support with revolutionary or nationalistic appeals for the overthrow of that system. The critical step in the evolution from faction into party is the linkage of the elite clique of political activists to a significant social force or interest group in society. This normally occurs only after a large number of small elite factions have become polarized over a major issue confronting the society and hence have found it necessary to compete for support among nonparticipant groups, thereby mobilizing them into the political arena. The sequence in the development of party systems is thus normally polarization of cliques, expansion of participation, and then institutionalization of the party system (Huntington, 1968; pp. 412ff).

The political party is the distinctive institution of modern politics because the most fundamental distinction between modern and traditional political systems concerns the scope of political participation. As participation expands political parties appear to organize that participation, and as political parties develop they promote the expansion of participation. In many modernizing societies, however, conservative, administrative, and even reformist groups view political parties with suspicion and attempt to maintain partyless regimes. So long as the primary need in the modernizing society is the centralization of power and the promotion of socioeconomic reform from above, the absence of a party system is compatible with modernization. Once significant new middle-class groups develop, however, and lower-class groups become politically conscious, the absence of a party system begins to impede the processes of modernization. Efforts are often made to develop alternatives to party through structures of elected councils or through provisions for the direct representation of corporate interests within the bureaucracy or legislature.

All of the most economically developed countries in the world have relatively highly developed party systems, either competitive or communist. Societies with authoritarian political systems in which parties play relatively minor roles, such as Spain or Brazil in the early 1970s, are faced with the question of whether they can develop a corporate party system as an institutional alternative to either a competitive party system or a revolutionary party system. Is there a "third way" of organizing political participation in a modern society? The greatest obstacle to the development of such a third institutional pattern is the problem of legitimacy. Both communist and competitive party systems are compatible with and can be justified in terms of the basic idea of equality. A corporate system, which may reflect the reality of power in a society, runs counter to the basic stress on human equality in modern society. The achievement of some solution of this problem of legitimacy would appear to be a prerequisite to the development of a third type of party system compatible with the needs of modern society. (See Huntington, 1970; Schmitter, 1971; and Linz, Chapter 3 of this *Handbook*.)

Administrative Institutions

During modernization the scope, complexity, and functions of the governmental administration expand tremendously. In a traditional society the government normally does not penetrate very far into society. The "law of the emperor stops at the village gate" and the tax collector who enters the village often is in the position of negotiating a collective tribute from a semiautonomous entity. The direct impact of the central government on the individual citizen, consequently, is relatively minor. The functions of the central government are primarily ceremonial, adjudicative, religious, and martial, but its ability to carry out the latter purposes is often limited by its inability to extract from society the needed resources in the form of men and money. Foreign war is, by far and away, the single most important cause for the expansion of governmental power and of the impact of government on society. The expansion of governmental functions and of the bureaucracies to perform them usually takes place in five areas.

1. *Regulative.* The government extends its controls over the economy, particularly as the economy becomes less agricultural and more commercial and industrial. Entry into business, methods of financing business activity, the supply of money, credit, prices and interest rates, wages and hours, rents and profits, imports and exports are all likely to become subject to some degree of governmental control.

2. *Distributive.* In due course the government not only regulates the activities of others but also plays a significant role in distributing benefits directly through transfer payments and by other means. Public monies raised by taxation or borrowing are paid out in a highly unequal fashion to individuals and groups within the society. Such distributive activities are found in any government, but as modernization progresses the scale of the distributions made, their legitimacy, and the number and diversity of their recipients expands tremendously.

3. *Productive.* In varying degrees governments undertake to perform productive functions in the economy. In a communist country, of course, an extraordinarily large portion of the economic activity in the society is performed by government agencies. Even in capitalist societies, however, governments are a major source of investment and often play the dominant role in communications, transportation, energy, metallurgy, construction, and armaments.

4. *Extractive.* To carry out their other functions governments have to increase their ability to remove money, resources, and, at times, labor from the society. The power to tax is the power to modernize. The ratio of taxation to total national income almost invariably increases with modernization, and the forms of taxation also change. As the economies of traditional societies become more complex, the principal form of taxation, taxes on land, is displaced in importance by taxes on trade, particularly imports and exports, which in turn are superseded in importance by taxes on income. (See Hinrichs, 1966.)

5. *Protective.* The defense and war-making capabilities of governments often increase in conjunction with but at a faster rate than the economic development of their societies. Between 1961 and 1970, for instance, the military expenditures of 93 developing countries increased at an average annual rate (in constant prices) of 8.5 percent per year, while their GNPs increased at a rate of 4.7 percent per year and their per capita GNPs at 2.2 percent. Similarly, the number of men in the military forces of these countries increased by 3.3 percent per year, while their total populations increased by 2.4 percent per year. This expansion of the military sector of government is probably considerably

greater for later developing countries than it was for those whose primary period of economic development occurred in the nineteenth century.

Political Institutions and Political Change

The political organizations and procedures appropriate for a small, simple, agrarian society are not normally appropriate for a large, complex, industrial society. Yet many different types of political organizations and procedures may be appropriate for simple societies, and many other different types of political institutions may be appropriate for complex, industrial societies. These institutions differ in their ability to respond to and meet different needs and challenges arising out of the societies' domestic and foreign environments. A society with one set of political institutions may be able to do some things more easily than another society that is otherwise very similar but has different political institutions.

In a very general sense modernization poses, more or less in sequence, three major challenges to political systems (Frey, 1965; Huntington, 1968). In the first phase the need exists to break down traditional institutions and practices and to inaugurate modernizing reforms designed to rationalize and secularize the system of authority, to develop an efficient bureaucracy and military force, to equalize the relations of citizens to government, and to extend the effective reach of the state. Achieving these modernizing reforms usually requires the centralization of power. The effect of such reforms, however, is to promote the development of political and social consciousness among existing groups and the emergence of new groups. In a second phase, consequently, the major challenge to the political system is to extend its scope so as to relate these groups to the system. In effect this means the overall expansion of power in the political system as the patterns of influence and control reaching out from the center encompass broader and more diversified sectors of the population. In a third phase these patterns of influence tend to become more reciprocal, and a dispersion of power takes place as the political system becomes more responsive to the needs and demands of those groups newly incorporated into it. One can thus think of political modernization as involving successively the concentration, expansion, and dispersion of power.

Different political institutions differ in their ability to provide for these changes in the amount and distribution of power. A highly simplified summary of the capabilities of different types of political institutions in this respect may be found in Table I. Crises in political modernization occur when the development of society imposes new demands on political institutions which those institutions are unable to meet. Absolute monarchies and military dictatorships may promote reforms in their societies and then be unable to expand the power in their political systems to assimilate the new social forces produced by the reforms. They fall victims to their own successes. At a higher level of modernization a similar challenge confronts one-party systems, which may successfully

TABLE 1   Hypothetical capacities of political institutions

Requirement of modernization	Absolute monarchy	Feudal system	Two-party system	Multiparty system	One-party system	Military dictatorship
Concentrate power	High	Low	Low	Low	High	High
Expand power	Low	Low	High	Low	High	Low
Disperse power	Low	High	High	High	?	Low

concentrate and expand power and then be confronted with an increasing need to accommodate themselves to the dispersion of power. (See Huntington and Moore, 1970.) Thus, as socioeconomic modernization takes place, either the existing political institutions adapt to meet the new needs, or the political institutions are themselves changed into or replaced by new political institutions more capable of meeting those needs, or the modernization of the political system grinds to a halt and severe stresses develop as a result of the gap between continuing socioeconomic modernization and aborted political modernization. The question is first whether and how existing political institutions can meet the demands of the next phase of modernization and second, if they cannot, whether and how those institutions can be modified or replaced so as to bring into existence new institutions that can meet those demands.

At particular points in the history of a society political elites may make critical institutional choices that will thereafter foreclose or impose high costs on certain subsequent political choices. Mustafa Kemal's decision in the early 1920s to create a republic in Turkey made it possible first to develop a one-party system, which provided for the effective centralization of power and reform, and then to shift in the 1940s and 1950s to a multiparty system, which furnished the institutional framework for the expansion and dispersion of power. In contrast, in Iran in the early 1920s Mohammad Reza Shah felt that the costs of attempting to introduce republican institutions were too high, and consequently he reinvigorated the Persian monarchy. As a result he and his successor were able to promote substantial modernizing reforms, including in the 1950s and 1960s a so-called "White Revolution," designed to improve the material lot of the peasantry, but Iranian political institutions remained ill-suited for accommodating the expansion and dispersion of political power.

The ability of traditional political institutions to meet the needs of modernization is decisively affected by their level of institutionalization and the extent to which they are pluralistic or monolithic. Political organizations and procedures in traditional society may be quite highly developed (and institutionalized) at the local level. The procedures for selecting village leaders and for making decisions on village issues are often established and sanctified by years and perhaps generations of usage. At this local level there is often fairly widespread political participation. At the societal or "national" level, on the other hand, the proportion of the population active in politics is almost always low, and political organizations and procedures are often at comparable low levels of institutionalization. Traditional political institutions do not provide organizations and procedures for large-scale mass participation in politics at the societal level. Like modern institutions, however, they can and do have to provide for either the centralization or the dispersion of power, and it is useful to analyze the traditional authority systems in these terms or in terms such as "pyramidal" and "hierarchical," such as David Apter has employed (Apter, 1965, pp. 81ff).

The most significant historical manifestations of the centralized (or hierarchical) and dispersed (or pyramidal) authority patterns are the bureaucratic empire and feudalism. In the bureaucratic empire or in oriental despotism (see Eisenstadt, 1963; Wittfogel, 1957) the emperor or monarch at the center is the source of legitimacy; he is often the formal and always the de facto religious as well as the political head of the society. He governs through an elaborate and highly differentiated bureaucracy. To maintain his authority he is continuously on guard against the emergence of autonomous centers of power. Consequently it is in his interest to maintain a high degree of mobility within the bureaucracy and not to let middle or higher level officials establish their own constituencies on either a geographical or a functional basis. An independent nobility, the hereditary transfer of property and office, and private ownership of real property all run counter to the total centralization that is in his interest to maintain.

In a feudal system, on the other hand, the ruling monarch is more likely to be first among equals. The position, office, and property of the nobility are theirs by right and inheritance and not simply at the dispensation of a supreme ruler. Society is likely to be more highly stratified and there is less social mobility between strata. Specialization and functional differentiation are less highly developed, with the feudal lords at all levels in the system combining political, military, economic, and social functions (Coulborn, 1965; Bloch, 1961). "The bureaucratic state thus tends towards the separation of functions and the concentration of power while the feudal state tends towards the fusion of functions and the division of power" (Huntington, 1968, p. 149). In reality, of course, traditional political systems seldom have all the characteristics of either the bureaucratic or the feudal ideal type. They often, however, tend strongly toward one institutional pattern or the other, and these tendencies have major implications for the future political evolution of their societies.

In terms of the political requirements of modernization, an absolute monarchy or bureaucratic empire clearly provides the centralization of power which is necessary to reform traditional society and to break up the power of traditional groups. It thus can meet the needs of the first phase of political modernization. Feudal institutions, on the other hand, obstruct the concentration of power and the initiation of reform. If, however, feudal institutions survive, at least in attenuated form, the pressures for centralization and reform, they can often be adapted into a competitive party system to meet the need for the expansion of power in the next phase of modernization. In this respect five common patterns of institutional evolution have dominated the experience of modernizing countries.

1. *Empire-Revolution Pattern.* Highly centralized bureaucratic empires often have many of the characteristics of modern political institutions with their highly articulated and differentiated bureaucratic structures and achievement-based recruitment of officials. They also, however, often have consummatory value patterns, and the combination makes it unlikely that such institutions can be adapted successfully to the needs of modernization. The consummatory value pattern makes it difficult for these systems to innovate policies; any reforms or piecemeal modernization appear to threaten the entire system. The centralization of power then makes it very difficult for these systems to assimilate new and newly self-conscious social forces produced by modernization. As a result, these systems, which may seem quite modern before modernization begins, collapse or are overthrown during the process of modernization. In Russia and in China the institutions of the centralized bureaucratic empire were replaced by the institutions of the Communist party dictatorship. The latter duplicated the centralization of the former. But it also possessed the capability both to innovate modernizing reforms and to mobilize and assimilate large masses of the population for its purposes at the same time that it repressed those groups that might have threatened it.

2. *Feudal-Absolutism Pattern.* Feudal systems usually encompass various strata and corporate bodies and hence have the potential capability of meeting the functional needs for group assimilation which modernization poses to political systems. Those needs typically are most critical after the state has begun to change the traditional social and economic order. In the feudal system, however, power is too widely dispersed to permit the state to play a decisive role in promoting modernization. Consequently, the early stages of modernization, as in seventeenth and eighteenth century France, typically involve the efforts of monarchs to strengthen the central state institutions and thereby to develop the capability to weaken the nobility and church, expand their own power, and innovate modernizing reforms. In destroying the dispersed institutions of feudalism and particularly the feudal assemblies, which might otherwise develop into modern parliaments, they also make it increasingly difficult for their system to adapt to the second requirement of modernization: the need to assimilate newly mobilized social forces into the political system. After centralizing power in the political system the monarch falls victim to his inability

to provide the channels for broader participation within the system and is deposed through coup d'état, revolt, or revolution.

3. *Feudal-Pluralism Pattern.* Alternatively, the drive to centralize power and introduce modernizing reforms in a more dispersed feudal system may be blunted or moderated. Under these circumstances fewer changes are likely to be made in the traditional social and economic institutions of the society, and there is likely to be greater continuity in political evolution. Feudal assemblies and councils are then able to evolve into modern representative parliaments and, of course, to furnish a vehicle for relating newly mobilized groups to the political system. The monarchy, in turn, shifts from being a ruling institution, although restricted in its powers, to being a ceremonial institution, important as a symbol of unity and continuity. The monarchy may continue to play a marginal and residual legitimating role in the political system, but it is not involved in the normal process of decision-making and is secondary to other, usually electoral, means of establishing legitimacy. Such has been the case in several northern European countries, including most notably Great Britain and Sweden. In this way two ancient institutions, parliament and crown, are adapted to meet the functional needs of a modern polity. In the modernization process the survivability of a parliament thus varies directly and that of a monarchy inversely with its power.

4. *Traditional Praetorian Pattern.* In all three of the above instances traditional political institutions were assumed to have reached fairly high levels of institutionalization. In societies in which traditional institutions at the societal level are not highly developed, modernization is likely to have a more disruptive impact. Traditional organizations and procedures may well be swept aside by the social forces brought into politics by the modernization process. At some point the scope of political participation is broadened beyond the traditional oligarchy, and more modern-oriented, middle-class groups emerge on the political scene. Their appearance frequently takes the form of a "breakthrough coup," in which modernizing elements in the army depose the traditional ruler, seize power, and set forth goals of reform and social change designed to make their society approximate the model of what a modern system is supposed to be (Huntington, 1968, pp. 198ff). Middle-class reformers in general and soldiers in particular, however, are normally not very successful at developing political institutions. The result is a chaotic and unstructured politics in which more and more diverse social forces become politically active and attempt to achieve their goals through the distinctive tactics that they can most effectively employ. Social cohesion is at a low level, and with the broadening of political participation the conflict among social groups more and more approximates a condition of subdued civil war of one against all. In such a "radical praetorian" society the development of political institutions capable of providing channels for the articulation and aggregation of interests becomes in-

creasingly difficult. In the early phases of such a system political parties are almost entirely urban based and usually have little stability in leadership, followers, program, or ideology. At the same time, efforts to develop more broadly based parties with roots among the rural masses are prohibited and repressed by the dominant groups in the system. Only in the rare instances in which such efforts succeed despite repression, such as those of the Acción Democrática in Venezuela, is the society able to move out of its praetorian condition and develop relatively highly institutionalized modern political structures.

5. *Colonial Bureaucracy Pattern.* Societies that are themselves small or weak or that have poorly developed traditional political institutions are open to conquest and colonial rule by more modern societies. It has, indeed, even been argued that in some sense colonialism in the nineteenth and twentieth centuries has been the "natural" relationship between modernizing European societies and the traditional societies of Asia and Africa (Kurth, 1970). In colonized societies whatever traditional political institutions may exist at the societal level typically disintegrate, are swept away, or are heavily subordinated to the control and direction of the imperial power. In varying degrees the latter rules through its own agents, and a relatively modern bureaucracy is imposed from the outside to govern a relatively traditional society. As a result, except in rare instances, a process of lopsided institutional development occurs, and these lopsided institutions are bequeathed to the newly independent state when the imperial control ends. Government is identified with bureaucratic rule, and the need to provide other institutional channels for the articulation and aggregation of the interests within the society is neglected. As a result the military frequently assume a dominant role, and politics tends toward a condition of low institutionalization comparable with that of the traditional praetorian pattern. Only in cases such as India, in which traditional society was relatively complex and a lengthy process of nationalist agitation and organization was permitted to develop slowly, were former colonies able to move into independence with relatively ·highly developed administrative *and* participatory institutions.

In all of these patterns key characteristics of the traditional political institutions survive or reappear in the modern system. Communist party dictatorships reproduce, on an expanded scale, the centralized power, bureaucratic structure, consummatory value patterns, arbitrary rule, and political repression characteristic of the earlier despotisms. In France, the Revolution, it has been aptly said, completed the process of centralization which the Bourbons had instigated. In those societies in which there has been a revolutionary discontinuity with the past, old patterns of political thought and behavior reappear in modern dress. In those societies in which institutional continuity is preserved, the extent to which old political institutions have been adopted to modern needs is often cloaked by the perpetuation of traditional ritual. Weakly institutionalized traditional political structures are likely to be succeeded by weakly institutionalized modern systems; and at least in the early years of independence the governmental institutions of new states often replicate the colonial institutions of the former masters. Only in the cases of full-scale communist revolution and of parliamentary democracy evolving out of feudal pluralism has modernization led to higher levels of political institutionalization. The overthrow of traditional institutions is thus not necessarily followed by the emergence of modern ones. And only in most unusual circumstances does modernization bring about a major and lasting change in the extent to which power is centralized or dispersed. The impact of modernization on the development of political institutions is thus clearly delimited by the nature of the existing traditional political system.

Political Institutions and Economic Development

The nature of the political institutions that exist in a modernizing society has significant implications for the processes of socioeconomic as well as political modernization. The overall level of political institutionalization and the degree to which those institutions are democratic or undemocratic affect the rate and character of economic growth and the distribution of wealth and income. By and large the following generalizations seem to hold on the relation between political institutions and economic development.

1. Societies with higher levels of political institutionalization tend to have higher rates of economic growth than societies with lower levels of political institutionalization.

2. Societies with less democratic political institutions tend to have higher overall rates of economic growth than societies with more democratic political institutions.

3. Societies with less democratic political institutions tend to have different patterns of economic development from those of societies with more democratic political institutions.

4. The extent to which variations in economic development tend to correlate with differences in political institutions itself varies inversely with the level of economic development in the society.

5. Societies in which the military play an active political role tend to have socioeconomic policies and patterns of development different from societies in which the military are not active in politics.

The following discussion summarizes some of the evidence relevant to these propositions.

Most empirical studies of the relationships between political institutions and economic development establish correlations between these two variables; in a few instances causal analyses have been attempted. Virtually every analysis of correlation, however, rests on an assumption about causation. The literature dealing with the relation between *level* of economic development and prevalence of democratic institutions is based on the assumption that the causal flow is from the former to the latter. In contrast, the literature dealing with the relation between *rate* of economic growth and the democratic or undemocratic character of political institutions assumes a causal flow from the latter to the former. There clearly are good commonsense reasons for thinking that levels of economic development should affect types of political institutions and types of political institutions should affect rates of economic growth. In most cases, however, the empirical evidence establishes only correlational and not causal connections.

Much controversy surrounds the question of the relationship of democratic and authoritarian political institutions to economic growth. In debunking the exaggerated claims that one-party systems are conducive to economic growth, S. E. Finer, for instance, concludes that "the proposition that the single-party system in any sense *guarantees* rapid economic advance must be rejected" (Finer, 1967). It surely must. But that was hardly the issue. The question is whether authoritarian systems in general or one-party systems in particular facilitate economic development more effectively than democratic or pluralistic party systems. In his own survey of African states Finer produces no evidence one way or another on this proposition; some one-party systems seem to have produced economic disaster, others did reasonably well economically. The difficulties of global comparisons that attempt to relate political systems to rates of economic development are obviously immense. The preponderance of the data that exists, however, suggests that, contrary to Finer's argument, authoritarian and one-party systems do have an edge, although not a great one, over other types of systems in promoting economic growth in the early phases of modernization.

In a competitive electoral system in a society in the early phases of modernization, the bulk of the voters live in the rural areas, and hence a party must win their support to stay in power. These voters are likely to be more traditional and resistant to change than urban groups, and if the system is really an operating democracy the rural voters will effectively prevent the government from exploiting the peasants to squeeze out a surplus for industrialization. Also in a democratic system in a newly modernizing society the interests of the voters generally lead parties to give the expansion of personal consumption a higher priority vis-à-vis investment than it would receive in a nondemocratic system. In the Soviet Union, for instance, the percentage of the GNP devoted to consumption was driven down from 65 percent in 1928 to 52 percent in 1937. It is most unlikely that a competitive party system could have sustained a revolution from above like this.

Methodological problems abound in attempting to relate political institutions to economic performance. Sufficient data exists from a sufficient variety of

TABLE 2   Party systems and economic growth
(countries with per capita GNP less than $500 in 1961)

Per capita growth rate in 1950s	Type of political system				Total
	One-party systems		Competitive-party systems	Unstable systems	
	Communist	Noncommunist			
4+ percent	7	1	2	0	10
2–3.9 percent	0	4	1	4	9
Below 2 percent	0	1	3	12	16
Total	7	6	6	16	35

Source: Bruce M. Russett *et al., World Handbook of Political and Social Indicators* (Yale University Press, 1964, pp. 160–61) ; Clair Wilcox, Willis D. Weatherford, Jr., and Holland Hunter, *Economies of the World Today* (Harcourt, Brace and World, 1962, pp. 16–19) .

sources, however, to suggest that the hypothesized relationship between institutionalization, democracy, and growth does indeed generally hold for less developed countries. During the 1950s, for instance, twelve of thirteen one-party systems in less developed countries maintained annual per capita growth rates of 2 percent or better (Bolivia being delinquent) and eight (mostly communist) had per capita growth rates of 4 percent or better. In contrast, competitive party systems were relatively evenly distributed in terms of growth rates, while weakly institutionalized, praetorian regimes had very low rates of economic growth. Similarly, during the years from 1961 to 1968 the average annual per capita growth rate of fifteen democratic countries with 1968 per capita GNPs of less than $950 was only 2.1 percent, ranging from a low of −1.4 percent for Uruguay to a high of 5.9 percent for Greece, which, of course, ceased being a democracy at the end of this time span (International Bank, 1970). The average annual growth rates for leading democracies in the developing world included India's 1.0 percent, Ceylon's 2.3 percent, the Philippines' 0.8 percent, Chile's 1.8 percent, and Costa Rica's 2.1 percent. In contrast, the average annual growth rate for seven conservative authoritarian regimes (Spain, Portugal, Iran, Nationalist China, South Korea, Thailand, and Pakistan) averaged 5.2 percent and varied from a low of 3.2 percent for Pakistan to highs of 6.5 percent for Spain and Nationalist China. The average growth rate for the ten less developed communist countries was 3.7 percent, with the eastern European countries and North Korea all doing very well, while the other Asian communist states did poorly, and Cuba (with an average annual growth rate of −2.0 percent) was an economic disaster. By and large, however, on a global basis, low rates of per capita economic growth prevailed among those less developed countries that were newly independent, lacked developed political institutions of any sort, and suffered from repeated political instability and violence.

In another cross-national analysis, focusing on the relationship between democracy and social and economic reform, Frey (1966) came to similar conclusions. He measured "reform" by the growth of GNP per capita and the decrease in the number of inhabitants per hospital bed. Democracy was measured by the Banks and Textor categories of constitutional status of regime, national horizontal power structure, representative character of regime, and freedom of group opposition. His analysis showed that "the more rapidly growing polities seem to be less democratic or, if one prefers again, the less democratic polities seem to be more rapidly growing. The absolute data suggest that democracy and reform go hand in hand—that they are positively associated. The growth data suggest that democracy and reform are incompatible—that they are negatively associated."

The analysis of Adelman and Morris suggests both the extent to which the rate of economic growth may vary with the democratic or authoritarian character of political institutions and the variations that exist in that relationship among different levels of economic development. They divided 74 "poor" countries (the wealthiest of which was Israel) into three subgroups according to their overall level of socioeconomic development. For the 28 countries (largely African) in the lowest group, they find "a weak but positive relationship between more autocratic, less representative forms of government and more rapid growth rates. . . ." Better economic performance is associated with "centralized political systems, less effective democratic institutions, greater restrictions on freedom of the press, and more severe limitations on the activities of the political opposition." The more rapidly developing of these countries tend "to be controlled by a single national unity party and to possess only very weak voluntary associations such as labor unions." For the 21 poor countries in the intermediate group, a similar "mild positive association" holds between more rapid economic growth and authoritarian government. In contrast, for the 25 poor countries at a "high" level of socioeconomic development, no significant relationship existed between the nature of the political system and the rate of economic growth. At that level "economic modernization appears to be compatible with a wide variety of political systems ranging from participatory democracy to pure dictatorship" (Adelman and Morris, 1967, pp. 197, 245). Thus for the 49 countries in the world at the lowest levels of socioeconomic development, authoritarian regimes seem to have some positive results for more rapid economic growth. Once countries reach a somewhat higher state of development—roughly a 1961 per capita GNP of $250 or more—authoritarian government begins to lose its comparative advantage.

The democratic or undemocratic character of political institutions may well have as much, if not more, effect on the nature of economic development as on the overall rate of growth. An authoritarian system, and particularly a one-party system whose leaders are committed to modernization, is more likely to be able to give high priority to the development of heavy industry and certain types of infrastructure, while political leaders in a competitive political system are more likely to be sensitive to the need to develop agriculture and consumer goods industry (Frey, 1966). Some illustration of the impact that the shift from a one-party to a competitive political system may have is afforded by the contrast between the economic policies in the 1950s of the Mexican and Turkish governments. In the 1930s both countries had one-party systems. The Mexican system was based on widespread popular support, including the organized participation of workers and peasants. The Turkish system, on the other hand, was based essentially on the urban middle class and presupposed apathy on the part of the peasants and effective controls on the very small minority of industrial labor. In this sense Mexico embodied an established and Turkey an unfinished revolution (Özbuden, 1970).

Both governments, however, were led by modernizing elites committed to economic growth, and both governments in the 1930s inaugurated vigorous measures to promote industrial development. In Turkey the Five Year Plan that went into effect in 1934 gave top priority to industrialization; it was, indeed, modeled on the Russian experience, an experience that would hardly have been relevant to a country with a competitive political system. Characteristic of this period was "the almost complete neglect of agriculture." As a result, "the greatest natural asset of the country remained unexploited, agricultural production did not increase, and only a limited labor force was released for urban industries" (Lewis, 1961, p. 282). From the Kemalist viewpoint, in the words of another analyst, "agricultural reform was not a prime necessity while the food supply remained satisfactory, and heavy steel plates, strategic railroad lines, and industrial power plants were more important than T-bars, an economically sound railroad network, or rural electrification." In Mexico, Cardenas did push agrarian reform, but he also gave high priority to industrial growth, and "manufacturing was the star performer in the Mexican economy during the decade of the 1930s" (Sugar, 1964; Vernon, 1963, p. 84). In both countries noncompetitive one-party systems were associated with a heavy emphasis on industrial development.

In the late 1940s Turkey shifted to a competitive political system, while in Mexico the single party remained firmly entrenched. Both economies continued to grow significantly, but the rate of economic development in Mexico clearly surpassed that in Turkey. Between 1950 and 1965 the annual per capita increase in Mexican GNP was 3.3 percent; for Turkey it was 2.81 percent. More importantly Mexico continued to give top priority to industrial development. In 1965–67 only 6 percent of the public sector budget went to agriculture as compared with 36 percent for industry, and the gap between urban and rural income apparently changed little during the 1940s and 1950s. The public funds that did go into agriculture were often used to promote private investment in large-scale cotton farming and other forms of commercial agriculture.

In Turkey, on the other hand, political competition led both major parties to make broad appeals to the countryside. The electoral victories of the Democratic party in 1950 and particularly in 1954 were in large part due to its ability to mobilize the support from the peasants. In part this support was a product of more traditionalist appeals, such as an easing of the Kemalist hostility toward religious practices. It was also in large part associated with a conscious change in the thrust of government economic policies. The Democrats aimed at "a shift in income distribution through increasing state support of commodity prices, continued tax exemption of agriculture, and a variety of other programs, all of which channeled income out of the city and into the village" (Robinson, 1965). Government funds went for agricultural credits, rural roads, tractors, seed, and fertilizer. As a result agricultural output rose by 41 percent, industrial output by only 25 percent (Grunwald and Ronall, 1960).

The increase in farm income, in turn, generated demands for consumer goods which the government had to respond to but found difficult to meet. As a result of the "deliberate channeling of an undue share of the national income into the pockets of the village farmers ... economic incentive began working with tremendous force at town and village level. The single most important political issue in Turkey became the availability of such key consumer goods as coffee, tea, sugar, kerosene, radios, batteries, lamps, glass, textiles, and shoes. ... And so long as democratic government continued, there seemed to be no method available to the leaders to curtail this enormous economic incentive.... The masters of Turkey were, in reality, the political slaves of the village farming masses and the new lower class urban group" (Robinson, 1965, pp. 208–9).

The masters of Turkey, however, had discovered the secret of political power in a competitive system. "What does it matter what the intellectuals of Istanbul think," Premier Menderes asked, "so long as the peasantry is with us?" And during the 1950s the peasants responded to the Democrats' efforts to win their support and provided the votes to give them overwhelming electoral majorities. "The peasants," it has been said, "were equally grateful for the largesse which Menderes distributed; they were unburdened by taxes, they were paid high support prices for their grain, and a few months prior to the 1957 election they received a one-year moratorium on all debts due the Government. To the bulk of the peasants, Menderes was a great hero" (Ross, 1960). Here indeed there was a dramatic contrast between the nationalist, urban, bureaucratic, intellectual, somewhat austere tradition of the Republican Peoples party, with its origins in the Ottoman bureaucracy, and the more popular, rural, traditionalist, local, and provincially oriented Democratic party, which supplanted the Republicans in power once party competition was allowed. In Mexico the continuation of the one-party system coincided with continued stress on industrial growth; in Turkey the shift from one-party to competitive politics coincided with the reorientation of governmental policy toward the agricultural sector.

Comparative studies of the states in the United States have generally shown that political participation and party competition are less significant than economic and ecological variables (particularly the level of economic development) in shaping policy outcomes. (See Dawson, 1967; Dawson and Robinson, 1965; Dye, 1966; Cnudde and McCrone, 1969; Sharkansky and Hofferbert, 1969.) The evidence among nations similarly suggests that level of economic development is critical but also that differences in political institutions play a significant role in shaping policy in a variety of economic areas. In his analysis of income distribution, Cutright (1967) found that representativeness of political institutions was second only to level of economic development in explaining variations in income distribution among 44 noncommunist countries. In similar fashion, when level of economic development was controlled for, Cutright (1965) also found that for 76 countries governments with more representative political institutions tended to provide more social security for their people than "governments whose rulers were less accessible to the demands of the population." In addition, in the economically more developed countries increases in the representativeness of political institutions tended to be followed by the innovation of new social security programs.

In analyzing the impact of political competitiveness and military regimes in Latin American countries, Schmitter (1971) found it desirable to differentiate between "outcomes," which indicate overall system performance, such as the rate of economic growth, and "outputs," which involve direct government actions, such as the level and distribution of public expenditures. The former were primarily affected by economic and ecological variables, particularly level of external economic dependence. Public taxation and expenditures, however, were "significantly associated" with variations in political institutions. "In short," Schmitter summarized, "politics or in this instance military intervention and party competitiveness are relevant to an understanding of the nature of public policy in this region of the world, definitely more so than in the more limited, homogenous area of North American state politics." Military regimes, by and large, tended to spend less on social welfare. Regimes with competitive institutions appeared to spend more on welfare, to have a more egalitarian tax system, to distribute the benefits of governmental spending more equally, and to have more unbalanced budgets and higher rates of inflation. Systems with weak political institutions, in which military and civilian regimes alternate in power, spent more on defense than either sustained military regimes or competitive civilian regimes. Nordlinger's parallel analysis (1970) in general provides support on a global basis for Schmitter's Latin American findings. In societies with a relatively small middle class, military rule is associated with high rates of economic growth, industrialization, and expansion of primary education. In more complex societies, with a larger and more influential middle class, these relationships tend to disappear.

The data from these varied sources suggest that the rate and character of economic development in countries in the process of modernization will be significantly affected by the political institutions of those countries. There is also the suggestion that the precise impact of the political institutions may vary with the level of economic development. It is possible, for instance, that at low levels of economic development, democratic political institutions may be associated with high levels of income inequality, while at higher levels of economic development democratic political institutions may go with greater economic equality. Those developing countries that have substantial middle-class participation in politics also often tend toward one or another of two political-economic models: the "technocratic model," which involves rapid economic growth, high economic inequality, authoritarian political institutions, and high levels of political stability; and the "populist model," which involves low rates of economic growth, greater economic equality, more open and democratic politics, and greater social conflict and political instability (Huntington and Nelson, 1976). The direction of the causal flow between the political and economic variables in these models needs further exploration, but the experience of Third World countries in Asia, Africa, and Latin America is evidence that the correlations themselves between political institutional variables and economic performance variables are beyond dispute.

VI. POLITICAL INTEGRATION

The term *political integration* most generally refers to the holding together of a political system. It has been used in various specific ways. Myron Weiner (1971) has identified five such usages. (1) National integration is the process of bringing together culturally and socially discrete groups into a single territorial unit and of establishing a national identity. This often involves plural societies, with distinct ethnic, religious, linguistic, or other groups and strata. National integration thus means the subjective feelings that individuals in different groups or strata have toward the nation. (2) Territorial integration is the establishment of national central authority over subordinate political units or regions. Territorial integration means objective territorial control. (3) Elite-mass integration is the linking of government with the governed, assuming that there is a gap between them. (4) Integration may also refer to the minimum value consensus necessary to maintain a social order: the common myths, symbols, beliefs, and shared history of a people. (5) Finally, integration may be the capacity of a people to organize for some common purpose. The last two usages have been discussed already in the section on political culture. Some aspects of elite-mass integration are discussed in the section on political participation; other aspects of elite-mass and territorial integration are discussed in the section on institutions. Therefore, in this section we will pay special attention to national integration.

National Integration: The Problem

Patterns of Stratification

Plural societies have more than one large culturally and socially discrete group, typically differentiated ethnically, linguistically, religiously, or through various combinations (Furnivall, 1948; Smith and Kuper, 1969; M. G. Smith, 1965). Politics in plural societies often take different courses depending on the structure of group differentiation.

In vertical, or hierarchical, structures social class stratification is synonymous with ascriptive strata membership (Gerth and Mills, 1958, pp. 188–90; Horowitz, 1971, pp. 232–37; van den Berghe, 1967, pp. 25–34; Frazier, 1965, pp. 253–87; Mason, 1970, pp. 55–65, 81–86, 124–36). Political and social mobility is often blocked by these ascriptive criteria. Castes typically develop from this condition. In horizontal, or parallel, systems parallel structures exist, each with its own criteria of social class stratification. Sociocultural groups coexist under conditions of mutual repulsion and disdain, but they allow each sociocultural community to consider its own honor the highest one. The caste structure of a hierarchical system, on the other hand, brings about a social subordination and an acknowledgment of "more honor" in favor of the privileged caste and status groups. Because of these differences in normative justification, ethnic systems may be either parallel or hierarchical, but religious systems of stratification tend to be parallel only. It is virtually impossible for a religious group to acknowledge more honor for another religious group.

Hierarchical systems, therefore, may possess more "social cement" and more normative justification than do parallel systems. When the cement cracks, however, the result is typically a social revolution. In parallel systems there is intermittent conflict but not necessarily of the kind that may lead to major social transformations. Hierarchical systems are typically the result of conquest; parallel systems may result from incomplete conquest or migration. As we shall see it is possible for hierarchical systems to become parallel in the long run, though ethnic hierarchies may also continue indefinitely. Each group in a parallel system does not have proportionate numbers of its members in all social classes, nor are mobility opportunities proportionate to the demand of each group. Discrepancies are a source of political conflict in the relations of parallel groups. But each group has its own elite, and each group considers its own "honor" the highest. Thus Ulster is an example of a parallel ethnic system because neither the Catholics nor the Protestants acknowledge more honor to the other group, and each has its own elite, although Catholics are more likely to be found in the lower classes and have found more obstacles to social mobility than Protestants.

Examples of originally hierarchical systems include the United States until the mid-1950s, South Africa, Liberia, Latin America, India, colonial Rwanda, and Burundi. The United States, South Africa, and Liberia have been additionally characterized by the prevalence of assimilative political cultures, while India and Latin America have been characterized by the prevalence of agglomerative political cultures. India and Latin America, in turn, differ in respect to the legitimacy accorded to sociocultural ascriptive *group* political behavior. Lebanon, Malaysia, Belgium, Canada, Nigeria, Uganda, and Pakistan are examples of parallel systems.

Social Mobilization and Political Change and Conflict

Social mobilization is the process by which major clusters of old social, economic, and psychological commitments are eroded or broken and people become available for new patterns of socialization and behavior. Karl Deutsch (1961, p. 501; see also Melson and Wolpe, 1970) has also argued that

> other things assumed equal, the stage of rapid social mobilization may be expected, therefore, to promote the consolidation of states whose peoples already share the same language, culture and major social institutions; while the same process may tend to strain or destroy the unity of states whose population is already divided into several groups with different languages or cultures or basic ways of life.

There appears to be a good deal of evidence for this proposition.[10]

Michael Hudson's study of Lebanon (1968, pp. 53–86) supports the hypothesis. Social mobilization in Lebanon's parallel religious structure has strained national integration. The concentration of people in the most modernized areas, where they are exposed to both mass communication and modern political organization, has enlarged the politically relevant population. The demand on social services and public housing has increased. Urban individuals have been fortified in their parochial and sectarian loyalties. Beirut has proved no more of a "melting pot" than has New York City. Social mobilization has worsened the distribution of wealth. Inequality in Lebanon is significant between both social classes and geographic regions. Exposure to modernity and in particular to the use of radio has politicized the population. Literacy is unevenly distributed throughout the population, with Christians more literate than Muslims. Social mobilization, in short, has not destroyed the national integration of Lebanon. But it has, indeed, placed considerable strains on the ability of politics to keep the system together.

Social mobilization has had a similar effect on India's hierarchical system. Weiner (1962, p. 72) has noted that "social changes accompanying modernization are facilitating the development and not the diminution of community interests in Indian politics." The number of caste, religious, tribal, linguistic, and ethnic associations is likely to continue to increase as the rate of social change increases, or even if it stays the same. These community interests may not exist at precisely the traditional level of fragmentation or cleavage. Social mobilization in India is not likely to lead to homogeneity, but it already seems to have aggregated some small groups into groups of somewhat greater size. Social mobilization, therefore, does not necessarily freeze the traditional system at the preexisting level of social cleavage. It may reinvigorate a social cleavage at a higher level of interest aggregation.

As Das Gupta (1970, p. 266) has argued, the language associations of contemporary India have grown as a part of India's contemporary political system. The associations have promoted social mobilization in their own language through literary and linguistic modernization. Language has provided for these associations a way of binding people drawn from narrower occupational or local group loyalties into wider regional linguistic frameworks. These associations have also used modern organizational methods of political recruitment and socialization. The politics of language associations in India, in short, illustrates the twin aspects of the effects of social mobilization on national integration. On the one hand, groups that shared cultural characteristics and language were able to put aside minor parochial differences and form a larger aggregate. But at this higher, albeit sub-nation-state, level of aggregation and cleavage in the traditional system, social mobilization reinforced the divisions with other cultural and linguistic aggregations in India.

It does not follow, however, that social mobilization would have the effect of promoting national disintegration wherever there is differentiation by language or skin color. In a hierarchical system of ethnic or linguistic stratification, with an agglomerative political culture, it is likely that social mobilization will not have disintegrating effects if the political culture of the system prior to the beginning of social mobilization did not legitimate ascriptive group political action. A hierarchical ethnic system includes the acquiescence by the social subordinates to the norm that more honor accrues rightfully to social superiors. An agglomerative political culture, moreover, has institutionalized patterns of social mobility over a long period of time. A long-term pattern of individual mobility renders new ethnic group political behavior by the social subordinates illegitimate and practically impossible. Social mobilization by itself does not automatically create ethnic group organizational capabilities. The social mobilization hypothesis alone is insufficient to predict the probable political outcome. It is also necessary to specify the prior context and experiences of ethnic group political behavior.

Latin America's historical development (Mörner, 1967, 1970; Pitt-Rivers, 1967) has emphasized a hierarchical ethnic system, an agglomerative political culture, and individual mobility. When social mobilization came, social subordinates did not organize politically as groups. Social mobilization opened new channels for individual change and thus reinforced, rather than changed, the preexisting pattern. The following figure illustrates Latin America's position in a comparative perspective.

Colonial and postcolonial Latin America have had mechanisms for social mobility of nonwhites. Mobility requires a cultural "whitening" and often ra-

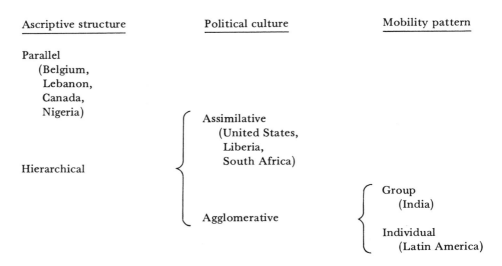

Ascriptive structure	Political culture	Mobility pattern

Parallel
    (Belgium,
    Lebanon,
    Canada,
    Nigeria)

Hierarchical

Assimilative
    (United States,
    Liberia,
    South Africa)

Agglomerative

Group
    (India)

Individual
    (Latin America)

Fig. 1. Typology of Ascriptive Structure, Political Culture, and Mobility Patterns

cial intermarriage. In a study of race relations in northeast Brazil, Donald Pierson (1967, pp. 178–81, 345–50) argued, somewhat controversially, that there is no race prejudice in Brazil—only class prejudice. His argument can be summarized with an old saying in Brazil: "A rich Negro is a white man, and a poor white man is a Negro." There can be, and there is, individual mobility for nonwhites *provided* they can become culturally, socially, and occupationally "white." Pierson provided quantitative data to show that middle and upper income occupations are overwhelmingly occupied by whites, while lower income occupations are occupied by nonwhites. The system of mobility for income and status, moreover, institutionalizes the normative inequality of color. White remains valued, black remains devalued. A common set of values and expectations are shared by Brazilian whites and blacks.

Individual mobility and social mobilization do not disrupt the traditional system. They reinforce it. The normative justification for the persistence of inequality has not been shaken, while new avenues for personal mobility have been opened. It does not follow, therefore, that the mere existence of racial differences indicates the existence of drastically different cultures within a country or that racial inequality leads automatically to violence. Brazil has had a single shared culture for blacks and whites, which includes the recognition that blacks and whites are unequal and that individual upward mobility —permissible and desirable—requires cultural whitening, while downward mobility leads to cultural blackening (Degler, 1971). This common inegalitarian and normatively justified culture has been reinforced by social mobilization.

In areas of Latin America which are linguistically differentiated, such as Mexico, Peru, Bolivia, and Guatemala, there is an additional factor. In these countries there are three categories of people: those who are assimilated into Spanish language and are also modernized, those who are assimilated into Spanish and are not modernized, and those who are not assimilated into Spanish and are not modernized. A fourth theoretically conceivable category, those who may not be assimilated into Spanish but may still be modernized, is virtually absent. The absence of a linguistically differentiated and modernized population characterizes the problem of integration for these countries.

Belgium, Canada, Nigeria, and India have competing ascriptive groups that are socially mobilized. Latin American countries, on the whole, do not. In Latin America change from the nonmodernized into the modernized category is virtually simultaneous with linguistic assimilation. In the 1940 Peruvian census (the last one to ask such embarrassing questions) the Pearson correlation between the proportion of literate persons in any one department of the country and the proportion of Spanish speakers was 0.85. Thus language alone explains 72 percent of the variance in adult literacy. The persistence of the correlation between ethnicity and social class can be seen in the following statistics from the 1940 Mexican census on the proportions of persons by language strata who wore shoes: 79.9 percent of Spanish monolinguals wore shoes, 47.7 percent of Spanish-Indian bilinguals wore shoes, and only 25.0 percent of Indian monolinguals wore shoes (Dirección Nacional de Estadística, 1944; Dirección General de Estadística, 1943, p. 71).

Although the premise of inequality has been stable and legitimate in modernizing Latin America, there have been two short-lived nonwhite political parties in recent times. Both clearly appeared under exceptional conditions. The Cuban Independent Party of Color appeared shortly after the country became independent from the United States; and the Brazilian Negro Front appeared after the Vargas revolution of 1930, at the bottom of the depression (Fernandes, 1969, pp. 189–233, 440–47; Fermoselle, 1974; Thomas, 1971, pp. 514–24). Both arose after the processes of social mobilization, commercialization of agriculture, and industrialization had begun in Cuba and in south-central and southeast Brazil, especially São Paulo city, where the Front was strongest. They are not the result of continued oppression. They appeared precisely at or after a process of change had begun. In Cuba 45 percent of blacks or mulattoes were already literate in 1907; by 1919 their literacy level rose to 52 percent, an average annual shift of 0.67 percent.

They both arose when the legitimacy of the dominant political system was in question. The Party of Color was founded in 1907, five years after the country had become independent. The Negro Front was founded in 1931, one year after the overthrow of the Republic by Vargas. Their life spans were brief. The first was drowned in a sea of blood in 1912; the second was more peacefully banned, along with all other parties, in 1937. The Negro Front was formed when prosperity was interrupted and the possibility of individual mobility blocked. As individual mobility became possible again, social mobilization and economic development in Brazil reinforced the traditional norm of individual, rather than group, mobility. These movements have not led to organized political behavior by nonwhites. Except for these two exceptions the dominant features of the Latin American system of ethnic and linguistic stratification have not been disrupted by social mobilization and may have been strengthened by it in the twentieth century.

The peculiarities of the Latin American situation can be specified further through comparisons. During the British industrial revolution Scottish Highlanders were socially mobilized and assimilated from Gaelic to English speech. The social mobilization of some Gaelic speakers in the cities did lead for a time to Gaelic-speaking social groups in Glasgow. But the absolute number of Gaelic speakers in the rural areas was not large, and assimilation into English proceeded apace during the nineteenth century (Deutsch, 1966, pp. 137, 231–34). Assimilation and social mobilization were not quite so simultaneous as in Latin America. The processes were sequential and related, but not identical. Indeed Scottish assimilation appears to have been less thorough than assimilation in Latin America, and Scottish nationalism seems livelier than Aztec or Inca nationalism. The Scottish National party got 5 percent of the Scottish vote in the 1966 parliamentary elections, jumping to 35 percent of the Scottish vote—more than any other party—in the 1968 municipal elections. Polls indicated that its strength in the late 1960s in Scotland varied between one-fifth and one-third of the electorate (Schwarz, 1970, p. 497). There is no Latin American analogue.

Different patterns obtain in hierarchical ethnic structures with assimilative political cultures (see Fig. 1). The United States has had an assimilative political culture in a hierarchical ethnic structure (white/black), within which there have also been parallel ethnic relations (WASP, Irish, Italians, Jews, etc.). The existence of parallel ethnic relations legitimized ethnic group political behavior in the political culture. Thus, when the subordinate nonwhite population was socially mobilized in a political system that had become ethnically more open and tolerant, the hierarchical features of the ethnic structure were transformed. The entire system became one of parallel ethnic relationships.

After the rise of the civil rights movement and its successors since the 1950s, the transformation of the ethnic system from hierarchical to parallel began in South Africa, though its development has been arrested. South Africa (van den Berghe, 1967, pp. 112–13) may have followed the assimilative pattern to its ultimate consequences. There has been an increasingly radical inclusion of all whites as competent citizens and exclusion of all nonwhites from competent citizenship. Unlike other assimilative political cultures the dominant South African group has not changed its world view. Especially in the last quarter century the radical conclusions of assimilation/exclusion have been relentlessly pursued. Social mobilization, however, has moved the system in South Africa, as in the United States, toward a parallel competitive ethnic structure. The level of tension increases because the maintenance of the ethnic hierarchy now requires much more coercion (Thompson, 1966).

For two reasons the South African political system is likely to continue these trends without drastic change. However divided white South Africans may have been on a host of issues, they agreed on white rule. The effect of protest against the system, mostly by nonwhites, has solidified this fundamental unity. It has enabled the government to curtail freedom and to turn from a government with an effective police force to an effective police-government (Feit, 1971, p. 324). The second reason is modernization—in particular, economic growth. The maintenance of political order by ruthless means has facilitated economic growth. The growth spillover has benefited those nonwhites who had acquired skills. Though income inequality between whites and nonwhites increased during the 1960s, the real economic gains of nonwhites served to satisfy and thus domesticate some of the potentially more troublesome nonwhites. Inequality was made tolerable by economic growth.

Moreover, in the short run, artificial labor shortages created by reserving certain categories of skilled jobs for whites can be resolved only by downgrading skilled work, paying off white workers, or simply officially exempting jobs from racial classification. There is no necessary incompatibility between rapid economic growth and a high degree of inefficiency that results from the economic consequences of social and political apartheid. Abundant cheap labor, abundant mineral resources, and economic expansion can yield considerable economic growth despite low productivity. It is still arguable that in the longer run continued low productivity could injure self-sustaining economic growth. And a systematic policy of incorporation of nonwhites into the more strategic skilled manufacturing blue-collar jobs would make the political system far more vulnerable to political nonwhite labor strikes than it is now. The onset of an economic recession could trigger off considerable turmoil. But the long run seems indeed far away (Adam, 1971, pp. 96–99, 145–59, 182–83).

Therefore, social mobilization does not have automatic political effects. A more automatic relationship appears in parallel ethnic systems or in those hierarchical ethnic systems with political cultures that legitimize ethnic, caste, or religious group behavior. But wherever these traditional legitimizing features have been lacking, as in Latin America, the political effects of social mobilization on ethnicity are minor. And where the coercive power of the state is put at the service of radical assimilation/exclusion policies, the dominant groups continue to rule. In Latin America dominant ascriptive strata rule with little apparent cost but also in the presence of considerable individual mobility; in South Africa they rule at considerable political, social, economic, and personal costs in order to freeze an ethnically immobile system with an uncertain long-term future.

Political Change and Conflict without Social Mobilization

Problems of national political integration are, of course, not new. They existed long before mass literacy and urbanization or industrialization began. The mere fact that a traditional system was not nationally integrated did not prove sufficient to doom its politics. For example, both the western and the eastern Roman empires were not nationally integrated. Yet at the very time that the western Roman empire collapsed, the eastern empire recovered. In the sixth century Emperor Justinian reconquered substantial parts of the western empire, making the eastern empire less nationally integrated though politically more capable (Jones, 1955, pp. 220–26). Indeed, S. N. Eisenstadt's hypotheses (1963, pp. 334–35) about the transformation of historical bureaucratic empires emphasize the patterns of elite values and institutionalization in these political systems. However, one key variable that may undermine institutionalization in these political systems is precisely the "growing importance of ethnically 'foreign' elements in the constitution of different elites." The task of the rulers of bureaucratic empires in balancing the traditional and more modern features of these systems is, *ceteris paribus,* more difficult in ethnically or religiously heterogeneous systems than in ethnically or religiously homogeneous systems. The elite is not the sole source of difficulty for national integration in traditional political systems. Upheavals have also occurred from below.

One such contemporary traditional political system is Rwanda. In the 1950s the Belgian colony of Ruanda-Urundi had a gross national product per capita (1957 U.S. dollars) of $70 (bottom decile of all countries of the world). Its adult literacy rate was 7.5 percent. Though these statistics must be used cautiously, they illustrate the lack of modernity (Russett *et al.,* 1964, pp. 157, 224). Rwanda was a classic case of hierarchical ethnic stratification: the Tutsi (8 percent of the population) had been the lords of the Hutu. The legitimacy of Rwanda's caste system was supported by the underlying premise of inequality. The maintenance of inferior-superior relationships was part of the "rightful" order of things. Deprivation in Rwanda, while objectively quite severe, was subjectively much less so. Belgium's colonial rule had been grafted on top of this traditional system and had supported Tutsi lordship. Belgium changed its policy drastically in 1959, responding to international pressures. It sought egalitarian democracy, shaking the roots of an institutionalized inegalitarian system. It purged many Tutsi from the civilian bureaucracy and the police. It evicted many Tutsi chiefs and subchiefs. And it supported the 1961 coup, which abolished the Tutsi monarchy and established the republic. Revolution occurred in Rwanda in fits and starts. It was first a localized *jacquerie.* It turned into a long struggle with large-scale peasant participation. The target of Hutu fury was the Tutsi population. The Hutu, though mostly poor, were not all poor. Yet the fury of the peasantry was not aimed at the rich, Tutsi or Hutu, but at the Tutsi, rich or poor. It was a war of national disintegration, not a class war. The dead came from an ethnic group, not a social class (Lemarchand, 1968; Kuper, 1971). Another Hutu effort to overthrow the Tutsi in neighboring Burundi in 1972 failed. However, the structural characteristics were the same: a bloody racial war after the cracking of the long-stable hierarchical ethnic system.

A historical example suggests the same characteristics of low modernization, hierarchical ethnic stratification, and externally induced drastic change in institutionalization followed by dispersed, though large-scale, ethnic peasant revolt. Such was the case of the Indian uprisings in southern Peru and northwestern Bolivia in the 1780s. These Indians had been at the bottom of the hierarchical ethnic structure. They were described as submissive and docile. There was the same underlying normative premise of inequality as in Rwanda. Abuses and oppression had been rampant but, as Viceroy Guirior reported to the Crown after the events of the 1780s, "They have not produced such troublesome and regrettable demonstrations." It was not the continuity of oppression or the increase of social mobilization that accounts for the revolts of the 1780s but the drastic change in institutionalization. The Crown, needing revenue to fight European wars, centralized public administration to better raise taxes. These bore heavily on the traditional structure, undermining its legitimacy. Government demands on the Indians' resources increased.

Indian riots, uprisings, and finally large revolts developed from 1780 to 1782. When they had run their course some 100,000 people, or 5 percent of the estimated total populations of Peru and Bolivia, were dead. Although the white, traditionalist, urban upper and middle classes had stimulated Indian riots to oppose centralization of government, they held back when the largest rebellion was launched, led by Jose Gabriel Tupac Amaru. The intensity and the violence of this revolt got out of hand. Tupac Amaru claimed to be the special agent of the king of Spain *and* a restorer of the Inca royal tradition. His appeal to Indian symbols was strong and pervasive. If the whites closed ranks behind the royal government, the Indians—unlike the Hutu in Rwanda—did not become equally unified. Many Indians sided with the government, and the revolt eventually failed (Cornblit, 1970; Valcárcel, 1947; Kubler, 1967).

The crucial feature in Rwanda, Burundi, and southern Peru—northwestern Bolivia is that the social mobilization hypothesis does not apply. These are pre-social-mobilization revolts. They occur when the patterns of *institutionalization* are changed, with sharp, drastic consequences for those near the bottom of the ethnic hierarchy. Hierarchical ethnic structures exhibit the paradox of normative support for inequality for long periods of time and then large-scale, bloody social revolutions when the system's normative bases are eroded.

National Integration and Religious Politics

Historical religions perceive human history as real and central to the religious experience (Smith, 1970, pp. 246–79). The Semitic religions (Christianity,

Judaism, Islam) are historical. Historical events can be acts of divine revelation. All human history has meaning because there is a divine plan leading to a climax. History has a beginning and an end; salvation depends on what is revealed in history. Revelation and truth appear objectively rooted in historical fact; therefore, truth can be propositional or dogmatic. Under the impact of social mobilization, historical religions are likely to lead to ideological, change-oriented political parties with religious links. The Lord gets a little help from his adherents in advancing the divine plan to a just conclusion. Because salvation is linked to historical fact, large-scale mass political involvement is induced. Because truth is propositional or dogmatic, ideological partisan coherence is fostered.

For ahistorical religions, history has no divine purpose, no beginning, no end; it may be cyclical. Indic religions (Buddhism and Hinduism) are ahistorical. Individual salvation or self-realization is the point of the religious quest. Historical events are irrelevant to the process. There can thus be a great diversity of statements about the nature of the divine, which leads away from propositional or dogmatic truth. Consequently, ahistorical religions are much less likely to lead to ideological, change-oriented parties with religious links. The transcendental and the real worlds are not inextricably joined in a march to a simultaneous climax. At most, ahistorical religions, under the impact of social mobilization, will have parties that seek to defend the religious community.

Ecclesiastical religions (e.g., Christianity and Buddhism) emphasize the centrality of a particular structure, separate from government and society in theory and in organization, though with a special relation to both. Ecclesiastical religions are likely to lead to clericalism or the involvement of religious leaders in politics. Clericalism is typically independent of social mobilization. Unlike the ideological parties spawned in historical religious settings, clerical politics leads to a limited role for the laity. The laity often have no role in clerical politics. If laity are involved in a clerical organization, their role is secondary; the organization is not likely to have politically trained party workers or party discipline. Clericalism is not attached to a single party but seeks to put pressure on all parties. Clericalism, therefore, is an aspect of the politics of lobbies or interest groups, not of parties. Historical religions may have both parties and clericalism; ahistorical religions may have clericalism only. Organic religions (e.g., Hinduism and Islam) define their collective expression in terms of the structure of the entire society. Religion tends to be equated with society, and separate ecclesiastical organizations, if they exist, are of minor importance. Organic religions are thus much less likely to lead to clericalism. Islam provides a partial exception to this hypothesis.

An historical and ecclesiastical religion, Christianity, has spawned both partisan and clerical religious politics. The cleavages of the Reformation and the French Revolution, with their strong religious content, were reflected in the cleavage and party systems of Western European countries when the social and political mobilization of their populations began. Religion and religious politics did not wither away with modernity. They took different forms; institutionalized, mass-based religious parties or at least parties in which the religious bases of political programs and electoral support were very important have continued to exist in Europe (Lipset and Rokkan, 1967; Dahl, 1966).

In Latin America, with one exception, social mobilization reinforced the preexisting features of the religious political cleavages. Where a religious cleavage had been institutionalized into a Catholic conservative party, as in Chile, Ecuador, Colombia, and Mexico, mass-based religious parties would arise after social mobilization developed. Where a religious cleavage had not been institutionalized in the elite in the nineteenth century, such a cleavage did not tend to arise under social mobilization. Thus Argentina, Brazil, Peru, and Cuba, for example, did not develop large mass-based Catholic parties. The chief exception to this generalization is Venezuela, where a religious cleavage developed at about the same time (1940s) as there was a sharp acceleration of social mobilization. Small Christian democratic parties would develop by the 1970s virtually everywhere in Latin America, but they would have political significance in only two countries, Chile and Venezuela.

Some Latin American countries developed religious parties and others did not. This is different from the pattern in Western Europe, where religion-linked parties were more pervasive. A general hypothesis explains a fair number of cases. When the major political attacks against the Church were conducted by conservative agrarian elites, the Church became a lobby within the elite. No economic allies were available to it because the urban elites were typically just as much in favor of anticlericalism. The Church would change its allies and its support from party to party thereafter, and religious political cleavages were not institutionalized. In contrast, when the major political attacks against the Church were conducted by liberal, urban, commercial, professional, and incipient industrial elites, the Church allied with agrarian elites to form a conservative party, to which it would remain loyal for the next century. Religious political cleavages were institutionalized. The net effect of modernization in Latin America has been to reinvigorate these preexisting patterns of religious politics.

The two large Christian democratic parties—in Chile and Venezuela—arose under circumstances in which there were (1) a "conservative" religious cleavage, preexistent or newly developing, over such issues as public and religious education; (2) the availability of transnational change-oriented Catholic ideologies and (3) a prolonged period of very rapid social mobilization (especially expansion of adult literacy, which in turn raises social mobilization to a high level). The participation of the Catholic Church in politics was characterized, as it had been previously, by strong involvement by the bishops and priests. The mass-based political partisan dimension was an addition to, not a replacement of, the previous pattern of clerical politics (Vallier, 1970; Williams, 1967; Einaudi, 1969; Houtart and Rousseau, 1971; Mutchler, 1971; Mecham, 1966).

In the countries in which partisan religious cleavages had been institutionalized since the nineteenth century, religious differences still strongly affected political behavior. The chief difference that members of Mexico's official party, the PRI (Partido Revolucionario Institucional), and members of the main opposition party, the PAN (Partido Acción Nacional), perceived between them in the late 1950s was religion (Almond and Verba, 1965, p. 93). The most important difference between Conservative and Liberal party legislators in Colombia in the late 1960s was religion (Payne, 1968, pp. 82–88; Hoskin, 1971, pp. 41–43). In Chile, after a variety of controls for residence, occupation, and social class are introduced, religion is still a statistically significant predictor of changes in political behavior (Behrman, 1972). And where there had been no institutionalized religious cleavage, religion makes no political difference, as in Argentina (Kirkpatrick, 1971, pp. 133–42) or Cuba, where a religious cleavage almost took root in the early 1960s only to be defused by the end of the 1960s (Büntig, 1971; Domínguez, 1972a). In Brazil the Church continues to function as a lobby, not a party. It now lobbies, to a large extent, against the perceived excesses of the military government. But it has not formed a party as such, nor is it likely that it will (Sanders, 1967; de Kadt, 1967, 1971; Wiarda and Wiarda, 1970).

When modernization occurs in an ahistorical religion, the issues are whether a party of communal defense will appear, and whether there is an ecclesiastical structure. Hinduism and Theravada Buddhism, as ahistorical religions, have not had ideological parties with religious links. Hinduism has had parties of communal defense, while Buddhism has had no parties at all. Ecclesiastical structures have made a difference too. Churchless Hinduism contrasts sharply with the clerical politics of Buddhist monks.[11]

Theravada Buddhism in Burma has had an ecclesiastical structure but no political party. Since independence the Burmese organization of Buddhist monks has struggled to increase its influence in the society. Since the mid-1950s the monks sought to make Buddhism the state religion. After U Nu's political party split, the monks allied with U Nu; the 1960 election was waged, among other issues, on the role of religion in Burma. The successful coalition implemented an appropriate amendment to the Constitution in 1961. When U Nu sought to amend the Constitution further, to protect the beleaguered religious minorities, the militant monks of the Union Sangha League attacked the proposal bitterly. On the day of the final vote two thousand monks picketed the parliament, to no avail. This political mobilization reveals both the political strengths and weaknesses of Theravada Buddhism. It can mobilize many monks effectively for risky tasks. But there was no clear-cut role for the Buddhist laity in the religious system which could be made relevant to contemporary political problems. Therefore no political party would be mobilized (D. E. Smith, 1965, pp. 230–80; Smith, 1973; van der Mehden, 1963).

In Ceylon a coalition of Theravada Buddhist monks came together for the first time in the 1956 national election. It included laymen who were also interested in changing the government. This was an interest group, a political lobby, and not a party. It did not have politically trained party workers or party discipline. Although laymen were involved in the organization, the effective political activities were carried out by the monks, who sought to induce voters to support S.W.R.D. Bandaranaike's Sri Lanka Freedom party. This party won power and proceeded to increase the weight of Buddhism in Ceylon's public life. But not far enough. The Buddhist monks' interest group protested against the lack of fulfillment of religious-political promises in 1956 and 1958; in September 1959, a monk assassinated Prime Minister Bandaranaike. The Sri Lanka Freedom party, under both S.W.R.D. and Sirimavo Bandaranaike, was always more than a Buddhist party. It sought support from the Sinhalese-speaking population; it pursued an active language policy; it also sought to gain and hold onto labor support. It supported the interests of Buddhism but clearly was not a Buddhist lay party. It was criticized by Buddhist monks for its insufficient commitment to the religion. The organizations of Buddhist monks continued to operate as an interest group, not within a party (Wriggins, 1960, pp. 193–210, 342–48, 363–65; Wilson, 1966; Kearney, 1967). All the major Ceylonese parties sought Buddhist support. Party-Buddhist relations are in contrast to Christian religious parties in Western Europe and Latin America, which were much more capable of integrating laity and clergy over time in support of a political party. The Buddhist monks were rather capable of acting politically as an organized group for communal defense but less capable of mobilizing the laity into a party or into extensive subsidiary lay organizations with a change-oriented ideology.

Hinduism did not have a monastic organization like Buddhism or a priesthood or ministry like Christianity. Hinduism's ecclesiastical organization was weak. Brahmans, by the mid-twentieth century, were not primarily devoted to fulfilling their traditional priestly functions. The relative insignificance of clericalism meant that religious politics was limited mostly to communal defense. Ahistorical beliefs hindered the growth of ideological parties with religious links. Thus Hinduism gives rise to political parties of communal defense but not to clerical politics or ideological religious parties.

A variety of Hindu political parties arose in response to the political mobilization of Hindu and Muslim communities in India in the first half of the twentieth century, which eventually led to partition in the subcontinent. The oldest was the Hindu Mahasabha. It has always been a communal party; its membership is open only to Hindus. It stands for a Hindu, not a secular, state. A Hindu communal movement that did not become a party is Ram Rajya Parishad. It has emphasized militant, nonelectoral Hinduism. A more open and electorally successful party has been the Bharatiya Jana Sangh. It has joined the more radical communal parties in attacking the "Muslim appeasement" of the Congress party. It is also concerned with religious legislation such as the banning of cow slaughter and of foreign missionaries, total integration of Kashmir, and "toughness" toward Pakistan. It claims, unlike the Hindu Mahasabha, that its membership is open to all Indians; and it is more concerned with noncommunal issues than the Hindu Mahasabha is. As a modernized communal political party, the Jana Sangh recognizes that its probable supporters vote for it mostly, but not exclusively, because of communal issues. Therefore, its programs and election campaigns have tended to emphasize a more diverse view of the electorate. For electoral purposes, this appeal continues to rest on Hindu religious-political mobilization (Smith, 1963, pp. 405–89; Baxter, 1966).

These Hindu communal parties are parties of the laity, not of monks, as in Burma and Ceylon. The manifestations of religious politics in these three South Asian countries are rather different. Their effect on national integration, however, is fairly similar; they all inject an ascriptive, though sometimes modernized, issue into politics. Governments must deal not only with economic development for tomorrow but also with timeless questions, of rectitude and honor, of pride and prejudice, raised by religious politics.

Islam—like Christianity—has been a historically conscious religion. Although the ulamas differ in origin, roles, functions, and development from the Christian and Buddhist ecclesiastical structures, the ulamas' political behavior is comparable to clerical behavior in Christianity and Buddhism. Islamic theology does not have an organized priesthood as does Christianity. A direct relationship with God is emphasized. Mass religious instruction in school, a bulwark of clerical control in Christianity, is minimal. But Islam has had a stronger juridical-legal aspect than Christianity; the judges of the law and the commentators on the law have been as influential as the Christian clergy. This religious-legal approach, therefore, has thrust the ulamas into the midst of important political controversies (Abbott, 1968, pp. 5, 20–21). Therefore, one finds both ideological partisan politics and clericalist politics in Islam. The presence of clericalism in an organic religion is an exception to the hypothesis that predicts the contrary.

An example of the political role of the ulamas was the debate over an Islamic constitution for Pakistan. The ulamas provided an important link between the government and the people throughout the debates. Because political parties within Pakistan, especially during the immediate postpartition years, had a very weak mass base, the role of the ulamas in the politics of factions was enhanced. The ulamas were divided, for both religious and political reasons; this made it possible for other political groups to use religious appeals that were most self-serving. But it did not decrease the political significance of clerical politics, whereas it did make national integration more difficult because political bargaining ploys were endowed with religious significance.

Leonard Binder has noted that, paradoxically, an increase of both economic development and literacy in Pakistan may make Islam an issue in itself.
Some secularizing tendencies in Pakistani society may be strengthened. A likely
effect may be the renewed mobilization of more traditional clerical groups to
combat the possible downgrading of Islam in an Islamic state. Hence modernization in Pakistan, for the foreseeable future, may increase the salience of religious political conflicts; this, in turn, will make national political integration
a continuously elusive problem for an already rump Pakistan (Binder, 1963,
pp. 22–33, 277–380).

Pakistan also exemplifies the mass partisan aspects of Islam and politics.
The development of the Pakistan movement and the Muslim League as the
political party dedicated to the partition of India is one of the classic and mo-
mentous examples of mass-based religious politics. It brought the problem of
national integration to its tragic resolution, namely, the first partition of the
subcontinent. Moreover, by placing so much significance on a single religious
cleavage, in order to mobilize large numbers of people for the partition of
British India, it ignored or downplayed language and ethnic cleavages, which
would eventually lead to the partition of Pakistan itself in the early 1970s.
Such an emphasis on a religious cleavage made it extraordinarily difficult for
Muslim League politicians to organize politics in the new state once their goal
was achieved (Sayeed, 1967, pp. 31–59; Wheeler, 1970).

Finally, specialized problems for national integration are posed by religious sects. Max Weber's distinction between church and sect is a frequent
starting point for the sociology of religion. Sect membership has often been a
certificate of moral qualification. A sect is a voluntary association of only those
adults who, according to the sect's principles, are religiously and morally
qualified. Sects have typically been opposed to, in competition with, or at least
not supportive of established state religion. Churches, on the other hand, have
often been established by the state. One is often "born" into a church, where
the righteous and the unrighteous coexist. Everyone belongs, especially in a
state church. Sects emphasize a more direct relationship between one's conscience and God. Churches tend to emphasize more the role of the clergy and
the state, especially in the case of state churches. Sects emphasize, far more
than churches, a consummatory value pattern, in which the sacred and the
secular are not distinct but intimately related spheres of life (Gerth and Mills,
1958, pp. 305–6). In many ways the political consequences of religious sectarianism are not different from the more general cases of religious politics or
from the more general cases of parallel or horizontal patterns of sociocultural
stratification. But sects do differ from these in the intensity of belief which they
may generate to propel members either toward or away from politics.

Seven different types of sects have been identified (B. R. Wilson, 1969; B.
A. Wilson, 1963). Three of these pull their members away from politics. Con-
versionist sects emphasize that the world is corrupt, that it can only be changed

if man is changed, and that man must convert religiously. There is little interest in politics. Pentecostal movements throughout the world are of this sort. Introversionist sects, in contrast, do not emphasize conversion and proselytism but withdraw from the world to enjoy the security of their personal holiness. Holiness movements and eighteenth-century European pietism are examples. Thaumaturgical sects insist that the supernatural can be experienced by people in their daily lives. Normal reality can be suspended because of the operation of spiritual intervention. Response to the world, as in the gnostic sects, is not collective but individual; it is, however, less intellectualized than in gnostic sects. Spiritualist sects, in their varied forms throughout the world, belong here.

Gnostic or manipulationist sects insist on a particular and distinctive knowledge; they define themselves toward the world by accepting its basic goals. They try to change existing methods used for attaining the goals of the culture within which they live. Worldly activity is reinterpreted; the idea of a personal God or savior tends to be replaced by ethical principles to apply in one's daily life. Christian Scientists, Rosacrucians, Unitarians, and Scientologists are examples. Politics are welcome but as individual, rather than collective, acts. These sects do not emphasize religious links with political groups. Gnostic sects are a transition from the otherworldly to this-worldly sects.

Three kinds of sects, in contrast, may propel their members toward politics. Revolutionary sects want to get rid of the social order when the time is ripe, if necessary by force. The world is deterministically and eschatologically explained. Predictions about the future are important. Conversion is gradual and admission to the sect is not automatic. The members of the sect are God's instruments. The more extreme versions of revolutionary sectarianism have led to Sudanese Mahdism and the Taiping rebellion. Sharing a common belief structure, though without military features, are Jehovah's Witnesses. Sects may move away from revolution toward reformism, as the Quakers have through time. This sect type studies the world in order to involve itself in its reformation. It is in the world but untouched by impurity. It seeks to become a social and political conscience. Finally, utopian sects such as Tolstoyans, Christian Socialists, and the like partly withdraw from the world and partly seek to reform it. Their emphasis is on communitarianism for the entire world (Wilson, 1963).

The most potentially politically disruptive subset of sects are revolutionary sects that may accept violence. These millenarian movements hope for a complete and radical change in the world, which will be reflected in the millennium —a world without its present deficiencies. In addition to rejecting the present external world, these sects also have an eschatological, historical, future-oriented religious ideology, which is only somewhat vaguely perceived (Hobsbawm, 1959, pp. 57–107; Lanternari, 1963; Cohn, 1957).

Ahistorical religions such as Buddhism and Hinduism are not likely to generate many millenarian movements. The evidence suggests that when millenarian movements are derived from an apparently ahistorical religion they have either significantly altered the more orthodox religious beliefs or borrowed from other religious. This has happened, for example, in the development of the Cao Dai and the Hoa Hao in South Vietnam. These sects injected history into their view of Mahayana Buddhism—a history with a definable end point. The Cao Dai have broken further from Buddhism to present their faith as the only truly indigenous Vietnamese religion. The Cao Dai and the Hoa Hao have also turned to considerable political and military activity within South Vietnam, showing impressive powers of survival through a combination of the sacred and the secular in a typically consummatory approach to social life (Hill, 1971). The historical consciousness with an end point, which is typical of millenarian movements, is not limited to the world's main religions. Such sects have developed outside of the world's main religions—in Africa, the South Pacific, and other areas. But the common features remain a view of an impending catastrophe and the regeneration of the world thereafter and, in a good many cases, use of violence—for example, the destruction of the Europeans was an integral part of the political and religious mixture of anticolonial millenarianism (Mair, 1959).

In short, religious sectarianism can have very diverse effects on national political integration—apart from its impact on the development of political culture (Lipset, 1970, pp. 305–73). Some religious sects are so otherworldly that their main impact on politics is their own withdrawal from political concerns. Among this-worldly sects, a major distinction exists between gnostic sects, which do not emphasize collective religious and political behavior, and those that are strongly collective and link religion and politics in a consummatory fashion. Revolutionary sects are the most potentially disruptive among the latter. Within these, those that accept violence as an instrument to rid themselves and others of an evil world pose the most threats to national integration.

National Integration: Some Solutions

At least five different types of responses to the problem of national integration can be identified: social engineering, assimilation, institutional, genocide, and partition. Social engineering is the effort to submerge the cleavages of national integration into the cleavages of something else, typically but not only those of social class. This requires either the elimination of national integration cleavages, often by ignoring them, or their containment through cross-pressures, crosscutting cleavages, or political culture. The approach has often been tried, but it encountered difficulties in parallel systems of stratification. After the nationwide general strike of June 1964, for example, Nigerian workers became more politically prominent. Because federal elections were to be held in December 1964, political appeals to the working class were accelerated. Such appeals came both from the major political parties, which typically emphasized ethnic loyalties, and from politicians trying to develop a class-conscious

Nigerian Labor party. Therefore, the cross-pressures on Nigerian workers at this time had quasi-experimental characteristics. The result, not unlike those in other countries, was that ethnic loyalties prevailed over class loyalties in the crunch. Shortly after the strike 88 percent of workers surveyed indicated some support for a Labor party; shortly before the election this had dropped to 41 percent (Melson, 1971, pp. 161–66).

Class loyalties did claim the support of a sizable portion of Nigerian workers. As in the case of a great many Western and Eastern European countries (Lipset and Rokkan, 1967; Dahl, 1966; Janos, 1971; Burks, 1961), both class appeals and the appeals of linguistic, religious, and ethnic groups have resonance in the electorate. They are likely to coexist with different degrees of success at different times. But it is not likely that the industrial revolution and class consciousness will wipe the preexisting set of cleavages off the political map.

Hierarchical systems of stratification, by definition, show a very close correlation between social class and the position of particular communal and cultural groups. Elites in countries with such systems typically argue that the disabilities of a particular ethnic or linguistic group result from class obstacles, not from deliberate segregation, ignoring evidence that these two criteria for stratification are closely joined in these systems. This elite logic, moreover, is not limited to allegedly traditional regimes.

The Cuban system of ethnic stratification, for example, has been quite similar to those elsewhere in Latin America. There was a pattern of ethnic segregation in revolutionary Cuba, of which only very little was supported by legislation. There was also considerable individual mobility for blacks and mulattoes. The revolution repealed the meager ethnically discriminatory legislation. It has also stressed a class approach to policy and therefore claims to have solved whatever racial problem the country may have had. Therefore, intellectual, artistic, and mutual aid societies by blacks and for blacks which existed in pre-revolutionary Cuba have been forced to disband. Public concerns about the persistence of black-white inequality are strongly discouraged.

While the condition of Cuban blacks has probably improved because they had been disproportionately poor, the government publishes no data to verify or refute the point. One can still show that the proportion of nonwhite Cubans in the Central Committee of the Communist party in the late 1960s was no different from the nonwhite share of the Cuban Congress in the 1940s—about 9 percent, or one-third of what would be expected from population shares. Standards of beauty and status are still based on whiteness—in posters, beauty contests, and newspapers. In short, Cuba could use a class approach to submerge ethnic differences because class stratification was inherent in the ethnic stratification system. Yet the ethnic problem has not been solved—only wished away. The revolutionary government's insistence on having solved the racial question also means that no efforts are made to meet the special needs of Cuban blacks or to remedy the legacy of racial inequality as such. The Cuban revolution shares both its problem and its approach to ethnicity with its revolutionary predecessors, the Soviet Union and China. Russification, whether in Soviet Islamic central Asia or the Ukraine and the Baltic states, and Han "imperialism," especially in Tibet, suggest that communist governments have not succeeded where others have failed (Domínguez, 1975).

In general, tinkering with mass characteristics is not especially helpful in contributing to successful, long-term conflict regulation. Social engineering has more often failed than not; when it seems to succeed, it is typically because it has been mixed with another type of conflict regulating solution. Social mobilization is likely to yield an increase in the probability of conflict in unintegrated societies. Hypotheses about cross-pressures, crosscutting divisions, and political culture do not help to explain long-term successful conflict regulation in societies deeply troubled by cleavages of national integration. At most these hypotheses may indicate why some groups or strata are more or less likely than others to partake in intense conflict or violence, especially in the short term, under conditions in which such intense conflict or violence already exists and has broken down the regulative methods (Nordlinger, 1972, pp. 88–104, 110–16; Esman, 1973, pp. 69–72; Keech, 1972, p. 404; Domínguez, 1972b, pp. 138–40, 425–42).

The second type of solution is the effort to induce the assimilation of the politically subordinate subcultural group into the politically dominant cultural group.[12] This is more difficult to do when the differentiating symbol is skin color (Isaacs, 1969) than when it is religion or language. Over a period of time a people can convert from one religion to another, learn a new language, and even forget the old; but people find it much more difficult to shed their skin! Therefore this solution clearly applies much less well than others to the large number of cases in which color is at stake. But there are other cases in which assimilation has been tried.

Perhaps the most successful case of religious assimilation was Spain's and Portugal's conversion of the Indians and the Africans in America to the Iberian version of Roman Catholicism. Although religious syncretism has been extensively at work, undermining the orthodoxy of Latin American Catholicism, and Protestant missionaries have enjoyed some modest success, especially in Brazil and Chile (Willems, 1969), Latin America is one of the world's more homogeneous religious-political settings. Political cleavages of significance have existed not so much between religious communities as between secular and antisecular groups.

The record of linguistic assimilation in Latin America is more mixed. In Paraguay, Bolivia, Peru, Ecuador, and Guatemala large numbers of Indian-language speakers remain. They do not pose as severe a threat to national integration in these countries as they do in other countries, because the proportion of Indian monolinguals who are socially mobilized is nil. But they do retard the process of modernization and continue to be an issue in national politics.

The most conspicuous Latin American success in linguistic assimilation has been Mexico. Even prior to the Mexican revolution the proportion of Indian monolinguals in the Mexican adult population was far less than in other Latin American countries with large Indian populations at the end of colonial rule. The governments of the Mexican revolution have systematically promoted the expansion of rural educational systems and of language training to reach Indian monolinguals. Though the proportion of persons who might be classified as Indians on general cultural grounds in Mexico remains fairly high, the proportion of Indian monolinguals has been below 5 percent since 1940. Despite classic debates in Mexico concerning public policy toward the Indian question, the goal has been the linguistic assimilation into Spanish of the largely rural and traditional Indian monolingual population. This has been impressively successful, though often filled with human pain (Ruiz, 1963, pp. 123–72; Heath, 1972).

Another effort toward assimilation can be found in Ethiopia. The Amhara constituted about one-quarter of the people of Ethiopia in the 1960s, but their influence outstripped their numbers. Donald Levine (1965a, 1965b) has argued that the ideas, symbols, and values that govern Ethiopian politics are drawn from Amhara culture. The radical inegalitarianism of Amhara culture, at the same time, legitimates the dominant position of the Amhara in Ethiopian national life. This is not, moreover, a static condition; it is enhanced by the process of Amharization of Ethiopian life. The Amhara monarchy has been perpetuated; the Amhara have been predominant in the top political offices. Amhara customs are spread throughout Ethiopia by soldiers, settlers, officials, and teachers. Amharic has been the required language in all schools, courts, and government offices. Perhaps half of the population knows Amharic. Amharic names have replaced indigenous place-names in many parts of the country. The Christian Church and the Ethiopian state have been closely associated. Though Christians probably do not compose more than half the population, most political leaders of the country have been Christian—regardless of ethnic, tribal, or linguistic background.

It is arguable, of course, that the spread of modernization—now barely beginning—could severely strain Ethiopia's multiethnic society. Thus far, however, Amharization has continued with a modest degree of success to preserve the integrity of Ethiopia, except for the possible secession of former Italian Eritrea, with historically weaker links to core Ethiopia. Because many of the non-Amhara are also among the least modernized Ethiopians, it is possible that Ethiopia could encounter a "Latin American solution," in which modernization and assimilation occur simultaneously and modernization rarely occurs without assimilation. If so, yet another case of successful assimilation could be recorded.

Assimilation policies, however, may also lead to an increase of political conflict over national integration. The Constitution of India provided that the official language of the Union would be Hindi in Deva Nagari script, with international numerals. For a period of 15 years from the effective date of the Constitution (1950), English would continue to be used for all the official purposes of the Union. The first Official Language Commission reported in 1956 that it would be the duty of the Union to promote the spread of Hindi. Hindi was also supposed to assimilate the forms, style, and expressions of other languages in India to enrich its vocabulary and range of expression. The attempts to implement the language provisions of the Indian Constitution generated more intense rivalry than unity. Assimilation into Hindi and the end of the use of English as an official language were strongly fought by non-Hindi speakers through political parties and communal associations.

The 1967 amendment to the Official Languages Act guaranteed the continuation of a two-language policy (Hindi and English) for all official transactions. An accompanying resolution authorized a three-language policy for the school system. The following languages would be taught in school: (1) the regional and local languages, when they differ; (2) Hindi or, in Hindi-speaking areas, another Indian language; and (3) English or another modern European language. For Union civil service examinations regional languages could be used provided there was additional knowledge of English or Hindi. Assimilationism in India, therefore, not only did not succeed but threatens to increase India's national integration problem. Assimilationism became part of the problem, not the solution. A solution depended on other instruments (Das Gupta, 1970).

A related approach within this family of solutions is the effort to induce assimilation into a new integrated identity above the existing cultural or tribal identities. Esman (1973, p. 58) has called it syncretic integration. Thus the political salience of existing communal pluralism is to be reduced, transcended, and eventually eliminated. New overarching symbols that command effective allegiance must be created quickly. On the whole this approach has tended to fail, in part because it is often little more than a mask for the assimilation of subgroups into the symbols and identity of the dominant sociocultural group. Are the new symbols Yugoslav or Serbian, Javanese or Indonesian, Ceylonese or Sinhalese? It is often no more than a fraud, and it is perceived as such. The efforts to create a national identity in a short period of time are likely to be unsuccessful and will probably increase mass violence and governmental repression (Esman, 1973, pp. 58–60; Nordlinger, 1972, pp. 37–39). The successful cases of assimilationism occur over long periods of time (Merritt, 1966). "Building a nation-state," Joseph Strayer (1966, p. 25) has noted in his analysis of the development of the state in the European middle ages, "is a slow and complicated affair." The French African experience is an especially disappointing one (Foltz, 1965; Emerson, 1966).

The third type of solution stresses the importance of political institutions. Eric Nordlinger (1972) has argued that conflict group leaders play a critical role in the process of conflict regulation in already divided societies. Only they can make a positive contribution. Conflict group members typically have either a directly negative impact on conflict regulation in societies characterized by severe problems of national integration or an indirect impact (positive or negative). The structured predominance of elites over nonelites within their own conflict groups, therefore, is a necessary condition for conflict regulating outcomes. Nordlinger discusses his hypotheses with reference to four European countries (Belgium, the Netherlands, Switzerland, and Austria) and two Asian countries (Lebanon and Malaysia). The conflicts include both major types of national integration problems: ethnic-linguistic and religious.

A variant within this family of solutions is the institutionalization of the dominance of the leading sociocultural or communal group or stratum. This institutionalized dominance (Esman, 1973, pp. 56–57) regulates interaction among the various groups in a society to the systematic advantage of the dominant group. This is required for the long-term survival of hierarchical systems. From South Africa to the southern United States until the mid-twentieth century, from Liberia, Rwanda, Burundi, and Ethiopia to Latin America, such institutionalization of dominance has been a necessity for the political system.

Yet another variant within this family of solutions is federalism. Federalism can be interpreted as a bargain between prospective national leaders and officials of constituent governments for the purpose of aggregating territory. A necessary condition for the federal bargain may be the desire to expand territorial control—but without violence. Hence concessions must be made if such nonviolent expansion is to hold (Riker, 1964, pp. 11–12). Federalism can also be thought of as a bargain to prevent the fragmentation of an existing state through the granting of autonomy (especially territorial) to constituent groups or strata. On the whole this has not been a terribly successful solution either, but some cases of at least modestly successful conflict resolution can be explained in these terms (Nordlinger, 1972, pp. 104–10; Esman, 1973, pp. 63–66).

One of the more successful examples may be the reorganization of the Indian states primarily on a linguistic basis during the 1950s. The national government of India sought to prevent the reorganization of the Indian states for fear that it would destroy the Union; yet after the spread of linguistic protest, from Madras to Bombay and to the Punjab, the major threat to the preservation of the Union was the failure to act. The States Reorganization Commission of the Government of India reorganized state boundary lines. Though it refused to do so explicitly on linguistic grounds—and there were notable exceptions—the linguistic principle was followed in most cases (Weiner, 1962, pp. 56–60). This defensive federalism has not quieted all of India's national integration problems, but it seems to have made an important contribution to the management and regulation of the national integration problem.

The fourth and fifth types of solutions are also tragic outcomes. The fourth specifies that members of the dominant cultural group perceive the subcultural group as an international enemy, unfortunately and perhaps accidentally located within the same state boundaries. Genocidal war or forced emigration may then be tried. Rwanda, Burundi, Biafra, Northern Ireland, and Bangladesh are but recent names in this tragic and criminal story. The fifth solution is territorial partition into two independent states. The double partition of the Indian subcontinent in the late 1940s and in the early 1970s illustrates how the tragic outcome can become painful but by that time necessary. But partition is not always a definitive outcome. Indeed the need to partition Pakistan a quarter century after the partition of India and the continuing troubles of Northern Ireland illustrate the perilous insufficiency of this approach in important cases. Partition also often does no more than transform—without solving—an internal problem into an international one.

A less tragic and dramatic but more frequent and equally troubling outcome occurs through the "partition" of the people of a state by induced or forced emigration. The problem of refugees has plagued virtually every continent in the twentieth century—in Germany, the Middle East, Korea, Indochina, the Indian subcontinent. Since about 1960, however, Africa has been the main new source of refugees. As the problem has spread (Matthews, 1972), interstate conflict between states of origin and host states for the refugees has increased. A new national integration problem within the host state is created when refugees settle there permanently rather than return to their country of origin.

One well-known example of the mixed effects of emigration, involving some elements of a solution, has been that of Roman Catholics in Vietnam. Hundreds of thousands of Catholic Vietnamese fled the North (about 65 percent of all northern Catholics) after the 1954 Geneva partition. One effect in the North was to help consolidate Vietminh control over the countryside. Land that had been owned by the Catholics could be redistributed; an internal source of opposition was exported. The arrival of the Catholics in South Vietnam, on the other hand, had the effects of bolstering the short-term political position of President Ngo Dinh Diem while worsening the general political problems of national integration in South Vietnam. It also added a refugee-Catholic dimension to the North-South confrontation in Vietnam (Fall, 1967, pp. 153–54). The internationalization of an internal national integration problem can have some benefits for the expelling state, but it is likely to have problematic consequences for the host state.

Over the long run, emigration of large numbers of people from one country to another is likely to create a parallel system of ethnic, linguistic, or religious stratification. Therefore, it is likely to institutionalize a severe political problem. In many countries of Europe these parallel systems have been well contained within one state. In Africa and Asia the international and internal problems of national integration are likely to continue. In south Asia (Connor, 1969), for example, not only are the systems parallel but the subordinate sociocultural groups often populate the border regions and become strategically important for both domestic and international reasons. Thus the long-term effects of partitioning solutions—despite some possible short-term benefits, as in the case of North Vietnam—are likely to create new problems of their own.

In sum, national integration remains more of a problem than a solution. The solutions that have worked rely either on the slow evolution of political skills in the elites and on institutions or on the slow transformation of plural societies into societies with more homogeneous characteristics. When the latter has happened, many human costs have been incurred. National integration, for good or ill, is likely to continue to demand political statesmanship of the sort that is often in short supply.

VII. THE FUTURE OF POLITICAL DEVELOPMENT

The bulk of this essay has been devoted to identifying concepts, hypotheses, and substantive findings that are useful to understanding the development of political culture, participation, institutions, and integration in the context of socioeconomic modernization. We have focused not on the study of political development but on political development itself. Nonetheless, in our opening section we did discuss the origins of recent academic concern with political development in the 1950s and early 1960s; here, in conclusion, it would be equally appropriate to make a few comments on the possible and probable future of the study of political development.

Work in almost any scholarly field tends to evolve in a sequence of surge, pause, redirection, and new surge. In the early 1970s the initial surge, which had emerged about 1960, in the study of political development had about run its course. The key issues, concepts, problems that commanded the attention of Western (primarily American) political scientists during the early part of the decade had now been formulated, elaborated, debated, and refined. Empirical studies continued to be made of particular political development topics in individual countries and comparatively, but the theoretical impetus had clearly weakened. There was a pause in which new interests and concerns began to appear, stimulating a reconsideration of existing theory and a redirection of that theory toward new topics and issues.

Political Development as History

The elaboration of political development theories was stimulated in large part by the dramatic social, economic, and political problems and changes that seemed to exist in the contemporary Third World. Scholars had, of course, been aware of the historical experience of European and American political development and had often implicitly used that experience as a base point for analyzing political change in the Third World. But the principal geographical focus of empirical concern, particularly for American political scientists, was in the contemporary experiences of the countries of Asia, Africa, the Middle

East, and Latin America. In the middle and late 1960s, however, scholars began increasingly to return to the study of the historical political development of Europe and America, applying to that subject ideas and concepts that had been generated in the analysis of Third World experience. This shift in attention reflected the following.

1. A decline in American foreign policy interest in Third World problems and a renewed concern with the problems and prospects of change and stability in the United States and Western European countries.

2. The obvious methodological problem of attempting to study the how, why, and consequences of political change with reference only to the contemporary environment. Many of the studies that did attempt to generate developmental models were based on cross-national comparisons that implicitly or explicitly involved the assumption that the evolution of the currently less developed countries would recapitulate that of the more developed countries. This methodological problem pointed to the desirability of longitudinal analyses of the actual historical evolution of one or more countries.

3. The difficulties of research in the developing countries and the availability of substantial primary data and numerous secondary analyses relating to the historical evolution of Western countries over sustained periods of time.

4. The possibility of analyzing the consequences as well as the causes of different patterns of political development. This concern reflected a strong trend generally in political science to focus attention on the outputs and outcomes of the political process, that is, to look at politics as an independent as well as a dependent variable.

5. The simple desire to test the relevance and validity of theories of political development against the historical experience of the West and to compare that experience with the political evolution of Third World countries.

One major manifestation of this shift in focus among scholars was to be found in the work of the SSRC Committee on Comparative Politics. The first major product of the Committee was the Almond and Coleman volume, concerned exclusively with *The Politics of the Developing Areas* (1960). The Committee's second major effort was its series of seven brown-jacketed volumes, five of which dealt with the relation of political development to education, political culture, political parties, bureaucracy, and communications; one with the political modernization of Japan and Turkey; and one with the crises and sequences in political development (Coleman, 1965; Pye and Verba, 1965; LaPalombara and Weiner, 1966; LaPalombara, 1963; Pye, 1963; Ward and Rustow, 1964; Binder *et al.,* 1971). All of these were edited volumes and the bulk of the contributions dealt with Third World countries, although there were some articles dealing with the European and American experiences. Finally, in a third phase at the end of the 1960s, the attention of the Committee turned almost entirely to European history, leading to two volumes. One, edited by Raymond Grew (forthcoming) and authored almost entirely by historians, looks at the political development of individual European countries in terms of the Committee's concepts of crises and sequences. The second, edited by Charles Tilly (1975) and authored by both political scientists and historians, analyzes on a comparative basis the historical "state building" experiences of Western European countries in developing tax systems, armies, bureaucracies, police forces, and comparable accoutrements of the modern nation-state. In a sense the study of political development in the 1970s had returned to many of the questions that-had occupied Carl Friedrich and other scholars in the 1930s.

A second major focus of attention derived from a concern with the ways in which democratic government emerged in Europe. There were likely to be, as Dankwart Rustow argued, significant differences between the conditions necessary to give rise to democratic government and those necessary to sustain it. Some of these studies involved quantitative, longitudinal analyses of the social, economic, communications, and cultural correlates and prerequisites of democratic evolution. Others focused on the relation between the development of cleavages and "contestation," on the one hand, and the political mobilization and expansion of the electorate, on the other.[13]

Still other scholars were concerned more explicitly with the applicability of political development theories to the American experience. At first the focus of attention was on the relevance of the American historical experience to the problems of the Third World; in a second phase the stress was on the relevance of theories derived from Third World experience to American historical development. Lipset (1963) had argued that the United States ought to be considered "the first new nation" and had pointed to the problems of national integration and political legitimacy confronting the United States in the late eighteenth and early nineteenth centuries and the extent to which the charismatic leadership of Washington helped to resolve those problems. In a similar vein, Clinton Rossiter (1971) discussed pre–Civil War American history in terms of political modernization. Taking issue with Lipset, Huntington (1968) contended that twentieth-century developing countries were "old societies and new states," while America in the eighteenth century had been a "new society and an old state" with working political institutions and practices inherited from Tudor England and with few of the problems of disestablishing a traditional social structure confronting contemporary less developed countries. Consequently, political modernization theories are of only limited value in understanding the American experience outside the South (Huntington, 1974b). In this connection, H. Douglas Price (1964) and Lester Salamon (1972, 1973) showed the particular relevance of political development concepts to the modernization of the South as that sector of American society where a traditional social structure had been most deeply entrenched and was overthrown only by application of organized violence by the modernizing center.

The External Context of Political Development

The merging in the late 1950s of area interests in Asia, Africa, and Latin America with the behavioral interest in systemic analysis led to the development of political development work on essentially a comparative basis. The patterns of development in individual countries were studied and compared in order to arrive at generalizations through the comparison of the processes of change in discrete societies. As a result of these origins in the discipline of comparative politics, the study of political development paid relatively little attention to the impact of external factors (apart from the impact of colonial heritage) on the development of societies. The study of political development was divorced from the study of international relations and concern with the broader international context in which development was taking place.

Beginning in the early 1960s this tendency in American political science was more than compensated for by the emergence of a very different tendency in the social and economic ideas of a number of thinkers, many of whom were citizens of developing countries. The common concern of these theorists was to explain the absence of or deficiencies in the economic and political development of Third World countries resulting from the continuing impact of the developed countries. The "developed" status of some countries perpetuated or created "underdevelopment" in other countries. Many of these thinkers were Latin Americans, such as Raúl Prebisch, Theotonio Dos Santos, Cândido Mendes, Osvaldo Sunkel, André Gunder Frank, Henrique Cardoso, Helio Jaguaribe. In some instances, such as Gunder Frank, the framework was more or less explicitly Marxist; in other cases it was not. But in all instances the decisive influence on development was seen as sources external to the society concerned. The common concepts, worded in different ways, focused on the relation between the "metropole" and the "periphery," which was variously described as one of neoimperialism, dependence, neocolonialism, and the like. In the late 1960s these and related concepts caught on in some degree in New Left intellectual circles in the United States and were elaborated and, in some respects, diluted and politicized in the debates over the proper role of the United States in world affairs.

A situation thus existed in which, to oversimplify, Establishment political science ignored a phenomenon, while radical social theory exaggerated it. The mainstreams in political science clearly did not pay sufficient attention to the ways in which the external environment influenced and constrained the development of Third World countries; the radical social-economic theorists often overemphasized the role of such influences, attributing a determinative influence to them, more as a result of doctrine than of analysis. Subtle psychological factors may have been at work on both sides. American political scientists may have avoided external influences because they themselves were, in some measure, one of those influences. Third World radical theorists may have exaggerated the role of external influences, on the other hand, in order to rationalize and justify their own failures to develop their societies.

As we argued in the second part of this essay, however, the relative impact of external and domestic environments on political development deserves careful analysis. Such analysis, in turn, requires a theoretical framework that does not prejudge the issue and empirical studies of individual and comparative cases. In the late 1960s Rosenau's work on "linkages" (1969) and Kurth's concept of "hegemony" (1970) represented efforts to meet the conceptual need. Empirical analyses often focused on the means of external influence (e.g., the effects of military intervention, private investment, economic and military assistance) rather than on the objects of such influence. Descriptions of and statistics on the means were often taken to be ipso facto proof of the effects of such means. What was clearly needed were studies of the changes that did or did not occur in political culture, participation, institutions, stability, and integration, focused precisely on the relative impact of domestic and external influences. To what extent also were changes in the political leadership and governmental policies influenced by foreign actors? What factors help to explain differences in the role of foreign and domestic influences on political development in different societies and at different times in the history of the same society? To what extent, for instance, does the probable impact of the foreign versus domestic environment vary inversely with political participation, institutionalization, and integration? In the early 1970s these were the type of question toward which students of political development were beginning to turn.

Political Development, Modernity, and Change

The study of political development was, in its origins in the late 1950s, in some sense the political science reflection of a broader interest among social scientists in the general processes of societal change normally subsumed under the heading of "modernization." In fact, much of the early work identified political development with political modernization, and almost all the work nonetheless focused on political development in the context of the overall change from traditional, rural, agrarian society to modern, urban, industrial society. In the middle and late 1960s, however, it became increasingly clear that the problems of political development—of democracy, stability, integration, participation, institutional development, cultural change—were not limited to that particular context.

In the first instance, the particular issues on which political scientists focused when they studied political development might characterize a society when it was undergoing any fundamental socioeconomic change, not just the shift from rural tradition to urban modernity. During the 1960s, for instance, social scientists, led by Daniel Bell, began to formulate the concept of a post-industrial society as a distinct form of society as different from industrial society as the latter was from agrarian society (Bell, 1967, 1968, 1971; Brzezinski, 1970). The United States and some of the countries of Western Europe were said to be making the transition from industrial to postindustrial society with the growth of the service sector in their economies, the increasingly central role of technology and theoretical knowledge in the functioning of society, the growing preponderance of white-collar and particularly professional and scientific workers in the labor force, and overall rising levels of education and affluence. If this transition from industrial to postindustrial society was, indeed, of the same order as the transition from agrarian to industrial society, then presumably the accompanying political problems, dislocations, and needs might also be comparable in intensity and conceivably similar in nature (Huntington, 1974a). And a theoretical base could, indeed, be made for this proposition, which the political traumas and disruptions that characterized American and to some extent Western European society in the late 1960s and early 1970s certainly did nothing to disprove. In this sense the concepts and lessons that could be derived from the study of political development in the modernizing countries of the Third World might be applicable not just to the earlier history of the First World but to its contemporary and future evolution as well. The identification of political development with the peculiar historical process of modernization was thus loosened.

Somewhat the same result also arose from the extent to which social scientists in the middle and late 1960s began to see difficulties in the blunt dichotomy between tradition and modernity and the often implicit corollary assumption that the emergence of one meant the weakening or disappearance of the other. In the eyes of the "modernization revisionists," the distinctions between traditional and modern society were considerably less clear than had been supposed and, accordingly, the march of history from the one to the other became less identified with the march of progress.[14] The tendency to link political development with political modernization was thus further weakened, if only because the latter was seen to be a much more ambiguous and complex phenomenon than it had been assumed to be. In addition, if the change from tradition to modernity lost its distinctiveness, presumably the problems of political development which had been assumed specially to characterize that phase of world history might be found in almost any phase of history. Moreover, if the differences between traditional and modern society began to dwindle in theoretical importance, other distinctions might begin to assume greater importance and relevance. It could well be, for instance, that the politics of a society was more decisively affected by the continuing underlying culture of the society than by its level of modernity. Perhaps the most important political differences between societies coincide not with differing levels of per capita income but with the great cultural faults that divide men according to language, religion, ethnicity, race, and historical experience. Nakane (1970) impressively documented the persistence of certain patterns of social behavior in Japanese society in both its traditional and modern phases; Lipset (1963) and Huntington (1968) stressed the continuity of American political values and American political institutions. It would not be difficult to identify distinctive patterns of political beliefs and behavior for the Latin, Nordic, Hindu, Arab, Chinese, Slav, Japanese, Malay, African, and possibly other major cultural groupings.

If the tradition-modernity dichotomy becomes less useful for political analysis, it seems likely that the study of political development will become increasingly divorced from the study of modernization and more closely identified with broader study of political change. In the late 1960s and early 1970s, political scientists who had been talking about political development began to think in more general terms about theories of political change. In some measure this meant a focus on change in the particular components of the political system and on how change in one component related to changes in other components. It also, as in work by Gabriel Almond and his associates, could mean an effort to integrate into a general paradigm of political change the influence of environmental factors, political leadership and skills, choices and coalitions. In yet a different approach, Brunner and Brewer (1971) showed that it was possible to develop models of complex change relating demographic, economic, and political variables to each other through a series of equations which could be used to specify how change in one of the variables subject to governmental manipulation might affect the values of other variables. In effect, this model was for political development the same type of complex interaction model that economists had much earlier developed to analyze the functioning of economies. While the Brunner-Brewer work, dependent as it was on computer simulation, might seem to represent the opposite extreme from the "return to history" of other students of political development, in actuality the theoretical and practical links between the two approaches were very close. For both aimed at the analysis of change in a multiplicity of variables through extended periods of time, and the elaboration of additional models along the lines of the work by Brunner and Brewer could well be most usefully done in the context of the historical experience of the countries of Western Europe and North America. The combination of historical data, longitudinal analysis, computer simulation, and political development theory held the promise of opening new and deeper understandings of the causes, patterns, and consequences of political change.

NOTES

1. Among the bibliographies and bibliographical discussions of this literature are Montgomery (1969), Huntington (1971a), Hah and Schneider (1968), Deutsch and Merrit (1970), Pratt (1973), Packenham (1970, 1973).

2. Many of the most useful of these data have been collected and discussed in the two Yale handbooks of political and social indicators. See Russett (1964) and Taylor and Hudson (1972).

3. Lerner's study dealt with Egypt, Iran, Lebanon, Turkey, Syria, and Jordan. Probably the three most significant subsequent efforts at comparative survey studies relating to political development issues are those directed by (1) Gabriel Almond and Sidney Verba: United States, Great Britain, Germany, Italy, Mexico; (2) Sidney Verba, Norman Nie, and Jae-On Kim: United States, Japan, India, Austria, Nigeria; and (3) Alex Inkeles: Argentina, Chile, India, Israel, Nigeria, East Pakistan. For reports of some results of these studies see Almond and Verba (1963), Verba, Nie, and Kim (1971), Inkeles (1969a, 1969b), Inkeles and Smith (1974).

4. This sentence and a few others following are drawn from Huntington (1971b).

5. In part, perhaps, as a result of this, social and political analysts from less developed countries as well as more radical theorists in developed societies have stressed the impact, which they see as primarily negative, of "metropolitan" influences on "peripheral" developing countries. See Gunder Frank (1970), Bodenheimer (1971), and in general Petras and Zeitlin (1968).

6. For an analysis of the history and utility of the concept of culture in general, and in political science specifically, see Geertz (1964), Pye (1972), and Geertz (1973, pp. 3–83).

7. For further discussion of ideology as a cultural system, see Geertz (1973, pp. 193–233).

8. Huntington and Nelson (1976). For an elaboration of the concept of political participation see Chapter 1 and the essay by Verba and Nie on "Political Participation" in Volume 4 of this *Handbook*.

9. The interest of political scientists in patron-client relations blossomed in the late 1960s. Among the more important items are Landé (1965, 1971), Tarrow (1967), Weingrod (1968), Scott (1969), Powell (1970), Kaufman (1972), Lemarchand (1972), Lemarchand and Legg (1972).

10. For a critique of Deutsch's work on nationalism and of the field in general, see Connor (1972), who nevertheless agrees with the main lines of the hypothesis as cited. Moreover, although the assumption that other things may be equal can be reasonably sustained in many cases, there is one major exception: the Soviet Union. In the Soviet Union social mobilization and russification are related. Cities serve both as centers of assimilation into a Russian national identity *and* as centers of ethnic consolidation and resistance for the non-Russian nationalities. The political limitations on open ethnic conflict and the predominance of Russians in key decision-making structures have set important limits to the divisive effects of social mobilization while encouraging russification. See Silver (1974, especially note 26).

11. For a discussion of Mahayana Buddhism in China and Japan, see Reischauer and Fairbank (1960) and Fairbank, Reischauer, and Craig (1965); for a discussion of Maha-

yana Buddhism in Vietnam and the extensive practice of clericalism by Buddhist monks in South Vietnam in the 1960s, see FitzGerald (1972), Buttinger (1967), McAlister and Mus (1970), and Duncanson (1968). In this and the following paragraphs, references to Buddhism in the text apply to Theravada Buddhism.

12. For the Soviet case see Silver (1974).

13. See particularly Rokkan (1968), Rustow (1970), Lipset and Rokkan (1967), Dahl (1971), Pride (1970), Flanigan and Fogelman (1970, 1971), Sunshine (1972). These approaches added a welcome new dimension to the other stream of analysis generated originally by Lerner (1958) and Lipset (1959) relating democracy to level of socioeconomic development and referred to in Section I above.

14. For a discussion of this trend of thought, see Huntington (1971a).

REFERENCES

Abbott, Freeland (1968). *Islam and Pakistan*. Ithaca, N.Y.: Cornell University Press.

Adam, Heribert (1971). *Modernizing Racial Domination: South Africa's Political Dynamics*. Berkeley: University of California Press.

Adams, Richard N. (1960). "Social change in Guatemala and U.S. policy." In Richard N. Adams *et al., Social Change in Latin America Today*. New York: Published for the Council on Foreign Relations by Harper & Row.

Adelman, Irma, and Cynthia Taft Morris (1967). *Society, Politics, and Economic Development: A Quantitative Approach*. Baltimore: Johns Hopkins University Press.

Alker, Hayward R., Jr., and Bruce M. Russett (1964). "The analysis of trends and patterns." In Bruce M. Russett *et al* (eds.), *World Handbook of Political and Social Indicators*. New Haven: Yale University Press.

Alker, Hayward R., Jr. (1966). "Causal inference and political analysis." In J. L. Bernd (ed.), *Mathematical Applications in Political Science*. Dallas: Southern Methodist University Press.

Almond, Gabriel, and James S. Coleman, eds. (1960). *The Politics of the Developing Areas*. Princeton: Princeton University Press.

Almond, Gabriel A., Scott C. Flanagan, and Robert J. Mundt, eds. (1973). *Crisis, Choice, and Change: Historical Studies of Political Development*. Boston: Little, Brown.

Almond, Gabriel, and Sidney Verba (1965). *The Civic Culture*. Boston: Little, Brown.

Almond, Gabriel, and G. Bingham Powell (1966). *Comparative Politics: A Developmental Approach*. Boston: Little, Brown.

Almond, Gabriel (1970). *Political Development*. Boston: Little, Brown.

Apter, David E. (1963). "Political religion in the new nations." In Clifford Geertz (ed.), *Old Societies and New States*. New York: Free Press.

——————— (1965). *The Politics of Modernization*. Chicago: University of Chicago Press.

_____ (1971). *Choice and the Politics of Allocation*. New Haven: Yale University Press.

Apter, David E., and Charles Andrain (1968). "Comparative government: developing new nations." In Marian D. Irish (ed.), *Political Science: Advance of the Discipline*. Englewood Cliffs, N.J.: Prentice-Hall.

Banfield, Edward C. (1958). *The Moral Basis of a Backward Society*. New York: Free Press.

Barghoorn, Frederick C. (1966). *Politics in the USSR*. Boston: Little, Brown.

Baxter, Craig (1966). "The Jana Sangh: a brief history." In Donald E. Smith (ed.), *South Asian Politics and Religion*. Princeton: Princeton University Press.

Behrman, Lucy (1972). "Political development and secularization in two Chilean urban communities." *Comparative Politics* 4:269–80.

Bell, Daniel (1967). "Notes on the post-industrial society." *The Public Interest* 6:24–35, 7:102–18.

_____ (1968). "The measurement of knowledge and technology." In Eleanor Sheldon and Wilbert Moore (eds.), *Indicators of Social Change*. New York: Russell Sage Foundation.

_____ (1971). "The post-industrial society: the evolution of an idea." *Survey* 17, no. 2:102–68.

Bendix, Reinhard (1964). *Nation-Building and Citizenship*. New York: Wiley.

Benjamin, Roger W. (1972). *Patterns of Political Development*. New York: McKay.

Bienen, Henry (1974). *Kenya: The Politics of Participation and Control*. Princeton: Princeton University Press.

Binder, Leonard (1962). *Iran: Political Development in a Changing Society*. Berkeley: University of California Press.

_____ (1963). *Religion and Politics in Pakistan.*. Berkeley: University of California Press.

Binder, Leonard (1962). *Iran: Political Development in a Changing Society*. Berkeley: ton: Princeton University Press.

Black, Cyril E. (1966). *The Dynamics of Modernization*. New York: Harper & Row.

Bloch, Marc (1961). *Feudal Society*. Translated by L. A. Manyon. London: Routledge & Kegan Paul.

Bodenheimer, Susanne (1971). "Dependency and imperialism: the roots of Latin American underdevelopment." In K. T. Fann and Donald C. Hodges (eds.), *Readings in U.S. Imperialism*. Boston: Porter Sargent.

Brunner, Ronald D., and Garry D. Brewer (1971). *Organized Complexity: Empirical Theories of Political Development*. New York: Free Press.

Brzezinski, Zbigniew (1970). *Between Two Ages: America's Role in the Technetronic Era*. New York: Viking Press.

Büntig, Aldo J. (1971). "The church in Cuba: toward a new frontier." In Alice L. Hageman and Philip E. Wheaton (eds.), *Religion in Cuba Today*. New York: Association Press.

Burks, R. V. (1961). *The Dynamics of Communism in Eastern Europe*. Princeton: Princeton University Press.

Buttinger, Joseph (1967). *Vietnam: A Dragon Embattled*. New York: Praeger.

Bwy, Douglas P. (1971). "Political instability in Latin America: the cross cultural test of a causal model." In John V. Gillespie and Betty A. Nesvold (eds.), *Macro-Quantitative Analysis: Conflict, Development, and Democratization*. Beverly Hills, Calif.: Sage.

Cnudde, Charles F., and Donald J. McCrone (1969). "Party competition and welfare politics in the American states." *American Political Science Review* 63:858–66.

Cohn, Norman (1957), *The Pursuit of the Millennium*. Fairlawn, N.J.: Essential Books.

Coleman, James S. (1960). "Conclusion." In Gabriel Almond and James S. Coleman (eds.), *The Politics of Developing Areas*. Princeton: Princeton University Press.

_____ (1965). *Education and Political Development*. Princeton: Princeton University Press.

Collier, David (1972). "Timing of development and political outcomes in Latin America." Paper prepared for Annual Meeting, American Political Science Association, Washington, D.C.

Connor, Walker (1969). "Ethnology and the peace of South Asia." *World Politics* 22:51–86.

_____ (1972). "Nation-building or nation-destroying?" *World Politics* 24:319–55.

Cornblit, Oscar (1970). "Society and mass rebellion in eighteenth century Peru and Bolivia." In Raymond Carr (ed.), *St. Antony's Papers: Latin American Affairs No. 22*. London: Oxford University Press.

Cornelius, Wayne (1972). "Principal research findings relating to political participation among low-income rural migrants to Mexico City." Unpublished paper, Harvard University Center for International Affairs, Cambridge, Mass.

Coulborn, Rushton, ed. (1965). *Feudalism in History*. Hamden, Conn.: Archon Books.

Coulter, Philip (1971–72). "Democratic political development: a systemic model based on regulative policy." *Development and Change* 3:25–61.

Cutright, Phillips (1963). "National political development: its measurement and social correlates." In Nelson W. Polsby, Robert A. Dentler, Paul A. Smith (eds.), *Politics and Social Life*. Boston: Houghton Mifflin.

_____ (1965). "Political structure, economic development, and social security programs." *American Journal of Sociology* 70:537–50.

_____ (1967). "Inequality: a cross-national analysis." *American Sociological Review* 32:562–78.

Dahl, Robert A. (1961). *Who Governs?* New Haven: Yale University Press.

_____, ed. (1966). *Political Oppositions in Western Democracies*. New Haven: Yale University Press.

_____ (1971). *Polyarchy: Participation and Opposition*. New Haven: Yale University Press.

_____ (1975). "Governments and political oppositions." In Fred Greenstein and Nelson Polsby (eds.), *The Handbook of Political Science*, Vol. 3. Reading, Mass.: Addison-Wesley.

Das Gupta, Jyotirindra (1970). *Language Conflict and National Development: Group Politics and National Language Policy in India*. Berkeley: University of California Press.

Davies, James C. (1962). "Toward a theory of revolution." *American Sociological Review* 27:5–19.

_____ (1969). "The J-curve of rising and declining satisfactions as a cause of some great rebellions and a contained revolution." In Hugh Davis Graham and Ted Robert Gurr (eds.), *Violence in America: Historical and Comparative Perspectives*. New York: Bantam Books.

Dawson, Richard, and James A. Robinson (1965). "The politics of welfare." In Herbert Jacob and Kenneth N. Vines (eds.), *Politics in the American States*. Boston: Little, Brown.

Dawson, Richard (1967). "Social development, party competition and policy." In William N. Chambers and Walter Dean Burham (eds.), *The American Party Systems*. New York: Oxford University Press.

Degler, Carl N. (1971). *Neither Black nor White: Slavery and Race Relations in Brazil and the United States*. New York: Macmillan.

de Kadt, Emanuel (1967). "The church and social change in Brazil." In Claudio Véliz (ed.), *The Politics of Conformity in Latin America*. London: Oxford University Press.

_____ (1971). "Church, society and development in Latin America." *Journal of Development Studies* 8:23–43.

Deutsch, Karl W. (1961). "Social mobilization and political development." *American Political Science Review* 55:493–514.

_____ (1966). *Nationalism and Social Communication*, 2nd edition. Cambridge, Mass.: M.I.T. Press.

Deutsch, Karl W., and Richard L. Merritt (1970). *Nationalism and National Development: An Interdisciplinary Bibliography*. Cambridge, Mass.: M.I.T. Press.

Dirección General de Estadística (1943). *Sexto censo de población 1940: Resumen general*. Mexico: Dirección General de Estadística.

Dirección Nacional de Estadística (1944). *Censo nacional de población y Ocupación 1940*. Lima, Peru: Dirección Nacional de Estadística.

Domínguez, Jorge I. (1972a). "Cuban Catholics and Castro." *Worldview* 15, no. 2:24–29.

_____ (1972b). "Social mobilization, traditional political participation and government response in early nineteenth century Spanish America." Unpublished dissertation, Harvard University, Cambridge, Mass.

_____ (1975). "Revolutionary values and development performance: China,

Cuba, and the Soviet Union." In Harold Lasswell, Daniel Lerner, and John Montgomery (eds.), *Values in Development*. Cambridge, Mass.: M.I.T. Press.

Doob, Leonard (1960). *Becoming More Civilized*. New Haven: Yale University Press.

Duncanson, Dennis J. (1968). *Government and Revolution in Vietnam*. New York: Oxford University Press.

Dye, Thomas R. (1966). *Politics, Economics, and the Public*. Chicago: Rand McNally.

Easton, David (1953). *The Political System*. New York: Knopf.

——————— (1965a). *A Framework for Political Analysis*. Englewood Cliffs, N.J.: Prentice-Hall.

——————— (1965b). *A Systems Analysis of Political Life*. New York: Wiley.

Eckstein, Harry H. (1961). *A Theory of Stable Democracy*. Center for International Studies, Woodrow Wilson School of Public and International Affairs, Monograph No. 10. Princeton: Princeton University Press.

——————— (1966). *Division and Cohesion in Democracy: A Study of Norway*. Princeton: Princeton University Press.

Einaudi, Luigi *et al.* (1969). *Latin American Institutional Development: The Changing Catholic Church*. Santa Monica, Calif.: The Rand Corporation.

Eisenstadt, S. N. (1963). *The Political Systems of Empires*. New York: Free Press.

——————— (1966). *Modernization: Protest and Change*. Modernization of Traditional Societies Series. Englewood Cliffs, N.J.: Prentice-Hall.

Elkins, Stanley (1963). *Slavery*. New York: Grosset, Universal Library.

Emerson, Rupert (1960). *From Empire to Nation*. Boston: Beacon Press.

——————— (1966). "Nation-building in Africa." In Karl W. Deutsch and William J. Foltz (eds.), *Nation-Building*. New York: Atherton Press.

Erbe, William (1964). "Social involvement and political activity: a replication and elaboration." *American Sociological Review* 29:198–215.

Esman, Milton J. (1973). "The management of communal conflict." *Public Policy* 21:49–78.

Fagen, Richard (1969). *The Transformation of Political Culture in Cuba*. Stanford, Calif.: Stanford University Press.

Fairbank, John K., Edwin O. Reischauer, and Albert M. Craig (1965). *East Asia: The Modern Transformation*. Boston: Houghton Mifflin.

Fall, Bernard B. (1967). *The Two Viet-Nams*, 2nd revised edition. New York: Praeger.

Fanon, Frantz (1967). *Black Skin, White Masks*. New York: Grove Press.

Feierabend, Ivo K., and Rosalind L. Feierabend (1966). "Aggressive behaviors within polities, 1948–1962: a cross national study." *Journal of Conflict Resolution* 10:249–71.

Feierabend, Ivo K., Rosalind L. Feierabend, and Betty A. Nesvold (1969). "Social change and political violence: cross national patterns." In Hugh Davis Graham and Ted Robert Gurr (eds.), *Violence in America: Historical and Comparative Perspectives*. New York: Bantam Books.

Feit, Edward (1971). *Urban Revolt in South Africa 1960–1964*. Evanston, Ill.: Northwestern University Press.

Fermoselle, Rafael (1974). *Política y color en Cuba: La guerrita de 1912*. Montevideo: Ediciones Geminis.

Fernandes, Florestan (1969). *The Negro in Brazilian Society*. Translated by J. D. Skiles, A. Brunel, and A. Rothwell. Institute of Latin American Studies Series, Phyllis B. Eveleth, editor. New York: Columbia University Press.

Field, John (1971). "Panel discussion of elections and political development in Turkey, India, and Colombia." Unpublished remarks at Harvard/MIT Joint Seminar on Political Development, Cambridge, Mass.

Finer, S. E. (1967). "The one-party regimes in Africa: reconsiderations." *Government and Opposition* 2:491–509.

FitzGerald, Frances (1972). *Fire in the Lake*. Boston: Little, Brown.

Flanigan, William H., and Edwin Fogelman (1970). "Patterns of political violence in comparative historical perspective." *Comparative Politics* 3:1–20.

——————— (1971). "Patterns of democratic development: an historical comparative analysis." In John V. Gillespie and Betty A. Nesvold (eds.), *Macro-Quantitative Analysis: Conflict, Development, and Democratization*, Vol. 1. Beverly Hills, Calif.: Sage.

Foltz, William J. (1965). *From French West Africa to the Mali Federation*. New Haven: Yale University Press.

Fossum, Egil (1967). "Factors influencing the occurrence of military coups d'etat in Latin America." *Journal of Peace Research* 3:228–51.

Foster, George (1962). *Traditional Cultures and the Impact of Technological Change*. New York: Harper & Row.

Frank, André Gunder (1970). *Latin America: Underdevelopment or Revolution*. New York: Monthly Review Press.

Frazier, E. Franklin (1965). *Race and Culture Contacts in the Modern World*. Boston: Beacon Press.

Frey, Frederick W. (1965). *The Turkish Political Elite*. Cambridge, Mass.: M.I.T. Press.

——————— (1966). "Democracy and reform in developing societies." Unpublished paper given at the Seminar on Political Development, University of Minas Gerais, Belo Horizonte, Brazil.

Furnivall, J. S. (1948). *Colonial Policy and Practice*. London: Cambridge University Press.

Geertz, Clifford (1964), "A study of national character." Review of *Politics, Personality and Nation Building* by Lucian Pye. *Economic Development and Cultural Change* 12:205–9.

——————— (1973). *The Interpretation of Cultures*. New York: Basic Books.

Gerth, H. H., and C. Wright Mills (1958). *From Max Weber*. New York: Oxford University Press.

Goel, M. Lal (1970). "The relevance of education for political participation in a developing society." *Comparative Political Studies* 3:333–46.

Graham, Hugh Davis, and Ted Robert Gurr, eds. (1969). *Violence in America: Historical and Comparative Perspectives*. New York: Bantam Books.

Grofman, Bernard, and Edward N. Muller (1972). "The strange case of relative gratification and potential for political violence: the V-curve hypothesis." Paper prepared for Annual Meeting of American Political Science Association, Washington, D.C.

Grunwald, Kurt, and Juachim O. Ronall (1960). *Industrialization in the Middle East.* New York: Council for Middle Eastern Affairs Press.

Gurr, Ted Robert (1970). *Why Men Rebel.* Princeton: Princeton University Press.

——————— (1973). "The revolution–social change nexus: some old theories and new hypotheses." *Comparative Politics* 5:359–92.

Hah, Chong-do, and Jeanne Schneider (1968). "A critique of current studies of political development and modernization." *Social Research* 35:130–58.

Hardgrave, Robert L., Jr. (1969). *The Nadars of Tamilnad.* Berkeley: University of California Press.

Haring, C. H. (1963). *The Spanish Empire in America.* New York: Harcourt, Brace and World.

Hartz, Louis (1964). "A theory of the development of the new societies." In Louis Hartz (ed.), *The Founding of New Societies.* New York: Harcourt, Brace and World.

Heath, Shirley Brice (1972). *Telling Tongues: Language Policy in Mexico, Colony to Nation.* New York: Teachers' College Press, Columbia University.

Hibbs, Douglas A., Jr. (1973). *Mass Political Violence: A Cross-National Causal Analysis.* New York: Wiley.

Hill, Frances (1971). "Millenarian machines in South Vietnam." *Comparative Studies in Society and History* 13:325–50.

Hinrichs, Harley H. (1966). *A General Theory of Tax Structure Change during Economic Development.* Cambridge, Mass.: Harvard Law School International Tax Program.

Hirschman, Albert O. (1970). *Exit, Voice, and Loyalty.* Cambridge, Mass.: Harvard University Press.

Hobsbawm, E. J. (1959). *Primitive Rebels.* New York: Praeger.

Hodgkin, Thomas (1957). *Nationalism in Colonial Africa.* New York: New York University Press.

Horowitz, Donald L. (1971). "Three dimensions of ethnic politics." *World Politics* 23:232–44.

Horowitz, Irving L. (1966). *Three Worlds of Development: The Theory and Practice of International Stratification.* New York: Oxford University Press.

Hoskin, Gary (1971). "Dimensions of conflict in the Colombian national legislature." Unpublished paper given at the Shambaugh Conference on Legislative Systems in Developing Countries, University of Iowa, Iowa City.

Houtart, François, and André Rousseau (1971). *The Church and Revolution.* Translated by Violet Nevile. Maryknoll, N.Y.: Orbis Books.

Hudson, Michael C. (1968). *The Precarious Republic: Political Modernization in Lebanon.* New York: Random House.

Huntington, Samuel P. (1965). "Political development and political decay." *World Politics* 17:386–430.

——————— (1968). *Political Order in Changing Societies.* New Haven: Yale University Press.

——————— (1970). "Social and institutional dynamics of one-party systems." In Samuel P. Huntington and Clement H. Moore (eds.), *Authoritarian Politics in Modern Society: The Dynamics of One-Party Systems.* New York: Basic Books.

——————— (1971a). "The change to change: modernization, development, and politics." *Comparative Politics* 3:283–322.

——————— (1971b). "Civil violence and the process of development." International Institute of Strategic Studies, *Adelphi Papers* 83:1–15.

——————— (1974a). "Postindustrial politics: how benign will it be?" *Comparative Politics* 6:163–91.

——————— (1974b). "Paradigms of American politics: beyond the one, the two, and the many." *Political Science Quarterly,* 89:1–26.

Huntington, Samuel P., and Clement H. Moore, eds. (1970). *Authoritarian Politics in Modern Society: The Dynamics of One-Party Systems.* New York: Basic Books.

Huntington, Samuel P., and Joan M. Nelson (1976). *Socio-economic Change and Political Participation.* Cambridge, Mass.: Harvard University Press.

Hurwitz, Leon (1973). "Contemporary approaches to political stability." *Comparative Politics* 5:449–63.

Inkeles, Alex (1966). "The modernization of man." In Myron Weiner (ed.), *Modernization.* New York: Basic Books.

——————— (1969a). "Making men modern: on the causes and consequences of individual change in six developing countries." *American Journal of Sociology* 75:208–25.

——————— (1969b). "Participant citizenship in six developing countries." *American Political Science Review* 63:1120–41.

Inkeles, Alex, and Daniel Levinson (1969). "National character: the study of model personality and sociocultural systems." In Gardner Lindzey and Elliot Aronson (eds.), *The Handbook of Social Psychology,* Vol. 4. Reading, Mass.: Addison-Wesley.

Inkeles, Alex, and David H. Smith (1974). *Becoming Modern.* Cambridge, Mass.: Harvard University Press.

International Bank for Reconstruction and Development (1970). *World Bank Atlas: Population, Per Capita Product, and Growth Rates.*

Isaacs, Harold R. (1969). "Group identity and political change: the role of color and physical characteristics." In John Hope Franklin (ed.), *Color and Race.* Boston: Beacon Press.

Jackman, Robert W. (1973). "On the relation of economic development to democratic performance." *Midwest Journal of Political Science* 17:611–21.

Janos, Andrew C. (1971). "Ethnicity, communism and political change in Eastern Europe." *World Politics* 23:493–521.

Johnson, Gerald W. (1971). "Research note on political correlates of voter participation: a deviant case analysis." *American Political Science Review* 65:768–76.

Jones, A. H. M. (1955). "The decline and fall of the Roman empire." *History* 40: 209–26.

Kasfir, Nelson N. (1972). "Controling ethnicity in Ugandan politics: departicipation as a strategy for political development in Africa." Unpublished Ph.D. thesis, Chapter 8, Harvard University, Cambridge, Mass.

Kaufman, Robert R. (1972). "The patron-client concept and macro-politics: prospects and problems." Paper prepared for Annual Meeting, American Political Science Association, Washington, D.C.

Kautsky, John (1972). *The Political Consequences of Modernization*. New York: Wiley.

Kearney, Robert N. (1967). *Communalism and Language in the Politics of Ceylon*. Durham, N.C.: Duke University Press.

Keech, William R. (1972). "Linguistic diversity and political conflict: some observations based on four Swiss cantons." *Comparative Politics* 4:387–404.

Kirkpatrick, Jeane (1971). *Leader and Vanguard in Mass Society: A Study of Peronist Argentina*. Cambridge, Mass.: M.I.T. Press.

Kubler, George A. (1967). "The great revolt of Túpac Amaru." In Lewis Hanke (ed.), *History of Latin American Civilization,* Vol. 1. Boston: Little, Brown.

Kuper, Leo (1971). "Theories of revolution and race relations." *Comparative Studies in Society and History* 13:87–107.

Kurth, James R. (1970). "Modernity and hegemony: the American way of foreign policy." Unpublished paper, Harvard University Center for International Affairs, Cambridge, Mass.

Landé, Carl H. (1965). *Leaders, Factions, and Parties: The Structure of Philippine Politics*. New Haven: Yale University Southeast Asian Studies Monograph No. 6.

—————— (1971). "Networks and groups in Southeast Asia: some observations on the group theory of politics." Paper prepared for Annual Meeting, American Political Science Association, Chicago.

Lane, Robert E. (1959). *Political Life: Why People Get Involved in Politics*. New York: Free Press.

Lanternari, Vittorio (1963). *The Religions of the Oppressed: A Study of the Modern Messianic Cults*. New York: Knopf.

LaPalombara, Joseph, ed. (1963). *Bureaucracy and Political Development*. Princeton: Princeton University Press.

LaPalombara, Joseph, and Myron Weiner, eds. (1966). *Political Parties and Political Development*. Princeton: Princeton University Press.

Lemarchand, René (1968). "Revolutionary phenomena in stratified societies: Rwanda and Zanzibar." *Civilisations* 18:16–51.

——————— (1972). "Political clientelism and ethnicity in tropical Africa: competing solidarities in nation-building." *American Political Science Review* 66:68–90.

Lemarchand, René, and Keith Legg (1972). "Political clientelism and development: a preliminary analysis." *Comparative Politics* 4:149–78.

Lerner, Daniel (1958). *The Passing of Traditional Society.* New York: Free Press.

Levine, Donald N. (1965a). "Ethiopia: identity, authority, and realism." In Lucian W. Pye and Sidney Verba (eds.), *Political Culture and Political Development.* Princeton: Princeton University Press.

——————— (1965b). *Wax and Gold: Tradition and Innovation in Ethiopian Culture.* Chicago: University of Chicago Press.

Levy, Marion J., Jr. (1966). *Modernization and the Structure of Societies.* Princeton: Princeton University Press.

Lewis, Bernard (1961). *The Emergence of Modern Turkey.* London: Oxford University Press.

Liebenow, J. Gus (1969). *Liberia: The Evolution of Privilege.* Ithaca, N.Y.: Cornell University Press.

Lipset, Seymour Martin (1959). "Some social requisites of democracy: economic development and political legitimacy." *American Political Science Review* 53:69–105.

——————— (1960). *Political Man.* Garden City, N.Y.: Doubleday.

——————— (1963). *The First New Nation.* New York: Basic Books.

——————— (1970). *Revolution and Counterrevolution.* Garden City, N.Y.: Doubleday, Anchor.

Lipset, Seymour Martin, and Stein Rokkan, eds. (1967). *Party Systems and Voter Alignments: Cross-National Perspectives.* New York: Free Press.

Mair, L. P. (1959). "Independent religious movements in three continents." *Comparative Studies in Society and History* 1, no. 2:113–36.

Mannoni, O. (1964). *Prospero and Caliban: The Psychology of Colonization,* 2nd edition. New York: Praeger.

Martinez-Alier, Verena (1974). *Marriage, Class and Colour in Nineteenth-Century Cuba.* Cambridge, England: Cambridge University Press.

Mason, Philip (1970). *Patterns of Dominance.* London: Oxford University Press.

Matthews, Robert O. (1972). "Refugees and stability in Africa." *International Organization* 26:62–83.

Mathiason, John R., and John D. Powell (1972). "Participation and efficacy: aspects of peasant involvement in political mobilization." *Comparative Politics* 4:303–29.

McAlister, John T., Jr., and Paul Mus (1970). *The Vietnamese and Their Revolution.* New York: Harper & Row.

McCrone, Donald J., and Charles F. Cnudde (1967). "Towards a communications theory of democratic political development: a causal model." *American Political Science Review* 61:72–79.

Mecham, J. Lloyd (1966). *Church and State in Latin America,* revised edition. Chapel Hill, N.C.: University of North Carolina Press.

Melson, Robert (1971). "Ideology and inconsistency: the cross-pressured Nigerian worker." *American Political Science Review* 65:161–71.

Melson, Robert, and Howard Wolpe (1970). "Modernization and the politics of communalism: a theoretical perspective." *American Political Science Review* 64, no. 4:1112–30.

——————, eds. (1971). *Nigeria: Modernization and the Politics of Communalism.* East Lansing, Mich.: Michigan State University Press.

Merritt, Richard L. (1966). *Symbols of American Community, 1735–1775.* New Haven: Yale University Press.

Milbrath, Lester W. (1965). *Political Participation.* Chicago: Rand McNally.

Montgomery, John D. (1969). "The quest for political development." *Comparative Politics* 1:285–95.

Moore, Barrington, Jr. (1966). *Social Origins of Dictatorship and Democracy.* Boston: Beacon Press.

Mörner, Magnus (1967). *Race Mixture in the History of Latin America.* Boston: Little, Brown.

—————— ed. (1970). *Race and Class in Latin America.* New York: Columbia University Press.

Morse, Richard M. (1964). "The heritage of Latin America." In Louis Hartz (ed.), *The Founding of New Societies.* New York: Harcourt, Brace and World.

Muller, Edward N. (1972). "A test of a partial theory of potential for political violence." *American Political Science Review* 66:928–59.

Mutchler, David E. (1971). *The Church as a Political Factor in Latin America.* New York: Praeger.

Nakane, Chie (1970). *Japanese Society.* Berkeley: University of California Press.

Needler, Martin C. (1968). *Political Development in Latin America: Instability, Violence, and Evolutionary Change.* New York: Random House.

—————— (1972). "The causality of the Latin American coup d'etat: some numbers, some speculations." Paper prepared for Annual Meeting, American Political Science Association, Washington, D.C.

Neubauer, Deane E. (1967). "Some conditions of democracy." *American Political Science Review* 61:1002–9.

Nie, Norman H., G. Bingham Powell, Jr., and Kenneth Prewitt (1969). "Social structure and political participation: developmental relationships, Part I." *American Political Science Review* 63:361–78.

Nordlinger, Eric A. (1968). "Political development: time sequences and rates of change." *World Politics* 20:494–520.

—————— (1970). "Soldiers in mufti: the impact of military rule upon economic and social change in the non-western states." *American Political Science Review* 64:1131–48.

————————— (1972). *Conflict Regulation in Divided Societies.* Cambridge, Mass.: Occasional Paper No. 29, Center for International Affairs, Harvard University.

Orbell, John M., and Toru Uno (1972). "A theory of neighborhood problem solving: political action vs. residential mobility." *American Political Science Review* 66:471–89.

Orum, Anthony M. (1966). "A reappraisal of the social and political participation of Negroes." *American Journal of Sociology* 72:32–46.

Özbuden, Ergun (1970). "Established revolution versus unfinished revolution: contrasting patterns of democratization of Mexico and Turkey." In Samuel P. Huntington and Clement H. Moore (eds.), *Authoritarian Politics in Modern Society.* New York: Basic Books.

Packenham, Robert A. (1964). "Approaches to the study of political development." *World Politics* 17:108–20.

————————— (1970). "Political development research." In Michael Haas and Henry Kariel (eds.), *Approaches to the Study of Political Science.* San Francisco: Chandler Books.

————————— (1973). *Liberal America and the Third World.* Princeton: Princeton University Press.

Payne, James L. (1968). *Patterns of Conflict in Colombia.* New Haven: Yale University Press.

Petras, James, and Maurice Zeitlin, eds. (1968). *Latin America: Reform or Revolution?* Greenwich, Conn.: Fawcett.

Pierson, Donald (1967). *Negroes in Brazil: A Study of Race Contact at Bahia.* Carbondale, Ill.: Southern Illinois University Press.

Pitt-Rivers, Julian (1967). "Race, color, and class in Central America and the Andes." *Daedalus* 96:542–59.

Powell, John Duncan (1970). "Peasant society and clientelist politics." *American Political Science Review* 64:411–25.

————————— (1971). *The Political Mobilization of the Venezuelan Peasant.* Cambridge, Mass.: Harvard University Press.

Pratt, Raymond B. (1973). "The underdeveloped political science of development." *Studies in Comparative International Development* 8:88–112.

Price, H. Douglas (1964). "Southern politics in the sixties: notes on economic development and political modernization." Paper presented at Annual Meeting, American Political Science Association, Washington, D.C.

Pride, Richard A. (1970). *Origins of Democracy: A Cross-National Study of Mobilization, Party Systems, and Democratic Stability.* Comparative Politics Series, No. 01–012, Vol. 1. Beverly Hills, Calif.: Sage.

Putnam, Robert D. (1967). "Toward explaining military intervention in Latin American politics." *World Politics* 20:83–110.

Pye, Lucian W. (1962). *Politics, Personality, and Nation Building: Burma's Search for Identity.* New Haven: Yale University Press.

Pye, Lucian W., ed. (1963). *Communications and Political Development*. Princeton: Princeton University Press.

—————— (1966). *Aspects of Political Development*. Boston: Little, Brown.

—————— (1972). "Culture and political science: problems in the evaluation of the concept of political culture." *Social Science Quarterly* 53:285–96.

Pye, Lucian W., and Sidney Verba, eds. (1965). *Political Culture and Political Development*. Princeton: Princeton University Press.

Rabushka, Alvin, and Kenneth A. Shepsle (1972). *Politics in Plural Societies: A Theory of Democratic Instability*. Columbus, Ohio: Charles E. Merrill.

Reis, Fabio Wanderley (1974). "Political development and social class: Brazilian authoritarianism in perspective." Unpublished Ph.D. dissertation prepared for Department of Government, Harvard University, Cambridge, Mass.

Reischauer, Edwin O., and John K. Fairbank (1960). *East Asia: The Great Tradition*. Boston: Houghton Mifflin.

Riggs, Fred (1964). *Administration in Developing Countries: The Theory of Prismatic Society*. Boston: Houghton Mifflin.

Riker, William H. (1964). *Federalism: Origin, Operation, Significance*. Boston: Little, Brown.

Robinson, Richard D. (1965). *The First Turkish Republic: A Case Study in National Development*. Cambridge, Mass.: Harvard University Press.

Rokkan, Stein (1966). "Electoral mobilization, party competition, and national integration." In Joseph LaPalombara and Myron Weiner (eds.), *Political Parties and Political Development*. Princeton: Princeton University Press.

—————— (1968). "The structuring of mass politics in the smaller European democracies: a developmental typology." *Comparative Studies in Society and History* 10:173–210.

Rokkan, Stein *et al.* (1970). *Citizens, Elections, Parties: Approaches to the Comparative Study of Development*. Oslo, Norway: Universite/slforlaget.

Rosenau, James N., ed. (1969). *Linkage Politics*. New York: Free Press.

Ross, Irwin (1960). "From Ataturk to Gursel: what went wrong in Turkey?" *New Leader* 43, no. 47:14–18.

Rossiter, Clinton (1971). *The American Quest, 1790–1860*. New York: Harcourt Brace Jovanovich.

Rudolph, Lloyd, and Susanne Hoeber Rudolph (1967). *The Modernity of Tradition*. Chicago: University of Chicago Press.

Ruiz, Ramón E. (1963). *Mexico: The Challenge of Poverty and Illiteracy*. San Marino, Calif.: The Huntington Library.

Russett, Bruce M. *et al.* (1964). *World Handbook of Political and Social Indicators*. New Haven: Yale University Press.

Russett, Bruce M., and Alfred Stepan (1973). *Military Force and American Society*. New York: Harper & Row, Torchbooks.

Rustow, Dankwart A. (1967). *A World of Nations.* Washington, D.C.: The Brookings Institution.

_____ (1970). "Transitions to democracy: toward a dynamic model." *Comparative Politics* 2:337–63.

Salamon, Lester M. (1972). "Protest, politics, and modernization in the American south: Mississippi as a 'developing society.' " Unpublished Ph.D. dissertation, Harvard University, Cambridge, Mass.

_____ (1973). "Leadership and modernization: the emerging black political elite in the American system." *Journal of Politics* 35:615–46.

Sanders, Thomas G. (1967). "Catholicism and development: the Catholic left in Brazil." In Kalman Silvert (ed.), *Churches and States: The Religious Institution and Modernization.* New York: American Universities Field Staff.

Sayeed, Khalid B. (1967). *The Political System of Pakistan.* Boston: Houghton Mifflin.

Schmitter, Philippe (1971). "Military intervention, political competitiveness and public policy in Latin America: 1950–1967." In Morris Janowitz and Jacques van Doorn (eds.), *On Military Ideology.* Rotterdam: Rotterdam University Press.

Schneider, Peter R., and Anne L. Schneider (1971). "Social mobilization, political institutions, and political violence: a cross-national analysis." *Comparative Political Studies* 4:69–90.

Schneider, William (1968). *Political Development: Area and Country Studies.* Cambridge, Mass.: Center for International Affairs, Harvard University.

Schwarz, John E. (1970). "The Scottish national party: nonviolent separatism and theories of violence." *World Politics* 22:496–517.

Scott, James C. (1969). "Corruption, machine politics, and political change." *American Political Science Review* 63:1142–58.

_____ (1972). "Patron-client politics and political change in Southeast Asia." *American Political Science Review* 66:91–113.

Scott, Robert E. (1964). *Mexican Government in Transition,* revised edition. Urbana, Ill.: University of Illinois Press.

Sharkansky, Ira, and Richard Hofferbert (1969). "Dimensions of state politics, economics, and public policy." *American Political Science Review* 63:867–79.

Silver, Brian (1974). "Social mobilization and the russification of Soviet nationalities." *American Political Science Review* 68:45–66.

Smith, Arthur K., Jr. (1969). "Socio-economic development and political democracy: a causal analysis." *Midwest Journal of Political Science* 13:95–125.

Smith, Donald E. (1963). *India as a Secular State.* Princeton: Princeton University Press.

_____ (1965). *Religion and Politics in Burma.* Princeton: Princeton University Press.

_____ (1970). *Religion and Political Development.* Boston: Little, Brown.

_____ (1973). "The politics of Buddhism." *Worldview* 16, no. 1:12–16.

Smith, Michael G. (1965). *The Plural Society in the British West Indies*. Berkeley: University of California Press.

Smith, Michael G., and Leo Kuper, eds. (1969). *Pluralism in Africa*. Berkeley: University of California Press.

Srinivas, M. N. (1966). *Social Change in Modern India*. Berkeley: University of California Press.

Strayer, Joseph R. (1966). "The historical experience of nation-building in Europe." In Karl W. Deutsch and William J. Foltz (eds.), *Nation-Building*. New York: Atherton Press.

Sugar, Peter F. (1964). "Economic and political modernization: Turkey." In Robert F. Ward and Dankwart A. Rustow (eds.), *Political Modernization in Japan and Turkey*. Princeton: Princeton University Press.

Sunshine, Jonathan (1972). "The economic basis and consequences of democracy: the need to study the time dimension." Paper prepared for Annual Meeting of the American Political Science Association, Washington, D.C.

Tanter, Raymond (1967). "Toward a theory of political development." *Midwest Journal of Political Science* 11:145–72.

Tarrow, Sidney G. (1967). *Peasant Communism in Southern Italy*. New Haven: Yale University Press.

——————— (1971). "The urban-rural cleavage in political involvement: the case of France." *American Political Science Review* 65:341–57.

Taylor, Charles Lewis, and Michael Hudson (1972). *World Handbook of Political and Social Indicators,* 2nd edition. New Haven: Yale University Press.

Thomas, Hugh (1971). *Cuba: The Pursuit of Freedom*. New York: Harper & Row.

Thompson, Leonard M. (1966). *Politics in the Republic of South Africa*. Boston: Little, Brown.

Tilly, Charles (1969). "Collective violence in European perspective." In Hugh Davis Graham and Ted Robert Gurr (eds.), *Violence in America: Historical and Comparative Perspectives*. New York: Bantam Books.

——————— (1973). "Does modernization breed revolution?" *Comparative Politics* 5:425–47.

——————— ed. (1975). *The Formation of National States in Western Europe*. Princeton: Princeton University Press.

Tingsten, Herbert (1963). *Political Behavior: Studies in Election Statistics*. Totowa, N.J.: Bedminster Press.

Tsurutani, Taketsugu (1968). "Stability and instability: a note in comparative political analysis." *Journal of Politics* 30:910–33.

Valcárcel, Daniel (1947). *La Rebelión de Tupac Amaru*. Mexico: Fondo de Cultura Económica.

Vallier, Ivan (1970). *Catholicism, Social Control, and Modernization in Latin America*. Englewood Cliffs, N.J.: Prentice-Hall.

van den Berghe, Pierre L. (1967). *Race and Racism: A Comparative Perspective*. New York: Wiley.

van der Mehden, Fred (1963). *Religion and Nationalism in Southeast Asia: Burma, Indonesia, and the Philippines*. Madison, Wis.: University of Wisconsin Press.

Verba, Sidney (1965). "Conclusion: comparative political culture." In Sidney Verba and Lucian Pye (eds.), *Political Culture and Political Development*. Princeton: Princeton University Press.

Verba, Sidney, Norman H. Nie, and Jae-On Kim (1971). *The Modes of Democratic Participation: A Cross-National Comparison*. Comparative Politics Series, No. 01–013, Vol. 2. Beverly Hills, Calif.: Sage.

Vernon, Ray (1963). *The Dilemma of Mexico's Development*. Cambridge, Mass.: Harvard University Press.

Wagley, Charles (1963). *An Introduction to Brazil*. New York: Columbia University Press.

—————— (1965). "On the concept of social race in the Americas." In Dwight B. Heath and Richard N. Adams (eds.), *Contemporary Cultures and Societies of Latin America*. New York: Random House.

Ward, Robert E., and Dankwart A. Rustow, eds. (1964). *Political Modernization in Japan and Turkey*. Princeton: Princeton University Press.

Watanuki, Joji (1974). "Japanese politics in flux." In James William Morley (ed.), *Prologue to the Future: The United States and Japan in the Postindustrial Age*. Lexington, Mass.: Published for the Japan Society by D. C. Heath.

Weiner, Myron (1962). *The Politics of Scarcity: Public Pressure and Political Response in India*. Chicago: University of Chicago Press.

—————— (1965). "India: two political cultures." In Lucian W. Pye and Sidney Verba, *Political Culture and Political Development*. Princeton: Princeton University Press.

—————— (1971). "Political integration and political development." In Jason L. Finkle and Richard W. Gable (eds.), *Political Development and Social Change,* 2nd edition. New York: Wiley.

Weingrod, Alex (1968). "Patrons, patronage, and political parties." *Comparative Studies in Society and History* 10:377–400.

Welch, Claude E., Jr., and Arthur K. Smith (1974). *Military Role and Rule*. North Scituate, Mass.: Duxbury Press.

Wheeler, Richard S. (1970). *The Politics of Pakistan: A Constitutional Quest*. Ithaca, N.Y.: Cornell University Press.

Wiarda, Ieda Siqueira, and Howard J. Wiarda (1970). "The churches and rapid social change: observations on the differences and similarities between Protestants and Catholics in Brazil." *The Journal of Church and State* 12:13–39.

Wilcox, Clair, Willis D. Weatherford, Jr., and Holland Hunter (1962). *Economics of the World Today*. New York: Harcourt, Brace and World.

Willems, E. (1969). "Religious pluralism and class structure: Brazil and Chile." In Roland Robertson (ed.), *Sociology of Religion*. Middlesex, England: Penguin Books.

Williams, Edward J. (1967). *Latin American Christian Democratic Parties*. Knoxville, Tenn.: University of Tennessee Press.

Wilson, A. Jeyaratnam (1966). "Buddhism in Ceylon politics 1960–1965." In Donald E. Smith (ed.), *South Asian Politics and Religion*. Princeton: Princeton University Press.

Wilson, Bryan A. (1963). "Millennialism in comparative perspective." *Comparative Studies in Society and History* 6:93–114.

Wilson, B. R. (1969). "A typology of sects." In Roland Robertson (ed.), *Sociology of Religion*. Middlesex, England: Penguin Books.

Wittfogel, Karl A. (1957). *Oriental Despotism: A Comparative Study of Total Power*. New Haven: Yale University Press.

Wriggins, W. Howard (1960). *Ceylon: Dilemmas of a New Nation*. Princeton: Princeton University Press.

Zolberg, Aristide (1966). *Creating Political Order*. Chicago: Rand McNally.

2
GOVERNMENTS AND POLITICAL OPPOSITIONS

ROBERT A. DAHL

INTRODUCTION

Of the three great milestones in the development of democratic institutions—
the right to participate in governmental decisions by casting a vote, the right to
be represented, and the right of an organized opposition to appeal for votes
against the government in elections and in parliament—the last is, in a highly
developed form, so wholly modern that there are people now living who were
born before it had appeared in most of western Europe.

Throughout recorded history, it seems, stable institutions providing legal,
orderly, peaceful modes of political opposition have been rare. If peaceful
antagonism between factions is uncommon, peaceful opposition among organized, permanent political parties is an even more exotic historical phenomenon. Legal party opposition, in fact, is a recent unplanned invention that has
been confined for the most part to a handful of countries in western Europe
and the English-speaking world. Even more recent are organized political parties that compete peacefully in elections for the votes of the great bulk of the
adult population who can exercise the franchise under nearly universal suffrage. Universal suffrage and enduring mass parties are, with few exceptions,
products of the past century.

Because some conflict of views seems to be unavoidable in human affairs,
political societies have always had to deal somehow with the fact of opposition.
Nevertheless, that there might legitimately exist an organized group within the
political system to oppose, criticize, and if possible oust the leading officials of

---

This essay consists of passages excerpted, paraphrased, or otherwise adapted from my
chapters in *Political Oppositions in Western Democracies* (Yale University Press, 1966),
Polyarchy: Participation and Political Oppositions (Yale University Press, 1971), and
Regimes and Oppositions (Yale University Press, 1971).

government was until recently an unfamiliar and generally unacceptable notion. When the men at the American Constitutional Convention of 1787 expressed their fear of "factions" as the bane of republics, they spoke the traditional view. The most long-lived republic in history, the aristocratic Republic of Venice, deliberately inhibited the formation of enduring political organizations. Venice, like Rome before it, sought to provide in its constitutional arrangements sufficient checks and balances among officials to prevent arbitrary decisions and to ensure a large measure of consensus for the laws; thus organized opposition was seen as unnecessary and a danger to the stability of the Republic.[1] Not all the premodern democracies and republics went quite as far as Venice. Factions, coalitions, and alliances of one kind or another existed in and outside the popular assemblies of Athens,[2] and in the late Roman Republic political alliances sought votes both for candidates and for laws in the various popular assemblies. But evidently these groups were never highly organized, had no permanent structure, and even lacked definite names (Taylor, 1961; Adcock, 1959, pp. 60–61). Moreover, like the Guelphs and Ghibellines of medieval Italy or the Piagnoni and the Arrabiati of Savonarola's Florence, factions typically settled their differences sooner or later, as they came to do during the last century of the Roman Republic, by bloodshed.

The system of managing the major political conflicts of a society by allowing one or more opposition parties to compete with the governing parties for votes in elections and in parliament is not only modern; surely it is also one of the most unexpected social discoveries that man has ever stumbled onto. Up until two centuries ago, no one had accurately foreseen it. Today one is inclined to regard the existence of an opposition party as very nearly the most distinctive characteristic of democracy itself; and we take the absence of an opposition party as evidence, if not always conclusive proof, for the absence of democracy.

Yet there are signs that this new form, which was unknown before the nineteenth century and had spread to some 30 countries in the twentieth, is, nearly everywhere, undergoing profound changes.

The Meaning of Opposition

The term *opposition* is rather difficult to define precisely. A preliminary definition will, I think, prove satisfactory enough for our purposes. Suppose that *A* determines the conduct of some aspect of the government of a particular political system during some interval. We need not specify the interval exactly; it may be a period in the past, the coming year, etc. Suppose that during this interval *B* cannot determine the conduct of the government; and that *B* is opposed to the conduct of government by *A*. Then *B* is what we mean by "an opposition." Note that during some different interval, *B* might determine the conduct of the government, and *A* might be "in opposition." Thus it is the *role* of opposition that we are interested in; we are concerned with *A* and *B* only insofar as they perform that role in different ways.

This preliminary definition can be clarified a little. To begin with, the "conduct" of the government is deliberately broad and vague, and I propose to leave it undefined; it remains therefore what logicians sometimes call a primitive term. But it is intended to be comprehensive enough to include, for example, the mere fact that A comes from an ethnic, racial, or religious group that B is opposed to having in high government offices. What is meant by "oppose" might also be left undefined, but a few comments may help to specify the meaning. As the term is used here, B is opposed to A's strategy, S_a, if B believes that S_a will prevent B from successfully pursuing his own preferred action or strategy, S_b. It is useful to distinguish between active opposition, which occurs when B undertakes a deliberate course of action intended to modify the conduct of government, and *passive* opposition, which exists when B recognizes the conflict but does not deliberately undertake any action directed toward a change in the conduct of government. Although passive opposition is important, in this article I am almost entirely concerned with active opposition.

Second, in some political systems the role of opposition might be difficult to distinguish, either because one is uncertain whether it is A or B that determines the conduct of the government, or because both do. In systems like this, opposition is not distinctive; it dissolves into the system, so to speak.

Several questions arise:

1. What are the consequences of regimes for oppositions, and of oppositions for regimes?

2. What conditions increase or reduce the chances that a political entity— specifically, a country—will tolerate the existence of organized oppositions that are free to contest the conduct of the government in elections conducted honestly among a sizable electorate?

3. Among such systems—here called polyarchies—what are the significant variations in the patterns of organized party opposition, and how do we explain these variations?

I. REGIMES AND OPPOSITIONS

Assumptions

1. No government receives indefinitely the total support of the people over whom it asserts its jurisdiction. Certainly the government of a large collection of people, such as the government of a country, is never completely supported in all that it does by all the people whom it claims to govern. In no country, in short, does everyone have the same preference as to the conduct of the government, with the term *conduct* used in its broadest sense.

2. Because people are not in perfect accord as to their political preferences, every political system, if it is to endure, must provide ways for determining

which (or whose) political preferences the government responds to. It will be useful to consider two extreme possibilities. At one extreme, a government might respond to the political preferences of only one person (or perhaps to a tiny and wholly unified minority); it would ignore or override all other preferences. A system of this kind might be called a pure *hegemony*. At the other extreme, the political preferences of everyone might be weighted equally, and in conflicts the government would respond always to the preferences of the greater number. A system of this kind might be called a pure *egalitarian democracy*. In a moment I shall incorporate these extreme types into a somewhat fuller typology.

3. All political systems in some respects constrain the expression, organization, representation, and satisfaction of political preferences. Given the existence of disagreements as to what the government should do (that is to say, given the human condition, if my first assumption is valid), even an egalitarian democracy cannot respond fully to the preferences of both the greater number and the smaller number who disagree with the majority. During any given period, therefore, a political system will contain some people who, if there were no barriers or costs to their doing so, would be actively opposed to the conduct of the government.

4. Political systems vary a great deal, however, in the *barriers* or *opportunities* they provide for the expression, organization, and representation of political preferences, and thus for the opportunities available to potential oppositions.

Definitions

To cope adequately with these variations among different political systems poses some difficulties. For example, I have just offered two extreme types, hegemony and egalitarian democracy; yet both are purely theoretical types. Although neither exists in pure form, they do hint at a way of defining regimes. Suppose that we define maximal reduction in the barriers to oppositions to require that all full citizens have unimpaired opportunities:

> To formulate their preferences.
>
> To signify their preferences to their fellow citizens and the government by individual and collective action.
>
> To have their preferences weighted equally in the conduct of the government—that is, weighted with no discrimination because of the conduct or source of the preference.

Let me further, and without proof, assume that for these three opportunities to exist among a large number of people, such as the number of people who constitute most nation-states at the present time, the institutions of the society must provide at least eight guarantees.

For the opportunity to:	*The following institutional guarantees are required:*
Formulate preferences	1. Freedom to form and join organizations 2. Freedom of expression 3. Right to vote 4. Competition by political leaders for support 5. Alternative sources of information
Signify preferences	1. Freedom to form and join organizations 2. Freedom of expression 3. Right to vote 4. Eligibility for public office 5. Competition by political leaders for support 6. Alternative sources of information 7. Free and fair elections
Have preferences weighted equally in conduct of government	1. Freedom to form and join organizations 2. Freedom of expression 3. Right to vote 4. Eligibility for public office 5. Competition by political leaders for support a) Competition by political leaders for votes 6. Alternative sources of information 7. Free and fair elections 8. Institutions for making government policies depend on votes and other expressions of preference

I am going to make the further assumption that the connections between the guarantees and the three fundamental opportunities are sufficiently evident to need no further elaboration here.

Now upon an examination of the list of eight institutional guarantees, it appears that they might provide us with a theoretical scale along which it would be possible to order different political systems. Upon closer examination, however, it appears that the eight guarantees might be fruitfully interpreted as constituting *two* somewhat different theoretical *dimensions of democratization:*

1. Both historically and at the present time, regimes vary enormously in the extent to which the eight institutional conditions are openly available, publicly employed, and fully guaranteed to at least some members of the political systems who wish to contest the conduct of the government. Thus a scale reflecting these eight conditions would enable us to compare different regimes according to the extent of permissible *public contestation* or *political competition.* However, since a regime might permit opposition to a very small or a very large proportion of the population, we clearly need a second dimension.

2. Both historically and contemporaneously, regimes also vary in the proportion of the population entitled to participate on a more or less equal plane in controlling and contesting the conduct of the government—to participate, so to speak, in the system of public contestation. A scale reflecting the breadth of the right to *participate* in public contestation would enable us to compare different regimes according to their *inclusiveness.*

The right to vote in free and fair elections, for example, partakes of both dimensions. When a regime grants this right to some of its citizens, it moves toward greater public contestation. But the larger the proportion of citizens who enjoy the right, the more inclusive the regime.

Public contestation and inclusiveness vary somewhat independently. Britain had a highly developed system of public contestation by the end of the eighteenth century; but only a minuscule fraction of the population was fully included in it until after the expansion of the suffrage in 1867 and 1884. Switzerland has long had one of the most fully developed systems of public contestation in the world. Yet women did not gain the constitutional right to vote in national elections until 1972. By contrast, the USSR still has almost no system of public contestation; yet it does have universal suffrage. In fact, one of the most striking changes during this century has been the virtual disappearance of an outright denial of the legitimacy of popular participation in government. Only a handful of countries have failed to grant at least a ritualistic vote to their citizens and to hold at least nominal elections; and even the most repressive dictators usually pay some lip service today to the legitimate right of the people to participate in the government, i.e., to participate in "governing" but not in public contestation.

Suppose, then, that we think of *democratization* as made up of at least two dimensions: public contestation and the right to participate (Fig. 1). Doubtless most readers believe that democratization involves more than these two dimensions; in a moment I shall discuss a third dimension. But I propose to limit the discussion here to these two. For the point has already emerged, I think: developing a system of public contestation is not necessarily equivalent to full democratization.

To display the relationship between public contestation and democratization more clearly, let us now lay out the two dimensions as in Fig. 2.

Let me call a regime near the lower left corner of Fig. 2 a *closed hegemony.* If a hegemonic regime shifts upward, as along Path A, it is moving toward greater public contestation. Without stretching language too far, one could say that a change in this direction involves the *liberalization* of a regime; alternatively, one might say that the regime becomes *more competitive.* If a regime changes to provide greater participation, as along Path B, one might say that it is changing toward greater *popularization,* or that it is becoming *inclusive.* A regime might change along one dimension and not the other. If we call a

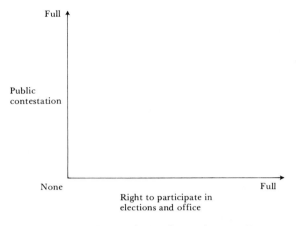

Fig. 1. Two Theoretical Dimensions of Democratization

regime near the upper left corner a competitive oligarchy, then Path A represents a change from a closed hegemony to a competitive oligarchy. But a closed hegemony might also become more inclusive without liberalizing, i.e., without increasing the opportunities for public contestation, as along Path B. In this case the regime changes from a closed to an *inclusive hegemony*.

Democracy might be conceived of as lying at the upper right corner. But since democracy may involve more dimensions than the two in Fig. 2, and

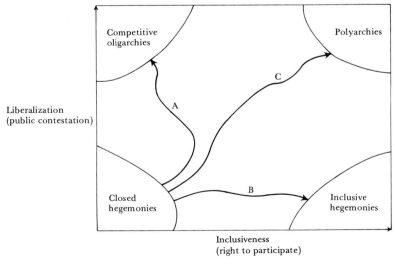

Fig. 2. Liberalization, Inclusiveness, and Democratization

since (in my view) no large system in the real world is fully democratized, I prefer to call real-world systems that are closest to the upper right corner *polyarchies*. Any change in a regime that moves it upward and to the right, e.g., along Path C, may be said to represent some degree of *democratization*. Polyarchies, then, may be thought of as relatively (but incompletely) democratized regimes, or, to put it in another way, polyarchies are regimes that have been substantially popularized and liberalized, i.e., are highly inclusive and extensively open to public contestation.

The large space in the middle of the figure is not named or subdivided. The lack of nomenclature does not mean a lack of regimes; in fact, perhaps the preponderant number of national regimes in the world today would fall into the middle area. Many significant changes in regimes, then, involve shifts within, into, or out of this important central area as the regimes become more (or less) inclusive and increase (or reduce) opportunities for public contestation. For our purposes, regimes in the large middle area can be called *mixed;* two subtypes might be referred to as a *nearly hegemonic* regime, which has somewhat more opportunities for public contestation than a hegemonic regime, and a *near polyarchy*, which could be quite inclusive but would have more severe restrictions on public contestation than full polyarchies, or it might provide opportunities for public contestation comparable to those of a full polyarchy and yet be somewhat less inclusive.

Table 1 shows the results of an attempt to locate 114 countries in a rough approximation to the scheme of Fig. 2. With 10 indicators of opportunities for political oppositions, it is possible to rank the countries in 31 scale-types. Because of irreparable limitations on available data, the dimension of inclusion is represented only by the extent of the suffrage, if any. The results correspond pretty much with one's impressions. The cutting points in the table are arbitrary, though the countries in the highest group, the polyarchies or near-polyarchies, are approximately the same as those classified as democracies by Rustow (1967, pp. 290–91).

TABLE 1   Extent of inclusion (suffrage only) in regimes in 114 countries, c. 1969

Extent of opportunities open to political oppositions	No elections	Percentage of adult citizens eligible to vote			Uncertain unascertained, transitional	Totals
		Under 20	20–90	Over 90		
Greatest	—	—	4	28	6	38
Intermediate	5	1	3	17	13	39
Least	16	—	1	16	4	37
Totals	21	1	8	61	23	114

Axioms

When hegemonic regimes and competitive oligarchies move toward polyarchy, they increase the opportunities for effective participation and contestation and hence the number of individuals, groups, and interests whose preferences have to be considered in policy-making.

From the perspective of the incumbents who currently govern, such a transformation carries with it new possibilities of conflict, as a result of which their goals (and they themselves) may be displaced by spokesmen for the newly incorporated individuals, groups, or interests.

The problem of their opponents is the mirror image of the problem of the incumbents. Any transformation that provides opponents of the government with greater opportunities to translate their goals into policies enforced by the state carries with it the possibility of conflict with spokesmen for the individuals, groups, or interests they displace in the government.

Thus the greater the conflict between government and opposition, the more likely it is that each will seek to deny opportunities to the other to participate effectively in policy-making. Stated another way, the greater the conflict between a government and its opponents, the more costly it is for each to tolerate the other. Since the opposition must gain control of the state in order to suppress the incumbents (at which point opposition and government have changed roles), we can formulate the general proposition as an axiom about governments tolerating their opponents.

Axiom 1. The likelihood that a government will tolerate an opposition increases as the expected costs of toleration decrease.

However, a government must also consider how costly it would be to suppress an opposition; for even if toleration is costly, suppression might be very much more costly and hence obviously foolish. Therefore:

Axiom 2. The likelihood that a government will tolerate an opposition increases as the expected costs of suppression increase.

Thus the chances that a more competitive political system will emerge or endure may be thought of as depending on these two sets of costs.

Axiom 3. The more the costs of suppression exceed the costs of toleration, the greater the chance for a competitive regime.

Axiom 3 can be illustrated graphically as in Fig. 3.

The lower the costs of toleration, the greater the *security* of the government. The greater the costs of suppression, the greater the *security* of the opposition. Hence conditions that provide a high degree of *mutual security*

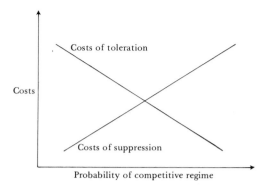

Figure 3

for government and opposition would tend to generate and to preserve wider opportunities for oppositions to contest the conduct of the government.

Some General Tendencies

Diversity, Not Polarity

It is a well-grounded observation, I believe, though one often denied, even in highly influential theories of politics, that differences in what people think they want from the government that rules over them tend *toward diversity and multiplicity rather than toward bipolarity: to many groupings rather than merely two.* Let me call what people think they want the government to be or to do their political preferences or, if you prefer, their *political interests.* Whenever the barriers to the expression and organization of political preferences are low, one should expect (as the usual result) the emergence of a multiplicity of camps, whereas polarization into two internally cohesive and unified camps would be rare.

It is rare for a country to divide into two camps along socioeconomic lines; it is rare, indeed, for a country to divide along any lines into only two camps. But it is commonplace for countries to display *more* than two sets of conflicting interests. The explanation seems to be that most countries have some conflicts based at least in part on differences in language, religion, race, or ethnic group. Frequently these conflicts cut, wholly or partly, across one another and across differences of status, function, or reward based on economic activity. And they do not disappear or become attenuated with modernization. It is, rather, the conflicts derived from economic differences that often become attenuated, leaving more room, so to speak, for the other conflicts to occur. What is more, different political preferences or interests stimulated by differences in economic function, status, or reward seldom divide a people into only two groups, each with more or less identical preferences. Much more often, it seems, when people respond to economic factors, they divide into more than two groups—frequently, in fact, into a bewildering multiplicity of contesting interests.

What seems to vary most from one country to another is not so much this tendency toward diversity rather than polarization as the extent to which the societal cloth is cut up into separate pieces by a succession of cuts or alternatively is woven with strong strands that hold one part to another. In language that is more familiar to social scientists (but that reverses the metaphor I have just used), I am of course speaking of the extent to which cleavages "reinforce" one another and hence produce "segmentation" or "fragmentation," or instead "cross-cut" one another and thus produce a greater tendency toward cohesion.

The important point is the comparative rarity of strongly bipolar social conflicts, particularly along an economic axis, and the comparative frequency of conflict involving more than two sets of contestants.

A hasty reader might be tempted at this point to jump to some unwarranted conclusions. To say that polarization, like the plague, is rare is obviously not to say that it presents no dangers. And because polarization, though rare, is dangerous, one should not leap to the conclusion that a multiplicity of political interests, though more common, inevitably produces cohesion and stability. For diversity, like polarization, can also create problems, even for polyarchies. In what follows it is the problems which seem to stem from diversity rather than from polarization that I want to stress. But first let me emphasize one further part of the argument.

The Lower the Barriers, The Greater the Variety

The lower the barriers to—or the greater the opportunities for—expressing, organizing, and representing political preferences, the greater the number and variety of preferences represented in policy-making. Hence the number and variety of interests represented in policy-making would be greater under a polyarchy than under a mixed regime and greater under a mixed regime than under a hegemony. Therefore the transformation of a hegemony into a mixed regime or polyarchy, or of a mixed regime into a polyarchy, would increase the number and variety of preferences and interests in policy-making.

If one is not careful about definitions, the argument can of course become circular. Even if a meticulous concern for definitions enables us to avoid the latent circularity, the hypothesis is not easy to test. Yet changes in regime occur, and the results do seem to bear out the argument. When hegemonic regimes are suddenly displaced by regimes that provide greater opportunities for oppositions—as in Spain after the flight of the king in 1931 and the establishment of the republic, or in Italy and Germany with the fall of their dictatorships, or more recently in Ghana with the fall of Nkrumah—political preferences and latent oppositions that had been dammed up spout forth like water through a collapsing dam. Thus Leiserson (1973, p. 366) reports that after the military dictatorship was defeated in Japan, "the profusion of political groups which burst into the open as soon as the wartime straitjacket had been removed showed that the eclipse of oppositions had been only temporary."

During its "interrupted revolution," as Skilling (1973b) calls it, Czechoslovakia provided an even more dramatic example of the abrupt surfacing of hitherto submerged interests and preferences. Ideological cleavages became visible as opponents of all change clashed with those who were ready to accept limited reforms, and moderate reformers differed not only with conservatives but with advocates of more radical, even revolutionary alterations. Organized groups and associations flourished, pressed for advantage, demanded changes. Long-dormant or merely formal associations took on life; pre-Communist organizations like the Boy Scouts were revived. The cleavage between Czechs and Slovaks appeared as a basic organizational principle. With the virtual suspension of censorship, existing journals became controversial, new papers sprang into existence, and conflicting views were heard on radio and television. Then, almost as abruptly as the revolution had begun, with the Russian occupation these processes were reversed, and hegemony was gradually restored.

Yet it is this very tendency for political interests to crowd against the barriers to expression and to participate in policy-making in increasing number and variety as the barriers are lowered that sometimes generates threats to regimes.

Threats to Regimes

Hegemonies: Self-fulfilling Prophecy

Hegemonies, by definition, are regimes that impose the most severe limits on the opportunities available to opponents of the government. Fully hegemonic regimes not only suppress all rival parties or convert them into mere appendages of the dominant party; they suppress factions within the dominant party as well. Internal party democracy, then, provides no alternative channel for expressing dissent. Nor are interest organizations permitted to function autonomously. The official organizations tend to be transmission belts for the regime—so much so that, as in Spain, the official trade unions have come to be displaced by illegal workers' councils.

Yet even in highly hegemonic regimes, opposition continues. Perhaps in all regimes, no matter how representative they may be, conflicts are bound to occur among the most powerful. These conflicts may be no more than surreptitious, lethal struggles by men who seek to win the dictator's favor and avoid his wrath. But beyond these struggles for power and place among the courtiers, there may also be, to quote Barghoorn (1973, p. 39), "efforts by members of the highest party and governmental decision-making bodies to change the personnel or policies of the party-state." Factionalism may spread beyond the inner circle as allies are sought in lower echelons of the party, in the bureaucracy, in the controlled press, or among intellectuals. In addition to the struggles among factions, there is the seemingly unavoidable maneuvering among leaders who wish to protect or improve the position of specific segments and institutions of the society: the military, heavy industry, consumer goods, education, sciences, the arts. Factional and interest-based opposition by leaders essentially loyal to the regime verges on a more fundamental opposition to basic policies or institutions—for example, by nationality groups who feel themselves unfairly treated, by intellectuals to whom a thaw following the harsh winter of repression is but a prelude to a libertarian regime, by economists who believe that a decentralized price-system economy must replace rigidly centralized planning. Beyond these oppositions, there are opponents who wish to subvert the regime and who are prepared to participate, if need be and if the opportunity arises, in conspiracies, violence, and revolution.

From the perspective of those who uphold a hegemonic regime, factional opposition may seem less dangerous than the others, but how can a line be drawn between "safe" and dangerous oppositions? The hegemonic regime, in fact, creates a self-fulfilling prophecy: *Since all opposition is potentially dangerous, no distinction can be made between acceptable and unacceptable opposition, between loyal and disloyal opposition, between opposition that is protected and opposition that must be repressed. Yet if all oppositions are treated as dangerous and subject to repression, opposition that would be loyal if it were tolerated becomes disloyal because it is not tolerated. Since all opposition is likely to be disloyal, all opposition must be repressed.*

I may have overdrawn the point. Yet highly hegemonic regimes seem unable wholly to escape the force of this self-fulfilling prophecy, particularly if they are endowed with an official ideology that claims a kind of divine right to rule based on the exclusive possession of political truth and virtue. They move within a small orbit of toleration and repression: as toleration begins to set free the latent forces of opposition, the regime's leaders become fearful and clamp down. Their fear is not necessarily irrational, for the hitherto repressed opposition *might* surge out of control. Thus, because toleration may sow the seeds of the regime's destruction, it contains the seeds of its own destruction.

The dilemma of mixed regimes: repression or explosion?   The frequency of mixed regimes partly reflects the fact that they make up a rather undiscriminating residual category in my classification. They vary from highly competitive oligarchies, where public contestation, including party organization, is well protected but restricted, to a small elite (as in Britain by the end of the eighteenth century) to systems like that of Tanzania, where under universal suffrage and the dominance of a single party, two candidates ran against each other in every parliamentary district, apparently in honestly conducted elections. During the late Meiji period and even under the Taisho Democracy, Japan was evidently ruled by a mixed regime. Yugoslavia should probably be classed as a mixed regime at the national level. During its brief revolution, Czechoslovakia was rapidly being transformed from a full hegemony into a mixed regime.

In mixed regimes, some oppositions can engage in at least some forms of public contestation, "loyal" oppositions are tolerated, and (as in late-eighteenth-century Britain or a century later in Japan) their leaders may even succeed from time to time in peacefully displacing some of the incumbents in the highest political offices.

If the barriers are, by definition, lower in mixed regimes than in hegemonies, and if as a result a greater variety of interests engage in public contestation, it is also true that, by definition, in mixed regimes the barriers are higher than in polyarchies. For example, even if opposition is well protected, the whole political game may be legally restricted to a tiny segment of the people, as in eighteenth-century Britain or in Japan until after World War II; and even if everyone is allowed to participate in the game (at least nominally), the rules of the game impose certain marked limits on the right to form political organizations, to contest elections, and so on. In Czechoslovakia under Dubcek, the Action Program of the Central Committee called for democratization of the party but rejected the more radical argument that socialist democracy would be impossible without a plural-party system.

Under mixed regimes, political preferences are repressed that would make themselves felt if the barriers to public contestation or participation were lower. In competitive oligarchies, the preferences of great mass segments—peasants, rural laborers, artisans, middle strata, and some commercial or industrial segments—are largely unorganized, unexpressed, and unrepresented. More typical is the mixed regime with a broad citizenship but limits on public contestation, particularly on the right to form opposition parties. Where one party is privileged and others are prohibited, intraparty democracy is sometimes offered as an alternative to plural parties. The catch in the theory of intraparty democracy in a one-party state, however, is that the kinds of guarantees that would fully protect the expression, organization, and representation of interests within a party would also allow the formation of de facto parties, even if they masqueraded as factions in the single party. Conversely, if opponents of government are not protected in their right to form opposition parties in order to challenge the conduct of the government in elections, it is difficult to see how opposition within the dominant party could be fully protected (Foltz, 1973, pp. 161–165; Finer, 1967).

In practice, it is probably not accidental, then, that organized party factions do not seem to exist in anything like the same degree in one-party states as they do in some countries where oppositions can express themselves not only in party factions but also in opposition parties. The highly organized factions in the Liberal-Democratic party of Japan or the Christian Democratic party in Italy seem to have no counterpart in one-party countries.

Thus in mixed regimes, as in hegemonies, when the barriers are lowered, oppositions, interests, and political preferences previously repressed or inhibited spring forth to engage in public contestation. Leaders in these countries of course know this perfectly well—whatever they may say in public. And the presence of these repressed forces creates a genuine danger to the regime, for which it can find no easy solution.

Viewed from the perspective of those who want to maintain a mixed regime and avoid both hegemony and polyarchy, the danger is that by yielding to the demands of oppositions for liberalization, they will trigger a runaway explosion out of which will emerge either polyarchy or, if repression is needed to bring liberalization to a halt, hegemony.

Can oppositions in a liberalized regime be expected to refrain from pressing demands for an opposition party and from mobilizing behind it those who feel inadequately represented? As we have seen, the doctrine of intraparty democracy in practice is unlikely to provide enough representation to satisfy all the major interests of a country. Some interests will therefore hope to organize a party more immediately responsive to their particular views. Democratic ideology also continues to exert a powerful force for plural parties.

Can the process of liberalization be launched and then checked just short of this critical threshold? In view of the danger inherent in arriving at this threshold and then trying to restrain the forces that would pull the country across it, it will often seem wiser—from the perspective of those who support a mixed regime—to confine public contestation to fairly narrow limits. Yet if repression is needed to maintain these boundaries, as it probably will be, the mixed regime confronts a painful and inescapable dilemma. By increasing discontent and disloyalty, repression also increases the chance for a runaway explosion—and so the need for even more repression.

Thus mixed regimes are prone to oscillate between liberalization and repression. By suitable dosages of each, skilled leadership may successfully avoid both full hegemony and polyarchy. Yet the moment of truth will arrive for any mixed regime if, in the process of liberalization, it should ever reach the threshold to polyarchy and a substantial group of spokesmen should begin to make a public demand for an opposition party.

Two Sources of Discontent in Polyarchies

By definition, polyarchies are systems that offer the lowest barriers to the expression, organization, and representation of political preferences and hence provide the widest array of opportunities for oppositions to contest the conduct of the government. But polyarchic regimes are not immune to discontent. For even in polyarchies, the political interests of some people—perhaps of many people—remain unsatisfied. Let me focus here on two of the reasons why this happens.

1. Inequalities.   In the first place, even in polyarchies some people have grounds for believing that their interests are inadequately expressed, organized, and represented. For one thing, there are no generally accepted, objective criteria for deciding when an interest is fairly or adequately taken into account. In addition, one obvious source of political inequalities is the massive differences in the political resources of different individuals and groups. In extreme cases, as in ancient Athens, the Venetian Republic, and the American South, within the confines of the same state one stratum of the population may govern itself through a polyarchy and at the same time impose a hegemony on other strata. These are anomalies, however, and not the main source of inequalities in polyarchies. Indeed, it is reasonable to argue that these anomalous cases do not indicate defects in polyarchy per se but simply demonstrate the existence of dual political systems in which hegemony is partly substituted for polyarchy. But even if we disregard these cases, no polyarchy has ever eradicated large differences in the political resources of its citizens. In every polyarchy, therefore, these differences help to generate inequalities in the effective representation of individuals and groups. In addition to these ancient and well-known causes of political inequalities, representation itself presents technical problems in ensuring equality that have never been satisfactorily solved.

To be sure, over a fairly extended period, so many people might be at least partly satisfied in so many of their most salient political preferences (even though they might be dissatisfied in particular cases) that discontent would not be particularly high. This result sometimes seems to be considered inherent in democratic procedures, but obviously it is not. I have already suggested the hypothetical case of the permanent minority for which no democratic rules provide a satisfactory solution. This of course represents an extreme form of persistent polarization, which, as I have argued earlier, is comparatively rare. In practice, discontent is less likely to be associated with polarization between a permanent majority and a permanent minority than with fragmentation or segmentation in political conflicts.

2. Polarization and segmentation.   Even if decisions were arrived at among political equals according to exact rules of democratic procedure, the outcome of decisions in a country with a great diversity of political preferences could rarely satisfy everyone.

To facilitate discussion, it will be helpful at this point to call attention to several aspects of political conflict: (1) The level of antagonism. Although antagonism is admittedly difficult to measure, particularly across countries or cultures, as a theoretical (and potentially operational) concept it seems indispensable. (2) The number of sets of antagonists involved in a single conflict. To simplify the discussion, I intend to consider only the distinction between conflicts involving two sets of antagonists (bipolarity) and those involving more than two (multipolarity). (3) The extent to which the composition of the sets of antagonists in one conflict is identical with the composition of the sets involved in other conflicts. If they are substantially the same, the conflicts are reinforcing or cumulative; if substantially different, the conflicts are cross-cutting. (4) The duration of any particular pattern, that is, the extent to which all of these aspects persist unchanged over time. In what follows, for the sake of simplicity I usually ignore the question of duration by assuming a more or less persistent pattern over a fairly substantial period of time. Although the possible patterns are innumerable, Table 2 shows some important possibilities.

TABLE 2   Some patterns of conflicts

Conflicts	Sets of antagonists	Levels of antagonism	
		Low	High
Reinforcing	Constant { Bipolar Multipolar	Moderate bipolarity Moderate multipolarity	Polarization Severe segmentation
Crosscutting	Changing	Moderate crosscutting conflicts	Moderate segmentation

Obviously, conflicts are relatively easy to handle as long as the level of antagonism remains low. They become dangerous to a regime when the level of antagonism is too high. Persistently high levels of antagonism seem to be less associated with purely socioeconomic differences than with differences in language, religion, ethnic or racial identity, and ideology.

Polarization seems particularly dangerous for polyarchies, since they lack the coercive forces and the willingness to repress severe antagonisms. If polarization occurs along regional lines, the best that can be hoped for as a solution consistent with polyarchy is peaceful separation, as between Norway and Sweden in 1905. But if separation is a threat to the prevailing concept of the nation, as the threat of secession was to the idea of the Union in the United States in the late 1850s, or as it would be in India today, the result is likely to be an attempt to coerce the separatists. Indeed, the most likely short-run consequence of polarization in a polyarchy seems to be civil war, as in the United States in 1861, in Austria in 1934, and in Spain in 1936. If polarization persists, a hegemony is likely to emerge as a kind of permanent means of coercion and, perhaps, of long-run pacification.

Yet if my earlier argument is roughly correct, segmentation is a good deal more likely than polarization. Like polarization, segmentation also carries with it a threat to polyarchy. For, like polarization, segmentation can also endanger nationhood whenever regional conflicts are reinforced by antagonism arising from such differences as those of language, religion, or socioeconomic condition. Language and region do often coincide, as in much of India; if these differences are reinforced by still others, such as socioeconomic condition, regions may seek not only autonomy but separation. For example, if Spain and Yugoslavia were to become polyarchies, they might be threatened by segmentation along regional lines, for in both countries differences of region, language, tradition, and economic status tend to reinforce one another.

Even where this is not the case and segmentation carries no threat to nationhood, it is likely to foster a form and style of politics that will produce discontent and cynicism about polyarchy. Such an enormous effort must be invested in building easily fragmented coalitions that the game of politics is reduced to—or is at least widely thought to be—little more than a narrow struggle for partisan advantage. Moreover, without some system of mutual guarantees, every major segment must live in perpetual fear lest a coalition from which it is excluded should override its most important interests. If, on the contrary, every major segment manages to win a veto over policy, no coalition can ever deal firmly with any pressing problem. Immobilism is the classic lot of the segmented policy. And immobilism combined with a total transformation of politics into the art of maneuvering for partisan advantage is likely to breed discontent, political cynicism, and in time, demands for a new political order more suited to decisive action.

Obviously, polyarchy is able to cope better with the dangers of segmentation if it can find more effective ways of reconciling the antagonistic groups. Reconciliation requires the investment of more energy and talent in the search for mutually satisfactory solutions to the issues in conflict. One system for mobilizing energy and talent in such a search is the large, catchall party that stands a good chance of putting together enough of the segments to win control of the government. In this situation, crass political incentives are mobilized in a search for solutions which, by being satisfactory to the various sectors, ensure the dominance of the party. The Congress party in India may be the world's leading example, as Kothari (1970, 1973) makes clear, and the Liberal-Democrats in Japan may well run a close second.

Another kind of incentive for mobilizing energy and talent in the search for mutually satisfactory solutions is provided by a system in which all the major segments have, de jure or de facto, a veto on the government's policies, as in Lebanon or the Netherlands. For the threat of a veto compels the leaders of all segments to throw themselves into the search for conciliatory solutions. Conceivably a country endangered by nationality conflicts, such as Yugoslavia, might be able to manage the transition to polyarchy if it were to develop some system of mutual veto among the nationalities.

Yet a system of mutual veto reduces one danger only to create another: immobilism. For often the only solution acceptable to everyone is the status quo; and even if this solution results in satisfactory short-run outcomes, the long-run outcome may be massive dissatisfaction with a system unable to confront and solve pressing problems of poverty, economic growth, welfare, redistribution, housing, and the like.

A special case of this system of mutual vetoes for reconciling antagonistic groups in a segmented polity requires a willingness to decentralize—investing a great deal of authority in the various cohesive segments—and at the same time to permit the settlement of the major issues by the leaders of various segments. In a broad sense, to be sure, this formula might be read as no more than a standard description of polyarchy; but what I have in mind is the system in the Netherlands as it has been described by Daalder (1966) and Lijphart (1968). A system like this does not, of course, spring up overnight, and probably not every segmented society could successfully engineer it. It requires a commitment all round, but particularly among the leaders, to the maintenance of the nation intact, to the seriousness of politics, to the importance of discovering mutually acceptable solutions, and to a process in which leaders are often allowed to negotiate solutions—in secret, outside the usual contentions of politics —which are then willingly accepted by their followers.

There may well be still other and better solutions to the dangers that segmented pluralism creates for polyarchies. Surely the invention of new institutions for political reconciliation—institutions consistent with democratic goals —should have a high place on the agenda of social scientists. For the prospect that existing polyarchies can do a better job in satisfying the claims of citizens, and that countries with hegemonic or mixed politics can in time be democratized, depends on the creation of institutions for reconciling diversities.

II. CONDITIONS FAVORING PUBLIC CONTESTATION AND POLYARCHY

At least seven sets of conditions appear to bear on the chances of public contestation and polyarchy.

Historical Sequences

Paths to Polyarchy

Consider three of the many possible paths from closed hegemony to polyarchy (Fig. 2).

Liberalization precedes inclusiveness:

> A closed hegemony increases opportunities for public contestation and thus is transformed into a competitive oligarchy.

> The competitive oligarchy is then transformed into a polyarchy by increasing the inclusiveness of the regime.

Inclusiveness precedes liberalization:

> A closed hegemony becomes inclusive.
>
> The inclusive hegemony is then transformed into a polyarchy, increasing opportunities for public contestation.

Shortcut:

> A closed hegemony is abruptly transformed into a polyarchy by a sudden grant of universal suffrage and rights of public contestation.

Probably the commonest sequence among the older and more stable polyarchies has been some approximation of the first path. The rules, practices, and culture of competitive politics developed first among a small elite, and the critical transition from nonparty politics to party competition also occurred initially within the restricted group. Although this transition was rarely an easy one and party conflict was often harsh and bitter, the severity of conflict was restrained by ties of friendship, family, interest, class, and ideology that pervaded the restricted group of notables who dominated the political life of the country. Later, as additional social strata were admitted into politics, they were more easily socialized into the norms and practices of competitive politics that had already been developed among the elites, and generally they accepted many if not all of the mutual guarantees that had been developed over many generations. As a consequence, neither the newer strata nor the incumbents who were threatened with displacement felt that the costs of toleration were so high as to outweigh the costs of repression, particularly since repression would entail the destruction of a well-developed system of mutual security.

The other two paths are more dangerous, and for the same reason: To arrive at a viable system of mutual security is a difficult matter at best; the greater the number of people and the variety and disparity of interests involved, the more difficult the task and the greater the time required. Tolerance and mutual security are more likely to develop among a small elite sharing similar perspectives than among a large and heterogeneous collection of leaders representing social strata with widely varying goals, interests, and outlooks. This is why the first path is more likely than the other two to produce stable transformations away from hegemony toward polyarchy. There seem to be few if any unambiguous cases in which the shortcut has been successfully taken. The explanation doubtless is that this path drastically shortens the time for learning complex skills and understandings, and for arriving at what may be an extremely subtle system of mutual security. The second path is also riskier than the first. When the suffrage is extended before the arts of competitive politics have been mastered and accepted as legitimate among the elites, the search for a system of mutual guarantees is likely to be complex and time-consuming. During the transition, when conflict erupts, neither side can be entirely confident that it will be safe to tolerate the other. Because the rules of the political game are ambiguous and the legitimacy of competitive politics is weak, the costs of suppression may not be inordinately high. The danger, then, is that before a system of mutual security can be worked out among the contestants, the emerging but precarious competitive regime will be displaced by a hegemony ruled by one of the contestants.

Although the first path seems to be the safest of the three, it is not likely to be available in the future, simply because the situation today, unlike that in previous periods, is that most countries with hegemonic regimes are *already* inclusive; consequently, if they move toward competitive politics they will have to do so in the presence of a mass electorate.

Inaugurating the Competitive Regime

By inauguration I mean the application of power, influence, or authority to introduce and to legitimize a regime. One way of deciding whether inauguration matters is to consider some of the important ways in which polyarchies or quasi-polyarchies have been inaugurated in the past. The chief forms seem to be as follows:

Within an already independent nation-state:

> The old regime is transformed by evolutionary processes. The new regime is inaugurated by incumbent leaders, who yield peacefully (more or less) to demands for changes and participate in the inauguration of polyarchy or quasi-polyarchy.

> The old regime is transformed by revolution. The new regime is inaugurated by revolutionary leaders, who overthrow the old regime and install a polyarchy or quasi-polyarchy.

> The old regime is transformed by military conquest. After a military defeat, victorious occupying forces help inaugurate a polyarchy or quasi-polyarchy.

In a hitherto dependent country subject to another state:

> The old regime is transformed by evolutionary processes. The new regime is fostered among the local population, whose leaders inaugurate polyarchy or quasi-polyarchy without a national independence movement or a serious struggle against the colonial power.

> The old regime is transformed as a part of the struggle for national independence, in the course of a "revolution" against the colonial power. The new regime is inaugurated by leaders of a national independence movement, who install polyarchy or quasi-polyarchy during or after a successful struggle for national independence.

Although there has been no uniform process of inaugurating polyarchies, the various alternatives may not be equally auspicious. A disproportionately large number of the stable high-consensus polyarchies seem to have come about in the first way, by peaceful evolution within an already independent nation state, or by the fourth, by peaceful evolution within a dependent country. The reason is probably that peaceful evolution is most likely to result in a polyarchy supported by a widespread sense of legitimacy. As the incumbents yield peacefully (on the whole) and participate in the changes, their consent is won, the legitimacy attached to the previous regime is transferred unbroken to the new regime, and the process of peaceful change, so important to polyarchy, gains in legitimacy. Inauguration by a revolutionary overthrow of the old regime is infrequent. In the three most notable cases—the French Revolution, Weimar Germany, and the Spanish Republic—revolution was followed by an unstable regime that soon regressed to hegemony. These reversals were probably not accidental, for where peaceful evolution cannot or does not take place and revolution occurs, the legitimacy of the new regime is more likely to be contested, and its own revolutionary inaugural helps to legitimate the use of revolution to overthrow it.

The third process has proved (so far) to lead to surprisingly stable polyarchies in the only four countries—Germany, Italy, Austria, and Japan—where inauguration of polyarchy by conquest has occurred in recent times. But these may prove to be historically unique cases.

The fifth process is probably most familiar to Americans. As in the United States, so, too, in Finland, Ireland, Israel, and India, the independence movement blended nationalism with the ideology of representative government and political liberalism. Thus the ideology of democracy was reinforced by the ideology of nationalism: to attack representative democracy was to attack the nation. The success of the movement for national independence largely liquidated the principal contenders for the legitimacy of the old regime. Mainly agents of the colonial power, they either returned to the home country or permanently exiled themselves from the new nation, as did the Tories who moved to Canada after the American Revolution.

However, world developments have made the fifth strategy obsolescent. With the disappearance of colonial empires, most of the world now consists of nominally sovereign states. In a world of independent states there are no longer many opportunities for movements of national independence to inaugurate more competitive regimes. The disappearance of colonial empires also reduces the opportunities for the fourth process of inauguration. If the third process —via military conquest—is unlikely, then the most likely alternatives are reduced to the first two: in existing hegemonic regimes, a more competitive system will have to be inaugurated either by evolution or by revolution. The simple fact that the revolutionary process carries a high risk of failure does not mean that it will not be tried; but revolutions will probably saddle new regimes with the serious conflicts over legitimacy and hence create from the start a serious danger of regression toward hegemonic rule.

In the future as in the past, then, tolerance of oppositions and enduring polyarchies or near-polyarchies are more likely to result from rather slow evolutionary processes than from the revolutionary overthrow of existing hegemonies.

Concentration in the Social and Economic Order

According to the more or less self-evident proposition introduced earlier (Axiom 3), a government is more likely to tolerate an opposition as the expected costs of suppression increase and as the expected costs of toleration decrease. Since the costs of toleration or suppression are in turn dependent on the relative resources available to the government and opposition, it is obvious that:

Axiom 4. The likelihood that a government will tolerate an opposition increases as the resources available to the government for suppression decline relative to the resources of the opposition.

Key resources used by governments to suppress oppositions are, broadly, *violent* means of coercion, persuasion, and inducement, typically wielded by military and police forces; and nonviolent means of coercion, persuasion, and inducement, or as they will be called here, *socioeconomic sanctions,* chiefly in the form of control over economic resources, means of communication, and processes of education and political socialization. Hence:

Axiom 5. The likelihood that a government will tolerate an opposition increases with a reduction in the capacity of the government to use violence or socioeconomic sanctions to suppress an opposition.

Two very general kinds of circumstances can reduce the capacity of a government to use violence or socioeconomic sanctions against an opposition. First, these factors sometimes cease to be available as political resources. Second, these (and other) political resources may be so widely dispersed that no unified group, including the government (or a unified group of leaders in the government), has a monopoly over them. Thus, in the eighteenth century, the professional military and police forces of Britain, other than the Navy, were not only dispersed throughout the counties, where they were subject to control by the local gentry, but they were, in fact, very nearly nonexistent. Britain's greatest instrument of organized violence was the Navy, over which the government enjoyed a monopoly control; but it was not an effective instrument for domestic coercion.

Consider now the possibilities suggested by Table 3.

The circumstances most favorable for competitive politics exist when access to violence and socioeconomic sanctions is either dispersed or denied both to oppositions and to government.[3] The least favorable circumstances exist when

TABLE 3   Relative access to violence and socioeconomic sanctions: government and opposition

		Available to government?	
		Yes	No
Available to opposition?	Yes	Dispersed	Monopolized by opposition; access denied to government
	No	Monopolized by government; access denied to opposition	Neutralized; access denied to both

violence and socioeconomic sanctions are exclusively available to the government and denied to the oppositions. But what of the remaining case, in which these key resources are a monopoly of the opposition? The pure case can hardly exist, since under such conditions a "government" would lack the definitional characteristics of a government. However, these conditions are roughly approximated in countries where economic resources are monopolized by a small group of local or foreign owners and managers, or where the military forces are politically committed to the defense of specific social strata or ideologies. Confronted by situations of this kind, a government is bound to be weak and unstable; whenever its conduct displeases the opposition, the government can easily be overthrown. A number of Latin American countries have provided a rough approximation to the circumstances I have in mind, not so much because of the monopoly of socioeconomic sanctions as because of military intervention.

It would be misleading to conclude, however, that violence and socioeconomic sanctions are necessarily distributed in the same way. Consider Table 4.

Clearly the most favorable situation for competitive politics is A, a *pluralistic social order*. It is equally obvious that the situation least favorable for competitive politics and most favorable for hegemony is D, a *centrally dominated social order*.

The other two situations are more ambiguous. Both are less favorable to political competition than a pluralistic social order; but both are less favorable

TABLE 4   Distribution of violence and socioeconomic sanctions

Access to socioeconomic sanctions is:	Access to violence is:	
	Dispersed or neutralized	Monopolized
Dispersed or neutralized	A	B
Monopolized	C	D

to a hegemonic regime than a centrally dominated social order. Contemporary Spain and Argentina roughly approximate B, which might be called a *quasi-pluralistic social order with repressive violence.* The remaining possibility, C, which might be called a *quasi-dominated social order without repressive violence,* seems to be rare, perhaps because a governing elite with such great resources for dominance would have no incentives for allowing *all* the major instruments of violence to be dispersed or politically neutralized, and it would probably possess enough resources (e.g., legal authority, promotions, pay, and wealth) to prevent such an outcome.

Agrarian Societies

Agrarian societies seem to fall roughly into two extreme types, with of course many variations. The most prevalent type, which might be called the traditional peasant society, has a very high propensity for inequality, hierarchy, and political hegemony (Lenski, 1966, Chapters 8 and 9; Svalastoga, Chapter 3). The other, a free-farmer society, is considerably more egalitarian and democratic. Although the free-farmer society is often ignored in discussion of agrarian societies, it furnishes too many important historical examples to pass it by: Switzerland, the United States,[4] Canada, New Zealand, and Norway—to cite the leading ones.

In the traditional peasant society, cumulative inequalities of status, wealth, income, and means of coercion mean a marked inequality in political resources, an inequality reinforced by prevailing ideas. A small minority with superior resources develops and maintains a hegemonic political system (often headed by a single dominant ruler) through which it can also enforce its domination over the social order and hence strengthen the initial inequalities even more. Limits on this potentially runaway cycle of ever-increasing inequalities are set by dangers of mass starvation, passive resistance, and even sporadic uprisings among the peasants, a decline in agricultural output, and, because of wide disaffection, vulnerability to foreign invasions. But for the great bulk of the population, life consists of hardship, deprivation, dependence, repressed dissent, and comparative ignorance, while a tiny minority enjoys exceptional power, wealth, and social esteem.[5]

The dynamics of the traditional peasant society might then be represented crudely as in Fig. 4.

In the contrasting society of free farmers, the distribution of land is closer to equal, even though it is always a far cry from perfect equality. If the norms are egalitarian and democratic, as Tocqueville insisted they were in the United States, then the one reinforces the other. Finally, in a number of cases both of these tendencies toward equality (or toward a lower limit on inequality) are strengthened by certain aspects of military technology. In the United States, the musket and later the rifle helped to provide a kind of equality in coercion for more than a century. In Switzerland the mountains, in Norway and New

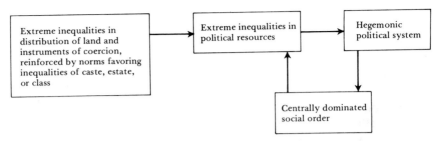

Fig. 4. Dynamics of the Peasant Society

Zealand the mountains and fjords, the continental proportions and the enormous length of Chile—all reduced the prospects for a successful monopoly of violence by any one stratum of the population. The way these factors interact in a society of free farmers is represented by Fig. 5.

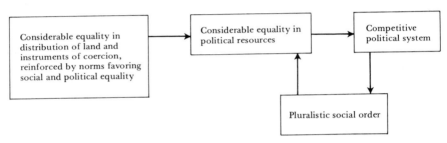

Fig. 5. Dynamics of the Free-Farmer Society

Commercial and Industrial Societies

Historically, commercial and industrial societies have been much more hospitable to competitive politics than agrarian societies. What might be called classic or orthodox liberal doctrine has explained this difference by establishing a connection between a pluralistic social order and a privately owned competitive economy: competitive politics requires a competitive economy. In effect, classic liberal doctrine set forth the following equation.

where ⟶ can be read as "requires."

For, it was argued, just as toleration of oppositions and the existence of a competitive representative government require a pluralistic social order, so a pluralistic social order in turn requires a competitive capitalistic economy. The twin equation was

A socialist   a centrally dominated   a hegemonic
economy   social order   regime.

However, numerous dictatorships—in Italy, Germany, Japan, Spain, and elsewhere—have shown that private ownership is no guarantee of a competitive economy or a political order that permits public contestation, much less polyarchy. Since the equations involve necessary and not sufficient conditions, strictly speaking these developments left the argument intact. But other developments have falsified the equations. One is the persistence of inclusive polyarchy in countries like Sweden, with mixed (not strictly competitive-capitalist) economies that employ an endless variety of techniques that preserve and may even strengthen a pluralistic social order.

Where the equations of classic liberalism went wrong was in supposing that every alternative to competitive capitalism necessarily requires a centrally directed economy, whereas in fact, competition among privately owned firms is by no means the unique method of decentralizing an economy. If decentralized socialist economies prove capable of handling major economic problems with a fair degree of success, then there is no inherent reason why decentralized socialism cannot produce and sustain a highly pluralistic social order and hence competitive politics.

The correct equations, in short, seem to be as follows:

Competitive politics ⟶ pluralistic social order ⟶ decentralized economy.

Highly centralized economy ⟶ centrally dominated
social order ⟶ hegemonic regime.

The argument can thus be summed up as follows:

A competitive political regime is unlikely to be maintained without a pluralistic social order. A centrally dominated social order is more favorable to a hegemonic than a competitive regime.

A competitive regime is unlikely to be maintained in a country where the military or police forces are accustomed to intervening in politics, even if the social order is otherwise pluralistic and not centrally dominated.

Agrarian societies seem to approach two extreme types, the traditional peasant society, characteristically associated with a hegemonic political regime, and the society of free farmers, characteristically associated with a competitive regime and evolution toward an inclusive polyarchy. The main factors determining the direction an agrarian society takes seem to be norms about equality, the distribution of land, and military techniques.

Private ownership of the economy is neither a necessary nor a sufficient condition for a pluralistic social order and hence for competitive politics.

A pluralistic social order and hence a competitive regime can exist, however, in a country with a decentralized economy, no matter what the form of ownership.

But a competitive regime is unlikely to exist in a country with highly centralized direction of the economy, no matter what the form of ownership.

The Level of Socioeconomic Development

Recent studies give impressive support to several propositions.

First, *various measures of socioeconomic level are all intercorrelated.* If a country is relatively poor or relatively rich, then its poverty or affluence shows up in all sorts of ways in addition to per capita income (Russett *et al.,* 1964, pp. 293–303; Russett, 1965, pp. 125–6). The commonsense notion that different countries are at different "stages" of economic and social development is amply confirmed by the data.[6]

Second, *there is unquestionably a significant association between socioeconomic level and "political development."* The data[7] show rather conclusively that:

> The higher the socioeconomic level of a country, the more likely it is to have a competitive political regime.

> The more competitive a country's political regime, the more likely that the country is at a relatively high level of socioeconomic development.

A relationship between socioeconomic development and inclusive or nearly inclusive polyarchy shows up perhaps even more sharply in the data. As with competitive regimes, so with polyarchy.

> The higher the socioeconomic level of a country, the more likely that its regime is an inclusive or near-polyarchy.

> If a regime is a polyarchy, it is more likely to exist in a country at a relatively high level of socioeconomic development than in one at lower levels.

Yet even though the argument up to this point is well supported by all the evidence now available, it does not take us very far. In fact, it leaves unanswered a number of crucial questions about the nature and strength of the very general relation between competitive politics and socioeconomic "level."

Are There "Thresholds?"

One such question is whether there are "thresholds" below or above which the chances for competitive politics or polyarchy do not change enough to matter. To pose the problem in a different way, is the relationship linear or curvilinear?

An inspection of the evidence strongly suggests that the relationship is not linear, and instead that:

> There exists an upper threshold, perhaps in the range of about $700–800 GNP per capita (1957 U.S. dollars), above which the chances of polyarchy (and hence of competitive politics) are so high that any further increases in per capita GNP (and variables associated with such an increase) cannot affect the outcome in any significant way.

> There exists a lower threshold, perhaps in the range of about $100–200 GNP per capita, below which the chances for polyarchy (although not

necessarily other forms of competitive politics) are so slight that differences in per capita GNP or variables associated with it do not really matter.

What about the Deviant Cases?

Yet even if we accept the idea of "thresholds," it is definitely not true that competitive regimes or even polyarchies exist only in countries at a high level of socioeconomic development. Nor is it true that all countries at a high level of socioeconomic development have polyarchies or even competitive regimes. Any ranking of a considerable number of countries along the dimensions of economic or socioeconomic development and political competition or polyarchy invariably displays a fair number of deviant cases in the contemporary world.[8]

History also provides its share of discrepant examples. How do we account for the early appearance of an inclusive polyarchy in the United States? The country already had created an inclusive polyarchy (for whites) by 1800, when per capita GNP was probably considerably less than $300.[9] What is more, according to the usual indicators of socioeconomic level, the United States in 1800 was definitely agricultural, premodern and nonindustrial.

What holds for the United States holds not only for Australia, New Zealand, and Canada, but in some degree for Britain, Norway, Sweden, and a number of other European countries where competitive politics (though not inclusive polyarchy) existed in the nineteenth century. By the indicators applied to the contemporary world, those countries were then at low levels of socioeconomic development.

That competitive politics is undoubtedly associated in some way with socioeconomic development is not, it seems, a very satisfactory—or perhaps even a very interesting—conclusion. What is more tantalizing is the fact that the association is weak, that the conclusion ignores a number of critical deviant cases, and that the relationship of one to the other is unexplained.

Explaining the Relationship

Assuming, however, that there is a relationship between competitive politics (and polyarchy) and level of socioeconomic development; that there are important exceptions, and that there may be thresholds below or above which the chances for polyarchy or competitive politics do not change significantly, how can we account for all this?

A very general hypothesis helps to establish the connection between political system and socioeconomic level:

The chances that a country will develop and maintain a competitive political regime (and, even more so, a polyarchy) depend on the extent to which the country's society and economy

a) provide literacy, education, and communication,

b) create a pluralistic rather than a centrally dominated social order, and

c) prevent extreme inequalities

   among the politically relevant strata of the country.

Literacy, education, and communication.   It is surely unnecessary to argue here that whenever the citizen body is large, the chances for polyarchy, and even for competitive politics of a less stringent sort, depend to some degree on the spread of reading, writing, literacy, education, and newspapers or their equivalents. The extent of literacy, education, newspapers, and other forms of communication is in turn related to urbanization and industrialization. The development of cities, commerce, industry, and the professions not only requires but also fosters these elemental requirements.

However, a moderately educated people with a generous supply of newspapers (or, today, access to radios and television sets) does not require a highly industrialized or urbanized society. After all, as Tocqueville pointed out, most white Americans were literate in the early nineteenth century; opportunities for a modest education were fairly widespread (though perhaps less so than Tocqueville thought), newspapers were generally available, and political communication seems to have been moderately efficient despite the great area over which Americans were spread. In other countries, too, widespread literacy and education have *preceded* extensive industrialization, the growth of cities, and high average per capita incomes; New Zealand, Australia, Canada, Norway, and Finland are all examples. For the costs of providing a general access to education and news media are not so high that they cannot be borne by moderately prosperous agrarian societies.

It seems reasonable, then, to conclude that:

> The hypothetical lower threshold for competitive politics could be accounted for—in part—by the difficulty countries below this level have in mobilizing the resources required for widespread literacy, education, and news media.

> Nonetheless, these minimal needs for competitive politics, and particularly for polyarchy, can be met by countries above the lower threshold, even though these countries are predominantly agricultural, rural, and unindustrialized.

> Thus the need to meet these minimal requirements helps to account for the lower threshold but does not account for the general relationship.

A pluralistic social order.   Because of its inherent requirements, an advanced economy and its supporting social structures automatically distribute political resources and political skills to a vast variety of individuals, groups, and organizations. Among these skills and resources are knowledge; income, status, and esteem among specialized groups; skill in organizing and communicating;

and access to organizations, experts, and elites. These skills and resources can be used to negotiate for advantages—for oneself, for a group, for an organization. Groups and organizations develop a thrust toward autonomy, internal and parochial loyalties, complex patterns of cohesion and cleavage. When conflicts arise, as they inevitably do, access to political resources helps individuals and groups to prevent the settlement of the conflict by compulsion and coercion and to insist, instead, on some degree of negotiation and bargaining—explicit, implicit, legal, alegal, illegal. Thus systems of bargaining and negotiation grow up within, parallel to, or in opposition to hierarchical arrangements; and these systems help to foster a political subculture with norms that legitimate negotiating, bargaining, log-rolling, give and take, the gaining of consent as against unilateral power or coercion.

Even within ostensibly hierarchical organizations, leaders learn that compulsion and coercion are often damaging to incentives. In an advanced economy, performance under threat or coercion is less productive at all levels than a more willing performance based on rewards for compliance. Even in markedly hierarchic organizations, then, the fear of punishment for bad performance is not merely supplemented but in many respects displaced by the expectation of rewards for successful performance. Just as slave labor is less efficient than free labor, so badly paid, discontented workers are less productive than highly paid, contented workers. For technicians, executives, scientists, and intellectuals the need for a measure of willing performance, based on their "consent," is even greater. And a large measure of autonomy and discretion are also found to produce better results than rigid, overcentralized supervision.

Thus an *advanced economy automatically generates many of the conditions required for a pluralistic social order.* And as a pluralistic social order evolves, at least in an elementary form, *some of its members make demands for participating in decisions by means more appropriate to a competitive than to a hegemonic political system.*

If we use a single arrow with a C to suggest the direction of causation, the argument might be represented as follows:

Advanced ⟶ C ⟶ pluralistic ⟶ C ⟶ demands for a
economy   social order   competitive political system.

Equalities and Inequalities

Equalities and inequalities in a society seem to affect the chances for hegemony or political competition by way of at least two different sets of intervening variables: the distribution of political resources and skills; and the creation of resentments and frustrations.

The Distribution of Political Resources and Skills

In allocating income, wealth, status, knowledge, occupation, organizational position, popularity, and a variety of other values, every society also allocates resources with which an actor can influence the behavior of other actors in at least some circumstances. These resources then become political resources. Who receives what and how much political resources is not, however, simply an inert output of socioeconomic institutions. Actors who influence or control the state with the aid of their political resources may use the various resources available to the state to rearrange the initial distribution that would result from the processes of the socioeconomic institutions, by income taxes, for example, or by imposing limits on campaign contributions; or they may actually create and allocate new political resources, such as the suffrage.

Extreme inequalities in the distribution of such key values as income, wealth, status, knowledge, and military prowess are equivalent to extreme inequalities in political resources. Obviously a country with extreme inequalities in political resources stands a very high chance of having extreme inequalities in the exercise of power and hence a hegemonic regime. So much for the axiomatics.

In agrarian societies, I suggested earlier, such key values as knowledge, wealth, income, status, and power are strongly intercorrelated: the well-off are well-off in all these respects, and the badly-off—who are the bulk of the population in many agrarian societies—are badly-off in all respects. Political resources, then, are strongly cumulative: if actor A outranks actor B with respect to one political resource—say, wealth or income—then A also outranks B with respect to all other political resources—say, knowledge or status. Yet, as we have seen, there are two major variants of the agrarian society. To put it simply, in the traditional peasant society there is extreme inequality in the distribution of values, hence in political resources, and consequently in the exercise of power. But in the free-farming society there is a considerably greater degree of equality in the distribution of values, hence in political resources, and so in the exercise of power. If the relatively greater condition of equality in a free-farmer society is also associated with a larger measure of political equality allocated through suffrage, competitive parties, elections, and responsive leaders, then the accumulation of inequalities is even further inhibited. By accumulating popularity, followers, and votes, leaders may offset some of the potential effects of differences in wealth and status, and they may use the regulatory powers of the state to curtail these differences or their consequences for political life.

As an agrarian society becomes industrialized, a profound change takes place in the nature of the equalities and inequalities among the citizens or subjects. Industrialization reallocates rewards and privileges in a drastic way. To be sure, these new allocations are often highly unequal. Yet, as I suggested earlier, the needs of an advanced industrial society and the aspirations it helps to create and to satisfy throw out on a very broad basis many political resources that in traditional peasant societies are the monopoly of tiny elites—literacy, education, technical knowledge, organizational skills, access to leaders, and the like. Although industrial societies do not eliminate inequalities, they significantly reduce many of them (cf. Lenski, 1966, p. 437). As average income rises with advancing technology and growing productivity, more and more advantages hitherto arrogated to small elites come within reach of an expanding proportion of the population.

In loose language, then, one might say that extreme differences in important political resources give way, if not to equality, at any rate to a greater *parity*.

Whether the development of an industrial society increases or decreases equality depends, then, on the type of agrarian society within which industrialization takes place. Introduced into a traditional peasant society, industrialization is sooner or later an equalizing force: it transforms a system of cumulative inequalities into a system of greater parity with respect to some key resources, and with respect to political resources in general it disperses (but does not eradicate) inequalities. Introduced into a free-farming society, however, industrialization may actually increase inequalities in political resources, even though these inequalities are dispersed rather than cumulative.[10]

The argument of this section is summarized schematically in Fig. 6.

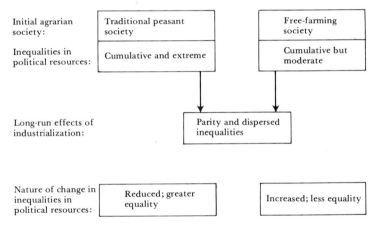

Fig. 6. Industrial Society and Inequality

Responses to Inequalities

Although inequalities may be less extreme and more dispersed in an industrial society than in a traditional peasant society, the remaining inequalities are very far from negligible. How, then, can we explain the fact that most polyarchies, presumably the very regimes most endangered by inequality, actually developed in the midst of severe and widespread inequalities? What is more, many polyarchal regimes exist even now in societies with enormous inequalities of some kinds, for example, with respect to incomes, wealth, or the chances for higher education. How, in these circumstances, can polyarchy endure?

The explanation, I think, has two parts:

When demands for greater equality arise, a regime may gain allegiance among the deprived group by responding to some part of the demands, though not necessarily all of them.

But a great deal of inequality does not generate among the disadvantaged group political demands for greater equality.

Responses by governments.   A situation of objective inequality may give rise to a demand that its causes be removed, but it also may not. If demands do arise, they may or may not be directed to the government. The inequality might be reduced or eliminated as a result of actions taken by the government, but unequal conditions might also be reduced even if the government takes no positive action—or sometimes even in spite of wrongly directed actions of the government. In some cases, even though the government's actions are misdirected, they may reduce further demands simply because these actions symbolize to the disadvantaged group that the government is concerned. Indeed, it is at least possible that sometimes a government's wrong-headed but seemingly well-intentioned policies may completely fail to reduce inequalities; yet the very fact that the government demonstrates its concern might be enough to hold, perhaps even to win over, the allegiance of the deprived group.

Among the various possibilities, however, two seem particularly relevant to the questions of this chapter. One moderately familiar path leads from an inequality to government responses that reduce the inequality and hence strengthen the allegiance of the deprived group to the regime. Here one thinks of the successful efforts of the Swedish government to reduce unemployment in the 1930s or, during the same decade, various actions taken by the government of Franklin Roosevelt to provide more economic security in the United States.

In fact, in a number of European and English-speaking countries that now have inclusive and seemingly quite stable polyarchies, competitive political regimes responded in the last century and this to demands for a reduction in inequalities. Typically, these demands at first emphasized and resulted in the extension of political rights to strata who were excluded from legal participation in the political system; the process was substantially completed in these countries by about 1920. Then the regimes became more responsive to demands, which had been made earlier, for an expansion of "social rights" to security, welfare, education, and the like. This process is still under way, though in a number of countries it has slowed down, as a result of extensive reforms already carried out. By responding to these demands for greater political and social equality, a number of countries seem to have won the long battle for the allegiance of hitherto disadvantaged groups, particularly, of course, the working classes. This is illustrated by Path A in Fig. 7. Because this process has been adequately analyzed elsewhere, I shall not discuss it further here (e.g., Marshall, 1950; Dahl, 1966).

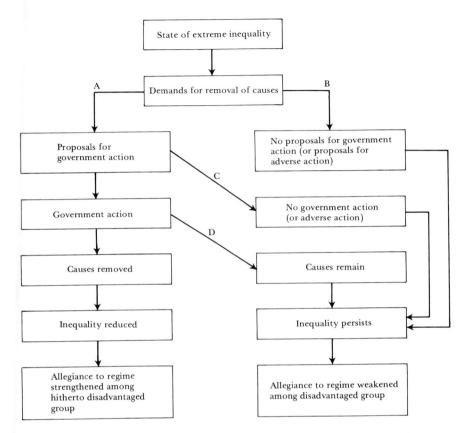

Fig. 7. Two Possible Effects of Inequality on Allegiance to a Regime

A second possibility, however, is that by its acts of commission or omission the government maintains the inequality and becomes the target for the hostilities of the disadvantaged group. Perhaps no proposals for government action arise, at least publicly. Or for whatever reasons, the government fails to act despite the demands made on it. Or if it acts, its policies are misdirected. Or it may even be that policies deliberately chosen by the government are perceived as a principal cause of deprivation (for example, racial discrimination imposed by state governments). These possibilities are represented in Fig. 7 by Paths B, C, and D. If, as a result, the inequality persists, then the allegiance of the disadvantaged group to the particular regime is likely to be weakened.

Responses by the disadvantaged.   Between a condition of objective inequality and the response of a disadvantaged person lie the perceptions, evaluations, expectations—in short, the psyche—of the individual. To the dismay and astonishment of activists who struggle to rouse a disadvantaged group to oppose their lot, the human psyche does not invariably impel those who are deprived of equality to seek it or, sometimes, even to want it (Lane, 1959).

Consider, then, a hypothetical path leading from objective inequality to demands for greater equality among the disadvantaged group (Fig. 8). Members of a disadvantaged group may not complete all the connections along our hypothetical path. For example, at (a) and (b) perceptions of inequality are sometimes clouded by changes in the conditions of one's "own" group. Moreover, people who are objectively disadvantaged generally do not compare themselves with the *most* advantaged groups, whose good fortune they simply do not consider to be relevant to their own condition, but substitute other comparisons instead. For one thing, a person in a disadvantaged group almost certainly will compare the *present* situation of his group with its own *past,* and if the group is now better off than it was in the past, that fact may be far more salient and relevant than the fact that certain other groups are currently very much better off (Runciman, 1966, p. 94). Then, too, many people identify themselves some of the time with large collectivities like the nation or the country; hence for the particular individual or group, past and present inequalities may be attenuated by the thought that the collectivity as a whole—the country, for example—is moving toward a richer or more just condition. Finally, when a person does compare himself or his "own" specific group with other individuals or groups, he is likely to make the comparison with others who are, socially speaking, not distant but quite *close* or adjacent to him.

Because of these various comparisons, in a society with extensive inequalities an individual may have a relatively favorable judgment of his own position

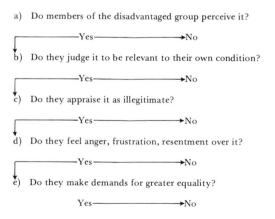

Fig. 8. A Hypothetical Path from Objective Inequality to Demands for Greater Equality

even though, objectively speaking, he is seriously disadvantaged in comparison with the elites.

The effectiveness of the connection at (c) depends on the prevailing ideas in the culture or subculture into which an individual is socialized. A deprived group may well believe that its present inferior condition is an inherent part of the order of things, justified by religion and cosmology (as Hinduism gave legitimacy to caste), subject to change only through some ultimate and perhaps apocalyptic redemption. A world view justifying and "rationalizing" inequality does not persist only because it is to the advantage of the elites who benefit from the status quo. Among the disadvantaged groups themselves, such a self-denying world view may help to make a miserable and often humiliating existence more bearable and understandable. A group confronted over a long period of time by seemingly ineradicable inequalities may learn to scale down its demands, to bring them more into line with the harsh limits of the possible—a process that one student of peasant societies has called "attenuation" (Bequiraj, 1966, pp. 31–33).

The connections at the end of the path at (d) and (e) may also break down. Frustration, resentments, and anger may not stimulate demands for greater equality but instead may turn into resignation, apathy, despair, hopelessness, self-denigration, fantasy, millennial dreams, pious acceptance, fatalism, the mentality of the "Uncle Tom," etc. Terms like these are used, in fact, to describe the psyche of the peasant in the acutely deprivational peasant society (Bequiraj, 1966, pp. 11–12, 19).

The argument of this section can be summarized in the following propositions:

In a society with a hegemonic regime, extreme inequalities in the distribution of key values reduce the chances that a stable system of competitive politics will develop.

In a society that already has a competitive regime, extreme inequalities increase the chances that the competitive politics will be displaced by a hegemony.

Inclusive polyarchies are particularly vulnerable to the effects of extreme inequalities.

Extreme inequalities in the distribution of key values are unfavorable to competitive politics because this state of affairs

is equivalent to extreme inequality in the distribution of key political resources; and

is likely to generate resentments and frustrations which weaken allegiance to the regime.

However, systems of competitive politics manage to survive a considerable measure of inequality because a great deal of inequality does not generate among the disadvantaged group political demands for greater equality or a change in the regime; and

when demands for greater equality do arise, a regime may gain allegiance among the deprived groups by responding to some part of the demands, though not necessarily all of them.

Subcultures, Cleavage Patterns, and Governmental Effectiveness

There are conflicts that a competitive political system does not manage easily and perhaps cannot handle at all. Any dispute in which a large section of the population of a country feels that its way of life or its highest values are severely menaced by another segment of the population creates a crisis in a competitive political system. Whatever the eventual outcome may be, the historical record argues that the system is very likely to dissolve into civil war or to be displaced by a hegemony, or both.

Thus any difference within a society that is likely to polarize people into severely antagonistic camps is a cleavage of exceptional importance.

A preoccupation with class conflict and often an unarticulated assumption, even among sophisticated social theorists, that classes are somehow the "real" basis of differences in an industrial society, to which all others are "ultimately" reducible, has tended to deflect attention from other differences that give rise to durable subcultures into which individuals are socialized. They are differences in religion, language, race or ethnic group, and region.

Because an ethnic or religious subculture is incorporated so early into one's personality, conflicts among groups divided along lines of religion, race, or language are specially fraught with danger, particularly if they are also tied to region. Such conflicts seem to threaten fundamental aspects of the self; opponents are readily transformed into a malign and inhuman "they" whose opposition justifies the violence and savagery common in such conflicts. The junction of race, language or religion with regional subcultures creates an incipient nation, demands for autonomy, even independence.

That subcultural pluralism often places a dangerous strain on the tolerance and mutual security required for a system of public contestation seems hardly open to doubt. Polyarchy, in particular, is more frequently found in relatively homogeneous countries than in countries with a great amount of subcultural pluralism (Table 5).

Nonetheless, if a competitive political system is less likely in countries with a considerable measure of subcultural pluralism, it would be going too far to say that it is impossible, or that subcultural pluralism necessarily rules out even an inclusive polyarchy.

One fact to keep in mind is that subcultural pluralism tends, at present, to be greatest among the less developed countries. Countries with extreme subcultural pluralism are predominantly new nations; 70 percent have achieved independence since 1945. Thus they bear all the typical disadvantages of the

TABLE 5   Polyarchy and subcultural pluralism[11]

	Amount of subcultural pluralism			
	Low	Moderate	Marked	Extreme
Total	26	28	27	33
Polyarchies	16	10	5	4
Percentage	62	36	19	12

new nations: low per capita GNP, high employment in agriculture, low urbanization, high illiteracy, low newspaper circulation. They are also relatively large in area (Haug, 1967, pp. 300–303).

As we have seen, low levels of socioeconomic development are themselves inimical to competitive politics. In fact, in the early stages of nation-building, a variety of factors typically interact to undermine the chances for a competitive regime and to produce hegemony instead; subcultural pluralism is only one of these factors. Hence some of the association between subcultural pluralism and hegemony can reasonably be attributed to other factors, such as the socioeconomic level.

Yet competitive politics *can* exist even in countries with a very considerable degree of subcultural pluralism. Indeed, Belgium, Canada, and India, among others, have managed to develop and sustain inclusive polyarchies. There is, in addition, the compelling example of the Netherlands. There, no significant part is played by differences in language, race, physical stock, ethnic identification, or region; hence, *numerically* speaking, subcultural pluralism is not extreme. Yet religion is a plane of cleavage that divides the country into three great spiritual families (Catholic, Protestant, and neither). These three subcultures have been voluntarily segregated to a degree unknown in any other inclusive polyarchy; yet the Netherlands has managed to sustain—and sturdily—a representative democracy. Finally, among the countries with a high degree of subcultural pluralism in the *numerical* sense is the impressive case of Switzerland.

At least three conditions seem to be essential if a country with considerable subcultural pluralism is to maintain its conflicts at a low enough level to sustain a polyarchy.[12]

First, conflict is more likely to be maintained at moderate levels if *no ethnic or regional subculture is "indefinitely" denied the opportunity to participate in the government*—i.e., in the majority coalition whose leaders form the "Government" or the Administration. This requires in turn that among a sufficient number of members of each subculture, and particularly among the leaders, there exist desires for cooperation that cut across the subcultures at least some of the time.

The condition that no subculture is indefinitely denied the opportunity to participate in the government can be met in two ways: a system oriented toward unanimity, in which, as in Switzerland, every party is represented in the government; or as in Belgium and the Netherlands, a system of shifting coalitions that, over time, allows each group to shift out of opposition into the government.

The second requirement is a set of understandings or engagements, not always codified into formal constitutional provisions, that provide a relatively high degree of security to the various subcultures. Among the most prevalent forms of mutual security arrangements are guarantees that the major subcultures will be represented in parliament in some rough approximation to their numerical weight, a guarantee which is frequently secured by using one of the various types of proportional representation for electing candidates. This kind of guarantee may extend even to the Executive, as in the all-party Federal Council in Switzerland, or under the *Proporz* arrangement used for some years in Austria under the Second Republic. Where participation in the Executive is ensured, the arrangement typically requires unanimity or (to put it differently) permits each minority to exercise a veto. Where the subcultures are more or less regional, mutual security may also be provided by federalism, as in Canada, India, and Switzerland. Finally, mutual guarantees may be provided by specific constitutional provisions, pacts, or understandings that impose limits on the constitutional authority of any parliamentary coalition to regulate certain matters important to one or more subcultures, e.g., language guarantees in Switzerland, India, and Canada, or the guarantees and understandings in the Netherlands that concede a large measure of autonomy to the three *zuilen* with respect not merely to religion, newspapers, political parties, trade unions, and farm organization, but also state-subsidized schools, social security programs, and the state-owned radio and television network.

The third requirement is not only more conjectural but also more difficult to state precisely. It appears, however, that a regime must be perceived as *effective* in responding to demands for coping with the major problems of the country, as those problems are defined by the population, or at least by the political stratum. For if demands on the government for "solutions" to major problems go unmet year after year, allegiance is likely to give way to disillusion and contempt, particularly when a "problem" involves extensive and acute deprivation among some considerable part of the population—galloping inflation, for example, extensive unemployment, acute poverty, severe discrimination, woeful inadequacies in education, and the like.

Although this requirement is not unique to polyarchy, the reason for emphasizing it here is that it may sometimes be inconsistent with the first two requirements. For governmental immobility is a likely consequence of a political system that works by unanimity and minority veto, or by shifting coalitions, and guarantees that no majority coalition will act adversely toward any of its subcultural minorities. Thus major problems, as these are defined by the political stratum, are likely to go unsolved because every possible solution is vetoed by some minority whose interests are threatened. Immobility is, in fact, a common complaint in systems of this kind.[13]

Foreign Domination

People in one country may deliberately seek to use their resources to impose a particular kind of political regime on another country. They will probably affect the *content* of politics, too; but the point I wish to emphasize here is that by their actions foreigners may massively affect the chances for hegemony or polyarchy, pretty much independent of any of the conditions discussed so far.

In an estimation of the chances for hegemony or polyarchy, therefore, it would obviously be important to know whether foreign powers were attempting to impose or intended to impose a particular regime. In the period immediately following the Second World War, a large number of European regimes were to some extent imposed: hegemonies in eastern Europe, polyarchies in Germany, Austria, and Italy. A purely autonomous political development over a long period has never been possible in Czechoslovakia; local circumstances favorable to a competitive political regime have too often been overridden by outside domination. Much the same has been true in Poland.

The interaction between local conditions and foreign domination is so complex that concrete historical statements or predictions based on a particular configuration of international forces at a specific time may be more fruitful than theoretical generalities about the interplay between foreign domination and polyarchy. Nonetheless, if we focus on *overt* rather than covert domination, and if we confine our attention exclusively to relatively *direct* consequences for polyarchy (and thus ruthlessly exclude from consideration a number of consequences that would be important from other points of view), it is possible to advance a few general statements that seem to be supported by the available evidence.

In the first place, a high proportion of the countries in which polyarchy existed in the early 1970s had been occupied or otherwise subject to foreign military intervention at least once since achieving independence. Most European countries that were polyarchies in 1974 had been overrun and occupied as a result of the Second World War (one of them, Belgium, had also suffered the same fate during the First). However, it should also be kept in mind that four of these countries, though governed by polyarchies as of 1974, had been ruled by hegemonic regimes at the time of capitulation.

Second, it does not appear to be true, as is sometimes thought, that a period of overt foreign domination by a hegemonic power inevitably wreaks irreparable damage on a polyarchy. In fact, a period of foreign domination may strengthen national unity, foster a climate of reconciliation among hostile groups, and speed the incorporation of strata struggling for more recognition and power.[14]

Needless to say, it would be utterly fatuous to draw the conclusion that overt foreign intervention is a good thing for a polyarchy. Even if one were to put to one side all the other costs, which have sometimes been enormous, not only is polyarchy superseded temporarily by hegemonic rule, but the longer-run consequences are by no means all beneficial. Some cleavages may be intensified. Lorwin (1966, p. 161) writes that in Belgium during the Second World War "the Germans encouraged Flemish separatism, leaving a train of political booby traps for the Belgian nation after the war." If reconciliation and national unity may sometimes facilitate the acceptance of hitherto excluded strata and greater generosity toward their demands, opposition leaders may be so fully drawn into coalition-building that they unduly soften their demands, leaving a legacy of relative inequalities and resentments as a cause of later crises.

Despite these qualifications, one must not lose sight of the simple proposition that overt foreign intervention is not *necessarily* fatal to an already existing polyarchy and may actually strengthen it in some respects.

In the third place, it is patently untrue that polyarchy has come about only through strictly autonomous developments within an already independent country. Of the 29 countries with polyarchal regimes in 1970, in only 12 was polyarchy inaugurated after independence and not during a period of overt foreign domination. In four countries, polyarchy was inaugurated during military occupation or intervention after the Second World War. In addition, in 10 countries, including some where polyarchy is now very deeply rooted, substantial strides toward polyarchy were taken while the country was at least nominally subject to a foreign power.

Fourth, foreign domination frequently produces a *boomerang effect*. Probably an important consequence of Nazism among countries where polyarchy was temporarily set aside by the occupiers was a temporary strengthening of attachments to democratic ideals and an increase in hostility to the antidemocratic ideology of Nazism.

Fifth, the circumstances in which it was possible for polyarchy to be inaugurated during a period of overt dependence (or to be preserved for subsequent revival) were historically unusual and seem much less likely to recur in the foreseeable future. To see why this is so, consider the rather schematic set of possibilities in Table 6.

The first situation is roughly comparable to that of Belgium, Denmark, the Netherlands, Norway, and France under Nazi domination. An important aspect of that domination was its comparatively short duration and limited scope. Most of the political leadership survived. Among the general population, the boomerang effect was powerful: Nazism came to be widely loathed; hegemony was the rule of the enemy and occupier, the cause of defeat, privation, humiliation, suffering.

TABLE 6   Some circumstances of foreign domination

	In the country subject to domination	
The previous regime was	The conditions favor	The dominant country seeks to inaugurate
1. Polyarchy	Polyarchy	Hegemony
2. Polyarchy	Hegemony	Hegemony
3. Hegemony	Polyarchy	Polyarchy
4. Hegemony	Hegemony	Polyarchy

In a country where polyarchy has existed for some time and the underlying conditions are favorable to it, if there is good reason for thinking that it is likely to be rapidly restored after a relatively brief period of overt domination, then the outcome is bound to be more uncertain if the period is long and the foreign power systematically wipes out everyone who holds democratic beliefs.

In the second situation envisaged in Table 6, the restoration of polyarchy would be very much less likely. The foreign power would find it easier not only to impose a hegemonic regime but also to withdraw in due time from overt domination, leaving behind a hegemonic ally. By going native, the hegemony would accommodate itself to the spirit of nationalism. Although there are no clear-cut cases, Poland provides at least a partial example. A country with only the briefest interludes of near-polyarchy during the French Revolution and its aftermath, dominated and divided for a century thereafter by Russia and Prussia, Poland had seen its latest experience with polyarchy already terminated in presidential absolutism before the country was overrun by the German and then the Russian armies (Skilling, 1966, p. 28). Unlike the situation in the occupied countries of western Europe, in Poland polyarchy is simply not there waiting to be revived; and the conditions for creating it anew are certainly far from favorable.

Turning now to situations in which the dominant power seeks to inaugurate polyarchy in a country where the previous regime has been hegemonic, we find that the third case in Table 6 pretty clearly poses much less of a challenge than the fourth. Even if conditions were by no means wholly favorable for polyarchy in Austria, Germany, Italy, and Japan in the wake of the Second World War, on a comparative basis each was a prime candidate for polyarchy.

On a comparative basis, however, practically all the countries that have achieved independence since 1945 have highly unfavorable conditions for polyarchy. Nonetheless, in 1970 Jamaica, Trinidad, India, the Philippines, and Lebanon were all governed by polyarchal regimes, and Malaysia and Cyprus by near-polyarchies. Although it would be folly to predict much stability for these regimes, their existence does raise the question as to the circumstances under which foreign intervention may facilitate the development of polyarchy in a country where many of the conditions are highly unfavorable to it.

Several factors seem to have helped the development of polyarchy in these countries. For one thing, a substantial proportion of the political activists were predisposed to favor the institutions of polyarchy. In India, for example, in the years preceding independence there was an astonishing degree of concurrence among leaders and activists on the proposition that India must be a democracy in the Western sense. So complex is the process by which political activists acquire their beliefs, however, that an outside power, particularly when it is itself a polyarchy, can have only limited success in generating support for a particular ideology: the foreign power is caught in a tough network of historical and cultural forces that it frequently can do very little to manipulate.

Moreover, in these countries prolonged and massive coercion was not employed by the foreign power against the subject population. Thus the boomerang effect was to some extent avoided. At any rate, polyarchy was not discredited by association with the brutalities of a hated outside force. Thus it was possible for the rudimentary institutions of polyarchy or near-polyarchy to be introduced and to function over a period long enough for the political activists to acquire skill in operating them and a vested interest in maintaining them.

These were historically uncommon circumstances, and today they seem to be absent in most countries where the underlying conditions are unfavorable to polyarchy. The end of formal colonialism means that the outside power today must move into a nominally independent country where nationalism is probably strong and the boomerang effect is likely to be powerful. A substantial proportion of political activists are likely to favor a hegemonic regime of some sort. Public contestation, which may allow deadly enemies to enhance their following, will seem at best to be luxury, at worst downright pernicious. Even if the outside power intervenes at the behest of the local government, the invitation will be issued precisely because that government cannot, unaided, put down its opponents. Thus the outside power is drawn into massive coercion, and the boomerang effect is amplified even further.

The Beliefs of Political Activists

The nature of a regime is clearly dependent on the beliefs of those who support or oppose it. A system of mutual guarantees is, at one level, a system of beliefs. Obviously polyarchy could not exist in a society where everyone believed in the desirability and practicality of hegemony. Nonetheless, the exact bearing of beliefs on the character of a regime is highly uncertain. Conflicting theories and assumptions abound; they are often neither clear nor testable, and satisfactory data are lacking.

However, it is reasonable to think that political activists and leaders are more likely than most other people

a) to have moderately elaborate systems of political beliefs;

b) to be guided in their actions by their political beliefs; and

c) to have more influence on political events, including events that affect the stability or transformation of regimes.

There is impressive evidence (mainly, to be sure, from the United States) for the validity of (a). Some of this evidence lends support to (b), though (b) is also a plausible inference from (a). The argument for (c) is more or less self-evident.

Evidence on variations in the political beliefs of activists among different countries is, unfortunately, still limited and often impressionistic, though research under way in a number of countries promises to remedy that deficiency fairly soon. The connection between variations in beliefs and difference in regime is even more in the realm of conjecture at present. Nonetheless, there is a scattering of evidence that the frequency of certain beliefs which it is reasonable to believe on theoretical grounds would affect the chances for polyarchy and political opposition does vary significantly among different countries.

To begin with the most direct and obvious set of beliefs, the *legitimacy of polyarchy* has pretty clearly varied *within* countries, particularly over lengthy historical periods, and *across* countries in recent decades. Widespread acceptance among political activists of the legitimacy of the major institutions of polyarchy, as I indicated earlier, is a rather late arrival even in many well-established polyarchies. How widespread such support needs to be in order to sustain polyarchy is unclear.

Beliefs about *authority* relationships vary among countries. Eckstein (1966) has argued that there must be a certain congruence, particularly in polyarchies, between patterns of authority in government and in other institutions, such as private associations, economic enterprises, educational institutions, and the like. Norway, according to Eckstein, furnishes an extreme case of highly democratic authority patterns permeating all associational life. By contrast, Levine (1965, pp. 276, 280) reports that among the Amhara of Ethiopia "there are only three alternatives: complete deference, acquiescence, and flattery; criticism by devious and covert means; or outright rebellion." As a consequence, ideas favoring the institutions of polyarchy fall on totally barren soil.

Countries also seem to vary in "the extent to which members of a political system have *trust* and *confidence* in their fellow political actors." LaPalombara (1965, pp. 290–97) has stressed the importance of distrust in the Italian political culture, Levine (1965, pp. 277–88) among the Amhara. Probably mutual trust favors polyarchy and public contestation, and extreme distrust favors hegemony, in three ways: polyarchy requires two-way or mutual communication, and two-way communication is impeded among people who do not trust one another; a certain level of mutual trust is required in order for people to join together freely to promote their goals; among people who distrust one another, conflicts are more threatening and hence less likely to be tolerated.

Trust is related to capacities for *cooperation*. At one extreme, relations among political actors may be viewed as strictly competitive or zero-sum, as is said to be true among Italians (LaPalombara, 1965, pp. 290–91). A strictly competitive outlook probably inhibits cooperation and intensifies conflict and fragmentation. In a polyarchy, a prevalent view that conflict is necessarily zero-sum is likely to impede cooperation so severely as to inhibit the formation of governments, the execution of policy, and the solution of public problems; indirectly, then, it will weaken the legitimacy of polyarchy. At the other extreme, relations may be seen as so strictly cooperative that they allow no proper place to antagonism, conflict, political parties, contestation. Such a view would logically entail a denial of legitimacy to the major institutions and processes of contestation and polyarchy, particularly the existence of rival parties. Weiner (1965, pp. 235–6) suggests that a strong insistence on the desirability of strictly cooperative relationships is characteristic of certain Indian elites. Thus it is interesting that in his concern for establishing—or as he would argue, reestablishing—harmony among Indians, the distinguished intellectual and onetime socialist leader Jayaprakash Narayan came to reject the desirability of political parties and parliamentary democracy and finally withdrew from political activity.

Relationships may also be seen as cooperative-competitive: conflict, competition, and cooperation are viewed as normal and even healthy aspects of sociopolitical relations. Belief in the fruitfulness of cooperative-competitive relations has been central to English liberal thought, and perhaps some such view comes closest to the assumptions held by most political scientists in the older polyarchies. However, although extreme beliefs in either extreme competition or strict cooperation probably generate an unfavorable environment for polyarchy, the range of beliefs about cooperation and conflict that are compatible with polyarchy may be quite broad.

Since compromise is a normal and desirable consequence of conflicts bounded by cooperation, it has often been suggested that polyarchy and the toleration of oppositions are more likely in countries where *compromise* is looked upon favorably—and correspondingly less likely where compromise is seen as evil or demeaning. Although the evidence is weak, there do seem to be significant differences among countries in beliefs about compromise. Certainly in some countries with long and sturdy traditions of polyarchy and public contestation, compromise is honorable in both word and deed, as it is, for example, in Sweden, the Netherlands, and Britain. It would be interesting to have more evidence about countries in which "compromise" is condemned or disdained, as is often said to be true in Latin American countries, where the cognate *compromiso* carries a meaning much more unfavorable than it does in English.

III. PATTERNS OF OPPOSITION IN POLYARCHIES

As Table 1 indicates, in 1969 the regimes in about 38 countries provided a fairly high degree (historically speaking, an extraordinarily high degree) of protection for oppositions. Of these, at least 28 were inclusive polyarchies; in addition, Switzerland was a full polyarchy in all but one respect (at that time): it excluded women from the suffrage in federal elections. Although all 29 have not been systematically studied and compared, the political systems of polyarchies are relatively accessible, and there is a good deal of data and analysis on many of them.

One of the most obvious and yet highly striking conclusions to emerge is that there exists a great variety of different patterns of opposition in polyarchies. Certainly no single pattern prevails.

Oppositions, it appears, differ in at least six important ways:

1. The organizational cohesion or concentration of the opponents
2. The competitiveness of the opposition
3. The site or setting for the encounter between the opposition and those who control the government
4. The distinctiveness or identifiability of the opposition
5. The goals of the opposition
6. The strategies of the opposition

Concentration

Opponents of a government may display varying degrees of organizational cohesion; they may all be concentrated in a single organization, for example, or they may be dispersed in a number of organizations operating independently of one another.

Probably in no country, and certainly in no polyarchy, are all the active opponents of government ever concentrated in one organization. If we concern ourselves with political parties, however, the situation is rather different. The extent to which opposition is concentrated depends on the party system of a country. The highest degree of concentration of opposition exists in two-party systems, where the out-party has a substantial monopoly of the opposition. In multiparty systems, opposition is likely to be dispersed among several parties.

In the English-speaking world, all thought about opposition has been dominated, at least in this century, by simple two-party models—to which multiparty systems are a kind of unsatisfactory and probably temporary exception. And this view, so confidently held in Britain and the United States, has often been accepted even outside the English-speaking world.

Yet the facts themselves are enough to discredit such a parochial notion. To begin with, the system of two dominant parties has not been much imitated outside the English-speaking world and its zones of influence. Among the 29 polyarchies in 1970 parties other than the two largest had more than 10 percent of the seats in all but nine. Moreover, in one of the nine, the German Federal Republic, neither major party could govern without forming a coalition with the Free Democratic minority. Of the eight remaining, all but two (Austria and Uruguay) are either English-speaking democracies or were launched politically under the influence of Britain or the United States.[15]

Moreover, even where there are only two dominant parties, the patterns of opposition are often radically different. Indeed, in the English-speaking world, the British two-party system as we now understand it seems to exist only in Britain and in New Zealand. The relative weakness of third parties throughout American history makes the United States an even more clear-cut example of two dominant parties than Britain; yet within this framework of two parties, the American pattern of dispersed opposition has nearly as much in common with some of the European multiparty systems as it does with the "concentrated" British pattern. Finally, the British two-party system as we know it today has not existed for much more than the last four decades.

In sum, it might be reasonable to consider multiparty systems as the natural way for government and oppositions to manage their conflicts in polyarchies whereas two-party systems, whether resembling the British pattern or the American, are the deviant cases.

In addition to the number of important parties, concentration has yet another dimension. Parties themselves vary enormously in internal unity, as measured, for example, by the way their members vote in parliament; what is formally a single opposition party may in fact disintegrate into a number of factions.

Competitiveness

How competitive an opposition is depends partly on how concentrated it is. On the analogy of an equivalent concept in the theory of games, two parties are in a strictly competitive (or zero-sum) relation if they pursue strategies such that, given the election or voting system, the gains of one will exactly equal the losses of the other. Because in any given election the number of seats in a legislative body is fixed, whenever only two parties run competing candidates in an election, they are necessarily engaged in a strictly competitive contest, since the seats gained by one party will be lost by the other. Applying the notion of strict competition to a legislative body presents some problems; but we can get around most of them by stipulating that two parties are strictly competitive in a legislature if they pursue strategies such that both cannot simultaneously belong to a winning coalition. As an empirical fact, of course, no legislature is strictly competitive all the time; some measures gain overwhelming or unanimous approval, and on others party leaders deliberately permit their followers to vote as they choose. In some legislatures, however, key votes are usually strictly competitive—votes on the formation of a government, votes of confidence, votes on the major legislative and budgeting measures submitted by the government, etc. We can regard parties as strictly competitive in parliament, then, if they are strictly competitive on key votes.

It might be conjectured that in a parliamentary or presidential system monopolized by two highly unified parties, competition would always be strictly competitive. The salient example is of course Britain. Yet the parties could deliberately decide to collaborate either in parliament or in elections, or in both. During most of two world wars the major parties in Britain agreed to substitute collaboration for competition: coalition cabinets were formed, and elections were delayed until after the end of the war. In Austria from 1947 onward, the People's party and the Socialist party formed a coalition government that left virtually no opposition in Parliament; yet at each election the two parties vigorously fought each other for votes. The most extreme displacement of competition by coalition has occurred in Colombia, where the two major parties deliberately entered into a pact to eliminate competition not only in Congress but in national elections.

The competitiveness of opposition (in the sense in which the term is used here) depends in large measure, though not completely, on the number and nature of parties, i.e., on the extent to which opposition is concentrated. The possibilities extend from a system in which the opposition is concentrated in a party that is strictly competitive, both in elections and in parliament, through various systems in which opposition strategies are both cooperative and competitive, to systems in which the minority party that would ordinarily constitute the opposition coalesces with the majority party, both in elections and in parliament (see Table 7).

Site

Because it seeks to bring about a change in the behavior of the government, an opposition will employ some of its political resources to persuade, induce, or compel a government to alter its conduct. The situation or circumstances in which an opposition employs its resources to bring about a change might be called a *site* for encounters between opposition and government.

All polyarchies offer oppositions the opportunity to challenge the government by influencing public opinion in order to increase support for themselves, by winning votes and parliamentary seats in elections, by entering into an executive coalition, by gaining support in parliament for legislation, by negotiating with other officials, and by negotiating with unofficial or quasi-official organizations.

TABLE 7   Competition, cooperation, and coalescence: types of party systems

	Opposition in:		
Type of system	Elections	Parliament	Examples
1. Strictly competitive	Strictly competitive	Strictly competitive	Britain
2. Cooperative-competitive			
a) Two-party	Strictly competitive	Cooperative and competitive	United States
b) Multiparty	Cooperative and competitive	Cooperative and competitive	France, Italy
3. Coalescent-competitive			
a) Two-party	Strictly competitive	Coalescent	Austria Britain (wartime)
b) Multiparty	Cooperative and competitive	Coalescent	
4. Strictly coalescent	Coalescent	Coalescent	Colombia

The relative importance of these sites varies from one system to another. In some systems one site is relatively decisive: victory in that encounter entails a rather high probability of victory in the rest. But other systems may not offer a decisive site; an opposition may win an encounter at one site and lose at another.

In one sense, to be sure, public opinion is a decisive site in every polyarchy; for each polyarchy it would be possible, in principle, to specify some amount and distribution of opinions that would be decisive. Nonetheless, the amount and distribution of public support required for an opposition to gain victory vary even among different polyarchies. Unfortunately, the theoretical and empirical patterns have not, as far as I know, been at all worked out, and I shall not attempt to do so here. However, it is possible to distinguish, in a rough way, four somewhat different patterns of "decisiveness."

First, in Britain, for example, parliamentary elections are relatively decisive. For a political opposition to succeed in changing important government policies, a condition that is ordinarily both necessary and sufficient is for it to win a majority of seats in a parliamentary election. By winning a parliamentary majority, the opposition is able to select the executive; and because of party unity, the onetime opposition, now the new government, can count on its majority in the House of Commons to support its policies. The consequences for opposition strategies are obvious. Ordinarily an opposition will concentrate on winning public opinion to its cause and its candidates so that it can win a future parliamentary majority. Every other use of its resources must be subordinated to this controlling purpose. Parliament itself is not, then, a site for genuine encounters so much as it is a forum from which to influence the next election. Parliamentary debate is not intended to influence Parliament as much as the public—and hence future elections; negotiations to enter the Cabinet would on the whole be futile, and everyone knows it.

Second, in some countries where, unlike the situation in Britain, elections are not decisive (even though they are important), the formation of the executive is relatively decisive: an executive coalition is moderately sure of gaining the necessary parliamentary support for the policies the coalition agrees on; a group not in the executive coalition is much less likely to gain support for its policies. This pattern exists in countries with multi-party systems where the parties are cohesive in parliamentary voting, as in Holland and Italy, and also in the unusual Austrian two-party coalition system. In these countries the parties attempt to influence public opinion and win parliamentary seats in elections, but they take it more or less for granted that they cannot govern except as part of a coalition. Hence, unlike the British parties, they shape their strategy to take advantage of opportunities for bargaining their way into the current coalition, replacing it with a different coalition, or forcing new elections that are expected to improve their bargaining position.

Third, some countries that might be placed in the second category because of the working of their parties and the regular governmental institutions have in fact moved closer to a system in which elections and the selection of the executive coalition are decisive only with respect to other *official* sites—parliament, the bureaucracies, local governments, and so on. But on a variety of key issues bargaining has been displaced from these official sites to "bargaining processes between the giant alliances of . . . associations and corporations," as Rokkan (1966, p. 56) says of the "two-tier system" in Norway. So important has this bargaining become in the Scandinavian countries that parliamentary democracy in the conventional sense has been to some extent replaced by a kind of democratic corporatism—or if one prefers terms less tainted by undemocratic connotations, by a pluralistic democracy with highly organized associations.

The fourth group of countries bears some similarity to the third category because of the dispersed or pluralistic character of key decisions; what distinguishes these countries, however, is the fact that even among official sites none is decisive. For the absence of a decisive site has been produced by a deliberate dispersion of legal authority through constitutional devices, such as federalism, separation of powers, and checks and balances. The United States and Switzerland are probably the extreme cases, though West Germany also falls into this category.

Distinctiveness

The distinctiveness of opposition in a political system is largely a result of the three factors we have just discussed: cohesion, competitiveness, and the relative importance of different sites.

In the classic model, the opposition is clearly identified. The principal sites for encounters between opposition and government are the national parliament, parliamentary elections, and the communications media; hence parliament enjoys a virtual monopoly over official, day-to-day encounters. There are only two major parties, both highly unified; hence the opposition is highly concentrated in a single party. Finally, the two parties are strictly competitive in parliament and in elections. As a result of all these conditions, opposition is so sharply distinguished that it is possible to identify unambiguously *the* opposition. In Britain, which has at various times most closely corresponded to this classic model, the distinctiveness of the opposition is symbolized by its very name, "Her Majesty's Loyal Opposition."

The United States and Switzerland both lie close to the opposite extreme. In the United States the sites at which conflict occurs between supporters and opponents of the conduct of government are scattered among the two houses of Congress, the bureaucracy, the White House itself, the courts, and the 50 states, to mention some of the main official sites. The two parties are decentralized; and in Congress they pursue cooperative-competitive strategies. Hence it is never easy to distinguish "opposition" from "government"; and it is exceedingly difficult, if not impossible, to identify *the* opposition.

Goals

An opposition may oppose the conduct of government because it wants to change (or to resist a possible change in) (1) the personnel of government; (2) the specific policies of government; (3) the structure of the political system; or (4) the socioeconomic structure. Although these are by no means sharply distinct categories, for the sake of simplicity we shall speak of them as if they were more clearly distinguishable than in fact they are. The seven most relevant patterns are shown in Table 8.

Strategies

The specific strategies used by opponents in order to change (or to prevent possible change) in the conduct of government are of almost infinite variety.

Nonetheless, some patterns do emerge. The strategy an opposition is likely to select depends, in part, on all the characteristics that have been examined up to this point. Thus strategies obviously depend to some extent on goals: a revolutionary opposition is not likely to follow the same strategy as a pressure group. But as we have seen, given roughly similar goals, a strategy that might make a good deal of sense in one system would be inappropriate in another.

TABLE 8   Patterns of opposition: goals*

| Types of opposition | Opposition to the conduct of government in order to change (or prevent change) in | | | | Example |
	Personnel of government	Specific policies of government	Political structure	Socioeconomic structure	
Nonstructural opposition					
1. Pure office-seeking parties	Yes	No	No	No	U.S. Federalists 1815–30
2. Pressure groups	No	Yes	No	No	U.S. Farm Bureau Federation
3. Policy-oriented parties	+	+	—	—	U.S. Republican party
Limited structural opposition					
4. Political reformism (not policy-oriented)	Yes or No	—	+	—	Britain: Irish Nationalists U.S.: Women's suffrage movement
Major structural opposition					
5. Comprehensive political-structural reformism	+	+	+	—	France: RPF
6. Democratic social-structured reformism	+	+	—	+	Democratic-Socialist parties
7. Revolutionary movements	+	+	+	+	Communist parties

* Note that limited structural opposition (4) includes two subpatterns, i.e., either the presence or absence of opposition to the personnel of government. There are 16 theoretically possible patterns. The remaining eight do not appear in the table because they were felt to be irrelevant or highly unlikely.

Putting goals momentarily to one side, then, one might deliberately oversimplify the actual variations in order to formulate the strategic imperatives of our various systems as follows:

Strategy 1. Opposition will concentrate above all on strict competition by seeking to gain enough votes in elections to win a majority of seats in parliament and then to form a government (cabinet or executive) consisting only of its own leaders. This strategy is encouraged by a system characterized by two unified parties, where opposition is highly distinctive and elections are decisive. The only system of this kind among our ten countries is Britain, where the strategy is in fact usually pursued by the opposition party.

Strategy 2. An opposition will try to convert additional voters and to gain additional seats in parliamentary elections, but it will assume that it cannot win a parliamentary majority; hence it will concentrate heavily on entering into a governing coalition and gaining as much as it can by intracoalition bargaining. This strategy is encouraged by a system with more than two major parties that have a high degree of party unity, and in which the selection of the government (i.e., cabinet or executive) is relatively decisive. This strategy is usually followed by oppositions in Belgium, France, Italy, and Holland.

Strategy 3. An opposition will adopt all of Strategy 2, but in addition it will assume that many important decisions will be made in quasi-official bargaining among giant associations; hence failure to get into the cabinet need not prevent it from gaining some of its goals by hard bargaining in these quasi-official encounters. This strategy is encouraged by multi-party systems, in which Strategy 2 is appropriate but in which there also exists a rather highly developed structure of democratic corporatism. Strategy 3 is followed most notably in Norway and Sweden, perhaps, but also in the Netherlands and, to some extent, in a good many other countries as well.

Strategy 4. Oppositions will assume that gaining public support and winning votes in elections are both important but neither is always necessary or always sufficient, since any one of a great variety of sites may prove decisive in a specific case and none will prove generally decisive. Hence an opposition will adapt its specific tactics to its resources and to the most vulnerable site or sites. It may concentrate on pressure-group activities, intraparty bargaining, legislative maneuvering, gaining favorable judicial decisions, actions at state and local levels, winning elections, or any combination of these. This kind of strategy is encouraged by a system in which constitutional rules and practice prevent any site from being decisive and in which opportunities for preventing or inhibiting government action are numerous. The most notable examples of this strategy are provided by the United States; however, among our 10 countries, West Germany also seems to approach it.

Strategy 5. Really a set of strategies, it is pursued by an opposition committed to the survival of the political entity when the opposition and the government believe that survival is seriously threatened by severe internal crisis, subversion, war, or the like. A great threat to the political entity encourages overtures by the government to opposition groups to enter into a broader coalition for the duration of the crisis; it encourages all oppositions committed to preserving the political entity (usually, therefore, all the nonrevolutionary oppositions) to adopt coalescent strategies. Coalescent strategies may vary somewhat from one system to another, but in general an opposition tries to enter into a coalition government on the most advantageous terms, seeks to confine conflicts within the cabinet and to prevent them from breaking out in parliament or in public, and keeps open the possibility of reverting to strict competition when the crisis has passed or at the next election. This is the strategy pursued in Britain in both world wars, by the Swedish parties in the Second World War, and in Italy during the immediate postwar period. Austria is the most interesting example, however, for the coalescent strategy was pursued by both the major parties long after the dangers that initially encouraged that strategy had declined.

Strategy 6. Also a set of strategies, it is often pursued by revolutionary oppositions committed to the destruction of the political entity or the main features of its constitutional system. The essence of this strategy is to use whatever resources the revolutionary opposition has available in order to disrupt the normal operation of political processes, to discredit the system, to impair its legitimacy, and, in general, to increase the vulnerability of the polity to seizure of power by the revolutionary opposition. This was the strategy pursued by the Nazis and the Communists in Weimar Germany.

Some Conclusions and Unsolved Problems

First, there exist a great variety of different patterns of opposition in democratic systems. Second, patterns of opposition differ, among other characteristics, in concentration, competitiveness, relative decisiveness of site, distinctiveness, goals, and strategies. Third, a choice among strategies is partly determined for an opposition by all the other characteristics of the pattern. The influence of these other characteristics on strategies can be represented schematically as in Fig. 9. Fourth, although this schema offers some explanation for the selection of opposition *strategies,* our analysis so far leaves the goals and the other system characteristics pretty much unexplained. Evidently, then, a fuller explanation of differences in strategy would require some explanation of the differences that exist with respect to goals, concentration, competitiveness, identifiability, and site. Moreover, ideally one would want to account not only for present differences in these characteristics among our 10 countries but also for any significant changes that have occurred, such as a decline in structural opposition. These are formidable tasks. In the present state of knowledge, explanations remain highly incomplete and conjectural.

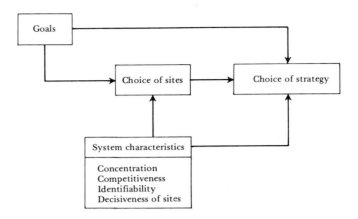

Fig. 9. A Schematic Representation of the Influence of Various Characteristics of Opposition Patterns on the Choice of Strategies

NOTES

1.   For a description of this constitution and the preoccupation of the aristocracy with the prevention of internal conflict, see Maranini (1927), particularly pp. 168–71. The highly complex method for electing the doge is described at pp. 187–90 and 324–50, and in Maranini (1932, pp. 99, 115, 122).

2.   "There were no parties in anything like the modern sense, either among the politicians or the general public. At the one end of the scale there were groups or cliques among the politicians. But such alliances were probably based on personalities rather than principles, and seem to have been temporary." However, "Athenian policy was really determined by mass meetings of the citizens on the advice of anyone who could win the people's ear" (Jones, 1957, pp. 130–32). See also de Coulanges (n.d.).

3.   To simplify the theory and exposition at this point, I treat "government" and "opposition" each as single, unified actors. Clearly this is rarely the case.

4.   The absence of a feudal past has been strongly emphasized by Louis Hartz (1955) as an explanation for the development of a liberal democracy in the United States.

5.   "For example, recent research indicates that in nineteenth century China, the gentry or degree holders, who formed the governing class, totaled about 1.3 percent of the population in the first half of the century and about 1.9 percent toward the end. In mid-nineteenth century Russia the nobility constituted 1.25 percent of that nation's population. In France, on the eve of the Revolution, the nobility of all ranks and grades constituted only 0.6 percent, despite the recent influx of many wealthy mercantile families. During the last days of the Roman Republic, the governing class is estimated to have included about 1 percent of the capital's population. Finally, in seventeenth century England, peers, baronets, knights, and esquires combined constituted roughly 1 percent of the total population" (Lenski, 1966, p. 219).

6.   For example, nine indicators applied to 107 countries yield five "stages" of economic and political development in Russett (1965, p. 127). Factor scores used as indi-

cators yield three levels of socioeconomic development for 74 "less developed countries," ranging from Niger with a 1961 per capita GNP of $40 to Israel with a 1951 per capita GNP of $814 (Adelman and Morris, 1967, p. 170).

7.   For example, see Lipset (1960, pp. 45–76); Cutright (1963); and Neubauer (1967).

8.   For examples, see Hagen's "Classification of Asian and African Countries by Type of Political Structure and Rank in Economic Development" and his similar classification of Latin American countries (1962, Chapter 1); and Cutright's "Relationships of Political Development to Communications Development: 71 Nations" (1963, Fig. 1, pp. 572–73). See also Coleman's "Composite Rank Order of Latin American Countries on Eleven Indices of Economic Development" and the similar rank ordering of Asian and African countries in Almond and Coleman (1960). See also Adelman and Morris (1967), "Scatter Diagram Relating Per Capita GNP and Country Scores on Factor Representing the Extent of Democracy," p. 262. One of the earliest systematic statements is Lipset (1960), pp. 45–76.

9.   Goldsmith (1969, Chapter 2, p. 357) has estimated real GNP per capita in 1839 as about $200 in 1929 prices. This would be about $380, converted to 1957 prices by means of the price deflators in U.S. Department of Commerce (1958), Table VII-2, pp. 220–1.

10.   In *Who Governs?* (1961), I interpreted historical evidence drawn from New Haven (which would be typical in this respect, I think, of most old cities of the eastern seaboard) as indicating a shift between the eighteenth and twentieth centuries from cumulative to dispersed inequalities. This is not inconsistent with the view that in agrarian America, as distinct from these few old urban centers, the shift from the early eighteenth to the twentieth century was from relative equality to dispersed inequalities.

11.   Sources for Table 5. The classification of polyarchies is from Dahl (1971, p. 248). The classification according to subcultural pluralism is from Marie R. Haug (1967). On Haug's index of pluralism, *low* is defined as 0 or 1, *moderate* as 2 or 3, *marked* as 4 or 5, *extreme* as 6, 7, or 8. The construction of Haug's index is shown in her Table 2, p. 297. The variables in the index are language, race, religion, sectionalism, and "interest articulation by non-associational groups," which include kinship, lineage, ethnic, regional, and religious groups. This purely numerical index unfortunately cannot register the depth or completeness of subcultural cleavages, as in the Netherlands.

12.   The analysis here has been strongly influenced by the experience of the Netherlands, described by Daalder (1966) and Lijphart (1968a) and Belgium, described by Lorwin (1966). In particular, see Daalder, pp. 216–20, Lijphart, pp. 197 ff., and Lorwin, pp. 174–85. See also Lijphart (1968b, pp. 3–44). For a critique and an alternative formulation, see Eric A. Nordlinger, *Conflict Regulation in Divided Societies* (Cambridge: Harvard University Center for International Affairs, 1972).

13.   On Lebanon, for example, see the comments of Hudson (1968, pp. 9–12 and 329–31) and Crow (1962).

14.   In Belgium, the German invasion and occupation during the First World War brought Socialists into the government for the first time; they remained even after the war was over. The war also led directly to universal suffrage in Belgium. Under the old system of plural voting, as Lorwin (1966) writes,

> Workers and peasants who had suffered in the trenches or in deportation could have cast one ballot each, while war profiteers could have cast two or three. Instead, the King and the government called the voters to the polls on a one man, one vote basis. The parliament they elected legitimatized the change by constitutional amendment.

Lorwin goes on to describe the impact of the Second World War:

> If the First War marked the full acceptance of the Socialist Party, the Second marked that of the Labor Unions. Under the Nazi occupation, clandestine personal contacts among leaders of industry and Catholic, Socialist, and Liberal trade unions produced a "pact of social solidarity" of symbolic and practical importance. The pact was implemented after the Liberation by wide advances in social legislation and collective bargaining.... Union and industry representatives came to exercise powers of administration in a number of quasi-public social welfare agencies. (pp. 158–65)

In the Netherlands, the first Socialist ministers came into the government in 1939 under the threat of Nazism, and in that country, Belgium, and Norway, invasion and occupation also produced all-party governments in exile.

15. The others are Britain, Jamaica, New Zealand, the Philippines, Trinidad and Tobago, and the United States.

REFERENCES

Adcock, F. E. (1959). *Roman Political Ideas and Practice*. Ann Arbor: University of Michigan.

Adelman, Irma, and Cynthia Taft Morris (1967). *Society, Politics and Economic Development*. Baltimore: Johns Hopkins Press.

Almond, Gabriel, and James Coleman (1960). *The Politics of The Developing Areas*. Princeton: Princeton University Press.

Barghoorn, Frederick C. (1973). "Factional, sectional, and subversive opposition in Soviet politics." In Dahl, 1973.

Bequiraj, Mehmet (1966). *Peasantry in Revolution*. Ithaca: Cornell University Center for International Studies.

Crow, Ralph E. (1962). "Religious sectarianism in the Lebanese political system." *Journal of Politics* 24:489–520.

Cutright, Phillips (1963). "National political development, its measurement and social correlates." In Nelson W. Polsby, Robert A. Dentler, and Paul A. Smith (eds.), *Politics and Social Life*. Boston: Houghton Mifflin.

Daalder, Hans (1966). "The Netherlands: opposition in a segmented society." In Dahl, 1966.

Dahl, Robert A. (1961). *Who Governs?* New Haven: Yale University Press.

——————— (1971). *Polyarchy: Participation and Opposition*. New Haven: Yale University Press.

——————— (1973). *Regimes and Oppositions*. New Haven: Yale University Press.

———————, ed. (1966). *Political Opposition in Western Democracies*. New Haven: Yale University Press.

de Coulanges, Foustel (n.d.). *The Ancient City*. Garden City, N.Y.: Doubleday, Anchor.

Eckstein, Harry (1966). *Division and Cohesion in a Democracy: A Study of Norway.* Princeton: Princeton University Press.

Finer, S. E. (1967). "The one-party regimes in Africa: reconsiderations." *Government and Opposition* 2:491–508.

Foltz, William J. (1973). "Political opposition in tropical Africa." In Dahl, 1973.

Goldsmith, Raymond (1969). "Long period growth in income and product, 1839–1960." In R. Andreano (ed.), *New Views on American Economic Development.* Cambridge, Mass.: Schenkman.

Hagen, Everett E. (1962). *The Development of the Emerging Countries.* Washington: Brookings.

Hartz, Louis (1955). *The Liberal Tradition in America.* New York: Harcourt, Brace.

Haug, Marie R. (1967). "Social and cultural pluralism as a concept in social system analysis." *The American Journal of Sociology* 73:294–304.

Hudson, Michael C. (1968). *The Precarious Republic, Political Modernization in Lebanon.* New York: Random House.

Jones, A. H. M. (1957). *Athenian Democracy.* Oxford: Blackwell.

Kothari, Rajni (1970). *India.* Boston: Little, Brown.

—————— (1973). "India: oppositions in a consensual polity." In Dahl, 1973.

Lane, Robert E. (1959). "The fear of equality." *The American Political Science Review* 53:35–51.

LaPalombara, Joseph (1965). "Italy: fragmentation, isolation, and alienation." In Pye and Verba, 1965.

Leiserson, Michael (1973). "Political opposition and political development in Japan." In Dahl, 1973.

Lenski, Gerhard (1966). *Power and Privilege.* New York: McGraw-Hill.

Levine, Donald N. (1965). "Ethiopia: identity, authority, and realism." In Pye and Verba, 1965.

Lijphart, A. (1968a). *The Politics of Accommodation.* Berkeley: University of California.

—————— (1968b). "Typologies of democratic systems." *Comparative Political Studies* 1:3–44.

Lipset, Seymour Martin (1960). "Economic development and democracy." In his *Political Man.* Garden City, N.Y.: Doubleday.

Lorwin, Val R. (1966). "Belgium: religion, class and language in national politics." In Dahl, 1966.

Maranini, Giuseppe (1927, 1932). *La Costituzione di Venezia,* Vol. 1, 1927. *Dalle Origini alla Serrata del Maggior Consiglio,* Vol. 2, 1932. *Dopo La Serrata del Maggior Consiglio.* Venice: La Nuova Italia Editrice.

Marshall, T. H. (1950). *Citizenship and Social Class.* Cambridge: Cambridge University Press.

Neubauer, Deane E. (1967). "Some conditions of democracy." *The American Political Science Review* 61:1002–9.

Pye, Lucian, and Sidney Verba, eds. (1965). *Political Culture and Political Development*. Princeton: Princeton University Press.

Rokkan, Stein (1966). "Norway: numerical democracy and corporate pluralism." In Dahl, 1966.

Runciman, W. G. (1966). *Relative Deprivation and Social Justice*. Berkeley: University of California Press.

Russett, Bruce M. (1965). *Trends in World Politics*. New York: Macmillan.

Russett, Bruce M., *et al.* (1964). *World Handbook of Political and Social Indicators*. New Haven: Yale University Press.

Rustow, Dankwart (1967). *A World of Nations*. Washington: Brookings.

Skilling, Gordon (1966). *The Governments of Communist East Europe*. New York: Crowell.

———————— (1973a). "Opposition in communist east Europe." In Dahl, 1973.

———————— (1973b). "Czechoslovakia's interrupted revolution." In Dahl, 1973.

Svalastoga, Kaare (1965). *Social Differentiation*. New York: McKay.

Taylor, Lily Ross (1961). *Party Politics in the Age of Caesar*. Berkeley and Los Angeles: University of California Press.

U.S. Department of Commerce (1958). *U.S. Income and Output*. Washington: Government Printing Office.

Weiner, Myron (1965). "India, two political cultures." In Pye and Verba, 1965.

3

TOTALITARIAN AND AUTHORITARIAN REGIMES

JUAN J. LINZ

I. INTRODUCTION

Variety and Prevalence of Nondemocratic Regimes

We all know that governments are different and that it is not the same thing to be the citizen or subject of one or another country, even in matters of daily life. We also know that almost all governments do some of the same things, and sometimes we feel like the pure anarchist, for whom all states, being states, are essentially the same. This double awareness is also the point of departure of our intellectual efforts as social scientists.

We obviously know that life under Stalin or Hitler, even for the average citizen but particularly for those occupying important positions in their society, was different than for citizens living in the United Kingdom or Sweden.[1] Without going to such extremes, we can still say that life for many people—but perhaps not that many—is different in Franco's Spain than in Italy. Certainly it is for a leader of the Communist party in either country. As social scientists we want to describe in all its complexity the relationship of people to their government and to understand why this relationship is so different in different countries. Leaving aside consideration of personal documents—the memoirs of politicians, generals, intellectuals, conspirators, and concentration camp inmates—and the literary works inspired by the human experience of man confronting power, often brutal and arbitrary power, we will consider the work of social scientists who have, by observation, by analysis of the laws, the judicial and administrative decisions, the records of the bureaucratic activities of the

This work has been made possible by my stay at the Institute for Advanced Study, Princeton, supported by NSF Grant GS-31730X2. I would like to acknowledge the invaluable assistance of Rocío de Terán and the help of Claire Coombs.

state, by interviews with leaders and sample surveys of the population, written excellent monographs on politics in many societies, trying to describe and explain how different political systems work.

Political theorists have given us the framework to ask relevant questions. However, we cannot be satisfied with even the best descriptive studies of political life in a particular society at a particular time. We, like Aristotle when he confronted the diversity of constitutions of the Greek polis of his time, feel the need to reduce the complexity to a limited number of types sufficiently different to take into account the variety in real life but also able to describe those elements that a certain number of polities share. Such an effort of conceptualization has to ask why these polities share some characteristics and, ultimately, what difference it makes. The classification of political systems, like that of other aspects of reality—of social structures, economic systems, religions, kinship structures—has been at the core of social science since its origins. New forms of political organizations, of creating and using power and authority, and new perspectives derived from different values have inevitably led to new classifications. The intellectual task is far from easy, confronted as we are with the changing political reality. The old terms become inadequate. As Tocqueville noted when he wrote about "a kind of oppression which threatens democratic nations that will not resemble any other form previously experienced in the world": "It is something new, I must therefore attempt to define it for I cannot name it." Unfortunately, we have to use names for realities that we are just attempting to define. Worse even, we are not alone in that process, since those who control political life in the states of the twentieth century also want to define, describe, and name their political system—or at least to define it according to what they want it to be or what they want others to believe that it is. Obviously the perspectives of scholarship and of political actors will not always coincide, and the same words will be used with different meanings. This makes the need for conceptual clarity even more imperative. In addition, societies differ not only in the way they organize political life but in the relations of authority in spheres other than politics. Certainly those who consider dimensions of society other than government more important for the life of people would prefer a conceptualization of the variety of societies in which politics would be only one and perhaps not a very important dimension. Our concern here is, however, the variety of political systems as a problem in itself.

One of the easiest ways to define a concept is to say what it is not. To do this obviously assumes that we know what something else is, so that we can say that our concept is not the same. Here we shall start from the assumption that we know what democracy is and center our attention on all the political systems that do not fit our definition of democracy. As Giovanni Sartori (1962a, pp. 135–57) noted, as he was reviewing the use of terms like totalitarianism, authoritarianism, dictatorship, despotism, and absolutism which over time had been opposed to democracy, in modern times it has become more and more difficult to know what democracy is not. We feel, however, that the work of many scholars has at least provided us with a definition of democracy that fits a large number of political systems sufficiently similar in the way of organizing political life and the relationship between citizen and government to be described by a single definition. We shall therefore deal here with the political systems that share at least one characteristic, that of not being like those we shall describe with our definition of democracy. Thus, we shall deal here with nondemocratic political systems.

This basic duality has been described traditionally with terms like polycracy and monocracy, democracy and autocracy. In the eighteenth century absolutism and despotism became the descriptive and ideological terms to describe governments that were free from restraint *(legibus solutus)*, even when there was an ambivalence such as the term enlightened despotism reflects. Late in the nineteenth century and early in the twentieth century, after constitutional governments had been established, at least on paper, in most Western countries and liberalism and the *Rechtstaat*—"state of law"—had become the symbol of political progress, the new autocratic forms of rule were generally called dictatorships. In the twenties Mussolini adopted Giovanni Gentile's neo-idealist conception of the state as an "ethical" and "totalitarian" state, and as he said: "The armed party leads to the totalitarian regime . . . . a party that governs totalitarianly a nation is a new fact in history." [2] Only shortly later the term would find echo in Germany, more among the political scientists like Carl Schmitt (1940), writing in 1931, than among the Nazi leadership. The success of the word was easily linked with the famous work by General Ludendorff (1935), *Der Totale Krieg*,[3] which turned around the old Clausewitz conception of "war as a continuation of politics with other means" to conceiving of peace as a preparation for war, politics as continuation of war with other means. An influential writer, Ernst Jünger (1930), at that time also coined the phrase *"Totale Mobilmachung."* Soon this idea of total mobilization would enter the political discourse and even legal texts like the statutes of the Spanish single party with the positive connotation. Already in the thirties, political scientists like Sabine (1934) would start using it for the new mobilizational single-party regimes, fascist and communist. Robert Michels (1928, pp. 770–72) already in 1928 would note the similarity between the Bolshevik and the fascist parties. Trotsky (1937, p. 278) in 1936 would write: "Stalinism and fascism, in spite of a deep difference in social foundations, are symmetrical phenomena. In many of their features they show a deadly similarity." And many fascists, particularly left fascists, would feel strongly the affinity between their ideals and those of a national Russian communism led by Stalin.[4] It was therefore not left to the liberal critics of the fascist powers and the Soviet Union to discover those affinities and the usefulness of a concept that would cover these two novel political phenomena. As we shall see, only recently a reaction has set in against the overextension and misuse of the concept, as well as its intellectual fruitfulness. Already in the thirties, however, some theorists who favored authoritarian, antidemocratic political solutions but were hostile to the activist mobilizational conceptions of the totalitarian state and were concerned about the autonomy of the state from society, even a society mobilized by a single party, formulated the contrasts among the authoritarian state, the totalitarian state, and what they called the neutral liberal democratic state (Ziegler, 1932; Voegelin, 1936). Those formulations did not find echo in political science after World War II. With the cold-war transition to democracy of some authoritarian regimes like Turkey and Brazil and the initial democratic form taken by the new independent nations, it appeared as if the dichotomy between democracy and totalitarianism could serve to describe the universe of political systems or at least the polar extremes toward which other systems would tend. It was at this point that the regimes that could not be classified either as political democracies or totalitarian systems tended to be conceived of either as tutelary democracies, that is, as regimes that have adopted the formal norms of a democratic polity and whose elites have as a goal the democratizing of their polities even though they might be unclear as to the requirements, or as traditional oligarchies surviving from the past (Shils, 1960). Even so, the regimes that found themselves between these two types, oriented either toward a democratic future or a traditional past, required the formulation of the type of modernizing oligarchies. Significantly, in that case the description focused more on the goal of economic development than on the nature of the political institutions to be created or maintained.

Only a few years later the great hopes for democracy in Latin America, particularly in the more developed republics of South America and those created by the apparently successful transfer of British and French democratic constitutions to former colonies that became independent, were disappointed. On the other hand, authoritarian regimes like Spain and Portugal unexpectedly survived the defeat of the Axis. Political scientists would discover that such regimes could not be understood as unsuccessful totalitarian regimes, since many, if not all, of their founders did not share a totalitarian conception of society and the state; they functioned very differently from Nazi or Stalinist regimes; and their rulers, particularly in the Third World, did not keep up the pretenses of preparing the nation for democracy with temporary authoritarian rule. They increasingly rejected explicitly the liberal democratic model and often pretended to imitate the Leninist model of the vanguard party for building the new states or nations. Soon social scientists would discover that the ideological pronouncements and the organization charts of the parties and the mass organizations in almost all cases did not correspond to any reality, as in the past the pseudofascism of Balkan, Eastern European, and Baltic states had not corresponded to the German or even the Italian model. Inevitably those developments would lead to the formulation, with one or another emphasis, of the idea of a third type of regime, a type *sui generis* rather than on a continuum between democracy and totalitarianism. On the basis of an analysis of the Franco regime, particularly after 1945, we (Linz, 1964) formulated the concept of an authoritarian regime distinct from both democratic governments and totalitarian systems.

Our analysis here will focus on totalitarian and authoritarian regimes that share at least one characteristic: they are nondemocratic. Therefore we shall start with a brief statement of an empirical definition of democracy that will allow us to delimit the subject of our research. We shall turn to the rich theoretical and empirical research on totalitarian political systems over the last decade as well as to the recent critiques of that concept in order to delimit the types of regimes that we shall call authoritarian by what they are not. However, those three types do not exhaust fully the types of political systems existing in the twentieth century. There are still a number of regimes based on traditional legitimacy whose nature we would misunderstand if we would classify them together with the modern authoritarian regimes established after the breakdown of traditional legitimacy or after a democratic period. We also feel that it would not be fully fruitful to consider certain types of tyrannical, arbitrary rule exercised by an individual and his clients with the help of the praetorian guard, without any form of organized participation in power of institutional structures, with little effort of legitimation of any sort, and in pursuit of more private than collective goals, in the same category with more institutionalized authoritarian regimes in which the rulers feel that they are acting for a collectivity. We therefore decided to deal with this type of regime separately, calling it "sultanistic," even when it shares some characteristics with those we have called authoritarian. The case of dual societies, in which one sector of the society imposes its rule on another, by force if necessary, while allowing its members to participate in political life according to the rules of political democracy except for excluding from discussion the issue of the relationship to the dominated group, supported by a wide consensus on that issue, poses a special problem. We have labeled that type of regime "racial democracy," conveying the paradox of democracy combined with racial domination. Recent developments in Eastern Europe after de-Stalinization and even some trends in the Soviet Union have raised the question of the nature of the post-Stalinist communist regimes. We have found that the emerging regimes in Eastern Europe have many characteristics in common with those we have described as authoritarian, but their more or less recent totalitarian past and the commitment of their elites to some elements of the totalitarian utopia makes these regimes quite distinct. We shall discuss them as a particular case of authoritarian regimes: as posttotalitarian.

The two main dimensions that we shall use in our definition of the authoritarian regime—the degree or type of limited political pluralism under such regimes and the degree to which such regimes are based on political apathy and demobilization of the population or limited and controlled mobilizations —lead us to distinguish a number of subtypes. Those subtypes are based fundamentally on the type of participants in the limited pluralism and on the way in which they are organized, as well as on the level and type of participation. We shall distinguish: bureaucratic-military authoritarian regimes; those forms of institutionalization of authoritarian regimes that we shall call "organic statism"; the mobilizational authoritarian regimes in postdemocratic societies, of which the Italian Fascism was in many ways an example; postindependence mobilizational authoritarian regimes; and finally the posttotalitarian authoritarian regimes. Certainly these ideal types in the Weberian sense do not fully correspond to any particular regime, since political systems are built in reality by leaders and social forces with contradictory conceptions of the polity and subject to constant changes in emphasis and direction. Regimes are the result of contradictory manifest and latent tendencies in different directions and therefore are all mixed forms. However, some regimes approach more one or another type. In that sense it would be difficult to locate precisely each country even in a particular moment in time within the boxes of our typology. Therefore our table and figure in this paper have to be taken as suggestive of a political attribute space in which regimes can be placed.

Social scientists have attempted to classify the independent states of the world using some operational criteria (Shils, 1960; Almond and Coleman, 1960; Almond and Powell, 1966; Huntington, 1970; Huntington and Moore, 1970; Moore, 1970; Lanning, 1974).[5] Political change, particularly in the unstable states of the Third World, obviously has quickly dated many of those classifications. In addition there has been little consensus on the few theoretical efforts to classify political systems into any more complex typology, largely because there are few systematic collections of data relevant to the dimensions used in formulating the typologies and because the politics of many countries has not been the subject of scholarly research. There is, however, considerable consensus on the countries considered by Dankwart Rustow to be democratic systems and by Robert Dahl to be polyarchies and those characterized as competitive by the contributors to the 1960 review of Politics of the Developing Areas. Many of those studies show that only between one-fourth and one-third of the political systems of the world at any time were political democracies. Robert Dahl, Richard Norling, and Mary Frase Williams (Dahl, 1971, Appendix A, pp. 231–49), on the basis of data from the *Cross Polity Survey* and other sources on eligibility to participate in elections and on the degree of opportunity for public opposition using seven indicators of required conditions, scaled 114 countries into 31 types. On the basis of those data, gathered around 1969, they classified 29 as polyarchies and 6 as near-polyarchies. The list of Dankwart Rustow (1967), which coincides with that of Dahl except for Mexico, Ceylon, Greece, and Colombia, included 31 countries. Both lists omit a few microstates that would qualify as polyarchies.

Among the 25 countries whose population in 1965 was over 20 million people only 8 at the time were considered polyarchies by Dahl and one, Turkey, a near-polyarchy, to which the list of Rustow would add Mexico.[6] If we consider that among those 25 countries Japan, Germany, and Italy for a considerable part of the first half of this century were under nondemocratic governments and that among the 5 largest states in the world only the United States and India have enjoyed continuously democratic rule since their independence, the importance of the study of nondemocratic political systems should be obvious. In fact, in some parts of the world even fewer are democracies. Only 7 countries, mostly small ones, of the 38 African nations that gained independence since 1950 remain multiparty states in which elections are held and parties can campaign. Seventeen of those 38 nations by 1973 had a military chief of state and 64 percent of the 266 million inhabitants in them were under military rule (Young, forthcoming). Even in Europe, excluding the USSR and Turkey, only 16 of 28 states were stable democracies, and 3, Portugal, Greece, and Cyprus, face at this moment an uncertain future. Of the European population west of the Soviet Union, 61.5 percent live under democracies, 4.1 percent live under unstable regimes, and 34.4 percent live under nondemocratic political systems.

There is certainly considerable diversity among democracies—diversity between those like the United States, where there have been continuous popular elections since 1788, and those like the Federal Republic of Germany, established in 1949 after twelve years of Nazi totalitarianism and foreign occupation; between states based on majority rule, like the United Kingdom, and those based on complex arrangements among ethnic religious minorities which combine competitive politics with the unity of the state, as in Lebanon; between highly egalitarian societies, as in Scandinavia, and a country with the inequality of India. Despite all those differences, the political institutions of these countries have many similarities that allow us to consider them democracies. That basic similarity becomes apparent when we consider the heterogeneity in the list of the 20 largest nondemocratic countries. No one would doubt that the Soviet Union, Spain, Ethiopia, and South Africa are politically more different from each other than are the United States and India, to take extreme cases, or to stay within Europe, Spain and East Germany. It shall be our task in this chapter to attempt a conceptualization that will allow us to make some meaningful distinctions among that great variety of political systems that no stretching of the concept would allow us to consider competitive democracies and under which at least half of humanity lives.

Certainly the richest countries, the 24 whose gross national product per capita around 1965 was over 1,000 U.S. dollars, were democracies—with the exception of Czechoslovakia, the Soviet Union, East Germany, Hungary, and the special case of Kuwait; but already among the 16 ranking behind them with over $500 per capita only 7 could be considered stable democracies. We are not therefore dealing only with poor, underdeveloped countries or with countries arrested in their economic development, since among 36 countries whose growth rate was above the mean of 5.1 percent for the period 1960–65 only 12 appear on Dahl's list of 35 polyarchies or near-polyarchies. If we were to take only those with a high per capita growth rate for the same period, that is, over 5 percent, only 2 of 12 countries would be on that list of Dahl.

Therefore, in spite of the significant relationship discovered between the stability of democracy in economically developed countries and the higher probability that those having reached a certain level of economic and social development would be democracies, there is a sufficient number of deviant cases to warrant a separate analysis of types of political systems, social systems, and economic systems. There is no doubt that certain forms of political organization, of legitimation of power, are more likely in certain types of societies and under certain economic conditions than others and that some combinations are highly unlikely. We feel, however, that it is essential to keep those spheres conceptually separated and to formulate distinct typologies of social, economic, and political systems. Unless we do so, important intellectual questions would disappear. We would be unable to ask, What type of social and economic structure is likely to lead with greater probability to the establishment of certain types of regimes and their stability? Nor could we ask, What difference does it make for the social and economic structure and its development to have one or another regime? Is there a greater likelihood of the society and perhaps the economy to develop under one or another type of political system?

Certainly there is no one-to-one relationship between those different aspects of social reality. Democratic governments are certainly compatible with a wide range of social and economic systems, and the same is true for the variety of autocratic regimes. In fact, in only the recent past German society has been ruled by the unstable Weimar democracy, Nazi totalitarianism, and the stable Bonn republic. Certainly the social and economic structures were considerably affected by those different regimes, in addition to other factors, but the political differences were certainly greater than those in the economic and even the social structure. It is for this reason that we shall center our attention on the variety of political systems without including in our conceptualization dimensions more directly relevant for a typology of societies or of economic systems.

We cannot emphasize enough how important such an analytical distinction is for raising meaningful questions about the relationship between polity, society, and economy, to which we should add a fourth aspect, the cultural and religious realm.

Democratic Governments and Nondemocratic Polities

It is relatively easy to define democratic government without implying that the social structure and social relations in a democratic state should enter into the definition.[7] We shall call a political system democratic when it allows the free

formulation of political preferences, through the use of basic freedoms of association, information, and communication, for the purpose of free competition
between leaders to validate at regular intervals by nonviolent means their claim
to rule; a democratic system does this without excluding any effective political
office from that competition or prohibiting any members of the political community from expressing their preference by norms requiring the use of force
to enforce them. The liberal political rights are a requirement for that public
contestation and competition for power and for the expansion of the right to
participate in elections for an ever increasing number of citizens an inevitable
consequence. The requirement of regular intervals excludes from the definition
any system in which the rulers at one point in time might have derived their
legitimacy from support in a free contest but refuse to be accountable at a later
date. It clearly excludes certain plebiscitarian authoritarian regimes, even if
we should accept the honesty and freedom of choice in the original plebiscite.
The requirement that all effective political offices should be directly or indirectly dependent on the election by the citizens excludes those systems in
which a traditional ruler, through inheritance, retains powers not controlled
or mediated by a popularly elected assembly or in which nonsymbolic offices
are for life, like Franco as head of state or Tito as president of the Republic.
A wide range of political freedoms that guarantee the freedom of minorities to
organize and compete peacefully for the support of the people are essential,
even when there are some legal or even de facto limits, for us to state that certain systems are more or less democratic (Dahl, 1971). Nondemocratic regimes,
however, not only impose de facto limits on minority freedoms but establish
generally well-defined legal limits, leaving the interpretation of those laws to
the rulers themselves, rather than to independent objective bodies, and applying them with a wide range of discretion. The requirement that no citizen
should be excluded from participation in elections, if that exclusion requires
the use of force, takes into account the fact that the expansion of citizenship
has been a slow and conflictual process from censitairy suffrage to universal
male suffrage and finally to the inclusion of women and young adults, as pressures developed from those sectors demanding the expansion of suffrage. Systems that at one point in time allowed more or less restricted participation but
refused, using force, to expand it to other groups would be excluded on that
count. South Africa would be a prime example of a political system that decades
ago might have qualified as a democracy but by excluding permanently and
in principle the blacks from the electorate and even depriving the Cape Town
Coloured of their vote has lost that characteristic. Whatever element of democratization the development of internal party democracy in a single-party regime
might represent, the limitation of "citizenship" to the members of a single
party, that is, to those agreeing with certain basic political preferences and
subject to party discipline and exclusion from it, would not qualify the regime
as democratic. Certainly a system with internal party democracy is more demo-

cratic than one without it, one in which the party is ruled by the *Führerprinzip* or "democratic centralism," but the exclusion from participation of citizens unwilling to join the party does not allow us to classify the political system as democratic.

In our definition we have not made any reference to political parties, because in theory it is conceivable that the competition for power could be organized without them, even though we know of no system without political parties which would satisfy our requirements. In theory, competition for leadership could take place among individuals within narrow constituencies, without organizations of some permanence committed to particular principles, aggregating a wide range of issues across many constituencies, which we call parties. This is the *theory of organic or corporative democracy,* which holds that representatives should be elected in primary social groups where people know each other and share common interests, presumably eliminating the need for political parties. In a later section on organic statism we shall discuss in detail the theoretical and empirical difficulties in the creation of a free competition for power in so-called organic democracies and the authoritarian character of such regimes. Therefore, the freedom to form political parties and of parties to compete for power and not a share in power offers a prima facie test of the democratic character of the government. Any system in which a party is de jure granted a special constitutional and legal status and its offices are subject to special party courts and granted special protection by the law, in which other parties have to recognize its leadership and are allowed to participate only insofar as they do not question that preeminent position or have to commit themselves to sustain a certain social-political order (beyond a constitutional framework in which free competition for power at regular intervals can take place by peaceful means), would not qualify. It is fundamental to keep clear the distinction between de facto predominant parties obtaining overwhelming support, election after election at the polls, in competition with other parties, from hegemonic parties in pseudo-multiparty systems. It is on this ground that the distinction between democratic and nondemocratic regimes cannot be made identical with single and multiparty systems. Another criterion often advanced for the distinction between democratic and nondemocratic regimes is that alternation in power provides a presumption of democracy but is not a necessary condition (Sartori, 1974, pp. 199–201).

The criteria mentioned allow an almost unequivocal classification of states as democracies without denying democratic elements to other states or the presence of de facto ademocratic or antidemocratic tendencies in those so classified. Only in a few cases has disagreement among the scholars about the facts about the freedom for political groups and competition among them lead to doubts.[8] Further evidence for the validity of the distinction is the resistance of nondemocratic regimes that claim to be democracies to introducing just the elements listed here and the ideological contortions into which they go to justify their reluctance. The fact that no democracy has been transformed into a non-democratic regime without changing one or more of the characteristics listed is further evidence. Only in rare cases has a nontraditional regime been transformed into a democracy without constitutional discontinuity and the use of force to remove the incumbents. Turkey after World War II (Karpat, 1959; Weiker, 1963 and 1973), Mexico (if we accept the arguments of those who want to classify it as a democracy), and perhaps Argentina after the 1973 election are cases in point. The borderline between nondemocratic and democratic regimes is therefore a fairly rigid one that cannot be crossed by slow and imperceptible evolution but practically always requires a violent break, anticonstitutional acts, a military coup, a revolution, or foreign intervention. By comparison, the line separating totalitarian systems from other nondemocratic systems is much more diffuse, and there are obvious cases in which systems lost the characteristics that would allow us to define them as totalitarian in any meaningful sense of the term without becoming democracies and in a way that does not allow the observer to say exactly when and how the change took place. Despite our emphasis on the importance of retaining the distinction of totalitarian and other nondemocratic types of polity, these have more in common with each other than with democratic governments, justifying nondemocratic as a more general comprehensive category. It is those regimes that constitute our subject.

A Note on Dictatorship

One term often used to designate nondemocratic and nontraditional legitimate governments, both in the literature (Sartori, 1962b), and common usage, is dictatorship. From its historical origins in Rome as *dictator rei gerundae causa,* designating an extraordinary office limited and foreseen in the constitution for emergency situations—limited in time to six months, which could not be extended, or in function to carry out a particular task—the term dictatorship has become a loosely used term of opprobrium. It is no accident, as Carl Schmitt (1928) and Sartori (1962b, pp. 416–19) have noted, that even Garibaldi and Marx should still have used it without that negative connotation.

If there is a point in conserving the term for scientific usage today, it should be limited to describe emergency rule that suspends or violates temporarily the constitutional norms about the accession to an exercise of authority. Constitutional dictatorship is the type of rule that is established on the basis of constitutional provisions for situations of emergency, especially in the face of widespread disorder or war, extending the power of some offices of the state or extending their mandate beyond the date it should be returned to the electorate through a decision taken by constitutionally legitimate authority. Such an extraconstitutional authority does not necessarily have to be anticonstitutional, that is, a permanent change of political institutions. But it might well serve to defend them in a crisis situation. The ambivalent character of the expression "constitutional dictatorship" has led Sartori and others to prefer the term "crisis government" (Rossiter, 1948). In fact, the revolutionary committees that have assumed power after the breakdown of traditional rule or authoritarian regimes with the purpose of calling free elections to instore democratic regimes, as long as they have remained provisional government without the ratification by an electorate, can be considered dictatorships in this narrow sense of the term. Many military coups against traditional rulers, autocratic governments, or democracies in the process of breaking down, due to efforts to assure a fraudulent continuity in power through manipulation or delay of elections, gain broad support on the basis of the commitment, initially honestly felt by some of the leaders, to reestablish free competitive democracy. The difficulty in the extrication process of military rule, so well analyzed by Samuel Finer (1962) and Huntington (1968, pp. 231–37), accounts for the fact that more often than not such military rule creates authoritarian regimes rather than assures the return to democracy. Overt foreign *domination* for the purpose of establishing the conditions for democracy by ousting from power nondemocratic rulers would be another very special case. Japan, Austria, and West Germany after World War II would be unique examples, since certainly the Allied High Commanders and Commissioners were not democratic rulers of those societies (Gimbel, 1968; Hirschman and Montgomery, 1968). But their success might also have been due to quite unique circumstances in those societies not likely to be found everywhere. In this restricted sense we are talking only about those dictatorships that Carl Schmitt (1928) has called *"Kommissarische Diktatur"* as distinct from the ones he called "sovereign dictatorships."

In the world of political realities, however, the return to constitutional democracy after the break with democratic legitimacy, even by so-called constitutional dictatorship or by the intervention of monarchs or armies as moderating power in emergency situations, is uncertain. One exception is perhaps national-unity governments in case of war, when all major parties agree on postponing elections or avoiding real electoral competition to assure almost unanimous support to the government to pursue a united war effort. Dictatorship as extraordinary emergency power limiting civil liberties temporarily and/or increasing the power of certain offices becomes hard to distinguish from other types of autocratic rule when it lasts beyond a well-defined situation. The political scientist cannot ignore the statements of those assuming such powers even when he or she might have doubts about their honesty or their realism in their expectations of devolving power to the people, because those statements are likely to have permanent consequences for the legitimacy of nondemocratic rule so established. The political scientist cannot decide *a priori* but only *ex post facto* that the rule of an individual or group was actually a dictatorship in this narrow sense of the term as derived from its historical Roman meaning. Dictatorships of this type are more often than not bridges toward other forms of autocratic rule, and it is no accident that the kings of the Balkan states that broke with constitutional rule should have been considered royal dictatorships rather than a return to absolute monarchies. Once the continuity of traditional legitimacy has been given up for democratic forms, the return to it seems to be impossible. Dictatorship as interim, extraordinary authority all too often is perpetuated in more or less institutionalized forms of authoritarian rule. Let us not forget that already the Roman constitutional institution was subverted and transformed into a more permanent authoritarian rule when Silla became in 82 B.C. *dictator reipublicae constituendae* and Caesar became in 48 B.C. dictator for a limited time and in 46 B.C. for ten years. Caesarism has been since then a term for the subversion of constitutional government by an outstanding leader.

We shall reserve the term dictatorship for interim crisis government that has not institutionalized itself and represents a break with the institutionalized rules about accession to and exercise of power of the preceding regime, be it democratic, traditional, or authoritarian. The temporary suspension of those rules according to rules foreseen in the constitution of a regime shall be called crisis government or constitutional dictatorship.

II. TOTALITARIAN SYSTEMS

Toward a Definition of Totalitarianism

In view of the central place in the study of modern noncompetitive democratic regimes of totalitarianism it seems useful to start with some of the already classical definitions of totalitarian systems and, after presenting them, attempt to push our knowledge somewhat further along the lines derived from the criticism they have been subject to (Jänicke, 1971; Friedrich, 1954; Friedrich and Brzezinski, 1965; S. Neumann, 1942; Aron, 1968; Buchheim, 1968a; Schapiro, 1972a, 1972b; Seidel and Jenkner, 1968). Carl Friedrich has recently reformulated the original descriptive definition he and Z. K. Brzezinski (1965) had formulated, in the following way:

> The features which distinguish this regime from other and older autocracies as well as from heterocracies are six in number. They are to recall what by now is a fairly generally accepted set of facts: (1) a totalist ideology; (2) a single party commited to this ideology and usually led by one man, the dictator; (3) a fully developed secret police and three kinds of monopoly or more precisely monopolistic control; namely, that of (a) mass communications, (b) operational weapons, and (c) all organizations including economic ones, thus involving a centrally planned economy . . . . We might add that these six features could if greater simplicity is desired be grouped into three, a totalist ideology, a party reinforced by a secret police and a monopoly of the three major forms of interpersonal confrontation in industrial mass society. Such monopoly is not necessarily exercised by the party. This should

be stressed at the outset in order to forestall a misunderstanding which has arisen in some of the critical commentaries in my earlier work. The important point is that such a monopolistic control is in the hands of whatever elite rules the particular society and thereby constitutes its regime. (Friedrich, 1969, p. 126)

Brzezinski has offered a more essentialist definition emphasizing the ultimate end of such systems when he writes:

Totalitarianism is a new form of government falling into the general classification of dictatorship, a system in which technologically advanced instruments of political power are wielded without restraint by centralized leadership of an elite movement for the purpose of affecting a total social revolution, including the conditioning of man on the basis of certain arbitrary ideological assumptions, proclaimed by the leadership in an atmosphere of coerced unanimity of the entire population. (Brzezinski, 1962)

Franz Neumann (1957, pp. 233–56) has provided us with a similar set of defining characteristics.

Let us stress that in these definitions the terror element—the role of the police, of coercion—is not central as, for example, in the work of Hannah Arendt (1966). In fact, it could be argued that a totalitarian system could be based on the identification of a very large part of the population with the rulers, the population's active involvement in political organizations controlled by them and at the service of their goals, and use of diffused social control based on voluntary, manipulated involvement and a mixture of rewards and fears in a relatively closed society, as long as the rulers could count on the loyalty of the armed forces. In some respects, communist China has approached this type of totalitarianism, and the Khrushchev experience of a populist rationalization of party control described by Paul Cocks (1970) would fit such a model.

Explicitly or implicitly those definitions suggest a tendency toward the destruction of the line between state and society and the emergence of "total" politicization of society by political organizations, generally the party and its affiliates. However, this dimension that differentiates totalitarian systems from various types of authoritarian regimes and particularly from democratic governments is unlikely to be fully realized and, consequently, the problem of tension between society and political system, while reduced, is far from disappearing under such systems. The shaping of the individual, the internalization by the mass of the citizens of the ideology, the realization of the "new man" of which ideologists talk are obviously even more unlikely, even when few social systems, except religions, have gone as far in this direction as the totalitarian systems.

The dimensions that we have to retain as necessary to characterize a system as totalitarian are an ideology, a single mass party and other mobilizational organizations, and concentrated power in an individual and his collaborators or a small group that is not accountable to any large constituency and cannot be dislodged from power by institutionalized, peaceful means. Each of those elements can be found separately in other types of nondemocratic systems and only their simultaneous presence makes a system totalitarian. This means that not all single-party systems are totalitarian, that no system in which there exists a fair competition for power between freely created parties can be totalitarian, and that no nondemocratic system without a single party, or more specifically an active single party, can be considered totalitarian. As Friedrich admits in his revised version, it is not essential that ultimate power or the largest amount of power should be found in the party organization, even when it seems highly improbable that such a single mass party and the bureaucracy controlling it should not be among the most powerful institutions in the society, at least in relationship to its members and to the common citizen.

There are certainly dictators—Caesaristic leaders, small oligarchies like military juntas, or coalitions of elites within different institutional realms not accountable to the members of their organizations and institutions—whose power we would not call totalitarian. Unless their power is exercised in the name of an ideology guided to a greater or lesser degree by some central ideas, or *Weltanschauung*, and unless they use some form of mass organization and participation of members of the society beyond the armed forces and a police to impose their rule, we cannot speak of a totalitarian system but, as we shall see later, of authoritarian regimes. Whatever its unity, infighting might exist in the top leadership around and under the top leader and between organizations created by the top leadership. Such group politics does not emerge from the society or take place between institutions or organizations that existed before taking of power. The conflicting men, factions, or organizations do not derive their power from structures of the society that are not strictly political, even when those engaged in such struggles for power might have closer links with some sectors of society than with others. In this sense it seems impossible to speak of class conflict in a Marxist sense in totalitarian systems. The initial power positions from which the competitors attempt to expand their base by linking with the diversity of interests in the society are part of the political system— political organizations like the party, affiliated mass organizations, regional organizations of the party, the party militia, or government and police bureaucracies. In stable totalitarian systems preexisting institutions like business organizations, the church, or even the army play a secondary role in the struggle for power, and to the extent that they participate they are brought in to support one or another leader or group within the political elite. Their leadership is not a legitimate contender for political power but only for influence on particular decisions and rarely capable of veto power. In this respect, the subordination of the military authority is one of the distinctive characteristics of totalitarian systems in contrast to other nondemocratic systems. To this day, no totalitarian system has been overthrown or changed fundamentally by the intervention of the armed forces, even when in crisis moments one or another faction might have reinforced its power by the support of the military.

Only the highly political People's Liberation Army (PLA) in China (Joffe, 1965, 1971; Pollack, 1974; Schurmann, 1968, pp. 12–13; Gittings, 1967) and the army in Cuba (Domínguez, 1974; Dumont, 1970) might have played such a role. It is only in a very relative sense that we can speak of particular leaders or factions or bureaucracies within the power structure as representing the managers, the farmers, linguistic or cultural groups, the intellectuals, and so on. Whenever leaders or groups represent to some degree the interests of such sectors of the society, they are not accountable to a constituency, do not derive their power base fundamentally from it, generally are not recruited from it, and often are not even co-opted as leaders emerging from such social groups. The destruction or at least decisive weakening of all the institutions, organizations, and interest groups existing before a new elite takes political power and organizes its own political structures is one of the distinguishing characteristics of totalitarian systems compared with other nondemocratic systems. In this sense we can speak of monopoly of power, monism, but it would be a great mistake to take this concentration of power in the political sphere and in the hands of the people and the organizations created by the political leadership as monolithic. The pluralism of totalitarian systems is not social pluralism but political pluralism within the ruling political elite. To give one example: the conflicts between the SA and the SS, the DAF (Labor Front) and the party, the four-year plan organization of Goehring and the Organization Todt of Speer, were conflicts within the Nazi elite and between its organizations. They certainly looked for and found allies among the military, the bureaucracy, and sectors of business, but it would be a great mistake to consider any of those leaders or organizations as representatives of the pre-Nazi structures of German society. The same could probably be said about the struggles among factions within the Politbureau or the Central Committee after the death of Stalin.

However, it might be argued that in a totalitarian system that is fully established and in power for a long time, members of the political organizations, particularly the party, become identified through a process of differentiation and division of labor with particular policy areas and are likely to identify increasingly with particular economic or territorial interests and represent their aspirations and points of view in the formulation of specific policies, particularly in peacetime, when no single goal is all-important, and at the time of succession or leadership crisis. Once basic decisions about the nature of the political system have been settled, preexisting social structures destroyed or decisively weakened, and dominant leaders displaced, a transformation of the system allowing a pluralism limited in scope and autonomy is not unlikely to take place. At that point, the degree of vitality of the ideology and the party or other organizations committed to its dominance and the strength of the leaders at the top will be decisive in characterizing the system as some variety of totalitarianism or as being transformed into something different. Certainly such transformations within totalitarian systems are not without tension and strain and therefore may be characterized by cyclical changes rather than a smooth continuous evolution.

Any typology of totalitarian systems will have to take into account the relative importance of ideology, party and mass organizations, and the political leader or leadership groups that have appropriated power—and the cohesion or factionalization of the leadership. In addition, it will have to analyze how those three main dimensions link with the society and its structure, history, and cultural traditions. Different totalitarian systems or phases of the same system might be characterized as more ideological, populist, or bureaucratic, depending on the character of the single party, and more charismatic, oligarchical, or even feudal, depending on the structure of the dominant center of power. The absence of any of those three factors or their weakening beyond a certain point will fundamentally change the nature of the system. However, the variety among those three dimensions certainly allows for quite different types of totalitarian systems.

It is the combination of those three dimensions that accounts for many of the other characteristics we are more likely to find in totalitarian than other nondemocratic systems. However, some of those other characteristics are neither necessary nor sufficient to characterize a system as totalitarian and can be found in other types of political systems.

In summary, I shall consider a system totalitarian when the following characteristics apply.

1. There is a monistic but not monolithic center of power, and whatever pluralism of institutions or groups exists derives its legitimacy from that center, is largely mediated by it, and is mostly a political creation rather than an outgrowth of the dynamics of the preexisting society.

2. There is an exclusive, autonomous, and more or less intellectually elaborate ideology with which the ruling group or leader, and the party serving the leaders, identify and which they use as a basis for policies or manipulate to legitimize them. The ideology has some boundaries beyond which lies heterodoxy that does not remain unsanctioned. The ideology goes beyond a particular program or definition of the boundaries of legitimate political action to provide, presumably, some ultimate meaning, sense of historical purpose, and interpretation of social reality.

3. Citizen participation in and active mobilization for political and collective social tasks are encouraged, demanded, rewarded, and channeled through a single party and many monopolistic secondary groups. Passive obedience

and apathy, retreat into the role of "parochials" and "subjects," character-istic of many authoritarian regimes, are considered undesirable by the rulers.

This third characteristic brings a totalitarian society closer to the ideal and even the reality of most democracies and basically differentiates it from most "nontotalitarian nondemocratic systems." It is this participation and the sense of participation that democratic observers of totalitarian systems often find so admirable and that make them think that they are faced with a democracy, even a more perfect democracy than one in which citizens get involved in pub-lic issues only or mainly at election time. However, the basic difference between participation in a mobilizational regime and in a democracy is that, in the former, in each realm of life for each purpose there is only one possible channel for participation and the overall purpose and direction is set by one center, which defines the legitimate goals of those organizations and ultimately con-trols them.

It is the constant feedback between the dominant, more or less monistic center of decision making, undergirded by the ideological commitments that guide it or are used or manipulated by it, and these processes of participation for those ideological purposes within those controlled organizations that char-acterizes a totalitarian system.

It should be possible to derive other characteristics frequently stressed in describing totalitarian systems from the three we just sketched, and we shall do so in discussing in more detail some of the main scholarly contributions to the study of specific totalitarian systems. Here we might give a few basic examples. The tense relationship between intellectuals and artists and the political authorities,[9] in addition to being the result of the personal idiosyncrasies of rulers like Hitler and Stalin, is certainly the result of the emphasis on an ideol-ogy and the exclusion by the commitment to it of other systems of ideas or the fear of the questioning of the values implicit in the ideology, particularly the collective and public goals versus individual and private ones. Privatized, inner-oriented man is a latent threat, and certainly many forms of aesthetic expres-sion search for that orientation. The same is true for the exacerbation of the normal conflicts between church and state to conflicts between religion and politics.[10] The importance of ideology also has positive aspects, in the sense of making education a highly valued activity, making selective cultural efforts and their mass diffusion highly desirable. This is, in contrast to most traditional autocracies, with the exception of religious indoctrination in religious autocra-cies and scientific and technological education in secular autocracies. Propa-ganda, education, training of cadres, intellectual elaboration of the ideology, scholarship inspired by the ideology, rewards for intellectuals identified with the system are more likely to be important in totalitarian than in other non-democratic systems. If we ignore the limited content of that effort, the limitations or denial of freedom, we find here a certain convergence with democratic systems, in which the mass participation in political life requires also mass education and mass communications and assigns to intellectuals an important, even when not always welcome, role.

The concentration of power in the leader and his collaborators or a distinct group of powerholders, formed by their joint participation in the struggle to gain power and create the regime, their socialization in the political organizations, or their co-optation from other sectors (keeping in mind criteria of loyalty and/or identification with the ideology), necessarily limits the autonomy of other organizations like industrial enterprises, professional groups, the armed forces, the intellectuals, and so on. The sharing to greater or lesser degree of the belief in the ideology, of the identification with its symbols, and the conviction that decisions should be legitimized or at least rationalized in terms of the ideology, separates this group from those more skeptical or disinterested in the ideology and from those who, because of their calling, like the intellectuals, are most likely to question those ideas. However, it also brings them close to those who, without challenging their power, are willing to elaborate the ideology. The element of elitism so often stressed in the analysis of totalitarian systems is a logical consequence of this search for a monopoly of power. It is also a source of the bitterness of many conflicts within the elite and the ostracism or purge of those who lose the struggle for power. Power, more than in democratic societies, becomes a zero-sum game.

The commitment to ideology, the desire for monopolistic control, and the fear of losing power certainly explain the propensity toward coercive methods in such systems and the likelihood for continuing terror. Therefore, terror, particularly within the elite rather than against opponents or even potential opponents to the system, distinguishes totalitarian systems from other non-democratic systems. The size of the society, stressed by Hannah Arendt, and the degree of modernization in terms of technology linked with industrialization, stressed by other scholars, are not as important as ideological zeal in explaining the drive for positive commitment rather than apathy of subjects or just external conformity of bureaucrats.

The nature and role of the single party is obviously the most important variable when we come to analyze in behavioral terms the impact of totalitarian systems on different societies. The importance assigned to the party organization, the specialized political organizations emerging from the party, and the mass organizations linked with it account for many of the basic characteristics of such systems. Foremost, their capacity to penetrate the society, to be present and influential in many institutional realms, to mobilize people for large-scale tasks on a voluntary or pseudo voluntary basis rather than just for material incentives and rewards allows such systems to carry out important changes with limited resources and therefore to serve as instruments for certain types of economic and social development. It also gives them a certain democratic character, in the sense of offering to those willing to participate (accepting the basic goals of the leadership rather than advancing alternative goals) a chance for active participation and a sense of involvement. Despite the bureaucratic character of the state and of many organizations and even the party, the mass membership in the party and in related sponsored organizations can give meaning, purpose, and a sense of participation to many citizens. In this respect, totalitarian systems are very different from many other nondemocratic systems—authoritarian regimes—in which the rulers rely fundamentally on a staff of bureaucrats, experts, and policemen, distinct and separate from the rest of the people, who have little or no chance to feel as active participants in the society and polity beyond their personal life and their work.

The party organization and the many minor leadership positions in it give many people a chance to exercise some share in power, sometimes over people who in other hierarchies of the society would be their superiors.[11] This obviously introduces an element of equality undermining other stratified structures of the society while introducing a new and different type of inequality. An active party organization with members involved in its activities also increases enormously the possibilities of control and latent coercion of those who are unwilling to join or are excluded. Many of the energies that in a democratic society are channeled into political life, but also into a myriad of voluntary associations that take an interest in collective goods, are used by totalitarian systems. Much of the idealism associated with collective orientation rather than self-orientation (idealism that in the past went into religious organizations and now in liberal democratic society goes into voluntary groups) is likely to be found in the party and its sponsored organizations, together, obviously, with the opportunism of those attracted by a variety of rewards and access to power or the hope of having it. This mobilizational aspect is central to totalitarian systems and absent in many, if not most, other nondemocratic systems. Some of the kind of people who in a totalitarian system become zealous activists on many of the tasks assigned to them by the leadership in other nondemocratic systems would be passive subjects only interested in their private narrow goals or alienated in view of the lack of opportunities for any participation in efforts directed at changing their societies. Certainly much of the attraction that the totalitarian model has comes from this participatory mobilizational dimension of the party and the mass organizations. But also much of the alienation and negative feelings about such systems are due to the absence of choice for the average citizen between alternative goals for the society and the limited freedom or lack of freedom in choosing the leadership of such organizations due to the bureaucratic character derived from norms like the leadership principle or democratic centralism.

Other characteristics often noted in describing totalitarian systems, like their expansionist tendencies, are much more difficult to derive from their more central characteristics. There is obviously an indirect relationship, since the emphasis on an exclusive ideology makes the persistence of alternative ideologies and belief systems a latent threat. However, much will depend on the content of the ideology, and certainly the character and direction of the expansionism will be shaped more by that than by other structural features.[12]

A search for conformity, a proscription of most forms of dissidence, particularly those that can reach larger segments of the population and that involve any attempt of organization, a reduction of the private realm, and considerable amount of half-free if not enforced participation are almost inevitable in totalitarian systems. The massive and/or arbitrary use of terror as we find in the concentration camps, the purges, the show trials, the collective punishments of groups or communities do not seem essential to a totalitarian system. However, we can say that it was not accidental that some of those forms appeared under Hitler and Stalin, that they were distinctive and widespread as they have not been in any democratic system, and that they should have been qualitatively and quantitatively different from other nondemocratic systems, except in their periods of consolidation in power either during or immediately after a civil war. Terror is neither a necessary nor sufficient characteristic of totalitarian systems, but there seems to be a greater probability that it should appear under such systems than under others, and certain of its forms seem to be distinctive of certain types of totalitarian systems. Some authors have rightly spoken of totalitarianism without terror.

Early studies of totalitarianism, particularly Sigmund Neumann's (1942) *Permanent Revolution,* emphasized the role of a leader. The fascist commitment to the *Führerprinzip* and the exaltation of the *Duce,* together with the cult of personality around Stalin, certainly made this an obvious element in a definition of totalitarian systems. However, in recent years we have seen systems that on many counts are still totalitarian in which we do not find such an undisputed leader at the top or a comparable cult or personification of leadership. On the other hand, there are many nondemocratic systems that would not fit into the type we have delineated above in which a single leader occupies a comparable place and the cult of personality has gone as far. Therefore we can legitimately say that the appearance of a single leader who concentrates vast amounts of power in his person, is the object of a cult of personality, and claims a charismatic authority and to a greater or lesser extent enjoys it among the party members and the populace at large is highly probable in totalitarian systems but not inevitable or necessary for their stability. Succession crises that some scholars thought threatened the stability and even survival of such regimes have not led to their downfall or breakdown even when they have been very critical for them.[13] It could be argued that the emphasis on personal leadership is characteristic of totalitarian systems of the fascist type, and this is certainly true of Italy and Germany as well as of some of the minor fascist regimes, but the role of Stalin in the Soviet Union shows that it was not a feature exclusive to fascist regimes. Obviously if we should argue, as some dissident communists and some left fascists do, that Stalin was the Russian functional equivalent to fascism, the difficulty would disappear. But this seems a sophistic solution. At this point we can say only that there is a higher probability that such leadership will appear in totalitarian systems than in other nondemocratic systems. Changes in the relationship between leadership, ideology, and organized participation are the variables likely to offer the best clue for the construction of the typology of totalitarian systems and for an understanding of the processes of consolidation, stability, and change—and perhaps breakdown—of such systems. It might be overambitious to attempt to formulate some propositions about those interrelationships among those relatively independent variables for any totalitarian system; and certainly only a theoretical-empirical analysis of particular types and even unique cases will facilitate such a theoretical effort at a higher level of abstraction. With all the risks involved, we shall attempt to sketch some directions in which such an analysis might move. Let us stress from the beginning that the relationships are likely to be two way without any of them being ever fully unidirectional, since unidirectional relationships would change decisively the nature of the system and bring into question the independent character of each of the variables, but also that the flow of influence of the variables might be stronger in one or another direction.

Ideology and Totalitarianism

As some of the scholars have noted, totalitarian systems might be considered ideocracies or logocracies, and Inkeles (1954) has developed the notion of totalitarian mystique to convey the importance of ideology as a powerful independent variable in such systems.[14] There can be no doubt that totalitarian leaders, individuals or groups, in contrast to other nondemocratic rulers, derive much of their sense of mission, their legitimation, and often very specific policies from their commitment to some holistic conception of man and society. Ideologies vary much in the richness and complexity of their content and in the degree to which they are closed, fixed, and can be action-related. The study of ideologies as systems of ideas, of meanings, and of the internal logical or emotional connections between those ideas is obviously essential to understanding different totalitarian systems. Such a study can be done from different perspectives: intellectual-cultural history, sociology of knowledge, and social psychology. The initial commitment of a ruler or ruling group to an ideology imposes constraints, excluding a greater or smaller number of alternative values, goals, and styles of thinking, and sets a framework limiting the range of alternative policies. There can be no question that an intellectually elaborate ideology like Marxism provides a more complex and heterogenous as well as rational starting point for ideological elaboration than the more simple, emotional, and less intellectually fixated elements of fascist ideology. Some of those who question the usefulness of the totalitarian approach to the study of fascist regimes and of Nazism do so because they question the ideological character of those movements reducing their ideas to those of their founders and rulers and engaging in purely pragmatic power seeking and opportunist manipulation of symbols. The existence of a printed and fixed and to some degree unambiguous corpus of writing of Marx, Engels, and Lenin, which can be doctored, partly suppressed, and reinterpreted but not fully abandoned, certainly differs from those regimes in which the leader or group in power claims identification with much less elaborate ideas or is in the process of giving ideological content to his rule. The autonomy or heteronomy in the control of ideological formulation is obviously a key to the autonomy and stability of different totalitarian systems and is one of the sources of conflict between them when they attempt to derive their legitimacy from identification with an ideological corpus. The hypothesis may be advanced that a fully autonomous totalitarian system cannot exist without almost full control over the formulation or interpretation of the ideological heritage or content. In this respect different fascist regimes found themselves in a better position in relation to the hegemonic powers in their camp than did the Eastern European communists, and the regimes of China and Cuba found themselves in a better position than those of other minor communist states. The heteronomous control of the ideological content of Catholic thought by a universal church and specifically by the Pope is one of the most serious obstacles to the creation of a truly totalitarian system by nondemocratic rulers claiming to implement Catholic social doctrine in their states. Among other factors this is one that has prevented the Austrian "clerical-fascists" and the regimes of Franco and Salazar from pursuing further the path toward totalitarianism (Linz, 1964, p. 303).

Ideologies in totalitarian systems are a source of legitimacy, a source of the sense of mission of a leader or a ruling group, and it is not surprising that one should speak of charisma of the leader or the party, for at least important segments of their societies, on the basis of that element. Many of the differences between systems or within the same system over time are to be understood in terms of the relationship of people in those positions to the ideology. However, while the ideology imposes some constraints, more or less narrow, on the rulers and their actions, the relationship is not one-sided, and much of the effort in such systems goes into the manipulation, adaptation, and selective interpretation of the ideological heritage, particularly in the second generation of rulers. Only a complete change in the relationship to the ideology—its substitution by pragmatic policy formulation and the acceptance of heteronomous sources for ideas and central policies, of evidence clearly and explicitly in conflict with the ideology—will lead to changes away from the totalitarian model. The ruling group might very well reach the conclusion that a fixed ideology limits its choices too much and that a scholastic reinterpretation of the texts can go only so far, but the fact that a simplified and vulgarized version of the ideologies has been central to the indoctrination of the middle levels of cadres of the single mass party and even the membership will certainly make it difficult to abandon certain policies and sometimes create real crises of legitimacy. The autonomy and importance of the party organization compared to the personal power of the leader or a small oligarchy is to some extent a function of the importance of the commitment to the ideology. Inversely, the constraining character of the ideological commitments for the ruling group is likely to be directly related to the active life of the party—intraparty discussion, elaboration of party thought, cadre training activities, agitprop activities, and so on. Important ideological changes rather than just manipulation of the ideology require some activation of the party structure and thereby impose pressures on the ruling group, contribute to crises within it, and might lead to important changes in its composition. Obviously, changes in the relationship between the ruling group or leader and the party organization, like those achieved by Stalin as first secretary, also make possible changes in the ideology and the displacement of those in the ruling group who had devoted their energies to the intellectual elaboration of the ideology and policies derived from it rather than to the development of an organizational base. The displacement and elimination of the original Bolshevik intellectual ideologists by the apparatchiki identified with Stalin certainly contributed to the debasement of the Marxist-Leninist ideological heritage. This process had some interesting parallels in fascist regimes, with the displacement of Rosenberg by Himmler and Bormann and of Gentile and Bottai by Starace. Such processes are not without consequences for the system, since the capacity to mobilize the loyalties of intellectuals, students, and young idealistic activists in the party and the mass organizations is to some degree a function of the capacity for creative ideological development as well as for continuity. This might account for waves of ideological fervor and with them mobilization of new members in some sectors of the regime. The intellectual elaborations sponsored by the SS, often neglected by scholars, might be a good example. The simultaneous weakening and ossification of the ideology and the party organization obviously tend to isolate the ruling group, weaken the dynamism of the society, and create a certain power vacuum that tends to be filled by more coercive bureaucratic control and the reliance on a more praetorian police. Ultimately this could lead to the transformation of a totalitarian system into other forms of authoritarianism.

The Totalitarian Party

The unique syndrome of totalitarian political systems resulting from the importance of ideology, the tendency toward a monistic center of power, and the emphasis on mass participation and mobilization finds its purest expression in the totalitarian party, its dependent organizations and affiliates, and the functions they perform in the society. The totalitarian party, as a unique type of organization, distinguishes most clearly the modern forms of autocracy from any traditional absolutist regime and from a great variety of other nondemocratic governments. Mussolini was right when he wrote: "The party that governs a nation totalitarianly is a new fact in history; similarities and comparisons are impossible" (Aquarone, 1965, p. 577).[15] In the mid-thirties Mihail Manoilesco (1938), a Rumanian scholar and cabinet member sympathetic to authoritarian regimes, wrote one of the first comparative analyses of single parties, including, together with the fascist parties that enjoyed his sympathies, the Communist party of the Soviet Union and the Turkish Republican party. The index of his book reflects some of the permanent intellectual problems in the study of such parties: the ideological-historical context in which they are born, their functions in the process of taking power and consolidating it, in established regimes the complex relationship between party, state, and nation, their organizational characteristics, and their special legal status. At that time there were six single ruling parties. Today their number has multiplied manifold and we are conscious that there are many different types of established single-party systems. In addition, in a number of communist countries, including China, one cannot speak of one-party systems but of dominant leading parties and subordinate parties under their aegis. The theoretical model of the totalitarian party has been widely imitated, but only under very special circumstances can we say that the single party is a totalitarian party. In many democracies we find parties that more or less explicitly have the goal of doing away with party competition. Such parties often by extension have been called totalitarian but we feel this is a misleading use of the term, since only after taking power can such a party realize its ambitions. In fact, it is debatable whether a party that shares an ideology and certain organizational characteristics with totalitarian parties would not be forced to function differently if it came to power in a stable democracy and might even become a loyal opposition or a legitimate participant in democratic politics.

The concept of the totalitarian party itself reflects some of the inherent tensions and ambivalence of the term, and it is no accident that some of the parties, particularly of the fascist and nationalist type and including many Nazi theoreticians, tried to substitute the word "party" by others like "movement." Party underlines that the organization is only part of the political life, while the adjective totalitarian indicates the more or less utopian goal of encompassing the whole individual, the whole society. Communist parties based on the Leninist conception of the vanguard party have always emphasized this part character. For example, Article 126 of the Stalin Constitution:

> The citizens of the USSR are guaranteed the right to unite in public organizations, trade unions, cooperative societies, youth organizations, sport and defense organizations, cultural, technical, and scientific societies. And the most active and politically conscious citizens in the ranks of the working class, working peasants, and working intelligentsia voluntarily unite in the Communist Party of the Soviet Union which is the vanguard of the working people in their struggle to build a Communist society and is the leading

core of all organizations of the working people, both societal and governmental. (Meyer, 1965, p. 107)

The party is therefore a minority, a vanguard in communist terminology, an elite in that of the fascist. In most communist countries it represents somewhat less than 5 percent of the population, and even where it is larger than that it does not get close to 25 percent.[16] Totalitarian parties fit the definition of party of Max Weber:

> The term "party" will be employed to designate associations, membership in which rests on formally free recruitment. The end to which its activity is devoted is to secure power within an organization for its leaders in order to attain ideal or material advantages for its active members. These advantages may consist in the realization of certain objective policies or the attainment of personal advantages, or both. (1968, Vol. 1, p. 284)

The goal of power within an organization highlights a major problem in the study of totalitarian parties, the relationship between party and state. In spite of all the bureaucratization of parties, the oligarchic continuity of leadership, and even the legally privileged status of its leaders and members, parties are deliberately distinct from the organization of a state, its offices and bureaucracy, whatever degree of overlap between their leadership. In the USSR ministers of the Soviet government have frequently not been members of the highest bodies of the Politbureau and even the Central Committee, and men highly placed in the party have never held government office. Fraenkel (1941), in his analysis of early Nazi rule, even when emphasizing some different aspects, spoke of the dual state. In principle, therefore, the totalitarian party retains the function of expressing the demands, aspirations, interests of the society or particular classes of society. In this sense it is a modern phenomenon, inconceivable without the duality of state and society. Despite the tendency of the totalitarian party to become a closed group, incorporated by law into the administrative staff, the formal criterion of voluntary solicitation and adherence distinguishes parties from state bureaucracies, modern or patrimonial, and from most modern armies. Membership involves whatever the psychic, social, and economic pressures to join there are, for example for civil servants, a commitment, a voluntary identification. It is no accident that a member of the Hitler cabinet would for reasons of conscience refuse even an honorary membership in the Nationalsozialistische Deutsche Arbeiterpartei (NSDAP) (Peterson, 1969, p. 33).[17] This part character contrasts with the totalitarian goal expressed in a 1958 edition of the official *Primer of Soviet Philosophy:*

> Only the party expressing the interest of the entire nation embodying its collective understanding, uniting in its ranks the finest individuals of the nation, is qualified and called to control the work of all organizations and organs of power. The party realizes the leadership of all state and public

organizations through its members who work in these organizations and who enter into their governing organ. (Schurmann, 1968, p. 109)

Hitler (1924–26) in *Mein Kampf* expressed this ambition of totality of the party in this revealing text:

> Every philosophy of life, even if it is a thousand times correct and of highest benefit to humanity, will remain without significance for the practical shaping of a people's life as long as its principles have not become the banner of the fighting movement which for its part in turn will be a party as long as its activity has not found completion in the victory of its ideas and its party dogmas have not become the new state principles of a people's community. (p. 380)

Ideas valid for the whole community or a class cannot be realized without a militant organization. Significantly, the party had to conquer and retain the power in the state. The state is an indispensable means for its realization but no totalitarian leader conceives that the state could realize his utopia. It is significant that only in Italy, where the Fascists tended, after taking control of the state, to subordinate the party organization and its leaders to Fascist state officials and where the corporativist ideology offered an alternative way to organize society, the possibility of dissolving the party would be discussed briefly. Despite the constant use by the Fascists of the term totalitarian, the Fascist conception of the party as an organization of the political administrative forces of the regime, as a voluntary civil militia, at the order of the *Duce,* at the service of the Fascist state, tended to undermine the totalitarian conception of the party and make it more comparable to the many single parties created by a ruler or ruling group from above.[18]

The totalitarian party is a mass party. It is not just an organization of officeholders based on the co-optation by a ruling group of officials, local notables, army officers in civilian garb, and perhaps some functionaries and a few office-seeking members, as many single parties in authoritarian regimes can accurately be described. It is also not an organization based on indirect membership in trade unions, cooperatives, professional associations, and so forth. Certainly, totalitarian parties have a close relationship with such functional organizations. The NSDAP, for example, made a clear distinction between the party as a cadre and membership organization, its divisions (*Gliederungen*), the Hitler Youth, (*Jugend*), the SA, the SS, and the large number of affiliated organizations, (*angeschlossene Verbände*), that is, professional and interest groups including the giant labor organization, the *Deutsche Arbeitsfront* (DAF) (Orlow, 1973, pp. 6–7, 92). Those organizations for the communists are transmission belts, and as Stalin put it:

> To forget the distinction between the advanced detachment and the whole of the masses which gravitate towards it, to forget the constant duty of the

advanced detachment to raise ever wider strata to this most advanced level means merely to deceive oneself. (1924, p. 174).

As one *Gauleiter* (regional head of the party) representing the popular Nazi farmers organization, the *NS Landvolk,* put it, the purpose of the *NS Landvolk* is not to represent the farmers but to make National Socialists out of them (Orlow, 1973, p. 59). Membership in theory and very often in practice involves much more than paying dues, like in many democratic parties and even social democratic parties. It is no accident that the definition of party membership should have been one of the basic disagreements between Martov and Lenin, between the Mencheviks and the Bolsheviks, by requiring personal participation in one of the party organizations. The acceptance by the party member of party discipline and the intolerability of any criticism undermining or obstructing the unity of action decided on by the party, extended even to activities outside of politics in the professional sphere, even in conflict with the hierarchical authority relationships in the state or the army, characterize totalitarian parties. Admission to membership is not automatic; parties reserve for themselves the right to admit or to reject. They often establish a probationary or candidate period, formally grant different rights to new members and provide for expulsion, which means, as the statutes of the PNF *(Partito Nazionale Fascista)* stated, "The Fascist who is expelled from the party must be outlawed from public life" (Aquarone, 1965, p. 510). Deliberate planning of the composition of the membership and purges by the leadership characterize those parties,[19] and, consistent with the conception of the organization as voluntary and self-regulating, there is no recourse in the absence of other parties against the decision to any outside authority or court despite the privation of political citizenship (Rigby, 1968; Buchheim, 1958). Many positions in the state and societal organizations are formally or de facto accessible only to party members.

Totalitarian parties are bureaucratic in a way that even the most bureaucratized democratic parties are not. As Lenin stated it in *One Step Forward, Two Steps Back:*

> The party link must be founded on formal "bureaucratically" (from the point of view of the disorganized intellectual) worded rules strict observance of which alone can guarantee us from the willfulness and the caprices of the circle spirit, from the circle scramble methods which are termed the free "process of the ideological struggle." (Daniels, 1969, p. 11)

The life of the party is regulated by innumerable rules. Written norms are constantly enacted, extensive files are kept, decisions go through channels, and party officials control that apparatus. Both at the center and at the periphery there is a large number of full-time officials, who often have distinctive training and sometimes with privileged legal status and enjoy not only power but other rewards comparable to those of civil servants; in addition there are others who exercise leadership functions on a part-time basis. In the Communist party the expression "cadre" is used to designate party members who exercise leadership roles with distinctive ranks included in the *nomenklatura* (list of key job categories and descriptions used in elite recruitment) (Harasymiw, 1969). In the case of the Nazis the equivalent was the *Hoheitsträger,* the political leadership of the party from the *Gauleiters* down to the local leaders. In 1934, in Germany, the territorial cadre organization, *Politische Organisation,* had 373,000 functionaries for a party membership of some 2.5 million, while the Weimar Social Democratic party, with 1 million members, needed only 10,000 (Orlow, 1973, p. 42). At that time the Hitler Youth had 205,000 functionaries and the NSDAP, including all its affiliates, had 1,017,000, not all of them necessarily party members. Jerry F. Hough (1971, p. 49), on the basis of the size of the apparatus of various city and district party committees, estimates the number of party apparatchiki in the Soviet Union between 100,000 and 125,000. A 1956 breakdown of party membership by occupation in China lists 1,039,419 "organs," which seems to refer to party members employed full time in the party bureaucracy among the party's 10.7 million members. The penetration by the party into the society to perform the multiple functions assigned to it is achieved by a large number of functionaries close to the masses, the heads of cell and local organizations. The figures for the NSDAP in 1939 show 28,376 leaders of local groups, 89,378 cell leaders, and 463,048 block leaders, without counting those of the affiliated organizations. Obviously the degree of ideological consciousness, dedication to political activity, and willingness of these cadres to put loyalty to the party ahead of other loyalties vary enormously from party to party and over time. However, we cannot underestimate the degree to which the cadres of a party are perceived by the members as leaders and by the citizens as representatives of the power of the party, for good and evil, to help them solve many problems (like a ward heeler in urban America) or to supply information to those in power about their doings and attitudes (Inkeles and Bauer, 1959, p. 321–37). Nor can we ignore the sense of participation in politics, in a collective effort, or the petty gratifications of these leaders, which are so characteristic of totalitarian systems. It is this cadre structure that allows totalitarian parties to pursue successfully their functions, and many of the achievements in transforming the society have to be attributed to the cadres. Without them the mobilization for the large number of campaigns, actions, problems, policies, would be impossible. Even if the party did not play a decisive role, as it does in communist systems, in the management of the society and the economy, the availability at short notice of such cadres and those they can influence or control can assure a massive and visible expression of support for the regime in plebiscitarian elections and mass rallies. If we keep in mind the findings about opinion leaders as mediators between the mass media and the individual in democratic societies and the impossibility of creating any comparable network of personal influences, except in some cases the churches, we can understand the success of propaganda, the appearance of enthusiasm and support, and the pervasive conformity in totalitarian systems. Many of those who in pluralistic societies devote their time and energy to diverse voluntary associations do so in totalitarian societies in the activities of the party and its affiliated organizations, often with the same motivation and sincerity. Their actions contribute to the efficacy of the system and through it to its legitimacy. It is the absence of either pluralistic or single-party forms of voluntary participation and of a complex organizational network that characterizes most authoritarian regimes (except for short periods of mobilization through single parties).

Since the totalitarian party assumes a growing number of functions of a technical character in the management of complex industrial societies, the cadres experience a slow process of transformation, not infrequently accompanied by reversals, in the course of the stabilization of totalitarian systems. Initially, the cadres are recruited from the old fighters, the people who joined the party while it was in the opposition and sometimes in the illegal underground, who often made great sacrifices for the cause. Their loyalty, except for those disappointed by the absence of a second revolution, tends to be unquestionable but their competence to manage large-scale organizations in normal rather than exceptional circumstances is often limited. If the party wants to retain its momentum and not abdicate its revolutionary ambition and become dependent on the civil service, it has to recruit and socialize those who are experts and in due time train loyal party members as experts. The creation of party schools (Orlow, 1965; Scholtz, 1967; Ueberhorst, 1968; Mickiewicz, 1967), the promotion of activists from the youth organization through educational channels and through stages in different sectors of party activity into elite positions, the efforts to commit and even to compromise in the party those with expert knowledge are some of the techniques used. The dilemma of red or expert, which has been central to the Communist parties in power, is a perfect example. In the case of communist regimes the problem is compounded by the fact that the party plays a decisive role in the management of industry, agriculture, and services. The problem of preventing red expert cadres from also becoming professionals with a less political conception of their role, particularly devoting less attention to the social and political mobilization dimension of the party, has been particularly well analyzed in the Chinese case by Franz Schurmann (1968, pp. 75–76, 163–67, 170–72; Townsend, 1972). The Italian PNF, despite some efforts to create party schools, never fully faced this dilemma, due to the limited ideological thrust of the movement, the compatibility of its authoritarian nationalism and corporativism with a reliance on the state, and Mussolini's identification with the state, whose ministries and prefectures he had taken over, leaving to the party officials a secondary role. We do not know how the Nazis would have ultimately solved this dilemma, except that the social recruitment by the party before takeover and the ideological affinity of conservative, nationalist, authoritarian experts allowed the Nazis the partification of many sectors of the society. Even so, the men in the administration of the party felt unhappy about the situation and made generally unsuccessful attempts to train the Nazi elite in special schools. The irrational, romantic, anti-intellectual, militaristic, genetic, and racist components of the ideology were an obvious obstacle for the training of party men as experts. The SS as an elite within the party, with its pseudoreligious, pseudofeudal, semisecret, and terroristic character, opted for a process of co-optation and compromise in the "order"; these were men who had made their career not in the street fights and propaganda activities of the party before 1933, but in the establishment (Krausnick, 1968; Höhne, 1969). We do not know how a stable Nazi regime, victorious in the war, would have handled this problem. We know, however, how the Soviet Union and other communist countries have, in the course of their longer and more stable, peaceful development, moved toward combining *partiinost* ("partyness") with expertise. What we do not know exactly is the answer to the question raised so well by Jerry F. Hough (1971, pp. 47–92) of to what extent the apparatchiki of the contemporary Soviet Union in their multiple functions and career lines, with their professional education and expertise, their frequent shifts from state administration to party work, share a distinctive ideological outlook, and have common interests, have a different party perspective than their counterparts in the governmental and economic hierarchies. As he writes:

> It would certainly simplify the comparative study of political systems if we could assume that the elite members of the institutional groups which comprise "the gigantic bureaucracy party organizational complex" in a country such as the Soviet Union represent essentially their own interests and not those of farmers, workers, and clerks whom they supervise. (Hough, 1971, p. 89)

Franz Schurmann, in the context of his analysis of the Cultural Revolution in China, has suggested the need to make a distinction between professional and expert when he writes:

> Expertise means a technical capacity (e.g., in science, technology, or administration). Professionalism means commitment to an occupational position. I have noted that two elites appeared to be developing in China, the body of organizational leaders with political status deriving from ideology and the professional intellectuals with status deriving from education. If occupational position gives rise to status, then professionalism will lead to the formation of elites. The accusations directed against "the authoritarian clique following the capitalist road" have aimed at the elite status, and not at the expertise. That has also been at the root of the attacks on the tendencies for a professional officer corps to develop. The intellectuals are the men of expertise in China, its scientists, technicians, and administrators. There are, have been, and undoubtedly continue to be tendencies

toward the formation of an expert elite. However, since the brunt of the attack of the Cultural Revolution was on the Party, of gravest concern to Mao Tse-tung and his followers was the emergence of a professional red elite—that is, an elite whose power and status derived from Party position. (Schurmann, 1968, p. 565)

The commitment in a totalitarian society to the ideology of "politics takes command," to the control and preferably guidance of the society by a group of dedicated people committed to collective interests and to a utopian vision (however muddleheaded it is), accounts for the basic ambiguity in the role of the cadres of a party. It might well be that what starts as total politicization through the mobilization of a party might end, except for permanent revolution against the party or within the party, in the administration of a posttotalitarian society with its limited bureaucratic pluralism.

Party leadership. Many scholars in their analysis of totalitarian parties have emphasized as the ultimate key to our understanding the role of the leader, be it the *Duce, Führer,* or First Secretary, and the unique concentration of power in his hands and the cult of personality, *Führerprinzip,* the distorted interpretation of democratic centralism that from the top down permeates the party (Schapiro, 1972a; Tucker, 1965; Vierhaus, 1964).[20] Others go even further and find the explanation in the unique personalities of men like Hitler and Stalin.[21] It would be an obvious mistake to ignore those factors, but the question will still remain, Why were those men capable of exercising such power and how did those principles emerge and become accepted by their staff and many party members? Michels (1962; originally published 1911) in his sociology of the modern party lists many of the factors that account for the exercise of such power, which are far from absent in competitive democratic parties but do not have the same consequences due to the pluralism of parties. Rosa Luxemburg in 1904 already noted that "the ultra centralism advocated by Lenin is not something born of the positive creative spirit but of the negative sterile spirit of the watchman" (Daniels, 1969, p. 12), and Trotsky felt that Lenin would have the party and its prescribed theology substitute for the mass movement in order to force the pace of history, concluding prophetically:

> These methods lead, as we shall yet see to this: the party organization is substituted for the party, the Central Committee is substituted for the party organization, and finally the "dictator" is substituted for the Central Committee. (Daniels, 1969, p. 13)

He concludes that the complicated task of cleaning out deadwood and bourgeois thinking "cannot be solved by placing above the proletariat a well-selected group of people, or still better one person and with the right to liquidate and demote." Those tendencies toward an all-powerful leader and the destruction even of a collective leadership are perhaps, as recent trends show, not inevitable in a communist party. They were, perhaps, in fascist parties, given some of their basic ideological orientations—the voluntarism, irrationalism, and appeal to emotion so congruent with the appeal to charisma, the admiration of military organization and leadership, the appeal of the great man in history idea, and in the German case the romantic yearning for a saviour with particular virtues based on a fascist, feudal, or Germanic imagery. However, it should be noted that fascist party statutes provided for elected leadership and that one of the few changes in *Mein Kampf* from the first edition was a radical formulation of the *Führerprinzip*.[22] The commitment to an indisputable ideology that expresses inexorable laws of history with substantive rather than procedural content makes the emergence of that kind of leadership more likely. Such commitment can easily justify the search for unanimity and the outlawing of any opposition within the party. The degree of free discussion before reaching a decision and the tolerance for loyal support of dissenters not convinced in such a context would depend on the personality of the leader or leaders rather than, in a more relativist conception of politics, based on normative limits of authority and pragmatic skepticism. The leadership principle, the charismatic demand of obedience, and the truly charismatic or pseudocharismatic loyalty of the followers are congruent with the totalitarian party but perhaps not inevitable. The model of concentration of power in a rational bureaucratic organization, the creation of a single center of decision making, is often used in describing such regimes. In fact, the contrary is true, and Franck, the Nazi governor of Poland, was right in stressing the anarchy in Hitler's rule. No centers of power challenging the authority of the leader are allowed to emerge, but the struggle for power between subleaders and organizations is one of the central characteristics of totalitarian systems, tolerated, if not encouraged, by the leader, following a policy of divide and rule. In a pure totalitarian system that struggle takes place mainly within the party and its affiliate organizations, which seek alliances with pretotalitarian structures or the emerging social interests of complex societies. As Orlow (1973, pp. 7–12) has noted, Hitler subcontracted (with the understanding that the contract could be terminated at will) segments of his authority to his individual agents, rather than to officers or institutions, on the basis of intensely personal relationships. Since, on the same principle, those agents developed strong power bases with different interests and goals and with poorly defined areas of competence, conflicts between them were endemic and required either arbitration by the *Führer*, or by those able to speak in his name, or efforts of coordination by creating complex interdependencies between agencies, new organizations under someone the rivals could agree on, or the like. The system, despite the appearance of monocentrism, could not be further from rational bureaucratic organization principles, and only arbitrary interventions of the leader or his spokesmen could disentangle it. In the German case the importance of certain ideological elements derived from the romantic idealization of the Middle Ages and the hostility to law contributed to giving it, as Robert Koehl has noted, a feudal aspect (Koehl, 1972), understanding by feudalism, in the words of Coulborn, a system in which "the performance of political functions depends on personal agreement between a limited number of individuals . . . since political power is personal rather than institutional, there is relatively little separation of function" and in which "a dispersal of political authority amongst the hierarchy of persons who exercise in their own interests powers normally attributed to the state, which are often in fact derived from its breakup." In other systems in which the emotional bond between the leader and most of his followers was less stable than in the case of Hitler, the political process approached more the model of court politics in a degenerate patrimonial regime. Sometimes the withdrawal of direct intervention of the leaders leads to stalemates, greater bureaucratization, and rationality, but as long as the leader retains legitimacy and/or control of coercion he can impose his will without being restrained by norms or traditions. This is one among the many factors accounting for the unpredictability so often noted in the analysis of totalitarian politics. It is also one of the factors that ultimately may account for the instability of pure totalitarianism and the emergence of posttotalitarian patterns, the rejection of the cult of personality and the emergence of collective leadership, and the search for greater rationality in the allocation of competencies by the leadership that has experienced working with such a leader. It accounts for an effort to institutionalize the charisma of the leader in the party as a corporate body.

Functions of the party. The totalitarian party, however, is defined not only by its unique structure but by its functions. Functions obviously change from one period in the development of the regime to another. They are different in the stage of creating a power vacuum in a previous regime, particularly a democratic one, in the takeover phase, the phase of consolidation (often combined with considerable tactical compromises with the existing power structure, social interests, and pretotalitarian institutions in a two-step-forward, one-step-backward pattern to neutralize them), in the phase of purging itself from those co-opted in that consolidation process, in the renewed efforts of mass mobilization followed by more stable domination of an atomized society (Kornhauser, 1959; Dallin and Breslauer, 1970), to a final phase of administering society without basis for principled opposition but facing complex policy decisions leading to a moderate degree of pluralism among decision makers even within the party. The scholarly literature focusing on politics in totalitarian regimes rather than on the process of their establishment, particularly in the case of Nazi Germany, and the more monographic work on particular policy areas make us more conscious of those phases and the very different functions performed by the party and its organization in each of them. It is impossible to summarize here in a comparative perspective these problems, and therefore we have to describe the functions of the party without taking into account the high and low tides in their performance (Orlow, 1973).

Foremost among its functions is the politicization of the masses, their incorporation, in-cadration, integration, conscientization, and conversion, and their reciprocals, the detachment from other bonds, the destruction of the autonomy of other organizations, uprooting of other values, and desocialization. This process is achieved by a mixture, which is very different in various totalitarian systems, of propaganda, education, and coercion. It is here where the different styles of totalitarian systems become most visible. There is an abyss between the brutal regimentation of the Nazis in their mass organizations and the sophisticated combination in China of coercion in the land reform and the "speaking bitterness," the small groups organized by party cadres and activists for thought reform, propaganda, and coercion, in very different proportions in different phases (Townsend, 1972; Schurmann, 1968). This function of integration and conscientization also accounts for the importance assigned in such parties to the youth organization, as the recruiting ground for future leaders and to counteract the socializing influences of family and church (Brandenburg, 1968; Klönne, 1957; Kassof, 1965; Germino, 1959). The in-cadration of masses not ready to join the party and participate in its many activities is to be achieved by the many functional organizations to which people have to belong to achieve other ends. In the case of Nazi Germany, this, given the large number of organizations and their high rate of penetration into their constituencies (which contrasts with the theory of mass society of Kornhauser, 1959, as Lepsius, 1968, has noted), required either the destruction or the infiltration and *Gleichschaltung* of those organizations. An example: the *Doppolavoro* and *Kraft durch Freude* organizations of leisure time in Italy and Germany show how even the free time can, by voluntary participation on apolitical grounds, be used for political socialization. In the case of less developed countries one of the great achievements of totalitarian parties is to create such functional organizations that can serve as transmission belts. It is important to stress that participation is not passive but involves active engagement in campaigns for the benefit of community, from welfare to beautification, sports to culture, and, in developing countries, for production on the basis of moral incentives. Organizations like a voluntary or compulsory labor service, *Arbeitsdienst,* capture motivations such as in the United States led young people to join the Peace Corps. Brigades of volunteers also serve as a recruiting ground of activists and future leaders. In fact, one of the threats to the totalitarian ideological socialization is that many participants become more interested in the substantive functions of such organizations and activities than in ideological schooling (Pipping, 1954, pp. 324–25). In a stabilized totalitarian society the careful screening and indoctrination of educators obviously lowers the saliency of these socialization functions of the party and probably weakens the responsiveness of those tired of indoctrination.

The integrative function explains the importance assigned to elections and plebiscites in totalitarian systems and their use to test the effectiveness of the party and its mass organizations in their success of getting out the vote.[23] Voting is not just a duty but an opportunity to express publicly, visibly, and preferably joyously the identification with the regime. Many types of authoritarian regimes less concerned with democratic legitimation and ideological conversion just put off elections or tolerate apathy as long as their candidates get elected.

The second central function of the totalitarian party is the recruitment, testing, selection, and training of the new political elite. This is obvious in the phase of the struggle for power in opposition, underground, revolution, and civil war. In the process of consolidation, co-optation into the party of experts and people of the establishment swells its ranks, often leading to the closure of admission and even purges of the newcomers (Rigby, 1968, pp. 178–81; Aquarone, 1965, pp. 379–81; Orlow, 1973, pp. 202–5; Buchheim, 1958). Ideally, once the party has consolidated itself in power, the recruitment should take place through socialization in the youth organizations, a so-called *leva fascista,* literally "fascist draft," by which those who graduate from the youth organizations are admitted into the party. The compulsory or at least mass character of those youth organizations, however, limits their effectiveness as a selection mechanism, and more stringent and specialized systems of recruitment tend to be devised. The dilemma of expert versus red and the search for the red expert often leads to lateral entry, particularly through active participation in party-affiliated mass organizations. Success of the party ultimately depends in a stabilized totalitarian system on its capacity to attract people in different sectors of society who are loyal to the regime but uninterested in political activism, contact with the masses, and political responsibilities. Recruitment and cadre selection in a stabilized totalitarian system finds itself between the Scylla and Charybdis of professionalization, with the consequent loss of representativeness by emphasizing educational requirements, and the promotion of activists without qualification with the risk of incompetence. The efforts to combine a broad recruitment, particularly in communist systems from the working class in the factories, with rapid and intensive training in party programs in organizational and managerial skills reflect this dilemma (Rigby, 1968, pp. 115–25; Ludz, 1968 and 1970). In communist systems the important role of the party in the management of production and economic planning makes this problem central. It also accounts for the more rapid routinization of totalitarianism in advanced industrial communist societies.

One major function of totalitarian parties is to control a variety of specialized functions that can become independent, nonpolitical centers of power. The party is a recruiting ground for the political commissars in the army (Kolkowicz, 1967 and 1971), and in this respect it is interesting to remember that the Nazis in the last period of their rule were moving to partify the army (Orlow,

1973, pp. 460–62). The importance of coercion of opponents in the struggle to gain power, the tradition of secrecy developed in the period of illegality under repressive regimes, the international tension that has often surrounded the new regime, and the emergence of many of them in a civil war lead to an almost projective fear of subversion, conspiracy, and aggression, and consequently to a propensity for terror. Since a defense of order involves political considerations, a strictly professional police is largely inadequate, and therefore the politicization of police forces and the creation of party militias are characteristic of totalitarian systems. The organizations involved tend to be heavily recruited through party channels.

However, the main function of the party is to be present in the many sponsored organizations and those that have been taken over—trade unions, cooperatives, professional and interest groups. In a socialized economy this control function acquires a special sense. There is a great variety in the way of conceiving this "leading and guiding function" of the party, and volumes have been written on the shifting conception of the relationship between party and society, both in ideology and practice, particularly in communist countries.

Even among the Nazis, as Orlow (1973, pp. 14–16) has pointed out, two conceptions of the role of the NSDAP emerged, identified with Hess, the "representative of the *Führer*," and Ley, the head of the Party Organization Office and the Labor Front. The key terms in the differing approaches were "control" and *"Betreuung"* ("welfare, taking care"), signaling two different ways of responding to a complex, sophisticated, industrialized society, ways that largely remained intact during the years of struggle for and after the seizure of power. According to Ley, the synthetic party community, *Gemeinschaft,* created in the course of the struggle, should merge with the remaining, now politicized segment of the German social organism and form a *Volksgemeinschaft,* a people's community, through *Betreuung* ("taking care of the needs of the people through a politically motivated welfare state"), emphasizing less the elite status of membership and the cadre organization by ultimately fusing the party with the Labor Front into a single mass organization. His opponents felt that far from becoming a *Volksgemeinschaft,* Germany should remain a society *(Gesellschaft)* in which the key activity of the party was controlled through a tightly knit centralized organization with an elite co-opted membership and a fanatic but technically and administratively competent functionary corps. Neither of the two conceptions won the endorsement of Hitler, but basically the regime was closer to the second alternative.

State and party. The important role of the party in providing leadership to many affiliated or sponsored organizations that control other institutions should not lead us to forget that the main function of the party is to fill political offices at all levels of government through elections or appointments. Since the officeholders in totalitarian systems, in contrast to competitive political systems, are assured their position as long as they enjoy the confidence of the party, basically the party has its own extensive and often specialized bureaucracies and the relation between government and party is central to these systems. The extent to which the party in government is or is not independent from the party as an organization, attempts to subordinate or ignore the party, or the party organization attempts to give orders to its representatives at all levels of government is perhaps the most interesting question in the study of totalitarian parties. Only when the party organization is superior or equal to the government can we speak of a totalitarian system.[24] Without that tension the system degenerates into bureaucratic authoritarianism, losing its linkage with the society and much of its mobilization and dynamic potential. Mao's statement that the party is the instrument that "forges the resolution of the contradiction between state and society under socialism" is a very exact formulation of this novel phenomenon (Schurmann, 1968, p. 112). The superiority of the state apparatus even when manned by party members characterizes a pretotalitarian phase of the regime, a failure of the totalitarian drive, as in the case of Italy, or the transition to a posttotalitarian system. It is fundamental to remember that in the Marxist ideological tradition there is no legitimacy in the post-capitalist society for the state apparatus and that ultimately the utopian stage will represent the withering away of the state. What is less known and almost deliberately forgotten is that Hitler in *Mein Kampf* expressed his hostility to the state and the traditional German *Staatsgläubigkeit*. As he writes:

> It is therefore the first obligation of the new movement standing on the ground of the folkish world view to make sure that the conception of the nature and purpose of the state attains a uniform and clear character.

> Thus the basic realization is: that the state represents no end but a means. It is, to be sure, the premise for the formation of a higher human culture, but not its cause, which lies exclusively in the existence of a race capable of culture. . . . thus the precondition for the existence of a higher humanity is not the state but the nation possessing the necessary ability . . . of course as I have said before, it is easier to see in state authority the near formal mechanism of an organization, than the sovereign embodiment of a nationality's instinct of self preservation on earth. (1924–26, p. 391)

The chapter goes on from here into a rambling discourse on race, biological selection, and a socialization informed by those values. The radical community is basically counterposed to the state, particularly a state like the German that does not coincide with that community. As Hannah Arendt (1966, pp. 257–66) rightly noted, the totalitarian movements cannot be understood without reference to the hostility to the state, and to conventional patriotism and the substitution by a loyalty to a larger social unit. She rightly links totalitarianism with the pan-movements that appeared in Central and Eastern Europe, where state and national boundaries did not tend to coincide like in the West. Hitler, born Austrian, deserter from the Imperial Army, serving in that of his adopted country, Germany, clearly reflects this disjunction between state and broader social community. The international proletariat and the identification of socialism in one country with leadership of a world political movement beyond its borders is the Marxist equivalent. In this context the ideological and organizational development in Italy and in Mussolini's mind put inherent limits to a totalitarian development. Hitler's confused idea in the second book of *Mein Kampf* of a distinction between subjects and citizens of the state, which found its legal expression in the Nuremberg racial laws, differentiates his regime from both the civic culture of democracies and traditional and authoritarian conceptions of the state.

The party in theory and reality. The description of both manifest and latent functions of the party we have presented is based largely on the ideological conception, pragmatic statements, ideal typical descriptions, and research on the overlap between parties and other institutions. The question is, To what extent do party cadres, particularly at the middle and lower levels, and party members behave as expected? There are obvious variations from one totalitarian system to another, from one period or phase to another, which monographic research, particularly studies of regional and local life under such regimes, is revealing every day.[25] The research points out that, for a variety of reasons, there is considerable degree of policy diversion, that is, alteration of policies from within the power structure in directions not wanted by the rulers. It also shows that particularly on the periphery the local organs of the party, far away from the centers of ideological infighting at the top, might concentrate their attention on a function that appears in the theory of totalitarian parties but tends to be less emphasized, to represent the interests of the constituencies before higher-up party, and government, bureaucracies. This point has been particularly emphasized by Jerry F. Hough (1969) for the Soviet Union, but a reading of literature on Nazi local party activities would probably show the same pattern, even when in a more limited sphere, in view of the function of the Soviet party in the economy. The representation of the interests of territorial communities (perhaps facilitated because of a relatively centralized system with a national policy and monocentrism for major decisions) by the local party organizations, is not unlike democratic parties and democratically elected lower government units. Less divided over and involved in overall policy formulation and resource collection, they can agree on demanding as much as possible from the center for the benefit of their constituents. Successful, influential, old-time party leaders can obviously act as mediators between a variety of local, special, and even private interests and the higher bureaucratic structures, and this, as in democratic government, is obviously an opportunity for corruption and for diversion of policy.

Somewhat similarly, the ideologically assigned functions of a party at the higher levels become often secondary to those of bureaucratic infighting between organizations, both in the party and in the government controlled by party officials, interested, like their civil servants, in protecting the autonomy of the organization from the party. Totalitarian politics, despite its mobilizational component, very often gets clogged down in endless bureaucratic infighting, which in the German case, given the very personal direct relations of many of the top leaders with Hitler, led to feudal infighting and court politics and consumed most of the energies of the elite. Thus the limited span of attention of the top levels of leadership, even their work habits, the shifting goals and policies often hastily decided, run counter to any image of totalitarian politics as an efficient machine frictionlessly transmitting decisions from the top to the bottom. However, a superficial reading of Peterson's book (1969) *The Limits of Hitler's Power* should not lead us to forget that many, and particularly the really important, wishes of the *Führer* were ultimately implemented without the possibility of any effective opposition to them, and that the "rule of anticipated reactions" made the whole system responsive to decisions congruent with the image of his power and his basic policies, or of those close to him. In a sense, an image of an all-powerful leader making all the decisions is empirically false, but in another sense it is true, since the men chosen by him or tolerated around him will act in such a system largely as they think he expects them to do. In this sense, contrary to finding in the total power of the leader an alibi for the party and other organizations, they have to share in the responsibility for decisions (Speer, 1971, pp. 649–50). Without them there cannot be even the attempt to create a totalitarian society, nor can there be the attempt without the responsiveness to their expectations of a large number of middle and lower cadres, party members, and citizens whatever the motivation, even if as minimal as the security of the individual and his or her family. The lesser commitment of many of the top leaders to such a total control for the sake of certain utopian goals of social mobilization, and as a result the lesser commitment throughout the structure of the state, explains that Italian Fascism never reached the level of control and mobilization that the pronouncements of the *Duce* and the legal enactments would lead us to expect. This in turn might have been a reflection of the degree to which Italians felt more strongly other loyalties and interests, even particularistic ties embedded in the culture, than loyalty to the PNF. In our discussion of the conditions for the emergence of totalitarianism we shall note some of the social, economic, cultural, and psychological conditions that make it possible for a totalitarian organization to approach even remotely its utopian self-image that has served us to construct the ideal type. We have seen, however, that it is dangerous to lose sight of the degree to which a limited number of political systems, in particular historical phases, approach the totalitarian utopia, both for evil and for good.

Communist and fascist parties. There are many important differences between communist and fascist totalitarian parties, not only in the ideology and policies, as we noted before, but in the organizational structure. The most important difference is the emphasis in the fascist parties on the *Führerprinzip* (Vierhaus, 1964; Nyomarkay, 1967; Horn, 1972), specifically in the Nazi case, which contrasts with the democratic component of democratic socialism, whatever similarities emerged in practice in the Stalinist period. The different ideological and formal principle is of central importance. Some degree of internal party democracy is possible in communist parties and there is ideological basis for those who want to move in that direction, while there was none in the National Socialist case.

Another major difference between the national socialist totalitarian party and Stalinist parties is the formal institutionalization of paramilitary organizations like the SA and the SS. Already the Italian Fascists had attempted, with the creation of the *Milizia volontaria per la sicurezza nazionale* (MVSN), to absorb the more unruly elements of the party *squadrismo* and to give a legal and institutional basis to the repression in support of the regime. In Italy its subordination to the head of the government and the coordination with the army for the appointment of officers did not allow it to become a real political army. The evolution of the SA (Werner, 1964) and particularly the SS (Höhne, 1969; Krausnick *et al.,* 1965), which in the course of the war became a real party army, parallel to the army of the state but not subject to its control and influence, was one of the basic differences with Italy that assured the turn toward totalitarianism of the Nazi regime. There have been similar tendencies in communist countries, but the total control by the political leadership of the regular army and its politicization, as well as the politicization of the police, have prevented the emergence of organizations of violence as part of the party and distinct from those more professional organizations. The difference, while congruent with the ideological romanticization of violence in fascism and the nationalist admiration for the armed forces, can also be explained by the different process of takeover of power. The fascist parties emerged in liberal democratic societies that allowed the opponents a large degree of freedom of organization and tolerated, if not indirectly encouraged, for a variety of reasons (reaction to communist revolutionary attempts or fear of a highly organized and mobilized working class, illegal rearmament in violation of the Versailles treaty), the emergence of paramilitary organizations and armed party groups. Once the fascist leadership had taken over a state thanks largely to the violence and the threat created by those organizations, it was not ready to disband them even when they were forced to compromise with the establishment, particularly the military, which was suspicious of them. Such a compromise and fear of a second revolution led in Germany to the bloody purge of the SA in 1934, which, however, initiated the rise of the SS and, contrary to formal promises to the army, broke the monopoly of armed forces (Mau, 1953). Those organizations based on a voluntary recruitment attracted a strange mixture of violence-prone persons—fanatical idealists, mercenaries, and sadists—who nonetheless could feel, on the basis of elaborate rituals, the comradeship of the barracks; the romantic, pseudofeudal rhetoric of "loyalty is mine honour" plus their rejection by civil society produced a sense of being the vanguard of the movement, a mixture of monastic and chivalry order. It was this organization that implemented the most monstrous aspects of the totalitarian utopia. As Himmler said:

> These measures could not be carried out by a police force consisting simply of officials. A body which had merely sworn the normal official oath would not have the necessary strength. These measures could only be tolerable and could only be carried out by an organization consisting of the staunchest individuals, of fanatical, deeply committed National Socialists. The SS believes it is such an organization, considers that it is fitted for this task and so has assumed this responsibility. (Buchheim, 1968, p. 366)

In the communist countries the party was born in secrecy without opportunity to organize freely—and even less so its strong arm. The takeover of power took place either in societies in which the existing establishments had disintegrated or under the sponsorship of the Soviet army. In most cases the takeover required a more or less prolonged civil war often mixed, like in China or Vietnam, with a national independence struggle. In such circumstances the party acted as a core organizing element of a new army, the Red Army, the People's Liberation Army, and in the areas controlled by the revolutionaries the party was able to establish its own police, the *Cheka,* and its successor organization staffed by loyal party members. Neither the army nor the police had to compete with organizations created before the takeover, with their distinct professional status and self-conception and therefore perceived as unreliable from a political point of view. Even though there is evidence of idealization of the role of the *chekist,* there was no need to develop a distinctive ethos for the instruments of coercion and make them elitist, voluntary, ideological organizations (Barghoorn, 1971). It was possible to conceive of them as part of the state apparatus, intimately coordinated with the party but never equal or potentially superior to the party mass organization. It is no accident that the revolutionaries in the SA would have preferred a militia type of army in which they would have played a leading role and that a segment of the SS, the Waffen SS, showed tendencies to drift apart from the more terroristic *Verfügungstruppe* and were less interested in ideology, seeking ultimately the respectability of the armed forces. In authoritarian regimes with totalitarian tendencies, particularly with a fascist party, the failure to build an independent armed militia to challenge the monopoly of force in the hands of the army and traditional police corps is one of the best signs of the limit to the total politicization and control of the society.

Excursus on Terror

The claim of the modern state to monopolize the use of force is one of its defining characteristics, but certainly regimes differ widely in the amount, type, and ways of using coercion. Totalitarian systems, at least in some of their phases, have been characterized by massive coercion—police acting unrestrained by any outside controls, concentration camps and torture, imprisonment and executions without proof of guilt, repressive measures against whole categories of people, the absence of public trial and even any opportunity for defense, the imposition of penalties totally out of proportion to the actions of the accused, all on a scale without precedence in recent history (Solzhenitsyn, 1973).

Political terror, defined by Dallin and Breslauer (1970, p. 7) as "the arbitrary use, by organs of the political authority of severe coercion against individuals or groups, the credible threat of such use or the arbitrary extermination of such individuals or groups," has certainly characterized totalitarian rule. This has led Hannah Arendt (1966, p. 474), to define totalitarianism as "a form of government whose essence is terror and whose principle of action is the logicality of ideological thinking." However, it is undeniable that the forms of coercion we have mentioned and political terror can be found in political systems that otherwise, without stretching the term, could not be called totalitarian (Chapman, 1970). Certainly, nondemocratic systems not characterized by "the logicality of ideological thinking" have shown their capacity for terror and the violation of the most elementary human rights. We only have to think of the rule of Trujillo in the Dominican Republic, where the arbitrary terror exercised by one man did not have or need ideological justification and was not characterized by modern forms of political mobilization.

On the other side, we can conceive regimes with the characteristics we have used in defining totalitarianism, and which distinguish them from those we characterize as authoritarian, without political terror. Certainly in such regimes we cannot expect the political freedoms enjoyed by a citizen of a democracy, but we can expect limits on the arbitrary power of the police, certain legal, particularly procedural, guarantees, and a return to the principle of *nullum crimen sine lege,* which makes it possible for those not willing to take the risk of violating the laws to enjoy a modicum of security. Even with laws that punish behavior considered legal in other societies, like publishing criticism of the government, associating for political purposes or the defense of interests, participating in strikes, etc., the definition of such acts as crimes, the exclusion of retroactive application of the law, combined with a minimum of procedural guarantees for the defendant, independence of the judiciary from direct intervention of the authorities, and restraints on the police, would allow the citizen who does not contest the regime to live without fear. A regime with those characteristics could still be highly monopolistic in its power structure, be guided by ideological commitment, and demand and reward active participation in its organizations. It would be, in our view, totalitarianism without terror. Its legal system would be repressive rather than liberal but certainly different from Stalinism or the rule of the SS under Hitler. The Soviet Union in recent years, with the introduction of what is called "socialist legality," is moving in this direction (Barghoorn, 1972, Chapter 10; Lipson, 1968; Weiner, 1970; Berman and Spindler, 1972).

To summarize our argument, while terror acquired a unique importance in totalitarian systems, many of its manifestations are not absent in regimes that lack many of the characteristics used by most authors to characterize totalitarianism, and we can conceive of particularly stabilized systems with all the characteristics of totalitarianism except widespread and all-pervasive terror. It is for that reason we have not included terror in our definition of totalitarianism.

We cannot ignore, however, the distinctive forms and scale of repression under totalitarianism and have to raise the question: Was the terror that accompanied it, without being a necessary consequence, a likely result of that type of regime rather than of the personality of men like Stalin and Hitler? We would argue that the system made those leaders possible but not inevitable. We also have to ask if and why terror in those systems had some characteristics not found elsewhere. Does the terror of different totalitarian systems differ? Which were functions and consequences of terror? Can we distinguish different types of terror, corresponding to different phases in those regimes? These and other questions would bring us closer to an answer to the question, How was it possible? In addition we shall ask the question, What forms does terror and coercion take in authoritarian regimes? Are they different, and if so, can we link the differences to the characteristics defining totalitarian and authoritarian regimes?

Coercion in totalitarian systems has shown the following characteristics: (1) its unprecedented scale, (2) its use against social categories without consideration of guilt for specific acts, (3) the disregard for even the appearance of legal procedures, the formalities of the trial, and the opportunity for some kind of defense, in imposing penalties, (4) the moral self-righteousness and often the publicity surrounding it, (5) the extension of the terror to members of the elite, (6) the extension to members of the family of the accused not involved in the crime, (7) the emphasis on the intent and social characteristics of the accused rather than on his actions, (8) the use of organizations of the state and/or the party rather than of so-called uncontrolled elements, and the size and complexity of those organizations, (9) the continuing and sometimes growing terror after the consolidation of the regime in power, and (10) the nonexclusion of the leadership of the armed forces from the repressive policy.

In addition, with the all-important position of the party in the society, a new form of sanction emerges: the exclusion from party membership, the purges that affect decisively the life chances of people and their social relations.

The scale in number of lives lost, man-years in concentration camps, and people arrested and subject to limitations of freedom of movement not resulting from strictly military operations is unique in modern repressive societies. While there can be debates about the exactness of statistical estimates, the magnitude is beyond discussion. Conquest (1968) has brought together the scattered evidence on the number of arrests, executions, and prisoners and death in camps and the estimates that can be derived from population census data. The estimate for executions in the late 1930s runs into around 1 million persons. Calculations for the number of inmates in camps around 1940 range between 6.5 and 12 million, depending on the year and the method of estimate. Taking the conservative figure of an average over the period 1936–1950, inclusive of an 8 million population of the camps and a 10 percent death rate per annum, we get a total casualty figure of 12 million dead. Adding to them the million executions of the period, the casualties of the pre-Yezhov era of Stalin's rule (1930–1936), those sent to camps who died, and the 3.5 million victims of the collectivization, Conquest reaches the figure of 20 million dead in 23 years of Stalin's rule. The figures for China in the consolidation phase are lower, but Mao admitted in February 1967 that in the first five years of communist rule some 800,000 "enemies of the people" had been killed, while others estimate the number between 1 and 3 million, that is, between $\frac{1}{3}$ and $\frac{1}{2}$ of 1 percent of the population (Dallin and Breslauer, 1970, p. 55). Reitlinger (1968, pp. 533–46) estimates that the number of victims of the Nazi "final solution of the Jewish problem" ranges between 4.2 and 4.5 million persons, with a total loss of Jewish life estimated at 6 million. It Italy, despite strong tendencies toward totalitarianism, terror except in the struggle for power and the short-lived Republic of Salo period was more limited. The Special Tribunal for the Defense of the State sentenced over the years 33 persons to death, of whom 22 were executed, and tried 5,619, sentencing 4,596 to an average of five years (Aquarone, 1965, p. 104). Undoubtedly the scale of repression in a number of regimes approaching far less the totalitarian model than Italy has been greater.

As significant, if not more, than the scale of the terror in some totalitarian systems has been its use against whole categories of people irrespective of any evidence of guilt or even intention of threatening the political system. The deprivation of human rights, wholesale arrests, and extermination as a result of deliberately formulated government policy by the agents of the state or the party of those identified, in the case of the Nazis, as Jews, gypsies (Döring, 1964), members of religious sects, biologically unfit, certain prisoners of war, or sectors of the population of occupied territories (Institut für Zeitgeschichte, 1958) and, in the case of communist countries, as belonging to certain social categories that could be labeled counterrevolutionary, like landlords, the clergy, and kulaks, and as members of ethnic groups on the basis of collective guilt (Conquest, 1960), have been unique in modern times. In those cases, the victims did not need to be personally guilty of any acts against the state or the social order, nor did their persecutors have to attempt to make a case against them based on any charges, trumped up or real, nor could they represent in many cases any real threat even if they had wanted to do so. Their fate was the result of ideological preconceptions, often, like in the case of Hitler, formulated before coming to power, which deprived those people of their human character and linked the creation of a better society with their destruction. The holocaust was in the eyes of a Himmler (Bracher, 1970, Krausnick *et al.*, 1968) a painful duty at the service of historical tasks for which future generations would be grateful.

In every political system there are miscarriages of justice, violations of procedural guarantees, obstacles to an adequate defense, biased courts, unfair trials, as well as illegal violence against political opponents ordered or condoned by those in power. But the systematic, large-scale, formally organized imposition of penalties, including death, without even the semblance of an adversary procedure and in the absence of an emergency situation, has been characteristic of totalitarian systems. The power of the special boards of the Ministry of Internal Affairs in the Soviet Union, on the basis of the 1934 statute, effective until 1953, to sentence people in absentia and without trial or counsel to labor camps is only one example. The executions ordered by the *Führer* without intervention of any regular or extraordinary courts that began with the purge of the SA leadership and other opponents in "the night of the long knives" in 1934, legalized by a law as emergency defense of the state, officially of 77 persons but perhaps three times as many, was only the beginning of the legalization of lawlessness (Bloch, 1970; Bracher, 1970; Mau, 1953). The terror of totalitarianism is not only the perversion and misuse of justice in the courts or the unofficial tolerance for illegal acts of the authorities that we find in many authoritarian regimes, and sometimes in democracies, but the normative institutionalization of such practices and their ideological justification sometimes even in the learned commentaries of jurists. The writing of Soviet and Nazi legal theorists, sometimes men of intellectual distinction—like Carl Schmitt—reflect and articulate that break with a long legal tradition. When Vyshinsky, the attorney general of the USSR, wrote in 1935,

> The formal law is subordinate to the law of the revolution. There might be collisions and discrepancies between the formal commands of laws and those of the proletarian revolution. . . . This collision must be solved only by the subordination of the formal commands of law to those of party policy (Berman, 1963, pp. 42–43),

he was expressing a thought that we will not find so frequently and authoritatively stated in any authoritarian regime.

The most striking characteristic of terror under totalitarianism and perhaps the explanation for its pervasiveness and scope is the moral self-righteousness with which it is justified by the rulers and their supporters, sometimes publicly, other times in the inner circle. Often it even conflicts with more pragmatic goals of the system. The nonpurely instrumental character of the terror derived from the passion for unanimity, the ideal of conflictlessness, the need to eradicate totally social groups defined as evil as a historical task, the explicit rejection of traditional moral standards that would make other men hesitate or feel guilty, and the demand of abdication of personal responsibility constitute some of the unique characteristics of totalitarian terror (Arendt, 1963; Cohn, 1966; Jäger, 1967; Barghoorn, 1971; Dicks, 1972). They ultimately are derived from the strength of ideological commitments. They also explain why many of the agents of terror could be otherwise normal men in their daily life, rather than psychologically defective persons. Let us not forget that Khrushchev in his secret speech of February 1956 concludes, after his appalling revelations and his negative portrayal of Stalin's personality, saying:

> Stalin was convinced that it was necessary for the defence of the interests of the working class against the plotting of the enemies and against the attack of the imperialist camp. He saw this from the position of the working class, the interests of the working people, the interests of the victory of Socialism and Communism. We cannot say that these were the deeds of a giddy despot. He considered that this should be done in the interests of the Party, of the working masses, in the name of defence of the revolution's gains. In this lies the whole tragedy. (Conquest, 1968, p. 66)

Another unique feature is the extension of the terror to members of the elite, in fact, the harsher punishment particularly under Stalin of those who had made the revolution with him and those who had positions of responsibility and whose loss of favor or trust in other systems would lead to their demotion, return to private life, and often to powerless but well-paid or prestigeful sinecures. In the case of Stalin, the victims were not only Soviet citizens but the leaders of foreign Communist parties living in the USSR and the satellite countries (Kriegel, 1972; Oren, 1973). Few data could tell the grim story of political terror better than those of Weber (1969, pp. 36–37) on the fate of the 504 leading cadres of the German Party (KPD) before Hitler: of the 136 who died violently, 86 (17 percent) were victims of the Nazis and 43 (9 percent) of Stalinist and East German purges. Members of the elite that lose in the struggle for power, even when they cannot represent a real threat, are to be destroyed, dishonored, and under Stalinism made to confess crimes they did not commit and to become nonpersons even in the writing of history (Leites and Bernaut, 1954; Brzezinski, 1956; Kriegel, 1972; Levytsky, 1974). As a result of the subordination of the military to the political leadership and the capacity of the party or police units to challenge the monopoly of force of the army, even the military leadership cannot escape political repression and a nonmilitary jurisdiction. The figures given by Conquest (1968, p. 485) for the Stalinist purges—3 of the 5 marshalls, 14 of the 16 army commanders Class I and II, 60 of the 67 corps commanders, 136 of the 199 divisional commanders, and about half of the officer corps, some 35,000 either shot or imprisoned—are testimony of that capacity. In the case of Germany, 20 generals of the army executed among 675 do not represent comparable figures, particularly considering the actual involvement in the plot of July 1944 against Hitler, but show the capacity to punish even in wartime the high command (Zapf, 1966, p. 164). Another unique characteristic is the extension of legal responsibility to the members of the family of the accused irrespective of complicity in their acts, both in the Nazi *Sippenhaft* (arrest of the family) and in the provisions of Article 58 (i.c.) of the criminal code of the RSFSR that punished "in the event of flight abroad of a member of the armed forces, the adult members of his family if they assisted him . . . or even if they knew about the crime but failed to report," and made "the remaining members of the family, and those living with him or dependent on him at the time of the commission of the crime liable to exile to the remote areas of Siberia for a period of five years" (Conquest, 1968, p. 558). The Nazi taking away the children of those involved in the 20th of July plot and the praise given to members of the youth organizations ready to denounce their parents are examples of the disregard for family bonds under totalitarian terror.

The ideological basis of totalitarian coercion leads to a rejection of legal formalism even in the definitions of crime, in the formulation of the accusation by the prosecutors, the argumentation of the judges of their sentences, and the variations in the punishment. Rather than strict laws and draconian but clearly established penalties, the tendency is to introduce subjective considerations, diffuse standards, and unpredictable sentences more dependent on who the defendant is than on his legally typified actions. Even the harshest military summary justice, by contrast, tends to be formalistic and even legalistic, paying little attention to the motive and not trying to justify its decisions except on the basis of repressive legislation and inarticulated, pragmatic considerations. Political justice in totalitarian regimes tries to show the base motives of the actor, to punish his intention rather than just his acts. The punishment is to reflect substantive ideological criteria, like the *gesunde Volksempfinden* ("the healthy sense of the people") or "socialist legal consciousness," and the pedagogical and exemplary rather than retributional aspects. The emphasis on the actor and his motive rather than the act itself is closely linked with the consideration given to the social background of the defendant and the ideological characterization of entire social groups. This explains the paradox that legal positivism in authoritarian settings serves the repressive state and in totalitarian systems is substituted by a sociological conception of law with legal positivism becoming an obstacle to the desires of the rulers (Schorn, 1959; Staff, 1964; Johe, 1967; Weinkauff, 1968).

Another tendency is the greater implication of the whole society in the repressive process, which is not left in the hands of a professional police and the courts but tends to involve actively or passively many members of the society through participation in the party and its formations, typically commanding those among high-status groups who had joined the SS to a tour of concentration camp duty, by making party members informers on their neighbors, by widespread publicity of selected political trials, and particularly in China through participation of the whole community in the process of repression—the "speaking bitterness" against landlords and efforts toward "thought reform" with the participation of the work group or the community. The Moscow show trials, the great purge, and the trial before the *Volksgerichtshof*—People's Court—of those involved in the plot against Hitler and their propagandistic exploitation are examples of this pattern without many parallels in authoritarian regimes (Travaglini, 1963). This does not exclude on the other hand the utmost secrecy surrounding other manifestations of the terror. Without accepting the thesis of Hannah Arendt that terror under totalitarianism increases with the consolidation of the regime and the weakness of its opponents, we can say that it certainly is not limited to or greatest in the takeover stage, as it tends to be in most authoritarian regimes. Perhaps because terror is not just instrumental in the way that Lenin and Trotsky conceived it when the latter wrote:

> The question as to who is to rule . . . will be decided on either side not by references to the paragraphs of the constitution, but by the employment of all forms of violence . . . war like revolution is founded upon intimidation, a victorious war generally destroys only an insignificant part of the conquered army intimidating the remainder and breaking their will, the revolution works in the same way, it kills individuals and intimidates thousands. . . . (Dallin and Breslauer, 1970, p. 77)

That type of terror in the takeover stage would be found in most authoritarian regimes, particularly when confronted with a well-organized opponent whose defeat is not assured, as in the case of Spain after the Civil War or in Chile today.

Totalitarian terror acquires its unique character from the centrality of ideology for many of those participating in it. As Hitler had remarked, "Any violence which does not spring from a firm spiritual base will be wavering and uncertain, it lacks the stability which can only rest in a fanatical outlook." However, it would not be possible without the organizational resources provided by the cadres and activists of a party committed to the defense of the regime. Without those factors it would not reach the intensity and scope or the systematic character that it can but does not necessarily reach under totalitarianism. Terror under some authoritarian regimes can be widespread, and under those that we shall call sultanistic, equally if not more arbitrary, but as we think we have shown it is likely to be very different.

In accounting for that difference one major factor is that in most authoritarian regimes the repressive function is left to the armed forces, which, while far from reluctant to use violence and expeditious methods of justice, tend to have a bureaucratic mentality emphasizing rules and procedures and none of the interest of intellectually more sophisticated men in motives and ideological justifications and little desire to explain their actions to the people and to gain their support. Unfortunately, we have no comparative analysis of political trials under different types of political systems to capture the different styles of the proceedings under totalitarianism and authoritarian regimes. A reading of the reporting in the mass media and systematic observation would certainly reveal some of the basic differences.

In totalitarian systems the independence of the regular courts is likely to disappear and their politicization to be the goal of the regime (Wagner, 1968), while most authoritarian regimes tend to leave to the regular judiciary its traditional degree of independence while they shift the politically relevant cases to special courts, generally the military justice (Toharia, 1974). We find here another example of the breakdown of the differentiation between state and society, politics and administration under totalitarianism.

There are undoubtedly major differences in the forms of repression under different totalitarian systems that should not be ignored but that we cannot fully develop here. It is not always clear to what extent those differences are due to national culture and legal traditions, to the idiosyncrasies of the leadership, to the patterns of behavior acquired in the process of takeover of power, and last but not least to a learning process based on the experience of similar regimes preceding them. Nazi and communist terror are certainly different in many respects, and despite many similarities between communist regimes, Stalinist and Chinese methods differ in many fundamental respects. In Cuba the possibility of emigration (estimated to be 7.1 percent of the population) to Spain and the United States probably limited the need for repression (Fagen, Brody, and O'Leary, 1968). The Nazis, having come in to power in a society whose institutional order had not been destroyed, initially relied much more on manipulated spontaneity and uncontrolled but planned actions than on the normal machinery of the state, which they only slowly transformed to serve their purposes. It also meant the emergence of a dual state and ultimately a parallel state of the SS, as well as a much greater secrecy surrounding their actions. The Nazis never developed the same urge to have the victims confess their guilt and to recognize the rightness of those in power. The self-criticism of the victims of the purges under Stalin has no parallel in Germany. Undoubtedly the communist conception of man as perfectable and the biological determinism underlying the Nazi ideology account in part for the difference. The Chinese, with their idea of the recuperability through "thought reform" and "coercive persuasion" even of class enemies, tend toward a "voluntarism" and "activism" and an emphasis on consciousness that substitutes a sophisticated assault on the individual's identity through self-criticism, confession, self-degradation, punishment, and rehabilitation for strictly physical punishment (Lifton, 1968; Schein, 1961; Townsend, 1972; Vogel, 1967). In this the

Chinese carry to the ultimate consequences certain tendencies implicit in the Soviet party. The contrast between Soviet Stalinism and the Chinese communists might also reflect the different process of conquest and consolidation in power, the different relationship to the rural masses in both systems. The patterns of behavior acquired during the revolution and the civil war by the *chekists* could be extended under Stalin to the kulaks by basically urban cadres and created the habits of brutality that would be institutionalized in the *Yezhovshchina*. Perhaps the Chinese also became aware of the fact that certain forms of terror provoke hostility that only terror can repress, that is, of the dysfunctional consequences of terror. Finally, the experience of Stalinist terror accounts for the efforts of the post-Stalinist leadership in the Soviet Union to do away with his excesses, to introduce forms of "socialist legality" while maintaining patterns of coercion very different from those in most authoritarian regimes through the creation of comrades courts and other forms of popular participation in enforcing social and political conformity (O'Connor, 1963; Lipson, 1967). The Committees for the Defense of the Revolution in Cuba, with their multiple social functions, also represent a system of collective vigilance capable of arresting those threatening the political order (Fagen, 1969). Undoubtedly, the 110,000 CDR, with 2 million members, represent a capacity of political integration, socialization, and organizational implementation of various programs that goes far beyond the vigilance activities for which they initially were created to face the counterrevolutionary challenge in the 1960s, but their presence in each neighborhood and work place contributes to providing the coercive organs of the state and party with information it would otherwise not have. In the last analysis, the compliance and efficacy of consolidated totalitarian systems is likely to depend more on such a penetration of the society and the coercive atmosphere it can provide than on the police and indiscriminate terror. It could be argued that initially the Stalinist form of terror was the result of the loss of revolutionary enthusiasm combined with low capacity to satisfy demands and the lack of penetration of the Communist party in many rural areas. Paradoxically, it could be argued that coercive compliance under totalitarianism is more likely to be achieved by the penetration of the party and its mass organizations in the whole society along Chinese lines than the excesses and the surplus of Stalinist police terror.

The great question on the prison walls and one that has no easy answer is, Why? Why did terror take the forms it took, how was it possible to create the machinery to implement it, and why was no one able to stop it? Dallin and Breslauer (1970), those who have written about the great purges (Leites and Bernaut, 1954; Brzezinski, 1956; Conquest, 1968; Gliksman, 1954; Kriegel, 1972) and those who have written on Nazism and the SS (Bracher, 1970; Arendt, 1963, 1966; Cohn, 1966; Krausnick *et al.,* 1968; Höhne, 1969; Dicks, 1972) have all asked these questions. The answers, sometimes conflicting, cannot be discussed in detail here. Undoubtedly terror and its different manifestations have to be explained differently in the variety of systems and historical situations. Any political system established by a minority or even a majority against the will of others who decided to use force to oppose its consolidation will turn to a greater or lesser extent to terror. The greater the conviction of those involved in the conflict and the weaker the support in the whole political community in the absence of a normative framework regulating conflict accepted by both sides, the more coercion. Violence has its legitimate place in revolutionary thought and tends to go with a takeover of power as "measures of suppression and intimidation towards determined and armed counter-revolution," to use Trotsky's words, and "the scientific concept of dictatorship means nothing else but power based directly on violence unrestrained by any laws, absolutely unrestricted by any rules," to use Lenin's expression (Dallin and Breslauer, 1970, pp. 10–11). Without theorizing as much about it, any counterrevolutionary would agree with those formulations substituting the word counterrevolution by revolution. The takeover phase directed at breaking the backbone of the opposition and punishing those collaborating with it, particularly in a civil war, leads to mass violence without concern of hurting innocents. The weakness of the minority attempting to impose a new order is likely to heighten its repression. Terror in turn leads to counterterror and the consequent spiral of violence. The justifications then formulated create the "habit of violence" among those involved in the repression. At this stage the terror can be seen as purely instrumental, even when many of its manifestations go far beyond such a "means-ends" relationship to become ends in themselves, as a purifying act carried out by idealists or as a source of gratification of the base motives of its agents. But terror continues and even in many political systems, particularly totalitarian ones, it seems to increase to become more rationalized and bureaucratically controlled when the regime seems most consolidated and counts on at least a passive compliance of most of the population. Dallin and Breslauer (1970) and many others have attempted to explain the continuity and rise in terror by describing its functions for the regime in this new phase, in which the regime attempts to achieve a decisive breakthrough toward critical goals. The more a regime attempts to transform the social order to create the "new man," to change the values of the people, and the greater the speed with which it attempts to achieve those ends, the greater the perception of the resistance to those changes, the more terror. They describe this period as a mobilization phase. The fewer the positive incentives in terms of rewards and the greater the deprivations required to implement the policies of the ruling elite, the greater the terror in the mobilization phase. We find this type of analysis among those who argue that the rapid industrialization of the Soviet Union, which required the transformation of the rural economy and society and consequently deprivations for the peasantry, was at the root of Stalinist terror. In such a view terror is still instrumental and rational, at least for those who accept the goals of the rulers and their timetable as valid and cannot conceive alternative ways to achieve the same goals. Those assumptions undoubtedly do not remain unchallenged and are not easy to prove or disprove. It is certainly difficult to argue that the goals achieved justified the cost in human misery, but it is possible to think that rulers could feel the need to sacrifice one generation for the sake of goals highly valued. Here the ideology, "the spiritual base," of which Hitler spoke, becomes decisive in the fanatical implementation through terror, and we can find here the root of the high probability of terror in totalitarian systems. In this context the emphasis has been on the functions of terror in establishing the monopoly of authority and organization, eliminating all autonomous subgroups, destroying physically and morally not only actual but potential opponents, creating an atomized society in which individuals feel unable to trust others, disrupting even the most elementary solidarities like the family and friendship, creating a widespread sense of personal insecurity leading to compliance and even overcompliance (Moore, 1954). Terror is conceived as social prophylaxis (Gliksman, 1954) and as educational—"unfreezing" the individual's perceptions, assumptions, and attitudes, particularly in the Chinese conception of "thought reform," with a combination of public accusation, confession, and reeducation in small groups. Significantly Kriegel (1972) subtitles her book *La Pédagogie infernale*. It is no accident either that the imagery used in describing the victims so often refers to the opponents as carriers of sickness; we have only to think of the expressions used by Hitler (Jäckel, 1972) to describe the Jews and Mao Tse-tung's view of "the citizen as a patient in need of treatment." In one case the cure required the destruction of its carrier, in the other a complex process labelled "coercive persuasion." In either case the victims are not considered normal members of the community. The "passion for unanimity" that follows from the commitment to a single belief system, a single hierarchy, and the concomitant definition of orthodoxy and heterodoxy requires the use of coercion within the elite and particularly against intellectuals. Since the right policy goals are presumably linked to the orthodox political beliefs, that kind of terror becomes presumably functional to their implementation. A latent function that often is neglected in the analysis but has been noted particularly for the SS state is that of compromising those connected with the terrorist system and even many ordinary citizens, to assure ultimately their loyalty as fearful accomplices.

The emphasis on those functions runs the risk of making the whole process far too rational and purposive, ignoring that it has a dynamics of its own that cannot be explained by the alleged functions in the mobilization phase. First of all, one cannot ignore the carry-over of the habit of terror from the revolutionary takeover period among policemen and activists, nor can one ignore the personal grievances and vendettas and just plain human nastiness that find a now-legitimate outlet. The bureaucratic apparatus itself ends having to justify its existence, and compliance and overcompliance with directives from above produce more and more victims. The assignation to the labor camps of certain economic functions ends creating the need to supply more inmates (Dallin and Nicolaevsky, 1947). The criticism, the hatred, the resistance created by terror and the fear that they arouse in its agents in turn spiral the wave of terror. Finally the Khrushchev speech reminds us of the personality of the top leader and the obedience he can find as a major factor in initiating and maintaining a system of terror. In view of all those noninstrumental reasons for widespread terror we should not overestimate the extent to which it is a prerequisite for the deep social transformations that totalitarian systems want to achieve. That is why we can conceive similar totalitarian systems and comparable social transformations with very different amounts, degrees, and forms of terror, and the same would be true for authoritarian regimes. A frightening and rationally difficult to explain characteristic of Nazi and Stalinist terror was the degree to which it was unnecessary and even dysfunctional for the achievement of the goals those systems had set themselves, the extent to which it had become an evil end in itself (Nove, 1964). This also accounts for the fact that the "decompression" of terror could be introduced relatively easily in the post-Stalin era without serious threats to the system, except in its Eastern European periphery, without a radical change in the nature of the political and socioeconomic system and probably with considerable gains in legitimacy. Certainly the introduction of calculated rather than arbitrary forms of coercion allows for new and before-unknown expressions of dissidence (Tökés, 1974) and with it the need for renewed coercion, but it should not be forgotten that those manifestations of dissidence were made possible by the end of terror. Undoubtedly, as Dallin and Breslauer (1970, p. 90) note, terror may generate alienation, and the abandonment of terror may paradoxically permit the expression of such alienation in the form of organized resistance or revolt, or more mildly in various forms of dissidence. This is why the phase of decompression is a dangerous one for totalitarian and authoritarian regimes that have been highly coercive and not able to create stable bases of legitimacy. Often, if it were not for the fears of the members of the elite of becoming themselves victims of terror and probably for the loss of faith in the ideological commitment, we would expect an increase in coercive measures after such a liberalization phase.

The Internal Dynamics of the Totalitarian System

A systematic analysis of the relative independent contribution of ideology, party, and ruling group or leader to the legitimacy, the formulation of policies, and the mobilization of the population in different totalitarian systems might be one way to conceptualize different types of totalitarian systems and to understand better the processes of change within them. Without ignoring the significance of the other factors we might then distinguish ideological totalitarian systems, power-centered ones, of which those in which the leadership principle becomes dominant would be a specially important subtype, and party-centered ones, which might vary from more bureaucratic to more populist-participatory. We might suggest very tentatively that the dynamics of such regimes move from a highly ideological phase, in which often there is a spectre of a second revolution of those ideologically committed but disappointed with the compromises the leadership had to make with reality in the process of consolidation of power, to more personalized leadership or oligarchic control. In a second phase a more instrumental attitude toward ideology, despite protestations to the contrary, is likely. In a later one the staff of the ruling group, to assure its continuity, safety, and a certain degree of predictability, tries to limit the power of the leader or ruling group and institutionalize it within the party organization by various attempts of rationalization of the party along a variety of strategies, from populism to an emphasis on technical expertise, and ultimately to the development of more reciprocal links between the middle levels of the party organization and the larger society and its differentiated structures. The more remote the ideological initial thrust and commitment becomes and the more scholastic the use of the ideology, the more the system will either turn to personal power or, once the staff in a Weberian process proceeds to the routinization of charisma and its institutionalization in the party, toward a process of deideologization. This process in turn should open the way to nontotalitarian forms of autocratic rule, though sometimes the rule would be threatened by ideological revivals. This process has to some extent been described in the recent literature on "posttotalitarian" Soviet-type politics[26] as the emergence of the "administered society" by Kassof (1969), "organizational society" by Rigby, the "regime of clerks or bureaucratic politics" by Brzezinski, less descriptively as posttotalitarian by Tucker, and "populist totalitarianism" by Paul Cocks. In the same direction we find a model in which leaders in the party organization, the mass organizations, and other bureaucracies establish for the formulation of policies closer links with different interests. A model for the emergence of group politics is a limited pluralism not only of political factions and organizations but of a variety of economic and professional and even class or regional interests, which ultimately should lead to the transformation into a kind of system that would no longer deserve the name of totalitarian. Gordon Skilling in his work has very hesitantly and imprecisely described the kind of system that might emerge this way in the womb of a totalitarian system. However, there would be some serious difficulties with such a transformation, given the importance of the ultimate legitimation of the system in the absence of a linkage with the ideology or a more aggregating central political organization like the party (and in the absence of true and independent choices by the population giving a democratic legitimacy for such a mixture between technocratic and interest group power). Unfortunately, the number of cases in which we could observe and study such a life cycle of totalitarian systems is limited, due to the relatively recent instoration of a number of them, the imperfect realization of the totalitarian model due to the resistance of the society to its implementation in other cases like Fascist Italy, and the premature disappearance of the Nazi regime.

Those changes are likely to be associated also with the very different composition in terms of social, educational, and career background of the ruling elite and the middle-level cadres in such systems. They are likely to have some interesting correlation with the types of legitimacy formulated by Max Weber. After an initial phase, which in some respects we should consider pretotalitarian, in the center of ideological formulation some type of charismatic authority is likely to appear supported by a group of disciples. The weaning of the belief in the uniqueness of the leader or of his immediate successor might give rise to a combination of patrimonial bureaucratic features, which can degenerate into the sultanistic type, while the posttotalitarian phase would show a combination of patrimonial bureaucratic characteristics with the emergence of legal authority, and a distrust or fear of the reemergence of charismatic leadership together with attempts to institutionalize the charisma in the party. The institutionalization of interest or group politics might lead, as it seems to have happened in the case of Yugoslavia, to the emergence of certain forms of corporative representation on an occupational basis, for which obviously the ideology of the Soviets provides a legitimacy not available for an individualistic representation that would be closer to the model of competitive democracy. The party organization might fight back in this context by reinforcing the more plebiscitarian elements of direct mass participation. In this context it is interesting to note that even those totalitarian systems that dabbled with corporative ideological elements in their totalitarian phase were suspicious of corporative organic representation and that the party leadership rejected such tendencies to reinforce the more charismatic plebiscitarian component.

Totalitarianism of the "Left" and the "Right"

Many critics are right in noting that works using the totalitarian model tend to focus on formal similarity in the way power is organized, created, and used, somewhat like the term democracy is used to cover such different political social systems as Scandinavia, Italy, and the United States, neglecting the content of the policies formulated and implemented through institutions that in other respects might have considerable similarities. To some extent the critics are right in noting that the emphasis on how things are done tends to neglect for whom and to whom. Unfortunately the literature comparing different totalitarian systems, particularly communist and fascist, is not rich. Talmon (1961, pp. 6–8), in a few pages, has stressed some basic differences in the ideological assumptions of both totalitarianisms, and Groth (1964) has attempted a more empirical analysis of some basic differences, noting at the same time some of the difficulties for a systematic analysis. While it might sound scholastic, we cannot avoid an emphasis on some of those methodological problems that he could not fully resolve.

The first difficulty lies in the fact that fascist totalitarian systems, particularly the only one that strictly speaking can be called totalitarian, had a short life span compared to the Soviet Union. Is a totalitarian system in the process of consolidation, like that of Hitler before World War II, comparable to a regime in its second and third decade, like Stalin's Soviet Union? A second difficulty is to isolate the impact of war on the German, and to a lesser extent the Italian, society. Were certain features of the Nazi regime a result of the war? Did the war accelerate the process toward totalitarianism or was it a temporary obstacle? Would we have had to wait to see the development of the regime after the war to evaluate better its totalitarian potential?

Another series of methodological difficulties emerge from the analysis of fascism. To what extent is Nazism a very special type of fascism or a model example of fascist regimes? To what extent were the ideological commitments of fascism realizable in a complex, advanced society with a long history of institutionalization and with masses of the population, to which fascism wanted to appeal, largely preempted by previously successful political movements, particularly socialism and Catholic social movements, limiting therefore its appeal to other strata of society? The left fascists, whose ideological formulations have recently received more attention (Kühnl, 1966), were aware of this problem. Other fascist movements with the more popular and less middle-class or upper-middle-class support, like those in some Balkan countries (Nagy-Talavera, 1970) and Peronism (Germani, 1965, 1973; Kirkpatrick, 1971), arose in societies where part of the lower classes had not developed such strong partisan loyalties. An analysis in terms of the initial social base of fascist parties limited to the Italian and the Nazis, as we find in Marxist literature, obviously ignores the possibility of a broader *Volksgemeinschaft* and a less class-bound fascist movement. There is also an ambivalence built into the analysis about the degree to which a totalitarian party in power reflects in its policy its original social composition and class appeal (Schoenbaum, 1967; Dahrendorf, 1965; Kele, 1972). Here again the length of the German experiment imposes serious limitations on the comparison.

Much of the value of the comparison depends on the narrowness or inclusiveness of the policy areas considered. It is significant that those who argue for the similarity of the systems pay special attention to the coercive aspects of the regimes, their impact on the legal systems and the role of the judiciary, their relation to education and youth, some of the impact on the family, and perhaps more than anything else on mass media, culture, and the arts, and the relation to religion. On the other hand they are very sketchy on the relationship between the national socialists and the economy, aspects like the role of owners, managers, and planners, as well as the role of the government and party-related sector, in economic policy formulation and the direction of production (Schweitzer, 1965; Mason, 1968; Milward, 1966; Eichholtz, 1969; Hennig, 1973). Even more complicated is the analysis of the impact of totalitarian systems on the distribution of income and power between social classes and particular social groups in relationship to economic decisions and daily work life (Schoenbaum, 1967; Schumann, 1958; Uhlig, 1956; Bauer, Inkeles, and Kluckhohn, 1956; Inkeles and Bauer, 1959; Lipset, 1973; Lipset and Dobson, 1973). It is in this area where Groth and other authors find essential differences, arguing that fascist totalitarianism did not intend to change the class structure, while communism deliberately aimed at such a change. The argument is obviously easy to make if we consider exclusively the variable of private ownership of large enterprises but ignore the separation between ownership and control and the degree to which such control shifted into the hands of state or party-related bodies.

Given the initially different basis of the Communist party and the supporters of the Bolshevik Revolution in the Soviet Union and those supporting the rise to power of Hitler, the social composition of the elites of both regimes was very different, with the working class providing fewer of the leaders among the Nazis than among the Bolsheviks, particularly at the middle levels (Linz, forthcoming; Lerner, 1965; Zapf, 1966). We know how the leadership of the Soviet Union in recent years has changed considerably in its composition (Farrell, 1970; Barghoorn, 1972), but we cannot know what that of a second generation Nazi elite would have been. Certainly we could have expected a certain amount of convergence of the two systems, given the greater emphasis on education and with it a certain transmission of positions within the intelligentsia in the Soviet scene, while in Germany the Nazification of the whole society would perhaps have provided for a broader recruitment of the elite and a dispossessing of some of the traditional strata whose values and style were in conflict with the Nazis.

The question of the elite composition, however, has to be kept quite separate from that of distribution of income and other advantages among major social strata like managers, employees, workers, and farmers as well as nonproductive groups like youth and the old. Such a comparison in societies in which many advantages are not distributed through wages and salaries is particularly difficult, and much research needs to be done in the comparison of political and social systems, holding constant economic development levels, the business cycle, and relations of international dependency even within ideological blocs. Undoubtedly such differences cannot be deduced simply from the social composition of the political elite or from the continuity in certain positions of the old elite. Nor are such differences in a modern economy exclusively dependent on the distribution of property.

The fact that the Soviet Union was built on a war-ravaged country after a revolution that had often physically destroyed the old social structure obviously contrasts with the imposition of Nazi rule on a society that acquiesced in its taking of power and therefore did not need to be restored and rebuilt to the same extent.

An obvious difference between communism and fascism is the latter's almost insane commitment to nationalism, even pan-nationalism, against the state when its frontiers do not coincide with the nation, in contrast with the ideological internationalism of the Bolsheviks and the formal commitment to federal, multination states. In practice, however, this rigid ideological distinction, which served the fascists to attack communism even while admiring many aspects of it, is not such a neat criterion to distinguish the two types of totalitarianism. Totalitarian Russia and China have not given up the appeal to national loyalties and traditions, particularly in the Stalinist patriotic war, and the Soviet leadership has not neglected its national interest in relation to other communist countries, which in turn have increasingly strengthened their legitimacy, like Rumania (Jowitt, 1971), by turning to nationalism without either democratization or liberalization. On the other side, in the original fascist movements, particularly in some of the German left National Socialists, some strains of Italian Fascism, and in the ideologists of the SS, we find elements of internationalism (Ledeen, 1972; Kluke, 1973).

Obviously the racism in Nazism was a crucial difference between its totalitarianism and that of the Soviet Union, but the emphasis on the Nordic or Aryan race was latently in conflict with the traditional conception of nation. Fascism in a number of its manifestations was not racist or even anti-Semitic, except the Hungarian Arrow Cross and the Rumanian Iron Guard. Fascist leaders were even capable of identifying with non-Western fascist movements (Kühnl, 1966). In fact, fascism was not exclusively European. The lack of success of Japanese fascists (Maruyama, 1963; Morris, 1968) confronted with the bureaucratic, military, authoritarian state and the failure of Chandra Bosse's Indian fascism as well as of Latin American fascism of the Brazilian *Integralistas* (Trindade, 1974), have obscured this fact. Even when communist anti-Semitism under the label of anti-Zionism and anticosmopolitanism is not racist and is a minor feature in its politics—and some of the appeals to non-Western races by the Chinese are more a part of political-economic conflict—those secondary strains show how the apparently neat distinction on this ideological dimension between the two historical antagonists is not so neat.

A major difference in the ideological formulations of both movements can be found in the emphasis on elitism and the leadership principle, with its charismatic connotation in fascism from its beginning in contrast to the fundamentally democratic commitments of communism, even in the form of democratic centralism. However, the Stalinist version of cult of personality led to considerable convergence but its ultimate ideological illegitimacy was important for the reforms of Khrushchev. The "vanguard" notion of the party in turn introduced an important elitist element reinforced by the special education of party schools. In making this important contrast we should, on the other hand, not forget that leadership in the fascist doctrine and party statutes initially had a democratic legitimation rather than a purely traditional one, even when democracy was to be limited to the party. The elitism of race, party, and followers of the leader ultimately was based in fascism on an idea of identity with the nation, the *Volksgemeinschaft*. This ultimately introduced into traditional status- and class-based societies certain egalitarian features, like the use of the second person in its familiar form among party members irrespective of rank, the subversion of traditional status and class differences by a new hierarchy in the party, and the sense of solidarity across class lines expressed symbolically. Actually, fascist regimes, given their social base and the unrevolutionary way in which they generally took power, did not fully activate those commitments and therefore in reality the two systems were very different. Both ideologies ultimately pursued, by different ways, a classless society rather than an institutionalization of class conflicts as it has become characteristic of societies under democratic governments. The critics of totalitarianism have seized on this aspect, stressing the negative side of a mass society undifferentiated, subordinated, and manipulated by the rulers, but in doing so have neglected the appeal that this renewed sense of community had for those living in societies in which class conflicts had become bitter, societies in which it was obvious that the dictatorship of the proletariat was not to be, in the sense of Marx, the dictatorship of the majority but of the minority, since important segments that Marx would have considered proletarian, like the white-collar workers, did not want to consider themselves proletarians.

The contrast between communism and fascism highlights both the importance of certain ultimate social and philosophical assumptions that differentiate them and also certain common responses to modern society and the strains it imposes with its pluralism, conflict of interests, absence of a shared comprehensive system of values after secularization. Those ultimate differences in intellectual origins, however, became crucially important for the different development of both systems and the basis of immanent critique. In turn, the relationship between the ideology and the realities of the society in which it was to be implemented politically, as well as the way in which the two movements came to power, made for very different consequences for different social strata. The realities of fascist and communist rule cannot be confused, whatever affinity at some level of analysis we might find in the ideological assumptions. However, some of those ideological assumptions were very important for the way of organizing political power and thereby to the common totalitarian features: the role of ideology, the concentration of power in a ruling group, the role of the party, and the emphasis on mobilization.

For a better understanding of both systems, however, it is interesting to compare specifically how those three aspects differ between the Soviet Union and Nazi Germany.

Probably the most important difference between communism and fascism can be found in the nature of the ideology and the way in which it affected the political process. We do not accept the position of those who deny to fascism the character of an ideology and reduce it exclusively to the arbitrary pronouncements of the leadership adapting ideas to Machiavellian power seeking. Recent work on fascism, particularly Gregor, Mosse, Nolte,[27] has again delineated clearly the difference between fascism and other political ideologies. The reader of fascist ideology and literature, party programs, and slogans can certainly distinguish them from other ideologies like conservatism or Catholic corporativism, to mention two of a certain affinity (Schmitter, 1974; Wiarda, 1973a, 1973b, 1974), the same way that he can distinguish a Marxist-Leninist formulation from the variety of African socialisms and similar ideologies of the Third World. The fact that fascism is a latecomer on the political scene and therefore defines itself largely in negative terms as antiliberalism, anticommunism, anticlericalism, antiinternationalism, antiproletarianism, etc., should not obscure the fact that there was a distinctive style, rhetoric, and sensibility that had a positive appeal in its time. The argument that an antirationalist conception and emphasis on action and emotion rather than intellectual and scientific thought cannot constitute an ideology ignores the fact that much of modern and respected philosophy and thought has an irrationalist strain. A more serious difference is that communism links with the work of Marx, who in addition to being a man of action was a philosopher and a learned social scientist. Despite the use by fascists of the name and the ideas of a number of philosophers, thinkers, and writers, none achieved similar importance for them and therefore no thought formulated before and independently of taking power became equally binding as a source of legitimacy and criticism within the movement. This, together with the irrationalist emphasis on action, not fully absent from Leninism, allowed infinitely wider scope to political opportunism and therefore made fascist totalitarianism much less an ideocracy and more the rule of a leader and his loyal followers, more often than not without ideas. Totalitarianism in both cases meant manipulation of the ideological heritage, in the case of Stalin even the elimination of the intellectuals in the movement, like Bukharin, in the case of Hitler the loss of influence of Rosenberg, or in that of Mussolini, of Gentile. The enshrinement of Marx and Lenin and of their printed work, however, ultimately allows some intellectual criticism and further elaboration of communist thought and thereby of vitality of the ideology. The ultimate ideas underlying both ideological movements are a lasting part of our intellectual heritage and respond to some needs of modern man, but undoubtedly Marxism, being closer to a modern science of society and economy, offers a better basis for the formulation of rational policies. Even when some outstanding intellectuals could feel a temporary sympathy or affinity with fascism (Hamilton, 1973), fewer could explain away its negative aspects; and the absence of a corpus of thought like that of Marx ultimately limited its appeal beyond committed followers and party hacks. The fact that Marx could be interpreted in a noncommunist-democratic and even liberal-humanist direction makes it possible for the non-Marxist-Leninist and particularly for the non-Stalinist to appreciate the ideology of communist systems. This in turn can be and has been a stimulus for ideological evolution, polycentrism (Labedz, 1962; Laqueur and Labedz, 1962; Drachkovitch, 1965; Shaffer, 1967; Triska, 1969), and therefore tension with a strict totalitarianism. In Nazism the combination of social Darwinism and totally unscientific racism with an irrationalist voluntarism in the hands of an uneducated autodidact led to a parochial and crude ideology whose implementation brought out the worst potentialities of ideological totalitarian rule. This makes it difficult to conceive a post-Hitler evolution.

The difference between the two totalitarianisms is based not on the fact that one has an ideology and the other does not but on the different quality of the two ideologies. This allows us to separate communism from its worst manifestations under Stalin but makes it almost impossible to separate national socialism from Hitler and his final solution. The fact that the fate of non-Nazi fascism became tied during the war to the leader of the fascist camp in a way that communism after Yugoslavia, China, and Cuba is not tied to the Soviet Union and Stalin is decisive for the future of both ideologies. We are likely to find fascist ideological elements in many nondemocratic regimes, but it is doubtful that we will find a true fascist regime and even less a true fascist totalitarianism. The lack of success of neofascist parties cannot be explained only by military defeat and discrimination against its representatives.

In spite of important similarities in the conception and organization of the totalitarian parties in communist and fascist systems, there are important differences between them that should not be neglected, differences that are not exclusively a result of the different social composition of the membership and/ or elite and the different social, economic, political, and historical contexts in which they came to power. The organizational conception of the Bolsheviks, after all, emerged out of the mass socialist parties more or less linked with the trade union movement of nineteenth-century Europe; and the Leninist conception of an elite of professional revolutionaries was an adaptation to the particular circumstances of czarist autocracy, even when it became rationalized in terms of incapacity of the working class masses to go beyond trade union consciousness (Schapiro, 1965; Daniels, 1969; Meyer, 1957). Fascist parties, in contrast, emerged out of the experiences of World War I and/or as a response to the success of communist parties. The war experience of the *arditi*, the *Frontkämpfer,* was the basis of the emphasis on military models of organization and discipline, the "community" of elite units, and the love of uniforms and symbols, exalted by the ideology. Reinforced by organizational forms and social composition, including the young and the veterans, the movement turns from instrument into an end in itself. The romantic element of the *Bund,* a sociological category invented by Schmalenbach to distinguish a type of group from both *Gesellschaft* ("association") and *Gemeinschaft* ("community"), is characteristic of fascist parties (Duverger, 1963, pp. 124–32). The ideological concern for personalized relations based on a search for meaning, a rejection of individualism, etc., reflects the concerns of the secularized bourgeoisie for a modern society without its insecurities (Merkl, 1975). It leads in the Nazi case to emphasize the pseudoreligious and therefore the ritual, the indoctrination, the style, the creation of a feeling of membership. A distinction, in military terminology, between a first and a second line, between the active militant member of the fascist squad and the regular party member, introduces into the party the elitist element and is the source of the characteristic heterogeneity of organizations in fascist totalitarianism. In Germany, with the pseudoreligious groups of the *völkisch* movement, with its romantic, mystic images of peasant-military democracy, medieval teutonic knights, and its semilegal or illegal paramilitary *Kampfbünde,* combined with Hitler's hate-love attitude toward the Jesuits, this tendency reaches its paroxysm (Gamm, 1962). There is nothing comparable in communist countries to the plurality of organizations, with distinctive uniform styles and outlook—the party, the SA, the SS, and ultimately the internal divisions within the SS—that we find in Germany. The Red Guard always remained basically instrumental rather than an elite of the party superior to the regular member. This plurality of organizations introduces into Nazi totalitarianism an element of heterogeneity and thereby of feudal rather than bureaucratic characteristics (Koehl, 1972). The infighting of the elites is not only of individuals but of political organizations, not of factions necessarily identified with different sectors of the society or the administration but of political organizations tied together only by their identification with the leader. Another consequence was that the terror became even more directly tied with the party with the strange fusion between the police and a party elite, the SS.

Ideological components reflected in organizational forms reinforce the fundamentally antidemocratic and antipopulist character of Nazism. They also reinforce the cult of masculinity, which, separating men and women, has a latent homosexual component. Without using the Nazi exaggeration, this style element also explains why in none of the fascist parties women would play a prominent role compared to some of the communist movements. The organizational form of the militia party organization also made it difficult for fascist parties to maintain their drive when they were out of power, to become electoral opposition parties, and accounts for the urgency they felt to gain power rather than to disintegrate. This kind of activism of the SA man or the *squadristi* could not be maintained in the same way as could the loyalty of party members and voters of a communist party. The organizational form of the militia party organization also accounts for the initial collaboration of army officers, their active involvement in fascist parties, but also for the suspicions and even hatred by the army of some fascist movements, reflected for example in the suppression of the Iron Guard by Marshall Antonescu. The exclusivist character of such paramilitary political organizations also accounts for the very different way the fascists and communists handled membership in the party of army officers in active service; the communists drove to affiliate officers with the party (Weinberg, 1964; Berghahn, 1969; Messerschmidt, 1969), while Franco went to the opposite extreme, making all officers party members. It is also at the root of the emergence of a party army like the Waffen SS, which cannot be compared to the special NKVD (People's Commissariat of Internal Affairs) troops under Beria, since such units did not have an equally ideologically justified status in the communist system. The multiorganizational structure of Nazism and the elitism within the elite movement led to a multiplication of channels of recruitment and an internal differentiation, which contrasts with the model of monolithic authority of some descriptions of totalitarianism. Nazi career lines took place not within the party and through missions of the party in different organizations but within the feudal structure of party organizations, in turn characterized by identification with different subleaders. However, this multiplicity, which some have likened to feudalism and others have described as a quasi-anarchy, while menacing the unity of the ruling group during the period of Hitler (who benefitted from playing one off against the other) and particularly after Hitler, did not imply the kind of pluralism we find in authoritarian regimes, or even the type of group politics that Skilling and others want to see in posttotalitarian communism. The articulation of these leader-follower structures and bureaucracies with the rest of the society was quite different. It was based not on functional specialization and a division of labor like that of party workers with experience in agriculture or industry but on personal linkages and affinities of style, cutting even more across the social structure than do factions in the communist party. The comparison between totalitarian and semitotalitarian parties shows how organizational principles are related to the ideology and interact constantly with it.

The characteristics of the ruling group and particularly the role of the leaders are probably the most important differentiating variables between totalitarian systems but also the least theoretically relevant. Historical context, particularly the process of taking power and consolidating it, and personality factors stand out more. These obviously are less susceptible to generalizations, more idiosyncratic, and to a certain extent accidental. It is difficult to say to what extent the pattern of interaction between Stalin and his intimate collaborators and that of Hitler were a reflection of the ideology and the organizational forms or of their personalities. The fact that Stalin had been only one among the initial leaders of the Bolshevik Revolution, far from loved by many of his peers who he wanted to make subordinates, accounts for the deep-seated suspicions in the relations and for the fact that purges affected much of the leadership of the politbureau (Schueller, 1966; Levytsky, 1974). In contrast, Hitler over a number of years in the opposition had been able to shape the party, and the departure of the dissidents had left only the loyal comrades; even so he felt the need to purge Roehm and his SA leaders. Where the difference between the two ruling groups might become more apparent is in the relationships between the top leader, his lieutenants, and the rank and file. Those relationships obviously depend very much on the process of growth of the party and the leadership group, as the works of Orlow (1973) and Nyomarkay (1967), the description of the relationship of the *Gauleiters* with Hitler by Peterson (1969), and the works on communist elites in Eastern Europe and in China (Farrell, 1970; Barton, Denitch, and Kadushin, 1973; Beck, 1970; Lewis, 1963; Scalapino, 1972) show. The date of joining the party, the shared experiences like jail, the international brigades, or regional party organizations, guerrilla versus underground activity in the cities, fusion of related parties or organizations, etc., become important factors in understanding the internal life of movement parties. They are—and this shows the importance of the political socialization and organizational experiences—generally more important than the standard sociological background variables used in the study of democratic elites. They also account for the different climates and styles of different totalitarian systems within the communist camp as well as among the fascists.

As Groth has stressed, the alliances made in the process of taking power have considerable impact on the system at least until its full consolidation and maturity. The fact that the fascists and Nazis came to power through a silent revolution under pseudolegal forms (Linz and Stepan, forthcoming), with the support of institutions and parties that hoped to use them for their own purposes and with a passive support or at least submission of many potential antagonists, accounts for a more complex relationship with the pre-takeover social structure than in communist systems that gained power by revolution, civil war, or support of the Soviet army (Seton-Watson, 1952; Gripp, 1973, pp. 19–39). Many of the differences between totalitarian systems, both communist and noncommunist, can be explained by how they gained power and their strength and cohesion before gaining power (Huntington, 1970, p. 14). The type of society in which they took over the government and the circumstances under which they did so also account for the more or less totalitarian character of their rule and, in cases like Italy and Spain, for the failures to establish a fully totalitarian regime despite the ambitions of many fascist leaders. The coexistence between fascist and prefascist or pseudofascist, if not antifascist, elements naturally affected the ideology, the organization, and the character of the party and its affiliates and many of its policies in the process of consolidation in power. The relative ease with which fascists gained power in contrast to the Russian, Chinese, Yugoslav, and even Cuban communists accounts for the much greater range of policy diversion even under the Nazis, so well described by Peterson (1969). We could establish some interesting parallels in Eastern European communist countries, particularly in the case of Poland, where the relative weakness of the Communist party and the strength of the Church led to patterns very different from those of Hungary. Azrael (1970) in his analysis of the varieties of de-Stalinization, Zvi Gitelman (1970) in his "Power and Authority in Eastern Europe," and Roger W. Benjamin and John H. Kautsky (1968) in their "Communism and Economic Development" have convincingly shown how the background of the society and the process of taking power and consolidating it have modified the nature of communist regimes. For our comparative purposes, however, we do not have a communist regime created by a silent revolution taking power by semi- or pseudolegal processes within a competitive democracy and once in power transforming its rule into a nondemocratic control except Czechoslovakia (Korbell, 1959). It would be interesting to see if in such a system there would develop some forms of cooperation between the preexisting institutions and elites in the Church and the managers and the military that would lead to a less total transformation of the social structure than other communist regimes have carried through. In the case of fascist regimes and particularly Nazism it is always difficult to distinguish the coincidence of interests between pre-takeover institutions and groups, the shared ideological commitments, the co-optation and corruption of those institutions by the yielders of political power, and the cooperation obtained by the coercion and fear. Certainly those factors all operated at one time or another, and the differences between totalitarian systems often are based on focusing on one or another phase of such systems. The persistence of pre-takeover social structures, institutions, and interests and the conservative character of the system, which Groth rightly stresses, would be true for the early years of Nazi rule and perhaps the first years of the War but not after July 20, 1944, and it might have disappeared after victory in World War II or under a Himmler or Bormann succession of Hitler and the elimination of other leaders like Goering.

As in all macrosociological phenomena, generalizations are made difficult by the fact that previous experiences are known. Scholars studying Chinese communism, Eastern European collectivization, terror in the Soviet Union and China, etc., all note how the knowledge of the Stalinist period has led communist rulers elsewhere to modify their tactics and attempt to avoid some of the worst features of Stalinism, to invent other methods of social control emphasizing, for example, voluntarism and thought control rather than police terror (Schurmann, 1968, pp. 311–13). In this sense it becomes dangerous to overgeneralize from any historical experience, and certainly no totalitarian system will be fully identical to any that has preceded it in time except when it is, like some Stalinist Eastern European systems for a short time, a dependent system. In this sense every totalitarian system—every political process—carried out by people who know about the recent past will not be identical to a previous one. No attempt of model building can ignore the historicity of macrosocial phenomena.

The Critiques of the Concept of Totalitarianism and Some Suggested Alternatives

In recent years important contributions have been made to the critique of the writings using the term totalitarianism and suggestions have been made to replace it by other concepts. With the exception of the use of the term "mobilization regimes" or "parties," none of the latter has gained equal acceptance. The critique has many valid points that should be extremely fruitful in a more careful elaboration of the model of the totalitarian system and even more so in advancing our knowledge of the variety of totalitarian systems in time and space. A somewhat systematic exposition of the many critiques and a sifting of their valid contributions and their less useful negative aspects seems to be a first step in preparing the ground for future thinking and research by those who want to retain the term.

Explicitly or implicitly many of the critics stress that the concept was formulated and gained acceptance in the context of the cold war with a pejorative evaluative connotation and that its polemic significance makes it intellectually useless (Barber, 1969; Curtis, 1969; Spiro, 1968; Burrowes, 1969). However, this could be said about many of the most important concepts in political science, and the alternative would be to renounce all the terms that have entered the political discourse and struggle and to formulate a distinctive formal terminology, which would lead to the opposite accusation of being scholastic and ivory-towerish and difficult for the layperson to understand. Another alternative would be to use the terminology used by the actors to describe their systems with their evaluative connotations and to describe the realities so often covered up by those terms. Neither of those solutions seems adequate. The critics, in addition, forget that the term totalitarian was formulated before the cold war (Jänicke, 1971) and that many scholars and politicians—and not only liberal democrats—had discovered the common elements between fascist and communist systems: Robert Michels is just one distinguished name among the scholars, and on the political scene there are the left wings of a number of fascist movements and some dissident communists. The critics also forget that the term totalitarian was formulated and accepted without negative connotation by many fascists. Therefore the critique is rather, Can the same term be used to describe certain common features of fascist and communist regimes rather than to be limited to fascism, in which case we might not need the term? Certainly the concept has become associated, particularly in some definitions, with some of the most negative aspects in the evaluation by most people of those regimes, specifically terror, neglecting those that can be considered more positive from a variety of value perspectives. It is no accident that Hannah Arendt should practically limit the use of the term to the rule of Hitler and Stalin. If, however, it should turn out that a number of political systems in addition to those two share a sufficient number of characteristics to distinguish them from other autocracies, we should be allowed to retain the term. Ultimately, much hinges on the interpretation of the rule of those two men as being the result either of their idiosyncratic personalities or of the possibilities that the particular form of organization of political life and the ideological assumptions justifying it offered them.

The critics are on solid ground when they reject the indiscriminate use of the term to describe all nondemocratic systems or at least all those the author does not like, a critique that also would deprive us of any scholarly use of the term fascism. Certainly if the term has any use it is to describe a very specific type of autocracy and not to serve as a synonym for dictatorship, despotism, or just nondemocratic regimes. There are certainly regimes we would not in any meaningful use of the term call totalitarian which from most value perspectives would be considered equally or more negative than the rule of Hitler, especially the rule of Trujillo.

Another argument of revisionists is to stress that some of the features used in characterizing totalitarian systems are also found in societies under different political systems, including advanced Western democracies. Similarly, the work of Barrington Moore (1965, pp. 30–88) on totalitarian elements in preindustrial societies has shown the usefulness of the concept totalitarian beyond the study of the political systems we would call totalitarian. Certainly a distinction between totalitarian political systems and totalitarian elements in other systems is a fruitful one, but does not invalidate characterizing as totalitarian those systems in which totalitarian elements are dominant and central to the political system. The recent critique of liberal democracy by the new left certainly introduces confusion in the use of the term totalitarian but indirectly is evidence of its usefulness (Marcuse, 1964, 1969).

Another criticism is that totalitarianism refers only to a reality that has been metamorphosized by time. Regimes that have been vanquished to the realm of historical controversy and others that have undergone fundamental changes seem to relinquish the term to the field of historical scholarship, like those of feudalism, absolute monarchy, enlightened despotism, and the police state. In that case the question would be: Is the study of such systems only of historical interest, or are they close enough to our own political life and reality to be significant in understanding contemporary political systems in a way quite different from the concept of feudalism (using the term in a strictly historical sense)?

Much of the criticism justifiably centers on the number, different character, and lack of precision of the definitions. Unfortunately that criticism can be directed against most concepts in political science dealing with complex phenomena. Certainly the different definitions and descriptions have contributed to our knowledge by highlighting different dimensions of the phenomena and probably providing elements for further conceptualization, distinguishing types of totalitarian systems that share only a limited number of crucial common characteristics. The effort of Benjamin R. Barber (1969) to classify the phenomenological and essentialist definitions is useful but somewhat scholastic. Most such definitions underline some of the qualitative or quantitative dimensions on which the political systems that are to be subsumed are different from a variety of others. Certainly the more descriptive rather than essentialist definitions make it easier to identify empirically a particular system as totalitarian, or at least as more or less totalitarian. Certainly most of the scholars have not gone very far in operationalizing the dimensions to the extent that would allow an empirical researcher to make an unambiguous decision that a system at any particular point in time is or is not totalitarian or to transform an attribute space into a continuum allowing measures of totalitarianism using some quantification of a series of indicators. This has been and certainly is one of the great obstacles in the use of the concept. One possibility, naturally, is to conceive totalitarianism as an ideal type, which will not correspond exactly to any concrete historical reality. In fact, some of the essentialist's definitions include normative elements in the minds of the leaders of totalitarian parties and the ideologists of what a totalitarian political system and a society dominated by it should be, rather than what it is likely to be. As we have seen and Giovanni Sartori (1962) has stressed, this is also true for the concept of democracy and perhaps is inherent to many political science concepts. To some extent our insights into the nature of totalitarian systems will come from an analysis of these tensions between the ideal type and the reality it partly describes. It is no accident that some of the essentialist concepts would be acceptable to the leaders that have shaped those systems and often, from their value perspective, do not involve a negative connotation as some of the more descriptive concepts almost inevitably do.

A much more substantial criticism is that the term totalitarian attempts to cover too much, to characterize political systems that on many important aspects are fundamentally different. The burden of proof must be on those who advocate the term to show the extent to which some communist systems, at least in some of their phases, share a sufficient number of important characteristics with the Nazi system to warrant the inclusion under a common concept, to show that both subtypes respond to some similar preconditions in their emergence, and that the use of the concept allows us to understand better the way they handle some invariant problems of political life. It is also the burden of advocates of the concept to show that the systems so characterized share characteristics that differentiate them from other types of autocracies which would not be highlighted without the use of such a concept. Much of this has been and can be done, but it also demands as a counterpart more thorough analysis of the basic differences between totalitarianism of the Stalinist era and that of the National Socialists or Fascists. This has unfortunately not been done systematically in the literature.

A more thorough analysis of the subtypes of totalitarianism—communist, fascist, and perhaps nationalist—and of stages of development of totalitarian systems and the modification of soviet totalitarianism in different social contexts, especially the USSR, China, some of the Eastern European communist states, and perhaps Cuba, should lead us to a more elaborate typology of totalitarian systems. It also should bring the term totalitarianism down from its fairly high position on the ladder of abstraction to produce middle-range theories (Sartori, 1970). The most general and abstract construct of a totalitarian system should serve as a point of reference to understand and describe better the various subtypes of communist and fascist systems and to contribute to a theory about the processes leading to the consolidation and establishment of a totalitarian system and those leading to their transformation, like the recent efforts by Azrael (1970) to understand types of de-Stalinization, or posttotalitarian systems in communist countries.

A serious limitation of some of the definitions of totalitarianism has been the static and rigid character of many of the conceptualizations, which ignored the dynamic element, the tensions inherent in the ideal and almost normative models, the resistance that societies offer to the full development of the totalitarian system, and therefore the stages, phases, degrees, of totalitarianism. A central theme on the agenda of the study of totalitarianism has to be the study of change in and of them. Unfortunately for the scholar, the limited time that the most pure totalitarian fascist system existed and the fact that there was no successor regime to Hitler, in contrast to the long period of Soviet rule and the variety of communist systems, make it difficult to formulate generalizations about the processes of change in totalitarian systems rather than only within communist totalitarian systems.

A very different type of criticism is one we might label "historicist," which underlines the unique social or cultural preconditions and traditions of the country in which regimes we labelled totalitarian emerged. The "Slavophile" interpretation of Soviet communism[28] or the analysis of the unique German political, cultural, and social history that accounts for the rise of national socialism[29] are powerful alternatives to a political science conceptual analysis. Certainly scholars have made important contributions stressing the continuities between modern totalitarian systems and the premodern or preindustrial traditions of their societies. Others have rightly stressed how the unique personality of certain leaders accounts for some essential features of the political systems they created or shaped. Some would go so far as to argue that without those leaders those systems would never have emerged, particularly in the cases of Mussolini and Hitler, to which we certainly could add the role of Lenin in the victory of bolshevism. However valid such an approach might be to a point, it is certainly not fruitful to reduce such a complex historical phenomenon as national socialism or Stalinism to their personalities and to treat them as accidents not requiring explanation by social scientists. In this respect the

Marxist or Marxist-Leninist inability to explain in general categories, in their case sociological/economic, the phenomenon of Stalinism stands in clear contrast to their scientific ambitions. Obviously it should be the task of any in-depth analysis of the systems under the rule of these men to attempt to describe the impact of their personal leadership on the system and to separate the more structural components from the more idiosyncratic ones. Probably the specific form that terror took under Stalin cannot be fully explained without reference to his personality. However, the historicist critique of totalitarianism as a conceptual approach is implicitly a critique of any effort of social science conceptualization of ultimately unique historical phenomenons. While such a critique can moderate the illegitimate claims of social scientists, it cannot be accepted without loss of knowledge and of understanding of social phenomena.

A more fruitful criticism comes from those scholars who have studied carefully the reality of totalitarian rule, particularly at the local level and due to the openness of the archives in Germany. Those scholars have rightly stressed, as has Edward N. Peterson (1969), the limits of Hitler's power, the heteronomy rather than monism of power, the changing role of the party and other organizations struggling for power, the diversion of decision making, the survival of opposition in and under the system—the islands of separateness, as Inkeles called them. These are facts that are incompatible with some of the more simplistic and overdrawn characterizations of totalitarian systems. But those scholars who emphasize them risk losing sight of the forest for the trees, missing the more central tendencies that differentiate the systems from other autocracies. The work of Skilling (1973) stressing the group politics element in communist systems, particularly after Stalin, is a welcome corrective of overstatements of the monism of such regimes, as long as it does not fall into the pitfall, stressed by Sartori, of neglecting the essential difference between such relatively pluralistic group politics within the framework of a totalitarian or even an authoritarian system and analogous processes in democratic regimes.

The theories of convergence between the Soviet Union and the United States, summarized by Alfred G. Meyer (1970), more or less explicitly question the usefulness of the totalitarian category. By pointing out common tendencies and problems in advanced industrial societies, particularly the Soviet Union and the United States—the similarity in bureaucratic organizations, large-scale economic units, certain types of economic decision making and military organization, the similar impact of such societies on common people and the resulting psychological attitudes of conformity, powerlessness, etc.—these theories represent a welcome corrective of a tendency to make black and white contrasts between societies. However, much of the writings in this direction focus more on the similarities in social structure than in political institutions. Ideological motives are not absent, nor are the desires to overcome the cold war or, particularly among some new-left critics, to question both advanced, industrial, democratic and communist societies from a distinct value perspective. These analyses, while discovering the similarity in certain key decision-making processes at the top—the kind of processes analyzed by Mills in his *Power Elite*—and certain similarities in the daily life of common citizens in their factories or in their dealings with bureaucracies, tend to ignore some of the fundamental differences in a whole middle range of decision making, institutions, and roles in different political systems.

Undoubtedly the most serious challenge to the construct of totalitarianism comes from the difficulty of defining in clear operational terms the difference between totalitarian systems and other types of autocracy, particularly in empirical terms, because of the difficulty of documentation. The problem is much more complex than the problem of defining the boundaries between competitive democracies, as we define them, and various transitional authoritarian regimes. It is certainly more difficult because the changes are more likely to be matters of degree and generally do not involve the discontinuities created by revolutions, coups, or foreign intervention which with rare exceptions have characterized the transition between democracy and authoritarian regimes or totalitarian systems.

The critique of theories of totalitarianism has not been limited to questioning those theories; there are some attempts to offer alternative conceptualizations. In some cases it is difficult to distinguish clearly the alternative concepts from the old definitions of totalitarianism. Others, like Tucker's (1965) concept of "mobilization regimes," seem to us to fall into some of the same difficulties that the critics of the loose use of the term totalitarian have noted, specifically, covering too wide a range of autocracies and ignoring important differences among them. In addition, the term mobilization, as Azrael (1970a, pp. 136–37) has noted, is in itself ambiguous, is used as a distinctive criterion rather than as one of a number of dimensions to characterize political systems, and is very difficult to use empirically. Other attempts of conceptualization, like Meyer's (1967) "administrative totalitarianism," "totalitarianism without terror," or "rationalization" and "populist totalitarianisms" describing certain features of post-Stalinist Russian political life, are more fruitful but do not imply a rejection of the broader category of totalitarianism. Other conceptualizations, like that offered by Rigby (1969) of "traditional market and organizations societies," seem to deal more with social and economic systems than with political systems. Certainly the alternative concepts offered in recent years have not gained as wide an acceptance as the old concept of totalitarianism.

The efforts of the critics have not led us to give up some concept of totalitarianism, even though we might accept the suggestion of finding another term less loaded with the connotations that have become attached with it through the rule of Hitler and Stalin, which might be considered quite unique. The critics have, however, made evident that the term should not be used loosely if it is going to be of any use, that a theory of totalitarianism or totalitarianisms does not exhaust the understanding and description of particular historical political systems, that there is urgent need for careful systematic comparison between totalitarian systems to discover their common and their differential elements, that we need a typology of totalitarian systems, and that the theory has to include a more dynamic analysis of change within and of totalitarian systems rather than, as up to now, theories about the origin of totalitarianism. Certainly much of our thinking and research has been centered on the rise of totalitarian movements and the takeover of power after the breakdown of democracies, particularly the rise of fascism. Even in the case of the Soviet Union there has been little theorizing about how the system evolved from the February Revolution to the dominance of the Bolsheviks, the displacement of other radical parties (Schapiro, 1965; Daniels, 1969) from Lenin to Stalin, and at what point we can consider the system totalitarian and why it should have become so. A comparative study of the rise to power of autochthonous communist movements in the Soviet Union, China, Cuba, and North Vietnam would certainly tell us more than some of the more abstract models like Kornhauser's *Politics of Mass Society* (1959). The military defeat of fascism and particularly Nazism has prevented scholars from analyzing change in totalitarian systems after succession crises, but since the death of Stalin and de-Stalinization an analysis of the dynamics of change in and of totalitarian systems has become imperative. In addition, more monographic research and theoretical conceptualization of nondemocratic regimes that cannot be meaningfully labeled totalitarian should help us in conceptualizing more precisely different types of autocracy. The discovery of multiple dimensions that distinguish types of totalitarianism and clarify the distinction between totalitarianism and other nondemocratic regimes should also allow us a more complex evaluation of such regimes. Certainly totalitarian systems must have many positive features that make them attractive to people who are not ignorant of some of their worst features. The ultimate result of the criticism should be a more complex theory of totalitarianisms rather than the initial model of a totalitarian system. In the same way, contemporary political science is beginning to think about types of democracies and the internal dynamics of democratic regimes rather than of a single type (identified preferably with one or another of the great Anglo-Saxon democracies).

The Conditions for Nondemocratic, Particularly Totalitarian, Systems in Modern or Modernizing Societies

A superficial analysis would suggest that the absence of the conditions making competitive democracies possible and stable[30] would be the first answer to the question of what conditions must exist for nondemocratic regimes and more specifically for totalitarianism. However, this might not be true even for nondemocratic regimes, since those, as the critics have noted, have appeared in countries that according to many analysts should have had a high probability of having democratic regimes. Obviously the introduction of the time dimension, analyzing the conditions that existed when the regimes were installed rather than at any specific point in time, would have eliminated some apparent exceptions. If we accept the distinction between a variety of nondemocratic regimes and the totalitarian systems, we still have to answer the question, What are the specific conditions for totalitarianism? A more fruitful accounting scheme would require answers to the questions that follow.

1. A first step in the analysis would be to specify the conditions leading to the crisis and final breakdown of pretotalitarian regimes, distinguishing various types of nondemocratic regimes and democracies, since at least one of the most outstanding models of totalitarianism emerged in a former democracy. It is perhaps this aspect that has been studied best by scholars, particularly the outstanding work of Bracher and his collaborators Sauer and Schulz on the rise to power of Hitler (Bracher, 1957; Bracher, Sauer, and Schulz, 1960), the works on the crisis of Weimar democracy (Matthias and Morsey, 1960; Eschenburg, 1966; Conze and Raupach, 1967; Kaltefleiter, 1968; Lepsius, 1966, 1971; Jasper, 1968), as well as the excellent study of the process at the local level by Allen (1965). The less theoretical but richly informative studies on the rise of fascism in Italy (De Felice, 1965, 1966, 1968), the origins of the Spanish Civil War,[31] the end of party government in Japan (Scalapino, 1953), the decline of constitutional democracy in Indonesia (Feith, 1962), and some of the studies of the fall of Latin American democracies, particularly Brazil in 1964 (Schneider, 1971; Stepan, 1971), should allow the formulation of some model or theory of the breakdown of democracies (Linz and Stepan, forthcoming). However, the analysis of the crisis and the breakdown of democracy does not tell us what kind of regimes will emerge or what conditions will make for its consolidation and stability. In fact, ignoring the cases of reequilibration of democracy, like France in 1958, in only one of the cases mentioned was the outcome a pure totalitarian system and in another an incipient one. Breakdown of democracy therefore is not identical with the establishment of totalitarianism, but it can be one of the conditions. It should not be forgotten, however, that the other outstanding model of totalitarian system did not result from the breakdown of a relatively stabilized democracy, since the regime born in the February Revolution of 1917 in Russia can certainly not be considered a minimally institutionalized democracy.

2. A question that coincides in part with that of the crisis and breakdown of democratic regimes is the analysis of the conditions leading to the emergence and growth of antidemocratic mass parties.[32] Since such parties have appeared and gained widespread support in a number of democracies without having been able to provoke or contribute decisively to their breakdown, the study of the emergence of fascist and communist parties and their appeal, organization, leadership, policies, legal and illegal activities, etc., can contribute only one element to the causal chain. In fact it might be misleading to speak of totali-

tarian parties, since the term can refer only to the type of political system such parties might intend to create, and we know that a number of them have been unable even after the breakdown of democracy to create totalitarian systems. Some parties committed to ideologies and to some degree to models like the Soviet Union, which would lead us to label them totalitarian, in democracies of sufficient stability over long periods of time might undergo a process of change that could in the long run make them legitimate participants in a democratic political system.[33] The case of Italy in the near future might be particularly interesting from this perspective (Blackmer, 1968; Blackmer and Tarrow, forthcoming).

3. If the breakdown of democracy and even the existence of a party committed to an ideology and having many of the organizational characteristics that should make it the single party of a totalitarian regime are not sufficient to establish such a regime, we have to ask an additional question: Which are the conditions that lead to the establishment of a more or less totalitarian system rather than to other forms of nondemocratic government once a democratic regime has broken down? Given the definition of totalitarian system, it is highly unlikely that such a system will be created in a short time, and therefore we can expect a period of transition of nondemocratic rule that does not become fully institutionalized and leads to the emergence of a totalitarian system. In this sense it is more difficult to date the establishment of totalitarianism than the breakdown of democracy. Therefore the most important and specific question that has to be raised is: How does a nondemocratic situation or regime develop the specific features we have identified as totalitarian? How do the ruling groups conceive totalitarian institutions or is it an accident that they should have developed such a model of society? What factors make some of them successful and prevent other groups from transforming their political systems and societies into truly totalitarian systems?

4. What accounts for the stabilization and persistence of totalitarian systems over longer periods of time? In this context it is important to note that to this day no totalitarian system has been overthrown by force internally, but those that have lost some of their distinctive totalitarian characteristics have done so by a complex process of transformation.

5. Is totalitarianism a stable type of political system like democracy or many traditional forms of autocratic rule? And if not, which are the factors leading to transformation into other forms of nondemocratic rule?

The first two questions are not specific to the problem of totalitarianism but to the problem of the breakdown of democracies and the emergence of potential leaders and parties that could, under favorable circumstances, become the core of a totalitarian system. It seems difficult to conceive an analysis of the conditions making for the emergence of the more specific features of a totalitarian system without reference to the particular subtypes, most importantly by the communist and fascist ones. In addition it becomes difficult to analyze those conditions without explaining why in some situations in which there were many elements favoring the establishment of a totalitarian system this was not possible. In this respect the comparison of the evolution of the Nazi regime and that of Mussolini would be extremely revealing, as would be a comparison of the evolution of the different communist systems, particularly in the Stalinist phase. Many of the analyses of these processes were written at the time or shortly after the event and therefore could assume that certain conditions were unique to the societies under study, when events years later would show that some similar processes would be possible in very different societies. In this respect it is interesting to see how the initial interpretation of the rise of fascism and the consolidation of Mussolini in power looked for distinctive characteristics of Italian society and history, and interpretations of a number of relatively underdeveloped countries of Eastern Europe and Turkey asserted that similar developments would not be possible in advanced industrial societies and particularly in Germany, in spite of the strength of the National Socialist party (Borkenau, 1933; Matossian, 1958). The literature derived from the experience of Germany and the Soviet Union, in turn, underlined certain characteristics of industrial society that would seem irrelevant in the case of China. Perhaps it would be better to proceed through the analysis of particular cases of successful and unsuccessful drives toward totalitarianism, and only after the variables most relevant in each case have been analyzed to attempt a generalization at a higher level of abstraction.

Just as the analysis of the conditions for the instoration of democracy, has to face the problem of endogenous processes as distinct from exogenous factors, so does the analysis of totalitarianism.[34] We cannot forget the external imposition of democratic systems in the case of Italy, Germany, and Japan after World War II, even when there were many endogenous factors favorable for the success of the regime so instored (Dahl, 1971, pp. 189–201). In the case of Stalinist totalitarian or semitotalitarian systems we also have to be aware of such exogenous factors like the presence of the Soviet army. Those cases, however, show how important the endogenous factors were for the full consolidation of such a regime when we consider the later evolution of the different Eastern European countries.

Cutting across many of the questions we have raised, we encounter different intellectual perspectives, the contribution of different disciplines, and a variety of theoretical approaches, which, unfortunately, have not been applied to all cases but only to some so that it is impossible to test their validity for others. For example, in the literature on the origins and the development of Nazi totalitarianism we have a number of studies that emphasize psychological variables, culture, personality, even psychoanalytical perspectives (Greenstein, Handbook, Vol. 2), but relatively few studies have applied the same perspective to the rise and consolidation of power of Stalin. Marxism has provided the students of fascism with many of their hypotheses, but few have applied a Marxist theoretical perspective to Stalinism. Most of the theoretical orientations and hypotheses developed for the cases in which totalitarian systems consolidated themselves in power have not been tested, *a contrario,* in those cases where the drive toward totalitarianism was unsuccessful or only partly successful. We shall deal with those theories in other sections in accounting for the emergence of a variety of types of authoritarian, but not totalitarian, regimes, which should complement our review of the theories on the origins and conditions for totalitarianism.

Two Historico-Sociological Analyses: Wittfogel and Barrington Moore

Some of the analyses of totalitarianism, rather than focussing on the particular historical crisis that led to the breakdown of a predecessor regime, the concurrent social disorganization, and the rise to power of a new elite with a totalist commitment, place the problem in a macrohistorical context of basic socioeconomic and organizational structures resulting from a long evolution. Outstanding works in this tradition are Wittfogel (1957) and Moore (1966). For Wittfogel, *Oriental Despotism,* as a form of total power resulting from the requirement of a bureaucratic rule to regulate the use of water in the societies he calls hydraulic—described by Marx as the "Asiatic mode of production"— serves as a basis for despotic institutions. Societies in which "the state is stronger than society" limit the development of autonomous secondary groups of political significance and lead to the development of a stratification system based on political control rather than property, that is, bureaucratic capitalism and landlordism. Significantly, in his view, communist scholars have ignored Marx's analysis of this type of society, presumably because it could serve to interpret contemporary realities in the communist world. The theory has not remained unchallenged, particularly by Eberhard with respect to the role of the Chinese gentry (for a review see Eisenstadt, 1958).

More directly linked with contemporary political realities—though in my view there are important missing steps—is the thesis of Moore (1966) about alternative paths to modernity in his *Social Origin of Dictatorship and Democracy,* significantly subtitled: *Lord and Peasant in the Making of the Modern World.* The first path has been the great revolutions and civil wars that led to the combination of capitalism and Western democracy. The second route has also been capitalist, but culminated during the twentieth century in fascism. Germany and Japan are the obvious cases, called the capitalist and reactionary form, revolution from above due to the weakness of the bourgeoisie. The third route is communism, exemplified in Russia and China, countries in which the great agrarian bureaucracies inhibited the commercial and later industrial impulses, even weaker than in Germany and Japan. The then-large remaining peasantry provided the destructive revolutionary force that overthrew the old order under communist leadership, which later made the peasants its primary victims. The ways in which the landed upper classes and the peasants reacted to the challenge of commercial agriculture were the decisive factors in determining the political outcome.

The fusion of peasant grievances with those of other strata has been decisive for revolutions, but the success of revolutions has been negative for peasants although decisive in creating new political and economic conditions. Those revolutions have been the result of the absence of commercial revolution in agriculture led by the landed upper classes and the survival of peasant social institutions into the modern era, with consequent stresses particularly when traditional and capitalist modes of pumping surplus out of the countryside were added to each other. This and the loss of functions of the landlord with the growth of centralized monarchy was the cause of revolutions. One outcome was conservative modernization and fascism, with a separation of government from society and modernization from above at the expense of the lower classes after unsuccessful attempts at parliamentary liberal democracy. In it the landed upper class will use a variety of levers to hold down a labor force on the land.

Moore's effort—to whose richness in specific analyses, complexity, and limitations we cannot do justice—by offering an explanation of the conditions for democracy, fascism, and communism, places the problem of nondemocratic politics in an ambitious historical framework worth testing and refining (Moy, 1971). In our view the neglect of the smaller European democracies that did not undergo the great revolutions, the equation of Japanese authoritarian rule with Nazi totalitarianism under the common label "fascism," and the ambiguous answer to the question Why democracy in India? pose serious problems to his analysis. Even greater are the problems raised by the time gap between the agrarian developments in Germany in the nineteenth century and the rise of Nazism to power in the thirties, the neglect of the tensions created within urban industrial society with the rise of an organized working class, and the impact of World War I and its aftermath on the middle classes. The same would be true for the impact of war and defeat on the semitraditional agrarian societies of Russia and China in making possible the rise to power with opportune peasant support of communist revolutionaries, a process not explainable exclusively in terms of socioeconomic structure and labor repression.

III. TRADITIONAL AUTHORITY AND PERSONAL RULERSHIP

Introduction

The main types of modern political systems—democratic, totalitarian, and authoritarian—are at the center of our attention in this chapter. There are, however, still political systems that would not fit, by any stretching of concepts, into those three main types, particularly various forms of traditional authority (sometimes combined, it is true, with more modern bureaucratic-military elements). Traditional rule of more or less patrimonial or feudal character still enjoys considerable legitimacy, even though its future is in doubt. Those traditional elements are even more important at the regional and local level in many countries in the Maghreb, Southeast Asia, and Subsaharan Africa. On the periphery of the modern Western world, particularly Latin America after independence, under formally democratic constitutions, forms of nonstrictly traditional personal rulership emerged: *caudillismo* and the oligarchic rule of local notables, landowners, and *políticos*, sometimes in alliance with a more modern center, a system known as *caciquismo*. In fact, the combination of traditional and modern elements in economically underdeveloped countries with an unmobilized population (sometimes ethnically and culturally distinct like the Andean and Middle American Indians) and with limited civil liberties made possible what we might call "oligarchic democracies," often alternating with more open authoritarian rule (for example in Peru, see Bourricaud, 1967). In a few societies relatively unique circumstances allowed the emergence of more centralized, in some respects more modern forms of personal rulership (to use the expression of Guenther Roth, 1971) not based on tradition, or charisma, or organized corporative institutions, or a modern single party. We shall discuss this type of highly arbitrary personal rule as "sultanistic," borrowing the term from Max Weber.

The regimes just mentioned—*caudillismo, caciquismo,* oligarchic democracy, sultanistic—show many similarities with those we label authoritarian (*strictu sensu*). The coercion and fear under sultanistic regimes reminds one of totalitarianism but the roots and function of the regimes are radically different. All this leads us to discuss these types of political systems separatedly in the next few pages.

Traditional and Semitraditional Legitimate Authority

It is beyond our scope to review the extensive literature on premodern political systems, except for brief references to the few states still under traditional rule and to the persistence of traditional elements, legitimation, and institutions in partly modernized systems. Political anthropologists, particularly the students of African politics, have significantly broadened our understanding of how the state and primitive political systems emerge.[35] Historians, and in their footsteps sociologists, have made major advances in the systematic typological and comparative study of a multiplicity of political forms—from gerontocracy, patriarchalism, and patrimonialism to kingship in different societies, from ancient city-states like the Greek polis in its various manifestations to the medieval city-states of the Renaissance.[36] Feudalism in the West, in Japan, and elsewhere, the evolution of representative institutions and estate societies in the West and the centralized traditional polities (particularly the bureaucratic empires), and the emergence of the modern state have been the object of historical and social science scholarship for decades. The great political and legal thinkers, moralists, and churchmen throughout the ages have added their perspectives. Thus many disciplines have contributed to our understanding of that variety of *premodern, predemocratic political forms* which with few exceptions were autocratic and devoid of a free and peaceful competition for power among all the members of the political community, even less among all the inhabitants of a political unit.

That scholarship has crystallized, notably in the work of Max Weber, in a series of typological and analytical concepts of more than historico-descriptive value for the social scientist, concepts that are of great use in understanding contemporary political systems, particularly those in transition from tradition to modernity in the non-Western world. The historico-sociological scholarship has also contributed much to our understanding of the historical, institutional, and legal conditions for the emergence of representative institutions and, with them, of liberal democratic regimes. The persistence of traditional political culture, most evident in the great non-Christian civilizations, and the role of religious values and institutions in many societies make the understanding of the traditional political culture essential in the study of diverse regimes.[37] Authoritarian rule outside of communist countries, and perhaps even in them, in non-Western and largely rural societies cannot ignore the traditional elements in their politics. These elements are apt to be strongest at the local community level, and scholars focusing on the authoritarian structures at the center—single parties, military establishments, bureaucracies—risk underestimating the extent to which government and politics take place in traditional or mixed institutions according to traditional values, legitimated by religion and tradition, through traditional channels, and at the margin or outside the controls of central authorities. The growing body of scholarship on politics at the local, tribal, community, or regional level in those countries is likely to correct or, more exactly, to complement the description of both democratic and authoritarian governments in many parts of the world.

The small and diminishing number of Third World traditional political systems whose rulers enjoy continuing legitimacy and govern through patrimonial bureaucracies, feudal authoritative structures, tribal organizations, or some combination of traditional forms should be distinguished from those in which such elements have been mixed with nontraditional, generally Western institutions, often in uneasy coexistence. Some of those relatively pure traditional politics have shown considerable stability as compared with semimodern states, though it is difficult to say if it is the persistence of traditional legitimacy beliefs, the traditional or premobilized social structure, or isolation and economic underdevelopment (or in the Middle East disproportionate wealth) that accounts for the stability of the regimes, for example, of the emperor of Ethiopia (Perham, 1947; Hess and Loewenberg, 1964; Levine, 1965; Abraha, 1967; Hess, 1970), and the king of Nepal (Rose and Fisher, 1970), or some of the kings, emirs, and sheiks on the Arabic peninsula. Even after their formal overthrow or abdication such rulers may continue to exercise power under pseudo-modern forms copied from the West. Yet Thailand (Wilson, 1962; Riggs, 1967) and Iran (Binder, 1962; Zonis, 1971), two Asian countries never subject to colonial rule, have commingled modern authoritarian or democratic forms and the remnants of traditional legitimacy to sustain apparently stable social orders without undergoing radical breaks with tradition. Malaysia too is proof that such partial continuity with the past is not fully incompatible with the introduction of democratic institutions (Milne, 1967), even when the number of semitraditional regimes with bureaucratic-military-authoritarian governments seems to be growing. Traditional authority of monarchs and their patrimonial bureaucracies has and can facilitate the introduction of modern political institutions, a process with historical precedents in Japan in the Meiji restoration or the more recent institution of democracy under the American occupation.[38] Traditional authority can persist in mixed political systems but there is no evidence that it can be fully restored once elements of discontinuity have appeared. Attempts at restoration may only lead to various forms of neotraditional authoritarian rule, often, as in the case of Morocco,[39] with considerable instability.

The societies of the Maghreb exemplify very well how a historical heritage of a traditional, precolonial political and social structure and its transformation under different patterns of colonial rule, in turn partly a response to preconquest structures, can affect political developments after independence. The excellent study by Elbaki Hermassi (1972) comparing national development, both political and economic, in Morocco, Tunisia, and Algeria explains how the dominance of the monarchy, the party, and the army in each case is the result of structural factors and elite development, elite coalitions, and cleavages resulting from that historical background, precolonial and colonial. Hermassi shows how the Moroccan monarchy proved too powerful to be weakened by the political parties and too entrenched to allow expansion of the political system. He notes, following Samuel Huntington, three possible strategies open to the monarchy: to reduce its authority and promote movement toward a modern constitutional monarchy, to combine monarchical and popular authority in the same political system, or to maintain the monarchy as the principal source of authority and minimize the disruptive effects on it by the broadening of political consciousness (Huntington, 1968, pp. 40–91). The king attempted the third by assuming personal command of the army and the police and placing the ministry of interior in the hands of a former head of his private cabinet. This solution has led to a quasi-vizierial system without having opted initially for a purely vizierial or purely ministerial system. This unstable arrangement based on a council dominated by nonparty technicians, not responsible before political groups—which could make their work impossible—and not committed by collective responsibility for the government, ultimately forced Mohammed V and his successor, Hassan II, to vizierial governments with their members separately designated and individually responsible to the king, to use the description of Zartman (1971).

The rejection of the second strategy—direct monarchical rule leavened by some popular participation, for example, by the *Istiqulal* party and a variety of organized interests represented in the National Assembly—led to the split of the nationalist movement and the formation of a new opposition to the regime. To play off this new opposition the king summoned counterelites, such as the supporters of the rural Berber cause and the advocates of pluralism (who argued that the complexity of Moroccan society made one-party rule unworkable and a royal arbitrator a necessity). After the elections under a constitution promulgated in 1962 gave the monarchical forces only 69 seats of 144, the king suspended the constitution and reverted to government through his ministry of interior, first under a state of emergency and later under a new fundamental law that legalized his absolute power. The regime, as the repeated attempts to overthrow it and its ineffectiveness in economic policy making show, finds itself largely isolated from the political elite. It is an interesting example of the impossibility of return to stable traditional rule after a period of considerable political mobilization. In the Moroccan case the situation was compounded by the absence of success in economic development due largely to the constraints imposed by the limited power basis of the regime.

Hermassi's analysis of the historical development of Morocco before independence exemplifies well the kind of conditions that can lead to the stalemate of neotraditionalism. Colonial rule often reinforces traditional social structures and institutions at the same time as it produces the mobilization of new social forces in a struggle for independence. In the nineteenth century the Maghrebi states were all characterized by patrimonialism—private appropriation of army and administration, total discretion in appointments of officers, dynastic appropriation of the land, and imitation of the same traits in the provinces. Even so, the personal exercise of power was to greater or lesser extent circumscribed by religious and traditional restraints. Another constraint on the patrimonial domination emanated from the tribal grounding of the rural society, which created constant problems in territorial and social unification for the state apparatus. In Morocco the state remained dependent on armed tribes until the middle of the nineteenth century, and the establishment (*Makhzen*) remained a rudimentary organization dependent for its effectiveness on the existence of a venerate personage, an institution unto himself, the sultan. Patrimonial rule faced the almost unsolvable problem of maintaining in a quasi-subsistence economy a taxation system capable of meeting the needs of the bureaucracy and the army. The resultant rebellion of the notables and the grand chiefs in the marginal zones left the sultan no other recourse but to make use of French assistance to maintain his empire. Thereafter, colonization interrupted any autonomous form of political and economic development, whether feudalistic, capitalistic, or whatever.

The French, entering each of the three Maghreb societies at different times with different methods, manipulated the existing tensions to their advantage, maintaining and at the same time changing the traditional social structure. While in Tunisia the Berber element had almost disappeared and in Algeria had continued to be 30 percent of the population, with half of those Berbers being rural, it represented 40 percent of the Moroccan population and two-thirds of the total rural population. The nineteenth century was a period of change in which the sultan attempted to stabilize his control over the tribes using firearms, his religious monopoly, and the conflict between *Bled el Makhzen,* or "land of government," and *Bled es-Siba,* or "land of dissidence." This territorial conflict, in which the intensity of tribal connections, difficulties of communication, and the oscillation between nomadic and sedentary forms of life had sheltered marginal populations from the central power, eventually evolved from a twofold to a threefold cleavage. This change came about with the institutionalization of intermediary powers of chiefs, who presented themselves to the regime as integrators of anarchical tribes and to the tribes as an ultimate resort against a fatal submission. Those chiefs eliminated local, more or less democratic institutions and substituted a personal despotic patrimonial form of government. The sultanate had to limit the arbitrariness of its notables and encourage intermediary chiefs to face dissident units without letting their power become strong enough to be a temptation to disloyalty in times of crisis. In doing so the sultanate seized on traditions of political legitimacy in Islam, meeting the aspirations of rural Muslims by emphasis on individual charismatic authority of a descendant of the prophet and gaining urban legitimation by seeing that no investiture was actually carried out without the notables and religious scholars (*Ulama*) assenting and making binding arrangements in the name of the community. As Geertz (1968) has noted, the Alawites in Morocco managed to combine in their sultanate principles of political and religious organization that remain antithetic in most parts of the Muslim world. The religious legitimacy extended even to the marginal population officially considered politically dissident.

In Morocco the French administered neither directly nor through a partial control, as in Tunisia, but by a complicated administrative structure that dissociated the symbols of legitimacy, the loci of power, and the instrument of authority. The monarchy was preserved; administration lay in the hands of Europeans, who acted in the name of the monarchy, and a body of qaids formally appointed by the sultan. The French protected the Berber qaids and their tribal solidarities, encouraging chieftaincies and keeping alive the old Marabout confraternities. In contrast to Tunisia, Morocco did not continue in the process of centralization of government, due to the absence of tribal segmentation and dissent. Nor did the French destroy the existing administration, as in Algeria, where they had arrived much earlier and erased all existing signs of Algerian sovereignty in the name of an ideology of integration, making the indigenous population a dust of individuals. The protectorate policy in Morocco was based on using the ancient ruling cadres instead of dissolving them. The greater functional weight of the Moroccan monarchy compared with the Tunisian dynasty led the French to undertake the modernization of the sultan's administrative apparatus. The tribes, which for a long time had refused to submit to France, were willing to surrender to the French-supported sultan, bringing the unexpected benefit of unification of the society, to the advantage of the monarchy. The traditional religious universities of Morocco and Tunis were left undisturbed, and the learned strata of the old urban cities continued to exert leadership in a way that was impossible with the deculturation of Algeria. The homogeneity and openness to cosmopolitan influences in Tunisia and the greater historical weakness of the bey compared with the sultan of Morocco undermined the bey's authority and permitted the creation of a secular one-party state engaged in considerable mobilization. In Morocco the Berber Dahir of 1930, which attempted to isolate the Berber rural society through the maintenance and restoration of customary law and legalization of the dual conception of the land of government and the land of dissidence, thus structuring the divisions between Berbers and Arabs, led against their goals to the emergence of modern nationalism. The protest movement expressed the liberals' fear of partition of their society but also enlisted the support of politico-religious leaders, who, with the backing of urban bourgeois families and in the name of primordial Islam, clustered their energies around the restoration of integral power in the hands of the monarch. French-sponsored educational institutions for the sons of urban bourgeois families and Berber students, a military academy oriented to the children of rural notables, and the persistence of traditional Islamic education further divided the elite. The nationalist movement, *Istiqlal,* was led by a coalition of heterogenous elites, whose aims were approved by the sultan. Simultaneously accused of capitulation by some nationalists and of obstructionism by the French, reproached by Chief El Glawi of being the king only of the *Istiqlal* and the marginal elements of urban society, Mohammed V became allied with the national elites. This led to counteralliances from the apparently civic to the fundamentally primordial, particularly around the rural notability. To counteract the growing urban opposition, the French attempted to ruralize politics by expanding the suffrage. With the boycott of the elections by the *Istiqlal,* the French began a policy of reactivation of tribal dissidence combined with the repression of the urban elite. Mobilization of religious chiefs and qaids, and through them of traditional masses, against the sultan effected his deposition and exile. Nothing better might be imagined to bring together such diverse factions as the Marxists and the *Ulama* for the restoration of the monarch in place of the broader goals of independence, forcing even the sultan improvised by the French to demand the return of the legitimate ruler. Through this complex process the monarchy emerged as the major beneficiary of independence, with the national elite forced to a secondary role, and the unitary party drowned in a morass of pluralistic tendencies. As Geertz notes (1968, p. 78), "there is probably no other liberated colony in which the struggle for independence so centered around the capture, revival, and renovation of a traditional institution." At the same time the rapidly expanding state power undermined the traditionalist, scripturalist, Islamic forces.

The Moroccan case well exemplifies trends found in different degrees and forms in many transitions from colonialism to independence, trends sometimes masked by semi- or pseudomodern authoritarian forms. The particular historical development in the colonial policy of segmentation, traditionalism, and praetorianism, the structural incapacity of the elite to undertake rural mobilization, and the functional weight of the monarchy resulted in the unstable and ineffective semitraditional system we have described above. Unfortunately, we cannot extend ourselves in the comparative analysis that Hermassi develops with Tunisia, one of the most stable and successful mobilizational single-party systems, and with Algeria, where the colonial rule, most destructive of indigenous society due to its direct rule, the large white settlement, and the deculturation, probably created the difficulties of political institutionalization that have led to the rule by the army. His analysis shows how important a thorough understanding of the historical background, precolonial and colonial, is to a grasp of the diversity of authoritarian regimes emerging in non-Western societies. The example of Morocco should indicate how superficial some of the typological efforts to understand such regimes can be. It also shows, considering the degree to which the countries of the Maghreb share a common Islamic culture and common European influences, the limits of a cultural interpretation underlying so many area approaches to comparative politics and the importance of structural, social, historical, and economic factors.

Sultanistic Regimes

We encounter a few regimes based on personal rulership (Roth, 1971) with loyalty to the ruler based not on tradition, or on him embodying an ideology, or on a unique personal mission, or on charismatic qualities, but on a mixture of fear and rewards to his collaborators. The ruler exercises his power without restraint at his own discretion and above all unencumbered by rules or by any commitment to an ideology or value system. The binding norms and relations of bureaucratic administration are constantly subverted by personal arbitrary decisions of the ruler, which he does not feel constrained to justify in ideological terms. In many respects the organization of power and of the staff of the ruler is similar to traditional patrimonialism as described by Weber (1968, pp. 231–32). But the lack of constraint derived from tradition and from continuing traditional legitimacy distinguishes it from the historical types of patrimonial rule. The staff of such rulers is constituted not by an establishment with distinctive career lines, like a bureaucratic army or civil servants, recruited by more or less universalistic criteria, but largely by men chosen directly by the ruler. They are neither the "disciples" nor old fighters of a movement party or conspiratorial group. They are often men who would not enjoy any prestige or esteem in the society on their own account but whose power is derived exclusively from the ruler. Among them we very often find members of his family, friends, cronies, business associates, and men directly involved in the use of violence to sustain the regime. The army and the police play a prominent role in the system, but assassination, attacks, and harassment against opponents are often carried out privately with the knowledge of the ruler but without using the police or the courts. Certainly such arbitrary use of power and the fear of it can also be found in the worst phases of totalitarianism. However, there is an essential difference between these regimes and totalitarian systems: the lack of ideological goals for the society on the part of the ruler and his collaborators as well as of any effort of mobilization of the population in a mass single party. The personalistic and particularistic use of power for essentially private ends of the ruler and his collaborators makes the country essentially like a huge domain. Support is based not on a coincidence of interest between preexisting privileged social groups and the ruler but on the interests created by his rule, the rewards he offers for loyalty, and the fear of his vengeance. The boundaries between the public treasury and the private wealth of the ruler become blurred. He and his collaborators, with his consent, take appropriate public funds freely, establish profit-oriented monopolies, and demand gifts and payoffs from business for which no public accounting is given; the enterprises of the ruler contract with the state, and the ruler often shows his generosity to his followers and to his subjects in a particularistic way. The family of the ruler often plays a prominent political role, appropriates public offices, and shares in the spoils. It is this fusion between the public and the private and the lack of commitment to impersonal purposes that distinguishes essentially such regimes from totalitarianism. The economy is subject to considerable governmental interference but not for the purposes of planning but of extracting resources.

The position of the officials derives from their purely personal submission to the ruler, and their position vis-à-vis the subjects is merely the external aspect of this relation, in contrast to bureaucracies, both civil and military. Even when the political official is not a personal dependent, the ruler demands unconditional administrative compliance, for the official's loyalty to his office is not an impersonal commitment to impersonal tasks that define the extent and content of his office, but rather a servant's loyalty based on a strictly personal relationship to the ruler and an obligation that in principle permits no limitation. In this description we have paraphrased some of Weber's description of patrimonial officialdom. Those officials enjoy little security; they are promoted or dismissed at will and enjoy no independent status. They may even, in extreme cases, be subject to dishonor and persecution one day and return to the graces of the ruler the next. The legal and symbolic institutionalization of the regime is pure facade and likely to change for reasons external to the system, like the availability of models enjoying legitimacy abroad.

Such regimes are obviously dependent on the economic situation, since the rewards the ruler can offer to his staff depend on it, and opposition to his regime is likely to come from disappointed members of the staff rather than from social strata, institutions, or political organizations of the regime. The sudden collapse of such regimes as well as their equally sudden reestablishment manifest the fundamental instability of such domination based on force.

Such regimes are unlikely to be established in advanced industrial societies but are compatible with an agrarian economy with commercial and some industrial enterprises. Their stabilization and continuity require a certain degree of modernization of transportation and communications as well as of the military and police organizations, to provide the funds to sustain the rule and to prevent threats to it from the periphery. The isolation of the rural masses, their lack of education, and their poverty are probably necessary to assure their passive submission, which results from the combination of fear and gratitude for occasional paternalistic welfare measures made possible by a modicum of economic development. The rulers' policies are likely to encourage certain types of capitalist enterprise, particularly commercial and plantation types, but can be a serious obstacle to rational calculability, required by enterprises with heavy investments in fixed capital and oriented toward a consumer market. It is also probable that a small-sized country with few urban centers might facilitate this type of rule, making difficult the emergence of alternative elites and of uprisings in the periphery. Certainly the regimes of Trujillo (Wiarda, 1968; Galíndez, 1973; Crassweller, 1966) and Duvalier (Rotberg, 1971; Diederich and Burt, 1969; Fleischman, 1971), which in many ways fit this model, were made possible by the fact that the Dominican Republic and Haiti are on an island, which, combined with their economic dependence on export crops, facilitated both the control of resources like trade and the isolation from external threats.[40] Outside of underdeveloped economies and societies, sultanistic regimes, like some traditional autocracies, have a chance of survival only when they can dispose of considerable economic resources produced by enterprises that do not require a modern industrial labor force and entrepreneurial class, a modern administration, urbanization, expansion of education, etc. Obviously, easily exploitable natural resources whose production is in the hands of one or few enterprises with high profits can provide the resources for such a regime. In the case of Trujillo,[41] the limited modernization of the country under his longtime rule facilitated both the appropriation of resources and the use of some modern techniques of control that most nineteenth-century Latin American *caudillos* could not count on, making their rule so often unstable and often contested by other *caudillos*. The discovery of oil in Venezuela certainly made possible the consolidation of the rule of the *caudillo* Gómez and later of Pérez

Jiménez, even when at that point Venezuelan society had already reached a level of complexity that ultimately made his rule impossible despite some populistic components. The plantation economy of some Central American republics has also served as a basis for such regimes. However, it would be a mistake to consider such regimes as the inevitable result of the economic structure, ignoring many other factors contributing to their emergence and stability, including the interests in "order" of foreign investors that have established stable "business" relations with the ruler.

This type cannot be always neatly distinguished from other types of authoritarian regimes, particularly those without a real single party. But certainly any student of the Dominican Republic or Salazar's Portugal, to take just two relatively small countries, becomes immediately sensitive to the fundamental difference between two types of authoritarianism. The rule of a Stalin or Hitler would never have produced the admiration and loyalty of the masses, and even of intellectuals and foreign observers identified with very different types of regimes, if they had not put their rule at the service of impersonal purposes. Under totalitarianism, even when some of the members of the ruling group like a Göring enjoy life and when corruption is not absent, the rule of a Stalin or a Hitler was not directed at the personal enrichment of the ruler and his family, nor was power exercised simply in the benefit of the ruling group. In fact, under such a sultanistic system what is at stake is the maintenance and furtherance of the privileges, not of the social class or stratum, but of a group of power holders, often by exploiting even the privileged, landowners, merchants, or foreign capitalists who buy their peace in that way.

Obviously, the costs of such a regime fall mainly on the masses of the population, since the privileged are likely to revert their contributions to the maintenance of the system back onto the masses, who lack of any organization to resist exploitation due to the atomization created by the autocratic rule and whose only recourse is to turn to the benevolent paternalism of the ruler. Sometimes the ruler, out of status resentment and to consolidate his power against economically or socially privileged oligarchies or institutional groups like the army officers, might combine his rule through patrimonial officials and mercenaries with populistic gestures. This seems to have been the pattern of Duvalier in Haiti in his exploitation of racial and social tensions.

The overthrow of sultanistic authoritarian regimes without considerable prior social and economic change is not likely to lead to anything but another sultanistic regime or at best to more rational authoritarian rule with the support of the privileged oligarchies. However, with outside support it is not impossible that a revolutionary regime, which might have some totalitarian features, could emerge, while the transition to a stable democracy seems extremely difficult. Batista's Cuba is a very special case, since it shared many of the characteristics of the model just described, even though it also had some of those of the authoritarian regime, combining the rule of the military with that of politicians and interest groups (Solaún, 1969). The fact that Batista was ruling over a country with many modern characteristics in its urban sector contributed to its basic illegitimacy and its ultimate downfall when its military could not suppress the Castro rebellion. The unwillingness of the establishment of Cuban society—parts of the judiciary, the Church, etc.—to support Batista's rule made his overthrow and his flight possible without a real civil war, which is more likely to accompany revolutionary challenges against traditional autocratic rule, like in Yemen, or nonsultanistic authoritarian regimes.

Caudillismo and Caciquismo

In nineteenth-century Latin American politics the disintegration of larger political units and the difficulties of establishing a new type of legitimate rule led to the rule of *caudillo*—"chieftain"—politics. *Caudillaje* politics has been defined by Eric Wolf and Edward Hansen by the following four characteristics:

> (1) the repeated emergence of armed patron-client sets, cemented by personal ties of dominance and submission, and by a common desire to obtain wealth by force of arms; (2) the lack of institutionalized means for succession to offices; (3) the use of violence in political competition; and (4) the repeated failures of incumbent leaders to guarantee their tenures as chieftains. (Wolf and Hansen, 1967, p. 169)

It was a system that emerged with the broad diffusion of military power among wide strata of the population, as it could not be found in modern Europe, and that deranged the predictable interplay of hierarchical class relations. Its base was the traditional *hacienda*, the labor and economic dependencies based on it, the social ties of kinship and friendship, and a personal capacity for the organization of violence (Gilmore, 1964). It was an essentially unstable system, due to the limited resources to impose one's rule, the competition among *caudillos*, the instability of personal loyalties. This instability and changes in the international economic situation as reflected in Latin America led to "order and progress" dictatorships, exhibiting many *caudillo* features but achieving greater centralization, more stable relations with certain social forces, and international links, of which the Mexican Porfiriato (1876–1911) was a prototype. The "order and progress" dictatorship was on the boundaries between the sultanistic and the military-bureaucratic authoritarian regime. However, at the local level the power structures that served as the basis of *caudillaje*, became the support of *caciquismo, coronelismo* systems (Kern, 1973), which were based on alliances between central power holders and those at the local level who "delivered" the votes in exchange for patronage, pork barrel, or just exemption from interference in their arbitrary or paternalistic authority over laborers, tenants, and local government.

Caciquismo has been defined by Kern and Dolkart (1973, pp. 1–2) "as an oligarchical system of politics run by a diffuse and heterogenous elite whose common denominator is local power used for national purposes." Its base is predominantly agrarian but not exclusively so, since professionals, merchants, industrialists, and urban bosses of political machines are often involved. The basis has been "strong local power organized pyramid-fashion so that the 'boss' systems or 'chiefdoms'—*cacicatos*—interlock with one another to form the political infrastructure in many Luso-Hispanic states," with a restricted oligarchy of nationally influential men at the top connected consciously through social ties, formal and informal, with the local *caciques*.

Such structures, through constant transformations,[42] have survived under both authoritarian and semidemocratic regimes at the center up to our days. Sultanistic authoritarianism reproduces at the national level some of the worst features of local nineteenth-century *caciquismo*, perhaps due to the absence of some of the social controls by a local community.

IV. AUTHORITARIAN REGIMES

Toward a Definition of Authoritarian Regimes

In an earlier essay we attempted to define a variety of nondemocratic and nontotalitarian political systems as authoritarian if they were

> political systems with limited, not responsible, political pluralism, without elaborate and guiding ideology, but with distinctive mentalities, without extensive nor intensive political mobilization, except at some points in their development, and in which a leader or occasionally a small group exercises power within formally ill-defined limits but actually quite predictable ones. (Linz, 1964, p. 255)

This definition was developed by contrasting those systems both with competitive democracies and with the ideal type of totalitarian systems (Linz, 1964, 1970a, 1973a, 1973b). It implies clear conceptual boundaries with democratic polities but somewhat more diffuse ones with totalitarianism, since pre- and posttotalitarian situations and regimes might also fit the definition. A further delimitation is the exclusion of traditional legitimate regimes, on account of the different sources of legitimacy of the leadership, or oligarchies ruling authoritarianly. The type of regimes we have labelled sultanistic-authoritarian regimes have much in common with those we intend to cover with our definition of authoritarian but differ from them in the importance in sultanistic-authoritarian regimes of arbitrary and unpredictable use of power and the weakness of the limited political pluralism. For other reasons we find it convenient to exclude from our definition the nineteenth-century semiconstitutional monarchies, which were halfway between traditional legitimate and authoritarian rule (with monarchical, estate, and even feudal elements mixed with emerging democratic institutions), and the censitary democracies, where the restricted suffrage represented a step in the process of development toward modern competitive democracies based at least on universal male suffrage. The oligarchic democracies that, particularly in Latin America, have resisted pressures toward further democratization through the persistence of suffrage limitations based on illiteracy, control or manipulation of elections by *caciques,* frequent recourse to the moderating power of the army, undifferentiated parties, etc., find themselves on the borderline between modern authoritarian regimes and democracy. They are closer to democracy in their constitutional and ideological conception but sociologically more similar to some authoritarian regimes. Our delimitation by exclusion still leaves us with a large number of contemporary political systems fitting our definition and therefore requiring, as we shall see, the characterization of a number of subtypes.

Our concept focuses on the way of exercising power, organizing power, linking with the societies, on the nature of the belief systems sustaining it, and on the role of citizens in the political process without, however, paying attention to the substantive content of policies, the goals pursued, the *raison d'être* of such regimes. It does not tell us much about the institutions, groups, and social strata forming part of the limited pluralism or about those excluded. The emphasis on the more strictly political aspects exposes the concept to some of the same criticism of formalism advanced against a general concept of totalitarianism, or for that matter of democracy. We feel, however, that by characterizing regimes independently of the policies they pursue we tend to deal in a distinctive way with problems faced by all political systems, for example, the relationship between politics and religion and the intellectuals. The conditions for their emergence, stability, transformation, and perhaps breakdown are also quite distinct. The general and abstract character of our definition makes it even more imperative to go down on the ladder of abstraction into the study of the variety of sub types, as we shall do here.

We speak of authoritarian regimes rather than authoritarian governments to indicate the relatively low specificity of political institutions: they often penetrate the life of the society, preventing, even forcibly, the political expression of certain group interests (as religion in Turkey and in Mexico after the revolution, labor in Spain) or shaping them by interventionist policies like those of corporativist regimes. In contrast to some analysts of totalitarianism, we speak of regimes rather than of societies because the distinction between state and society is not fully obliterated even in the intentions of the rulers.

The pluralistic element is the most distinctive feature of these regimes, but it cannot be strongly enough emphasized that in contrast to democracies, with their almost *unlimited* pluralism, their institutionalized political pluralism, we are dealing here with *limited* pluralism. In fact, it has been suggested that we could also have characterized these regimes as of limited monism. In fact, these two terms would suggest the fairly wide range in which those regimes operate. The limitation of pluralism may be legal or de facto, implemented more or less effectively, confined to strictly political groups or extended to interest groups, as long as there remain groups not created by or dependent on the state which influence the political process one way or another. Some regimes go even so far as to institutionalize the political participation of the limited number of independent groups or institutions and even encourage their emergence without, however, leaving any doubt that the rulers ultimately define which groups they will allow to exist and under what conditions. In addition, political power is not legally and/or de facto accountable through such groups to the citizens, even when it might be quite responsive to them. This is in contrast to democratic governments, where the political forces are formally dependent on the support of constituencies, whatever de facto deviations the Michelsian "iron law of oligarchy" might introduce. In authoritarian regimes the men who come to power reflecting the views of various groups and institutions derive their position not from the support from those groups alone but from the trust placed in them by the leader or ruling group, which certainly takes into account their prestige and their influence. They have a kind of constituency; we might call it a potential constituency, but this is not solely or even principally the source of their power. A constant process of co-optation of leaders is the mechanism by which different sectors or institutions become participants in the system, and this process accounts for the characteristics of the elite: a certain heterogeneity in its background and career patterns and the smaller number of professional politicians, men who have made their career in strictly political organizations, compared with the number of those recruited from the bureaucracy, technically skilled elites, the army, interest groups, and sometimes religious groups.

As we shall see, in some of these regimes an official or a single or privileged party is one more-or-less important component of the limited pluralism. On paper such parties often claim the monopolistic power of the totalitarian parties and presumably perform the same functions, but in reality they have to be kept clearly distinct. The absence or weakness of a political party often makes lay organizations sponsored by or linked with the Church, like Catholic Action or the Opus Dei in Spain, a reservoir of leadership for such regimes not too different from their function in the recruitment of elites of Christian democratic parties (Hermet, 1973). The single party more often than not is what the Africans have called a *parti unifié* rather than a *parti unique,* a party based on the fusion of different elements rather than a single disciplined body (Foltz, 1965). Often such parties are a creation from above rather than from the grass roots, created by the group in power rather than a party-conquering power like in totalitarian systems.

In the definition of authoritarian regimes we use the term mentality rather than ideology, from the distinction of the German sociologist Theodor Geiger (1932, pp. 77–79). For him ideologies are systems of thought more or less intellectually elaborated and organized, often in written form, by intellectuals, pseudointellectuals, or with their assistance. Mentalities are ways of thinking and feeling, more emotional than rational, that provide noncodified ways of reacting to different situations. He uses a very graphic German expression: mentality is *subjektiver Geist* (even when collective); ideology is *objektiver Geist*. Mentality is intellectual attitude; ideology is intellectual content. Mentality is psychic predisposition, ideology is reflection, self-interpretation; mentality is previous, ideology later; mentality is formless, fluctuating—ideology, however, is firmly formed. Ideology is a concept of the sociology of culture, mentality is a concept of the study of social character. Ideologies have a strong utopian element, mentalities are closer to the present or the past. Ideological belief systems based on fixed elements and characterized by strong affect and closed cognitive structure, with considerable constraining power, important for mass mobilization and manipulation, are characteristic of totalitarian systems. In contrast, the consensus in democratic regimes is based on a procedural consensus, the commitment to which acquires some of the qualities of ideological beliefs.

The utility and validity of the distinction between mentality and ideology has been questioned by Bolivar Lamounier (1974). He notes that as an actual political variable, as cognitive forms of consciousness actually operative in political life, particularly in the communication process, they are not really that different. He feels that the distinction implies a hasty dismissal of the ruling ideas of authoritarian regimes as an object worth study. Nothing could be further from our intent. He rightly notes the effectiveness of symbolic communication, the multiplicity of referential connections between symbol and social reality, in authoritarian regimes.

Much of the argument hinges on the philosophical assumptions about the definition of ideology, an aspect into which we shall not go. Both ideologies and mentalities as characterized above are part of a broader phenomenon of ideas leading to action-oriented ideals—which are an aspect of the institutionalization of power relationships for which Lamounier prefers to use the term ideology.

The important question is, Why do ideas take a different form, different coherence, articulation, comprehensiveness, explicitness, intellectual elaboration, and normativeness? On those various dimensions ideologies and mentalities differ. Those differences are not without consequences in the political process. It is more difficult to conceive of mentalities as binding, requiring a commitment of the rulers and the subjects irrespective of costs and of the need of coercion to implement them. Mentalities are more difficult to diffuse among the masses, less susceptible to be used in education, less likely to come into conflict with religion or science and more difficult to use as a test of loyalty. The range of issues for which an answer can be derived from them, the degree of precision of those answers, the logic of the process of derivation, and the visibility of the contradictions between them and policies are very different. Their constraining power to legitimate and delegitimate actions are very different. The student of an authoritarian regime would be hard pressed to identify explicit references to ideas guiding the regime in legal theorizing and judicial decisions in nonpolitical cases, in art criticism and scientific arguments, and would find only limited evidence of their use in education. He or she certainly would not find the rich and distinctive language, the new terminology and esoteric use of an ideology, all difficult to understand to the outsider but important to the participants. Nor would he or she find in the libraries stacks of books and publications of an ideological character elaborating endlessly and in a variety of directions those ideas.

Let us admit that the distinction is and cannot be clear-cut but reflects two extreme poles with a large gray area in between. Certainly bureaucratic-military authoritarian regimes are likely to reflect more the mentality of their rulers. In others we are likely to find what Susan Kaufman (1970) has called a programmatic consensus and in others a set of ideas derived from a variety of sources haphazardly combined to give the impression of being an ideology in the sense we have described in the totalitarian systems. Certainly the authoritarian regimes on the periphery of ideological centers feel the pressure to imitate, incorporate, manipulate dominant ideological styles. This can often lead scholars to serious misunderstanding of such regimes, to misplaced emphases. The real question to ask is, What power arrangements seem to prevent ideological articulation in such regimes? In our view the complex coalition of forces, interests, political traditions, and institutions—part of the limited pluralism—requires the rulers to use as symbolic referent the minimum common denominator of the coalition. In this way the rulers achieve the neutralization of a maximum of potential opponents in the process of taking power (in the absence of the highly mobilized mass of supporters). The vagueness of the mentality blunts the lines of cleavage in the coalition, allowing the rulers to retain the loyalty of disparate elements. The lack of an assertion of specific, articulated, and explicit commitments facilitates adaptation to changing conditions in the nonsupportive environment, particularly in the case of authoritarian regimes in the Western democratic sphere of influence. The reference to generic values like patriotism and nationalism, economic development, social justice, and order and the discreet and pragmatic incorporation of ideological elements derived from the dominant political centers of the time allow rulers who have gained power without mobilized mass support to neutralize opponents, co-opt a variety of supporters, and decide policies pragmatically. Mentalities, semi- or pseudoideologies reduce the utopian strain in politics and with it conflict that otherwise would require either institutionalization or more repression than the rulers could afford. The limited utopianism obviously is congruent with conservative tendencies.

Such regimes pay a price for their lack of ideology in our sense of the term. It limits their capacity to mobilize people to create the psychological and emotional identification of the masses with the regime. The absence of an articulate ideology, of a sense of ultimate meaning, of long-run purposes, of an *a priori* model of ideal society reduces the attractiveness of such regimes to those for whom ideas, meaning, and values are central. The alienation of intellectuals, students, youth, and deeply religious persons from such regimes, even when successful and relatively liberal compared with totalitarian systems, can be explained in part by the absence or weakness of ideology. One of the advantages of authoritarian regimes with an important fascist component was that this derivative ideology appealed to some of those groups. But it also was one of the sources of tension when the disregard of the elite of the regime for those ideological elements became apparent.

In theory we should be able to distinguish this content of ideas of the regime, including its style, from the ideas guiding or influencing the political process as an actual political variable. It could be argued that the first aspect, to which we will be looking for the objectivization, is ultimately less central than the subjective appropriation, the various forms of consciousness actually operative in political life. However, we feel that the distinction between mentality and ideology is not irrelevant for the way in which they affect activities and communication processes in politics and society. The complex interaction between both levels of analysis precludes any *a priori* statement about the direction in which the relationship operates. Probably in totalitarian systems the actual political processes are more deeply affected by the content of the ideology, while in authoritarian regimes the mentalities of the rulers, not having to be equally explicit, might reflect more the social and political realities.

The elusiveness of mentalities, the mimetic and derivative character of the so-called ideologies of authoritarian regimes, has limited the number of scholarly studies of this dimension of such regimes. Only interview studies of the elites and surveys of the population, of great sophistication given the limited freedom of expression and the obstacles in the communication processes, make this an important dimension in the study of such regimes. The typology of authoritarian regimes we will present relies more on the character of the limited pluralism and the degree of apathy or mobilization than on an analysis of types of mentalities.

In our original definition we emphasized the actual absence of extensive and intensive political mobilization but admitted that at some point of the development of such regimes there could be such mobilization. The characteristic of low and limited political mobilization is therefore a factual characteristic on which such regimes tend to converge, for a variety of reasons. As we shall see in the discussion of the subtypes, in some regimes the depoliticization of the mass of the citizens falls into the intent of the rulers, fits with their mentality, and reflects the character of the components of the limited pluralism supporting them. In other types of systems the rulers initially intend to mobilize their supporters and the population at large into active involvement in the

regime and its organizations. Their public commitments, often derivative ideological conceptions, push them in that direction. The historical and social context of the establishment of the regime favors or demands such a mobilization
through a single party and its mass organizations. The struggle for national
independence from a colonial power or for full independence, the desire to
incorporate into the political process sectors of the society untapped by any
previous political leadership, or the defeat of a highly mobilized opponent in
societies in which democracy had allowed and encouraged such a mobilization
lead to the emergence of mobilizational authoritarian regimes of a nationalist,
populist, or fascist variety. In reality there is a likelihood of convergence of
regimes starting from such different assumptions following quite different
routes. That convergence should not, however, obscure many important differences derived from those origins in terms of the type of pluralism emerging,
the legitimacy formulae chosen, the response to crises situations, the capacity
for transformation, the sources and types of opposition, etc.

Ultimately the degree of political mobilization and with it the opportunities for participation in the regime of those among the citizens supporting it
are a result of the other two dimensions used in the definition of authoritarian
regimes. Mobilization and participation ultimately become difficult to sustain
unless the regime moves in a more totalitarian or democratic direction. Effective mobilization, particularly through a single party and its mass organizations,
would be perceived as a threat by the other components of the limited pluralism, typically the army, the bureaucracy, the churches, or interest groups. To
break through those constraining conditions would require moves in the totalitarian direction. The failure to break through those conditions and the limited
pluralism standing in the way to totalitarianism has been well analyzed by
Alberto Aquarone, who quotes this revealing conversation of Mussolini with
and old syndicalist friend:

> If you could imagine the effort it has taken me to search for a possible
> equilibrium in which I could avoid the collision of antagonistic powers
> which touched each other side by side, jealous, distrustful one of the other,
> government, party, monarchy, Vatican, army, militzia, prefects, provincial
> party leaders, ministers, the head of the Confederazioni [corporative struc-
> tures] and the giant monopolistic interests, etc. you will understand they are
> the indigestions of totalitarianism, in which I did not succeed in melting
> that "estate" that I had to accept in 1922 without reservations. A pathological
> connecting tissue linking the traditional and circumstantial deficiencies of
> this great, small, Italian people, which a tenacious therapy of twenty years
> has achieved to modify only on the surface. (Aquarone, 1965, p. 302)

We have described how the maintenance of equilibrium between those
limited pluralisms limits in reality the effectiveness of the mobilization to a
single party and ultimately has to lead to the apathy of the members and activ-

ists, since such a party offers limited access to power compared with other channels. Underdevelopment, particularly of a large rural population living in
isolated areas and engaging in subsistence agriculture, often linked with traditional or clientelistic power structures integrated into the unified party, despite
the ideological pronouncements, the organization charts, and the machinery of
plebiscitarian elections, does not create a participatory political culture, not
even controlled or manipulated participation.

As we shall see in more detail, the authoritarian regimes that emerge after
a period of competitive democratic participation that created an unsolvable
conflict in the society opt for depoliticization and apathy, which is felt by many
citizens as a relief from the tensions of the previous period. Initially this is the
apathy of those defeated by the new regime, but in the absence of a disciplined
totalitarian mass party and its mass organizations combined with terror, little
effort will be made to integrate them to participate in the system. As the tensions and hatreds that produced a mobilization for the system diminish, the
supporters are also likely to lapse into apathy, which often the rulers might
welcome to avoid pressures to make good the promises they made in the process
of mobilization.

The absence of an ideology, the heterogeneous and compromise character,
and often mimetism of the guiding ideas, and above all the mentality of the
rulers, particularly military elites, bureaucrats, experts, and co-opted politicians
of pro-regime parties, are serious obstacles in the process of mobilization and
participation. Without an ideology it becomes difficult to mobilize activists for
voluntary campaigns, regular attendance at party meetings, face-to-face propaganda activities, etc. Without an ideology with utopian components it is difficult to attract those interested in politics as an end in itself rather than a means
for more pragmatic and immediate interests. Without ideology the young, the
students, the intellectuals are not likely to get involved in politics and provide
the cadres for politicization of the population. Without the utopian element,
without the appeal to broader constituencies that would require a participatory
pluralism rather than the limited, controlled, and co-opted pluralism of elites,
the appeals based on a consensual, nonconflictive society, except in moments
of upsurge of nationalism or of danger to the regime, tend to reduce politics to
administration of the public interest and to the de facto expression of particular
interests.

The limited pluralism of authoritarian regimes and the different share that
the tolerated pluralistic components have in the exercise of power in different
moments lead to complex patterns of semiopposition and pseudoopposition
within the regime (Linz, 1973a). There is semiopposition by groups that are
not dominant or represented in the governing group and that engage in partial
criticism but are willing to participate in power without fundamentally challenging the regime. Without being institutionalized such groups are not illegitimate, even when they lack a legal framework in which to operate. They might

be highly critical of the government and some aspects of the institutional order, but they distinguish between these and the leader of the regime and accept the historical legitimacy or at least necessity of the authoritarian formula. There are groups that advocate different emphases and policy, groups that join in supporting the establishment of the regime but in the hope of achieving goals not shared by their coalition partners. There is dissidence among those who initially identified with the system but did not participate in its establishment, typically the Young Turks of the regime, and among those within the regime who want to work for goals that are not illegitimate, like the restoration of a previous regime initially announced but never realized. There are those who had stronger ideological commitments but accepted seeing them postponed to gain power against an enemy, those with a foreign model and/or even loyalty from which the rulers attempt to distance themselves, and in the late stages of such a regime those who oppose its transformation, specifically its liberalization and the abandonment of its exclusionary character. Semiopposition is likely to appear among men of the older generation who joined in the establishment of the regime to pursue goals they had already formulated before the takeover. But it also appears among the intellectuals and the young, particularly students who have taken seriously the rhetorical pronouncements of the leadership and who in addition find that there are no effective channels for political participation. Not infrequently the semiopposition within the regime becomes an alegal opposition. It has given up hope of transforming the regime from the inside but is not yet ready to move into illegal or subversive activities and finds intermittent tolerance sometimes based on the personal ties established in earlier years. The weakness of the efforts of political socialization and indoctrination in authoritarian regimes also accounts for the fact that when the third generation, never incorporated in the regime, discovers politics it might turn to an alegal opposition. The autonomy left by the regime to certain social organizations, the limited efforts of liberalization and increased participation in the regime organizations, and the relative openness to other societies create opportunities for the emergence of an alegal opposition, which sometimes serves as a front for an illegal opposition that is ready to infiltrate the organizations of the regime, rejecting the moral qualms about participating in it held by other opponents. Opposition is often channeled into formally apolitical organizations of cultural, religious, or professional character. In multilingual, multicultural societies, where the regime is identified with one of the national groups, cultural manifestations such as the use of languages other than the official language become an expression of opposition. The special position of the Catholic Church in many societies under authoritarian rule and the legal status of many of its organizations in the concordats between the Vatican and the rulers allow priests and laymen a certain autonomy to serve as a channel for opposition sentiments of social classes, cultural minorities, generational unrest, etc., and for the emergence of new leaders. In the case of the Catholic Church the trans-

national character, the moral legitimation of the relatively wide range of ideological positions by the refusal on the part of the Pope to condemn them, the
legitimacy for moral prophetic indignation against injustice, particularly after
Vaticanum II, together with the concern of the hierarchy for the autonomy
of religious organizations and the freedom of priests account for the role of
religious groups in the politics of authoritarian regimes. Paradoxically, the
Church has provided the regimes through its lay organizations with elites but
has also protected its dissidents and occasionally played the role described by
Guy Hermet (1973) as tribunicial against the regime by being witness of moral
values against abuses of power. The Church as an institution that will outlast
any regime, even those with which it becomes identified in the particular historical moment, is likely to disidentify and regain its autonomy when signs of
crisis appear. The same is true for other permanent institutions that might have
retained considerable autonomy under authoritarian rule, like the judiciary or
even the professional civil servants.

Let us emphasize here that the semioppositions—the alegal but tolerated
opposition, the relatively autonomous role of various institutions under conditions of semifreedom—creates a complex political process of far-reaching consequences for the society and its political development. The liberalization of
authoritarian regimes can go far, but without a change in the nature of the
regime, without the institutionalization of political parties, is likely to be quite
limited. The semifreedom under such regimes imposes on their opponents certain costs that are quite different from those of persecution of illegal oppositions and that explain their frustration, disintegration, and sometimes readiness
to co-optation, which contribute to the persistence of such regimes sometimes
as much as does their repressive capacity. The ambiguity of opposition under
authoritarian regimes contrasts with the clear boundaries between regime and
its opponents in totalitarian systems. However, let us emphasize that the limited
pluralism, the processes of liberalization, and the existence of the tolerated opposition, in the absence of institutional channels for political participation and
for the opposition to reach the mass of the population, allow a clear distinction
between authoritarian and democratic regimes.

Before closing our general discussion of authoritarian regimes we want to
call attention to one difficulty in their study. In a world in which the great
and most successful powers are and have been either stable democracies or communist or fascist political systems, with the unique attraction given to them
by their ideologies, their organizational capacity, their apparent stability, their
success as advanced industrial nations or in overcoming economic backward-
ness, and their capacity to overcome international second-rank status, authoritarian regimes are in an ambiguous position. None of them has served as a
utopian model for other societies, except, perhaps for special historical reasons,
Nasser's Egypt in the Arab world. Possibly Mexico, with its combination of
the revolutionary myth and the pragmatic stability of its hegemonic party

regime, could serve rulers as a model. None of the authoritarian regimes has fired the imagination of intellectuals and activists across the borders. None has inspired an international of parties supporting such a model. Only the original solutions attempted by the Yugoslavs have created a noncritical interest among intellectuals. Under those circumstances authoritarian regimes and their leaders have felt constrained to take the trappings of the appealing totalitarian models, avoiding or unable to incorporate the substance of the model. Only the thirties, as we shall see, with the ideology of corporativism combining a variety of ideological heritages and linking with Catholic conservative social doctrine, seemed to offer a genuine nontotalitarian and nondemocratic ideological alternative. The visible failure of such systems, the fact that no major power followed that route, the diffuse boundaries between conservative or Catholic corporativism and Italian fascism, and, finally, the disengagement of the Church from its commitment to organic theories of society have ultimately undermined this third model of politics. Authoritarian regimes, whatever their roots in the society, whatever their achievements, are ultimately confronted with two appealing alternative models of polity, which limit the possibilities of full and self-confident institutionalization and give strength to their opponents (Linz, 1973b).

The Problem of a Typology of Authoritarian Regimes

The social science literature offers many ideas for developing typologies of such regimes: Almond and Powell's (1966) distinction of conservative, modernizing, and premobilized authoritarian systems, of which respectively Spain, Brazil, and Ghana would be examples, and the many inchoate typologies in the chapters of Samuel Huntington and Clement Moore (1970) in their analysis of the dynamics of established one-party systems, particularly Huntington's distinction between exclusionary and revolutionary one-party systems and between revolutionary and established one-party systems. Nor should the pioneer effort of Edward Shils (1960), distinguishing tutelary democracies, modernizing oligarchies, and traditional oligarchies, be forgotten. Giovanni Sartori, in an unpublished study of political parties, with his unexcelled ability to make clear logical distinctions has differentiated the variety of party state systems, that is, noncompetitive-party systems, distinguishing one-party and hegemonic-party systems and, further down on the ladder of abstraction, totalitarian and authoritarian parties, single or hegemonic parties, and finally ideological and pragmatic parties (Sartori, 1970b). The four-fold typology of single-party ideologies of Clement Moore follows.

It is based on a distinction between instrumental and expressive functions, whose operationalization seems to offer certain difficulties. The distinction resulting between totalitarian and chiliastic systems is particularly hazy, and it is not fully clear why the tutelary should be considered instrumental and the administrative expressive (Moore, 1970).

It is, however, far from our intention to dismiss or ignore such typologies

	Transformation Goals	
Functions	Total	Partial
Instrumental	Totalitarian	Tutelary
	Stalinist Russia, Maoist China, Nazi Germany, "Stalinist" East Europe	Tunisia, Tanzania, Yugoslavia, Ataturk's Turkey
Expressive	Chiliastic	Administrative
	Fascist Italy, Nkrumah's Ghana, Mali, Guinea, Cuba, Ben Bella's Algeria	Mexico

that highlight certain aspects of authoritarian regimes and that might be particularly valuable for the analysis of such regimes in the new and old states of the non-Western world or certain cultural areas like Africa south of the Sahara.

Since many authoritarian regimes have been founded by military coups and are headed by military men, it would seem that a typology distinguishing military and nonmilitary authoritarian regimes would be fruitful, distinguishing further the political nature and purpose of the military intervention in assuming power. Certainly the writers on military in politics like Finer (1962) and the many specialists on Latin America and the Middle East have made valuable contributions to our understanding of authoritarian regimes. However, a category of military authoritarian regimes would include too many, quite different regimes, as the mention of the names of Ataturk, Pétain, Franco, Perón, Nasser, Odria, Medici, and Cárdenas suggests. Military regimes, with some significant and interesting exceptions, undergo a process of civilization, if they are stable, and the military origin or military background of the head of state does not tell us enough about their nature. Military men can carry out a deep cultural revolution like Ataturk, important social and economic changes like Nasser, displace traditional regimes like they did or prevent a continuing process of change toward democracy and perhaps social revolution after a break with tradition with a counterrevolutionary intent, like Franco. Certainly the military mentality of men at the top would give such regimes certain common features, which, however important, are not sufficient for any meaningful typology.

Scholars are likely to be confused in studying authoritarian regimes because of the frequent inauthenticity of their claims. Since the founding group or leader has no or few ideological commitments before taking power except some vague ideas about defending order, uniting the country, modernizing the nation, overthrowing a corrupt regime, or rejecting foreign influences, they find themselves without ideological justification, without ideas attractive to the intellectuals, removed from the mainstream of international ideological confrontations. In that vacuum the rulers will search for acceptable symbols and ideas to incorporate them into their *arcana imperi*. Those ideas are likely to be the ones dominant at the time and congruent with the "march of history." It is no accident that Ataturk should have chosen progressive, secularist, democratic ideas and symbols; that the Eastern European royal dictators, bureaucrats, and officers, and Franco, should have mimicked fascism; that contemporary authoritarian regimes should claim to be socialist and to introduce "democratic centralism" or "participatory democracy" and "workers' councils" rather than corporativism. No scholar should accept such claims at face value—not that the claims are irrelevant, since such initially vague commitments largely condition the international response to such regimes and influence their later development, opening certain possibilities and excluding others (Linz, 1973b). However, it would be dangerous to base our classifications on those claims. Actual policies and the operation of political institutions might be very similar despite such pseudoideological differences, and the similarity in mentality of the rulers might make possible an understanding and affinity between leaders of systems apparently dissimilar.

The ideological elements used, far from central to the understanding of such systems, would allow us to distinguish the following main types.

1. Authoritarian regimes claiming to carry out basic processes of modernization, particularly secularization and educational reforms, to create the preconditions for constitutional democracy like that of the more successful Western nations. Regimes born in the eve of World War I, like Turkey and Mexico, were committed to such a pattern, which was reflected in the institutional rules, ignored in practice, but ultimately is making possible an evolution in that direction.

2. Fascist- or semifascist-nationalist authoritarian regimes.

3. Authoritarian regimes that we shall characterize as "organic statism," attempting to link with the Catholic corporativist social doctrine mixed with fascist elements but distinct from the fascist-populist-nationalist totalitarian conceptions. Often these types of regimes that attempt to institutionalize a particular type of pluralism have been confused with fascism, and the term "clerical fascism" reflects both the bias of the observers and the ambiguity of that type of authoritarianism in the late twenties and early thirties.

4. The authoritarian regimes born in the aftermath of World War II in the newly independent states claiming to pursue a different national way toward participation, including a single party or subordinating the existing parties, characterizing their regimes as tutelary democracies, like Sukarno in Indonesia, or institutionalizing "basic democracies" in Pakistan.

5. More recently, African new nations and Islamic countries rejecting traditional religious conceptions of authority, impressed by the success of com-

munist countries and sometimes searching for their sympathy, have claimed to be socialist, to build mass parties and to reject Western individualism for a new sense of community based on identification with the leader and the party. In the case of Islamic countries an attempt has been made to link those ideological imitations with a genuine national cultural tradition, the Islamic notion of community, sometimes fusing modern ideas with traditional religious conceptions. It is no accident that some political scientists like James Gregor should have noted some of the similarities between African socialism (and similar ideologies) and fascism in semideveloped agrarian societies in the thirties (Gregor, 1968 and 1974a).

6. Communist posttotalitarian authoritarian regimes, described by Gordon Skilling as "consultative authoritarianism, quasi-pluralistic authoritarianism, democratizing and pluralistic authoritarianism and anarchic authoritarianism."

Despite the usefulness of the six types briefly delineated above, except for the sixth one, I would argue that this is not the most fruitful approach to the development of a typology of authoritarian regimes as defined above.

Toward a Typology of Authoritarian Regimes

If our definition is useful, it should also allow us to develop subtypes of such regimes. The limited pluralism, as opposed to the tendency toward monism, should lead us to typologies taking into account which institutions and groups are allowed to participate and in what way, and which ones are excluded. If rejection of mobilization along totalitarian lines or failure to achieve such mobilization distinguishes such regimes from totalitarianism, the reasons for and the nature of the limited mobilization should provide another dimension of a typology. Since mentalities in contrast to ideologies are elusive to study, that dimension, particularly due to the importance of mimicking of ideologies, should turn out in practice to be less helpful. Even when in theory it should provide important elements for typologies.

The limited pluralism of authoritarian regimes takes a variety of forms, and within it different groups or institutions take a more or less preeminent place. The participation of groups in political power is controlled by certain social forces and channeled through different organizational structures. On that account authoritarian regimes range from those dominated by a bureaucratic-military-technocratic elite that preexisted the regime, to a large extent, to others in which there is a privileged political participation and entry into the elite through a single or dominant party emerging from the society. In other regimes we find that a variety of social groups and institutions defined by the state are created or allowed to participate in one or another degree in the political process under the forms we shall call organic statism, which often is ideologically described as corporatism or organic democracy. A very special

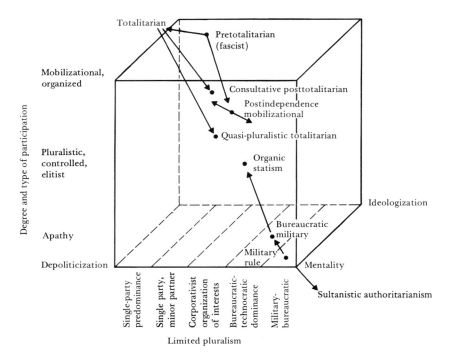

Fig. 1. A Typology of Authoritarian Regimes

case of limited pluralism is the one in which a large part of the society is excluded from organized participation in influencing major decisions on the basis of an ascriptive characteristic like race or ethnicity while other citizens enjoy the political freedoms of democracy, except insofar as advocating the inclusion into the body politic of the excluded segment of the society. We shall discuss this very special type of authoritarian regime under the paradoxical label of "racial democracies."

If we turn to the other dimension of our definition of authoritarian regimes —the limited participation, the controlled participation, the tendency toward political apathy of most citizens and the toleration or encouragement of such apathy—we find that in bureaucratic-military-technocratic regimes there are few, if any, channels for participation of the mass of the citizens and that the rulers have no particular interest in even manipulated participation. On the other hand we have regimes that attempt to mobilize the citizens to participate in well-defined, more or less monopolistic channels created by the political leadership, most characteristically through a mobilization of single or dominant party and its dependent mass and functional organizations. Insofar as such a single party is not conceived to exclude other organizations and institutions from a limited political pluralism and does not thoroughly penetrate them, we are dealing with an authoritarian regime. Such regimes would then be characterized as mobilizational authoritarian regimes and in this respect would be different from both bureaucratic-military-technocratic regimes and those we have labeled organic statism. They would also be different from the much freer political pluralism within the privileged racial community of the racial democracies.

Taking into account the circumstances under which such relatively mobilizational authoritarian regimes have appeared historically, we have two main types. In the first type the mobilizational single party or dominant party has emerged from the society in the course of the struggle for independence from foreign domination and has established in the process of taking power a dominant position, which it will protect from any competitors that might emerge either by outlawing the political freedoms that would lead to the emergence of other parties or by co-opting or even corrupting the leaders of such potential competitors. Initially such regimes are based on a considerable mobilization and, under conditions different from those of postcolonial underdeveloped societies, could move in a totalitarian direction but, for reasons to be analyzed later, become authoritarian regimes in which the originally mobilizational party becomes one important component in the structure of power. The second main type of mobilizational authoritarian regimes can be found in postdemocratic societies, in which a purely bureaucratic-military rule or one based on the representation of a well-defined, limited number of social groups and institutional interests in organic statism is not feasible because of the expectation of a large part of the society of some form of opportunity for participation for the average citizen. In addition, such regimes emerge when the struggle to exclude from the political process particular sectors of the society, to destroy the organizations of those sectors, has required something more than a coup d'etat, when a mobilization was necessary to proceed with the exclusion of those sectors by the creation of a mass party, a variety of mass organizations, and even coercive organizations beyond the bureaucratic structures of the police or any army. This kind of exclusionary mobilizational authoritarian regime in postdemocratic societies was one of the outcomes of the fascist mobilization of a variety of interests and ideological and emotional commitments among the citizens of the democracies in crisis in the Europe of the interwar years. To the extent that such mobilizational authoritarian parties and movements aimed at a totalitarian monopoly of power and *Gleichschaltung* of a variety of social groups, interests, and organizations and a total political neutralization of others like the churches and armed forces, but did not succeed in so doing, we can speak of defective or arrested totalitarian systems. Since the process of establishing a truly totalitarian system is not achieved the day of takeover of power, we can also characterize as an authoritarian situation the pretotalitarian phases of certain political systems.

Finally, the way in which the limited pluralism in certain political systems emerges after a period of totalitarian rule leads us to speak of the post-totalitarian societies as a very distinct type. In such systems the dominant position of the party has not fully disappeared. The limited pluralism of other institutions, groups, and interests that share or influence political power is to a large extent emerging out of the social and political structure created by the new regime rather than from the preexisting society, politics, and history. To the extent that these groups are not simply parts of the single-party, controlled political structure and that the competition for power among them is not simply the result of bureaucratic or factional infighting within the elites and the institutions of the system but links with broader segments of the society, we are dealing with posttotalitarian authoritarian regimes. However, the legacy of organizational patterns, political culture, and memories of the past of the totalitarian period makes such regimes distinct from those listed before.

It would be surprising if the types we have derived from our analysis of the nature of the limited pluralism and the degree and type of participation or apathy would not also have some affinity with different ways of articulating ideas to legitimize the system. Certainly such ideas are least articulated intellectually in the case of the bureaucratic-military rule; it is in those cases that we can speak mostly of mentalities of the rulers and should pay least attention to the ideological formulations offered, which are likely to be simple and often derivative. In contrast, the mobilization of authoritarian regimes, particularly when they assign an important role to the single or dominant party and attempt to encourage the participation of at least a certain number of citizens in that party, is likely to rely on ideological formulations. Those ideological formulations, while they do not play a role comparable to the role of ideology in totalitarian systems, are an important factor in the political process. However it is their relative lack of articulation and complexity and often their derivative character that contribute to the relatively rapid decay of the mobilizational component, that is, of the role of the party and of mass participation. This process was particularly visible in many of the African one-party states, that initially appeared as regimes based on an ideology and moving in a direction that would have placed them closer to the totalitarian systems that some of their leaders might have thought as a model. The outcome has been obviously to bring many mobilizational authoritarian regimes closer to either the bureaucratic-military type or the organic-statism type. Only in the mobilizational-postdemocratic-exclusionary authoritarian regimes in Western societies with a fascist party that had become an important political force before taking power did ideology remain an important independent factor that could not be fully reduced to what we have described as mentality. This is even truer for the posttotalitarian systems, for those we have called defective or arrested totalitarianism systems, and the pretotalitarianism phase of some regimes.

In the following pages, therefore, we will describe in some detail the characteristics of a variety of types of authoritarian regimes, the conditions for their emergence, some of the consequences of the political processes, and the lives of citizens of those types. Let us note here that they have not been logically derived from the dimensions of our concept of authoritarian regimes, but derived largely inductively from an extensive descriptive literature on such regimes, which did not offer a comparative typological conceptualization. We feel, however, that the types inductively derived fit our definition of authoritarian regimes and that the salient differences used to characterize them are found along the dimensions of the definition.

Congruently with our emphasis on the relatively well defined boundary between nondemocratic and democratic systems, in terms of our definition, only those systems we have conceptualized as racial or ethnic democracies could at one point or another have been considered democratic, that is, as long as they did not need to use considerably repressive force to prevent the excluded racial group from demanding participation and do not increasingly have to do so with the members of the privileged racial community who would advocate such an extension of political rights. On the other hand, the boundary between authoritarian regimes and those approaching the ideal type of a totalitarian system is much more difficult to operationalize. This fact is reflected in the need we felt to describe as types of authoritarian regimes posttotalitarian political systems, the defective or arrested totalitarian regimes, and the pretotalitarian phases of another set of regimes.

To some extent the bureaucratic-military authoritarian regimes, which have developed neither a more complex institutionalization of the limited pluralism in the form of organic statism or a single party contributing to the recruitment of the top-level elite serving as an instrument of control and as a channel for participation of citizens so motivated, are in some ways the paradigmatic authoritarian regimes. They are those furthest removed from any similarity to democratic political systems but also from modern totalitarianism. The question might be raised: Which of the other types more closely approach the model of democratic politics? In some respects it might be argued that the opportunities for participation in political life and through it access to positions of power in mobilizational authoritarian regimes bring those closer to the ideal type of democratic politics. On the other hand such mobilizational organizations like the single party and the various mass organizations controlled by it are an obstacle for the survival and political influence of the pluralism in the society, and to that extent will run counter to the freedom of organization for social and political purposes that characterizes democratic policies in societies. On the other hand, organic statism, by institutionalizing, even when in a controlled form, the existing social pluralism and incorporating it into the political process without creating or granting a monopoly to a single political organization, is closer to the social pluralism that develops spontaneously within a free society but at the cost of broader opportunities for participation of average citizens in contrast to various elites. In this respect organic statism is further removed from the idea of citizen participation than are the more mobilizational regimes. On one or another count both mobilizational authoritarian regimes and organic statist regimes are therefore clearly distinct from democratic regimes and societies. Even more difficult to answer is the question to what extent either of these types has potential to transform itself into a competitive democracy. It could be argued that the organic statism leaves more freedom for the articulation of specific interests and more autonomy to institutions, makes less effort to politicize in a particular direction the mass of the citizens, and therefore creates a society that is better prepared to accept the unlimited pluralism, the multiple and conflicting leadership of democratic politics. However, within the framework of organic statism, the privileges granted to the recognized organizations and institutions are likely to lead their leadership to perceive the opportunities for political mobilization of citizens through political parties as particularly threatening and therefore to cling to the authoritarian framework to defend them. In contrast, a mobilizational authoritarian regime, if it feels that the single or dominant party has penetrated the society sufficiently to be assured, even in a more competitive framework created by the extension of political freedom of its dominant position might be tempted to explore the possibility of retaining its power within such a framework. In fact, an initial chance of retaining its dominant position might encourage, given the legitimacy of competitive democracy, a slow transformation in that direction. In the long run or by a miscalculation such a move could ultimately lead to the installation of competitive democracy. A mobilizational authoritarian regime also retains institutionally and ideologically the principle of direct participation of individual citizens in the political process, a principle that is essential to competitive democracies. In view of this we can understand that the Turkey of Ataturk, in which a bureaucratic-military regime had become a single-party, moderately mobilizational authoritarian regime, could transform itself after World War II into a competitive democracy. The same would be true to some extent for the transformation of Estado Novo in Brazil into a populist democracy in which the elites of the preceding authoritarian regime could continue playing an important role. Mexico would be another case in point.

Some observers have placed considerable hope on the development of internal democracy within single parties in mobilizational authoritarian regimes and particularly in posttotalitarian regimes. We feel that the possibilities of transformation into competitive democracies of such regimes are more dubious than those observers have thought, since ultimately that participation through the single dominant party assumes a commitment to the party, its program and ideology, and the exclusion of any opportunity for alternative competing political conceptions that would be a requisite for competitive politics and that could always be rejected on the basis that there are opportunities for political participation within the boundaries of the party and its mass organizations.

Unfortunately we cannot develop at any length, with the information available and the space given to us, an analysis of the many regimes that are on the borderlines between the ideal types we have described. Many of the regimes combine in a more or less planned or accidental way elements from the different types, giving more or less importance to one or another in different phases of their history. It would seem that many authoritarian regimes are established as bureaucratic-military but after consolidating themselves in power explore the other alternatives and attempt with more or less success to transform themselves into organic-statist regimes and, generally unsuccessfully, into mobilizational regimes. On the other side many regimes that start as mobilizational authoritarian, either postindependence or postdemocratic, seem to drift into a combination of bureaucratic and organic statism, when they are not overthrown by a combination of military and bureaucratic power that soon rules with the help of technocratic elites and attempts to institutionalize some degree of organic statism. Each phase in the development of authoritarian regimes, from their emergence of the preauthoritarian society, their installation, their search for legitimate models to imitate, their hesitant efforts of institutionalization, is likely to leave an imprint on the system. Authoritarian regimes in reality, therefore, are likely to be complex systems characterized by heterogeneity of models influencing their institutionalization, often contradictory models in uneasy coexistence. It is this that accounts for the difficulty to subsume particular regimes under the types we shall describe here. Certainly many of the regimes, being nondemocratic, at one or another point in time would be closer to one or another of the types described. This fact is to some extent neglected in our emphasis on the analysis of the developmental aspect, the genesis of such regimes, and their location on a particular point in time in relationship to the preceding or subsequent regime. It is no accident that years after having been established such regimes are still, in the view of their rulers, in a constituent stage, that constitutional law after constitutional law is being enacted, and that the political edifice remains unfinished for a long time, giving hope to a variety of political forces of building it according to their particular blueprints. Paradoxically, democratic regimes seem to have a shorter period of constitution making, which prejudges in many, often unexpected, ways the future development of the regime. Paradoxically, the phase of installation of a new democracy offers to the democratic elites the temptation to use their power to constitutionalize their political preferences, with the result that social forces weak at that point in their organization in competing for political power might later be placed in the situation of having to challenge the constitutional order using the freedoms that democracy grants them. The rationalistic streak in Jacobinic democracy in this respect contrasts with the often very pragmatic way of creating political institutions in authoritarian regimes. Perhaps here we might find one of the clues to the relative stability of many authoritarian regimes despite considerable change in the regime and the instability of newly established democracies in the same societies.

Our effort to conceptualize and understand the variety of authoritarian regimes—strictly defined—encounters considerable difficulties due to the tendency to study political systems, outside of both the Western democratic world and communist systems, within the framework of geographic cultural areas like Latin America, the Middle East, Southeast Asia, and Africa rather than using analytical categories.[43] On the other hand, the tendency of scholars to group the Eastern European communist countries for comparative analysis and to specialize in the study of communist politics has led them to ignore potential comparisons with noncommunist authoritarian regimes.[44] Similarly, the dominant attention to Nazi Germany in the study of interwar fascist Europe has led to the neglect of the authoritarian regimes of the twenties and thirties as a distinct type of polities, leaving us mainly with excellent historical accounts but few systematic studies. In that context the neglect of Portugal, the most long-lived authoritarian regime in a Western society, is striking.[45] On the other hand, the analysis of many authoritarian regimes has been limited by the perspective introduced by a one-sided emphasis on the origins of such regimes as cases of military intervention in politics without further analysis of their functioning after having been established by a coup. The lack of a broader comparative perspective has been particularly damaging in the case of Latin America, where a regional grouping on the basis of certain cultural, historical, and international politics has prevented scholars from potentially fruitful comparisons with Latin-European politics, for example, the comparable economic and social development of some of the more advanced Latin American countries and those of Europe and the important ideological influences coming from Europe.

More recently the overemphasis on sociological categories, very often based on relatively simple indicators of economic development, and even more recently simplified Marxist analyses have led to a neglect of the most distinctively political variables in the study of many political systems of the Third World. The same is true for the emphasis in the literature on grand theories of political development or modernization, often at a high level of abstraction, which do not build bridges between the descriptive case studies and empirical comparative research, focusing on particular variables and their interrelationships. Lately the quantitative global studies based on the data, of dubious quality for these types of political systems and societies, accumulated in the data banks have tended to ignore the differences between types of political systems by treating them all on a single continuum of social-economic development, political development, and democratization used in a very loose sense of the term, leading to findings of specious scientific accuracy.

These various intellectual perspectives certainly have not encouraged scholars to undertake systematic comparative studies of a limited number of political systems with middle-range theoretical problems, or paired comparisons, or the systematic collection of hard data for comparisons.

We would argue that such a middle-range comparative analysis of authoritarian regimes in different cultural and geographic areas and under the influence of different ideological systems should allow the scholar to identify more clearly the distinctive impact of cultural traditions as well as of ideological models rather than attributing to both or either of them patterns that might be found in a great variety of systems where those variables might not be present.

Obviously there is considerable overlap between the study of authoritarian regimes and of the processes of political development, particularly in the so-called Third World of economically underdeveloped societies and new states, since so many of them are neither competitive democracies nor communist totalitarian systems. Since there is a chapter in the *Handbook* (this volume, Chapter 1) devoted to political development, we have deliberately neglected this fruitful perspective.

1. Bureaucratic-Military Authoritarian Regimes

Authoritarian regimes in which a coalition predominated by but not exclusively controlled by army officers and bureaucrats establishes control of government and excludes or includes other groups without commitment to specific ideology, acts pragmatically within the limits of their bureaucratic mentality, and neither creates nor allows a mass single party to play a dominant role are the most frequent subtype. They may operate without the existence of any parties, but more frequent is the creation of an official government-sponsored single party, which, rather than aiming at a controlled mobilization of the population, tends to reduce its participation in political life even in a manipulated form—to use the fortunate expression of Schmitter (1974), "to occupy political space." In quite a few cases such regimes allow a multiparty system but make sure that the elections do not offer an opportunity for a free competition for popular support, even among the limited range of parties allowed, and attempt by a variety of manipulations, going from co-optation and corruption to repression, to assure the collaboration, subservience, or ineffectiveness of such parties (Janos, 1970a).

In the more polemic literature such regimes tend to be labeled fascist, particularly since in the years between the two World Wars they adopted some fascist slogans, symbols, and style elements and when possible co-opted some of the more opportunist elements of the fascist movements in their countries. Some countries in Eastern Europe were led by geographical and foreign-policy imperatives to align with the Axis powers, who often preferred them to more sincere, and therefore nationalist, fascist movements like the Iron Guard in Rumania. The essentially pragmatic character of such regimes allowed some of them to be allied with the Western democracies against their rising fascist neighbors (Seton-Watson, 1967). The prominent role of the army as a supporter of the regime and the fact that many officers played an important role in those regimes in which the army as an institution did not assume power lead other authors to describe them as military dictatorships. Some of them were born as military dictatorships, and the military continued in a few of them to play the dominant role, but it would be a mistake to ignore the much more complex political structure and the important role of civilian leaders, mainly higher civil servants but also professionals and experts as well as politicians of the precoup parties, in such regimes (Janos, 1970a; Roberts, 1951; Tomasevich, 1955; Cohen, 1973; Macartney, 1962). In many of them traditional institutions like the monarchy and to a much lesser extent the Church, or premodern social structures like large landowners, aristocratic or bourgeois, played an important role, but it would be a mistake to describe such systems as traditional. To start with, the traditional legitimacy of the monarchy in the countries with such regimes with a few exceptions was and is relatively weak (Clogg and Yannopoulos, 1972). In a number of them it had been established only a few generations back and the kings came from an alien royal house. In one case, that of Iran, the dynasty has been established by a successful general after a coup. It is very doubtful that in most of these regimes any significant sector of the population gave its allegiance to such rule, on account of the sacredness of tradition, of a belief in the divine right of kings, or strong loyalty to a dynasty like that of feudal retainers. Even the traditional social structures like the aristocratic landholders were often more the beneficiaries of the rule of more modern elites recruited from other social strata, who generally exercised political power and often attacked some of the symbolic privileges of the traditional ruling strata that often saw their power limited to the rural communities. In the typology proposed by Edward Shils, and let us not forget it, formulated mainly for non-Western developing nations, such regimes would logically fall into the category of traditional oligarchies. While the borderline between the type of regime we are describing and the more traditional oligarchies and the purely traditional political systems is somewhat difficult to define, it should not be forgotten that a large number of the powerful leaders of such regimes do not come from the families of the traditional oligarchy and have no strong ties with them. Their policies, while not attacking seriously the privileges of the traditional oligarchy, serve a much greater variety of social groups.

In terms of the Weberian types of legitimacy, such regimes tend to be very mixed. Very few of their supporters think of the man heading the government, or of the single party, as a unique personality endowed with a mission and as having a personal attraction that would deserve the label of charismatic leadership. More often than not the personalities at the head of the government are, in their own style, their own conception of their task, and in the appeal they have to their supporters, acharismatic if not the opposite from charismatic, or sometimes pseudocharismatic. While we find many features in the exercise of their rule that we could call patrimonial or characteristics of a patrimonial bureaucracy, the element of traditional legitimacy is too weak to fall into the pure type of traditional authority in the Weberian sense. Redefined in the sense of personal rulership, as has been done in the work of Guenther Roth, quite a few would fit that characterization. Despite the many arbitrary elements in the exercise of authority not only in relationship to an illegal opposition or just opponents and critics of the system, such regimes made and make a considerable effort to operate within a legalistic framework: enacting constitutions modeled after the Western liberal democratic type, holding on as long as possible to pseudoconstitutional parliamentary forms, using and abusing legal procedures and the courts, and above all demanding obedience from civil servants and officers not on the ground of an identification with their policies, programs, or charisma but on the basis of legal authority. This legalism, congruent with the training of many of those holding power—civil servants and politicians of a previous, more liberal democratic period—often leads to odd contradictions in such regimes. It assures surprising areas of individual freedom but also accounts for some of the more outrageous misuses of power, like political assassination, the execution of opponents while "attempting to escape" (rather than after a trial or, like in totalitarian systems, a show trial), and the use of private violence with the connivance of the authorities. Rather than "revolutionary legality," we find the distortion or perversion of legality.

In the typology offered by Shils these regimes would sometimes, if we were to trust some of their programmatic statements, appear as tutelary democracies. But probably the majority would fit the type of modernizing oligarchies that he proposes, particularly when they make their appearance in preindustrial societies with a low development of the urban bureaucratic, professional, and commercial middle classes. In other cases it would be misleading to speak of modernizing except in a relative sense. Certainly some of the men who take control of such systems are higher civil servants, quite often experts in fiscal matters, committed to tax reforms, a certain degree of government intervention in the economy, and encouragement of industrialization without, however, creating a large-scale public sector (Janos, 1970a, pp. 212–16). Their policies are pragmatic and responsive to business cycles and the international economic system and therefore are likely to use a variety of measures often not too dissimilar from those of countries with other political systems.

Such regimes have appeared in societies that had an incipient industrialization and not highly modernized agriculture and consequently had a large rural population, generally of poor peasants and/or farm laborers or tenants. They have appeared in those societies that, despite their now low level of economic development, generally were characterized by considerable urbanization, particularly in a capital city, by an expansion of education beyond what we could expect in terms of economic development, and therefore by the growth of a stratum of middle-class professionals seeking government employment or dependent directly or indirectly on government activities, a stratum in which we would find both intelligent upwardly mobile persons and others who were downwardly mobile trying to hold on to their social status. While other social groups might have been the beneficiaries of the policies of such regimes, particularly some of the wealthier rural strata or the few well-connected business sectors, the main support for the regime and the recruiting ground for the elites of the system were found largely in what the students of Eastern European societies like Seton-Watson (1967) called state bourgeoisie and Linz and De Miguel (1966) in the study of Spanish society have called *clases medias,* in contrast to bourgeoisie with its connotation of a stratum linked with a modern economy. The middle-class coup of José Nun (1968) would also fit to some degree into this model.

Politically such regimes made their appearance in societies in which liberal democratic institutions, particularly parliamentary institutions, had been introduced but no true party system attracting the loyalties of the population had emerged and/or the parties were unable to produce stable governments. The incapacity of the parties to mobilize democratically the population outside of a few urban centers reflected the persistence of landlord power in some parts of the country, the low level of education of the masses, and clientelistic politics at the local level. However, in contrast to the nineteenth century, they had been sufficiently mobilized to create a threat to a system of traditional oligarchic rule through parties of notables.

In Eastern Europe the peasant parties that emerged as powerful political movements after World War I, stimulated by mobilization in the war, the hopes and results of agrarian reform, the expansion of suffrage, the self-consciousness of the peasantry when confronted with what they perceived as the wickedness of urban life particularly of a bourgeoisie oriented toward foreign life styles, appeared as a threat to the crown, the old liberal political oligarchies tied with landlords, financiers, large merchants, and a few industrialists. In some cases (like Croatia) such parties also threatened the state-supporting ethnic-cultural community (like the Serbs). The leaders of the peasant parties, when confronted with the world depression and its impact on the farmers, could not find satisfactory solutions. Their support failed, and in some cases more aggressive fascist movements competed for their constituency and contributed with their violence to the crisis atmosphere. The bind of agricultural countries in the process of industrialization in relation to advanced industrial nations created unsolvable problems (Roberts, 1951). The moral intransigence of peasantist leaders did not contribute to consensual solutions. The outcomes were the royal dictatorships and an alternation between elections allowing participation of all parties but assuming the victory of some, the outlawing of some and toleration for others, and sometimes the creation of a single national party with the participation of many politicians of the old parties and some co-opted from the opposition parties, peasantist or fascist. Ultimately the tensions led to military takeovers, in the case of Rumania first incorporating the Iron Guard and later brutally suppressing it.

In the more economically, socially, and culturally advanced societies the dislocations produced by war and/or the model of foreign revolutions created pockets of protest and in crisis moments revolutionary attempts condemned to failure or waves of terrorism and counterterrorism. The experience of a revolutionary threat gave to many of the systems a strong counterrevolutionary and reactionary character.

The purpose of such regimes is to exclude from independent, uncontrolled opportunities to participate in power and to organize to that effect the masses demanding a greater share in the goods of the society, particularly workers, farm laborers and underprivileged peasants, and sometimes religious, ethnic, or cultural minorities. Such systems allow more or less pluralism within other sectors of society and assure a prominent role to the military and the bureaucrats capable of enforcing that exclusion and implementing policies that will prevent the excluded strata from exasperation. In that process they are unlikely to introduce major structural changes in the society, but often they will also limit the power, organizational capacity, and autonomy of privileged elites: business, professional groups, foreign capitalists, even the churches, and in rare cases the army. Some quotations of a study by Manuel Lucena (1917) of the Portuguese regime selected by Philippe Schmitter (1973a) reflect the ambivalent relation of such systems, even of one of the most conservative and least "populistic" ones, with the class and economic structure. He writes, for example:

> The State, in the course of this (evolutionary) process, dealt with capitalists with a velvet but heavy hand. Using capitalism it remained ahead (but not brilliantly) of most capitalists. It assisted the most powerful, but it also obstructed them. It captured all of them, large and small in the thickest of regulatory nets. Finally, it is itself, a large entrepreneur, against the wishes of its founder, but in agreement with the imperative laws of the economic system.... One must never forget that, especially in its beginnings, this (corporatist) system was a creature of the State. It was not created by the dominant class which had to be carefully reassured.... Portuguese corporatism controls the sphere of labor without, however, obeying that of capital. It is the State which created *de toutes pieces* their forced agreement which benefited capital. The latter had neither unity nor clear ideas. And, it does not always show itself properly appreciative.... The New State has been the avant garde of a bourgeoisie that did not support it. (Lucena, 1971, pp. 56, 75bis, 126, 292)

Such regimes generally emerge after a period of liberal democracy has allowed a more or less high level of mobilization of the underprivileged strata. They will vary in the degree of autonomy they are ready to grant the more

privileged, in social economic terms, strata, in view of the threat that dominance of those strata might represent for those who have assumed the task of
protecting the regime and themselves from the revolutionary radical claims of
the underprivileged. Depending upon the strength of the regime, traditional
notables would be allowed a share in power. Economic development will determine to what extent those controlling the means of production will be
allowed a place in the coalition or dominant influence. The degree of preauthoritarian regime mobilization of the underprivileged will largely determine
the degree to which those committed to the maintenance of the system—
bureaucrats and military—will play a dominant role and the extent to which
they will attempt to incorporate them through controlled organizations for the
underprivileged, official trade unions, corporative organizations, or populist or
fascist-type parties. We will discuss those types of authoritarian regimes later.
Despite their initially reactionary purpose and the conservative character of
many of their supporters, they are not unlikely to engage in social welfare and
economic development policies, thereby often threatening or limiting the interests of the economically privileged and powerful. As Philippe Schmitter has
shown in his use of the Bonapartist model as developed by Marx, such authoritarian regimes can go far in making the state itself completely independent and
breaking the political power of the middle class, daily anew, protecting at the
same time the material power of those strata.[46] Obviously, where there is a
politically unmobilized or secure and contented peasantry, such a stratum provides much support to such regimes. The limits imposed on the economically
privileged strata and the obstacles placed on the free articulation of the interests of most of the middle class, particularly its intellectually most sophisticated
sectors and sometimes including sectors of the bureaucracy and the army, lead
to the paradox that such regimes are more threatened in their stability by the
strata that brought them to power and that largely benefit of their rule than by
those excluded from the limited pluralism.

Another problem that many of the liberal democratic regimes had been unable to solve were the deep-seated ethnic and nationality cleavages, particularly
in Eastern Europe, where every country had its irredenta abroad and its more
or less oppressed minorities at home, sometimes loyal to a neighboring country.
Such nationality conflicts reinforced chauvinistic nationalism and the political
role of the army. As Janos (1970a) and Nagy-Talavera (1970) have shown, the
social position of the Jews in a number of Eastern European societies, particularly their overrepresentation among those with university education in societies with large-scale intellectual unemployment, created strong feelings of
anti-Semitism. The important role of the Jews in the financial and business
elite in some of the countries contributed to the popular anti-Semitism, while
on the other hand it favored secret coalitions that corrupted political life.

It is no accident that in Hungary and Rumania the true fascist movements,
with a populist ideology attempting a mobilization of the masses and succeed-
ing like the Arrow Cross in gaining the support of many workers in Budapest

and the Iron Guard mobilizing peasants of the least developed areas of Rumania, should have been the most active and dangerous opposition movements to those bureaucratic authoritarian regimes. The fact that in both Hungary and Rumania some of the more dispossessed social groups had not become identified with a Marxist protest movement before the establishment of an authoritarian regime allowed the fascists to appeal to them, something they could not do in some of the more socially and economically advanced and integrated countries, like Spain. Therefore, the co-optation of fascism into the authoritarian regime depended more on the external situation, its own weakness, and a desire to share in power rather than to present the oligarchic structure with the challenge of a national fascist revolution. It is no accident either that some of the fascist leaders would come from an ethnically marginal background and that some of the fascist movements would be appealing to nationalities that were not part of the ruling oligarchical authoritarian elite, like the Croats in Serb-dominated Yugoslavia.

Andrew Janos has very well summarized some of the factors that account for

the survival of pluralism in the face of totalitarian tendencies inherent in the ideology of the single party. If and when revolutionary movements seize power in an insufficiently mobilized society, or in a society in which the commitments of the mobilized strata of the population are sharply divided, the new elite may be forced to seek at least temporary accommodations with autonomous groups and organizations. Thus the emerging one party state will often be totalitarian in ideology and form, but not in reality. On the other hand the precepts of the revolutionary ideology will militate against bargaining, compromise and reconciliation, and the development of institutional mechanisms for the resolution of conflict. In such political contexts (the term "system" appears to be inappropriate here) tensions between ideology and structure will produce considerable randomness in the political process and may result in recurrent attempts by competing groups to eliminate one another from the political scene. These types of party state are pluralistic *de facto* but not by custom or by explicit agreement. This is pluralism by default and not by design. If one may borrow a term from the vocabulary of administrative theory, they are neither pluralistic nor monolithic but "prismatic." By definition these prismatic configurations of political forces are unstable and they best be conceived of as representing a transitional stage in the process of political change. The prismatic condition of a polity may lead to full-fledged totalitarianism, intraparty institutionalization, a multiparty system, or further and complete disintegration, to mention only some of the possible alternatives. (Janos, 1970a, p. 233)

As we will see later, in more complex societies, with higher levels of social mobilization, a Catholic intellectual tradition, and less concern about complex links between foreign and internal policy, stabilized military-bureaucratic authoritarian regimes moved further in their institutionalization, in the explicit break with liberal-democratic constitutional forms, and in the incorporation of the old political elite. Some opted for various mixes between what we shall call organic statism and experimentation with mobilizational single parties of fascist inspiration. This was the case of Spain in 1926, Portugal in the early thirties, Austria in 1934, Brazil under Vargas, 1937–1945, and Spain under Franco.[47]

The victory of the allied powers in World War II provided countries faced with the task of nation building and the crisis of modernization with two basic political models: Western competitive democracies and movement regimes after the Soviet model. Those two powerful paradigms seemed to exclude the bureaucratic authoritarian pattern developed in the interwar years in the then new nations of Eastern and Southeastern Europe. Initially only Portugal appeared as the survival of the bureaucratic-authoritarian reactions to the failure of democracy in interwar Europe. The defeat of fascism had discredited any mobilizational single-party authoritarian regime not based on the model of the Communist vanguard party. Certainly the Franco regime,[48] with its mixture of bureaucratic authoritarianism with weakened fascist-single-party-mobilizational elements and the later (1942) developments of organic statism, survived ostracism by the United Nations. Argentine nationalism, reacting to foreign pressures and to the opportunities created by a new working class emerging from industrialization due to wartime import substitution, led to the transformation of a military-oligarchic regime into a populist authoritarianism with some fascist components in the form of Peronism. That model was not without attractiveness to young Latin Americans dissatisfied with unsuccessful or oligarchic democracies, but for sometime political scientists could predict that with economic development, social and cultural modernization, the professionalization of traditional armies, and the shift of the Church from a democratic corporativism to Christian democracy, the countries of the Western hemisphere would move toward competitive democracy. The successful transfer of democratic institutions in India led those unaware of the long and complex historical process leading to the creation of Indian political institutions by the Congress party (after all, the party was founded in 1885 and participated in representative semisovereign institutions since 1937) to hope for a similar transfer in the other areas being decolonized by Britain. The initial deviations from that transfer model were sometimes interpreted as transitional stages that would ultimately prepare society for democracy as tutelary democracies. However, two decades later those hopes would be shattered in a few places by a successful revolution, like in Cuba, or by a combination of a national struggle for independence and social revolution, first in China and particularly in North Vietnam, and by the attempt to create mobilizational single-party regimes in Africa and Arab countries.

More unexpectedly, the optimistic model of social-economic developments increasing political pluralization and as a result of it the likelihood of political democracy was to be disproved in two of the most advanced Latin American countries. Guillermo O'Donnell (1973), building on the earlier work of Stepan (1971, 1973) on Brazil, on the basis of a case study of Argentina in recent decades has advanced an alternative model linking a higher state of economic and social development with the emergence of bureaucratic authoritarianism aimed at excluding activated popular sectors, particularly urban working classes, on the basis of the coalition between a new type of military elite—the incumbents of technocratic roles in the public and private sectors, in the more dynamic and efficient sectors—with the support of social strata threatened by mobilization. As Stepan has shown, technocratic roles in the military, the bureaucracy, and the modern enterprises share a common view of the requirements for development, particularly the need to exclude and deactivate the popular sector, and have international linkages with similar elites in advanced industrial societies, which have led them to a favorable assessment of their combined social-problem-solving capabilities and to a greater control of crucial sectors of their societies. Their emerging coup coalition will aim at reshaping the social context in ways envisioned as more favorable for the application of technocratic expertise and for the expansion of the influence of social sectors that they have most densely penetrated as a result of modernization.

O'Donnell notes with some hesitation the similarities between this model and that of the developing societies on the periphery of the industrial heartland of Europe in the interwar years, but the relative weight of the experts, technocrats, and new managers, with their emphasis on development rather than economic stability and protectionism, would suggest some important differences. They might be characterized as military-technocratic-bureaucratic authoritarian regimes in contrast to the more bureaucratic-military-oligarchical authoritarian regimes of Eastern Europe. There are other differences not stressed by O'Donnell but worth notice, like the absence in the former type of regime of even a weak monarchical legitimacy capable of shifts in policy in crisis situations (particularly as in Rumania and Yugoslavia, but also Spain under Primo de Rivera). Another difference is the absence of nationality, linguistic, and cultural conflicts, which both strengthened and weakened Eastern European and Balkan authoritarian regimes. However, in our view a basic difference is the absence of fascist coalition partners or models to mimic that on occasion gave a legitimacy to those regimes among intellectuals, students, and youth. The crisis of Catholic corporativist ideology compounds the problem of institutionalization of the new bureaucratic authoritarian regimes in Latin America. Both authoritarian responses share the fear of revolution from below, stimulated by radicalized intellectuals, a fear that was stimulated in Europe by the Russian and Hungarian communist revolutions, the peasant populist mobilization in Bulgaria, and isolated revolutionary or pseudorevolutionary outbreaks in other European countries. In Latin America in the mid-60s the Cuban Revolution and the minor efforts of guerrilla or peasant mobilization stimulated by it, particularly by Che Guevara, contributed to that fear. More realistically, important segments of the more advanced Latin American societies were concerned about the pressures coming from a popular sector, initially mobilized from above by preceding populist authoritarian regimes that had created organized forces like trade unions and parties linked with them capable of expressing their demands in democratic or quasidemocratic political systems after the fall of the Estado Novo and Peronism. In our view O'Donnell neglects to emphasize the impossibility of controlled mobilization by modernizing elites after fascism had been discredited and in societies in which populist authoritarian regimes had (perhaps incorporating fascist elements) achieved a nationalistic, more or less antioligarchical mobilization. The demobilization of those forces required coercion, like in Brazil, or produced an unstable authoritarian regime, like in Argentina, where the costs of coercion as well as those of an open society seemed too high, leading to a constant experimenting between exclusion and co-optation, particularly in the quasi-democratic stage that preceded the coup by General Onganía in 1966 and that was resumed in the last stages of bureaucratic military rule before the recent election that brought the Peronistas to power.

O'Donnell has described at length and documented carefully the structural constraints at a particular level of economic development in the specific Latin American international economic-dependency relation and their social consequences that lead to an unsolvable problem and what he calls (following Apter) a "ceiling effect," which seems to leave no other way out than bureaucratic authoritarianism. We cannot summarize here his dynamic model in all its richness, which can serve as an example of how the analysis of the conditions and processes leading to the emergence of authoritarian regimes should be done, combining economic, sociological, and political analysis. Nor can we present his comparative analysis of the conditions contributing to the instability of that solution in the Argentine case and its temporal stability and success in Brazil. Space also excludes an analysis based on the work of Alfred Stepan (1973) of the factors accounting for the different types of authoritarian institutionalization achieved by the military that took over power in Brazil in 1964 and in Peru in 1968. Their analyses, those by a distinguished group of Brazilian scholars, and the recent study by John S. Fitch III (1973) of the variety of patterns of military intervention in Ecuador have advanced our knowledge of the conditions leading to authoritarian regimes under the leadership of the army far beyond the traditional literature, with its liberal perspective of "generals versus presidents," and beyond the cultural-historical interpretations of Latin American politics. The model of O'Donnell tends to overemphasize the structural constraints and to underestimate the possibilities of political engineering (to pick up an idea of Giovanni Sartori, 1968). He also underestimates the possibility of responsible democratic leaders preventing the crisis situation that crystallized the coup coalition, gave it an apparent legitimacy, and broadened its initial basis of support. Alfred Stepan's brilliant analysis of the fall of Goulart (Stepan, 1971) and the comparison with several crises preceding it that did not lead to a change of regime is complementary and in part corrective of the macropolitical, social, and economic model of O'Donnell.

A sophisticated documented and reasoned analysis of modernization of South America, examining critically the indicators and the internal heterogeneity of societies and the degree of modernization in centers, suggests that the higher and lower levels of modernization are associated with nondemocratic political systems, while political democracies are found at the intermediate level of modernization, with the exception of Peru. Argentina and Brazil, contrary to the expectations of many analysts, have moved toward bureaucratic authoritarianism in a period that Venezuela and with some reservations Colombia moved toward democracy, while Chile, despite economic difficulties, still seemed to be holding on to its embattled democracy.

Brazil and Argentina moved in the mid-60s to exclude the already-activated urban popular sector (working class and segments of the lower middle class) from the national political arena by refusal to meet the political demands made by the leaders of this sector and denying its leaders access to positions of political power from where they could have direct influence on national decisions. Exclusion can be achieved by direct coercion and/or by closing the electoral channels of political access. Those attempts have varying degrees of success. At one extreme the political deactivation of an excluded sector may be achieved; it becomes politically inert through destruction of its resources (especially its organizational basis). At the other extreme this deactivation might not be achieved. These countries moved from an incorporating political system that purposefully attempted to activate the popular sector and allowed it some voice in national politics in a period of populism and horizontal industrialization, to exclusion. They were countries in which the world crisis of the thirties and World War II accelerated the emergence of domestic industry and an urban working class, which changed the distribution of political power away from the nationally owned agrarian areas producing exportable goods and the largely foreign-owned network of financial and export intermediaries. The basis of that process was a broad populist coalition, led by powerful leaders like Vargas and Perón, against the old oligarchies and the highly visible foreign-owned firms mediating the international-domestic market and the traditional policies of free trade. The coalition favored industrialization and the expansion of the domestic market. Socially it meant the broadening of the functions of the state and providing employment for many middle-class, white-collar workers and technicians. Nationalism and industrialization appealed to the military, benefitted the urban workers, fostered migration to the urban centers, extended the market economy, raised consumption levels, and increased unionization and benefits for the domestic-consumption-oriented agrarian sectors. The tradi-

tional export-oriented sector, provider of international currency, lost its traditional hegemony and the government extracted a significant portion of its income to redistribute for the benefit of domestic expansion and consumption.
The economic importance of exports, however, allowed this sector to retain
political influence disproportionate to its decreasing share in the gross national
product. Nationalistic-populist policies never went much further than recurring
deprecation of the oligarchy and expropriation of the more visible symbols of
foreign presence. Industrialization was horizontal or extensive, and few inroads
were made into the production of intermediate and capital goods; a consequence was a heavy dependence on imports of those goods as well as of technology. After an exhaustion of the easy stages of industrialization based on
substitution for imports of finished consumer goods, import substitution proved
to be an import-intensive activity in a period of erratic prices for exports that
aggravated the poor productivity of the export sectors, which were paying the
bill for the populist policies. This led to severe foreign exchange shortages.
At the same time, Vargas and Perón encouraged workers' unionization as the
basis for allegiance and to facilitate governmental control over newly incorporated segments of the popular sector. Even though union leaders were dependent on those leaders, the urban popular sector was given its first chance
to have an effective weight in national politics and to bargain within the populist coalition, developing a high degree of organization. Initially all participants
in the populist coalition were receiving payoffs roughly proportionate to their
expectations in a period of exultation and hope for takeoff into sustained
growth. However, the economic dynamics, described before, led to an end of
the expansion. Horizontal industrialization left a schedule of supply, which included a disproportionate share of consumption and luxury items as well as
a myriad of small producers coexisting with a few big firms, under an umbrella
of minimum competition and maximum state protection. Consumption expectations consolidated, and vertical industrial projects became more dependent
on capital and technology transfers from abroad and an increasing penetration
of technocratic roles, which consolidated linkages of dependency with originating
societies from which such roles had been transplanted. A new need for a high
degree of stabilization and predictability in the social context was perceived
with growing modernization. After reaching in this way the high point of
modernization of their centers, new problems emerged that led to the breakdown of populist or developmentalist alliance. The need to clear the market
of marginal producers, eliminating restrictions on the more technologically
advanced or more capital intensive and financially powerful enterprises, combined with appeals to nationalism and preservation of the social peace, led to
opposition to expert advice, stabilization plans, and the interests of more powerful producers. This issue had special significance for the military and *técnicos*
in strategic points for national economic planning and decision making. In
more open democratic political systems, like those that succeeded Vargas, with

distributionist-populist economic policies, the electoral weight, the capacity to strike, demonstrate, and disrupt, and intensified political activation were perceived as profoundly threatening by most other social sectors. As a result, most propertied Argentine and Brazilian sectors agreed that the popular sectors' demands were excessive, both in terms of consumption and power participation, and that capital accumulation would be impossible if they were not controlled. The class component of the polarization led to the acceptance of a political solution that supposedly would eliminate such threats, which became particularly (we might say disproportionately) salient with the spector of socialist revolution that arose with the Cuban Revolution. The changed mentality of the officer corps, as the result of antisubversive training in the United States, and the impact of French military thinking on political-warfare and civic-action doctrines led to the national-security doctrines that included socioeconomic development as a response to internal subversion. The deterioration of the income of the large salaried middle class during the years preceding the 1964 and 1966 coups led to their disaffection from a formally democratic system and their response to a law and order appeal. The popular sector, suffering from unfavorable income redistribution, engaged in increasing political activation to obtain decreasing returns. The demands-performance gap and the differentiation-integration gap led to the situation that Samuel Huntington described as "mass praetorianism" (Huntington, 1968, pp. 192–343). Political institutions, partisan parliaments, which had never been particularly strong, were further weakened and the executive became the primary focus of a flood of demands. Governments were victimized by and collaborated in "praetorianism." The situation became a stalemate, with high levels of unrestrained conflict; sharp differences in demands, the weakness of government preventing the implementation of any policy, and concern for survival in office led to sequences of policies designated to placate the more threatening political actors with little concern for general problem solving. Competition was increasingly zero-sum, gains were precarious, and the threshold for a definitive crisis was reached when most of the political actors focused on changing the rules of the political game altogether instead of trying to obtain gains within the existing rules. The existing political system had reached its ceiling.

The process of modernization in a variety of sectors had led to the emergence of technocratic roles, particularly in larger organizations of persons trained in techniques of production, planning, and control. The incumbents of those roles have expectations derived from role models of the "originating" societies. This new group has been particularly important in the discussion by Brazilian social scientists of social change, some of whom speak of a technobureaucracy. Their consciousness and their expertise convince them that by molding the social context to serve their own aspirations they would at the same time improve the social situation. Potential planners and civil servants yearn for governments that will follow their advice and grant them effective decision-making power. In addition—and in this development Latin America in the sixties probably differed from the European developments in the twenties and thirties—these elites met in a new context, new business schools and advanced military schools like the *Escola Superior de Guerra* in Brazil, and new opinion-making publications emerged. As Stepan (1973) has shown, a new mentality appeared. The training of these elites emphasized technical problem solving, a rejection of emotional issues, a perception of the ambiguities of bargaining, of politics as hindrances to rational solutions, and a definition of conflict as dysfunctional. A common technical language, or jargon, facilitated communication, and the density of interaction of this group despite the small numbers led them to play a dominant role in the new coup coalition rather than, like in less modernized contexts, to withdrawal from political involvement. High confidence in their capabilities for governing led to their crucial influence in the 1964 Brazilian and the 1966 Argentine coups.

In a highly modernized context, the attempt to exclude and eventually deactivate the popular sector in the absence of the possibility of offering psychological or economic payoffs inevitably required strong and systematic coercive measures. Bureaucratic authoritarianism—eliminating political parties and elections and the political personnel sensitive to the demands of the popular sector, domesticating labor unions by co-optation, if not by coercion, and attempting to bureaucratically encapsulate most social sectors to maximize control—was the answer. Bargaining and interest representation would be limited to leaders at the top of these organizations, and spontaneous modes of demand formulation as well as dissent would have no legitimate place.

O'Donnell links his model with that offered by Barrington Moore (1967) as the third historical path toward industrialization, in addition to the bourgeois and communist revolutions, a path that involves the coalition of the public bureaucracy and the propertied sectors (including a subordinate industrial bourgeoisie) against the peasantry and an emerging proletariat. It is a conservative reaction to the strains of advancing industrialization and to a weak push toward parliamentary democracy and the entry of the masses into the political scene. Such regimes attempt to consolidate traditional forms of domination in the rural areas and accelerate industrialization, minimizing the chances of social revolution. Incidentally, we might note that here Barrington Moore and O'Donnell converging with him coincide with the insightful analysis by Franz Borkenau (1933) of the conditions for the rise of fascism. Borkenau characteristically linked fascism with the problems of semideveloped societies reaching the point of industrialization as latecomers and therefore combining the natural tensions created by change from rural to urban society, from small to modern enterprise with its new type of discipline, with the diffusion of socialist political demands, which threatened the development of national capitalism in a way that it did not in the early industrializing societies.

After developing this general model O'Donnell analyzes the differences between Brazil and Argentina after the successful military coups, particularly the
different degrees of coercion applied. For him the difference can be found in
the fact that in Argentina the level of activation was higher than in Brazil,
even though the rate of increase in the precoup period was lower. While in
Argentina the impulse came mainly from below, with the governing Radicales
not encouraging it, in Brazil the inducement for political activation came from
above in the Goulart government. The Peronista allegiance was perceived by
established sectors as relatively less threatening than the suggestion of socialist
tendencies among Brazilian governing personnel, a perception that fostered
an initially tighter degree of cohesion in the ruling coalition as well as an increase in the influence of its more *antisubversive* and *"efficientist"* members.
The hostility of the Radicales in power against the Peronistas led the unions
and Peronistas to welcome the 1966 coup for a short period before the policy
implications of the new political system were spelled out, a factor that delayed
and lessened the degree of coercion, while in the Brazilian case the initial
antagonistic position of the populist sector led to a more coercive response.
The result was the success in the deactivation of the popular sector in the
Brazilian case and the retention of the relatively high level of political activation in the Argentine modern area and accounts for the different degree of
consolidation of the two systems.

In bureaucratic authoritarian regimes the incumbents of technocratic roles
tend to emphasize those aspects that their socialization has best taught them
to measure and deal with. Reality may be confounded with hard data indicating performance, like growth in GNP, diminished inflation, and fewer
strikes, neglecting hard-to-decode information coming from noisier channels
for the expression of popular preference and the fact that those achievements
have been made at the cost of repression, income redistribution, elimination
of national entrepreneurship, liquidation of political institutions, increased
poverty of the urban and rural popular sectors, and alienation of intellectuals
and students. However, if the indicators to which those elites are sensitive show
satisfactory performance, the political rule will be easily rationalized, the assessment of their capabilities for solving problems reinforced, and the coalition
consolidated. This accounts for the hardening and *continuismo* in the Brazilian
system and the fact that in the Argentine case influential members of the original coalition seem willing to attempt a return to democracy in view of the
blatant failure of the system using the set of indicators preferentially monitored.
The coups that deposed Generals Onganía and Levingston and the election
that the Peronists won after the interregnum of Lanusse are a reflection of the
different success, in the opinion of the ruling elites, of the postcoup regimes in
Brazil and Argentina. This does not mean that the effort of extrication of the
military and the democratizing of bureaucratic authoritarian rule are assured
success. Nor does the relative success in certain respects of the Brazilian mili-

tary-technocratic-bureaucratic authoritarian regime imply that it has found a stable institutional form and legitimacy (Linz, 1973b). The strains caused by recent developments do not exclude the possibility that some military officers might appeal to domestic entrepreneurs and organized labor, using nationalistic pleas and promises of protectionist and more distributionist policies, in their efforts to reconstruct the political system along populist lines, even when in O'Donnell's opinion the chances for such solutions are slim.

He recognizes that his model stresses unidirectional effects, produced by socioeconomic factors on the political side, and the need for further research on the effects that political action can have on socioeconomic factors. Our feeling is that his analysis, while rightly underlining the negative political consequences of bureaucratic authoritarianism, tends to underestimate the broader social impact that success in economic development of the technocratic elite can have through a trickling-down process from the initial beneficiaries to larger population segments, and the possibility for such regimes to selectively implement welfare policies through the expansion of social security and enforced company paternalism, particularly in favor of critical urban working-class sectors, once an initial accumulation stage has been achieved. Even Marxist critics admit that this has been the case in Spain, and survey data show that large segments of the society (except significantly in the most modern and highest-income regions) show a feeling of improvement, which, however, might result in heightened expectations and tensions at a later date but which also carries with it a change in the pattern of social and class relations.

On the basis of my analysis of the Spanish case I would argue that the problems of stabilized bureaucratic authoritarianism are likely to be derived more from its ambiguous legitimacy and the difficulties of political institutionalization than from economic constraints and their impact on the society. I would particularly emphasize that in the Western world, in the absence of an ideological single party, important elites use either the competitive liberal democracies or the dynamic single-party mobilizational regimes as ideals assuring participation of citizens. The international linkages with stable democratic advanced industrial societies, while contributing through the linkages of the technocratic elites to the emergence and/or success of those regimes, at the same time also constantly undermine their legitimacy through the critique to which they subject them and through the cultural influences that conflict with their values. While contributing to the basis of their success, they in the same process contribute to the basis for future crises; while justifying their existence on technical and economic grounds, they every day contribute to undermining their legitimacy by offering to their citizens an alternative political model and by encouraging them not to give their full allegiance to the authoritarian regime, not to give up hope for a democratic political development. Even with considerable achievements, bureaucratic authoritarian regimes in the West might not be assured the same stability as posttotalitarian authoritarian regimes in Eastern Europe, partly due to the different nature of their linkage with a hegemonic power in whose sphere of influence they find themselves.

Excursus on military intervention in politics. Our analysis of authoritarian regimes with a military component could be misleading without a reference to other aspects of the military in politics. First of all, not all interventions are aimed at the creation of such regimes, nor do they all lead to their establishment. Secondly, it would be wrong to derive the motives of the officers and the circumstances leading to the overthrow of a democratic regime from the nature and politico-social functions of the regime, established with the military's help, ignoring "internal," specifically military, factors—the mentality of officers, institutional interests, organizational problems—that shaped the military's response to the actions of political leaders. It is because of this that it often is difficult to predict the course to be followed in political, economic, and social matters by a military junta after taking power. Thirdly, we should not forget that more often than not it is the civilians who call at the barracks for support either to overthrow or defend constitutional government, and that in many societies the civilian and "democratically" enacted constitutions attribute to the military a "moderating" power that "legitimizes" their intervention. Ultimately, even weak democratic governments in crisis situations become dependent on military support. Fourthly, the role of the military in internal politics does not exhaust the topic of civilian-political-military relations, since there is the whole problem area of the role of the military in international affairs and the pressures for military and political considerations and leadership in the conduct of war, so brilliantly formulated by Clausewitz (1911; originally published 1832) which will not concern us here. Nor can we devote the attention it merits to the question of the relation between different regimes and their armed forces (Huntington, 1956, 1964), or to the complex process of extrication from power and civilianization of the military after interventions in politics. All these themes would certainly deserve another chapter.

The analysis of military intervention has shifted between two perspectives: one emphasizing the characteristics of the military establishment motivating and facilitating its intervention, with little concern for the actions of other actors in the political and social system; the other emphasizing that the most important causes are not military but political and reflect not the social and organizational characteristics of the military establishment but the political and institutional structure of society (Fitch, 1973). There is also a difference in emphasis between those who center their attention on the level and type of social and political development and the importance of certain cultural traditions—sometimes summarized under the label of "political culture"—and those who turn to a more careful analysis of the particular historical crisis leading to a specific intervention—the process of formation of a coup coalition, the broadening of its support and neutralization of potential opponents—and the distinctive political outcome of the intervention. Others tend to ignore or dismiss the explicit justifications and pronouncements of the participants, searching for the "real" interests of the military—as a social group or as an "instrument" or "representative" of social and economic interests. Another difference found in the literature is between those who stress the political strengths of the military and those who note their political weaknesses. In addition, the increasing importance of global political conflict—the cold war and patterns of international dependency, the links established between the military of different countries (through training, military missions, expeditionary forces, supply of weapons, diffusion of military doctrines)—leads to increased emphasis on the role of foreign influences (Einaudi, 1969; Pauker, 1963). In part those differences reflect the fact that much of the literature is centered on the role of the military in particular parts of the world or countries, but there are also differences between comparative and sometimes quantitative analyses (Schmitter, 1973a; Nordlinger, 1970; Putnam, 1967) and case studies, as well as ideological and cultural preconceptions. The scarcity of systematic, theoretically oriented empirical case studies has often led to premature generalizations. Certainly all the perspectives noted should be taken into account even when one or the other might be more fruitful in the study of particular cases.[49]

The different dimensions of the problem are also likely to be of different importance in different phases of the process: the period preceding the formation of a conspiratorial group, the phase of the expansion of its appeal, the crucial period of the decision to act, the immediate aftermath of a coup, and the political process in the months and years after taking power. In fact, the main actors—within the military—at each of those stages might be quite different persons reflecting different outlooks. It is important to realize that it is difficult, if not impossible, to explain why any particular coup occurred by reference to the propositions advanced by cross-national statistical analyses in order to answer the question why some countries have higher incidence of coups than others. In the analysis of a set of variables in which the meaning of any detail depends on its relation to the whole context of which it is a part we are confronted with a higher degree of complexity than can be easily dealt with by cross-national regression analysis.

It would be risky to say that any state is immune to overthrow and even more so to a change of government under pressure of the military, but certainly political systems have quite different probabilities of maintaining subordination of the armed forces to the political leadership. In serious political, social, or economic crises, defeat in war or loss of prestige, irrespective of types of regime the military are likely to play a more influential role. With wars, or the possibility of war, as well as any potential internal disorder, it will probably increase. Different parties or factions are likely to find greater sympathy among officers, and the interests of the armed forces are likely to find a more or less responsive ear among them. However, in certain societies the political role will not easily go beyond the threshhold of insubordination, while in others that point will easily be reached. Among the models, based on different patterns of value congruence and/or control mechanisms, that have assured a high probability of subordination we find the aristocratic, the liberal, the traditional professional, and the communist, formulated by Huntington (1956, 1964).

There are, however, two models that involve a high probability of military intervention in politics and with it the establishment of authoritarian regimes, described by Alfred Stepan (1971, 1973) as the moderating pattern of civil-military relations and the new professionalism. Neither of them represents a deviation from a well-established pattern of subordination of military to political authority resulting from exceptional crisis situations in the body politic but an institutionalized response that is likely to be successful when a broad consensus develops among the leadership of the armed forces that the circumstances are such as to legitimize their intervention. To Stepan's two models we might add a third, attentivism, in which the military stand outside the political process without an explicit commitment to any regime, as a neutral power, making their loyalty or support of governments in crisis situations conditional and avoiding any support that would divide the armed forces. This was the position of von Seckt under the Weimar Republic (Carsten, 1967; Vogelsang, 1962) and of Franco in the thirties (Payne, 1967), a position that undermines the authenticity of democratic regimes and indirectly can contribute to their breakdown.

The liberal model based on objective civilian control is impossible as long as civilian groups are unwilling simply to accept a politically neutral officer corps and as long as there are multifarious civilian groups anxious to maximize their power in military affairs. It is also unlikely when the professional goals of the military as an instrument in international conflict are questioned or are of limited relevance. Under those circumstances the moderating pattern appears. In it the norms encourage a highly political military whose political acts are nonetheless limited to certain boundaries. The key components in this pattern of civil-military relations have been summarized by Stepan (1971, p. 64) as follows:

1. All major political actors attempt to co-opt the military. A politicized military is the norm.

2. The military is politically heterogeneous but also seeks to maintain a degree of institutional unity.

3. The relevant political actors grant legitimacy to the military under certain circumstances to act as moderators of the political process and to check or overthrow the executive or to avoid the breakdown of the system, especially one involving massive mobilization of new groups previously excluded from participation in the political process.

4. Approval given by civilian elites to the politically heterogeneous military to overthrow the executive greatly facilitates the construction of a winning coup coalition. Denial by civilians that the overthrow of the executive by the military is a legitimate act conversely hinders the formation of a winning coup coalition.

5. There is a strong belief among civilian elites and military officers that while it is legitimate for the military to intervene in the political process and exercise temporary political power, it is illegitimate for the military to assume the direction of the political system for long periods of time.

6. This rough value congruence is the result of civilian and military socialization via schools and literature. The military doctrine of development is also roughly congruent with that of parliamentary groups. The military officers' social and intellectual deference facilitates military cooption and continued civilian leadership.

In this model, found frequently in Latin America in the past and even formalized in constitutional provisions about the role of the army, the propensity to intervene is not pathological, as it would be if the agreed model were the liberal one, but normal. That propensity correlates with the cohesion of the relevant political strata; the propensity is high when civilian cohesion is low, low when civilian cohesion is high. The success of the coups is related to the degree of public legitimacy ascribed to the executive and the military. A typical situation of low cohesion of relevant political strata is given by the frequent conflicts between the president and the legislature, heightened in recent decades by the different electoral and popular bases of support for populist national leaders and legislators with local bases of power. Under the circumstances the attitudes of pro-regime strata toward executive become decisive. Good indicators of that lack of cohesion of relevant civilian strata are the low percentage of votes of winning candidates, the absence of a broad consensus on a compromise candidate, the belief in the legitimacy of the institutions (particularly of the executive and the conformity of his actions with the constitutional provisions) and in the personal qualifications of the president, the trust in his willingness to abide by legal or conventional rules, for example the exclusion of *continuismo,* his respect for the autonomy of institutions including the armed forces, which becomes decisive for the response of the armed forces in a crisis situation (Fitch, 1973; Solaún, 1973). In a context in which the military activists, for or against the government, are always in the minority, that minority needs to convince the great majority of officers who are either strict legalists or simply nonactivists. Activists do not wish to risk bloodshed or military splits, so they wait until a consensus has developed. Public opinion, or at least some form of expression of public opinion (as reflected for example in the editorials of leading independent newspapers), and the position of influential social groups become decisive to convince the military itself. The success or failure of attempted coups is closely correlated with that legitimation. The moderating pattern is dependent on the belief in the constitutional forms of government itself, on a military confident that the crisis could be effectively resolved by returning the government to civilian control, and on the belief that the military had no legitimacy to rule in comparison to civilians. Under such circumstances the military do not create or at least aim to create a new regime but an interim regime of exception, which has a lot in common with the Roman concept of dictatorship. The leniency with the opponents, both civilian and military, not joining in the coup and the readiness of those defeated to abandon office without resistance allowed in the past the moderating pattern to function without a permanent discontinuity in regime legitimacy.

In the last decade some of the conditions that made the moderating pattern possible have disappeared. The degree of mobilization that populist presidents, democratic or semiauthoritarian, had achieved and with it the real or misplaced confidence in their capacity to challenge the moderating role of the military have increasingly prevented the bloodless coup and the easy extrication from power. The prolonged ineffectiveness of civilian leadership, the emergence of increasingly difficult-to-solve problems, the growing social unrest and problems of public order characteristic of what Huntington has called praetorian politics, which give encouragement or tolerance to the articulation of demands that cannot be satisfied by the system operating within the constraints of the institutions, have all led to the emergence of a new pattern of intervention. A new professionalism, very different from that of the military in advanced stable societies with major foreign-policy responsibilities, has emerged. The success of revolutionary warfare techniques against conventional armies and the subsequent diffusion of ideas of counterrevolutionary internal warfare created a new type of social and political consciousness among the military. Confronted with the need or the possibility of having to fight against internal subversion that articulated demands that appeared just and could not be satisfied by the civilian authorities and whose suppression required political skills, the military expanded the scope of their preoccupations. Criticism of the uselessness of costly military establishments led to the involvement in civic action projects that made officers aware of the problems created by underdevelopment. A new type of training in military educational institutions changed the scope of attention and professional capacity of the military. That training, contact with other societies, and interaction with other elites, particularly experts and managers, led to the new professionalism in internal security and national development. The consequent role expansion led the military, when they perceived failure of civilian leadership, not to intervene in the moderating pattern but, once they believed in their capacity to rule and distrusted the politicians, to assume power *sine die*. In addition, their perception that the political leadership was mainly an instrument of special interests, of well-organized groups be they latifundia owners, exporters and foreign investors, or the trade unionists and activist intellectuals, led them to feel that their duty was to assume power to objectively serve the national interest. The new professionalism has led to the establishment of authoritarian regimes that in response to different national contexts pursue quite different policies, as the cases of Brazil and Peru exemplify, but in both cases do so in response to similar assumptions about the role of the army in societies in crisis.

2. Organic Statism

Authoritarian regimes pursuing quite different policies in terms of class interest and organization of the economy have attempted to go beyond the bureaucratic-military-technocratic authoritarian rule by a controlled participation and mobilization of the society through "organic structures." The rejection of the individualistic assumptions of liberal democracy, combined with the desire to provide an institutional channel for the representation of the heterogeneity of interests in modern or modernizing societies, while rejecting the model of class conflict, has led to a great variety of theoretical-ideological formulations and attempts to implement them through political institutions. Such attempts have been conceived as an alternative to the mobilizational single party, as an instrument or complement to single party rule, or even as a way to link a single party with society.

In competitive democracies political parties serve to articulate and aggregate a wide range of interests rather than serving as a channel for very specific interests. Political parties aiming at holding power have an inevitable tendency to search for a majority, either by representing a cross section of society agreeing at least *pro tempore* on certain goals, like the modern catchall parties, or maximizing their support in a social class or otherwise numerous sector of a society. Only parties with limited access to power identify with specific interests, as Max Weber noted for the parties in Imperial Germany, except for minor parties in a fragmented multiparty system, which generally act as minor allies of major parties. Single parties in this respect are, once again, closer to the assumptions underlying democratic politics. It is therefore not surprising that authoritarian conceptions born in a climate of rejection of political parties, of the bitterness of ideological partisan conflict in unstable democracies but in societies of some degree of economic and social complexity and having reached a certain level of political mobilization, should turn to corporativist solutions.

The ideological heritage of nineteenth-century counterrevolutionary conservatism, with its rejection of both individualistic liberalism and state absolutism and its ideological identification with the Middle Ages—the response of preindustrial strata like artisans, peasants, and sometimes even professionals to advancing industrial and financial capitalism—gave rise to a variety of corporativist ideologies (Schmitter, 1974; Manoilesco, 1934; Elbow, 1953; Bowen, 1947; Pike and Stritch, 1974). The antiliberal, anticapitalist, and antistatist—

specifically of the secularizing state—response of the Catholic Church in encyclicals like the *Rerum Novarum* was another stream contributing to its appeal (Azpiazu, 1951; Vallauri, 1971). The syndicalist tradition in the labor movement, which rejected the authoritarianism of Marxism; the persistence of the state as an instrument of oppression; and the co-optation of the social democratic labor movement by participation in electoral and parliamentary politics also contributed to the search for formulas of participation through independent councils of producers at the factory and community level which would freely agree, through pacts that could be revoked, to create larger organizations. Even some democratic liberals, fearful of the growing power of the state and of the anomie of lonely isolated individuals as a result of the growing division of labor and the crisis of traditional institutions, felt that corporative professional organizations could serve social control (Durkheim, 1902). The availability of conservative antirevolutionary; Catholic; syndicalist; and liberal solidarist traditions had its fruits in the crisis of the twenties and thirties. Italian and other fascists, in theoretical formulations, laws and learned legal commentaries, and efforts of institution building, made corporativism an influential political-ideological current.[50]

It is conceivable in theory that corporativism would have offered an alternative way to organize free and spontaneous participation to that through election of individuals or candidates of parties to a national parliament on the basis of territorial constituencies. Actually, "organic democracy" in contrast to individualist "inorganic democracy" of parties has in every case been combined with authoritarian imposition and lack of accountability of the rulers to the ruled. The reality of corporativism has been defined by Philippe Schmitter (1974) as

> a system of interest representation in which the constituent units are organized into a limited number of singular, compulsory, noncompetitive, hierarchically ordered and functionally differentiated categories, recognized and licensed (if not created) by the state and granted a deliberate representational monopoly within their respective categories in exchange for observing certain controls on their selection of leaders and articulation of demands and supports. (p. 93)

In ideal-type terms he contrasts this system with the pluralism in democracies described as

> a system of interest representation in which the constituent units are organized into an unspecified number of multiple, voluntary, competitive, non-hierarchically ordered, and self-determined (as to type or scope of interest) categories which are not specially licensed, subsidized, created or otherwise controlled . . . by the state and which do not exercise a monopoly of representational activity within their respective categories. (p. 96)

Obviously, in reality we do not find these pure ideal types; interest pluralism in democratic societies often takes corporativist characteristics, and the reality of corporativism in authoritarian regimes has some tolerance for unfettered pluralist tendencies, particularly for business and professional interests.

Why should corporativism have become identified with authoritarian regimes, become, as Alfred Stepan has aptly characterized it, organic statism? Three reasons seem to account for it: first, logical and practical difficulties in organizing political life exclusively as an expression of "corporate" interests; secondly, the socio-political purpose pursued in the particular historical-social context in which such solutions have been implemented; and thirdly, the nature of political community and the state as well as the intellectual and legal traditions on which the idea of the state is based.

The theoreticians of organic democracy all emphasize that people are naturally members of numerous groups based on primary social relations, at the work place, farmers' cooperatives, professional associations, universities, neighborhoods, parishes, etc., in contrast to artificially created larger groups, like political parties, which divide people in those primary contexts and lead to the emergence of professional politicians, party bureaucrats remote from the life of the citizen. Why not organize representation on the basis of such primary units? Obviously the representatives of such more or less face-to-face groups would be close to the people and subject to their daily control. Social science research has shown that contrary to the expectations of those theories, private governments are characterized by strong oligarchic tendencies and membership apathy.[51] Leaving this aside, the question arises, How can participation in larger units of decision making, required in urban industrial societies with large-scale organizations interacting with other large social, economic, and political units, be organized on this basis? The theory responds with multi-tier, that is, indirect, elections within a series of constituencies based on grouping such primary units up to a national chamber of corporations (Aquarone, 1965; Fraga, 1959; Fernández-Carvajal, 1969, pp. 77–124; Esteban, 1973, pp. 127–255) or a series of specialized chambers. In principle it should be possible to organize a national democratic polity on this indirect democracy basis, even when accountability of the national leadership to the individual citizen would seem difficult to achieve. However, a number of false assumptions make the model questionable: foremost, that such primary units share common interests rather than being internally conflictual; secondly, that there should be no cleavages crosscutting on a national level those units of greater saliency than the common interest of their members—that neighbors should have more interest in local problems than in, let us say, secularization versus clericalism, or war and peace, and those issues would not divide the society and require representation. If such broader issues would exist in the society, we could assume that ultimately, particularly at the national level, parties based on the aggregation of a large number of issues would emerge without the corporatively elected representatives having any basis to make their decision and without having been chosen on account of their position on them.

Even more serious is the problem of delimiting in a rational way the constituencies and the share in representational power to be attributed to them. To recognize spontaneously emerged, preexisting organizations would show the very unequal organizational mobilization of various interests, and therefore the state inevitably assumes the task of defining noncompetitive and functionally predetermined categories by certifying them or licensing them and granting them a representational monopoly. Even more difficult is the decision of what weight to assign in the decision making to the variety of organized interests. There are no obvious criteria for such a decision. The number of members would make impossible the representation of functionally important groups of numerical insignificance. The weight in the economy (a criterion used in assigning seats in the Yugoslav chamber system) again disenfranchises numerically important but economically weak sectors, like agriculture in semideveloped societies. There is no easily defensible criterion to assign representation to noneconomic, nonoccupational interests, and ultimately even the best decisions would be subject to constant revisions with changes in the economic and social structure which would make the conflicts about reapportionment in inorganic democracies children's play. The authoritarian decisions by the state, that is, by bureaucrats and/or ruling political groups, would in all cases predetermine the nature and composition of the decision-making bodies, which would then be anything but an organic outgrowth of the society. Whatever deviations from fair representation almost inevitably exist in democracies based on population and territorial constituencies (except for a single national constituency with strict proportional representation), they are incomparably smaller than those that even the most rational and equitable corporative system of representation would produce.

Sociologically, as Max Weber (1968) noted in a short section on "representation by agents of interest groups," any such system has as a latent function to disenfranchise certain strata.[52] As he notes, it is possible for such a system to be extremely conservative or radically revolutionary in its character. It can be the former by distributing mandates among the occupations and thus in fact disenfranchising the numerically superior masses, or the latter by openly and formally limiting suffrage to the proletariat and thus disenfranchising those strata whose power rests on their economic position (the case of a state of soviets). It is this that has recommended corporative representation to authoritarian regimes, particularly in societies in which the masses of workers, farm laborers, and peasants are a potentially majority support for mass class parties. This and the opportunity for electoral manipulation with indirect, multi-tier, elections accounts for the realities of political systems based on such principles. In addition, interests are often highly antagonistic and hence majority voting among elements that in status and class affiliation are highly heterogeneous is exceedingly artificial. The ballot as a basis of final decision is characteristic of settling and expressing the compromise of parties. It is not, however, characteristic of occupational interest groups. In addition, on many issues representatives of interests would have no reason to have an opinion and therefore they would be logically willing to exchange their vote on most issues for measures favoring their narrow specific interests. In such a context power ultimately ends up in a ruling group that organizes the system, delimits its constituencies, assigns the share in representation, arbitrates conflicts between interests, and decides all those issues on which the representatives have no basis for choice. Even in systems ideologically committed to organic democracy, the realities can be better described as "state organicism," with bureaucratic-military-technocratic elites and/or the leaders of a single party having the largest share of power. The corporative structure at best becomes one element in the limited pluralism of such authoritarian regimes. However, even weak corporative structures represent a limit, particularly at the grass-roots level, to the monistic ambitions of a disciplined political elite attempting to mobilize a society for its utopian purposes. It is therefore no accident that there should have been in the fascist regimes ambivalence and tension on how far those institutions should have been developed at the cost of the power of the single party, and that the Nazis, with their perception of plebiscitarian, classless *Volksgemeinschaft,* should have rejected early the corporativist ideas of German conservatism (Rämisch, 1957).

No political system has made the highest and most powerful decision-making bodies—the cabinet and head of government—accountable to its corporative-type legislatures (Aquarone, 1965; Fraga, 1959; Fernández-Carvajal, 1969). In our sense of the term there has not been any democracy without political parties, even though in pure theory popular participation could be organized through corporative constituencies and elections rather than parties.

Once the ideas of institutionalized or tolerated class conflict and of a classless society in its utopian ideological versions of Marxism or Nazi *Volksgemeinschaft* are rejected, the idea of building political institutions through corporate interest representation becomes an obvious alternative. It is one that is particularly tempting for bureaucratic, military, and technocratic elites that reject the idea of open conflict and believe in a rational, ultimately administrative solution of conflicts of interests but are not guided by a utopian vision of society but by pragmatic considerations. It should allow the expression of the heterogeneity of interests, of the pluralism of society, but also serve to limit the conflictual expression of that heterogeneity, particularly in the form of class conflict. De facto the emergent systems had many elements of class imposition.

It is no accident that the National Socialists, impelled toward a more totalitarian model of society, after toying with corporativist ideas of a *Ständestaat* should have rejected it, and that democratic parties, inclined to create second chambers based on corporative principles like the *Reichswirtschaftsrat* or the

Conseil Economique et Social, ultimately never infused real life into those bodies. In all political systems we find some elements of corporativism, of institutionalized and regulated representation of interests, particularly economic and occupational, but only in authoritarian regimes has a serious effort been made to organize a political regime according to a corporativist ideology. In reality those authoritarian regimes claiming to be corporativist have ultimately been bureaucratic, technocratic, or single-party mobilizational authoritarian regimes. However, corporativism—organic democracy—has served as an important ideological alternative to competitive democracy. It has been an important component of the institutional pluralism of regimes ruling over a society that had reached a level of social and economic complexity and social and political mobilization that could not be managed by sheer administration, and thus needing to provide for some opportunity for political participation but unable to create or sustain an ideological mass party led by a politically conscious elite or vanguard. It was also a solution particularly congruent with an economic system that rejected a free-market, entrepreneurial capitalism but also public ownership of all the means of production and centralized planning. The disillusion in a number of European and Latin American societies with liberal democracy and a pure capitalist economic system was fertile ground for the acceptance by many groups, including business elites, of corporativist solutions.

There have been and exist a significant number of authoritarian regimes that have turned to ideas of organic democracy to legitimize their rule and to organize a more or less limited participation of carefully delimited and weighted sectors of the population. Theoretically the Portuguese Estado Novo built by Salazar, with its weak single party created from above, is the purest case of such a regime (Schmitter, 1973a). There, as in Austria (Voegelin, 1936; Diamant, 1960; Busshoff, 1968) between 1934 and 1938 under Dollfuss (Bärnthaler, 1971), and in Spain under Franco after a pretotalitarian fascist period,[53] the rulers, using a Catholic ideological heritage combined with the Italian Fascist experience, created systems with a component of organic democracy. Mussolini, linking originally with the syndicalist tradition, reinforced by the intellectual heritage of rightist nationalists, and searching for the approval of Catholics, built a corporativist superstructure that served conservative interests well by disenfranchising a highly mobilized working class and providing a channel for the complex interest structure of a relatively developed society. The strong pretotalitarian tendencies of many Fascist leaders and the conception of an "ethical state" above interests derived from an idealistic tradition, however, created an uneasy balance between the corporativist and the single-party mobilizational components of the regime.[54] Authoritarian regimes in Latin America, particularly of the populist variety, found corporativist policies particularly congenial (Wiarda, 1973a, 1974). The absence of widespread political mobilization of a large working class organized by socialists or other independent labor movements before the assumption of power allowed rulers like Vargas (Schmitter, 1971), Cárdenas, and to some extent Perón to use corporativist interest representation, including powerful trade unions in their authoritarian regimes. The Mexicans, through the sector organization of the party and its reflection in candidate selection for legislature and other offices, have also incorporated into a dominant party structure corporative elements (Scott, 1964). Nowadays the military in Peru are attempting an interesting experiment of the same character by encouraging the creation of the *Sinamos* (*Sistema Nacional de Apoyo a la Mobilización Social*, "national system of support to social mobilization") in several spheres like (Cotler, 1972; Palmer, 1973; Malloy, 1974): the *pueblos jóvenes* and urban slums; rural organizations; youth; labor organizations (trade unions and labor communities); cultural; professional; and economic (cooperatives, self-managed enterprises). In an initial phase after the Russian Revolution the ideas of Soviets (councils of workers or of workers, peasants, and soldiers) had considerable attraction for revolutionaries who rejected the Marxist social democratic party, which had been ready to participate in parliamentary democratic regimes, as a method to disenfranchise other sectors of society and to provide a particularly effective arena to revolutionary activists ready to displace the leadership of other leftist parties and movements (Kool, 1967). However, ultimately the vanguard party dispensed with this form of participation. Yugoslavia, with workers' management and local self-government, has also created a system of chambers of corporative character, which complement the political structure based on the party and its functional organizations and the revolutionary oligarchy.

It is important to emphasize that many pluralistic systems with competitive democratic political institutions and parties institutionalize or encourage directly or indirectly corporative arrangements to handle particular problems, especially in the field of management and labor of relations. Many have attempted to complement the political chambers with advisory corporative chambers, but they generally have lacked vitality when interest groups were divided along political, ideological, or religious lines. Only in the Scandinavian democracies (Rokkan, 1966) and in some of the consociational smaller European democracies, particularly Austria, have these institutions gained a considerable share in power. This has, perhaps, been possible because of the high degree of overlap of a moderate, centripetal, multiparty system with the basic interest cleavages in the society and the integration between party system and interest-organization system. However, we should not forget the basic difference between the presence of corporative tendencies in systems based on the political pluralism of parties and in systems claiming to organize the political process through corporative structures. Nor should we ignore the differences between such organizations having grown out of the society, even when often encouraged and privileged by the state, and those authoritatively created by the state. The first development is the result of a liberal period, sometimes historical continuity, and a culture and economic development encouraging the "art of association"; the other is a result of imposition in the absence of those factors or of control of them by one sector of society holding authoritarian power.

In spite of all the ideological emphasis on corporativism and organic democracy, none of the regimes identifying themselves as "organic" has renounced to a single party, which often results from a fusion of a variety of antidemocratic organizations and/or is created from above. Those single parties in Europe—with the exception of Fascist Italy—were weak organizations, while in Latin America, perhaps because of the oligarchic character of previous political systems, the new officially created parties—often closely linked with the corporative structures like "recognized" trade unions—became important institutions capable of survival after a transition to more democratic politics.

3. Mobilizational Authoritarian Regimes in Postdemocratic Societies

The Western European democratic revolution initiated in the eighteenth century spread liberal democratic institutions to societies of very different economic, social, cultural, and institutional development. In many of them there was no possibility of returning to traditional legitimate rule after political revolutions and often major social and economic changes. In a number of them the sequence of development crises—state-building legitimation, participation, incorporation of new social forces, representation in legislative organs, and ultimately share in executive power—cumulated in a short period of time. More often than not economic development did not keep pace with political change. Protest ideologies formulated in more advanced societies diffused and new movements combined demands for redistribution and participation with the hostility to the changes resulting from early industrialization and disruption of traditional economic and social patterns (Borkenau, 1933). Other countries, particularly those that had not experienced the Protestant Reformation and the disestablishment of religion that went with religious pluralism in earlier centuries, faced a crisis of secularization. Some like Italy and Germany as latecomers to statehood, whose boundaries did not coincide with those of the culture nation, experienced a heightened need for a sense of national cohesion (Allen, forthcoming). The success of the United Kingdom and France and to a lesser extent the Netherlands and Belgium in the colonial expansion created in other medium-sized powers the consciousness of the "proletarian nation." The loss of the last remnants of Spain's empire and the English veto of Portugal's expansion also created crises of national consciousness. The coincidence of these quite different but cumulated crises through the period of rapid political democratization, particularly in the absence or weakness of traditionally legitimate institutions and elites, prevented the successful and slow institutionalization of democratic political processes capable of incorporating the demands of new social groups awakened to class or cultural consciousness. In contrast to the Eastern European societies, those of Western Europe already before World

War I had experienced the introduction of liberal freedoms, constitutional or semiconstitutional government, and an increasing importance of modern political parties, including Marxist, syndicalist, and Christian labor movements. The crisis caused by war interventions, postwar economic dislocations, and the psychological impact on the underprivileged masses of the Russian Revolution and with it the split of the socialist movement led to the delegitimation and ineffectiveness of democratic regimes in process of consolidation. In contrast to the less politically, economically, and socially developed Eastern European nations, purely bureaucratic-military-oligarchical authoritarian solutions could not be the response to the crisis. It could not be because even the oligarchic institutions of the establishment had accepted the notion that politics could not be reduced to administration and realized that a purely coercive repression was condemned to failure because in all social classes, including the privileged middle class, democratic ideas had gained considerable loyalty. In such societies the crisis of democracy would lead to new political formulas including the plebiscitarian pseudodemocratic component: the mass single party. On the other hand, those societies had reached a level of development and complexity that made it difficult for the leadership of such a single party to move in a totalitarian direction, except in the case of Nazi Germany. It is no accident that the first manifestation in Europe of a plebiscitarian, nonliberal authoritarian solution to the crisis of democracy should have been Bonapartism, considering that France was the country of Europe in which revolutionary change had brought the biggest break with traditional authority and had led to the highest political mobilization with the 1848 revolution. It is no accident that some Marxists like Thalheimer (1930) should have turned to Marx' analysis in the *Eighteenth Brumaire* to understand the novel authoritarian regimes created by fascism.[55]

The crisis of European societies at the end of World War I led to the emergence of two political movements that broke with the liberal democratic systems that seemed on the ascendancy: Leninism and fascism. Both were based on the rule by the minority, by an elite, self-appointed to represent the majority, the proletariat or the nation, at the service of an historical task. Parties led by a self-confident elite defined not by ascriptive characteristics or by professional achievements but by its will to gain power and to use it to break through social and historical constraining conditions, appealing for the support of the masses but unwilling to allow them to interfere in the pursuit of its goals. The strength of the democratic heritage of Marxism and the scientism of Marxist social science, while allowing a break with the liberal tradition, assured the persistence of an ideological commitment to democracy. Fascism as a nationalistic response to the ideological internationalism of Marxism, by linking with other ideological traditions of the nineteenth century—romantic irrationalism, social Darwinism, Hegelian exultation of the state, Nietzschean ideas, Sorelian conceptions of the role of the myth, imagery of the great man and the genius—turned explicitly antidemocratic (Gregor, 1969; Nolte, 1969; E. Weber, 1964). In contrast to other conceptions of authoritarianism as a modern response to the crisis of society, it searched for a new and different form of democratic legitimation, based on the emotional identification of the followers with the leader, in a plebiscitarianism that had found its first postrevolutionary manifestation in Napoleonic Caesarism. In a complex way we cannot analyze here, fascism combined and perverted many strains of Western intellectual tradition that directly or indirectly put into question the assumptions of liberal democratic pluralist society and politics.

The special circumstances of Italian society after World War I led to the emergence under the leadership of Mussolini of a new type of nontraditionalist, popular antidemocratic movement, initially carried by a small number of activists recruited among the interventionists; nationalists; the veterans of the war who found reintegration into civil society difficult; a certain type of intelligentsia heady with nationalism, futurism, and hostility for the clientelistic politics of Giolittian *transformismo* and for the selfishness of the bourgeoisie; together with revolutionary syndicalists who had discovered their national identity (De Felice, 1966a, 1969, 1970; Delzell, 1970). The poet D'Annunzio discovered a new style, new symbols for this generation of rebels (Hamilton, 1971). It was, however, the mobilization of the Italian working class by a Maximalist social labor movement, unable to implement a revolutionary takeover of power and still unwilling to follow a reformist path toward integration into democracy in the making, that created the conditions for success of this minority of activists. The red domination of the northern Italian countryside, which scared landowners and wealthier peasants, and occupation of factories in the industrial centers, particularly Torino, led a scared bourgeoisie to join and support the incipient movement (Salvemini, 1961). Its leaders, hostile to the socialists on account of their antiinterventionism and to the workers who had stayed in the factories and received with hostility the returning veterans, were ready for the alliance. The ambivalent attitude of the state and its representatives toward the terrorist activities of the *squadrismo,* the failure of the reformists to turn to support the demo-liberal state, and the tensions between the old liberal parties and both the socialists and the new democratic Christian populist party, combined with the ruthlessness and opportunism of Mussolini, led the new movement to power. A new and multifaceted ideology, a new form of political action, and a new style had been born and would find echo in much of Europe (Nolte, 1966, 1968a; Laqueur and Mosse, 1966; Rogger and E. Weber, 1966; Woolf, 1969; Carsten, 1967; Kedward, 1969; Hayes, 1973) and even in Latin America (Trindade, 1974) and Asia (Maruyama, 1963; Morris, 1968). Initially it was possible to conceive of fascism as a peculiar outcome of the Italian crisis (De Felice, 1966a, 1969, 1970; Nolte, 1967). Later, even as far as the 1930s, it could be interpreted as a response to the problems created by late and unsuccessful economic development and modernization (Borkenau, 1933). But with the success of Hitler it became necessary to explain it in terms of certain basic characteristics of Western society (Nolte, 1967, 1969; Gregor, 1968, 1974a, 1974b; Woolf, 1968; Turner, 1972).

In the context of our analysis of types of political systems we cannot enter into an analysis of the variety of forms the fascist antidemocratic ideology and movement took, nor an explanation of the conditions for its success (Lipset, 1960; Nolte, 1968a; Linz, forthcoming). The nature and definition of fascism itself is a subject of lively debate. We would characterize fascism as an ideology and movement defined by what it rejects, by its exacerbated nationalism, by the discovery of new forms of political action and a new style. The anti-positions of fascism are essential to its understanding and its appeal, but they alone do not account for its success. Fascism is antiliberal, antiparliamentarian, anti-Marxist, and particularly anticommunist, anti- or at least aclerical, and in a certain sense antibourgeois and anticapitalist; while linking with the real or imagined historical national tradition, it is not committed to a conservative continuity with the recent past or a purely reactionary return to it but is future-oriented. Those negative stances are a logical outcome of its being a latecomer on the political scene, trying to displace liberal, Marxist, socialist, and clerical parties and win over their supporters. They are also the fruit of the exacerbated nationalism that rejects the appeal to class solidarity across national boundaries and puts in its place the solidarity of all those involved in production in a nation against other nations, seizing on the notion of the proletarian nation: the poor countries against the wealthy plutocracies, which happened to be at that time also powerful democracies. Communist internationalism is defined in this context as the enemy. The latent hostility to a church that transcends the national boundaries and whose devisive effect on the national community with the struggle between clerical and secularizers interferes with the goal of national greatness, hostility that becomes bitter hatred in cases like Nazism, is another logical consequence that differentiates the fascist from other conservative antidemocratic parties. To the extent that modern capitalism is, particularly in its financial institutions, part of an international system, fascists tend to idealize preindustrial strata like the independent peasant, the artisan, and the entrepreneur, particularly the founder directing his own firm (Mosse, 1964; Winkler, 1972). Masonry, as an organization emphasizing links across nations and closely identified with the liberal bourgeois, secularized strata that created the democratic liberal regimes, is another obvious enemy. Anti-Semitism in the Europe of the turn of the century, particularly Eastern Europe (Pulzer, 1964; Massing, 1949), had a long tradition, and wherever there were Jews fascism seized on those tendencies, stressing the anational, cosmopolitan character of the Jews and particularly of Zionism.

Those negative appeals, however, had a kind of distorted positive counterpart. The anti-Marxism is compensated by an exultation of work, of the producers of *Faust* and *Stirn*, "hand and brain," in that way appealing to the growing white-collar middle class, which rejected Marxist demands that it should identify with the proletariat (Kele, 1972). The populism of fascism leads it to support welfare-state policies and to engage in loose talk of national socialism, socialization of the banks, etc., which justifies in fascist authoritarian regimes economic interventionism and the development of an important public sector in the economy. The anticapitalism that appeals to precapitalist and petit bourgeois strata is redefined as hostility to international financial stock exchange and Jewish capitalism and as exultation of the national entrepreneurial bourgeoisie. The emphasis on a national common good, which rejects the assumptions of individualism, is easily combined with hostility to the free play of interests of economic liberalism and finds expression in protectionist and autarchic economic policies that appeal to industrialists threatened by international competition. The hostility of a secularized intelligentsia of exacerbated nationalists to clerical politics and their competition with Christian democratic parties for a similar social basis account for the anticlericalism that gets combined with an affirmation of the religious tradition as part of the national, cultural, historical tradition. Already the Action Française in secularist France had taken this path, appealing to the Catholics who rejected the secularizing, liberal democratic state. The Iron Guard, the only successful fascist movement in a Greek Orthodox country, confronted with the denationalized, secularized bourgeoisie and an influential Jewish community, was the fascism that most directly linked with religious symbolism. In the case of Germany the confused programmatic statements about positive Christianity and the identification of many Protestants with a conservative state religion were used by the Nazis, but ultimately the racist ideology became incompatible with any commitment to Christianity (Lewy, 1965; Buchheim, 1953). The antireligious stands of Marxism and particularly communism in the Soviet Union allowed the fascists to capitalize on the ambivalent identification with the religious heritage. The anticlericalism facilitated the appeal to secularized middle classes unwilling to support the clerical and Christian democratic middle-class parties, while their antiliberalism, anti-Masonic, and even anti-Semitic stands, combined with their anticommunism, facilitated the collaboration with the churches when they came to power. The antibourgeois affect, the romanticization of the peasant, the artisan, the soldier, contrasted with the impersonal capitalism and selfish bourgeois rentiers, appealed to the emotional discontent of the sons of the bourgeoisie, the cultural critics of modern industrial and urban society. The rejection of the proletarian self-righteousness and the bourgeois egoism and the affirmation of the common national interests above and beyond class cleavages exploited the desire for interclass solidarity developed among veterans of the war (Linz, forthcoming; Merkl, forthcoming) and the guilt feeling of the bourgeoisie, and served well the interests of the business community in destroying a labor movement that threatened its privileges and status. The populist appeal to community against the pragmatism of society, *Gemeinschaft* versus *Gesellschaft,* had considerable appeal in democratic societies divided by class conflict and mobilized by modern mass parties.

The deliberately ambiguous and largely contradictory appeals we have just described would have been, and were, unsuccessful in those societies in which war and defeat had not created a serious national crisis. In the defeated nations or those, like Italy, being victors, felt unjustly deprived of the fruits of their victory, an upsurge of nationalism was channeled by the new parties. The efforts to establish an international political order through the League of Nations under the leadership and to the benefit of the Western, capitalistic, plutocratic democracies became another issue in the armory of the fascists. The lack of coincidence between the national-cultural boundaries and those of the states, the irredenta on the borders, and the existence of nationalities that had not become nation-states, combined with the pannationalist movements, were another source of strength for fascism, particularly in the case of Nazis.

Fascist ideology had to reject totally the assumptions of liberal democratic politics based on pluralist participation, the free expression of interests, and compromise among them rather than the assertion of the collective interests above individuals and classes, cultural and religious communities. The obvious distortion of the idea of democracy in the reality of the early twentieth century and the incapacity of the democratic leadership to institutionalize mechanisms for conflict resolution provided the ground for the appeal of fascism. On a less lofty level, all the interests threatened by a powerful labor movement with revolutionary rhetoric, particularly after some of its revolutionary attempts had been defeated, could support the fascist squads as a defense of the social order. In societies that had reached the level of political, economic, and social development of Western Europe, that defense could not be left to the old institutions —the monarchy, the army, the bureaucracy, and the oligarchical political elites. In that context the fascist ideology offered a new alternative, which promised the integration of the working class into the national community and the assertion of its interests against other nations, if necessary through military preparedness and even aggression (Neumann, 1963). This position would appeal to veterans not reintegrated into civil society and army officers and would neutralize the armed forces in the course of the struggle for power.

Neither the ideological appeals nor the interests served by or expected to be served by fascism are sufficient to account for its rapid success. Fascism developed new forms of political organization, different from both the committee electoral-type of parties and the mass-membership, trade-union-based socialist parties, as well as the clerically led religious parties. It was the type of organization that, like the communist counterpart, offered an opportunity for action, involvement, participation, breaking with the monotony of everyday life. For a generation that had lived heroic, adventurous actions of war and even more for the one that had lived that experience vicariously, due to its youth, the *squadrismo* and the storm troopers offered welcome relief. Many of those who found their normal careers and education disrupted by the war and economic crisis, and probably some of the unemployed, provided the party with many of its activists, whose propaganda and direct action in support of specific grievances—of farmers to be evicted, peasants onto whom the labor unions were imposing the employment of labor, industrialists threatened by strikers—gained them support that no electoral propaganda could have achieved. This new style of politics satisfied certain psychological and emotional needs like no other party could except some forms of cultural protest and to some extent the communists.

Finally, fascism is characterized by a distinctive style reflected in the uniforms—the shirts—which symbolized the break with bourgeois convention, the individualism of bourgeois dress; and the mass demonstrations and ceremonies, which allowed individuals to submerge in the collective and escape the privatization of modern society. The songs, the greetings, the marches, all gave expression to the new myth, the hopes, and illusions of part of that generation.

This ideal-typical description of fascism as a political movement ignores national variants in ideology, appeal, social basis, and alignments on the political scene. We cannot go into the complex question of whether National Socialism, with its extreme racism, its biologic conception of man, fits into the broader category of fascism (Nolte, 1963; Mosse, 1964, 1966), particularly since many fascists felt quite critical of Nazism and many Nazis felt ambivalent toward Mussolini and his movement (Hoepke, 1968). Our view is that National Socialism, particularly the northern left wing of the movement, rather than "Hitlerism," fits into the more general category (Kühnl, 1966). Nazism did not reject the identification as fascism, but it also acquired unique characteristics making it a quite different branch of the common tree into which German ideological traditions (Mosse, 1964; Sontheimer, 1968; Lukácz, 1962) had been grafted and one that had its own distinct fruits.[56] The strength of that branch growing with the resources of German society made it an appealing competitor of the first fascist state.

The ambiguities and contradictions of the fascist utopia, combined with the inevitable pragmatic compromises with many of the forces it initially criticized, account for the failure of the model, except in Italy (to a certain point) and in Germany. To have been successful the initial nucleus would have had to gain support in all strata of the society and particularly among the working class in addition to the peasantry. However, the organizational penetration, except perhaps in Hungary, Rumania, and (if we consider Peronism as a deviant of fascism) in Argentina, of the socialist, communist, and anarcho-syndicalist (in Spain) labor movements was such that such hopes were condemned to failure. In some countries the Catholic peasantry, middle classes, and even many workers had identified with clerical and/or Christian democratic parties in the defense of religion and found in the social doctrine of the Church an answer to many of the problems to which fascism presumed to be a response. Unless deeply scared by unsuccessful revolutionary attempts, disorganized by continuous economic crises—inflation, depression, unemployment, and bankruptcies—or uprooted by war, the middle and upper-middle classes remained loyal to old parties (including, before the March on Rome, most of the Italian south) in countries like France, Belgium, the Netherlands, Scandinavia, and the UK (Linz, forthcoming; Kaltefleiter, 1966; Lepsius, 1968). Fascism's success in these countries was a minority, largely generational phenomenon, strengthened in nationalist border areas and gaining broader support in crisis periods. The heterogeneous basis and the failure to gain strata to which its appeal was directed, ultimately explainable by its latecomer role on the political scene, led the leaders to an unremitting struggle to gain power and to a policy of opportunistic alliances with a variety of established groups and a- or antidemocratic conservative forces, which in turn hoped to manipulate its popular appeal and youthful activist following for their own purposes. In societies that had experienced a serious crisis but no political, social, and economic breakdown comparable to czarist Russia, this meant that the way of power was open only in coalition with other forces, particularly the conservative authoritarian parties like the Partito Nazionalista in Italy and the DNVP in Germany, the powerful antilabor interest groups, and the army, and by neutralizing the churches. Such groups well entrenched in the establishment and the state could provide men more capable of governing than were the activists of the first hour. The result was the establishment of authoritarian regimes—with a seriously limited and muted pluralism—with a single party whose rule ranged from fairly dominant and active, approaching in some moments the totalitarian model, to regimes in which it was only a minor partner in the coalition of forces, or absorbed like in Portugal, or suppressed, like in Rumania. Only in Germany would the party and its many—and competing—organizations become dominant. In all of them fascism introduced a mobilizational, populist component, a channel for some degree and some types of voluntary political participation, a source of ideological discontent with the status quo and justification for social change, which differentiates authoritarian mobilizational regimes from other types. Even where that mobilization was ultimately deliberately demobilized, like in Spain (Linz, 1970), the half organic-statist, half bureaucratic-expert-military authoritarian regime emerging after the 1940s would never be the same as for example the regime of Salazar, where fascism as we have characterized it never had taken root.

The struggle against a powerful, particularly a social democratic, labor movement and the effort to undermine the authority of a democratic state exacerbated the romantic love for violence into an end in itself and generally, consciously or unconsciously, transformed the movement into an instrument of vested interests (often verbally and even sincerely denounced), transforming the "national integrative revolution" into hateful counterrevolution. The Marxist interpretation (Abendroth, 1968; Mansilla, 1971; *International Journal of Politics,* 1973; Galkin, 1970; Lopukhov, 1965 [57]), while inadequate to explain the emergence of the ideology, its complex appeal, and its success in capturing the imagination of many youthful ideologists and misunderstanding the motivation of the founders and many leaders, is largely right in the analysis of the "objective" historical role played by fascism (F. Neumann, 1963). This obviously does not mean to accept the thesis that the fascists were the hirelings of capitalism based on subsidies that started coming only when the party had gathered strength and in proportion to its success relative to other anti-Marxist parties, or that fascism was the last possible defense of capitalism, or that in power it only and always served its interests. Even less does it absolve the Marxist movement of having undertaken and failed in revolutionary attempts to gain power in relatively democratic societies or of holding onto a maximalist revolutionary rhetoric that mobilizes its enemies and prevents the democratic governments from functioning effectively—a policy that prevents the government from imposing the order desired by those supporting it, while not making a serious effort to impose (at least in part) the policies favored by those movements by participating actively in democratic policymaking by either supporting or even entering government. Fascism, among other things, is a response to the ambivalence of the Marxist ideological heritage toward the importance of political institutions, toward "formal" liberal democracy, toward reform rather than revolution. Mussolini reflected this dialectical relationship when he said that if the red menace had not been there it would have had to be invented. The anti- or at least ademocratic behavior of the left made possible the more effective one of the right, even when in turn the manipulative attitude of the liberals toward democratic institutions explains the reaction of the left.

Fascist-mobilizational authoritarian regimes are less pluralistic, more ideological, and more participatory than bureaucratic-military or organic-statist regimes with a weak single party. They are further from "liberalism" and closer to "democracy," further from individual freedom from political constraint but closer to offering citizens a chance to participate, less conservative, and more change oriented.[58] Probably the greater ideological legitimacy and the greater mobilization of support made them less vulnerable to internal opposition and overthrow than other types of authoritarian rule, and in fact only external defeat destroyed them.

4. Postindependence Mobilizational Authoritarian Regimes: Theory and Reality

Mobilizational authoritarian regimes have appeared in states gaining independence from colonial rule or asserting themselves against foreign dependency. Countries in black Africa[59] and the Maghreb,[60] among the countries of the Third World, provide examples of this type. Contrary to the expectations of many political scientists, not many have proven stable over the last decade, particularly since 1964 military coups swept civilians from office in many of them (Bienen, 1968, 1974; Lee, 1969; C. E. Welch, 1970; Young, forthcoming). In others a process of decline set in, leading in many places to a no-party state (Wallerstein, 1966; Potholm, 1970, pp. 272–96; Bretton, 1973).

Single-party mobilizational authoritarian regimes created by political leaders emerging from and mobilizing the grass roots, and not from above by the ruler, were possible in societies of low economic development, particularly with the relatively egalitarian peasant rural structure, where the modern economic elite was small and often composed of foreigners or members of an outside ethnic group and where the colonial rulers had not allowed or encouraged the growth of a professional middle class, a civil service with distinctive status and honor, and a professional army (Apter, 1963). In the case of sub-Saharan Africa one might add the absence of a native hierarchically organized religious leadership. Colonial rule had often destroyed or, in the case of indirect rule, discredited traditional precolonial authorities, at least for the emerging urban-educated, more modernized sectors. In this context a new nationalist leadership emerged among those trained abroad or in the few educational institutions created by the colonial power, sometimes encouraged by the parties of the left in the metropolis as leaders of trade unions or representatives in emerging self-government institutions and stimulated by a few nationalist intellectuals and their contacts abroad (Wallerstein, 1961; Hodgkin, 1961; Carter, 1962; Coleman and Rosberg, 1964). These leaders sometimes seized successfully the representation of grievances of the native population, the workers and peasants affected by the dislocations of the traditional order resulting from economic change or the introduction of Western legal institutions and in some cases European settlement. The colonial rulers confronted with those incipient movements shifted between repression and co-optation, policies that, particularly when inconsistently applied, contributed to strengthening this emerging nationalist leadership. The desire for independence, at least initially, obscured the importance of other cleavages; the underdevelopment and the foreign character of the modern economic sector limited the importance of class politics. In the representative assemblies elected shortly before or immediately after independence the representatives of the nationalist movements obtained pluralities or majorities, which they often expanded by co-opting those representing more particularistic constituencies like tribal, religious, or traditional groups. Initially there was hope that the transfer of British or French constitutional arrangements would lead to new democratic states. However, soon after independence the actions of the opposition, or the perceptions of them by the leaders of the governing party; the governing party's conception of nation building as excluding peripheral, sectional, tribal demands (particularly in states with artificial boundaries imposed by the colonizers); the difficult economic problems; and the problems caused by new expectations of the people led those leaders to prevent, limit, or exclude free political and electoral competition. In many of the states created by decolonization, independence and statehood became symbolically identified with a leader and his party, who often claimed a charismatic authority, which was recognized by his followers. The weakness of traditional authority and the lack of understanding of the complexities of legal rational authority made the emergence of at least a semblance of charismatic leadership possible. The artificial character of many of the state boundaries, the ethnic, linguistic, and religious diversity of the population, the great difference in social development of the few urban centers and coastal areas and the rural periphery, and the weakness of administrative institutions led the leaders of the new independent states to believe that their party could serve as a nation-building instrument. Faced with the problems of national integration, the not-always loyal opposition, and the fear of foreign influences, the dominant party, in the context of a political culture that had not institutionalized liberal democratic values, soon became a single party.

Significantly, some of the leaders rejected the idea of a single monolithic party: "We are against the *parti unique*. We are in favor of a unified party [*parti unifié*]," to use the expression of Senghor (Foltz, 1965, p. 141). Many leaders of dominant parties encouraged the entry into the party of leaders with a strong regional, communal, tribal, or sectional following who initially supported the defeated opposition parties or were prominent in them. They bring into the loosely organized *parti unifié* their following and electorate.

In analyzing African one-party systems and their mobilizational capacity, we should keep in mind some facts stressed by Aristide R. Zolberg (1966, pp. 15–33) about their penetration in the society. In Ghana the first test of the strength of the Convention People's party (CPP) came in the 1951 election, two years after its founding, in which it obtained 92 percent of the votes cast in Accra, 94 percent in other municipalities where elections were direct, and 72 percent of grand electors of other areas. However, in the five municipalities, 64 percent of the qualified population registered to vote and, of these, 47.2 percent voted. Hence, the voters represented about 30 percent of the eligible population, itself somewhat smaller than the total number of adults. This was a startling achievement but one that cannot be taken as an indication of territorial saturation by the CPP. Similarly, Zolberg notes that in the Ivory Coast the organization of Houphouet-Boigny (the PDCI) in 1946 obtained 94 percent of the votes in the election to the territorial assembly, which amounted to 53 percent of the eligible electorate that had registered, but since the electorate was a very restricted one these votes represented about 6 percent of the estimated adult population. In 1952, in an election that the leaders acknowledged to be fair, Houphouet-Boigny's opponents obtained only 28 percent of the votes cast and the PDCI represented only 33 percent of the enlarged electorate. A similar calculation leads to an estimation of the support for Leopold Senghor's party in Senegal, with 68 percent of the votes cast in 1951 and similarly in 1952, of perhaps 10 to 15 percent of the adult population. Certainly such voting strength is not comparable to that achieved by mass parties, democratic or antidemocratic, in critical elections preceding the breakdown of several European democracies, particularly the massive vote for the NSDAP in the early thirties. Such figures should have given pause to those who feared or hoped for a totalitarian control by a movement regime and its leaders in African states, including Ghana, where the rhetoric, the organization charts of the party, and the cult of the leader gave the impression of moving in such a direction.[61]

The single-party regimes in the newly independent nations, given the social structure and the economic development, could not extract enough resources to sustain their vision of radically transforming the society by organizational methods. The collecting of dues or taxes to sustain those organizations was unfeasible. The few politically conscious and relatively educated leaders were needed to staff the government and numerous agencies, to the detriment of the party oragnization. Primordial and personal loyalties deflected the party organization in the periphery from the tasks that the center wanted to assign to it. The discrepancies between the ideological rhetoric (Friedland and Rosberg, 1964) and the achievements and realities of politics, together with the discontent of new generations, particularly those returning from abroad and not finding positions of power commensurate to their ambitions, often created factional tension with the youth organizations, trade-union leadership, etc., which could be best avoided by placing less emphasis on the party. The ideological formulations were largely derivative, ambiguous, and in contradiction with the pragmatic policies to which the leadership felt bound by social and economic realities, and therefore did not provide clear and immediate goals to the membership. As a result, the single party, rather than becoming a totalitarian instrument of mobilization, the monistic center, became one more factor in the power structure, achieving only limited participation. Ironically, it has been argued that single parties had the best chances of survival in the least mobilized, most backward societies, like Mali (Snyder, 1965) and Tanzania (Bienen, 1970), rather than in countries like Ghana with greater resources, where, as a result, an inflationary process of demand formation is likely to develop (Zolberg, 1966, pp. 145–50). In very backward societies revolutionary blueprints affecting the modern sector of the economy caused little disruption.

Another alternative was the transformation of the single party from a disciplined, ideological mass movement into a flexible machine that maintained solidarity among its members by appealing to their self-interest while allowing for the play of factions and for recurrent reconciliation, relying characteristically on the attraction of material rewards rather than enthusiasm for political principles. Leaders who some observers and perhaps some sectors of their society had conceived of as charismatic appeared to others as political bosses. The opportunities for corruption contributed further to the crisis of the ideological single party but often cemented a machinelike organization. While the opposition and the dissidents had to be silenced, there was no need, given their numbers and their resources, for the type of paramilitary organizations developed in the advanced European societies by fascist parties. The coercion would also take the form of machine politics (Zolberg, 1966, 1969; Bretton, 1973).

Few mobilizational single parties retained any function only a few years after independence. Those that had not been ousted by military coups experienced considerable transformation. The typologies initially formulated (Morrison *et al.,* 1972; Hodgkin, 1961; Carter, 1962) have been misleading because they were often based on images that the African parties wanted to convey to the world and themselves. They are based on relatively formal structures, that is, they relate to real phenomena but are limited to an account of how they would work if they worked according to the normative expectations of the elites. The people who articulated those ideologies were often not very close to the center of power within the party. However, the single party often remained as an objectified, tangible symbol of the unity of the society. From having been a means, the political monopoly becomes a self-justifying goal. As Zolberg (1966, pp. 62–63) has noted, the mood underlying the emphasis on the single party in such essentially plural societies as those of Africa is somewhat like that of the Jacobins when faced with the *Fédérés.* The faith in planning, in rational control of the economy, rather than in a complex and little visible process like the market, is parallel to and reinforces the symbolic commitment to community. Zolberg in *Creating Political Order* (1966) has noted the functions that can be performed by machine parties appealing to the self-interest of members, allowing for the play of factions and recurrent reconciliation, and providing for formal and informal representation of a multitude of relatively modern and not-so-modern groups in the society, including those based on common origin and on explicit economic and political interests. Its informal inner workings allow patterns of behavior and norms that might otherwise be dismissed as unmodern, allow participation to individuals who do not possess expert or bureaucratic skills but are interested in politics, and sustain a powerful central authority while the party remains popular, facilitating a contact between the mass and the leadership.

One hope of some single-party leaders was that they would provide a channel for democratic participation of the population without the tensions of multiparty systems in unintegrated societies. In this context, the attempt of Nyerere to use TANU, the Tanganyika African National Union, for the establishment of a democratic one-party state, with the sponsorship of two candidates by the party in national legislative elections, has been particularly interesting (Bienen, 1970; Hopkins, 1971). The experiment of TANU not as an elite but as a mass party through which any citizen of good will can participate in the process of government is faced with a dilemma well formulated in this official report: "To insist on narrow ideological conformity would clearly be inconsistent with the mass participation in the affairs of the party which we regard as essential" (Bienen, 1970, p. 242). On the other hand, if membership involves no political commitment of any kind, TANU would become coextensive with the nation and would cease to function as a political party in any serious sense.

Preselection of candidates within the party but competition between them should allow the people to reject an individual without appearing to reject TANU. But the initial idea of Nyerere, that TANU hold completely open elections in which patriotic individuals could run as candidates, was not accepted. In fact, tendencies have appeared demanding a more elitist and tightly organized TANU, imposing qualitative criteria for membership. In September 1965 the voters in the former Tanganyika, except in five constituencies, could choose between two candidates with the result that 22 out of 31 officeholders were unsuccessful and 16 out of 31 MPs lost. The lack of clear relationship between success or failure and the share of votes received in district preference polls in the party suggest that while only those close to the party could run, they did not enjoy oligarchic control of the outcome, in an election in which 50 percent of the adult population voted. Tanzania is an interesting experiment of combining a single-party system with a freedom of choice for the electorate (Cliffe, 1967). The open, rather than ideological and disciplined, mass-party character of TANU combined with the importance of local concerns in the electorate and the absence of deep, mobilized nationwide cleavages seem to have made it possible. However, it is dubious that any experiment of a democratic one-party state could succeed in an urban industrial or even semiindustrial society.

5. Racial and Ethnic "Democracies"

With this deliberately paradoxical concept we want to refer to regimes in which the political process among those belonging to a racially defined group, particularly a minority of the population, satisfies our definition of democracy but permanently excludes another racial group (or groups), legally or by de facto coercive means. That exclusion does not allow us to fit such regimes into our definition of democracy. The Republic of South Africa is the prime example of such a regime. In many respects regimes that exclude from a limited pluralism a large part and even a majority of population on the basis of race could be described as racial oligarchies or authoritarian regimes. On account of the importance of the ideology of apartheid and the pervasive impact of the racial caste system on the daily life of citizens, including the racial dominant minority, the level of political and social mobilization against potential dangers to its supremacy, and the actual and, even more important, the future need for coercion to maintain the status quo, those regimes could be considered pretotalitarian or totalitarian in potential. Why should we then label them as racial democracies and place them in our attribute space on the borderline with democratic regimes? This paradox is reflected in the ranking of South Africa among 114 countries, according to eligibility to participate in elections and degree of opportunity for public opposition, in scale type 14 (when the least opportunity ranks 30), far above most authoritarian regimes in the world (Dahl, 1971). The paradox is the result of the strange juxtaposition of two societies and political systems, which in the utopian ideology of the defenders of apartheid would be parallel and separate but which inevitably, due to a number of economic, social, and historical constraints, find themselves in a castelike hierarchical relation sustained politically by authoritarian and ultimately coercive domination.

This type of relation has been characteristic of colonial rule[62] and still survives in the few territories under colonial government but diverges from it in several respects. The rule is not exercised in the name of a metropolitan government through its appointed agents ideologically and legally for the benefit of the whole population but is exercised in the name and actually for the benefit of a self-governing racial minority. The history of colonization in a few areas of the world led to sizable white settlements in areas where large nonwhite populations were not decimated, where racial prejudices, sometimes supported by religion and ideology and the migration of families rather than males ready to establish sexual relations with the natives, created castelike societies based on race. Those white settlers brought with them values and institutions in the mainstream of the liberal democratic tradition. In this respect they were like the societies described by Louis Hartz (1964) that resulted from fragmentation of Western European empires, particularly the United States, Australia, New Zealand, and Canada. Those traditions and their institutionalization, sometimes with the support of and other times against the metropolitan authority, could have led to the establishment of stable democracies, particularly considering the economic resources available in the case of South Africa. As long as the native population was socially nonmobilized, under traditional authority structures maintained as indirect rule, nonurban and illiterate, unexposed to Western culture, religion, and mass media, and more or less resigned to that marginal and subordinate status, the white settlers could develop representative institutions and enjoy civil liberties and the rule of law. The result was the development of a competitive party system, parliamentary government, and many of those characteristics that still in 1968, using ten characteristics of political life among the white population, place South Africa very close to the polyarchies.

However, the racism of the whites, the numerical proportions of whites and nonwhites in the population, the economic, social, and cultural inequality between the races, the fears resulting from racist prejudice and the demographic and other inequalities between the races, and the inevitable polarization resulting from the initial segregation and rejection of a policy of integration have prevented the emergence of any form of multiracial nation and consequently multiracial democratic state (Thompson, 1966; Van den Berghe, 1967; Adam, 1971; Potholm and Dale, 1972). Even the limited participation of the Cape Town Coloured in the electorate and representative institutions was slowly restricted and practically eliminated through a complex and long legal process.

The metropolitan power was unwilling and/or unable (in the case of Rhodesia) to impose some form of multiracial democracy. The tensions between the large, long-time resident, Afrikaans-speaking whites and the more recent English-speaking population, based on the memories of the Great Trek and the War of 1899–1902 and the persistent differences in social structure, economic power, religion, and culture, led to the mobilization of the white Afrikaners behind the Nationalist party and its policy of apartheid. It also accounts for the electoral weakness of moderates and the practical insignificance of the Progressive party and the enlightened minority among the elite opposing that policy. The enactment over the years of repressive legislation, culminating in the general law amendment acts of 1963 and 1965, has banned and served to destroy any African opposition to full white domination and second-class citizenship. The exclusion from the electorate of the 68.3 percent Bantus, 9.4 percent Coloureds, except for a small minority allowed to elect four representatives, and the 3 percent Asians, requiring after the Sharpeville incident an increasing use of force, places South Africa according to our definition among the nondemocratic regimes. On the other hand, the persistence of liberal democratic institutions, a wide range of civil liberties, and of parties competing for power in free elections among the white minority justifies the label racial democracy. The political freedom among whites is based on the unity among whites, on the widespread consensus among them on the policy of racial domination, and particularly on the support by a majority of the electorate of the Nationalist party.

A racial democracy, however, is not only an authoritarian rule over the nonwhites but inevitably leads to increasingly authoritarian rule over those whites who question the policy of the majority and increasing limitations and infringements of the civil liberties and political expression of the dissidents. The Suppression of Communism Act of 1950, the Public Safety Act of 1953, the Criminal Law Amendment Act of the same year, the Prison Act of 1959, the Publications and Entertainment Act of 1963, etc., in their loose formulation include restrictions that can be and have been increasingly applied to white dissidents who protest against the law or support any campaign against it, reflecting the policy approved by the majority. Ultimately racial democracy leads to authoritarian rule with majority support regularly expressed through elections, allowing democratic political competition on nonracial issues and guaranteeing, at least for the time being, other freedoms like the equality of the Afrikaans and the English languages.

The supporter of the South African regime would argue that this description is incomplete and even distorted. He would stress that apartheid in principle, even when not perhaps in its present practice, implies the separate development of racial communities, in fact of separate nations, in their own area with their own democratic self-government. Ignoring for the moment the difficulty of applying that model to the populations intermingled in the great urban centers without a distinct territorial basis, particularly the Asians, most of the Coloured, and a very large proportion of the Bantu population, the attempts to create democratic, nonwhite states have not and are not likely to succeed to fit our definition of democracy. The case of the Transkei, in which 400 white inhabitants were deprived of a say in local government, consistent with the ideology that non-Africans may not become citizens, does not fit. It does not fit not only because of the presence in the legislative assembly of the 4 paramount chiefs and 60 chiefs of the Transkei, among whom vacancies are filled by the regional authorities subject to the confirmation of the state president, in addition to 45 elected representatives, but because of the number of important legislative subjects excluded from its competence, among them the amendment of the Transkei Constitution enacted by the South African Parliament. The basic law is therefore similar to that of a colony under the system of dyarchy, in which the metropolitan power retains control over everything that is vital while allowing the indigenous people the qualified management of a limited range of local affairs mainly through the medium of chiefs, whom the metropolitan power can influence in many overt and covert ways.

Even ignoring that fewer than 40 percent of the African inhabitants of the republic are physically present in Bantu areas, in which, according to government policy, such black racial democracies would be established, the fact that constitutionally they would have only a share in power and no institutionalized mechanisms to participate in the decision making for the whole South African Republic would not allow us to call the African Bantustans parallel democratic political units. The development of a Coloured representative council and of an Indian representative council and the stripping of provincial and municipal authorities of many of their powers over nonwhites, considering the powers allocated to the departments of the central government and the share of power assigned to such councils and the executive committee chosen by them, show the legal and de facto limits to the experiment of a single state with segregated racial communities, whatever degree of formal self-government allowed to them. The social and economic realities in South Africa, described at greater length in the chapter by Duane Lockard (Volume 6 of this *Handbook*), particularly the social and economic interdependence among the races in the urban economy, and the legally established inferiority of the nonwhites are even more impressive evidence of the authoritarian character of white racial "democracy."

Ultimately the political future of South Africa and Rhodesia depends on the level of political consciousness and the intensity of opposition and resistance of the nonwhite, particularly the African, majorities. That opposition by definition has to be principled and disloyal, illegal or at least alegal, and is not unlikely to be violent. Its strength and character will largely depend on the external support and the response of white South Africans. Open and violent conflict between the races, particularly with foreign support, would transform white racial democracy into a strictly authoritarian majority rule over dissident whites, which, considering the widespread support for apartheid, the strong consensus of the Afrikaners, and the support given to the policy by the Dutch Reform Churches, could lead to a totalitarian system with majority support, formal democratic institutions, and a strong component of legalism, based on a radical racist ideology.

Fortunately, the social and historical conditions that have led to the establishment of the racial democracy in South Africa are not found today in many parts of the world. Outside of Rhodesia, where the Salisbury government declaring its independence from Britain has established a similar regime, few colonies presented the combination of the large white settler population surrounded by a majority of nonwhites and having no intention or possibility of returning to the metropolitan homeland. Only Algeria, with a little over a million Europeans, many of them born there, many without roots in metropolitan France, among 8.5 million Maghrebi nationals, could have led to such a regime if the colons and the OAS had succeeded against the Algerians and the French. Perhaps in Angola could the white settler population, independent from metropolitan Portugal and under South African influence, have been tempted to establish such a regime. The American South, if it had gained its sovereignty in the war of secession, would have been another case. Undoubtedly other racially, ethnically, religiously, or culturally multinational or community societies in the non-Western world could in the future develop political forms similar to the racial democracies. But today some are experimenting with multinational democratic regimes or with a variety of authoritarian regimes with little semblance of democracy for any of the national groups. In most of them the low level of social mobilization and political organization, and consequently of coercive capacity of any group, is more likely to lead to political fragmentation and secession.

Multiethnic democracies without consensus. Paradoxically, Israel (Fein, 1967; Eisenstadt, 1967), with its democratic political culture, its democratic institutions, including proportional representation, which maximizes party pluralism, and the equal vote for all citizens, faces a future somewhat similar to the racial democracies in spite of the commitments of its leaders. It exemplifies the difficulties of creating a democratic, multiethnic, multicultural, and multilinguistic state when there is a dominant community conscious of its identity facing a demographically important minority also attached to its identity, separated by great cultural, religious, linguistic, and economic social differences. Only class and other divisions that could lead to majorities cutting across communal boundaries would make possible a democratic multinational state with real rather than formal equality of Jews, Arabs, and other minorities. Such a development in Israel, however, would run counter to the basic assumptions that have led to the creation of a Jewish state by the Zionists and of the religious characteristics introduced by the disproportionate influence of the minor religious parties in the policies of the dominant coalition since statehood. Only the cultural-ideological secularization of the state would make possible its acceptance within a democratic framework by the Arab minority and the return of the Palestinians and their loyalty to the state. It could be argued that a more federative structure that would leave considerable self-government to areas inhabited by each cultural community could, under democratic rule, facilitate such a development; but this ignores a basic presupposition of any democratic political system: the loyalty to the state and the rejection of any loyalty to another political system across its borders, any thought of secession, and any responsiveness to irredentist appeals from the outside. Those conditions do not seem likely to develop in the immediate future in Israel and in a number of other multiethnic, multicultural states whose boundaries cut across cultural, ethnic, or linguistic communities. Under such circumstances the participation of the minority in the national political process, even with full citizen rights, is likely to be partial, conditional, and suspect both to the state-sustaining majority and to those in the minority actually or potentially disloyal to it. Democratic institutions under such circumstances can work well within the majority community, particularly as long as it feels threatened, but it will be the democracy of the privileged. It could be argued that the formulas devised in those democracies not based on the strict application of majority of rule, called by Lijphart (1968a, 1968b, 1969) "consociational," should be able to handle such problems, but any reader of the now extensive literature on such systems (Daalder, 1973; McRae, 1974) is conscious of the numerous requirements for their success, unlikely to be found in many cases like that of contemporary Israel.

The case of Northern Ireland (Rose, 1971; Lijphart, 1975), with its formally democratic constitution and more or less real guarantees for political freedom for those willing to recognize its regime, is another example of the practical impossibility of making democratic processes work in divided societies without loyalty to the constitution and the regime on the part of the minority and a willingness of a large part of the majority to face the fact that a formally democratically legitimated majority rule under such circumstances becomes oppressive and has to turn to increasingly authoritarian responses.

Paradoxically, nationalism, the doctrine of self-determination of nationalities and cultural communities, born historically in the West at the same time as democratic ideals and with increasing social mobilization of the whole population, has become incompatible with democracy in many societies. The first victim of that process was a multinational Austro-Hungarian empire, which assured under autocratic rule a considerable degree of coexistence to its national components but which almost inevitably fell apart in the process of democratization. There is no easy solution within the framework of traditional democratic theory of government for the problem of permanent self-conscious minorities rejecting a common loyalty to the state and its institutions for the sake of independence or secession to join another state. The fact that in many parts of the world such communities do not coincide with any meaningful geographic boundaries, that they live interspersed in their cities or enclaves without geographical continuity, often leads to conflicts that are solved by authoritarian means or at least by the limitation of freedoms de jure or de facto for those in the minority questioning the legitimacy of a state. Their permanent frustration is likely, under certain conditions, to lead them to turn in their desperation to violence, against both members of the dominant community and those in the minority willing to participate in a democratic framework in more or less consociational formulas, reinforcing the authoritarian response of the majority. Democracy seems to have been more successful in the institutionalization of class conflicts, in the channeling through parties of economic interest conflicts and even of conflicts between religion and secularism, than in the resolution of conflicts among ethnic, linguistic, and cultural communalism. Such conflicts are one of the important factors accounting for the emergence and, paradoxically, the stability of many nondemocratic regimes (Fishman, 1968).

Racial democracy represents a theoretically interesting case of transition from democratic liberal institutions to authoritarian rule without discontinuity and by formal democratic procedures. Theoretically, other oligarchic democracies based on a restricted suffrage could have followed the same path when confronted with growing demands for expansion of political participation from the lower classes. However, the different level of social integration in racially homogeneous communities, despite other deep cleavages, and the consequent sense of community have prevented the combination of democratic liberal forms with minority rule. In such societies, inevitably, a minority of the politically privileged classes advocated the expansion of political rights and those opposed had to make concessions or give up any semblance of democratic freedoms, even within the privileged sector of the society. This provides indirect evidence for the difficulties and instability of attempts of partial liberalization and democratization within authoritarian regimes, like internal democracy in a single party. Ultimately, without a relatively rigid barrier like race defining those with the right to participate and those excluded and without an extraordinary fear of all those who deprive others of citizen rights, it becomes impossible to limit participation beyond the level of social mobilization without explicitly authoritarian institutions. However, as the case of ethnic-cultural-religious minorities shows, the extension of suffrage alone does not assure real opportunities for political participation nor real social integration and loyalty to a state needed for stable democratic politics.

6. "Defective" and "Pretotalitarian" Political Situations and Regimes

In an effort to understand the dynamics of nondemocratic political systems we have attempted to define totalitarianism fairly strictly, to keep it clearly distinct from the variety of authoritarian regimes. However, the transitions between both types do not involve the same basic discontinuity and, with rare exceptions, violent breaks, revolutions, civil wars, and military coups as do the transitions from democracy to authoritarianism. The diffuseness of the boundary is reflected in the increasing use of terms like quasi-totalitarian, posttotalitarian, rationalized-totalitarian, totalitarianism without terror, etc., to describe the gray zone between both. Our typological effort has been based on the assumption that in the process of instoration of nondemocratic governments some basic initial characteristics determine if the outcome will be closer to the totalitarian or the authoritarian pole. The analysis of the breakdown of competitive democracies (Linz and Stepan, forthcoming), traditional regimes, or colonial rule should tell us something about the dynamics leading to one or another outcome. We have also emphasized how the initial characteristics of the leader or group taking over power—their ideology or mentality, their organizational base in the existing social structure or in a new mass movement or conspiratorial party, and perhaps personality—prefigure, together with situational variables, the outcome. Since the complex structure of a totalitarian political system is not developed in a short time, except in societies suffering extreme disorganization after prolonged war, foreign occupation, or civil war, we can posit a stage that might be best described as pretotalitarian. We know still little about the way in which new, revolutionary rulers break through constraining conditions, to use the expression of Otto Kirchheimer (1969, pp. 385–407), and the circumstances under which they fail. We still need a theory of consolidation of new regimes. It is noteworthy that an insightful fascist politician, the Spaniard Ramiro Ledesma Ramos (1935), in a political essay comparing European one-party states, including the Soviet Union in the mid-30s, should have devoted much of his attention to the constraining conditions that, unless overcome, limited, in his view, a real totalitarian revolution. We would consider as pretotalitarian those situations in which there are important political, social, and cultural factors favorable to a totalitarian outcome: basically a situation in which there is a political group of sufficient importance pursuing a totalitarian utopia but that has not yet fully consolidated its power and given the system its institutional structure; a situation in which institutions like the armed forces, the churches, business organizations, interest groups, notables or tribal rulers, the courts, or even a monarch, not clearly committed to a system excluding all pluralism even though largely favoring a limitation of pluralism, still retain considerable autonomy, legitimacy, and effectiveness; and a situation characterized by an uneasy balance in which predictions go one way or another, where some expect the totalitarian movement to be co-opted by the preexisting social structure, while others look forward to or fear its ultimate success.

The reader of early descriptions of the Nazi system—particularly those by Marxists, which emphasize the multiple compromises the regime made with the conservative structures of German society, particularly the bureaucracy and the military (F. Neumann, 1963) and even, in some accounts, with the churches, and the betrayal of the petty-bourgeois revolutionary ideals against modern industrial and financial capitalism, large-scale cartels, department and chain stores, etc.—should keep in mind descriptions of the Soviet Union in one of the phases of its consolidation. For example, this summary by Jeremy R. Azrael:

> After a brief period of left wing militancy, the revisionism of "Bread, Land, and Peace" gave way to the far-reaching compromises of the New Economic Policy or NEP. The free market was revived; concessions were made to foreign investors; material incentives were restored to their paramount position; and individual peasant proprietorship was actively encouraged. Similarly, "workers' control" and "workers' management" were drastically curtailed, and administrative efficiency, technical rationality, and stringent labor discipline became hallmarks of official policy. In the same vein, the regime granted more authority to holdover "bourgeois specialists" and ordered communist executives to solicit and defer to expert advice. Moreover, these developments were accompanied by definite symptoms of decay within the party itself. In particular, there was a manifest decline of "class vigilance" and revolutionary ardor among the rank and file members of the party, and the upper strata of the party showed clear signs of "regrouping" into administrative pressure groups and bureaucratic cliques. (Azrael, 1970b, p. 263)

Had the Soviet regime been destroyed at this point, the capacity of the revolutionary forces to transform Russian society and to move toward the totalitarian utopia would certainly have been questioned. It also explains that many observers at the time predicted quite different outcomes than Stalinism. The very different interpretations of Hitler's rule in early years reflect that same intermingling. The uneasy balance between such contradictory tendencies might be prolonged for many years, with moves in one or another direction, as was the case with Fascism in Italy.

A typical pretotalitarian situation is that in which a party that is bent toward more or less totalitarian control with its mass organizations and, in the fascist case, its paramilitary organizations can exercise pressures on a government in which its leaders participate in coalition with representatives of other parties.[63] Such a coalition was formed in Italy after the March on Rome and in Germany by a presidential decision under the chancellorship of Hitler, with the participation of the authoritarian-nationalist DNVP and with Papen as Vice Chancellor. The parties participating were either opposed or semiloyal to the democratic regime, or, in the case of Italy, minority representatives of other parties willing to collaborate in a compromise with the Fascists. In Germany the Enabling Act, by which the parliament, under pressure, and with the exclusion of the Communists and the opposition of the Socialists, granted the government extraordinary powers and attempted to tie those powers to the continuity of that particular coalition government as an authoritarian "presidential government." The change represented the last break with Weimar constitutionality. In Eastern Europe after 1945 the pressures of the Soviet Union, its military presence, the desire for national unity in face of the Germans, the availability of collaborationist socialists, and the compromise between Western allies and the Soviet Union led to the formation of coalition national front governments in which all antifascist parties participated according to a prearranged proportion, not necessarily reflecting their strength in the electorate and parliaments after elections (Kase, 1968; Seton-Watson, 1968; Ionescu, 1967; Oren, 1973). Such still nominally "constitutional" governments often proceed to outlaw some parties (communist or fascist, or those presumably guilty of collaborating with them), restrict civil liberties (generally with the ministry of interior in the hands of the dominant party), and co-opt some leaders of the different parties, politically neutralizing others, ending with the dissolution of all or most parties and the fusion of some—or sections of some— in the totalitarian-bent party (Korbell, 1959). The relative weight and the linkage of those co-opted elements with independent power bases is obviously decisive for the ultimate totalitarian or authoritarian outcome. In economically or militarily dependent countries, foreign influences become decisive at this stage (Black and Thornton, 1964; Triska, 1969).

In those situations the coalition partners find themselves in the position of wanting to oppose some of the policies of the totalitarian-bent party but in doing so allowing that party to question their loyalty to the government and the new regime and facilitating its goal of ousting them. On the other hand, approval or passivity in face of policies of which they disapprove contributes to legitimating the transition to every day more authoritarian rule and to preventing an active opposition by institutions or social groups still capable of it. In such situations there is much room for opportunists ready to join the stronger armies by advocating the fusion of their party with the increasingly dominant coalition partner. This was the case with many conservative authoritarian organizations in Germany and with parts of the socialist parties that fused into communist-dominated united parties, like the East German *Sozialistische Einheitspartei* (SED). In a number of communist countries this phase of national front is still reflected in a multiparty system under the leadership of the communists, with the minor parties serving to co-opt representatives of other groups and in the post-Stalinist phase serving as controlled channels for the representation of certain interests and as a legitimizing façade. A system in which the development toward totalitarianism is arrested and stabilized and in which the forces aiming at totalitarian control become one—often very important—component of the limited pluralism of the regime, their ideology affects considerable spheres of social life, and participation in their organizations is significant, might be described as "defective totalitarianism." The term pretotalitarian, in contrast, might be reserved for the (more or less prolonged) phase leading to the

instoration of a totalitarian system. Situations in which the strength of pro-
totalitarian forces is reversed might be labelled "arrested totalitarianism."

The analysis of Spain as an authoritarian regime (Linz, 1964) has tended
to emphasize the variables that led to the ultimate failure of the totalitarian
tendencies within the Falangist movement, but it should be possible to re-
analyze Spanish politics in the later phases of the civil war and the first years
after 1939 as a defective totalitarian system. In many respects the insightful
analysis by Ernst Fraenkel (1941), *The Dual State: A Contribution to the
Theory of Dictatorship,* could be considered a study of the pretotalitarian aspects of the Nazi regime. The study of pretotalitarian situations and defective
totalitarian regimes in connection with the theory of the process of consolidation of new regimes would be a step toward a better understanding of the
uniqueness of totalitarianism and at the same time would prevent us from
underestimating the totalitarian tendencies that often accompany the emergence of authoritarian regimes. Such an underestimation is perhaps one of the
weaknesses of my analysis of the Franco regime as an authoritarian regime.

Historical studies like the monumental work by Bracher, Sauer, and Schulz
on the Nazi *Machtergreifung,* the history of fascism in the biography of Mussolini by De Felice (1965, 1966a, 1968), Leonard Schapiro's (1965) *The Origin of
the Communist Autocracy,* and Robert V. Daniels' (1969) *The Conscience of the
Revolution* would be the obvious sources together with studies of systems whose
totalitarian potential was weaker, like Robert Scalapino's (1953) *Democracy
and Party Government in Pre-War Japan* (there are, unfortunately, few works
of similar importance on the years after takeover in other nondemocratic systems). They could be the basis for a theory of emergence and consolidation of
totalitarianism rather than authoritarian regimes. Such a theory would complement those analyses that focus on social, cultural, psychological, and political
crises preceding the breakdown of democracy. It would also tell us the extent
to which totalitarianism is not predetermined but is the result of critical choices
made in such a transition period.

7. Posttotalitarian Authoritarian Regimes

The death of Stalin and the consequent de-Stalinization both in the Soviet
Union and the Eastern European countries that had followed the Soviet model
led to changes in those political systems which rightly made political scientists
question the applicability of the classical model of a totalitarian system. Research on interest groups in Soviet politics (Skilling and Griffiths, 1971; Janos,
1970b), on specific processes of policymaking (Ploss, 1965; Stewart, 1968), on
the changing composition of the Soviet elite (Armstrong, 1967; Fischer, 1968;
Farrell, 1970; Fleron, 1969, 1970; Barghoorn, 1972; Beck, 1970), on intellectual
life and the expression of dissent or contestation (Barghoorn, 1973) have shown
important changes from the Stalinist model despite some signs of "neo-Stalin-
ism." The comparative study of East European Communist regimes (Brzezinski,

1960; Brown, 1966; Skilling, 1966, 1973; Ionescu, 1967; Schöpflin, 1970) has also highlighted the increasingly differentiated development in response to national-cultural, historical, social-structural, and economic factors. The Czech spring of 1968 and the reforms proposed by and under Dubcek (Zeman, 1968; Gueyt, 1969; James, 1969; Remington, 1969; Tigrid, 1969; Windsor and Roberts, 1969; Skilling, 1970, 1973b) and before that the independent evolution of Yugoslavia from the administrative phase to self-management have raised the question of the condition and limits of change in Soviet-type political systems. The terms liberalization and democratization have been used freely, often interchangeably, and unfortunately with little precision. It is indicative of the train of thought of the discussion that the question could be raised: "Is Mexico the future of East Europe?" (Croan, 1970). It could be argued that those changes indicate a tendency in political systems that at one point in time could have been considered approaching the totalitarian model to show some of the characteristics we have used to characterize authoritarian regimes. This would be congruent with our emphasis on the relatively open and diffuse boundary between totalitarian systems and authoritarian regimes.

However, we feel it would be misleading to consider posttotalitarian authoritarian regimes as having the same characteristics as those that never were conceived by their founders to become totalitarian or that never went beyond a "defective" totalitarian stage despite the efforts of some of their founders. The totalitarian phase, even when imposed from the outside, as in some of the East European people's democracies, has left many structures—political as well as economic and social—that can be transformed but are unlikely to disappear and has created an image of a type of polity to which some of the elites still feel attached and whose "positive" aspects they might wish to retain or attain. It also has left memories, particularly of its worst features—the terror and the purges—which condition the responses of those participating in the political process and therefore affect the evolution of those systems. It is on these grounds that we find it necessary to consider posttotalitarian authoritarian regimes a distinct type, obviously with considerable national variations. The alternative would be to argue that the processes of change taking place after Stalin are really only a more visible manifestation of patterns already present (which would imply that totalitarianism was never as total and that the concept can be applied to the present reality too, despite changes, or that it never had any validity) or to deny any basic change. The vexing question, How much change *in* the system is required for change *of* the system? is obviously empirically difficult to answer, particularly when scholarship in the past might have been blind to deviations from the utopian totalitarian model and in recent years might have been too eager to see change and overestimate its importance. Unfortunately, for a more comparative analysis of what we might call "routinization" of totalitarianism—of its transformation—we are limited to communist countries, since none of the fascist totalitarian states were allowed by their military defeat to undergo such a process. There was no post-Hitler Germany, with Himmler executed, Dönitz as *Führer* displacing Bormann with a coalition of army officers loyal to the Reich, and civil servants and industrialists supporting some reasonable *Gauleiter* as head of the party.

For those who interpret Soviet totalitarianism as a reflection of Stalin's paranoic personality it is easy to consider the totalitarian phase as a passing aberration, and this might well be true for some of the most monstrous aspects of the system. This has been the official line of the de-Stalinizers. Implicit in this interpretation is a denial of a pretotalitarian character to Leninist rule and a totalitarian intent in Bolshevik revolutionary ideology. For the social scientists such an approach seems unsatisfactory or at least incomplete. They are likely to emphasize changes in the external environment, in the social-economic structure confronting the successors of Stalin: the complexity of managerial and technical decision making requiring greater rationality, decentralization, autonomy of experts, substitution of ideological *apparatchiki* by others with more education and expertise, fewer constraints with greater economic development, etc. Those writing about the convergence of postindustrial societies would certainly emphasize these factors and support the argument with reference to the role of economists and the reforms advocated by them in the process of change. Others, including some Soviet authors, would note the different international environment of a Soviet Union surrounded by allies in Eastern Europe, safe behind the atomic deterrent in a world in which the capitalist enemies find themselves challenged in the Third World and in which the mutual interests of security dictate a détente. To those factors we might add the emerging polycentrism of communism showing alternative and creative solutions linking with different national, cultural, and political traditions, which makes the original model of the first socialist state more questionable (Blackmer, 1968). The position taken by powerful nonruling communist parties toward changes in the Soviet Union and its Eastern European sphere of influence would be another factor. Certainly in the Eastern European countries the shift toward greater independence as national communist states, as the case of Yugoslavia shows, was decisive in the change. However, Rumania shows that a more nationalist policy within the bloc is not necessarily accompanied by deep internal changes (Jowitt, 1971). Without denying the decisive importance of all or some of these factors in the particular development toward posttotalitarianism in communist countries, I would agree with Gordon Skilling when he writes:

> No doubt there *are* social and economic forces at work which encourage interest group activity in the USSR. It seems clear, however, that this later development has been the consequence of certain conscious decisions of individual leaders and other participants in Soviet political life, decisions which were not necessarily pre-determined and which might be reversed in the future. The rise of group activity under Khrushchev was, in the first

place, the result of an initiative from above, representing an effort by Stalin's successor to make the political system more rational in its process of decision making and more responsive to the actual needs and demands of the people, especially of the influential elites. (Skilling and Griffiths, 1971, p. 403)

The work of Max Weber provides indirectly interesting insights into the process at work. In his analysis of charismatic authority he noted that its character is specifically alien to everyday routine structures, the strictly personal character of social relationships involved. He continued:

> If this is not to remain a purely transitory phenomenon, but to take on the character of a permanent relationship, a "community" of disciples or followers, or a party organization, or any sort of political or hierocratic organization, it is necessary for the character of charismatic authority to become radically changed ... it cannot remain stable, but becomes either traditionalized or rationalized, or a combination of both.

> The following are the principle motives underlying this transformation: (a) the ideal and also the material interest of the followers in the continuation and the continual reactivation of the community, (b) the still stronger ideal and also stronger material interests of the members of the administrative staff, the disciples, the party workers, or others in continuing their relationship ... but they have an interest in continuing it in such a way that both from an ideal and a material point of view, their own position is put on a stable everyday basis. (Weber, 1968, Vol. 1, p. 246)

In the subsequent discussion of the routinization of charisma particularly after the succession crisis, Weber notes that a process of traditionalization or of legalization takes place and that one of the possible outcomes is a greater bureaucratization. For Weber, one of the decisive motives underlying all cases of the routinization of charisma is naturally the striving for security, the objective necessity of adapting the order and the staff organization to the normal everyday needs and conditions of carrying on administration, and the necessity that there should be some definite order introduced into the organization of the administrative staff itself.

There can be no doubt that the desire for security in the top elite after Stalin, the surrogate Stalins, and the experience of the purges, decisively influenced the top elite's decisions. The weakening of the police as a key political factor, perhaps its neutralization by the army, the emphasis on collective leadership and the rejection of the cult of personality, the distrust of an emerging powerful leader that led to the ouster of Khrushchev, the desire even on his part to use the procedures of the party statutes to resolve the leadership crisis, the growing concern for socialist legality, are all reflections of this desire for security in the top elite. Some of those changes were made easier by the formal rules and the conception of leadership institutionalized before Stalin, and in this respect it is doubtful that a post-Hitler *Fuhrerstaat* would have had as easy a transformation. The desire for security, however, also explains the reaffirmation of the role of the party, the reactivation of the party as a source of legitimacy of the leadership, even the slowing down of the de-Stalinization and of efforts to revise it, as well as the decisive reaction to the Czech reform. To be stable, posttotalitarianism can reject the totalitarian heritage only selectively and gradually, if it is not to lead to a revolutionary outbreak that could lead to a radical change of the system, endangering the continuity in power of the elite. The literature suggests, even when it provides only limited and indirect evidence, that the cleavages between conservatives and reformists cut across practically all organizations, groups, opinion milieux, or whatever units of analysis are used, largely along generational lines. There seems to be a difference between this and the crisis of succession or approaching succession in authoritarian regimes, in which in addition to such crosscutting and generational differences we find a greater tension between the elements constituting the limited pluralism of the regime on a more institutional basis, possibly with some of them breaking out of the system and contributing to its final crisis or overthrow (Linz, 1973a). Significantly no one expects in any of the communist countries a military intervention or coup that would establish a noncommunist regime.

Once the great break through constraining conditions had been accomplished, with destruction of traditional society by war communism, the secure establishment of Communist party rule without any need to share power with other leftist parties, collectivization of agriculture and forced industrialization, destruction of the sanitary cordon intended by the West, and a more complex society requiring greater expertise and consequently autonomy of individuals and groups had emerged, the leadership was probably right in assuming that a system could be run more efficiently and equally securely without the constant affirmation of moral political unity, emphasis on ideological orthodoxy, fear of "groupism," constant assertion of the power of the party, and the recurrent mobilization for radical changes. The fact that, perhaps due to Stalin's idiosyncrasies, the totalitarian effort had been accompanied by massive terror even against the elite, obviously legitimated a transition to what Tucker (1963) has called an "extinct movement regime" and others "administrative totalitarianism" (Kassof, 1969) or "rationalized totalitarianism" (Cocks, 1970). The transition to a posttotalitarian state implies less emphasis on the goal culture and greater concern for the functional requisites of the social system. This allows a process that had been described as liberalization: the emergence of group interest, or at least the expression of it by a few outstanding individuals (Skilling, 1971, p. 382); "the free expression and collision of opinions" while rejecting "groupism" (*gruppovshina*); the ideological recognition of "non-antagonistic contradictions"; and the effective and to some extent visible manifestation of group influences in decision making (Skilling, 1971, p. 401). A limited monocentrism, a less ideological politics, and a greater tolerance for depolitization show a tendency toward an authoritarian regime. Let us note that while most noncommunist authoritarian rulers insistently warn against the return of political parties, rulers of the Soviet Union warn against "groupism" and factionalism—a recognition of tendencies within the party—showing the different starting points of change. These processes are accompanied by bureaucratization and professionalization, tendencies that run counter to the ideological tradition of participation and mobilization of the party activists and the citizens, a tradition that is potentially suspicious of the emerging social pluralism and legitimizes demands for greater participation. The initial posttotalitarian legitimacy of an emerging authoritarian regime is therefore likely to be questioned, not only by neo-Stalinists but by those wanting to return to some of the hopes in the Marxist-Leninist tradition for a more socially egalitarian, active, and participatory society. It is possible that some of the different paths followed after de-Stalinization and the tensions in this period are the result of these two, somewhat different, pressures. In fact, contrary to what many analysts believe, liberalization and "democratization" (in the sense of greater participation) are in tension. This is because, as other authoritarian regimes show, the pursuit of both tendencies would lead ultimately to a nonauthoritarian regime, endangering the position of the present ruling elite, but also because of an ideological heritage ambivalent on this point.

Richard Lowenthal has formulated very well the contradictory pressures leading to posttotalitarian authoritarianism when he writes:

> The Communist Party can no longer claim that its task is to use state power to transform the social structure in accordance with its utopian goals; it knows it must react to the pressures and demands of society. But wishing to keep its monopoly of power, it is not resigned to conceive of government as a mere representative of the needs of society—for a truly representative regime would have to be a pluralistic regime, permitting independent organized groups to struggle for their opinions and interests and to reach decisions by coalitions and compromise. Rather, the postrevolutionary party regime sees itself as an indispensable, authoritative, arbiter of society's various interests, recognizing their existence but regulating their expression and limiting their representation while retaining for itself the ultimate right of decision. Unable to continue its revolutionary offensive against society and unwilling to be reduced to a mere expression of the constellation of social forces at a given moment, it is neither totalitarian nor democratic, but *authoritarian:* it is on the defensive against the forces of autonomous social development, a guardian clinging to a role after his ward has reached adulthood. (Lowenthal, 1970, pp. 114–15)

It might be argued that the emergence of posttotalitarian tendencies after stabilization of the revolutionary regime in China, specifically bureaucratization of the party, etc., led Mao, the old revolutionary still formally in power, to reverse the trend with the mobilizational response of the Great Cultural Revolution and the Red Guards, as the analysis of Schurmann (1968) suggests. Let us not forget that Khrushchev combined the detotalitarianization of the thaw with the revitalization of the party and new efforts to engage citizens in political participation, through activities like the citizens' courts and the activation of local volunteers, people's guards (*druzhiny*), and the Komsomol in functions of social control described by Leon Lipson (1967). To the extent that the mass of the population and the more active sectors of it share many of the values of a deprivatized, collectively oriented society, they might question the tendencies toward greater autonomy advocated by intermediate strata and support more consensually than terroristically imposed totalitarian tendencies. This would account for the quite different posttotalitarian character of the Soviet Union and the German Democratic Republic compared to those societies in which the totalitarian phase was much shorter and was largely imposed from outside and in which pluralistic elements of the pretakeover society and culture had survived.

In the literature we find a variety of attempts to conceptualize and describe posttotalitarian communist systems which reflect some of the dilemmas pointed out above.[64] Since the Soviet Union was in many ways, under Stalin, the most totalitarian, it is still not clear how far it will move in the authoritarian direction. In fact, it could be argued the Stalinist regime in its last stage had become a system characterized by considerable conservatism, inflexibility, inertia, and stagnation, which ran counter the mobilizational aspects of a totalitarian movement regime. The kind of "late totalitarianism" characterized by a highly ritualized adherence to ideological formulae, a curbing of utopian expectations, extreme bureaucratic rigidity and few organizational innovations, a theoretical and actual downgrading of the party relative to the state and the police, and highly formalized popular participation with little real involvement could be conceived as a "totalitarian authoritarianism."

From that baseline the post-Stalinist development showed two somewhat different tendencies, one reflected in the scholarly discovery of interest and group politics and the other, well described by Azrael (1970a), "a populist model of rationalized totalitarianism" initiated by Khrushchev with his extensive use of the policy of "public participation." In this line we find the creation of so-called nonstaff party commissions by the district and city party committees, consisting of party volunteers who were not on the paid rosters of the party apparat assisting in the review of admission, discipline, and appeals. This contrasted with the pattern since 1934 in which such questions had been the privileged domain of party secretaries. Those instructors were also to observe party members who had been disciplined for "endlessly looking after their words" (Cocks, 1970, p. 172), an excellent example of why democratization and rationalization in the Soviet sense could not be equated with liberalization. Another example is control function assigned to "Komsomol Searchlight" detachments, of which in 1964 there were more than 260,000 groups and 500,000 posts of assistants (Cocks, 1970, p. 172). These activities under the Party State Control Committee (PSCC) implementing the policy described as *obshchestvennye nachala* (Cocks, 1970, pp. 165–66), or "public principles," with its dimension of "public participation" was naturally regarded with distrust by the *apparatchiki* and the economic managers. This trend toward "communist self-government" was reexamined and curtailed after the fall of Khrushchev by his successors, who turned toward a more bureaucratic formula for rationalization, deemphasizing the voluntarism and the populism with a turn to *nauchnaia organizatsiia truda* ("scientific organization of labor"). This policy, linked with another component of the Leninist tradition, his enthusiasm for scientific management, and practically with the needs of a socialist economy meant in practice an emphasis on retraining of party and government workers. The new spirit was reflected in a greater concern with information gathering and office organization, and technological aides aimed at administrative reform from above by experts. Cocks, whom we are following in this analysis of Soviet policies, concludes: "The alliance of economic managers and party bureaucrats which was forged out of the common interest and desire to maintain their own institutional structures against democratic intrusions and mass pressures, gives no guarantee of being long-lasting" (Cocks, 1970, p. 185). Zvi Gitelman also reflects this tension when he writes:

> Clearly the role of the party is a more delicate issue for systems opting for authentic participatory strategies since those opting for national performance strategies could retain the structure and the political position of the party while altering the content of its ideology, thus making it a party of "experts" for example. (Gitelman, 1970, p. 261)

This alternative course leads toward what Allen Kassof (1969) has called "the administered society, totalitarianism without terror." The aim was well expressed in 1969 by the editors of *Partiinaia Zhizn* as "systematic and fundamental control prevents mistakes and slips, holds people in constant state of creative stress and does not leave room for such manifestations as placidity, complacency, and conceit" (Cocks, 1970, pp. 186–87). Cocks notes that there is some tendency to fuse the two main trends we have just been discussing, to strike a balance between the populist and the bureaucratic formulas for rationalization. All this leads us to the question, How posttotalitarian (ignoring obviously the Stalinist idiosyncrasies and terror) is Soviet society?

Gordon Skilling's extensive writings and a number of monographic studies on policymaking and local politics have emphasized the role of group conflict. Much of the discussion hinges on what is meant by groups and to what extent the five types that he mentions—"leadership groups or factions, official or bureaucratic groups, intellectual groups, broad social groups, and opinion groups"—are comparable to the groups we discover in pretotalitarian or stable authoritarian regimes. He rightly notes that the first question is that of legitimacy or, rather, the presumed lack of legitimacy of political groups in Marxist-Leninist theory. There is obviously a thin line between the existence of such groups de facto and the limited legitimacy granted to them in pure authoritarian regimes. Certainly the talk about "nonantagonistic contradictions" opens the door to convergence. Skilling lists three additional major considerations: the question of group autonomy in the defense of its interest and opinions, the extent to which political groups have become organized or institutionalized, and the range of purposes and specific objectives of such groups. These dimensions lead him in a comparative analysis of communist systems to a classification of communist states in five types, to which in passing he adds the pretotalitarian (pre-Stalinist) phase. Let us quote briefly his characterization of these types.

> In the quasi-totalitarianism state political groups are treated in theory as illegitimate, and in practice are severely limited in their capacity for independent action. In some cases, the leadership consciously sets out to destroy political groups, in others to infiltrate and emasculate them. If organized groups such as trade unions exist, they are manipulated and controlled by the leadership and do not articulate the interests of their constituency. In general the official groups, especially the party, are superior in power and influence to the intellectuals who are bereft of any real power. Even the official groups are relatively weak and are used as instruments by the leadership. (Skilling, 1970, pp. 222–23)

As he notes, this category coincides with totalitarianism except for the definitions that overstress the monopoly of power and make terror an essential characteristic. Stalin's Russia from 1929 to 1953, Hungary, Poland, Czechoslovakia after 1947–48, and Albania to the present might be in this category.

A second type may be called "consultative authoritarianism," to use the term suggested by Peter Ludz (1968) in reference to the German Democratic Republic, in which Skilling would include Rumania (Jowitt, 1971), Bulgaria (Oren, 1973), and in certain respects Hungary in the sixties, Poland (Wiatr, 1967; Lane and Kolankiewicz, 1973) after March 1968, and the Soviet Union after Khrushchev. In it:

> When group activity occurs spontaneously and expresses fundamental opposition, it is firmly repressed, and the dominant role of the top leadership is kept intact. Although the police remain an important force, the prominent position they held in the quasi-totalitarian state is occupied here by such bureaucratic groups as the party and state administrators. These groups are valued for their expertise and thus acquire an opportunity to articulate

their own and other groups' interests. There is also an increasing willingness to bring some of the professional groups, such as the economists and scientists, into the decision making process, although the party apparat continues to play the superior role, both in theory and in practice. Creative intellectuals . . . are subject to strict control but occasionally slip the leash and assert their own viewpoint. Broader social groups continue to be impotent, and their interests are expressed, if at all, by more powerful official groups. (Skilling, 1970, p. 223)

Skilling notes how in response to particular crises and wishes of the leadership this type moves back and forth. Probably in terms of our general typology at a higher level of abstraction, this type is still closer to the totalitarian pole using our definition.

The third category of Skilling is "quasi-pluralistic authoritarianism," in which he includes Hungary and Poland during the thaw of 1953–56, the Soviet Union under Khrushchev, and Czechoslovakia and Poland in the mid-1960s. He characterized this type

as distinguished by a greater degree of group conflict, resulting usually from the initiative of the groups themselves. Although the party leadership remains the dominant factor in politics, there is greater interaction between the leaders and political groups and greater likelihood of some influence by the latter on the political process. Group conflict is often accompanied, and may be encouraged, by sharp factional conflicts among the leaders and serious divisions of opinion within the party as a whole. Although bureaucratic groups, especially the party hierarchy, remain powerful, they cannot entirely exclude the intellectual and opinion groups in general from participation. Both types of group show a greater determination to express interests and values in opposition to the party line, advancing alternative policies, criticizing official decisions and actions, and in some cases challenging frontally a whole series of official policies. Ironically, these active groups continue to be for the most part noninstitutionalized, whereas organized groups such as the trade unions remain impotent. (Skilling, 1970, p. 224)

It is in this context that we find for the first time a preregime institution mentioned as a significant group, the Catholic Church in Poland. His effort to locate a number of communist countries in the typology shows the instability of this type but also its frequency. It is perhaps the most dominant type of posttotalitarian communist regime.

A fourth type, characterized as "democratizing and pluralistic authoritarianism," includes Czechoslovakia between January and August 1968 and Yugoslavia after the break with the Soviet Union and most particularly after 1966. They are systems in which "with the endorsement of the leadership, political groups were to a substantial degree institutionalized and they played a significant role in policy making" (Skilling, 1970, p. 225). Czechoslovakia under Dubcek represents an interesting example "in which both centrally directed change designed and elaborated by the party leaders and powerful spontaneous forces from below with considerable freedom of expression, particularly for change oriented intellectual groups articulating a wide variety of group interests and opinions," a revitalization of dormant associations like trade unions and even distinctive opinion groups like the "club of the non-party committee" urged alternative policies on the leadership and even institutional change (Skilling, 1973a). However, the Soviet invasion cut short this development. Yugoslavia, in a more gradual way over the fifties and sixties, moved toward this type through the decentralization of public administration and the introduction of workers councils, institutionalizing expressions of local and regional interests and giving representation of economic interests in elected assemblies, on the basis of a kind of corporativism. Skilling suggests that this pluralistic development affected the cultural and intellectual sphere less in Yugoslavia than in Czechoslovakia and even in a short period in Hungary and Poland.

Yugoslavia, which would deserve more discussion in this context, would be in our basic typology an authoritarian regime, and the different degree of autonomy granted to various groups and their institutionalization fits well with our notion of limited pluralism (Neal, 1957; Hoffman and Neal, 1962; Zaninovich, 1968; Horvat, 1969; Barton, Denitch, and Kadushin, 1973). However, we should not ignore the opportunities for participation provided by self-management and workers' control (Roggemann, 1970; Pusic, 1973; Supek, 1973) and the potential for mobilization of the League of Communists. This participatory element is in conflict with bureaucratic and technocratic tendencies (Milenkovitch, 1971) and should—in principle—counteract the pressures of nationalism. A sign of the legitimacy gained by the new institutions is that criticism is often articulated in terms of discrepancies between ideal and reality of self-management. Yugoslavia also exemplifies that in the dynamics of authoritarian regimes there might be two alternative paths: one, liberalization, which might benefit particularly intellectual, cultural groups, opinion groups, making the pool from which the professional politicians are recruited more heterogeneous; and another path emphasizing more the ideology, retaining an important function for the party but allowing a greater democratization at the local and factory level. From this perspective a comparison of Yugoslavia with the Partido Revolucionario Institucional (PRI) regime in Mexico and even with Franco's Spain would be fruitful. It is our assumption that stable communist regimes created by a national revolution, fully independent of the USSR, are more likely to progress in the direction of partial democratization than of liberalization. Posttotalitarian, and in the case of Yugoslavia postadministrative-phase, independent communist regimes are likely to take this form. Or perhaps, if the break through the constraining conditions has not yet been achieved and the original ideologically committed leadership is still in power, the form will fit the Chinese model with its antibureaucratic mobilizational features under the cultural revolution.

It is this last model that is described by Skilling as "anarchic authoritarianism," in which few of the groups that clashed in the cultural revolution were institutionalized or "legitimate." Also they were permitted and even encouraged by Mao, using spontaneous and coercive methods that had little in common with the organized processes of group action in Czechoslovakia or Yugoslavia. It is this last type in Skilling's classification that seems less useful. His typology raises a basic question, which is not easy to answer: Under what conditions does "quasi-pluralistic authoritarianism" become "democratizing and pluralistic authoritarianism"?

John Michael Montias' (1970) "Types of Economic Systems," based on three coordinates—the degree of mobilization for the promotion of regime goals of participants in the system, particularly of peasants, workers, and employees by lower-level party cadres; the degree of reliance by central authorities on hierarchically transmitted commands for furthering regime goals; and the relative importance of markets for producer goods—makes little reference to other political and cultural changes in communist systems. However, in view of the central importance of the organization of the economy in the development of communist politics, the changing role of the party in the economy, the nature of incentives as they affect the citizen, the sources of discontent, etc., it would be most interesting to relate his types with other political changes. On the basis of the three mentioned coordinates, he distinguishes four main types of socialist economic systems: (1) mobilization, (2) centralized administered, and (3) decentralized administered, both of which are characterized by having hierarchically structured bureaucracies for affecting the party's economic policies, and (4) market socialist. The mobilization system, high on the mobilization coordinate and on that of command, is certainly in the economic sphere the most congruent with totalitarianism. This probably would be true for a mobilization system not relying heavily on hierarchically transmitted commands as it might have existed in China in the Great Leap Forward campaign. It seems reasonable that the posttotalitarian authoritarian systems will run the economy either as decentralized administered systems or in the form of market socialism.

In connection with the typology offered by Montias the question might be raised whether a totalitarianism aiming at a utopian transformation of society in spheres not directly related to the economy and social structure but to cultural and religious values, the mobilization for an imperialist policy, and changing the status structure rather than the class structure (as it was in the case of the Nazis) was totalitarian with an economic policy that would not fit in the mobilizational or centralized administrative system types. Perhaps this was the case because the German economy at that time was much further advanced. It seems, however, that given the close interconnection between the political and economic system in communist societies, changes in the economic system toward greater autonomy of various units will tend to have also political consequences. Montias in his analysis stresses that the transitions from one to another type of economic system are reversible and that there are cases of remobilization. He also seems to suggest that the dismantling of centralized systems and particularly the shift to market socialism is hard to achieve without "revolution from above" buttressed by suitable changes in ideology. In that context he notes that in Yugoslavia the ideological support for the economic reform was provided by inveighing against state capital monopoly and bureaucratization, which were made to be hallmarks of Soviet "degeneration," a process that did not take place in Czechoslovakia and Hungary, where the reforms were grafted to the old system. Without a change in political leadership it seems that the transformation to market socialism could not occur. Certainly the question of the relative weight of economic developments, social changes, and strictly defined political factors, in the process of transition from totalitarianism to a variety of posttotalitarian systems, deserves further analysis.

Certainly a number of social, economic, political, and historical variables would account for these different developments in posttotalitarian communist states, but as the case of Czechoslovakia shows, the international linkages with the Soviet Union are a far from negligible variable. We should not forget either, in any comparative analysis, the different ways in which the communists achieved power in different countries: the combination of national and social revolution in China, Yugoslavia, North Vietnam, Cuba, and Albania; and the largely externally imposed rule in Poland, Czechoslovakia, Rumania, Bulgaria, and East Germany. Nor can we neglect the characteristics of the Communist party before taking power: its size, its respectable showing in free elections in Czechoslovakia, and the ways in which it had developed in exile, illegality, and resistance in other countries like the Southern Balkans. In the case of East Germany the transition of a society from one totalitarian system to another obviously contributed to its stability, despite the discontent and the competition with the Federal Republic that before the Berlin Wall undermined its development. Nor can we ignore the demonstration effect of changes in one communist country on others, particularly the impact of the Yugoslav example and in a quite different direction of the Chinese.

In the short run we would argue that the stabilized Soviet sphere of influence, the Soviet intervention in Hungary and Czechoslovakia, and the détente with the United States should discourage those favoring a more open discussion of political institutional alternatives and questioning the dominant role of the party. On the other hand the complexity of tasks undertaken by the political system and the party should, in a less tense atmosphere and with greater economic resources, favor a more participatory authoritarian regime, in which at the local level, perhaps at the factory level, a certain decentralization would be combined with a freer participation of those loyal to the system. This would favor a "democratizing authoritarianism" at the lower levels and the "consultative authoritarianism" of Peter Ludz at the higher level rather than a further institutionalization of "quasi-pluralistic authoritarianism." It would favor economic rather than political reform even when these are obviously difficult to separate in communist states. Despite the convergence in many respects with other types of authoritarian regimes, particularly the "mobilizational one-party states" in the Third World and some of the "statist-organic authoritarian regimes" in the Western sphere of influence, we do not expect them to evolve in the same direction. In the West the pressures for liberalization are likely to be stronger than those for greater participation, while in the East those for liberalization are likely to be curtailed and those for participation, strengthened, at least at the lower levels, where they can be controlled. It depends very much on the values of the observer which of these two developments he or she would consider closer to the model of competitive democracy. But neither is likely to lead ultimately to competitive democracy. The possibility of a reversal of post-totalitarian authoritarianisms in the communist world to "populist" or "bureaucratic" totalitarian tendencies cannot be excluded, but at present does not seem likely.

The question of posttotalitarianism, particularly in the Soviet Union, is intimately linked with the theories of convergence of industrial or postindustrial society.[65] Alfred G. Meyer has summarized very well the intellectual and ideological context in which such theories have been formulated:

> Theories of convergence are as old as the Russian revolution itself, if we think of Waclaw Machajski's wry Saint-Simonian prognosis of the development of a stratified industrial society in which the educated and skilled would emerge as the new ruling class. Machajski was a disillusioned Marxist; and theories of convergence seem to suggest themselves easily to disillusioned Marxists, or at least to Marxists who have become disillusioned about the Soviet Union. Consider the theories of Trotsky, Achminov, Djilas, Mao, and the European and American New Left. In some fashion or other, they all describe the Soviet system as one in which a proletarian revolution gone wrong has resulted in the society reverting to some form of capitalism. Conversely, in the manner of James Burnham, another disillusioned Marxist, theories of the revolution betrayed correspond to assumptions about the end of capitalism and democracy in the West and foretell the emergence of a "managerial" society much like that projected by Saint-Simon, Machajski, and others. (Meyer, 1970, p. 319)

In addition to the disillusioned Marxists, writers disappointed with or suspicious of democracy, particularly among sociologists, starting with Tocqueville, have also noted the totalitarian tendencies of democracy. Another group is some economists who argue that the command economy has become dysfunctional and must be replaced by new and more rational planning methods. In their work, as in that of Isaac Deutscher, there is a strong element of technological economic determinism, which assumes a given technology causing a functionally corresponding social structure or system of social relations and similar systems of social relations developing similar political systems. The tendency from the days of the founding fathers of sociology to allow only limited autonomy to politics from the socioeconomic system and their areas of interest explain the favor that this perspective has found among them. The collection of readings edited by Paul Hollander (1969), *American and Soviet Society,* shows the fruitfulness and also the limitations of this perspective. Another source has been pacifist moralizing, wishful thinking, and sheer impatience with the cold war, based on the somewhat dubious assumption that similar systems are more compatible with each other than dissimilar ones. A newer theory of convergence proceeds from the assumption that industrial societies will converge in the form of bureaucratization rather than liberalization and democratization, which represented passing stages in the development of Western societies. Alfred G. Meyer (1970), without calling it convergence, contributes to that perspective when he asserts that the Soviet Union can be best understood as a giant bureaucracy, something like a modern corporation extended over the entire society, a "General Motors at large," even when he warns against pushing the analogy too far considering that in real life General Motors still exists within a larger society, culture, and political system.

The convergence theories, optimistic or apocalyptic, often on the basis of the opposite of ideological premises, have the merit of highlighting certain aspects of the study of societies and political systems that the type of analysis offered in this chapter tend to neglect but that cannot be fully dismissed.

V. THE PLACE OF THE WORLD'S STATES IN THE TYPOLOGY: AN ATTEMPT AND ITS DIFFICULTIES

It would have certainly been highly desirable to further operationalize our three main dimensions: the degree of monism versus limited pluralism, mobilization versus depoliticization of the population, and centrality of ideologies versus predominance of what we have called mentalities. The next step would have been to find systematic, valid, and reliable indicators of those three dimensions and to locate the countries of the world in the resulting attribute space. Finally, by selecting meaningful cutting points we would be able to define operationally the types and subtypes of nondemocratic regimes. The end product of such efforts would be a list of countries that at any particular point in time could be placed in each type.

Any reader of the now extensive literature on the conditions and measures of democracy, well summarized by John D. May (1973), will be fully aware of the difficulties in carrying out such an operation, even for the limited number of countries that generally are considered democratic or borderline cases. In spite of the availability of easily measurable indicators like the percentage of population eligible to vote, percentage voting, electoral support of majority and minority parties, share in seats of those parties, and constitutionally legitimate turnover of executives, as well as much richer information and other indicators like mass media control and the usual indices of economic development, no generally accepted classification or measure of the degree of democracy has resulted. The data that we would need to operationalize the dimensions of our typology are much more elusive, and in addition no one has yet made a deliberate effort to collect them systematically. To take just one obvious dimension, political mobilization of the citizens versus depoliticization, there is no easily available measure comparable to the percentage of citizen voting in competitive democracies.[66] Even leaving aside the differing meaning of the vote when there is no freedom to articulate and organize alternative opinion, it seems somewhat strange to find that in the Ivory Coast, Guinea, Gabon, the United Arab Republic, and Niger over 98 percent of the electorate actually votes, according to official reports (a similar report is made for seven communist countries), while among the polyarchies only the Netherlands reaches that high level of participation. It is, however, worth notice that among all the countries that we would not consider democracies according to our definition, those claiming an electoral participation rate above 90 percent happen to be totalitarian, posttotalitarian, or those we would have classified at the time as mobilizational postindependence regimes, generally with an officially established single party.[67] However, such an indicator would be useless for those countries that have not had national elections, like Cuba and China, obviously based on a high level of mobilization, and others like traditional Arab sheikhdoms, nor would such an indicator with its gross distortions and falsifications be of much value to classify countries between those extremes. Another possible indicator of mobilization, as we suggested in our discussion, would be the actual membership and participation in the activities of the officially established single party and its mass organizations for youth, women, etc. No one has systematically collected such data, and it is likely that the figures reported would in many cases be a wishful distortion of reality. Certainly the 1.1 million members claimed in the early sixties by Falange Movimiento in Spain can in no meaningful way be compared with the 2.5 million members of the NSDAP in 1935, if we would consider even the most minimal indicators of involvement in the party. Actually in proportion to the population of each country, those figures would not be far apart. If this is the case with the most easily quantifiable indicator, the situation becomes even worse when we consider ones like the degree of limited pluralism or the monopoly of political power. Scholars unfamiliar with this type of system have fallen into the trap of considering the proportion of members of the government or high officeholders who are members of the party as an indicator, forgetting that they were legally considered members by the fact of holding such offices and their reaching those positions had nothing to do with previous involvement in the party but was based on quite different criteria, like military or bureaucratic careers, technical expertise, membership in influential religious associations, etc. Only a case-by-case sifting of the evidence for which the monographic research is often unavailable would allow us to make intelligent use of such operational criteria. We would obviously wish to have quantitative indicators of the importance of the official single parties in the political process of totalitarian and authoritarian regimes, and we would not deny that such indicators could be devised, like the ratio between government nonparty officials and paid officials of the party; the presence of men who made their careers in the party in other sectors of the political system like government, bureaucracies, the military, the academy, etc.; and the share of the party in the control of mass media. It would seem as if the degree of autonomy, development, interest articulation, and aggregation as defined by Gabriel Almond could serve to measure the degree of pluralism. But the efforts of Banks and Textor (1963; Banks and Gregg, 1965) to operationalize those concepts show the difficulty in using them outside of the democratic and a few other well-known countries. In fact, their coding of those dimensions is based not on any hard indicators but on the judgment of experts, using probably quite different frames of reference in classifying the country they know best.

In view of all these problems it seems unwarranted to attempt to place all the countries of the world within the types and subtypes we have developed here. But it seems appropriate, using our best judgment, to place a number of polities in the types we have theoretically and inductively developed. Certainly even more than in the case of the measurement of democracy found in the literature, scholars will disagree with our typology, but even accepting its usefulness they will question the placing of particular countries at a particular time in it, on account of a different reading of the available evidence or using different indicators than those implicitly used by us. Therefore our classification should be considered indicative and illustrative and be perfected by other scholars before it is used in sophisticated computer analysis in search for correlations with other nonpolitical variables. Our distinctions are qualitative rather than quantitative, and often quite far apart from those resulting from perhaps premature efforts of quantification of some relevant dimensions, like the scaling by Dahl and his associates of 114 countries in 31 types by the opportunities to participate in national elections and to oppose the government. This does not mean that the clusters of countries discovered by them using the admittedly debatable coding of Banks and Textor do not show significant coincidences with the groupings reached by us. When there could be such a profound disagreement as that between Banks and Textor and Dahl about the classification of a well-known country like France, we can imagine how precarious the data base for such refined classifications must be in the case of most countries that have reached independence recently and are characterized by unstable governments that have not been the object of monographic research from a comparative perspective. All this would account for the relatively low level of coincidence between the classifications in our typology and the scaling of those same countries by Dahl, Norling, and Williams (Dahl, 1971, Appendix A, pp. 231–45) disregarding changes in the nature of the political regime even over short periods of time. The difficulties encountered by Marvin E. Olsen, Dick Simpson, and Arthur K. Smith in measuring democratic performance, noted by John D. May (1973), should serve as warning against premature and specious quantification of any typological effort like ours. Elegant statistical operations built on weak foundations seem to us more misleading than a frankly qualitative judgment based on a mental and hopefully intelligent summation of a large amount of information.

VI. CONCLUDING COMMENTS

After our panoramic overview of the variety of political systems that are not based on a regular free competition for power among organized groups emerging with more or less spontaneity from the society, that is, of all the regimes that cannot be called competitive democracies, it is difficult to discern some general trends about the prospects of different forms of government.[68] On the one hand, the successful stable democracies, with their political freedoms, the opportunities for political participation of the average citizen, particularly those with a calling for politics, and the predictability and relative peacefulness in handling political and social crises, continue to be a pole of attraction to people living under the variety of nondemocratic regimes. This accounts for the tendencies toward greater pluralism and more opportunities for participation to which the rulers in authoritarian regimes pay lip service or more or less sincerely and incompetently aim. On occasion we have noted how the processes of liberalization and democratization (in the sense of greater opportunities for active political participation) do not seem to have equally favorable prospects in different authoritarian and totalitarian systems. We can certainly expect the emergence of many transitional types of polities that, without losing their authoritarian character, might have a potential for becoming competitive democracies under favorable circumstances. In a small number of countries the fact that only recently they were ruled as competitive democracies creates pressures both from below and within the elite in that direction. However, we should not forget that the majority of countries we have been considering never have been under liberal democratic rule, never have had an opportunity to develop the traditions and values of a *Rechtstaat* ("state of law") or the pluralism of institutions and corporate groups of the type that the West developed in centuries of feudalism, estate representation (*ständische-Verfassung*), and autonomous corporate cities. Let us not forget that many of the regimes we have been considering have been established as successors of monarchical traditional despotisms or traditional political systems, where authority was limited by custom rather than by law and in which no other groups including religious organizations and authorities could challenge or limit political authority. A large number of polities, particularly in Africa, have emerged as a result of external colonial territorial divisions imposed upon smaller traditional political units, premodern tribal organizations, and communal structures. In those cases the modern and pseudomodern political systems have been imposed not upon a national community with civic consciousness but upon successors of an external authoritarian rule of the colonizer, and the task of building a civic and perhaps national consciousness may have to precede any attempt to organize a democratic state in which horizontal cleavages would crosscut and integrate vertical, territorial, and/or ethnic cleavages. In such societies we can expect a variety of authoritarian and perhaps occasionally totalitarian efforts to create stable regimes. In those societies in which authoritarian rule has succeeded with practically no discontinuity traditional premodern authoritarian forms or colonial rule, we can expect only limited popular pressures toward competitive democracy. Certainly, elites educated and/or oriented toward Western advanced societies are likely to be discontented with authoritarian rule and feel that modernization requires either competitive democracy or an imitation of the utopian totalitarian model. That discontent of sectors of the elite undoubtedly will contribute to the instability of authoritarian regimes, but it is doubtful that it will not lead to the successive reproduction of new and different authoritarian regimes. The transition from a desire by the elites for constitutional democratic forms after independence—first imitated and externally imposed or genuinely desired—to mobilizational or machine-type single parties and then to bureaucratic-military authoritarian rule in so many African states reflects those dilemmas. Authoritarian regimes of one or another type appeared to intellectuals, leaders, and even citizens of competitive democracies as basically illegitimate, and that value judgment in many ways contributes to delegitimize those regimes for important sectors in the elite of their societies but not necessarily for the masses. We therefore should be careful not to confuse the instability of authoritarian regimes with favorable prospects for competitive democracy. The alternative to a particular authoritarian regime might be change within the regime or from one type of authoritarian rule to another, if not permanent instability or chaos (of which the Congo after independence was an outstanding example; see Willame, 1972).

We should not forget either that even established competitive democracies in a period of social change and revived ideological passion might undergo crises that lead to authoritarian rule unless a last minute and deliberate effort of reequilibration succeeds (Linz and Stepan, forthcoming). The circumstances accompanying a breakdown of democracy, as cases in Latin America show, make the reestablishment very difficult. Competitive democracy seems to be the result of quite unique constellations of factors and circumstances leading to its inauguration and stability. Many developments in modern societies and in the not-so-modern, particularly in terms of economic well-being, should make stable democracies possible, but those same conditions do not assure a successful process of inauguration of such regimes. Certainly many societies satisfied the requirements for stable democracy we find in the literature, but did not become competitive regimes.

When Robert Dahl raised the question about the future of polyarchies he wrote, "As with a great many things, the safest bet about a country's regime a generation from now is that it will be somewhat different but not radically different from what it is today." We can make the same statement about today's nondemocratic regimes. We would, however, have to add that in contrast to the stabilized democracies, we would expect considerable change in the types of authoritarian regimes and within the regimes themselves. Paradoxically, great shifts in mass electorates in advanced societies, except in extreme crisis situations, are unlikely, and therefore evolutionary rather than basic change characterizes democratic politics. Since in authoritarian regimes change depends on few actors, less constrained by constituencies difficult to convince by persuasion rather than imposition, important changes can take place more unexpectedly and can change the system considerably. Perhaps the particular types of authoritarian regimes are less likely to be fully institutionalized, and therefore we can expect many changes within the genus authoritarian. Since the end of World War II and even earlier, the list of countries fitting into the basic subtypes of majoritarian and consociational democracies has changed little. Neither has that of nondemocratic political states over the same period. But the lists of countries fitting at different moments in time into the various subtypes has been far from stable. Irregular and violent changes have been frequent, as the overthrow of the postindependence single-party regimes in Africa by military coups establishing military-bureaucratic regimes shows. There are also evolutive tendencies within authoritarian regimes which seem to lead to a certain convergence toward some form of institutionalization of a limited pluralism based on a controlled and irresponsible representation of interests, limited and controlled forms of participation, and limited efforts of ideological justification of such institutional arrangements. That point of convergence in the development of authoritarian regimes seems to be relatively close to the model we have described as organic statism.[69] The regimes established as military dictatorships in the narrow sense of emergency interim rule by the army very quickly tend to become bureaucratic-military if not bureaucratic-technocratic-military. With the passing of time the variety of interests in society, particularly economic, professional, and sectorial, and to a certain degree labor and territorial, are included in one way or another into the limited and controlled pluralism. On the .other hand, systems established by and through political parties gaining or aspiring to the monopoly of control or at least dominance over other pluralistic components with the effort of mass mobilization and declared ideological commitments seem to lose that dynamism and increasingly share their power with a variety of selected interest groups. Their totalitarian and arrested totalitarian tendencies are deflected toward various forms of conservative quasi-pluralistic or pluralistic authoritarian regimes, some of which seem to show a growing affinity to the model of organic statism. At some point the observer could think that the future was in the hands of mobilizational single parties that would hold at least dominant or predominant, if not exclusive, power. Contrary to that expectation we have seen the overthrow, transformation, or decay of single-party rule and organizations. Bureaucratic rule in cooperation with recognized organized interests seems to be the dominant model, sometimes supported by the military with its coercive capacity and organizational resources, other times legitimated by the continuing presence and influence at the top of a single party that provides some opportunity to organize a well-controlled mass participation and to recruit politically ambitious persons. It is important to be aware of the range and direction of dynamic tendencies within authoritarian regimes. It is this fact that makes it so difficult to place different countries in the types delineated above without reference to a particular moment in their development.

As to the future of totalitarianism, predictions are even more difficult. Certainly two of the historically most salient and well-known cases, the rule of Hitler and Stalin, seem to have weakened its attractiveness. But there can be no question that some of the underlying utopian ideological assumptions that made those distorted forms with their terror possible are still there. Ultimately, once the pluralistic conflict and accommodation model underlying democratic politics has been rejected in favor of a consensual society based on a deliberate active search for the common good according to a rational or irrational ideal conception under a leadership defined as competent and self-confident about achieving it, this model is not likely to lose its appeal. The totalitarian utopia is, for modern man, a pole of attraction not easily forgotten and is comparable in this respect to that of freedom for the individual to participate in democratic politics. Almost inevitably the elites in authoritarian regimes will feel the attraction of those two poles, even when the confining conditions of reality make it unlikely that most authoritarian regimes will evolve in one or another of those directions. Totalitarianism is ultimately as much if not more a result of a unique constellation of factors as is competitive democracy. Perhaps, fortunately, it is not easy to establish totalitarian systems. In spite of their many failures, and their lack of a distinctive legitimacy formula and ideology attractive to intellectuals, authoritarian regimes rather than totalitarian systems and democratic governments are the regimes most easily established and function under conditions neither too favorable nor unfavorable to the stability of government. Contrary to the hopes of free men and those of the *terribles simplificateurs* of which Burckhardt wrote, many if not most states will be ruled in the immediate future by authoritarian regimes, neither fully subordinating the individual to a great historical task of building a perfect society nor allowing him a free choice among a large set of alternatives or an opportunity to convince his fellow citizens to support him to implement those goals.

NOTES

1.   An excellent comparative study of two societies under different political systems and the implications for the individual of living in the USSR and the U.S. is Hollander (1973). However, the impact of the generational and liberal-radical intellectual protest around 1970 colors some sections on the U.S. too much.

2.   For Mussolini's and the Italian use of the term totalitarian see Jänicke (1971), pp. 20–36. This work is also the best review of the history of the uses of the term, its variants, and the polemics surrounding it, and includes an extensive bibliography. It should be noted that the use of the term for both fascist and communist regimes was not exclusive of liberals, Catholics, or conservatives, but that socialists like Hilferding already in 1939 did so. Hilferding also in 1936 abandoned a Marxist analysis of the totalitarian state (see Jänicke, 1971, pp. 74–75 and Hilferding, 1947b, p. 266).

3.   On the concept of total war see Speier (1944).

4.   For a discussion of the perception of the similarities of the Soviet and the fascist regimes by Trotsky and Italian Fascists see Gregor (1974, pp. 183–88). For another example see the analysis by a Spanish left fascist, Ledesma Ramos (1935, pp. 288–91 passim). See also footnote 55.

5.   For a review of the current typologies of political systems see Wiseman (1966, pp. 47–96). Almond and Coleman (1960) was a pioneer work in which Pye, Weiner, Coleman, Rustow, and Blanksten study politics in Asia, Africa, and Latin America. The typology by Shils is used in connection with the functional analysis by Almond. Almond and Powell (1966, chapters 9–11) present a typology according to the degree of structural differentiation and secularization, from primitive political systems to modern democratic, authoritarian, and totalitarian. Another interesting contribution is Finer (1971, pp. 44–51 passim). Blondel (1972) organizes his comparative analysis of political systems, distinguishing traditional conservative, liberal democratic, communist, populist, and authoritarian conservative systems. Rustow (1967) distinguishes (1) traditional, (2) modernizing—personal charismatic, military, single-party authoritarian, (3) modern democratic, totalitarian and (4) absence of government.

   Organski (1965) has formulated another typology of regimes on the basis of their relation to stages of economic development, the function of politics in that process, and the type of elite alliances and class conflicts. Among them we might note the type he calls "syncratic" (from the Greek 'syn,' together, rule) in semideveloped countries based on a compromise between industrial and agrarian elites stimulated by a threat from below.

   Apter (1965), on the basis of his extensive research experience in Africa, has developed a highly stimulating and influential typology of political systems based on two main dimensions: the type of authority and the values pursued. The first dimension distinguishes systems of hierarchical authority (centrally controlled systems) and of pyramidal authority (systems with constitutional representation); the second distinguishes consummatory (sacred) and instrumental (secular) values. The resulting types are, among the hierarchic authority systems: (1) mobilizational systems (like China) and (2) either modernizing autocracies or neomercantilist societies (of which Morocco and Kemalism in Turkey would be examples); among pyramidal authority systems: (3) theocratic or feudal systems and (4) reconciliation systems. Mobilization and reconciliation systems are compared in relation to coercion and information, which are in inverse relation. Unfortunately it would be too complex to present here how Apter relates these theoretically developed types to the analysis of concrete political systems and to problems of modernization.

6.   The calculations used in this section on the ranking of countries by population, gross national product, GNP growth rates, and the population under different types of regimes in Europe are based on tables 5.1, 5.4, and 5.5 in Taylor and Hudson (1972).

7.   Our delimitation and definition of democracy has been derived from the following major works: Sartori (1962a), Kelsen (1929), Schumpeter (1950), and Dahl (1971). On Dahl's contribution to the theory of democracy, or—as he now prefers to call it—polyarchy, see the critical review essay of Ware (1974). It refers to criticisms of what has been called "elitist theory of democracy." See for example Bachrach (1967). Since these critiques focus more on the "democratization" of polyarchies than on their distinction from nonpolyarchies, we shall not enter further into these important discussions. We have developed our ideas about democracy further in the context of a discussion of R. Michels' pessimistic and ultimately misleading analysis; see Linz (1966).

8.   The most debated case is Mexico, where a presidential candidate only in 1952 obtained less than 75 percent of the vote and generally obtains close to or over 90 percent. Opposition leaders are fully aware that they are doomed to lose any election for the 200 governorships and 282 senatorial seats. The opposition party's only hope (a recent development) is to obtain, in exchange for a few positions as representatives or municipal presidents, recognition by the government for its leaders in the form of contracts, loans, or services. Parties are financed in many cases by the government, and they support the government candidates or provisionally fight them in exchange for concessions for their supporters. "Thus they have participated in the political game and the ceremony of elections," as a Mexican social scientist puts it. See González Casanova (1970). Another critical analysis is Cosío Villegas (1972). An earlier analysis that emphasizes the oligarchic characteristics is Brandenburg (1964). The best monographic study of policymaking in Mexico as an authoritarian regime is Kaufman (1970). For an analysis of elections see Taylor (1960). However, there are other interpretations that emphasize the democratic potential, either within the party or as a long-term development; see Scott (1964, 1965), Needler (1971), Padgett (1966), and Ross (1966). The fact that elections do not serve as a channel to power and that the Partido Revolucionario Institucional (PRI) is a privileged party does not mean that there is not considerable freedom of expression and organization. For a study of the leading opposition party, its electoral support, and the handicaps it faces see Mabry (1973), pp. 170–82. On the continuing disagreement of scholars on the nature of the political system see Needleman and Needleman (1969).

9.   On intellectual and cultural life in the Soviet Union see Pipes (1961), Swayze (1962), Simmons (1971), and P. Johnson and Labedz (1965). For East Germany see Lange (1955). For communist China, MacFarquhar (1960) and Chen (1967). An interesting case study is Medvedev (1969) on Lysenko. For Nazi Germany, Brenner (1963), Mosse (1966), Wulf (1963a, 1963b, 1963c, 1964), and Strothman (1963). For further particularly revealing bibliographic references to education, the world of knowledge, see Tannenbaum (1972). While not a theoretically significant contribution, the illustrations showing the heterogeneity and eclecticism in official Italian art contrast with the German equivalents and are another indicator of the doubtful totalitarian character of Italian

Fascism. See Silva (1973). The contrast between totalitarian and authoritarian regime cultural policy should become apparent to the reader of the study of Spanish intellectual life under Franco by E. Díaz (1974).

10. On religion and the state in the Soviet Union see Curtis (1960). For more recent times see Bourdeaux (1968, 1969) and Hayward and Fletcher (1969). For communist China see Baier (1968), Bush (1970), MacInnis (1972), and H. Welch (1972). For Germany see Conway (1968), Zipfel (1965), Lewy (1965), Buchheim (1953). For a regional study rich in documentation see Baier (1968). The contrast with Italy can be found in Webster (1960).

11. Already in the SA, ranks were given without regard to wartime rank in the army; see Gordon (1972, pp. 84–85). This ideology breaking through the status structure of the society was reflected in the SA oath: "I promise that I will see in every member . . . without thought of class, occupation, wealth or poverty, only my brother and true comrade, with whom I feel myself bound in joy and sorrow." Later this meant that a high civil servant might have been quite intimidated by his janitor holding the position of party *Blockwart*.

12. We cannot enter into the complex problem of the relationship between political systems and foreign policy. Certainly, aggressive policies, intervention in the internal affairs of other countries, political and economic imperialism are no monopoly of any type of regime. There can be no question either that national-socialism and its ideological conceptions and the internal dynamic of the German regime led to aggressive expansion, war, and the creation of an hegemonic system of exploited and oppressed countries and dependent satellites. There are distinctive Nazi components in that policy, particularly its racist conception, that cannot be confused with those derived from German nationalism (regaining full sovereignty after Versailles, the Auschluss, incorporation of border ethnic minorities) and those of a Mitteleuropa economic dominance policy. See Bracher (1970, pp. 287–329, 400–8, and the bibliographic references on pp. 520–23); Jacobsen (1968), Hillgruber (1971), and Hildebrand (1973). Deakin (1966) and Wiskemann (1966) study the very revealing relationship between Hitler and Mussolini. Undoubtedly, Fascist Italy also pursued a policy of expansion in the Adriatic and Africa, but it could be argued that—leaving aside rhetorical claims—its goals were those of prefascist imperialism. All fascist movements are characterized by their exacerbated nationalism, antiinternationalism, antipacificism, exultation of military values, irredentism, and often pannationalism, contrasted with the ideological commitments of democratic parties of the left and center, even when some of those parties were not opposed to colonialism and national power and prestige politics.

The question of foreign policy of communist states presents the same problem of isolating national interests of the USSR—inherited from the Russian Empire—from those derived from the dynamics of the regime (particularly as the result of the civil war and foreign intervention, encirclement, isolation) and finally from those derived from international revolutionary solidarity and ideologically based perceptions of the international scene. The different points of view expressed by scholars can be found in Hoffman and Fleron (1971, part 3), in addition to Schulman (1969) and Ulam (1968). The literature on the Sino-Soviet dispute (Zagoria, 1969) brings out the complex interweaving of national interest and ideological conflicts. Obviously the literature on Eastern European communist countries (Seton-Watson, 1968; Ionescu, 1967; Brzezinski, 1960) reveals the inseparability of foreign and internal policy considerations with the Soviet hegemonic sphere. The relations of communist parties with the CPSU, particularly when the Soviet Union served as model socialist country, make it impossible to separate (specifically in the Stalin era) the politics of a worldwide revolutionary movement from those of the only country in which the party was in power. Polycentrism has obviously changed and complicated things. In spite of the affinities between fascist parties, influences and imitations, they never were linked by a common discipline comparable to the communists. Ideologically linked parties, ignoring any more direct dependency, are undoubtedly a factor in the foreign policy of movement regimes. The style and capacity for certain types of international political responses of regimes subject to free public criticism and overt dissent and of those not facing them must be different. However, it would be a mistake to deduct (for any type of regime) foreign policy at any point in time from ideological commitments, as the flexibility shown in the Hitler-Stalin pact or U.S.-communist China relations prove; but it might be more valid to take them into account in long-range strategies of regimes. A related topic we have ignored (perhaps too much) is the link between foreign policy crises and the crises and breakdown of democratic regimes, particularly in the rise of fascism but also the turn to authoritarian solutions in the Third World, as well as the link between preparedness for war, more specifically total war, and totalitarian tendencies.

13. The problem of succession of leaders in nondemocratic constitutional regimes has been considered one of their weaknesses in contrast to hereditary monarchies and parliamentary or presidential democracies (Rustow, 1964). The succession of Lenin and the consequent struggle for power influenced that discussion, as well as the very personal leadership and life-long tenure of many single-party regime leaders. Already in 1933 Farinacci in a letter to Mussolini (Aquarone, 1965, pp. 173–75) raised the question of succession of a unique leader who would not allow the emergence of other leaders as a problem in this type of regime. In fact, the expectation was that in the absence of an heir apparent no smooth transition could be expected and that any effective legal method to remove leaders in life or after limited tenure could be institutionalized. Events did not allow us to see the succession of the founders of fascist regimes, and the longevity of other founders has left us with speculations about the future of their regimes. The rise of Khrushchev (Swearer, 1964; Rush, 1968) despite the conflicts involved proved that succession did not need to lead to a breakdown of the system or even another purge and reign of terror. For the problems surrounding the succession of Mao see Robinson (1974). However the relatively institutionalized and peaceful succession of Khrushchev and Ho Chi Minh, and that of Nasser and Salazar, among others, suggest that the institutions of such regimes might be better able to handle the problem than was thought. Even more noticeable is the tendency of newly established authoritarian regimes, like the Brazilian military, to forestall the emergence of personal leadership and to establish time limits for tenure of office. The not too distant passing away of a number of founders of authoritarian regimes should allow a comparative analysis of the problem.

14. A good measure of the importance of ideology is the growth of a distinctive language (for example in case of Germany see Berning, 1964, and Klemperer, 1966) and the frequency of its use.

15. Aquarone (1965). Quoted from the "Statuto del partito del 1938," Appendix 63, pp. 571–90; see page 577. The work of Aquarone is essential for the study of the ideology and organization of the Italian Fascist party and state and includes a wealth of documents and legal texts.

16. On the ruling and nonruling communist parties see the *Yearbook on International Communist Affairs* (Allen, 1969); on their strength see the annual reports of the U.S. Department of State. For the Soviet Union (Rigby, 1968); for China the figures are: 57 in 1921 to 300,000 in 1933, 40,000 in 1937, 1,211,128 in 1945, 4,438,080 in 1949, 7,859,473 in 1955, 17,000,000 in 1961. Ratios to population in other communist countries around

1961 range from 3.2 percent in Albania to 15.5 percent in North Korea, with most countries between 4 and 5 percent, and 4.2 percent in the USSR Schurmann (1968, pp. 129, 138). See also Brzezinski (1971, p. 86). For the Italian Fascist party see Germino (1959), De Felice (1966a, pp. 6–11); for the NSDAP, see Schäfer (1957), Buchheim (1958), Orlow (1973, pp. 136–38), and the extremely useful and neglected *Parteistatistik*, published by the Reichsorganisationsleiter der NSDAP (1935); and Linz (1970a, pp. 202) for other fascist parties.

For those who would argue that intraparty democracy could be an alternative to political competition in the society at large, it is worth remembering that party membership ranges from 1.3 to over 1.5 percent of the population in Cuba (1969), 2.5 percent of population in China, 4.2 percent in the USSR, to a high of 11.6 percent in Czechoslovakia (all in 1961) (Schurmann, 1968, p. 138). The figure of the PNF in Italy was 5.3 percent (1937) and the maximum for the NSDAP, 9.9 percent in 1943 (Linz, 1970a, p. 202).

17. See also Buchheim (1968a, pp. 391–96) on resignation from the SS, which confirms the in principle voluntary character of membership.

18. This point is well analyzed in Aquarone (1965, pp. 31–34, 262–63), with reference to the conflicts between prefects and party secretaries, and mayors and political secretaries, which generally (but not always) were decided in favor of the state authorities. In 1938 a confidant reported: "In the frequent changes of the guard the active, disinterested and revolutionary elements are substituted by elements that narcotize all activity of the party . . . the tendency to appoint secretary of the [local] Fasci, municipal employees that lack the necessary freedom to activate [potenziare] the party and control the activity of the administrative Enti [organizations]. The party loses, in those cases, its revolutionary activism, the possibility to reinvigorate and make the static element constituted by bureaucracy of the various Enti march in fascist step. In summary, there is lacking that healthy dualism between political and administrative power, indispensable factor in the revolutionary affirmation of fascism" (p. 263). The state-party relation was the object of constant debate among fascist theorists and constitutionalists (F. Neumann, 1963, pp. 75–77; for review of the literature see Conde, 1942, pp. 299–318; Manoilescò, 1938, pp. 97–108). The communists have constantly grappled with this difficult problem (see for example Schurmann, 1968, pp. 109–14). Mao's formulation: "The Party is the instrument that forges the resolution of the contradiction between state and society in socialism" is a response to this problem, as are the principle of vertical and dual rule (Schurmann, pp. 57, 88–89, 188–89) and the conflicts about decentralization. The Yugoslavs significantly criticized the early phase of the regime with the term "statism," and sophisticated Italian fascists like Bottai see in the statism that undermined corporativism and even the party the end of spontaneity and participation in the regime (Aquarone, pp. 216–21). It is no accident that the idea of a "withering away" of the party should have been discussed (Aquarone, p. 35) once the state would be fascisticized and the corporative system fully developed. Such ideas have also appeared with the emphasis on self-management in Yugoslavia and the development of a broadly based Marxist commitment. The Yugoslavs attempted to implement the principle of "separating the party from power," making state and party office incompatible, assigning to the party the role of leading ideological—"conscience of the revolution"—and political force of a society organized along the lines of self-management of workers councils and communes (Zaninovich, 1968, pp. 141–46; Supek, 1973). The party was conceived as the unifying factor in a self-managed society bridging other cleavages and restraining bureaucratic, technocratic, as well as particularistic interests, even when in practice the older, bureaucratically entrenched party cadres resisted the "pluralization" of society. An interesting possible development is a role for the army-

party members as a "vanguard" of the party, counteracting the nationalist tendencies in the society (Remington, 1974). It would be interesting to speculate if the duality state-party is not a functional analogue (equivalent would be too strong a statement) to the duality of state and church and the duality of authority in many traditional empires.

19. On the membership policy of the PNF see Aquarone, 1965, pp. 177–87. The purge of 1930–31 affected 120,000 members, but in 1932–33 the opening raised the membership from 1,007,231 to 1,413,407. (See also Germino, 1959.) On the NSDAP purge of SA members and the left wing particularly among the Politische Leiter, see Orlow, 1973, pp. 120–25, and Schäfer, 1957. See Orlow, pp. 204–7, on the disappointing 1937 membership drive, pp. 236–37 on membership composition and "planning," pp. 342 on difficulties in recruiting youth, p. 408 on membership figures for 1942.

For the USSR see the excellent monograph by Rigby (1968) who gives the official figures from 1917 to 1967 of full and candidate members, which show the impact of purges and membership drives, data on social and sex composition over time, regional variations, members in the armed forces, etc. The purge from May 1929 to May 1930 affected 170,000 members, about 11 percent of the membership, and in 1935, 16 percent.

20. The conception of democratic centralism formulated by Lenin in 1906 in these terms, "The principle of democratic centralism and autonomy of local institutions means specifically *freedom of criticism*, complete and everywhere, as long as this does not disrupt the unity of *action already decided upon*—and the intolerability of any criticism undermining or obstructing the *unity* of action decided on by the party," arouse the comments of Rosa Luxemburg and Trotsky, quoted by R. V. Daniels (1969, p. 12).

21. For excellent analyses of leader personality in totalitarian systems see Tucker (1965) and Vierhaus (1964). The general context of personal leadership in modern politics can be found in Hamon and Mabileau (1964), Willner (1968), and Schweitzer (1974). The peculiar hold of Hitler of the Nazi party before even taking power is studied by Nyomarkay (1967). See also Horn (1972). An obvious source not to be neglected are the biographies like the Bullock (1964) and the description of the world around the *Führer* by an insider like Speer (1971). The phenomenon of "court politics" that exists at the top in any political system but acquires special importance in authoritarian and totalitarian systems would deserve serious comparative analysis.

Some of the analyses of totalitarian systems, like the recent book by Schapiro (1972b), seem in our view to overemphasize the role of leadership. The blaming of Stalin has obviously excused many analysts from attempting to understand the conditions for "Stalinism." They should heed the advice in this criticism by Marx of Victor Hugo's *Napoleon the Little*: "He does not notice that he makes this individual great instead of little by ascribing to him a personal power of initiative such as would be without parallel in world history" (Karl Marx and Friedrich Engels, 1851, Vol. 1, p. 221).

22. For the change in *Mein Kampf* between the 1925 (second edition) and post-1930 editions, on the election of leaders in the party see Maser (1970, pp. 56–57).

23. The role of elections and the party in managing them in noncompetitive politics would deserve comparative analysis. Some interesting material can be found for the Soviet Union in Gilison (1970), Mote (1965), U.S. Department of State, Division of Research for Europe, Office of Intelligence Research (1948). For East Germany, Bundesministerium für Gesamtdeutsche Fragen (1963). For Poland, Pelczynski (1959). Yugoslav elections offer an interesting contrast; see Burks and Stanković (1967). The elections after Hitler's *Machtergreifung* have been analyzed by Bracher, Sauer, and Schulz (1960).

There is unfortunately no comparable analysis of elections after Mussolini's March on Rome. Elections under authoritarian regimes (outside of Yugoslavia) could deserve more analysis in terms of their functions for the system, the responses of citizens, the patterns of participation, voiding of votes in relation to the social structure, as well as the techniques to discourage candidates of the "tolerated" opposition, electoral coercion, and falsification. The contrast between the election process in totalitarian and authoritarian pseudo- or "semi-"democratic regimes (that some would even claim to be democratic) can be seen in Penniman (1972) and the election factbooks for Latin American countries published by the Institute for Comparative Study of Political Systems. For a theoretical paper that could serve as a starting point see Rose and Mossawir (1967).

24. The problem of relationship between party, state, and society has always been discussed in the ideological literature of totalitarian regimes. For a good analysis in the German case, see Franz Neumann (1963, pp. 62–68, 71–80, an interesting comparison with Italy; and pp. 467–70).

25. For the USSR see Fainsod (1963). For China, Yang (1965) and Vogel (1971). For Cuba, Yglesias (1969). For Germany, Allen (1965), Peterson (1969), Heyen (1967), Meyerhoff (1963), and Görgen (1968). For a contrast with an authoritarian regime see Ugalde (1970), Fagen and Tuohy (1972), and Linz (1970b).

26. See below.

27. See below.

28. An approach that cannot be ignored is the emphasis on the historical and cultural continuity with prerevolutionary Russia (Berdyaev, 1948; Simmons, 1955; Pipes 1967; Vaker, 1962; and the excellent collection of essays edited by Black, 1967). Bell (1961) reviews this "Slavic" interpretation in his essay on "Ten Theories in Search of Soviet Reality," which also discusses (pp. 51–56) Leites' *A Study of Bolshevism* (1953), which sees Bolshevism as a conscious attempt to reverse traditional patterns of Russian character, in an interesting attempt of pyscho-history. On cultural continuity and Chinese communism see Solomon (1971) and Pye (1971).

29. The particular German historical and cultural-ideological background that made the rise of national socialism and its successful drive to power possible has been highly debated. A balanced view by a sociologist is Dahrendorf (1967). The ideological-cultural roots are studied by Stern (1965), Mosse (1964), Sontheimer (1968), Faye (1972), Struve (1973) and the earlier and less focussed studies by Butler (1941), Viereck (1961), and Vermeil (1955). Interesting but overstated is Lukács (1955). The essays by Buchheim (1953) and Plessner (1959) deserve mention. However, the general European climate of opinion cannot be ignored either, as the study by Hoepke (1968) on the German right and Italian Fascism shows. Anti-Semitism, which fueled the totalitarian drive of the Nazis and some other fascist movements, has been the subject of considerable research we cannot review here; see Massing (1949), Pulzer (1964), and the more psychological interpretations of Fromm (1941), Adorno *et al.* (1950), Bettelheim and Janowitz (1950), and more recent German sources quoted by Bracher (1970, pp. 506–7). A related problem is that of social Darwinism; see Conrad-Martius (1955) and Zmarzlik (1973).

30. For a review of the literature and bibliography see May (1973) and the already classic analyses by Lipset (1959), Neubauer (1967), Eckstein (1966), and Dahl (1971). A more general analysis of stability of regimes is Eckstein (1971).

31. For a detailed historical account see La Cierva (1969). For historical accounts in English see Jackson (1965) and Carr (1971). More directly relevant for a political scien-

tist is the analysis by Malefakis (1970, Chapter 15, "Could the Disaster Have Been Avoided?" pp. 388–400). The chapter on Spain in Linz and Stepan (forthcoming) will attempt to draw the theoretical implications.

32. We have already referred to the writings of S. M. Lipset, S. Rokkan, S. Neumann. W. Kornhauser, R. Lepsius among others. The specific conditions for the rise of fascism are discussed in Linz (forthcoming). See also below for references to the literature on fascist movements and regimes.

33. The slow process of transition from negative integration, to use the expression of Guenther Roth (1963), to participation of socialist parties is particularly illuminating in this respect. The monographs by Schorsky, Berlau, Gay, and G. A. Ritter on the German Social Democratic party and the theoretical analysis of Robert Michels are the most salient contributions.

34. In this section we have analyzed only the internal processes leading to the establishment or overthrow of one or another type of regime. Obviously, all types of regimes have been overthrown by external defeat (we have only to think of Nazi totalitarianism, Japanese bureaucratic-military, semitraditional authoritarianism after World War II) or established, maintained, or overthrown with foreign assistance playing more or less decisive role (communist regimes in Eastern Europe, the GDR, North Korea, authoritarian rule in Spain with fascist help, not to mention the impact of American aid or hostility on regime changes in Latin America). Certainly in economically dependent countries outside influences and the reactions to them, even short of direct intervention, are one more factor accounting for internal crises and through them for the success or failure of different regimes. However, the interests of outside economic forces might be equally well served—in different cases—by democratic and a variety of authoritarian regimes, so that it is difficult to establish a direct link between *dependencia* and type of regime.

Another factor contributing to the emergence, consolidation, and permanence of authoritarian rule is a hostile international environment that makes the open debate of foreign policy alternatives of a democracy undesirable and justifies the outlawing of parties linked with a neighboring foreign power or the discrimination against irredentist minorities supported by it. This was a factor that contributed to the strengthening of antidemocratic tendencies in Finland in the thirties and the transformation of the three Baltic democracies into presidential dictatorships. Similar problems contributed to authoritarianism in Poland and a number of Balkan countries in the interwar period.

35. Among the extensive literature see Winckler (1970), Krader (1968), Eisenstadt (1959), Mair (1962), Cohen and Middleton (1957), Turner and Swartz (1966), Fortes and Evans-Pritchard (1940), Fallers (1965), Evans-Pritchard (1940 and 1948), Gluckman (1965a and 1965b).

36. The reader edited by Eisenstadt (1971) contains many contributions on premodern political systems and references to the literature. The same is true for Bendix (1968). The classic work in this field is Weber (1968), *Economy and Society*. Bendix (1960) is the best exposition in English of Weber's comparative historical-political sociology. The contemporary relevance of Weber's categories has been noted by Roth (1971, pp. 156–69). The major comparative study of classical empires is Eisenstadt (1962). For a typology of traditional systems see Apter (1965, pp. 85–122).

37. For essays showing the persistent significance of tradition for understanding contemporary politics see *Daedalus* (1973) on "Post-Traditional Societies." As examples of monographs showing the complex interaction between traditional and more modern political institutions we can mention Gellner and Micaud (1972) and Behrman (1970).

See for example the collection of papers edited by Swartz (1968) and the essays in *Political Systems and the Distribution of Power*, A.S.A. Monographs, No. 2.

38. The role of tradition in the political and social modernization of Japan has been the object of considerable research. As examples of different interpretations of modernization under the Meiji see Norman (1948), Craig (1961), and Jansen (1961). One of the few paired comparisons in social science is *Political Modernization in Japan and Turkey*, Ward and Rustow (1964). For the continuous role of the emperor and the court in modern times see Titus (1974).

39. There are a number of excellent studies on Moroccan politics: Ashford (1961, 1965a, 1967), Waterbury (1970), Zartman (1971), Moore (1970b), and Gellner and Micaud (1972). The latter focusses on the interaction between sectors of society—Arabs and Berbers—and its implications, including a discussion of the coup of 10 July 1971.

40. For a less extreme example see Anderson (1964). These regimes are classified as cases of "personal control" in the typology of Lanning (1974), based on the two dimensions: power relationships between authorities and groups (distinguishing group dominant, power balance, and authority dominance) and organizational basis (distinguishing functional, interest groups, and personal relations). The sixth of the resulting types is based on authority dominance and personal relations and includes Haiti, Nicaragua, and Paraguay and in the past Trujillo.

41. For life and politics in a rural community under Trujillo see Walker (1972, pp. 11–31).

42. Recent sociological and anthropological studies of local politics and even national politics in many societies have conceptualized them with the term *"clientela"*—from the Italian and Spanish—and described the patterns as "clientelism"; see for example Lemarchand (1972), Lemarchand and Legg (1972), Powell (1970), Heidenheimer (1970), Lande (1965), Leeds (1964), Leff (1968).

43. The descriptive literature on Latin American politics and particular countries in the area is extensive and we cannot refer to it in detail. A good exposition with country chapters by specialists (with bibliographies) is Needler (1970). See also Anderson (1967), with special emphasis on the relation between politics and economic development. R. H. McDonald (1971) is informative on party systems and elections. See also our notes in this chapter on military in politics, corporativism, and Mexican politics. On the problem of instability see Kling (1956) and chapters in Linz and Stepan (forthcoming).

There are a number of books on Middle East politics (Binder, 1964; Halpern, 1963; Karpat, 1968; Hurewitz, 1969; Abboushi, 1970; Rustow, 1971; Landau, 1972) that provide a wealth of descriptive information, bibliographic references, and analysis of ideological tendencies. These works and those on Egypt and the Maghreb (see note 60), particularly Morocco (see note 39), should provide the basis for a more comparative and theoretical analysis of the authoritarian regimes in Islamic societies and the variety of patterns of transition from traditional or colonial rule to more modern political systems in them. Our focus in this chapter precludes discussion of the link between cultural traditions, values, and even a culture-personality-psychological approach to the emergence of authoritarian rule in these societies in contrast to, let us say, the Hispanic or Southeast Asian societies, which would complement our analysis.

For reviews of Southeast Asian politics see Kahin (1964) and Pye (1967).

44. The comparative study of communist systems and the variety of theoretical approaches has a long tradition; for recent bibliographic essays see Cohen and Shapiro (1974, pp. xix–xliv) and Shoup (1971). Kanet (1971), after others like Tucker (1969)

and Fleron (1969), has argued that the study of communist systems should be incorporated more into a broader comparative framework. Without rejecting this point we would argue that a more systematic theoretical comparative analysis of communist systems, not limited to the USSR and Eastern Europe or to paired comparisons of the USSR and China like those in the volume edited by Treadgold (1967) and implicitly in the better monographs on China, but including Cuba, North Vietnam, and North Korea, would be perhaps a prior step. The different phases in those regimes could provide us with even greater opportunities for "multivariate" comparative study, like the paper by Yeh (1967) on industrialization strategies in the USSR 1928–37 and China 1953–62. Area specialization, perhaps imposed by the linguistic skills required and the difficulties of access to data, has been an obstacle to such an effort. Cuba for example has attracted mostly the attention of American sympathizers and critics, French leftists, and a few Latin Americanists, but almost no students of other communist regimes. It has been the object of descriptive-historical studies (Huberman and Sweezy, 1969; Draper, 1965; Suárez, 1967; Dumont, 1970; Karol, 1970; Thomas, 1971; Halperin, 1972) and of collections of papers edited by MacGaffey and Barnett (1965), Mesa Lago (1971), and Horowitz (1972). Except for a study by Tang and Maloney (1962) on the Chinese impact and the greater similarity in patterns of participation with China than the Soviets (Fagen, 1969, p. 259), there has been little effort to study the regime in a comparative perspective, even among communist countries. The charismatic authority of Castro (Fagen, 1965; Lockwood, 1967), the relatively slow institutionalization of the party organization, the shifts in policy, the dependence on the USSR, the U.S. hostility, the growing militarization (Dumont, 1970; Domínguez, 1974), and the highly polemical responses to the revolution have probably contributed to this lack of comparative analyses.

It is impossible to present here an adequate bibliography on communist China. For a basic list of sources, Berton and Wu (1967), Schurmann (1968), Waller (1971, pp. 172–82). The excellent collections of papers edited by Treadgold (1967), Barnett (1969), Baum (1971), Lindbeck (1971), and Scalapino (1972), and the *Handbook* edited by Wu (1973) can serve as introduction to the best scholarship, in addition to monographs quoted in this essay, like those of Lewis (1963), Townsend (1972), Vogel (1971), and the classic works of Schram (1967, 1969) on Mao and his thought.

A useful review is Shaffer (1967), with chapters by Marxist and non-Marxist authors, including countries generally neglected (like Albania, Korea, Vietnam, Mongolia) in a comparative analysis, and bibliographic references, particularly to specialized periodicals.

45. On the long-lived Estado Novo of Salazar see Kay (1970), Lucena (1971), Schmitter (1973b, 1974), Wiarda (1974), as well as the primary sources they quote, including basic books on organization of the state published in Portugal.

46. To use the expression of Karl Marx in the *Eighteenth Brumaire of Louis Bonaparte* (1851–52, revised 1869; see 1955 edition, pp. 243–344, especially 333–34). Thalheimer (1930) (quoted from 1968 edition, pp. 19–38) is an interesting application of the ideas of Marx in the *Eighteenth Brumaire* to fascism, more sophisticated than most Marxist, particularly communist, interpretations. See also note 55 for Trotsky's use of "Bonapartism" in his analysis of Stalinism.

47. The difference between mobilizational authoritarianism and the military-bureaucratic variants is well reflected in this quote from a report by Guariglia, Italian ambassador and top Fascist leader, arguing for support for Spanish fascists in May 1933: "We may be at its side. We have to help them for the moment to overcome their purely Catholic, Monarchist and even reactionary prejudices. We must aid them to avoid taking up the ideology of Action Française, and to forget *primoderiverismo*. Military

pronunciamientos like Sanjurjo's must be avoided. Propaganda among the agricultural and laboring masses is essential. In a word, they must leave behind the antiquated mentality of 1848 revolutionaries, and adopt the modern ideal of unanimous collaboration of all classes, united by the single superior principle of the authority of the State" (Report of May 16, 1933, quoted by Coverdale, forthcoming).

48. On the Franco regime after the phase we might describe as "arrested totalitarianism" in addition to Linz (1964, 1970a, 1973a, 1973b) the work of von Beyme (1971), significantly entitled *From Fascism to Development Dictatorship: Power Elite and Opposition in Spain,* and Medhurst (1973) provide excellent overviews. In Spanish, Esteban *et al.* (1973) analyze the constitution from the point of view of possible changes in the system leading to changes of the system. Iglesias Selgas (1968, 1971) offers a useful "orthodox" description. Anderson (1970) analyzes the economic policymaking in the regime and Linz and De Miguel (1966b) study the business community, its formal and informal leadership and the disjunction between both in the corporative institutions, and the realities of organic statism and interest group politics in an authoritarian regime. On local politics and community power see Linz (1970a).

49. Andreski (1954, revised 1968), S. E. Finer (1962), and Janowitz (1964) offered the first systematic and comparative analyses, which should be read together with the collections of papers edited by Huntington (1962), Gutteridge (1965), Van Doorn (1968), Janowitz and Van Doorn (1971), Kelleher (1974), and the work of Feit (1973). An early bibliography is Lang (1965). For a typology of military regimes see Perlmutter (1969). The frequency of intervention in Latin America has led to area-wide analyses from the early writings of Lieuwen (1960, 1964), Germani and Silvert (1961), Johnson (1964) to those of Needler (1966), Horowitz (1967), Putnam (1967), Nun (1969), Ronfeldt (1972), Solaún (1973), Stepan (1973), Schmitter (1973a), and the bibliographic essays of McAlister (1966) and Lowenthal (1974). Among the country monographs we can mention North (1966) on Argentina, Chile, and Peru; Potash (1969), Evers (1972), O'Donnell (1973) on Argentina; Hector (1964) on Argentina and Bolivia; Puhle (1970) also on Bolivia; Stepan (1971, 1973) and Schneider (1971) on Brazil; Gilmore (1964), Needler (1964), Fitch (1973) on Ecuador and Einaudi (1969), Lowenthal (1974) and a forthcoming collection of papers edited by him on Peru. Also on Peru and Brazil, Einaudi and Stepan (1971). The interventions and postcoup regimes in the Middle East have been studied by N. Fisher (1963), Hurewitz (1969), and Perlmutter (1970); in Egypt by Vatikiotis (1961) and Dekmejian (1971), in Iraq by Vernier (1963) and Dann (1969). For Indonesia see Feith (1962) and Pauker (1963), and for Korea, Kim (1971). The long history of the army in politics in Spain is covered by Payne (1967) and in the literature mentioned in the note on the origins of the civil war.

50. The literature on Italian corporativism is very extensive and little of it sociological. Among the many sources Sarti (1968, 1970, 1971) deserves special notice, in addition to Aquarone (1965) and Ungari (1963). Among studies published before the end of World War II see Schneider (1928 and 1936), Finer (1935), Schmidt (1938, 1939), Welk (1938). An interesting analysis of how the Italian experience was perceived by different sectors in Germany, from Conservatives to Nazis, see Hoepke (1968). For a contrast among the Catholic, Fascist, and Nationalist corporativist ideologies see Vallauri (1971).

51. The high member apathy and oligarchic control in a variety of voluntary associations, particularly trade unions and professional associations, has been noted by scholars inspired by the work of Michels (for references see Linz, 1966, pp. cv–cxiii).

52. Max Weber (1968), in *Economy and Society,* Vol. 1, pp. 297–99, in the section on "Representation by the Agents of Interest Groups" notes that "as a rule, this kind of

representation is propagated with a view toward disenfranchising certain strata: a) either by distributing mandates among the occupations and thus *in fact* disenfranchising the numerically superior masses; or b) by *openly* and *formally* limiting suffrage to the nonpropertied and thus by disenfranchising those strata whose power rests on their economic position (the case of a state of Soviets)." Weber continues commenting on the absence of effective individual leadership in such bodies, the difficulty of reaching nonartificial majority decisions, etc. These patterns obviously reinforce the "non-representative," "non-elective" elements in the political system, that is, the authoritarian non-accountable elements.

53. France under the Vichy government of Pétain also exemplifies the difference between an authoritarian regime with many characteristics of organic statism and a fascist mobilizational regime desired by some of those supporting it (Paxton, 1972).

54. On the three-cornered competition for power among the state—controlled by fascists, it is true, in alliance with the bureaucracy—the party organization and the *corporazioni*, as well as interests and ideological tendencies within them, ultimately decided in favor of the first, see Aquarone (1965, chapters 3 and 4, particularly pp. 151, 164–65, 188–89; and for those who argued that the *corporazioni* should substitute the party, pp. 220–21). On the conflicts between state and party, specifically the prefects and provincial party leaders, see pp. 262–63.

55. Significantly, Trotsky (1937, pp. 278–79), in attempting to describe and analyze Stalinism also uses the term Bonapartism in this text. We cannot resist quoting since it also reflects his view of the symmetry of Stalinism and Fascism "in spite of deep differences in social foundations."

> Bonapartism is one of the political weapons of the capitalist regime in its critical period. Stalinism is a variety of the same system, but upon the basis of a workers' state torn by the antagonism between an organized and armed soviet aristocracy and the unarmed toiling masses. . . .
>
> In the last analysis, Soviet Bonapartism owes its birth to the belatedness of the world revolution. But in the capitalist countries the same cause gave rise to fascism. We thus arrive at the conclusion, unexpected at first glance, but in reality inevitable, that the crushing of Soviet democracy by an all-powerful bureaucracy and the extermination of bourgeois democracy by fascism were produced by one and the same cause: the dilatoriness of the world proletariat in solving the problems set for it by history. Stalinism and fascism, in spite of a deep difference in social foundations, are symmetrical phenomena. In many of their features they show a deadly similarity. A victorious revolutionary movement in Europe would immediately shake not only fascism, but Soviet Bonapartism.

56. The literature on national socialism as an ideology, a movement and a party in power fills libraries. For a bibliography see Herre and Auerbach and supplement edited by Thile Vogelsang *Vierteljahrshefte für Zeitgeschichte* (since 1953). Basic in English is Bracher (1970), with bibliography, pp. 503–33. For annotated critical bibliography, Orlow (1969, 1973). See also Bracher and Jacobsen (1970). Useful reviews are Broszat (1966), Nolte (1963), the anthologies of documents with introductions by Hofer (1957), Remak (1969), and Noakes and Pridham (1974), and for the period 1933–35, Wheaton (1969). Still indispensable is the classic work by Franz Neumann (1963; originally published 1944), *Behemoth*. An interesting overview of German politics, society, and culture under the Nazis is Grunberger (1971). For excellent biographical sketches of the Nazi leadership, Fest (1970). To place Nazism in the context of German society and history see Dahrendorf (1965). An excellent documentary collection is Tyrell (1969). A

most stimulating review of conflicting or complementary interpretations of Nazism is Sauer (1967).

57. In addition to the more sophisticated Marxist analyses of fascism we cannot ignore the partisan interpretations of Aquila, Zetkin, Togliatti, Dutt discussed by Nolte (1967), De Felice (1969, 1970), and Gregor (1974b), the Trotskyite Guerin (1939), and more recent writings of Lopukhov (1965), Galkin (1970), and Vajda (1972), reviewed by Gregor (1974c, pp. 129–70), as well as the responses of the Third International (Fetscher, 1962; Pirker, 1965).

58. The relation of fascism to modernization is a complex issue, object of a recent debate (Turner, 1972; Gregor, 1974c; Turner, forthcoming). See also Organski (1965) and the early essay by Borkenau (1933).

59. The politics of particular countries have been the object of monographic study, although sometimes with little effort of comparison and theoretical conceptualization; see for example on the Ivory Coast, in addition to Zolberg (1969), Potholm (1970, pp. 230–71) for a more critical view, and for a comparison of the PDCI with Tanzania's TANU, Zeller (1969); on Mali, Snyder (1965); on Sierra Leone, Cartwright (1970); on Madagascar, Spacensky (1970); on Guinea under the leadership of Sékou Touré one of the few mobilizational single-party regimes left, see Ameillon (1964), Charles (1962), Voss (1971), and Zolberg (1966). On the authoritarian regime established in Congo (Zaire) by Mobutu after years of turmoil there is an interesting study (using the concept of patrimonialism) by Willame (1972).

60. The Maghreb and the Middle East countries after independence have experimented with military and single-party mobilizational regimes in addition to the survival of semitraditional rulers (like Morocco, see note 39). For an overview see Clement Moore (1970b) and Hurewitz (1969), who distinguishes in the Middle East military republics, military-civilian coalitions, traditional monarchies, modernizing monarchies, and nonmilitary republics. The most stable civilian single-party regime born in the struggle for independence has been Tunisia under the personal leadership of Bourguiba (Clement Moore 1965, 1970a; Camau, 1971; Hermassi, 1972), while Algeria, initially a mobilizational party regime, had from the beginning—due to the prolonged war with the French—a military component, which gained the upper hand when Boumedienne ousted Ben Bella (Quandt, 1969; Duprat, 1973). In Iraq (Vernier, 1963; Dann, 1969) and Syria (for bibliographic references see Hurewitz, 1969, p. 520), where the ideological Baathist party had considerable impact in alliance with the army, the military have attempted, like in Egypt, to create nationalist-socialist-populist mobilizational regimes, but ultimately personal rulership, the military and bureaucratic technocratic elements seem to have become dominant. The fate of the socialist Baath party has not been too different from minor fascist parties in authoritarian regimes. Ethnic and religious heterogeneity contributed to the instability of these regimes.

The politics of Egypt since the military coup against the monarchy, under Naguib, Nasser, and Sadat, has been the object of considerable analysis and debate. Among the main studies, Vatikiotis (1961), Lacouture and Lacouture (1958), Lacouture (1969), Wheelock (1960), Abdel-Malek (1968, first published 1962), Binder (1965), Moore (1970, 1973, 1974), Dekmejian (1971), Kosheri Mahfouz (1972), and Harik (1973) deserve mention. It is a perfect example of the changes "within" a regime approaching changes "of" the regime, from strictly military rule to the complex, shifting, and indecisive attempts to create a mobilizational single party, from a military mentality to efforts to develop an ideology, from popular passivity to efforts to create channels of participation. It shows the range of possibilities of change but also the difficulties of change within the framework of an authoritarian regime established by the army.

61. The case of Nkrumah, who moved from charismatic leadership to personal ruler-ship with the forms of a single-party mobilizational authoritarian regime (that some perceived as totalitarian in ambitions), is an example of how even the period of rule of one person cannot be pigeonholed into a typology but how different conceptualizations can serve the analysis: Wallerstein (1961), Apter (1963), Bretton (1966), Fitch and Oppenheimer (1966).

62. For references to different patterns of colonialism see Potholm (1970), pp. 70–77.

63. A decisive factor in the potential for mobilization, control, and participation of new regimes—and with it for totalitarianism—is the strength of the party conquering power before takeover. Let us not forget that the Italian Fascists in March 1921 already had 80,476 members, in December claimed 218,453, and by May 1922, 322,310 (the March on Rome would be at the end of October) (De Felice, 1966, pp. 10–11), even though those members were mostly north of Rome. The NSDAP in 1930 had 129,563 and on January 30, 1933, on the eve of the Machtergreifung, 719,446 (Schäfer, 1957, p. 17); the Hitler Youth at the end of 1931 had already organized 5.1 percent of those eligible (Orlow, 1969, p. 237). That kind of support can obviously be gained only in an open and relatively modern society, or one undergoing total disintegration, when war and revolution combine, like in Russia, Yugoslavia, China, and Vietnam.

64. In the context of the application to communist systems in Eastern Europe, including the Soviet Union, of the interest-group politics approach, the early and still very fruitful alternatives of "technical-rational traditionalist and ideological revolutionary" models of development offered by Barrington Moore (1954) have unfortunately been somewhat neglected.

65. For two reviews of the literature on convergence see Meyer (1970) and Weinberg (1969). Also, Halm (1969), Linnemann, Pronk, and Tinbergen (1965), Tinbergen (1961), Mills (1958), Sorokin (1964), Wolfe (1968), Black (1970), Aron (1967), and Brzezinski and Huntington (1964, pp. 9–14, 419–36), for a critical discussion of convergence. While far from accepting the convergence theory, the authors point to similarities, functional equivalents, and differences between the U.S. and the USSR in many spheres in a suggestive comparative study.

66. A basic source for comparative study of noncompetitive or semi- or pseudocompetitive elections under authoritarian regimes are the *Election Factbooks* for Latin American countries, published by the Institute for the Comparative Study of Political Systems, and the volumes edited by Sternberger and Vogel (1969–).

67. The empirical and systematic study of the organization, function, and composition of political parties (as reflected in the contribution to this *Handbook*) has tended to center on parties in a democratic competitive context (including antisystem parties) and the parties in power in communist noncompetitive regimes and Nazi Germany but has relatively neglected parties in authoritarian pseudo-multiparty, officially single party, and often de facto nonparty regimes. The International Comparative Political Parties Project covering 50 countries at Northwestern University directed by Kenneth Janda (with its careful coding of data and exhaustive bibliographic guides) is filling that gap (including countries like Guinea, Ecuador, Dominican Republic, Congo-Brazzaville, Greece, Iran, and among the communist countries Bulgaria, Hungary, and North Korea of those in our purview).

68. One objection that can legitimately be made to our analysis is that we have focussed on sovereign states, ignoring the clear and not so clear cases of foreign dependence. Certainly we did not include in our purview colonial rule in all its varieties, from intervention in fiscal affairs of state, protectorate of traditional rulers, to indirect

and direct administration by foreigners. Nor have we paid due attention to rule established by a foreign power by the threat of use of force—like the rest-Czech state under the Nazi *Reichsprotektorat*—or the creation of a regime headed by nationals of the country with the military and political assistance of another country, which even after withdrawing its forces exercises influence or veto of its policies and reserves itself the right to intervene by force to sustain the regime.

The satellite regimes that during WWII became identified with the name of Quisling accurately describe that relationship. Such rule of limited or practically no legitimacy is by definition nondemocratic in origin. Continuity, specific successes, and a growing autonomy might transform it into stable regimes not based only on coercion. The delimitation of international spheres of influence and the ideological affinities and personal links between national parties identified with an international movement, particularly in communist states, have contributed to the stabilization of such regimes. Internal political, social, and economic developments, even when not directly decided by the hegemonic power—as they were obviously by Hitler and Stalin—are deeply affected by changes in policy in the dominant power in the bloc or hegemonic area.

In addition there are more subtle types of linkages that affect the internal political development of many states, especially outside the major powers (Rosenau, 1969).

Intervention in internal crises and regime changes is not new, nor is the support for rebels and secessionist independence movements. Since the French Revolution, Napoleon, and the Holy Alliance, outside support on grounds of ideological affinity—not always easy to separate from power politics—has been normal. International parties made their appearance with the revolutionary movements—anarchism and socialism. Later, the ideological affinities created more or less tight relations between parties, from the Comintern and Cominform to the Christian Equipes Internationales and nowadays between nationalist terrorists. At each historical moment one or another successful regime kindles the admiration and desire of imitation by people in many countries, and without such an external reference internal political developments can not be understood. International and internation organizations have attempted to influence the development of regimes by mediation, nonrecognition, exclusion, political economic boycott, peace-keeping forces, etc., with varying degrees of success. Other nations, international movements, or organizations under their influence are therefore factors in the establishment of totalitarian, authoritarian, and on rare occasions democratic regimes, which we cannot ignore (even when we cannot discuss them here).

69. De facto, however, the process often leads to a more personal rule of the leader or the executive, who appoints, intervenes, or controls all institutions, preventing independent leadership and real institutional autonomy, but is without resources (given the deliberation of the single party) for mobilization of support and dynamic social change. These processes have been well described by Aquarone (1965).

REFERENCES

Abboushi, W. F. (1970). *Political Systems of the Middle East in the 20th Century.* New York: Dodd, Mead.

Abdel-Malek, Anouar (1968). *Egypt: Military Society. The Army Regime, the Left, and Social Change under Nasser.* New York: Random House (Vintage).

Abendroth, Wolfgang (1969). *Faschismus und Kapitalismus: Theorien über die sozialen Ursprünge und die Funktion des Faschismus.* Frankfurt: Europäische Verlagsanstalt.

Abraha, Gedamu (1967). "Wax and gold." *Ethiopian Observer* (Addis Ababa) 11:226–43.

Adam, Heribert (1971). *Modernizing Racial Domination: The Dynamics of South African Politics.* Berkeley: University of California Press.

Adorno, Theodor W., Else Frenkel-Brunswick, Daniel J. Levinson, and R. Nevitt Sanford (1964). *The Authoritarian Personality,* 2 vols. New York: Wiley.

Allen, Richard V., ed. (1968, 1969). *Yearbook on International Communist Affairs.* Stanford: Hoover Institution Press.

Allen, William Sheridan (1965). *The Nazi Seizure of Power: The Experience of a Single German Town 1930–1935.* Chicago: Quadrangle Books.

Almond, Gabriel, and James S. Coleman, eds. (1960). *The Politics of the Developing Areas.* Princeton: Princeton University Press.

Almond, Gabriel, and G. Bingham Powell (1966). *Comparative Politics: A Developmental Approach.* Boston: Little, Brown.

Ameillon, B. (1964). *La Guinée: Bilan d'une Independence.* Paris: Maspero.

Anderson, Charles W. (1967). *Politics and Economic Change in Latin America: The Governing of Restless Nations.* New York: Van Nostrand Reinhold.

—————— (1970a). "Nicaragua: The Somoza Dynasty." In Martin Needler (ed.), *Political Systems of Latin America.* New York: Van Nostrand Reinhold.

—————— (1970b). *The Political Economy of Modern Spain.* Madison: University of Wisconsin Press.

Andreski, Stanislav (1968). *Military Organization and Society.* Berkeley: University of California Press.

The Anti-Stalin Campaign and International Communism (1956). New York: Columbia University Press.

Apter, David E. (1963). *Ghana in Transition.* New York: Atheneum.

—————— (1965). *The Politics of Modernization.* Chicago: University of Chicago Press.

Aquarone, Alberto (1965). *L'organizzazione dello Stato totalitario.* Torino: Einaudi. Quoted by permission.

Arendt, Hannah (1963). *Eichmann in Jerusalem: a Report on the Banality of Evil.* New York: Viking Press.

—————— (1966). *The Origins of Totalitarianism.* New York: Harcourt, Brace & World.

Armstrong, John A. (1967). *The Soviet Bureaucratic Elite: A Case Study of the Ukrainian Apparatus.* New York: Praeger.

Aron, Raymond (1967). *The Industrial Society: Three Essays on Ideology and Development.* New York: Praeger.

—————— (1968). *Democracy and Totalitarianism.* London: Weidenfeld and Nicolson.

Ashford, Douglas E. (1961). *Political Change in Morocco*. Princeton: Princeton University Press.

_____ (1965a). *The Elusiveness of Power: The African Single Party State*. Ithaca, N.Y.: Center for International Studies, Cornell University.

_____ (1965b). *Morocco-Tunisia: Politics and Planning*. New York: Syracuse University Press.

_____ (1967). *National Development and Local Reform: Political Participation in Morocco, Tunisia and Pakistan*. Princeton: Princeton University Press.

Azpiazu, Joaquín (1951). *El Estado Corporativo*. Madrid: Fomento Social.

Azrael, Jeremy R. (1966). *Managerial Power and Soviet Politics*. Cambridge, Mass.: Harvard University Press.

_____ (1970a). "Varieties of de-Stalinization." In Chalmers Johnson (ed.), *Change in Communist Systems*. Stanford: Stanford University Press.

_____ (1970b). "The internal dynamics of the CPSU, 1917–1967." In S. Huntington and C. Moore (eds.), *Authoritarian Politics in Modern Society*. New York: Basic Books.

Bachrach, Peter (1967). *The Theory of Democratic Elitism: A Critique*. Boston: Little, Brown.

Baier, Helmut (1968). *Die Deutschen Christian Bayerns im Rahmen des bayerischen Kirchenfampfes*. Nurenberg: Verein für bayerische Kirchengeschichte.

Banks, Arthur S., and Robert B. Textor (1963). *A Cross-Polity Survey*. Cambridge, Mass.: M.I.T. Press.

Banks, Arthur S., and Phillip M. Gregg (1965). "Grouping political systems: Q-factor analysis of *A Cross-Polity Survey*." *American Behavioral Scientist* 9:3–6.

Barber, Benjamin (1969). "Conceptual foundations of totalitarianism." In Carl J. Friedrich, M. Curtis, and B. Barber (eds.), *Totalitarianism in Perspective: Three Views*. New York: Praeger.

Barghoorn, Frederick C. (1971). "The security police." In H. Gordon Skilling and F. Griffiths (eds.), *Interest Groups in Soviet Politics*. Princeton: Princeton University Press.

_____ (1972). *Politics in the USSR*. Boston: Little, Brown.

_____ (1973). "Factional, sectoral, and subversive opposition in Soviet politics." In Robert A. Dahl (ed.), *Regimes and Oppositions*. New Haven: Yale University Press.

Barnett, A. Doak, ed. (1969). *Chinese Communist Politics in Action*. Seattle: University of Washington Press.

Bärnthaler, Irmgard (1971). *Die Vaterländische Front: Geschichte und Organisation*. Vienna: Europa Verlag.

Barton, Allen H., Bogdan Denitch, and Charles Kadushin, eds. (1973). *Opinion-Making Elites in Yugoslavia*. New York: Praeger.

Bauer, Raymond A., Alex Inkeles, and Clyde Kluckholn (1956). *How the Soviet System Works*. Cambridge, Mass.: Harvard University Press.

Bauer, Otto, Herbert Marcuse, Arthur Rosenberg *et al.* (1968). *Faschismus und Kapitalismus*. Frankfurt: Europäische Verlag.

Baum, Richard, ed. (1971). *China in Ferment: Perspectives on the Cultural Revolution*. Englewood Cliffs, N.J.: Prentice-Hall.

Baylis, Thomas A. (1974). *The Technical Intelligentsia and the East German Elite: Legitimacy and Social Change in Mature Communism*. Berkeley: University of California Press.

Beck, Carl (1970). "Career characteristics of Eastern European leadership." In R. Barry Farrell (ed.), *Political Leadership in Eastern Europe and the Soviet Union*. Chicago: Aldine.

Beck, F., and W. Godin [pseuds.] (1951). *Russian Purge and the Extraction of Confession*. New York: Viking.

Behrman, Lucy C. (1970). *Muslim Brotherhoods and Politics in Senegal*. Cambridge, Mass.: Harvard University Press.

Bell, Daniel (1961). "Ten theories in search of Soviet reality." In Alex Inkeles and Kent Geiger (eds.), *Soviet Society: A Book of Readings*. Boston: Houghton Mifflin.

Bendix, Reinhard (1960). *Max Weber: An Intellectual Portrait*. Garden City, N.Y.: Doubleday.

——————, ed. (1968). *State and Society: A Reader in Comparative Political Sociology*. Boston: Little, Brown.

Berdyaev, Nicholas (1948). *The Origin of Russian Communism*. London: Geoffrey Bles.

Berghahn, Volker R. (1969). "NSDAP und 'Geistige Führung' der Wehrmacht 1939–1943." *Vierteljahrshefte für Zeitgeschichte* 7:17–71.

Berman, Harold J. (1963). *Justice in the USSR*. New York: Random House (Vintage).

—————— (1972). *Soviet Criminal Law and Procedure: the RSFSR Codes*. Cambridge, Mass.: Harvard University Press.

Berman, Harold J., and James W. Spindler (1972). *Soviet Criminal Law and Procedure: The RSFSR Codes*. Cambridge, Mass.: Harvard University Press.

Berning, Cornelia (1964). *Vom "Abstammungsnachweis" zum "Zuchtwart": Vokabular des Nationalsozialismus*. Berlin: de Gruyter.

Berton, Peter, and Eugene Wu (1967). *Contemporary China: A Research Guide*. Stanford: Hoover Institution on War, Revolution and Peace, Stanford University.

Bettelheim, Bruno, and Morris Janowitz (1950). *Dynamics of Prejudice*. New York: Harper.

Beyme, Klaus von (1971). *Vom Faschismus zur Entwicklungsdiktatur: Machtelite und Opposition in Spanien*. Munich: R. Piper.

Bienen, Henry (1970). *Tanzania*. Princeton: Princeton University Press.

—————— (1974). "Military and society in East Africa: thinking again about praetorianism." *Comparative Politics* 6:489–517.

——————, ed. (1968). *The Military Intervenes: Case Studies in Political Development*. New York: Russell Sage Foundation.

Binder, Leonard (1962). *Iran: Political Development in a Changing Society*. Berkeley: University of California Press.

——————— (1964). *The Ideological Revolution in the Middle East*. New York: Wiley.

——————— (1965). "Egypt: the integrative revolution." In L. W. Pye and S. Verba (eds.), *Political Culture and Political Development*. Princeton: Princeton University Press.

Black, Cyril (1970). "Marx and modernization." *Slavic Review* 29:182–86.

———————, ed. (1967). *The Transformation of Russian Society: Aspects of Social Change since 1861*. Cambridge, Mass.: Harvard University Press.

Black, Cyril E., and Thomas P. Thornton, eds. (1964). *Communism and Revolution: The Strategic Uses of Political Violence*. Princeton: Princeton University Press.

Blackmer, Donald L. M. (1968). *Unity in Diversity: Italian Communism and the Communist World*. Cambridge, Mass.: M.I.T. Press.

Blackmer, Donald L. M., and Sidney Tarrow, eds. (forthcoming). *Communism in Italy and France*. Princeton: Princeton University Press.

Bloch, Charles (1970). *Die SA und die Krise des NS-Regimes 1934*. Frankfurt am Main: Suhrkamp Verlag.

Blondel, Jean (1972). *Comparing Political Systems*. New York: Praeger.

Boberach, Heinz, ed. (1965). *Meldungen aus dem Reich: Auswahl aus den geheimen Lageberichten des Sicherheitsdienstes der SS 1939–1944*. Neuwied: Luchterhand.

Borkenau, Franz (1933). "Zur Soziologie des Faschismus." In Ernst Nolte (ed.), *Theorien über den Faschismus*. Cologne: Kiepenheuer & Witsch.

Bourdeaux, Michael (1968). *Religious Ferment in Russia: Protestant Opposition to Soviet Religious Policy*. New York: St. Martin's Press.

——————— (1969). *Patriarch and Prophets: Persecution of the Russian Orthodox Church Today*. London: Macmillan.

Bourricaud, François (1967). *Pouvoir et société dans le Pérou contemporain*. Paris: Colin.

Bowen, Ralph H. (1947). *German Theories of the Corporate State*. New York: Russell & Russell.

Bracher, Karl Dietrich (1957). *Die Auflösung der Weimarer Republik: Eine Studie zum Problem des Machverfalls in der Demokratie*. Stuttgart: Ring.

——————— (1970). *The German Dictatorship*. New York: Praeger.

Bracher, Karl Dietrich, and Hans-Adolf Jacobsen, eds. (1970). *Bibliographie zur Politik in Theorie und Praxis*. Düsseldorf: Droste Verlag.

Bracher, Karl Dietrich, Wolfgang Sauer, and Gerhard Schulz (1960). *Die nationalsozialistische Machtergreifung: Studien zur Errichtung des totalitären Herrschaftssystems in Deutschland 1933/34*. Cologne: Westdeutscher Verlag.

Bradenburg, Frank R. (1964). *The Making of Modern Mexico*. Englewood Cliffs: Prentice-Hall.

Brandenburg, Hans-Christian (1968). *HJ-Die Geschichte der HJ*. Cologne: Wissenschaft u. Politik.

Brenner, Hildegard (1963). *Die Kunstpolitik des Nationalsozialismus.* Reinbek bei Hamburg: Rowohlt.

Bretton, Henry L. (1966). *The Rise and Fall of Kwame Nkrumah: A Study of Personal Rule in Africa.* New York: Praeger.

_____ (1971). *Patron-Client Relations: Middle Africa and the Powers.* New York: General Learning Press.

_____ (1973). *Power and Politics in Africa.* Chicago: Aldine.

Broszat, Martin (1966). *German National Socialism, 1919–1945.* Santa Barbara: Clio Press.

Brown, J. F. (1966). *The New Eastern Europe: The Khrushchev Era and After.* New York: Praeger.

Brzezinski, Zbigniew (1956). *The Permanent Purge.* Cambridge, Mass.: Harvard University Press.

_____ (1960). *The Soviet Bloc.* Cambridge, Mass.: Harvard University Press. Enlarged and revised paperback edition, 1971.

_____ (1962). *Ideology and Power in Soviet Politics.* New York: Praeger.

_____ (1971). *The Soviet Bloc: Unity and Conflict.* Cambridge, Mass.: Harvard University Press.

Brzezinski, Zbigniew, and Samuel P. Huntington (1964). *Political Power: USA/USSR.* New York: Viking Press.

Buchheim, Hans (1953). *Glaubenskrise im Dritten Reich: Drei Kapitel Nationalsozialistischer Religionspolitik.* Stuttgart: Deutsche Verlags-Anstalt.

_____ (1958). "Mitgliedschaft bei der NSDAP." In Paul Kluke (ed.), *Gutachten des Instituts für Zeitgeschichte.* Munich: Institut für Zeitgeschichte.

_____ (1968a). *Totalitarian Rule: Its Nature and Characteristics.* Middletown, Conn.: Wesleyan University Press.

_____ (1968b). "Command and compliance." In Helmut Krausnik, Hans Buchheim, Martin Broszat, and Hans-Adolf Jacobsen (eds.), *Anatomy of the SS State.* New York: Walker.

Bullock, Alan (1964). *Hitler: A Study in Tyranny.* New York: Harper & Row.

Bundesministerium für Gesamtdeutsche Fragen (1963). *Die Wahlen in der Sowjetzone: Dokumente und Materialien.* Bonn: Deutscher Bundes-Verlag.

Burke, Melvin, and James Malloy (1972). "Del Populismo Nacional al Corporativismo Nacional: El caso de Bolivia 1952–1970." *Aportes* 26:66–97.

Burks, R. V. (1961). *The Dynamics of Communism in Eastern Europe.* Princeton: Princeton University Press.

Burks, R. V., and S. A. Stanković (1967). "Jugoslawien auf dem Weg zu halbfreien Wahlen?" *Osteuropa* 17:131–46.

Burrowes, Robert (1969). "Totalitarianism: the revised standard version." *World Politics* 21:272–94.

Bush, Richard C., Jr. (1970). *Religion in Communist China.* Nashville: Abingdon Press.

Busshoff, Heinrich (1968). *Das Dollfuss-Regime in Osterreich in geistesgeschichtlicher Perspektive unter besonderer Berücksichtigung der "Schöneren Zukinft" und "Reichs-post."* Berlin: Duncker & Humblot.

Butler, Rohan (1941). *The Roots of National Socialism 1783–1933.* London: Faber and Faber.

Camau, Michel (1971). *La notion de démocratie dans la pensée des dirigeants maghré-bins.* Paris: CNRS.

Cardoso, Fernando Henrique (1973). "As contradiçoes do Desenvolvimento-associado." Paper presented at the International Meeting on Sociology of Development: Dependency and Power Structure, Berlin, 1973.

Carr, Raymond, ed. (1971). *The Republic and the Civil War in Spain.* London: Macmillan.

Carsten, Francis L. (1967). *The Rise of Fascism.* Berkeley: University of California Press.

Carter, Gwendolen M., ed. (1962). *African One-Party States.* Ithaca: Cornell University Press.

Cartwright, John R. (1970). *Politics in Sierra Leone 1947–67.* Toronto: University of Toronto Press.

Chapman, Brian (1970). *Police State.* London: Pall Mall.

Charles, Bernard (1962). "Un parti politique africain: le Parti Démocratique de Guinée." *Revue Française de Science Politique* 12:312–59.

Chen, S. H. (1967). "Artificial 'flowers' during a natural 'thaw.'" In Donald W. Treadgold (ed.), *Soviet and Chinese Communism: Similarities and Differences.* Seattle: University of Washington Press.

Chen, Theodore H. E., ed. (1967). *The Chinese Communist Regime: Documents and Commentary.* New York: Praeger.

Clausewitz, Karl von (1911). *On War,* 3 vols. (Originally published 1832). London: Kegan Paul, Trench, Trübner & Co.

Cliffe, Lionel, ed. (1967). *One-Party Democracy.* Nairobi: East African Publishing House.

Clogg, Richard, and George Yannopoulos, eds. (1972). *Greece under Military Rule.* New York: Basic Books.

Cocks, Paul (1970). "The rationalization of party control." In Chalmers Johnson (ed.), *Change in Communist Systems.* Stanford: Stanford University Press.

Cohen, Lenard (1973). "The social background and recruitment of Yugoslav political elites, 1918–1948." In Allen H. Barton, Bogdan Denitch, and Charles Kadushin (eds.), *Opinion-Making Elites in Yugoslavia.* New York: Praeger.

Cohen, Ronald, and John Middleton, eds. (1957). *Comparative Political Systems: Studies in the Politics of Pre-industrial Societies.* New York: Natural History Press.

Cohn, Norman (1966). *Warrant for Genocide.* New York: Harper & Row.

Coleman, James S., and Carl G. Rosberg, Jr., eds. (1964). *Political Parties and National Integration in Tropical Africa.* Berkeley: University of California Press.

Conde, Francisco Javier (1942). *Introducción al Derecho Político actual.* Madrid: Escorial.

Conquest, Robert (1960). *The Soviet Deportation of Nationalities.* New York: St. Martin's Press.

———————— (1968). *The Great Terror: Stalin's Purge of the Thirties.* New York: Macmillan.

Conrad-Martius, Hedwig (1955). *Utopien der Menschenzüchtung: der Sozialdarwinismus und seine Fölge.* Munich: Kösel-Verlag.

Conway, John S. (1968). *The Nazi Persecution of the Churches, 1933–1945.* New York: Basic Books.

Conze, Werner, and Hans Raupach, eds. (1967). *Die Staats- und Wirtschaftskriese des Deutschen Reiches 1929/33.* Stuttgart: E. Klett.

Cornell, Richard (1970). *The Soviet Political System: A Book of Readings.* Englewood Cliffs, N.J.: Prentice-Hall.

Cosío Villegas, Daniel (1972). *El sistema político mexicano: las posibilidades de cambio.* Mexico city: Editorial Joaquín Mortiz.

Cotler, Julio (1972). "Bases del Corporativismo en el Perú." *Sociedad y Política* 1:3–11.

Coverdale, John F. (forthcoming). *Mussolini and Franco: Italian Intervention in the Spanish Civil War.* Princeton: Princeton University Press.

Craig, A. M. (1961). *Cho-Shu in the Meiji Restoration.* Cambridge, Mass.: Harvard University Press.

Crassweller, Robert D. (1966). *Trujillo: The Life and Times of a Caribbean Dictator.* New York: Macmillan.

Croan, Melvin (1970). "Is Mexico the future of East Europe: institutional adaptability and political change in comparative perspective." In S. Huntington and C. Moore (eds.), *Authoritarian Politics in Modern Society.* New York: Basic Books.

Curtis, John S. (1960). "Church and state." In Cyril E. Black (ed.), *The Transformation of Russian Society.* Cambridge, Mass.: Harvard University Press.

Curtis, Michael (1969). "Retreat from totalitarianism." In Carl J. Friedrich, M. Curtis, and Benjamin Barber (eds.), *Totalitarianism in Perspective: Three Views.* New York: Praeger.

Daalder, Hans (1974). "The consociational democracy theme: a review article." *World Politics* 26:604–21.

Daedalus (Winter, 1973). "Post-traditional societies." Essays by several authors.

Dahl, Robert A. (1971). *Polyarchy: Participation and Opposition.* New Haven: Yale University Press.

Dahrendorf, Ralf (1967). *Society and Democracy in Germany.* Garden City, N.Y.: Doubleday.

Dallin, Alexander, and George W. Breslauer (1970). *Political Terror in Communist Systems*. Stanford: Stanford University Press.

Dallin, David J., and Boris I. Nicolaevsky (1947). *Forced Labor in Soviet Russia*. New Haven: Yale University Press.

Daniels, Robert Vincent (1969). *The Conscience of the Revolution: Communist Opposition in Soviet Russia*. New York: Simon & Schuster.

Dann, Uriel (1969). *Iraq under Quassem: a Political History 1958–1963*. New York: Praeger.

Deakin, F. W. (1966). *The Brutal Friendship: Mussolini, Hitler and the Fall of Italian Fascism*. Garden City, N. Y.: Doubleday.

De Felice, Renzo (1965). *Mussolini il rivoluzionario: 1883–1920*. Torino: Einaudi.

_____ (1966a). *Mussolini il fascista. I: La conquista del potere. 1921–1925*. Torino: Einaudi.

_____ (1968). *Mussolini il fascista. II: L'organizzazione dello Stato fascista. 1925–1929*. Torino: Einaudi.

_____ (1969). *Le Interpretazioni del Fascismo*. Bari: Laterza.

_____ (1970). *Il Fascismo: Le Interpretazioni dei contemporanei e degli storici*. Bari: Laterza.

_____, ed. (1966b). *Il Fascismo e I Partiti politici Italiani: Testimonianze del 1921–1923*. Rocca San Casciano: Cappelli.

Dekmejian, R. Hrair (1971). *Egypt under Nasir: A Study in Political Dynamics*. Albany: State University of New York Press.

Delzell, Charles F., ed. (1970). *Mediterranean Fascism 1919–1945*. New York: Harper & Row.

Diamant, Alfred (1960). *Austrian Catholics and the First Republic: Democracy, Capitalism, and the Social Order, 1918–1934*. Princeton: Princeton University Press.

Díaz, Elías (1974). *Pensamiento español 1939–73*. Madrid: Edicusa.

Dicks, Henry V. (1972). *Licensed Mass Murder: A Socio-Psychological Study of Some SS Killers*. New York: Basic Books.

Diederich, Bernard, and Al Burt (1969). *Papa Doc: The Truth about Haiti Today*. New York: McGraw-Hill.

Domínguez, Jorge I. (1974). "The civic soldier in Cuba." In Catherine McArdle (ed.), *Political-Military Systems: Comparative Perspectives*. Beverly Hills: Sage.

Döring, Hans Joachim (1964). *Die Zigeuner im Nationalsozialistischen Staat*. Hamburg: Kriminalistik Verlag.

Drachkovitch, Milorad M., ed. (1965). *Marxism in the Modern World*. Stanford: Stanford University Press.

Draper, Theodore (1965). *Castroism: Theory and Practice*. New York: Praeger.

Dumont, René (1970). *Cuba est-il socialiste?* Paris: Editions du Seuil.

Duprat, Gérard (1973). *Révolution et autogestion rurale in Algérie*. Paris: A. Colin.

Durkheim, Emile (1902). *De la division du travail social: Etude sur l'organisation des sociétés supérieures.* 2nd ed., with a new preface: "Quelques remarques sur les groupements professionels." Paris: Alcan.

Duverger, Maurice (1963). *Political Parties.* New York: Wiley.

Eckstein, Harry (1966). *Division and Cohesion in Democracy: A Study of Norway.* Princeton: Princeton University Press.

——————— (1971). *The Evaluation of Political Performance: Problems and Dimensions.* Beverly Hills: Sage.

Eichholtz, Dietrich (1969). *Geschichte der deutschen Kriegwirtschaft: 1939–1945.* (East) Berlin: Akademie Verlag.

Einaudi, Luigi R. (1969). *The Peruvian Military: A Summary Political Analysis.* Rand Memorandum RM-6048-RC. Santa Monica: The Rand Corporation.

Einaudi, Luigi, and Alfred Stepan (1971). *Latin American Institutional Development: Changing Military Perspectives in Peru and Brazil.* Santa Monica: The Rand Corporation.

Eisenstadt, S. N. (1958). "The study of Oriental despotisms as systems of total power." *The Journal of Asian Studies* 17:435–46.

——————— (1959). "Primitive political systems: a preliminary comparative analysis." *American Anthropologist* 61:205–20.

——————— (1962). *The Political Systems of Empires.* New York: Free Press of Glencoe.

——————— (1967). *Israeli Society.* New York: Basic Books.

———————, ed. (1971). *Political Sociology: A Reader.* New York: Basic Books.

Elbow, Matthew H. (1953). *French Corporative Theory, 1789–1948.* New York: Columbia University Press.

Eschenburg, Theodor, et al. (1966). *The Path to Dictatorship 1918–1933: Ten Essays by German Scholars.* Garden City, N.Y.: Doubleday (Anchor).

Esteban, Jorge de, et al. (1973). *Desarrollo político y Constitución española.* Esplugues de Llobregat, Barcelona: Ariel.

Evans-Pritchard, E. E. (1940). *The Political System of the Annuak of the Anglo Egyptian Sudan.* London: London School of Economics.

——————— (1948). *The Divine Kingship of the Shilluk of the Nilotic Sudan.* Cambridge: Cambridge University Press.

Evers, Tilman Tönnies (1972). *Militärregierung in Argentinien.* Frankfurt am Main: A. Metzner Verlag.

Fagen, Richard R. (1965). "Charismatic authority and the leadership of Fidel Castro." *Western Political Quarterly* 18:275–84.

——————— (1969). *The Transformation of Political Culture in Cuba.* Stanford: Stanford University Press.

Fagen, Richard R., Richard A. Brody, and Thomas J. O'Leary (1968). *Cubans in Exile: Disaffection and the Revolution.* Stanford: Stanford University Press.

Fagen, Richard R., and William S. Tuohy (1972). *Politics and Privilege in a Mexican City*. Stanford: Stanford University Press.

Fainsod, Merle (1963). *Smolensk under Soviet Rule*. New York: Random House (Vintage).

Fallers, Lloyd A. (1965). *Bantu Bureaucracy: A Century of Political Evolution among the Basoga of Uganda*. Chicago: University of Chicago Press.

Farrell, R. Barry (1970a). "Top political leadership in Eastern Europe." In R. Barry Farrell (ed.), *Political Leadership in Eastern Europe and the Soviet Union*. Chicago: Aldine.

_____, ed. (1970b). *Political Leadership in Eastern Europe and the Soviet Union*. Chicago: Aldine.

Faye, Jean Pierre (1972). *Langages totalitaires*. Paris: Hermann.

Fein, Leonard J. (1967). *Politics in Israel*. Boston: Little, Brown.

Feit, Edward (1973). *The Armed Bureaucrats: Military-Administrative Regimes and Political Development*. Boston: Houghton Mifflin.

Feith, Herbert (1962). *The Decline of Constitutional Democracy in Indonesia*. Ithaca: Cornell University Press.

Fernández-Carvajal, Rodrigo (1969). *La Constitución Española*. Madrid: Editora Nacional.

Fest, Joachim C. (1970). *The Face of the Third Reich: Portraits of the Nazi Leadership*. New York: Pantheon Books.

Fetscher, Iring (1962). "Faschismus und Nationalsozialismus: Zur Kritik des sowjetmarxistischen Faschismusbegriffs." *Politische Vierteljahresschrift* 3:42–63.

Finer, Herman (1935). *Mussolini's Italy*. New York: Holt.

Finer, S. E. (1962). *The Man on Horseback: The Role of the Military in Politics*. New York: Praeger.

_____ (1971). *Comparative Government*. New York: Basic Books.

Fischer, George (1968). *The Soviet System and Modern Society*. New York: Atherton Press.

Fischer, Sydney Nettleton, ed. (1963). *The Military in the Middle East*. Columbus: Ohio State University Press.

Fishman, Joshua A. (1968). "Some contrast between linguistically homogeneous and linguistically heterogeneous polities." In Joshua A. Fishman, Charles A. Fergurson, and Jyatirindra das Gupta (eds.), *Language Problems of Developing Nations*. New York: Wiley.

Fitch, John S., III (1973). "Toward a model of the coup d'etat as a political process in Latin America: Ecuador 1948–1966." Ph.D. dissertation in political science, Yale University.

Fitch, Bob, and Mary Oppenheimer (1966). "Ghana: end of an illusion." *Monthly Review*. 18:1–130.

Fleischman, V. (1971). *Aspekte der Sozialen und Politischen Entwicklung Haitis.* Stuttgart: Klett.

Fleron, Frederic (1970). "Representation of career types in Soviet political leadership." In R. Barry Farrell (ed.), *Political Leadership in Eastern Europe and the Soviet Union.* Chicago: Aldine.

——————, ed. (1969). *Communist Studies and the Social Sciences: Essays on Methodology and Empirical Theory.* Chicago: Rand McNally.

Foltz, William J. (1965). *From French West Africa to the Mali Federation.* New Haven: Yale University Press.

Fortes, M., and E. E. Evans-Pritchard, eds. (1940). *African Political Systems.* London: Oxford University Press.

Fraenkel, Ernst (1941). *The Dual State: A Contribution to the Theory of Dictatorship.* New York: Oxford University Press.

Fraga Iribarne, Manuel (1959). *El reglamento de las Cortes Españolas.* Madrid: S.I.P.S.

Friedland, William H., and Carl G. Rosberg, Jr., eds. (1964). *African Socialism.* Stanford: Stanford University Press.

Friedrich, Carl J. (1969). "The evolving theory and practice of totalitarian regimes." In C. Friedrich, Michael Curtis, and Benjamin R. Barber (eds.), *Totalitarianism in Perspective: Three Views.* New York: Praeger.

——————, ed. (1954). *Totalitarianism: Proceedings of a Conference held at the American Academy of Arts and Sciences, March 1953.* Cambridge, Mass.: Harvard University Press.

Friedrich, Carl J., and Zbigniew K. Brzezinski (1965). *Totalitarian Dictatorship and Autocracy.* New York: Praeger.

Fromm, Erich (1941). *Escape from Freedom.* New York: Rinehart.

Galíndez, Jesús de (1973). *The Era of Trujillo Dominican Dictator.* Tucson: University of Arizona Press.

Galkin, Alexander (1970). "Capitalist society and fascism." *Social Sciences* (Published by the USSR Academy of Sciences) 1:128–38.

Gamm, Hans-Jochen (1962). *Der braune Kult. Das Dritte Reich und seine Ersatzreligion: Ein Beitrag zur politischen Bildung.* Hamburg: Rütten & Loening.

Geertz, Clifford (1968). *Islam Observed: Religious Development in Morocco and Indonesia.* New Haven: Yale University Press.

Geiger, Theodor (1932). *Die soziale Schichtung des deutschen Volkes.* Stuttgart: F. Enke.

Gellner, Ernest, and Charles Micaud, eds. (1972). *Arabs and Berbers: From Tribe to Nation in North Africa.* Lexington: D. C. Heath.

Germani, Gino (1965). *Política y sociedad en una época de transición.* Buenos Aires: Paidos.

—————— (1973). "El surgimiento del peronismo: el rol de los obreros y de los migrantes internos." *Desarrollo Económico* 13:435–88.

Germani, Gino, and Kalman Silvert (1961). "Politics, social structure and military intervention in Latin America." *Archives Européennes de Sociologie* 2:62–81.

Germino, Dante L. (1959). *The Italian Fascist Party in Power*. Minneapolis: University of Minnesota Press.

Gibson, Richard (1972). *African Liberation Movements: Contemporary Struggles against White Minority Rule*. London: Oxford University Press.

Gilison, Jerome M. (1970). "Elections, dissent, and political legitimacy." In Richard Cornell (ed.), *The Soviet Political System: A Book of Readings*. Englewood Cliffs, N.J.: Prentice-Hall.

Gilmore, Robert (1964). *Caudillism and Militarism in Venezuela 1810–1910*. Athens, Ohio: Ohio University Press.

Gimbel, John H. (1968). *The American Occupation of Germany: Politics and the Military, 1945–1949*. Stanford: Stanford University Press.

Gitelman, Zvi Y. (1970). "Power and authority in Eastern Europe." In Chalmers Johnson (ed.), *Change in Communist Systems*. Stanford: Stanford University Press.

Gittings, John (1967). *The Role of the Chinese Army*. London: Oxford University Press.

Gliksman, Jerzy G. (1954). "Social prophylaxis as a form of Soviet terror." In Carl J. Friedrich (ed.), *Totalitarianism*. Cambridge, Mass.: Harvard University Press.

Gluckman, Max (1965a). *Politics, Law and Religion in Tribal Society*. Chicago: Aldine.

_____ (1965b). *The Ideas of Barotse Jurisprudence*. New Haven: Yale University Press.

González Casanova, Pablo (1970). *Democracy in Mexico*. New York: Oxford University Press.

Gordon, Harold J., Jr. (1972). *Hitler and the Beer Hall Putsch*. Princeton: Princeton University Press.

Görgen, Hans-Peter (1968). "Düsseldorf und der Nationalsozialismus." Dissertation, Cologne University.

Greene, Nathanael, ed. (1968). *Fascism: An Anthology*. New York: Crowell.

Gregor, A. James (1968). *Contemporary Radical Ideologies*. New York: Random House.

_____ (1969). *The Ideology of Fascism: The Rationale of Totalitarianism*. New York: Free Press.

_____ (1974a). *The Fascist Persuasion in Radical Politics*. Princeton: Princeton University Press.

_____ (1974b). *Interpretations of Fascism*. Morristown, N.J.: General Learning Press.

_____ (1974c). "Fascism and modernization: some addenda." *World Politics* 26: 370–84.

Gripp, Richard C. (1973). *The Political System of Communism*. New York: Dodd, Mead.

Groth, Alexander J. (1964). "The 'isms' in totalitarianism." *The American Political Science Review* 58:888–901.

Grunberger, Richard (1971). *The 12-Year Reich: A Social History of Nazi Germany 1933–1945*. New York: Holt, Rinehart and Winston.

Gueyt, Rémi (1969). *La mutation tchécoslovaque*. Paris: Editions Ouvrières.

Gulijew, W. E. (1972). *Demokratie und Imperialismus*. East Berlin: Staats-Verlag der Deutschen Demokratischen Republik.

Gutteridge, William F. (1965). *Military Institutions and Power in the New States*. New York: Praeger.

Hale, Oron J. (1964). *The Captive Press in the Third Reich*. Princeton: Princeton University Press.

Halm, George N. (1969). "Will market economies and planned economies converge?" In Erich Streissler (ed.). *Roads to Freedom: Essays in Honor of Friedrich A. von Hayek*. London: Routledge & Kegan Paul.

Halperin, Maurice (1972). *The Rise and Decline of Fidel Castro: An Essay in Contemporary History*. Berkeley: University of California Press.

Halpern, Manfred (1963). *The Politics of Social Change in the Middle East and North Africa*. Princeton: Princeton University Press.

Hamilton, Alastair (1971). *The Appeal of Fascism*. New York: Avon.

——————— (1973). *The Appeal of Fascism: A Study of Intellectuals and Fascism 1919–1945*. New York: Avon.

Hammond, Thomas T. (1955). "Yugoslav elections: democracy in small doses." *Political Science Quarterly* 70:57–74.

Hamon, Léo, and Albert Mabileau (1964). *La personnalisation du pouvoir*. Paris: Presses Universitaires de France.

Harasymiw, Bohdan (1972). "Nomeklatura: the soviet communist party's leadership recruitment system." *Canadian Journal of Political Science* 2:493–512.

Harik, Iliya (1973). "The single party as a subordinate movement: the case of Egypt." *World Politics* 26:80–105.

Hartz, Louis (1964). *The Founding of New Societies: Studies in the History of the United States, Latin America, South Africa, Canada and Australia*. New York: Harcourt, Brace and World.

Hayes, Paul M. (1973). *Fascism*. New York: Free Press.

Hayward, Max, and William C. Fletcher eds. (1969). *Religion and the Soviet State*. New York: Praeger.

Hector, Cary (1964). *Der Staatsstreich als Mittel der politischen Entwicklung in Südamerika: Dargestellt am Beispiel Argentiniens und Boliviens von 1930 bis 1955*. Berlin: Colloquium Verlag.

Heidenheimer, Arnold J., ed. (1970). *Political Corruption: Readings in Comparative Analysis*. New York: Holt, Rinehart and Winston.

Hennig, Eike (1973). *Thesen zur deutschen Sozial und Wirtschaftsgeschichte 1933 bis 1938*. Frankfurt/a.M.: Suhrkamp.

Hermassi, Elbaki (1972). *Leadership and National Development in North Africa: A Comparative Study*. Berkeley: University of California Press.

Hermet, Guy (1973). "Les fonctions politiques des organisations religieuses dans les régimes à pluralisme limité." *Revue Française de Science Politique* 23:439–72.

Herre, Vorher F., and H. Auerbach (1955). *Bibliographie zur Zeitgeschichte und zum Zweiten Weltkrieg für die Jahre 1945–1950*. Munich: Instituts für Zeitgeschichte.

Hess, Robert L. (1970). *Ethiopia: The Modernization of Autocracy*. Ithaca: Cornell University Press.

Hess, Robert L., and Gerhard Loewenberg (1964). "The Ethiopian no-party state: a note on the functions of political parties in developing states." *American Political Science Review* 58:947–50.

Heyen, Franz Josef (1967). *Nationalsozialismus im Alltag*. Boppard am Rhein: Harald Beldt Verlag.

Hildebrand, Klaus (1973). *The Foreign Policy of the Third Reich*. London: B. T. Batsford.

Hilferding, Rudolf (1947a). "The modern totalitarian state." *Modern Review* 1:597–605. (First published under the pseudonym Richard Kern, "Die Weltwirtschaft in Kriegsgefahr," *Neuer Vorwärts* 289: January 1939.)

—————— (1947b). "State capitalism or totalitarian state economy." (Written in 1940.) *Modern Review* 1:266–71.

Hillgruber, Andreas (1971). *Kontinuität und Diskontinuität in der deutschen Aussenpolitik von Bismarch bis Hitler*. Düsseldorf: Droste Verlag.

Hitler, Adolf (1924–26). *Mein Kampf*. Page references are to the 1943 English edition, translated by Ralph Manheim. Boston: Houghton Mifflin.

Hodgkin, Thomas (1961). *African Political Parties: An Introductory Guide*. Harmondsworth, Middlesex: Penguin Books.

Höhne, Heinz (1969). *The Order of the Death's Head: The Story of Hitler's SS*. London: Secker & Warburg.

Hoepke, Klaus-Peter (1968). *Die deutsche Rechte und der italienische Faschismus*. Düsseldorf: Droste Verlag.

Hofer, Walther, ed. (1957). *Der Nationalsozialismus: Dokumente 1933–1945*. Frankfurt am Main: Fischer Bücherei.

Hoffmann, Erik P., and Frederic J. Fleron, Jr., eds. (1971). *The Conduct of Soviet Foreign Policy*. Chicago: Aldine-Atherton.

Hoffman, George W., and Fred W. Neal (1962). *Yugoslavia and the New Communism*. New York: Twentieth Century Fund.

Hollander, Gayle D. (1972). *Soviet Political Indoctrination*. New York: Praeger.

Hollander, Paul (1969). *American and Soviet Society*. Englewood Cliffs, N.J.: Prentice-Hall.

—————— (1973). *Soviet and American Society: A Comparison*. New York: Oxford University Press.

Hopkins, Raymond F. (1971). *Political Roles in a New State: Tanzania's First Decade*. New Haven: Yale University Press.

Horn, Wolfgang (1972). *Führerideologie und Parteiorganisation in der NSDAP (1919–1933)*. Düsseldorf: Droste.

Horowitz, Irving Louis (1967). "The military elites." In S. M. Lipset and A. Solari (eds.), *Elites in Latin America*. New York: Oxford University Press.

——————, ed. (1972). *Cuban Communism*. New Brunswick, N.J.: Transaction Books.

Horvat, Branko (1969). *An Essay on Yugoslav Society*. White Plains, N.Y.: International Arts and Sciences Press.

Hough, Jerry F. (1969). *The Soviet Prefects: The Local Party Organs in Industrial Decision-making*. Cambridge, Mass.: Harvard University Press.

—————— (1971). "The party apparatchiki." In H. Gordon Skilling and Franklyn Griffiths (eds.), *Interest Groups in Soviet Politics*. Princeton: Princeton University Press.

—————— (1974). "The Soviet system: petrification or pluralism?" In Lenard J. Cohen and Jane P. Shapiro (eds.), *Communist Systems in Comparative Perspective*. Garden City, N.Y.: Doubleday (Anchor).

Huberman, Leo, and Paul M. Sweezy (1969). *Cuba: Anatomy of a Revolution*. New York: Monthly Review Press.

Huntington, Samuel P. (1956). "Civilian control of the military: a theoretical statement." In H. Eulau, S. Eldersveld, and M. Janowitz (eds.), *Political Behaviour: A Reader in Theory and Research*. New York: Free Press.

—————— (1964). *The Soldier and the State: The Theory and Politics of Civil-Military Relations*. New York: Random House (Vintage).

—————— (1968). *Political Order in Changing Societies*. New Haven: Yale University Press.

—————— (1970). "Social and institutional dynamics of one-party systems." In S. P. Huntington and C. H. Moore (eds.), *Authoritarian Politics in Modern Society*. New York: Basic Books.

——————, ed. (1962). *Changing Patterns of Military Politics*. New York: Free Press.

Huntington, Samuel P., and Clement H. Moore (1970). "Conclusion: authoritarianism, democracy, and one-party politics." In S. P., Huntington and C. M. Moore (eds.), *Authoritarian Politics in Modern Society*. New York: Basic Books.

Hurewitz, J. C. (1969). *Middle East Politics: The Military Dimension*. New York: Praeger.

Iglesias Selgas, Carlos (1968). *La vía española a la democracia*. Madrid: Ediciones del Movimiento.

—————— (1971). *Comentarios a la Ley Sindical*. Madrid: Cabal.

Inkeles, Alex (1954). "The totalitarian mystique: some impressions of the dynamics of totalitarian society." In Carl J. Friedrich (ed.), *Totalitarianism*. Cambridge, Mass.: Harvard University Press.

Inkeles, Alex, and Raymond A. Bauer (1959). *The Soviet Citizen: Daily Life in a Totalitarian Society*. Cambridge, Mass.: Harvard University Press.

Inkeles, Alex, and Kent Geiger, eds. (1961). *Soviet Society: A Book of Readings*. Boston: Houghton Mifflin.

Institut für Zeitgeschichte (1958). *Gutachten des Instituts für* **Zeitgeschichte.** **Münich:** Institut für Zeitgeschichte.

Institute for the Comparative Study of Political Systems, A Division of Operations and Policy Research Inc. (from 1962 onwards). *Election Factbook* . . . (for different countries and dates). Washington, D.C.

International Journal of Politics (1973). Vol. 2, no. 4. "Critiques of fascism theory from the West German New Left." Several essays.

Ionescu, Ghita (1967). *The Politics of the European Communist States*. New York: Praeger.

Jäckel, Eberhard (1972). *Hitler's Weltanschauung. A Blueprint for Power*. Middletown: Wesleyan University Press.

Jackson, Gabriel (1965). *The Spanish Republic and the Civil War 1931–1939*. Princeton: Princeton University Press.

Jacobsen, Hans-Adolf (1968). *Nationalsozialistische Aussenpolitik 1933–1938*. Frankfurt a.M.: A. Metzner.

Jacobson, Jason, ed. (1972). *Soviet Communism and the Socialist Vision*. New Brunswick, N.J.: New Politics Publishing Company.

Jäger, Herbert (1967). *Verbrechen unter Totalitärer Herrschaft. Studien zur nationalsozialistischen Gewaltkriminalität*. Olten: Walter-Verlag.

James, Robert Rhodes, ed. (1969). *The Czechoslovak Crisis, 1968*. London: Weidenfeld and Nicolson.

Janda, Kenneth, ed. (1972). "International Comparative Political Parties Project: ICPP variables and coding manual." Multilith. Evanston: Northwestern University.

Jänicke, Martin (1971). *Totalitäre Herrschaft. Anatomie eines politischen Begriffes*. Berlin: Duncker & Humblot.

Janos, Andrew C. (1970a). "The one-party state and social mobilization: East Europe between the wars." In S. Huntington and C. Moore (eds.), *Authoritarian Politics in Modern Society*. New York: Basic Books.

_____ (1970b). "Group politics in communist society: a second look at the pluralistic model." In S. Huntington and C. Moore (eds.), *Authoritarian Politics in Modern Society*. New York: Basic Books.

Janowitz, Morris (1964). *The Military in the Political Development of New Nations: An Essay in Comparative Analysis*. Chicago: University of Chicago Press.

_____ (1971). *On Military Intervention*. Rotterdam: Rotterdam University Press.

Janowitz, Morris, and Jacques Van Doorn, eds. (1971). *On Military Ideology*. Rotterdam: Rotterdam University Press.

Jansen, M. B. (1961). *Sakamoto, Ryoma and the Meiji Restoration*. Princeton: Princeton University Press.

Jasper, Gotthard, ed. (1968). *Von Weimar zu Hitler, 1930–1933*. Cologne: Kiepenheuer & Witsch.

Joffe, Ellis (1965). *Party and Army-Professionalism and Political Control in the Chinese Officer Corps, 1949–1964*. Cambridge, Mass.: Harvard University East Asian Research Center.

——————— (1971). "The Chinese army under Lin Piao: prelude to political intervention." In J. M. H. Lindbeck (ed.), *China: Management of a Revolutionary Society*. Seattle: University of Washington Press.

Johe, Werner, ed. (1967). *Die gleichgeschaltete Justiz*. Frankfurt: Europäische Verlaganstalt.

Johnson, Chalmers, ed. (1970). *Change in Communist Systems*. Stanford: Stanford University Press.

Johnson, John J. (1964). *The Military and Society in Latin America*. Stanford: Stanford University Press.

Johnson, Priscilla, and Leopold Labedz, eds. (1965). *Khrushchev and the Arts: The Politics of Soviet Culture, 1962–1964*. Cambridge, Mass:. M.I.T. Press.

Jowitt, Kenneth (1971). *Revolutionary Breakthroughs and National Development: The Case of Romania, 1944–1965*. Berkeley: University of California Press.

Jünger, Ernst (1934). *Die totale Mobilmachung*. (First ed. 1930). Berlin: Junker und Dunnhaupt.

Kahin, Georg McTurnan (1964). *Governments and Politics in Southeast Asia*. Ithaca: Cornell University Press.

Kaltefleiter, Werner (1968). *Wirtschaft und Politik in Deutschland: Konjunktur als Bestimmungsfaktor des Parteiensystems*. Cologne: Westdeutscher Verlag.

Kanet, Roger E., ed. (1971). *The Behavioral Revolution and Communist Studies*. New York: Free Press.

Karol, K. S. (1970). *Guerrillas in Power: The Course of the Cuban Revolution*. New York: Hill & Wang.

Karpat, Kemal H. (1959). *Turkey's Politics: The Transition to a Multiparty System*. Princeton: Princeton University Press.

——————, ed. (1968). *Political and Social Thought in the Contemporary Middle East*. New York: Praeger.

Kase, Francis, J. (1968). *People's Democracy: A Contribution to the Study of the Communist Theory of State and Revolution*. Leyden: A. W. Sijthoff.

Kassof, Allen (1965). *The Soviet Youth Program*. Cambridge, Mass.: Harvard University Press.

——————— (1969). "The administered society: totalitarianism without terror." In Frederick J. Fleron, Jr. (ed.), *Communist Studies and the Social Sciences*. Chicago: Rand McNally.

——————, ed. (1968). *Propects for Soviet Society*. New York: Praeger.

Kaufman, Susan Beth (1970). "Decision-making in an authoritarian regime: the politics of profit-sharing in Mexico." Ph.D. dissertation, Columbia University.

Kautsky, John H., and Roger W. Benjamin (1968). "Communism and economic development." In John H. Kautsky (ed.), *Communism and the Politics of Development*. New York: Wiley.

Kay, Hugh (1970). *Salazar and Modern Portugal*. New York: Hawthorn Books.

Kedward, H. R. (1969). *Fascism in Western Europe 1900–45*. Glasgow: Blackie.

Kele, Max H. (1972). *Nazis and Workers: National Socialist Appeals to German Labor, 1919–1933*. Chapel Hill: University of North Carolina Press.

Kelleher, Catherine McArdle, ed. (1974). *Political-Military Systems: Comparative Perspectives*. Beverly Hills Sage.

Kelsen, Hans (1929). *Vom Wesen und Wert der Demokratie*. Tübingen: J. C. B. Mohr.

―――――――― (1948). *The Political Theory of Bolshevism: A Critical Analysis*. University of California Publications in Political Science, Vol. 2. Berkeley: University of California Press.

Kern, Robert, and Ronald Dolkart, eds. (1973). *The Caciques: Oligarchical Politics and the System of Caciquismo in the Luso-Hispanic World*. Albuquerque: University of New Mexico Press.

Kilson, Martin (1963). "Authoritarian and single-party tendencies in African politics." *World Politics* 15:262–94.

Kim, Se-Jin (1971). *The Politics of Military Revolution in Korea*. Chapel Hill: University of North Carolina Press.

Kirchheimer, Otto (1969). *Politics, Law, and Social Change*. New York: Columbia University Press.

Kirkpatrick, Jeane (1971). *Leader and Vanguard in Mass Society: A Study of Peronist Argentina*. Cambridge, Mass.: M.I.T. Press.

Klemperer, Victor (1966). *Die unbewältigte Sprach: Aus dem Notizbuch eines Philologen LTI*. Darmstadt: Melzer.

Kling, Merle (1956). "Towards a theory of power and political instability in Latin America." *Western Political Quarterly* 9:21–35.

Klönne, Arno (1957). *Hitlerjugend. Die Jugend und ihre Organisation im Dritten Reich*. Hannover: Norddeutsche Verlagsanstalt.

Kluke, Paul (1973). "National Socialist Europe ideology." In Hajo Holborn (ed.), *Republic to Reich: The Making of the Nazi Revolution*. New York: Random House (Vintage).

Koehl, Robert (1972). "Feudal aspects of National Socialism." In Henry A. Turner (ed.), *Nazism and the Third Reich*. New York: Quadrangle Books.

Kogon, Eugen (1950). *The Theory and Practice of Hell*. London: Secker and Warburg.

Kolkowicz, Roman (1967). *The Soviet Military and Communist Party*. Princeton: Princeton University Press.

―――――――― (1971). "The military." In H. Gordon Skilling and Franklyn Griffiths (eds.), *Interest Groups in Soviet Politics*. Princeton: Princeton University Press.

Kool, Frits, and Erwin Oberländer, eds. (1967). *Arbeiterdemokratie oder Parteidiktatur*. Olten: Walter Verlag.

Korbell, J. (1959). *Communist Subversion of Czechoslovakia, 1938–1948: The Failure of Coexistence.* Princeton: Princeton University Press.

Korbonski, Andrzej (1974). "Comparing liberalization processes in Eastern Europe: a preliminary analysis." In Lenard J. Cohen and Jane P. Shapiro (eds.), *Communist Systems in Comparative Perspective.* Garden City, N.Y.: Doubleday (Anchor).

Kornhauser, W. (1959). *The Politics of Mass Society.* Glencoe, Ill.: Free Press.

Kosheri Mahfouz, El (1972). *Socialisme et pouvoir en Egypte.* Paris: Librairie générale de droit et de jurisprudence.

Krader, Lawrence (1968). *The Origins of the State.* Englewood Cliffs, N.J.: Prentice-Hall.

Krausnick, Helmut, Hans Buchheim, Martin Broszat, and Hans-Adolf Jacobsen (1968). *Anatomy of the SS State.* New York: Walker.

Kriegel, Annie (1972). *Les grands procès dans les systèmes communistes.* Paris: Gallimard.

Kühnl, Reinhard (1966). *Die nationalsozialistische Linke 1925–1930.* Meisenheim am Glan: Anton Hain.

Labedz, Leopold, ed. (1962). *Revisionism: Essays on the History of Marxist Ideas.* New York: Praeger.

La Cierva, Ricardo de (1969). *Historia de la Guerra Civil española,* Vol. 1. Madrid: San Martín.

Lacouture, Jean (1969). *4 hommes et leurs peuples: Surpouvoir et sousdevelopment.* Paris: Editions du Seuil.

Lacouture, Jean, and Simonne Lacouture (1958). *Egypt in Transition.* New York: Criterion.

Lamounier, Bolívar (1974). "Ideologia em regimes autoritários: uma crítica a Juan J. Linz." *Estudos Cebrap* (São Paulo) 7:69–92.

Landau, Jacob M., ed. (1972). *Man, State, and Society in the Contemporary Middle East.* New York: Praeger.

Lande, Carl H. (1965). *Leaders, Factions, and Parties: The Structure of Philippine Politics.* New Haven: Southeast Asia Studies, Yale University.

Lane, David, and George Kolankiewicz, eds. (1973). *Social Groups in Polish Society.* New York: Columbia University Press.

Lang, Kurt (1965). "Military sociology: a trend report and bibliography." *Current Sociology* 13:1–55.

Lange, M. G. (1955). *Wissenschaft im Totalitären Staat: Die Wissenschaft der Sowjetischen Besatzungszone auf dem Weg zum 'Stalinismus.'* Stuttgart: Ring Verlag.

Lanning, Eldon (1974). "A typology of Latin American political systems." *Comparative Politics* 6:367–94.

Laqueur, Walter, and Leopold Labedz, eds. (1962). *Polycentrism: The New Factor in International Communism.* New York: Praeger.

Laqueur, Walter, and George L. Mosse, eds. (1966). *International Fascism, 1920–1945.* New York: Harper & Row.

Lasswell, Harold D., and Daniel Lerner, eds. (1966). *World Revolutionary Elites: Studies in Coercive Ideological Movements.* Cambridge, Mass.: M.IT. Press.

Ledeen, Michael Arthur (1972). *Universal Fascism: The Theory and Practice of the Fascist International, 1928–1936.* New York: Fertig.

Ledesma Ramos, Ramiro (1968). *¿Fascismo en España? Discurso a las juventudes de España.* Reprinted. (Originally published 1935). Esplugues de Llobregat, Barcelona: Ariel.

Lee, J. M. (1969). *African Armies and Civil Order.* New York: Praeger.

Leeds, Anthony (1964). "Brazilian careers and social structure." *American Anthropologist* 66:1321–47.

Lefever, Ernest W. (1970). *Spear and Scepter: Army, Police, and Politics in Tropical Africa.* Washington, D.C.: The Brookings Institution.

Leff, Nathaniel H. (1968). *Economic Policy-Making and Development in Brazil 1947–1964.* New York: Wiley.

Leites, Nathan C. (1953). *A Study of Bolshevism.* Glencoe, Ill.: Free Press.

Leites, Nathan, and Elsa Bernaut (1954). *Ritual of Liquidation: The Case of the Moscow Trials.* Glencoe: Free Press.

Lemarchand, René (1972). "Political clientelism and ethnicity in tropical Africa: competing solidarities in nation-building." *The American Political Science Review* 66:68–90.

Lemarchand, René, and Keith Legg (1972). "Political clientelism and development: a preliminary analysis." *Comparative Politics* 4:149–78.

Lenin, V. I., *One Step Forward, Two Steps Back,* as quoted in Daniels, Robert Vincent (1969). *The Conscience of the Revolution: Communist Opposition in Soviet Russia.* New York: Clarion Book.

Lepsius, Rainer (1968). "The collapse of an intermediary power structure: Germany 1933–1934." *International Journal of Comparative Sociology* 9:289–301.

—————— (1971). "Machtübernahme und Machtübergabe zur Strategie des Regimewechsels." In Hans Albert *et al.* (eds.), *Sozialtheorie und sozial Praxis.* Meisenheim am Glan: Verlag Anton Hain.

Lerner, Daniel, Ithiel de Sola Pool, and George K. Schueller (1966). "The Nazi elite." In H. Lasswell and D. Lerner (eds.), *World Revolutionary Elites: Studies in Coercive Ideological Movements.* Cambridge, Mass.: M.I.T Press.

Levine, Donald N. (1965). *Wax and Gold: Tradition and Innovation in Ethiopian Culture.* Chicago: University of Chicago Press.

Levytsky, Borys, ed. (1974). *The Stalinist Terror in the Thirties: Documentation from the Soviet Press.* Stanford: Hoover Institution Press.

Lewis, John Wilson (1963). *Leadership in Communist China.* Ithaca, N.Y.: Cornell University Press.

Lewy, Guenter (1965). *The Catholic Church and Nazi Germany.* New York: McGraw-Hill.

Lieuwen, Edwin (1960). *Arms and Politics in Latin America.* New York: Praeger.

Lieuwen, Edwin (1964). *Generals vs. Presidents: Neo-Militarism in Latin America.* New York: Praeger.

Lifton, Robert Jay (1968). *Revolutionary Immortality: Mao Tse-tung and the Chinese Cultural Revolution.* New York: Vintage Books.

Lijphart, Arend (1968a). "Typologies of democratic systems." *Comparative Political Studies* 1:3–44.

――――――― (1968b). *The Politics of Accommodation: Pluralism and Democracy in the Netherlands.* Berkeley: University of California Press.

――――――― (1969). "Consociational democracy." *World Politics* 21:207–25.

――――――― (1975). "Review article: the Northern Ireland problem: cases, theories, and solutions." *British Journal of Political Science* 5:83–106.

Lindbeck, J. M. H. (1967). "Transformation in the Chinese Communist Party." In Donald W. Treadgold (ed.), *Soviet and Chinese Communism: Similarities and Differences.* Seattle: University of Washington Press.

――――――――, ed. (1971). *China: Management of a Revolutionary Society.* Seattle: University of Washington Press.

Linnemann, H., J. P Pronk, and Jan Tinbergen (1965). *Convergence of Economic Systems in East and West.* Rotterdam: Netherlands Economic Institute.

Linz, Juan J. (1964). "An authoritarian regime: the case of Spain." In Erik Allard and Yrjo Littunen (eds.), *Cleavages, Ideologies and Party Systems.* Helsinki: Westermarck Society. Reprinted in Erik Allard and Stein Rokkan, eds. (1970), *Mass Politics: Studies in Political Sociology.* New York: Free Press. Page references are to the 1970 edition.

――――――― (1966). "Michels e il suo contributo alla sociologia politica." Introduction to Roberto Michels, *La sociologia del partito politico nella democrazia moderna.* Bologna: Il Mulino.

――――――― (1970a). "From Falange to Movimiento-Organización: the Spanish single party and the Franco regime 1936–1968." In S. Huntington and C. Moore (eds.), *Authoritarian Politics in Modern Societies: The Dynamics of Established One Party Systems.* New York: Basic Books.

――――――― (1970b). *Elites locales y cambio social en la Andalucía rural.* Vol. 2 of *Estudio Socioeconómico de Andalucía.* Madrid: Instituto de Desarrollo Económico.

――――――― (1973a). "Opposition in and under an authoritarian regime: the case of Spain." In Robert A. Dahl (ed.), *Regimes and Oppositions.* New Haven: Yale University Press.

――――――― (1973b). "The Future of an authoritarian situation or the institutionalization of an authoritarian regime: the case of Brazil." In Alfred Stepan (ed.), *Authoritarian Brazil: Origins, Policies, and Future.* New Haven: Yale University Press.

――――――― (1973c). "Continuidad y discontinuidad en la élite política española: de la restauración al régimen actual." In *Libro Homenaje al Prof. Carlos Ollero.* Madrid: Gráficas Carlavilla.

――――――― (forthcoming). "Some notes towards a comparative study of fascism in sociological-historical perspective." In Walter Laqueur (ed.), *A Guide to Fascism.*

Linz, Juan J., and Amando De Miguel (1966a). "Within-nation differences and comparisons: the eight Spains." In Richard L. Merritt and Stein Rokkan (eds.), *Comparing Nations*. New Haven: Yale University Press.

_____ (1966b). *Los empresarios ante el poder público: El liderazgo y los grupos de intereses en el empresariado español*. Madrid: Instituto de Estudios Políticos.

Linz, Juan J., and Alfred Stepan, eds. (forthcoming). *Breakdown and Crises of Democracies*.

Lipset, Seymour Martin (1959). "Some social requisites of democracy: economic development and political legitimacy." *American Political Science Review* 53:69–105.

_____ (1960). " 'Fascism'—left, right, and center." In S. M. Lipset, *Political Man: The Social Bases of Politics*. Garden City, N.Y.: Doubleday.

_____ (1973). "Commentary: social stratification research and Soviet scholarship." In Murray Yanowitch and Wesley A. Fisher (eds.), *Social Stratification and Mobility in the USSR*. White Plains, N.Y.: International Arts and Sciences Press.

Lipset, Seymour M., and Richard B. Dobson (1973). "Social stratification and sociology in the Soviet Union." *Survey* 3:114–85.

Lipset, S. M., and S. Rokkan (1967). "Cleavage structures, party systems, and voter alignment: an introduction." In Lipset and Rokkan (eds.), *Party Systems and Voter Alignments: Cross-National Perspectives*. New York: Free Press.

Lipson, Leon (1967). "Law: the function of extra-judicial mechanisms." In Donald W. Treadgold (ed.), *Soviet and Chinese Communism: Similarities and Differences*. Seattle: University of Washington Press.

_____ (1968). "Law and society." In Allen Kassof (ed.), *Prospects for Soviet Society*. New York: Praeger.

Lockwood, Lee (1967). *Castro's Cuba: Cuba's Fidel*. New York: Macmillan.

Lopukhov, Boris R. (1965). "Il problema del fascismo italiano negli scritti di autori sovietici." *Studi storici* 6:239–57.

Lowenthal, Abraham F. (1974). "Armies and politics in Latin America." *World Politics* 27:107–30.

_____, ed. (forthcoming). *Continuity and Change in Contemporary Peru*. Princeton: Princeton University Press.

Lowenthal, Richard (1970). "Development vs. utopia in communist policy." In Chalmers Johnson (ed.), *Change in Communist Systems*. Stanford: Stanford University Press.

Lucena, Manuel (1971). *L'Evolution du Systeme Portugais a travers les Lois (1933–1971)*, 2 vols. Paris: Institut des Sciences Sociales du Travail. Quoted by permission.

Ludendorff, Erich (1935). *Der Totale Krieg*. Munich: Ludendorff Verlag.

Ludz, Peter Christian (1964). "Entwurf Einer soziologischen Theorie Totalitär Verfasster Gesellschaft." In P. C. Ludz (ed.), *Soziologie der DDR*. Cologne-Opladen: Westdeutscher Verlag.

_____ (1970). *The German Democratic Republic from the Sixties to the Seventies: A Socio-Political Analysis*. Cambridge, Mass.: Center for International Affairs, Harvard University.

Ludz, Peter Christian (1972). *The Changing Party Elite in East Germany.* Cambridge, Mass.: M.I.T. Press.

Lukács, Georg (1955). *Die Zerstörung der Vernunft.* Berlin: Aufbau-Verlag.

Mabry, Donald J. (1973). *Mexico's Acción Nacional: A Catholic Alternative to Revolution.* Syracuse: Syracuse University Press.

Macartney, C. A. (1962). *October 15: A History of Modern Hungary, 1929–1944,* 2 vols. Edinburgh: Edinburgh University Press.

MacFarquhar, Roderick (1960). *The Hundred Flowers Campaign and the Chinese Intellectuals.* New York: Praeger.

MacGaffey, Wyatt, and Clifford R. Barnett (1965). *Twentieth-Century Cuba: The Background of the Castro Revolution.* Garden City, N.Y.: Doubleday (Anchor).

MacInnis, Donald E. (1972). *Religious Policy and Practice in Communist China.* New York: Macmillan.

Mair, Lucy (1962). *Primitive Government.* Harmondsworth: Penguin Books.

Malefakis, Edward E. (1970). *Agrarian Reform and Peasant Revolution in Spain: Origins of the Civil War.* New Haven: Yale University Press.

Malloy, James M. (1974). "Authoritarianism, corporatism and mobilization in Peru." *The Review of Politics* 36:52–84.

Manoïlesco, Mihail (1936). *Le Siècle du Corporatisme.* (Original ed. 1934.) Paris: Félix Alcan.

——————— (1938). *El partido único.* Zaragoza: Heraldo de Aragón.

Mansilla, H. C. F. (1971). *Faschismus und eindimensionale Gesellschaft.* Neuwied: Luchterhand.

Marcuse, Herbert (1964). *One-Dimensional Man.* Boston: Beacon Press.

——————— (1969). "Repressive tolerance." In Robert Paul Wolff, Barrington Moore, Jr., and H. Marcuse (eds.), *A Critique of Pure Tolerance.* Boston: Beacon Press.

Markovitz, Irving Leonard, ed. (1970). *African Politics and Society: Basic Issues and Problems of Government and Development.* New York: Free Press.

Maruyama, Masao (1963). *Thought and Behaviour in Modern Japanese Politics.* London: Oxford University Press.

Marx, Karl (1851–52; revised 1869). *The Eighteenth Brumaire of Louis Bonaparte.* Reprinted in Karl Marx and Frederick Engels, *Selected Works in Two Volumes.* Moscow: Foreign Language Publishing House, 1955.

Maser, Werner (1970). *Hitler's Mein Kampf: An Analysis.* London: Faber and Faber.

Mason, T. W. (1968). "The primacy of politics—politics and economics in National Socialist Germany." In S. J. Woolf (ed.), *The Nature of Fascism.* London: Weidenfeld & Nicolson.

Massing, Paul W. (1949). *Rehearsal for Destruction: A Study of Political Anti-Semitism in Imperial Germany.* New York: Fertig.

Matossian, Mary (1958). "Ideologies of delayed industrialization: some tensions and ambiguities." *Economic Development and Cultural Change* 6:217–28.

Matthias, Erich, and Rudolf Morsey, eds. (1960). *Das Ende der Parteien 1933*. Düsseldorf: Kommission für Geschichte des Parlamentarismus und der politische Parteien.

Mau, Hermann (1953). "Die 'Zweite Revolution' der 30. Juni 1934." *Vierteljahrshefte für Zeitgeschichte* 1:119–37.

May, John D. (1973). *Of the Conditions and Measures of Democracy*. Morristown, N.J.: General Learning Press.

McAlister, Lyle N. (1966). "Recent research and writings on the role of the military in Latin America." *Latin American Research Review* 2:5–36.

McDonald, Ronald H. (1971). *Party Systems and Elections in Latin America*. Chicago: Markham.

McRae, Kenneth D., ed. (1974). *Consociational Democracy: Political Accommodation in Segmented Societies*. Toronto: McClelland and Stewart.

Medhurst, Kenneth N. (1973). *Government in Spain: The Executive at Work*. Oxford: Pergamon Press.

Medvedev, Zhoros A. (1969). *Rise and Fall of T. D. Lysenko*. New York: Columbia University Press.

Merkl, Peter H. (forthcoming). *Political Violence under the Swastika: 581 Early Nazis*. Princeton: Princeton University Press.

Mesa-Lago, Carmelo, ed. (1971). *Revolutionary Change in Cuba*. Pittsburgh: University of Pittsburgh Press.

Messerschmidt, Manfred (1969). *Die Wehrmacht im NS-Staat*. Hamburg: v. Decker.

Meyer, Alfred G. (1957). *Leninism*. Cambridge, Mass.: Harvard University Press.

——————— (1964). "USSR, incorporated." In Donald W. Treadgold (ed.), *The Development of the USSR: An Exchange of Views*. Seattle: University of Washington Press.

——————— (1965). *The Soviet Political System: An Interpretation*. New York: Random House.

——————— (1967). "Authority in communist political systems." In Louis J. Edinger (ed.), *Political Leadership in Industrialized Societies*. New York: Wiley.

——————— (1970). "Theories of convergence." In Chalmers Johnson (ed.), *Change in Communist Systems*. Stanford: Stanford University Press.

Meyerhoff, Hermann (1963). *Herne 1933–1945—Die Zeit des Nationalsozialismus: Ein kommunalhistorischer Rückblick*. Herne: Stadt(verwaltung).

Michels, Robert (1928). "Some reflections on the sociological character of political parties." *The American Political Science Review* 21:753–72.

——————— (1962). *Political Parties: A Sociological Study of the Oligarchical Tendencies of Modern Democracy*. (Originally published 1911). New York: Collier Books.

Mickiewicz, Ellen Propper (1967). *Soviet Political Schools: The Communist Party Adult Instruction System*. New Haven: Yale University Press.

Milenkovitch, Deborah (1971). *Plan and Market in Yugoslav Economic Thought*. New Haven: Yale University Press.

Mills, C. Wright (1958). *The Causes of World War Three*. New York: Simon & Schuster.

Milne, R. S. (1967). *Government and Politics in Malaysia.* Boston: Houghton Mifflin.

Milward, Alan S. (1966). *Die Deutsche Kriegswirtschaft, 1939–1945.* Stuttgart: Deutsche Verlags-Anstalt.

Montias, John Michael (1970). "Types of communist economic systems." In Chalmers Johnson (ed.), *Change in Communist Systems.* Stanford: Stanford University Press.

Montgomery, John D., and Albert O. Hirschman, eds. (1968). *Public Policy* 17. Articles on military government and reconstruction by C. J. Friedrich, L. Krieger, and P. H. Merkl.

Moore, Barrington Jr. (1951). *Soviet Politics: The Dilemma of Power. The Role of Ideas in Social Change.* Cambridge, Mass.: Harvard University Press.

——————— (1954). *Terror and Progress USSR: Some sources of Change and Stability in the Soviet Dictatorship.* Cambridge, Mass.: Harvard University Press.

——————— (1965). *Political Power and Social Theory.* New York: Harper (Torch-books).

——————— (1966). *Social Origins of Dictatorship and Democracy: Lord and Peasant in the Making of the Modern World.* Boston: Beacon Press.

Moore, Clement H. (1965). *Tunisia since Independence.* Berkeley: University of California Press.

——————— (1970a). *Politics in North Africa, Algeria, Morocco, and Tunisia.* Boston: Little Brown.

——————— (1970b). "The single party as source of legitimacy." In S. Huntington and C. Moore (eds.), *Authoritarian Politics in Modern Society.* New York: Basic Books.

——————— (1973). "Raisons de la faillite du parti unique dans les pays arabes." *Revue de l'Occident Musulman et de la Méditerranée* 15–16:242–52.

——————— (1974). "Authoritarian politics in unincorporated society: the case of Nasser's Egypt." *Comparative Politics* 6:193–218.

Morris, Ivan, ed. (1968). *Japan 1931–1945: Militarism, Fascism, Japanism?* Lexington, Mass.: D. C. Heath.

Morrison, Donald George, *et al.* (1972). *Black Africa: A Comparative Handbook,* New York: Free Press.

Morton, Henry W., and Rudolf L. Tökés, eds. (1974). *Soviet Politics and Society in the 1970's.* New York: Free Press.

Mosse, George L. (1964). *The Crisis of German Ideology: Intellectual Origins of the Third Reich.* New York: Grosset & Dunlap.

——————— (1966). *Nazi Culture: Intellectual, Cultural and Social Life in the Third Reich.* New York: Grosset & Dunlap.

Mote, Max E. (1965). *Soviet Local and Republic Elections: A Description of the 1963 Elections in Leningrad Based on Official Documents, Press Accounts, and Private Interviews.* Stanford: The Hoover Institution on War, Revolution and Peace, Stanford University.

Moy, Roland F. (1971). *A Computer Simulation of Democratic Political Development:*

Tests of the Lipset and Moore Models. Sage Professional Papers in Comparative Politics, No. 01–019:2. Beverly Hills: Sage.

Nagy-Talavera, Nicholas M. (1970). *The Green Shirts and the Others: A History of Fascism in Hungary and Rumania.* Stanford: Hoover Institution Press.

Neal, Fred W. (1957). *Titoism in Action.* Berkeley: University of California Press.

Needleman, Carolyn, and Martin Needleman (1969). "Who rules Mexico? A critique of some current views of the Mexican political process." *Journal of Politics* 31:1011–34.

Needler, Martin (1964). *Anatomy of a Coup d'état: Ecuador 1963.* Washington, D.C.: Institute for the Comparative Study of Political Systems.

_____ (1966). "Political development and military intervention in Latin America." *American Political Science Review* 60:616–26.

_____ (1967). *Latin American Politics in Perspective.* Princeton: D. Van Nostrand.

_____ (1971). *Politics and Society in Mexico.* Albuquerque: University of New Mexico.

_____, ed. (1970). *Political Systems of Latin America.* New York: Van Nostrand Reinhold.

Neubauer, Deane E. (1967). "Some conditions of democracy." *American Political Science Review* 61:1002–09.

Neumann, Sigmund (1942). *Permanent Revolution: Totalitarianism in the Age of International Civil War.* New York: Harper.

Neumann, Franz (1957). *The Democratic and the Authoritarian State.* Glencoe, Ill.: Free Press.

_____ (1963). *Behemoth: The Structure and Practice of National Socialism 1933–1944.* (First ed. 1944). New York: Octagon.

Newton, Ronald C. (1974). "Natural corporatism and the passing of populism in Spanish America." *The Review of Politics* 36:34–51.

Noakes, Jeremy, and Geoffrey Pridham, eds. (1974). *Documents on Nazism 1919–1945.* London: Jonathan Cape.

Nolte, Ernst (1963). *Der Nationalsozialismus.* München: R. Piper & Co.

_____ (1966). *Die faschistischen Bewegungen.* München: Deutscher Taschenbuch Verlag.

_____ (1968a). *Die Krise des liberalen Systems und die faschistischen Bewegungen.* Munich: Piper.

_____ (1968b). *Der Faschismus von Mussolini zu Hitler: Texte, Bilder und Dokumente.* München: Verlag Kurt Desch.

_____ (1969). *Three Faces of Fascism: Action Française, Italian Fascism, and National Socialism.* New York: Mentor Book.

_____, ed. (1967). *Theorien über den Faschismus.* Cologne: Kiepenheuer.

Nordlinger, Eric A. (1970). "Soldiers in mufti: the impact of military rule upon economic and social change in the non-Western states." *The American Political Science Review* 64:1131–48.

Nordlinger, Eric A. (1972). *Conflict Regulation in Divided Societies.* Cambridge, Mass.: Center for International Affairs, Harvard University.

Norman, H. (1948). *Japan's Emergence as a Modern State.* New York: Institute of Pacific Relations.

North, Liisa (1966). *Civil-Military Relations in Argentina, Chile, and Peru.* Berkeley: Institute of International Studies.

Nove, Alec (1964). *Economic Rationality and Soviet Politics; Or Was Stalin Really Necessary?* New York: Praeger.

NSDAP, Reichsorganisationsleiter (1935?). *Partei-Statistik,* Stand: 1935, 4 vols. Munich: Internal publication.

Nun, José (1968). "A Latin American phenomenon: the middle-class military coup." In James Petras and Maurice Zeitlin (eds.), *Latin America: Reform or Revolution?* New York: Fawcett.

——————— (1969). *Latin America: The Hegemonic Crisis and the Military Coup.* Berkeley: Institute of International Studies, University of California.

Nyomarkay, Joseph (1967). *Charisma and Factionalism in the Nazi Party.* Minneapolis: University of Minnesota Press.

O'Connor, Dennis M. (1963). "Soviet People's Guards: an experiment with civic police." *New York University Law Review* 39:580–87.

O'Donnell, Guillermo (1973). *Modernization and Bureaucratic-Authoritarianism: Studies in South American Politics.* Berkeley: Institute of International Studies, University of California.

Oren, Nissan (1973). *Revolution Administered: Agrarianism and Communism in Bulgaria.* Baltimore: Johns Hopkins University Press.

Organski, A. F. K. (1965). *The Stages of Political Development.* New York: Knopf.

Orlow, Dietrich (1965). "Die Adolf-Hitler-Schulen." *Vierteljahrshefte für Zeitgeschichte* 23:272–84.

——————— (1969). *The History of the Nazi Party: 1919–1933.* Pittsburgh: University of Pittsburgh Press.

——————— (1973). *The History of the Nazi Party: 1933–1945.* Pittsburgh: University of Pittsburgh Press.

Padgett, Vincent (1966). *The Mexican Political System.* Boston: Houghton Mifflin.

Palmer, David Scott (1973). *"Revolution from Above": Military Government and Popular Participation in Peru, 1968–1972.* Cornell University Dissertation Series, No. 47. Ithaca: Cornell University.

Pauker, Guy J. (1963). *The Indonesian Doctrine of Territorial Warfare and Territorial Management.* Santa Monica: The Rand Corporation.

Paxton, Robert O. (1972). *Vichy France: Old Guard and New Order, 1940–44.* New York: Knopf.

Payne, Stanley G. (1967). *Politics and the Military in Modern Spain.* Stanford: Stanford University Press.

Pelczynski, Zbigniew (1959). "Poland 1957." In David E. Butler (ed.), *Elections Abroad*. London: Macmillan.

Penniman, Howard R. (1972). *Elections in South Vietnam*. Washington, D.C.: American Enterprise Institute for Public Policy Research.

Perham, Margery (1947). *The Government of Ethiopia*. London: Faber and Faber.

Perlmutter, Amos (1969). "The praetorian state and the praetorian army: toward a taxonomy of civil-military relations in developing polities." *Comparative Politics* 2:382–404.

——————— (1970). "The Arab military elite." *World Politics* 22:269–300.

Peterson, Edward N. (1969). *The Limits of Hitler's Power*. Princeton: Princeton University Press.

Pike, Frederick B., and Thomas Stritch, eds. (1974). *The New Corporatism: Social-Political Structures in the Iberian World*. Notre Dame: University of Notre Dame Press.

Pipes, Richard (1967). "Communism and Russian history." In Donald W. Treadgold (ed.), *Soviet and Chinese Communism: Similarities and Differences*. Seattle: University of Washington Press.

———————, ed. (1961). *The Russian Intelligentsia*. New York: Columbia University Press.

Pipping, Knut, Rudolf Abshagen, and Anne-Eva Brauneck (1954). *Gespräche mit der Deutschen Jugend: Ein Beitrag zum Authoritätsproblem*. Helsingfors: Akademische Buchhandlung.

Pirker, Theo, ed. (1965). *Komintern und Faschismus, 1920–1940: Dokumente zur Geschichte und Theorie des Faschismus*. Stuttgart: Deutsche Verlag-Anstalt.

Plessner, Helmuth (1959). *Die verspätete Nation: Über die politische Verführbarkeit bürgerlichen Geistes*. Stuttgart: W. Kohlhammer.

Ploss, Sidney I. (1965). *Conflict and Decision-Making in Soviet Russia: A Case Study of Agricultural Policy, 1953–1963*. Princeton: Princeton University Press.

Political Systems and the Distribution of Power. A.S.A. Monographs, No. 2. London: Tavistock.

Pollack, Jonathan D. (1974). "The study of Chinese military politics: toward a framework for analysis." In Catherine McArdle Kelleher (ed.), *Political-Military Systems: Comparative Perspectives*. Beverly Hills: Sage.

Potash, Robert A. (1969). *The Army and Politics in Argentina, 1928–1945: Yrigoyen to Perón*. Stanford: Stanford University Press.

Potholm, Christian P. (1970). *Four African Political Systems*. Englewood Cliffs, N.J.: Prentice-Hall.

Potholm, Christian P., and Richard Dale, eds. (1972). *Southern Africa in Perspective: Essays in Regional Politics*. New York: Free Press.

Powell, John Duncan (1970). "Peasant society and clientelist politics." *American Political Science Review* 64:411–25.

Puhle, Hans-Jürgen (1970). *Tradition und Reformpolitik in Bolivien.* Hannover: Verlag für Literatur und Zeitgeschehen.

Pulzer, P. G. J. (1964). *The Rise of Political Anti-Semitism in Germany and Austria.* New York: Wiley.

Pusić, Eugen, ed. (1973). *Participation and Self-Management.* Zagreb: Institute for Social Research.

Putnam, Robert (1967). "Toward explaining military intervention in Latin American politics." *World Politics* 20:83–110.

Pye, Lucian W. (1967). *Southeast Asia's Political Systems.* Englewood Cliffs, N.J.: Prentice-Hall.

——————— (1971). "Mass participation in Communist China: its limitations and the continuity of culture." In John M. H. Lindbeck (ed.), *China: Management of a Revolutionary Society.* Seattle: University of Washington Press.

Quandt, William B. (1969). *Revolution and Political Leadership: Algeria 1954–1968.* Cambridge, Mass.: M.I.T. Press.

Rämisch, Raimund (1957). "Der Berufsständische Gedanke als Episode in der nationalsozialistischen Politik." *Zeitschrift für Politik* 4:263–72.

Reitlinger, Gerald (1968). *The Final Solution: The Attempt to Exterminate the Jews of Europe, 1939–1945.* South Brunswick, N.J.: T. Yoseloff.

Remak, Joachim, ed. (1969). *The Nazi Years: A Documentary History.* Englewood Cliffs, N.J.: Prentice-Hall.

Remington, Robin A. (1974). "Armed forces and society in Yugoslavia." In Catherine McArdle Kelleher (ed.), *Political-Military Systems: Comparative Perspectives.* Beverly Hills: Sage.

———————, ed. (1969). *Winter in Prague: Documents on Czechoslovak Communism in Crisis.* Cambridge, Mass.: M.I.T. Press.

Rigby, T. H. (1968). *Communist Party Membership in the U.S.S.R. 1917–1967.* Princeton: Princeton University Press.

——————— (1969). "Traditional market and organizational societies and the USSR." In Frederic J. Fleron, Jr. (ed.), *Communist Studies and the Social Sciences.* Chicago: Rand McNally.

Riggs, Fred W. (1967). *Thailand: The Modernization of a Bureaucratic Polity.* Honolulu: East-West Center Press.

Roberts, Henry L. (1951). *Rumania: Political Problems of an Agrarian State.* New Haven: Yale University Press.

Robinson, Thomas W. (1974). "Political succession in China." *World Politics* 27:1–38.

Roggemann, H. (1970). *Das Modell der Arbeiterselbstverwaltung in Jugoslawien.* Frankfurt am Main: Europäische Verlagsanstalt.

Rogger, Hans, and Eugen Weber, eds. (1966). *The European Right: A Historical Profile.* Berkeley: University of California Press.

Rokkan, Stein (1966). "Norway: numerical democracy and corporate pluralism." In

Robert Dahl (ed.), *Political Oppositions in Western Democracies*. New Haven: Yale University Press.

Ronfeldt, David (1972). "Patterns of civil-military rule." In Luigi Einaudi (ed.), *Latin America in the 1970's*. Santa Monica: The Rand Corporation.

Rose, Leo E., and Margaret W. Fisher (1970). *The Politics of Nepal: Persistence and Change in an Asian Monarchy*. Ithaca: Cornell University Press.

Rose, Richard (1971). *Governing without Consensus: An Irish Perspective*. Boston: Beacon Press.

Rose, Richard, and Harve Mossawir (1967). "Voting and elections: a functional analysis." *Political Studies* 15:173–201.

Rosenau, James N., ed. (1969). *Linkage Politics: Essays on the Convergence of National and International Systems*. New York: Free Press.

Ross, Stanley R., ed. (1966). *Is the Mexican Revolution Dead?* New York: Knopf.

Rossiter, Clinton L. (1948). *Constitutional Dictatorship: Crisis Government in the Modern Democracies*. Princeton: Princeton University Press.

Rotberg, Robert I., with Christopher K. Clague (1971). *Haiti: The Politics of Squalor*. Boston: Houghton Mifflin.

Roth, Guenther (1963). *The Social Democrats in Imperial Germany*. Totowa, N.J.: Bedminster.

——————— (1971). "Personal rulership, patrimonialism, and empire-building." In Reinhard Bendix and Guenther Roth (eds.), *Scholarship and Partisanship: Essays on Max Weber*. Berkeley: University of California Press.

Rush, Myron (1968). *Political Succession in the USSR*. New York: Columbia University Press.

Rustow, Dankwart A. (1964). "Succession in the twentieth century." *Journal of International Affairs* 18:104–13.

——————— (1967). *A World of Nations: Problems of Political Modernization*. Washington, D.C.: The Brookings Institution.

——————— (1971). *Middle Eastern Political Systems*. Englewood Cliffs, N.J.: Prentice-Hall.

Sabine, George H. (1934). "The state." In Edwin R. A. Seligman and Alvin Johnson (eds.), *Encyclopedia of the Social Sciences*. New York: Macmillan.

Salvemini, Gaetano (1961). *Scritti sul fascismo*. Milano: Feltrinelli.

Sarti, Roland (1968). "Fascism and the industrial leadership in Italy before the March on Rome." *Industrial and Labor Relations Review* 21:400–17.

——————— (1971). *Fascism and the Industrial Leadership in Italy 1919–1940*. Berkeley: University of California Press.

——————— (1970). "Fascist modernization in Italy: traditional or revolutionary?" *American Historical Review* 75:1029–45.

Sartori, Giovanni (1962a). *Democratic Theory*. Detroit: Wayne State University Press.

——————— (1962b). "Dittatura." *Enciclopedia del Diritto*, Vol. 11. Milano: A. Giuffrè.

Sartori, Giovanni (1968). "Political development and political engineering." In John D. Montgomery and Albert O. Hirschman (eds.), *Public Policy*, Vol. 17. Cambridge, Mass.: Harvard University Press.

—————— (1970a). "Concept misformation in comparative politics." *The American Political Science Review* 64:1033–53.

—————— (1970b). "The typology of party systems—proposals for improvement." In Erik Allardt and Stein Rokkan (eds.), *Mass Politics: Studies in Political Sociology*. New York: Free Press.

—————— (1974). "Rivistando il 'pluralismo polarizzato.' " In Fabio L. Cavazza and Stephen R. Graubard (eds.), *Il Caso Italiano: Italia anni '70*. Milano: Garzanti.

Sauer, Wolfgang (1967). "National Socialism: totalitarianism or fascism?" *American Historical Review* 73:404–24.

Scalapino, Robert A. (1953). *Democracy and the Party Movement in Prewar Japan: The Failure of the First Attempt*. Berkeley: University of California Press.

——————, ed. (1972). *Elites in the People's Republic of China*. Seattle: University of Washington Press.

Schäfer, Wolfgang (1957): *NSDAP Entwicklung und Struktur der Staatspartei des Dritten Reiches*. Hannover: Norddeutsche Verlagsanstalt O. Goedel.

Schapiro, Leonard (1965). *The Origin of the Communist Autocracy: Political Opposition in the Soviet State, First Phase, 1917–1922*. New York: Praeger.

—————— (1972a). *Totalitarianism*. New York: Praeger.

——————, ed. (1972b). *Political Opposition in One-Party States*. London: Macmillan.

Schein, Edgard H., with Inge Schneier and Curtis H. Baker (1961). *Coercive Persuasion: A Socio-psychological Analysis of the "Brainwashing" of American civilian prisoners by the Chinese Communists*. New York: Norton.

Schmidt, Carl T. (1938). *The Plough and the Sword*. New York: Columbia University Press.

—————— (1939). *The Corporate State in Action: Italy under Fascism*. New York: Oxford University Press.

Schmitt, Carl (1928). *Die Diktatur: Von den Anfängen des modernen Souveränitätsgedankens bis zum proletarischen Klassenkampf*. München: Duncker & Humblot.

—————— (1940). "Die Wendung zum totalen Staat." *Positionen und Begriffe im Kampf mit Weimar—Genf—Versailles 1923–1939*. Hamburg: Hanseatische Verlagsanstalt.

Schmitter, Philippe C. (1971). *Interest Conflict and Political Change in Brazil*. Stanford: Stanford University Press.

—————— (1973a). *Military Rule in Latin America: Functions, Consequences and Perspectives*. Beverly Hills: Sage.

—————— (1973b). "Corporatist interest representation and public policy-making in Portugal." Paper presented at the Conference on Modern Portugal, October 10–14, 1973, University of New Hampshire, Durham, N.H.

Schmitter, Philippe C. (1974). "Still the century of corporatism?" *Review of Politics* 36:85–131. Quoted by permission.

Schneider, Herbert W. (1928). *Making the Fascist State*. New York: Oxford University Press.

_____ (1936). *The Fascist Government of Italy*. New York: Van Nostrand.

Schneider, Ronald M. (1971). *The Political System of Brazil: Emergence of a "Modernizing" Authoritarian Regime, 1964–1970*. New York: Columbia University Press.

Schoenbaum, David (1967). *Hitler's Social Revolution: Class and Status in Nazi Germany 1933–1939*. Garden City, N.Y.: Doubleday (Anchor).

Scholtz, Harold (1967). "Die 'NS-Ordensburgen.' " *Vierteljahrshefte für Zeitgeschichte* 15:269–98.

Schöpflin, George, ed. (1970). *The Soviet Union and Eastern Europe: A Handbook*. New York: Praeger.

Schorn, Hubert (1959). *Der Richter im Dritten Reich: Geschichte und Dokumente*. Frankfurt: Klostermann.

Schram, Stuart R. (1967). *Mao Tse-tung*. Harmondsworth: Penguin.

_____ (1969). *The Political Thought of Mao Tse-tung*. New York: Praeger.

Schueller, George K. (1966). "The politburo." In Harold D. Lasswell and Daniel Lerner (eds.), *World Revolutionary Elites: Studies in Coercive Ideological Movements*. Cambridge: M.I.T. Press.

Schumann, Hans-Gerd (1958). *Nationalsozialismus und Gewerkschaftsbewegung*. Hannover: Norddeutsche Verlagsanstalt O. Goedel.

Schumpeter, Joseph A. (1950). *Capitalism, Socialism, and Democracy*. New York: Harper & Row.

Schurmann, Franz (1968). *Ideology and Organization in Communist China*. Berkeley: University of California Press.

Schweitzer, Arthur (1965). *Big Business in the Third Reich*. Bloomington, Ind.: Indiana University Press.

_____ (1974). "Theory of Political Charisma," *Comparative Studies in Society and History* 16:150–81.

Scott, Robert E. (1964). *Mexican Government in Transition*. Urbana: University of Illinois Press.

_____ (1965). "Mexico: the established revolution." In Lucian W. Pye and Sydney Verga (eds.), *Political Culture and Political Development*. Princeton: Princeton University Press.

Seidel, Bruno, and Siegfried Jenkner, eds. (1968). *Wege der Totalitarismus-Forschung*. Darmstadt: Wissenschaftliche Buchgesellschaft.

Seton-Watson, Hugh (1967). *Eastern Europe between the Wars 1918–1941*. New York: Harper & Row.

_____ (1968). *The East European Revolution*. New York: Praeger.

Shaffer, Harry G., ed. (1967). *The Communist World: Marxist and Non-Marxist Views.* New York: Appleton-Century-Crofts.

Edward Shils (1960). *Political Development in the New States.* The Hague: Mouton.

Shoup, Paul (1971). "Comparing communist nations: prospects for an empirical approach." In Roger E. Kanet (ed.), *The Behavioral Revolution and Communist Studies.* New York: Free Press.

Shulman, Marshall D. (1969). *Stalin's Foreign Policy Reappraised.* New York: Atheneum.

Silva, Umberto (1973). *Ideologia e Arte del Fascismo.* Milano: Gabriele Mazzotta.

Simmons, Ernest J. (1971). "The writers." In H. Gordon Skilling and Franklyn Griffiths (eds.), *Interest Groups in Soviet Politics.* Princeton: Princeton University Press.

——————, ed. (1955). *Continuity and Change in Russian and Soviet Thought.* Cambridge, Mass.: Harvard University Press.

Skilling, H. Gordon (1966). *The Government of Communist East Europe.* New York: Crowell.

—————— (1970). "Leadership and group conflict in Czechoslovakia." In R. Barry Farrell (ed.), *Political Leadership in Eastern Europe and the Soviet Union.* Chicago: Aldine.

—————— (1971). "Group conflict in Soviet politics: some conclusions." In H. G. Skilling and F. Griffiths (eds.), *Interest Groups in Soviet Politics.* Princeton: Princeton University Press.

—————— (1973a). "Opposition in Communist East Europe." In Robert A. Dahl (ed.), *Regimes and Oppositions.* New Haven: Yale University Press.

—————— (1973b). "Czechoslovakia's interrupted revolution." In Robert A. Dahl (ed.), *Regimes and Oppositions.* New Haven: Yale University Press.

Skilling, H. Gordon, and Franklyn Griffiths, eds. (1971). *Interest Groups in Soviet Politics.* Princeton: Princeton University Press.

Snyder, Frank Gregory (1965). *One-party Government in Mali: Transition Toward Control.* New Haven: Yale University Press.

Solaún, Mauricio (1969). "El fracaso de la democracia en Cuba: un régimen 'patrimonial' autoritario (1952)." *Aportes* 13:57–80.

Solaún, Mauricio, and Michael A. Quinn (1973). *Sinners and Heretics: The Politics of Military Intervention in Latin America.* Urbana: University of Illinois Press.

Solomon, Richard H. (1971). *Mao's Revolution and the Chinese Political Culture.* Berkeley: University of California Press.

Solzhenitsyn, Aleksandr I. (1973). *The Gulag Archipelago 1918–1956: An Experiment in Literary Investigation.* Paperback ed. New York: Harper & Row.

Sontheimer, Kurt (1968). *Antidemokratisches Denken in der Weimarer Republik.* Munich: Nymphenburger Verlagshandlung.

Sorokin, Pitirim (1964). *The Basic Trends of our Times.* New Haven: College and University Press.

Spacensky, Alain (1970). *Madagascar: 50 ans de vie politique (de Ralaimongo à Tsiranana)*. Paris: Nouvelles Editions Latines.

Speer, Albert (1971). *Inside the Third Reich*. New York: Avon Books.

Speier, Hans (1944). "Ludendorff: the German concept of total war." In Edward Mead Earle (ed.), *Makers of Modern Strategy*. Princeton: Princeton University Press.

Spiro, Herbert J. (1968). "Totalitarianism." *International Encyclopedia of the Social Sciences*, Vol. 16. New York: Crowell, Collier and Macmillan.

Staff, Ilse, ed. (1964). *Justiz im Dritten Reich: eine Dokumentation*. Frankfurt am Main: Fischer-Bücherei.

Stalin, Joseph (1924). *The Foundations of Leninism*. Reprinted in Bruce Franklin, ed. (1972). *The Essential Stalin: Major Theoretical Writings, 1905–1952*. Garden City, N.Y.: Doubleday, Anchor.

Stepan, Alfred (1971). *The Military in Politics: Changing Patterns in Brazil*. Princeton: Princeton University Press.

––––––––––– (1973). "The new professionalism of internal welfare and military role expansion." In A. Stepan (ed.), *Authoritarian Brazil: Origins, Policies, and Future*. New Haven: Yale University Press.

Stern, Fritz (1965). *The Politics of Cultural Despair*. Garden City, N.Y.: Doubleday.

Sternberger, Dolf, and Bernhard Vogel, eds. (1969–). *Die Wahl der Parlamente und anderer Staatsorgane*. Vol. 1 for Europe, others in progress; with extensive bibliographic references. Berlin: De Gruyter.

Stewart, Philip (1968). *Political Power in the Soviet Union: A Study of Decision-Making in Stalingrad*. Indianapolis: Bobbs-Merrill.

Strothmann, Dietrich (1963). *Nationalsozialistische Literaturpolitik*. Bonn: H. Bouvier u. Co.

Struve, W. C. (1973). *Elites against Democracy: Leadership Ideals in Bourgeois Political Thought in Germany, 1890–1933*. Princeton: Princeton University Press.

Suárez, Andrés (1967). *Cuba: Castroism and Communism, 1959–1966*. Cambridge, Mass.: M.I.T. Press.

Supek, Rudi (1973). "The Statist and self-managing models of socialism." In Allen H. Barton, Bogdan Denitch, and Charles Kadushin (eds.), *Opinion-Making Elites in Yugoslavia*. New York: Praeger.

Swartz, Marc J. (1968). *Local-Level Politics: Social and Cultural Perspectives*. Chicago: Aldine.

Swayze, Harold (1962). *Political Control of Literature in the USSR, 1946–1959*. Cambridge, Mass.: Harvard University Press.

Swearer, Howard R., with Myron Rush (1964). *The Politics of Succession in the U.S.S.R.: Materials on Khrushchev's Rise to Leadership*. Boston: Little, Brown.

Talmon, J. L. (1961). *The Origins of Totalitarian Democracy*. New York: Praeger.

Tang, Peter S. H., and Joan Maloney (1962). *The Chinese Communist Impact on Cuba*. Chestnut Hill, Mass.: Research Institute on the Sino-Soviet Bloc.

Tannenbaum, Edward R. (1972). *The Fascist Experience: Italian Society and Culture, 1922–1945*. New York: Basic Books.

Taylor, Charles Lewis, and Michael C. Hudson (1972). *World Handbook of Political and Social Indicators*. 2d. ed. New Haven: Yale University Press.

Taylor, George E. (1967). "Communism and Chinese history." In Donald W. Treadgold (ed.), *Soviet and Chinese Communism: Similarities and Differences*. Seattle: University of Washington Press.

Taylor, Philip B., Jr. (1960). "The Mexican elections of 1958: affirmation of authoritarianism?" *Western Political Quarterly* 13:722–44.

Thalheimer, August (1930). "Über den faschismus." *Gegen den Strom: Organ der KPD (Opposition)*. Reprinted in O. Bauer, H. Marcuse, and A. Rosenberg (1967), *Faschismus und Kapitalismus*. Edited by Wolfgang Abendroth. Frankfurt: Europäische Verlagsantalt.

Thomas, Hugh (1971). *Cuba: The Pursuit of Freedom*. New York: Harper & Row.

Thompson, Leonard M. (1966). *The Republic of South Africa*. Boston: Little, Brown.

Tigrid, Pavel (1969). *La chute irrésistible d'Alexander Dubcek*. Paris: Calmann-Lévy.

Timashef, Nicholas S. (1960). "The inner life of the Russian Orthodox Church." In Cyril E. Black (ed.), *The Transformation of Russian Society*. Cambridge, Mass.: Harvard University Press.

Tinbergen, Jan (1961). "Do communist and free economies show a converging pattern?" *Soviet Studies* 1:133–41.

Titus, David Anson (1974). *Palace and Politics in Prewar Japan*. New York: Columbia University Press.

Toharia, José Juan (1974). "The Spanish judiciary: a sociological study. Justice in a civil law country undergoing social change under an authoritarian regime." Ph.D. dissertation in sociology, Yale University.

Tökés, Rudolf L. (1974). "Dissent: the politics for change in the USSR." In Henry W. Morton and Rudolf L. Tökés (eds.), *Soviet Politics and Society in the 1970's*. New York: Free Press.

Tomasevich, Jozo (1955). *Peasants, Politics, and Economic Change in Yugoslavia*. Stanford: Stanford University Press.

Townsend, James R. (1972). *Political Participation in Communist China*. Berkeley: University of California Press.

———— (1974). *Politics in China*. Boston: Little, Brown.

Travaglini, Thomas (1963). *Der 20 Juli. Technik und Wirkung seiner propagandistischen Behandlung nach den amtlichen SD-Berichten*. Berlin: Freie Universität. (Inaug. Diss.)

Treadgold, Donald W., ed. (1967). *Soviet and Chinese Communism: Similarities and Differences*. Seattle: University of Washington Press.

Trindade, Helgio (1974). *Integralismo: O Fascismo Brasileiro na Decada de 30*. Sao Paulo: Difusao Europeia do Livro.

Triska, Jan F., ed. (1969). *Communist Party-States: Comparative and International Studies.* Indianapolis: Bobbs-Merrill.

Trotsky, Leon (1937). *The Revolution Betrayed.* New York. Doubleday.

Tucker, Robert C. (1961). "Towards a comparative politics of movement-regimes." *American Political Science Review* 55:281–89.

——————— (1963). *The Soviet Political Mind.* New York: Praeger.

——————— (1965). "The dictator and totalitarianism." *World Politics* 17:555–84.

——————— (1969). "On the comparative study of communism." In F. J. Fleron, Jr. (ed.), *Communist Studies and the Social Sciences.* Chicago: Rand McNally.

Turner, Henry A. (1972). "Fascism and modernization." *World Politics* 24:547–64.

——————— (forthcoming). "Fascism and modernization: a few corrections." *World Politics.*

Turner, Victor, and Marc Swartz, eds. (1966). *Political Anthropology.* Chicago: Aldine.

Tyrell, Albrecht, ed. (1969). *Führer Befiehl . . . Selbstzeugnisse aus der "Kampfzeit" der NSDAP Dokumentation und Analyse.* Düsseldorf: Droste.

Ueberhorst, Horst (1968). *Elite für die Diktatur.* Düsseldorf: Droste.

Ugalde, Antonio (1970). *Power and Conflict in a Mexican Community: A Study of Political Integration.* Albuquerque: University of New Mexico Press.

Uhlig, Heinrich (1956). *Die Warenhäuser im Dritten Reich.* Cologne: Westdeutscher Verlag.

Ulam, Adam B. (1968). *Expansion and Coexistence: The History of Soviet Foreign Policy from 1917–67.* New York: Praeger.

Ungari, Paolo (1963). *Alfredo Rocco e l'Ideologia giuridica del Fascism.* Brescia: Morcelliana.

U.S. Department of State, Bureau of Intelligence and Research (1971). *World Strength of the Communist Party Organizations.* Washington, D.C.: Government Printing Office.

U.S. Department of State, Division of Research for Europe, Office of Intelligence Research (1948). *Direct Popular Elections in the Soviet Union.* OIR Report No. 4711. Washington, D.C.: Government Printing Office.

Vaker, Nicholas (1962). *The Taproot of Soviet Society.* New York: Harper & Row.

Vallauri, Carlo (1971). *Le radici del corporativismo.* Roma: Bulzoni.

Van den Berghe, Pierre L. (1967). *South Africa: A Study in Conflict.* Berkeley: University of California Press.

Van Doorn, Jacques, ed. (1968). *Armed Forces and Society.* The Hague: Mouton.

Vatikiotis, P. J. (1961). *The Egyptian Army in Politics: Pattern for New Nations?* Bloomington: Indiana University Press.

Vermeil, Edmond (1955). "The origin, nature and development of German nationalist ideology in the 19th and 20th centuries." In Maurice Baumont, John H. E. Fried, and Edmond Vermeil (eds.), *The Third Reich*. International Council for Philosophy and Humanistic Studies, with the assistance of UNESCO. New York: Praeger.

Vernier, Bernard (1963). *L'Irak d'aujourd'hui*. Paris. A. Colin.

Viereck, Peter (1961). *Metapolitics: The Roots of the Nazi Mind*. New York: Capricorn.

Vierhaus, Rudolf (1964). "Faschistisches Führerturm: Ein Beitrag zur Phänomenologie des europäischen Faschismus." *Historische Zeitschrift* 198:614–39.

Voegelin, Erich (1936). *Der Autoritäre Staat*. Vienna: Julius Springer.

Vogel, Ezra (1967). "Voluntarism and social control." In Donald W. Treadgold (ed.), *Soviet and Chinese Communism*. Seattle: University of Washington Press.

——————— (1971). *Canton under Communism: Programs and Politics in a Provincial Capital, 1949–1968*. New York: Harper & Row.

Vogelsang, Thilo (1962). *Reichswehr, Staat und NSDAP: Beiträge zur deutschen Geschichte 1930–1932*. Stuttgart: Deutsche Verlags-Anstalt.

Voss, Joachim (1971). *Der progressistische Entwicklungsstaat: Das Beispiel der Republik Guinea*. Hannover: Verlag für Literatur und Zeitgeschehen.

Wagner, Albrecht (1968). *Die Umgestaltung der Gerichtsverfassung und des Verfahrens- und Richterrechts im nationalsozialistischen Staat*. Stuttgart: Deutsche Verlags-Anstalt.

Walker, Malcolm T. (1972). *Politics and the Power Structure: A Rural Community in the Dominican Republic*. New York: Teachers College Press.

Wallerstein, Immanuel (1961). *Africa: The Politics of Independence. An Interpretation of Modern African History*. New York: Random House (Vintage).

——————— (1966). "The decline of the party in single-party African states." In Joseph LaPalombara and Myron Weiner (eds.), *Political Parties and Political Development*. Princeton: Princeton University Press.

Ward, Robert E., and Dankwart A. Rustow, eds. (1964). *Political Modernization in Japan and Turkey*. Princeton: Princeton University Press.

Ware, Alan (1974). "Polyarchy." *European Journal of Political Research* 2:179–99.

Waterbury, John (1970). *The Commander of the Faithful: The Moroccan Political Elite. A Study in Segmented Politics*. New York: Columbia University Press.

Weber, Eugen (1964). *Varieties of Fascism*. Princeton: Nostrand.

Weber, Hermann (1969). *Die Wandlung des deutschen Kommunismus: Die Stalinisierung der KPD in der Weimarer Republik*. Frankfurt am Main: Europäische Verlagsanstalt.

Weber, Max (1968). *Economy and Society*. Edited and translated by Guenther Roth and Claus Wittich, 3 vols. New York: Bedminster Press.

Webster, Richard A. (1960). *The Cross and the Fasces: Christian Democracy and Fascism in Italy*. Stanford: Stanford University Press.

Weeks, Albert L. (1970). *The Other Side of Coexistence: An Analysis of Russian Foreign Policy*. New York: Pitman.

Weiker, Walter F. (1963). *The Turkish Revolution: 1960–1961*. Washington: The Brookings Institution.

———————— (1973). *Political Tutelage and Democracy in Turkey: The Free Party and Its Aftermath*. Leiden: E. J. Brill.

Weinberg, Gerhard L., ed. (1964). "Adolf Hitler und der NS-Führungsoffizier (NSFO)." *Vierteljahrshefte für Zeitgeschichte* 12:443–56.

Weinberg, Ian (1969). "The problem of convergence of industrial societies: a critical look at the state of a theory." *Comparative Studies in Society and History* 11:1–15.

Weiner, Stephen M. (1970). "Socialist legality on trial." In Abraham Brumberg (ed.), *In Quest of Justice*. New York: Praeger.

Weinkauff, Hermann (1968). *Die deutsche Justiz und der Nationalsozialismus*. Stuttgart: Deutsche Verlags-Anstalt.

Welch, Claude E., Jr., ed. (1970). *Soldier and State in Africa: A Comparative Analysis of Military Intervention and Political Change*. Evanston: Northwestern University Press.

Welch, Holmes (1972). *Buddhism under Mao*. Cambridge, Mass.: Harvard University Press.

Welk, William G. (1938). *Fascist Economic Policy: An Analysis of Italy's Economic Experiment*. Cambridge, Mass.: Harvard University Press.

Werner, Andreas (1964). *SA und NSDAP. SA: "Wehrverband," "Parteitruppe" oder "Revolutionsarmee"?* Erlanden: A. Werner.

Wheaton, Eliot Barculo (1969). *Prelude to Calamity. With a Background Survey of the Weimar Era*. Garden City, N.Y.: Doubleday.

Wheelock, Keith (1960). *Nasser's New Egypt*. New York: Praeger.

Wiarda, Howard J. (1968). *Dictatorship and Development: The Methods of Control in Trujillo's Dominican Republic*. Gainesville: University of Florida Press.

———————— (1973a). "Toward a framework for the study of political change in the Iberic-Latin tradition: the corporative model." *World Politics* 25:206–35.

———————— (1973b). "The Portuguese corporative system: basic structures and current functions." *Iberian Studies* 2:73–80.

———————— (1974). "Corporatism and development in the Iberic-Latin word: persistent strains and new variations." *The Review of Politics* 36:3–33.

Wiatr, Jerzy J. (1962). "Elections and voting behavior in Poland." In A. Ranney (ed.), *Essays on the Behavioral Study of Politics*. Urbana: University of Illinois Press.

————————, ed. (1967). *Studies in Polish Political System*. Warsaw: Polish Academy of Sciences.

Wiatr, Jerzy J., and Adam Przeworski (1966). "Control without opposition." *Government and Opposition* 1:227–39.

Wiles, P. J. D., and Stefan Markowski (1971). "Income distribution under communism and capitalism." *Soviet Studies* 22:344.

Willame, Jean-Claude (1972). *Patrimonialism and Political Change in the Congo.* Stanford: Stanford University Press.

Willner, Ann Ruth (1968). *Charismatic Political Leadership: A Theory.* Center of International Studies Research Monograph 32. Princeton: Princeton University.

Wilson, David A. (1962). *Politics in Thailand.* Ithaca: Cornell University Press.

Winckler, Edwin A. (1970). "Political anthropology." In Bernard J. Siegel (ed.), *Biennial Review of Anthropology, 1969.* Stanford: Stanford University Press.

Windsor, Philip, and Adam Roberts (1969). *Czechoslovakia, 1968: Reform, Repression and Resistance.* London: Chatto and Windus.

Winkler, Heinrich August (1972). *Mittelstand, Demokratie und Nationalsozialismus, Die Politische Entwicklung von Handwerk und Kleinhandel in der Weimarer Republik.* Cologne: Kiepenheuer und Witsch.

Wiseman, H. V. (1966). *Political Systems: Some Sociological Approaches.* London: Routledge & Kegan Paul.

Wittfogel, Karl A. (1957). *Oriental Despotism: A Comparative Study of Total Power.* New Haven: Yale University Press.

Wolf, Eric R., and Edward C. Hansen (1967). "Caudillo politics: a structural analysis." *Comparative Studies in Society and History* 9:168–79.

Wolfe, Bertram D. (1968). "Russia and the USA: a challenge to the convergence theory." *The Humanist* 28:3–8.

Woolf, S. J., ed. (1968). *The Nature of Fascism.* London: Weidenfeld and Nicolson.

——————, ed. (1969). *European Fascism.* New York: Random House (Vintage).

Wu, Yuan-li, ed. (1973). *China: A Handbook.* New York: Praeger.

Wulf, Joseph (1963a). *Literatur und Dichtung im Dritten Reich: Ein Dokumentation.* Güterlosh: Sigbert Mohn.

——————— (1963b). *Die Bildenden Künste im Dritten Reich: Ein Dokumentation.* Güterlosh: Sigbert Mohn.

——————— (1963c). *Musik im Dritten Reich: Ein Dokumentation.* Güterlosh: Sigbert Mohn.

——————— (1964). *Theater und Film im Dritten Reich: Ein Dokumentation.* Güterlosh: Sigbert Mohn.

Yang, C. K. (1965). *Chinese Communist Society: The Family and the Village.* Cambridge, Mass.: M.I.T. Press.

Yeh, K. C. (1967). "Soviet and Chinese industrialization strategies." In D. Treadgold (ed.), *Soviet and Chinese Communism: Similarities and Differences.* Seattle: University of Washington Press.

Yglesias, José (1969). *In the Fist of the Revolution: Life in a Cuban Country Town.* New York: Random House (Vintage).

Young, William B. "Military regimes shape Africa's future. the military: key force." Unpublished paper.

Zagoria, Donald S. (1969). *The Sino-Soviet Conflict 1956–1961.* New York: Atheneum.

Zaninovich, M. George (1968). *The Development of Socialist Yugoslavia.* Baltimore: Johns Hopkins University Press.

Zapf, Wolfgang (1965). *Wandlungen der deutschen Elite: Ein Zirkulationsmodell Deutscher Führungsgruppen 1919–1961.* Munich: Piper.

Zartman, I. William, ed. (1971). *Man, State and Society in the Contemporary Maghreb.* New York: Praeger.

Zeller, Claus (1969). *Elfenbeinküste: Ein Entwicklungsland auf dem Wege zur Nation.* Freiburg: Rombach.

Zeman, Zbynek A. (1968). *Prague Spring: A Report on Czechoslovakia 1968.* Harmondsworth: Penguin.

Ziegler, Heinz O. (1932). *Autoritärer oder Totaler Staat.* Tübingen: J. C. B. Mohr (Paul Siebeck).

Zipfel, Friedrich (1965). *Kirchenkampf in Deutschland.* Berlin: de Gruyter.

Zmarzlik, Hans-Günter (1973). "Social Darwinism in Germany, seen as a historical problem." In Hajo Holborn (ed.), *Republic to Reich: The Making of the Nazi Revolution.* New York: Random House (Vintage).

Zolberg, Aristide R. (1966). *Creating Political Order: The Party-States of West Africa.* Chicago: Rand McNally.

_____ (1969). *One-Party Government in the Ivory Coast.* Princeton: Princeton University Press.

Zonis, Marvin (1971). *The Political Elite of Iran.* Princeton: Princeton University Press.

4
THE THEORY OF COLLECTIVE CHOICE

MICHAEL TAYLOR

Politics arises out of disagreement and scarcity—when people have different desires which cannot all be satisfied. Disagreement and scarcity are of course only necessary conditions for the occurrence of political activity. They are not sufficient, for the parties to a dispute may not do anything about their differences, or if they do, it need not be directly political: the dispute may be settled by the murder of one party by the other, or by an agreement to hold a pistol duel, consult an oracle, or flip a coin.

The outcomes of duels (and other contests), the judgments of oracles (and other authorities), and the results of coin-flipping (and other chance mechanisms) may be viewed as 'collective choices' or 'social decisions'. Even combat, including the use of murder, can be called a 'social decision procedure', Barry (1965, Chapter 5) uses 'social decision procedure' in this very broad sense, so that it includes *any* method of resolving disputes. The types of social decision to be discussed below will be more restricted. Decisions by contest, combat, chance, and appeal to authority will be of little direct interest. Rather, we shall be interested in social decisions which stand in some more or less determinate relation to the wants or preferences of the individuals concerned. Of course, *all* disputes occur because the individual preferences are what they are; but if a dispute is settled by recourse to contest, combat, chance, or authority, then the outcome does not necessarily bear any determinate relation to these preferences, except in the trivial sense that it 'ignores' all of them (or perhaps those of all but one of the individuals).

I am grateful to Hayward Alker, Brian Barry, and Amartya Sen for their helpful comments on a draft of the chapter, to Donald Moon for helping to rectify errors, and to Cambridge University Press for permission to use material from my article on "Mathematical Political Theory" in the *British Journal of Political Science* 1 (1971), pp. 339–82.

This still leaves a very broad range of social decision methods—in fact, probably all those which we usually think of as *political*. Generally speaking, those which remain and which will be of interest here are methods involving *voting* or *bargaining* or both.

Nevertheless, parts of the chapter (particularly the second section) are pitched at a level of generality and abstraction at which both the social decision method (or rule) and the type of collectivity are unspecified. Here we are interested in the *properties* of decision rules and in the compatibility of certain properties, and where there is compatibility, we are interested in finding decision rules (or classes of rules) which possess all the given properties. In principle, the set of individuals making the collective choice could be, for example, a jury, a committee, a legislature, an electorate, or two negotiators representing labor and management or their respective nations; it might also be an informal small group, a primitive tribe, or the entire population of a nation state, though making this characterization precise may sometimes be difficult. In specific contexts, the 'collective choices' referred to in these general sections would have more familiar names: verdicts, public policies, election outcomes, bargains, and so on.

It would not be too far-fetched to say that most political activity is a kind of collective decision-making. Yet most of the theoretical work described here is of very recent origin, having been done mainly in the 1960s and early 1970s, and is still at a very primitive stage of development. In the concluding section, I will briefly review some of the limitations and deficiencies of what has been done so far. Two points in particular should be mentioned here, because they are worth bearing in mind throughout.

First, in all the work described below, individual preferences are taken as given and assumed to remain constant, at least during the collective decision-making in question. The incorporation of variable individual preferences into formal theories of collective choice has hardly begun. Such incorporation presumably will enormously complicate explanatory theories of collective decision-making, though I believe that in some contexts the complication is a necessary one. In 'normative' theories of collective choice, however, the problem itself may have to be reformulated; for, as Arrow (1963) has remarked, "if individual values can themselves be affected by the method of social choice, it becomes much more difficult to learn what is meant by one method's being preferable to another" (p. 8).

Second, the very nature of these individual preferences is problematic, and the difficulties of empirically ascertaining them are in many situations formidable. These problems are of course evaded by those who would equate 'preference' with 'choice'. That a man's preferences may not be revealed by his choices has been noted by several writers, including Majumdar (1956). One important reason for this, *strategic* behavior, will be discussed later. The identification of 'preference' with 'choice' also ignores a number of interesting psychological problems, such as the possibility that preferences are 'rationalizations' of 'unpremeditated' choices.

Most of the theoretical work on collective choice is mathematical. I have tried to avoid using mathematics here (and proofs of theorems are omitted entirely), but a certain amount of formality was unavoidable in a highly compressed summary. Most of the propositions stated symbolically are also stated in ordinary English, though often, inevitably, with a consequent loss of precision and the introduction of some ambiguity. In this respect, the second half of the chapter (beginning with the section on two-party electoral competition) will probably be much more accessible to some and could be read first or by itself, although it is not completely independent of the first half; it contains only a very few mathematical statements (mainly in the section on cardinal preferences and 'Utilitarianism') and, furthermore, deals with subjects which should be more familiar to the nonspecialist than those of the first half of the chapter. But even in the more abstract first half, the only mathematical ideas used are the notions of a set and a function or mapping and the most elementary parts of formal logic. (Discussions of these topics can be found in most introductory texts on modern mathematics.) Finally, I suggest that the reader who has difficulty with this more formal material might profit from a preliminary reading of the chapter on political evaluation by Barry and Rae in Volume 1 of this *Handbook;* it deals nontechnically with problems closely related to those of the first half of the present chapter and in many ways is complementary to it.

The extent of my debt, mainly in the early sections, to Amartya Sen's *Collective Choice and Social Welfare* and Prasanta Pattanaik's *Voting and Collective Choice,* which appeared during the preparation of this chapter, should be obvious from my references to them. The nonmathematical reader wishing to go further can do no better than to begin with the informal chapters which Sen has interleaved with his mathematical presentation. For the mathematician, there is the new book, *The Theory of Social Choice,* by Peter Fishburn, who kindly made a draft available to me while I was working on this chapter.

PRELIMINARY DEFINITIONS

The Alternatives

The set of alternatives between which a collective choice is being made will be denoted by S. The members of S, denoted by $x, y, z, \ldots$, are assumed to be mutually exclusive. In general they will be 'social states', giving a complete specification of the state of every individual in the group or society throughout all future time. For most purposes, however, this specification need contain only a small number of relevant particulars, so that S may comprise, for example, the candidates in an election, or the choices facing a parliament in a series of divisions on one bill (the status quo, the original bill, the bill with an amendment, the bill with an amended amendment) or on a sequence of bills (cf. Arrow, 1963, pp. 17–18 and 87–88).

In much of the chapter, especially the first half, the alternatives will be 'unstructured' or 'arbitrary'; that is, no more will be said of them than has been said above. Sometimes, however, topological assumptions will be made about S: the alternatives will be points in N-dimensional Euclidean space. And in our discussion of the problem of constitutional choice, we shall be interested in *risky* alternatives. Of course, arbitrary alternatives do not have to be non-'spatial' and nonrisky. Occasionally, the distinction between a finite and an infinite set S may be important.

Individual Preferences

The individuals' preferences among the alternatives will usually be described by *binary relations* defined on the set S. We take as primitive the *weak preference* relations R_i, $i = 1, 2, \ldots, n$, where n is the number of individuals. For any pair of alternatives x and y, xR_iy means that the ith individual 'weakly prefers' x to y; that is, he considers x to be at least as good as y. The relations P_i of (*strict*) *preference* and I_i of *indifference* may be defined in terms of R_i:

$$xP_iy \text{ if and only if } \sim yR_ix,$$
$$xI_iy \text{ if and only if } xR_iy \text{ \& } yR_ix,$$

where $\sim$ denotes negation and & denotes logical conjunction (and). The symbol V will be used for logical disjunction (or), $\rightarrow$ for implication (if . . . then), and $\longleftrightarrow$ for bi-implication (if and only if). Throughout, each R_i is assumed to be reflexive and complete, as follows:

Definitions. R_i is *reflexive* if and only if, for all x in S, xR_ix; R_i is *complete* if and only if, for all x and y in S, $xR_iy \ V \ yR_ix$.

Reflexivity ('x is at least as good as itself') appears to be the only noncontroversial assumption made about preference relations. Completeness of individual preference has been criticized by Aumann (1962, 1964a, 1964b), though I am unaware of any study of collective choice which abandons this assumption.

Various assumptions can be made about the 'rationality' or consistency of individual preferences. In the early studies of collective choice, each R_i was required to be transitive.

Definition. R_i is *transitive* if and only if, for all x, y, z in S, $xR_iy \text{ \& } yR_iz \rightarrow xR_iz$.

A binary relation which is reflexive, complete, and transitive is called an *ordering*.

It follows from the transitivity of R_i that both strict preference P_i and indifference I_i are also transitive (for example, see Arrow, 1963, pp. 14–15). For reasons which will be discussed below, neither of these implications is wholly palatable. The transitivity of I_i is especially demanding, and later we shall abandon it, requiring only that the strict preference relation P_i be transitive. In this case, R_i is said to be quasitransitive.

Definition. R_i is *quasitransitive* if and only if, for all x, y, z in S, xP_iy and $yP_iz \rightarrow xP_iz$.

An even weaker requirement is acyclicity.

Definition. R_i is *acyclic* if and only if, for all $x_1, x_2, \ldots x_j$ in S, $x_1P_ix_2$ & $x_2P_ix_3$ & $\ldots$ & $x_{j-1}P_ix_j \rightarrow x_1R_ix_j$.

Note that acyclicity rules out intransitive strict preference but allows for a 'chain' of any number of strict preferences to 'cumulate' into mere indifference.

Decision Rules and Collective Choices

The term *Decision Rule* will be used for any method of aggregating individual preferences to produce collective choices. The collective choices will usually be represented by the binary weak collective preference relation R. If individual preferences are represented by $R_1, R_2, \ldots, R_n$ and collective preferences by R, then a Decision Rule is a function, f, which determines a unique R for any n-tuple $R_1, R_2, \ldots, R_n$. The *domain* of f is the set of values which the n-tuple $R_1, R_2, \ldots, R_n$ may take, and the *range* of f is the set of possible values of R. Later, however, individual preferences will be represented by ordinal or cardinal utility functions. In these cases a Decision Rule is a functional—a function of the set of individual utility functions.

A given collective decision or class of decisions may be viewed as the product of quite different Decision Rules, the specification depending on the object of the analysis. A parliament's decisions may be analyzed in relation to its members' preferences or in relation to the electorate's preferences (or in other ways). In the first case, the Decision Rule might be the simple majority rule; in the second, it could be specified as a multistage rule, being compounded of primaries, general elections, and the legislative voting itself.

Throughout, R is assumed to be reflexive. We may also require it to be complete and transitive; but as with the individual preferences, either of these requirements may be considered too demanding. If R is reflexive, complete, and transitive, it is an ordering. Following Arrow (1963, p. 23), a Decision Rule yielding orderings will be called a *Social Welfare Function* (SWF).

The work of Arrow (1951, 1963) and his immediate successors was concentrated on SWF's. But in many collective choice situations a complete ranking of all the alternatives is not required; a 'rational choice' can be made by merely establishing the 'best' alternative (or alternatives). A best alternative of the set S is one which is at least as good as every other alternative in S with respect to the collective preference relation R. More formally:

Definition. x in S is a *best* element of S with respect to R if and only if, for all y in S, xRy. The set of best alternatives in S with respect to R is called the *choice set* of S with respect to R and is denoted by $C(S, R)$.

For some purposes, a nonempty choice set for the whole set of alternatives S is all that is of interest. But the existence of a best alternative *in every subset of S* may also be required.

Definition. A *choice function* $C(S, R)$ defined over S is a functional relation specifying a nonempty choice set for every nonempty subset of S.

If R is reflexive and S is finite, it is easily shown that R must be complete if *every* subset of S is to have a nonempty choice set; but as we shall see, R need not be transitive. If fact, quasitransitivity of R is sufficient for the existence of a choice function; and a necessary and sufficient condition is that R be acyclic. We collect these results together for later reference.

Lemma 1. Given that R is reflexive and complete over the set S,

a) transitivity of R is a sufficient but not necessary condition for the existence of a choice function $C(S, R)$;

b) quasitransitivity of R is a sufficient but not necessary condition for the existence of a choice function $C(S, R)$;

c) acyclicity of R is a necessary and sufficient condition for the existence of a choice function $C(S, R)$.

For proofs of the last two results, see Sen (1970d, pp. 15–16).

A Decision Rule which always yielded a social ordering R was labeled an SWF. We now define a Social Decision Function (SDF) to be a Decision Rule yielding a collective preference relation which can generate a choice function. More precisely:

Definition. A *Social Decision Function* (SDF) is a functional relation which specifies for any set of individual preferences R_i a unique social preference relation R that can generate a choice function $C(S, R)$.

If S is finite, then clearly an SWF is always an SDF (since an ordering generates a choice function), but not conversely.

Criteria

A *criterion* is a way of evaluating a Decision Rule; it indicates a property which a Rule may or may not possess. A number of Criteria will be defined below. Some of them have been called in other studies "conditions," "principles," and "value judgments." Two (related) concerns of the next section and parts of later sections are (1) the relations between Criteria, and (2) the relations between Criteria and Decision Rules. Part of (2) is concerned with what elsewhere has been called "the relations between principles and institutions." These sections of the chapter are thus normative in this limited sense, although some of the 'models' may be interpreted as explanatory theories if certain additional assumptions are made.

GENERAL POSSIBILITY AND IMPOSSIBILITY THEOREMS

In this section, the alternatives are arbitrary (or 'unstructured'), and preferences are represented by no more than binary relations. The relations among certain Criteria are examined, mainly without reference to particular Decision Rules, which are the subject of the next section. We begin by listing and briefly commenting on various Criteria.

Let $C(S)$ be a choice function, not necessarily determined by a binary preference relation.

Criterion α.   If x is in S_1, a subset of S_2, and x is best in S_2, then x is best in S_1; or, more formally:

$$x \in S_1 \subset S_2 \to [x \in C(S_2) \to x \in C(S_1)], \text{ for all } x.$$

Criterion β.   If x and y are both best in S_1, a subset of S_2, then x is best in S_2 if and only if y is also best in S_2; or, more formally:

$$[x,y \in C(S_1) \ \& \ S_1 \subset S_2] \to [x \in C(S_2) \leftrightarrow y \in C(S_2)], \text{ for all } x \text{ and } y.$$

For comments on α and β, see Sen (1969). Property α was proposed by Nash (1950) in a slightly different form as a requirement of an Arbitration Scheme (which will be considered later) and by Arrow (1959) as a requirement of any choice function.

The Criterion of Decisiveness.   The range of the Decision Rule is restricted to complete preference relations R.

Criterion U: Unrestricted Domain.   The domain of the Decision Rule includes all possible n-tuples of individual preference orderings.

A Decisive Rule can compare any pair of alternatives. Criterion U is not met when some restriction is made on the admissible combinations of individual preferences; this possibility is considered later.

The Weak Pareto Criterion (P).   For all x and y in S, (1) if every individual strictly prefers x to y, then so does the society, and (2) if every individual is indifferent between x and y, then so is the society.

The Strict Pareto Criterion (P*).   For all x and y in S, (1) if every individual considers x to be at least as good as y and at least one individual strictly prefers

x to y, then the society strictly prefers x to y, and (2) if every individual is indifferent between x and y, then so is the society.

These are the terms used by Pattanaik (1971, p. 37). Arrow (1963, p. 96) refers to P as "the Pareto Principle"; Sen (1970d, p. 53) calls P^* "strong Pareto rule." Clearly P^* implies P. Both of these Criteria appear to be extremely weak (although Theorem 9 below may raise some doubts) and are satisfied by most Decision Rules actually in use in politics. Much of theoretical welfare economics consists of the study of the Pareto criteria and their ramifications.

Definition. A Decision Rule which satisfies the Strict Pareto Criterion is said to be *Pareto-inclusive*.

Definition. An alternative x is said to be *Pareto-optimal* in any set A if and only if there is no other alternative y in A such that yR_ix for all i and yP_ix for at least one i. The set of Pareto-optimal alternatives in A will be denoted by A^*.

Criterion I: Independence of Irrelevant Alternatives. The social preference between any two alternatives x and y depends on the individual orderings of *only* x and y.

Definition. A Decision Rule which satisfies Criterion I is said to be *binary*.

Criterion I was introduced by Arrow (1951). A type of Decision Rule which does *not* satisfy I is the rank-order procedure, or the "Borda method" as Black (1958, pp. 59 ff. and pp. 156–59) calls it. In the simplest version, each alternative is awarded a score equal to the sum of its ranks in the various individual preference orderings. The resulting scores determine the social preference ordering. The relative scores of any two alternatives are clearly sensitive to the positions in the individual orderings of the remaining alternatives. For an example, see Sen (1970d, p. 39).

Criterion I has met with a great deal of criticism, mainly because, the critics claim, it rules out the use of preference *intensities* in making collective decisions (Rothenberg, 1961, Chapter 6). The word "ordering" in the Criterion in fact ensures this. It is maintained that the alternatives which are deemed to be "irrelevant" in the social choice between x and y provide information about the individuals' preference intensities for x and y. Attempts to use the "irrelevant" alternatives to construct cardinal measures of preference intensity or cardinal utility will be discussed below. For the moment, we emphasize that if I is a Criterion for Decision Rules of the form $R = f(R_1, R_2, \ldots, R_n)$, then the insensitivity of the collective choice to individual preference intensity is already guaranteed in the definition of a Decision Rule: changes in individual intensities result in changes in the collective choice only if they lead to changes in individual preference *orderings*. Thus the criticisms of this Criterion (for example, by Rothenberg, 1961, Chapter 6) are to some extent misplaced. This is noted by Samuelson (1967) and Pattanaik (1971, p. 43). (Cf. also Hansson, 1969, and Fishburn, 1970g.)

This does not imply, however, that preference intensities should not be taken into account in collective decision-making. The difficulty of doing so will be discussed later. And Criterion *I* does not imply that an individual does not use the "irrelevant" alternatives in arriving at his ordering of *x* and *y*.

Criterion D: Non-dictatorship.   There is no individual *i* such that, for all *x* and *y* in *S*, $xP_iy \to xPy$, regardless of the preferences of all other individuals.

Criterion D*: Strict Non-dictatorship.   There is no individual *i* such that, for some *x* and *y* in *S*, either $xP_iy \to xPy$ or $xR_iy \to xRy$, regardless of the preferences of all other individuals.

Note that (1) *D** implies *D*; (2) *D* prohibits only a global dictator (one who dictates on every pair of alternatives), whereas *D** prohibits even a local dictator (one who dictates on just one pair of alternatives); and (3) *D** also strengthens *D* by prohibiting a dictatorship of the kind: $xR_iy \to xRy$ (Sen, 1970d, pp. 53–54).

Criterion S: Nonnegative Responsiveness.   For all pairs of n-tuples $(R_1, \ldots, R_n)$ and $(R'_1, \ldots, R'_n)$ in the domain of a Decision Rule f which maps them into R and R', respectively, and for all *x* and *y* in *S*,

$$\text{if } [\text{for all } i, (xP_iy \to xP'_iy) \ \& \ (xI_iy \to xR'_iy)],$$
$$\text{then } [(xPy \to xP'y) \ \& \ (xIy \to xR'y)].$$

Criterion S*: Positive Responsiveness.   For all pairs of n-tuples $(R_1, \ldots, R_n)$ and $(R'_1, \ldots, R'_n)$ in the domain of a Decision Rule f which maps them into R and R', respectively, and for all *x* and *y* in *S*,

$$\text{if } [\text{for all } i, \ \big\{ (xP_iy \to xP'_iy) \ \& \ (xI_iy \to xR'_iy) \big\}$$
$$\text{and there exists a } k \text{ such that } \big\{ (xI_ky \ \& \ xP'_ky) \text{ or }$$
$$(yP_kx \ \& \ xR'_ky) \big\}], \text{ then } (xRy \to xP'_y).$$

Note that *S** implies *S*. Criteria *S* and *S** are Sen's (1970d, pp. 72–74) adaptations of, respectively, Murakami's (1968, pp. 37 and 55) criterion of *monotonicity* and May's (1952) criterion of *positive responsiveness*. Criterion *S* simply stipulates that if an alternative *x* rises or remains in the same place, relative to *y*, in every individual's preference ordering, then it does not go down, relative to *y*, in the social ordering. Criterion *S** goes further and stipulates that if *x* rises above *y* in some individual's preferences while all other individuals' preferences remain unaltered, then the society should still prefer *x* to *y* if it did so previously or if it was indifferent between *x* and *y* previously.

Criterion A: Anonymity.   For all pairs of n-tuples $(R_1, \ldots, R_n)$ and $(R'_1, \ldots, R'_n)$ in the domain of a Decision Rule f which maps them into R and R', respectively, if $(R_1, \ldots, R_n)$ is a permutation of $(R'_1, \ldots, R'_n)$ then, for all x and y in S, xRy if and only if $xR'y$.

This is Sen's (1970d, p. 72) adaptation of May's (1952) criterion of *symmetry*. It requires that f be a symmetric function of its arguments; i.e., the collective preferences are independent of the labeling of the individuals. It thus expresses a certain kind of *equality*. This is the kind of equality which everybody would want, perhaps, when in "the original position"—a possibility which will be examined later. But once differences have become established, so that some people are more interested than others in preserving the status quo, Anonymity might no longer have great appeal for, say, a member of a permanent minority. He might reasonably believe that a more egalitarian test than Anonymity is the principle that an alternative's chance of becoming the social decision equals the proportion of individuals who most prefer it. As Wolff (1970, p. 44) suggests, a Decision Rule which meets this criterion consists of drawing at random from a basket containing every individual's first preference.

Criterion N: Neutrality. For all pairs of n-tuples $(R_1, \ldots, R_n)$ and $R'_1, \ldots,$ $R'_n)$ in the domain of a decision rule f which maps them into R and R', respectively, and for all x, y, z, w in S,

$$\text{if } [\text{for all } i, (xR_iy \longleftrightarrow zR'_iw) \,\&\, (yR_ix \longleftrightarrow wR'_iz)]$$
$$\text{then } [(xRy \longleftrightarrow zR'w) \,\&\, (yRx \longleftrightarrow wR'x)].$$

Again, this is Sen's (1970d, p. 72) adaptation of May's (1952) criterion of the same name. Neutrality requires that the Decision Rule be 'neutral' with respect to *alternatives*; in effect, the collective decisions should be independent of how the alternatives are labeled. Qualified majority rules, as they are used in practice, do not meet this Criterion: one alternative—the status quo—is distinguished, and another alternative must obtain the required majority over the status quo to win, whereas if neither alternative obtains the required majority against the other, then the status quo wins.

Criterion L: Liberalism. For each individual i there is at least one pair of alternatives (x, y) such that he dictates the collective choice between them in either order; that is, $xP_iy \rightarrow xPy$ and $yP_ix \rightarrow yPx$.

Criterion L*: Minimal Liberalism. There are at least two individuals k and j and two pairs of alternatives (x, y) and (z, w) such that k and j dictate the collective choices on (x, y) and (z, w), respectively, each pair taken in either order.

Criteria L and L^* were proposed by Sen (1970a; 1970d, p. 87). Clearly, L implies L^*. These Criteria express the idea that some collective choices should not be 'collective' at all, for they are about personal matters. Whether some individual should or should not be allowed to read a certain book, everything else in the society remaining the same, is for him to decide, and the preferences of all other members of the society should be disregarded. Neither Criterion says anything at all about *which* choices are personal or how to determine them in practice. It is only the *existence* of such choices that is required—for every individual in the case of *L* and for only two individuals in the case of the very weak *L**.

Of course, these Criteria may not be applicable in every problem of social choice. For example, they may not be required to hold of elections, viewed as Decision Rules.

This completes our initial list of Criteria. A few more will be introduced in later sections, in connection with specific types of Decision Rules. We turn now to a summary of most of the theorems establishing the relations between these Criteria.

Lemma 2.   (a) Every choice function $C(S, R)$ generated by a binary relation R satisfies Criterion α but not necessarily Criterion β. (b) A choice function $C(S, R)$ generated by a binary relation R satisfies β if and only if R is an ordering.

For proofs, see Sen (1969; 1970d, pp. 17–19). That all choice functions satisfy α is encouraging; α appears to be a minimal requirement for rational choice (cf. Arrow, 1959). Criterion β, on the other hand, is less appealing, and we need not be too discouraged to find that it is satisfied only by choice functions generated by a transitive R.

Our first theorem is the central result of Arrow's *Social Choice and Individual Values.*

Theorem 1 (Arrow's impossibility theorem).   There exists no SWF satisfying Criteria *U, P, I,* and *D.*

This rather startling result can be said to have been the inspiration of most of the work reported in this section. It has met with a great deal of criticism, mainly concentrated, on the one hand, on the very formulation of the problem of social choice, in particular the assumption that an SWF (entailing a transitive social preference relation R) is required, and on the other hand, the Criterion requiring Independence of Irrelevant Alternatives. There have also been attempts to modify Criterion *U,* i.e., to place restrictions on the admissible individual preferences in order to find a Decision Rule which will then satisfy Criteria *P, I,* and *D.* These will be discussed below and in the next section. Criteria *P* and *D* have been relatively noncontroversial.

Theorem 1 is perhaps the simplest formulation of Arrow's result. It is presented and proved in Arrow (1967). The original formulation (in Arrow, 1951) involved five Criteria: *I* and *D,* as in this version; in place of *U,* the requirement that there be three alternatives which the individuals can order in any way; and in place of *P,* the criteria of "positive association of social and individual values" and of "citizens' sovereignty." "Positive association" is similar to the Criteria S and S^* defined above, being weaker than S and implied by it. "Citizens' sovereignty" required, in effect, that the collective choice be not imposed; i.e., *some n*-tuple of individual preferences should be able to bring about any given collective choice on each pair of alternatives. As Arrow (1963, p. 97) notes, Criterion P is implied by Positive Association, Citizens' Sovereignty, and I. Blau (1957) showed that Arrow's original formulation was not quite correct. Arrow notes this in his second edition (1963, pp. 102–3). Blau's criticism applies also to Inada's (1955) version. Luce and Raiffa (1957, Chapter 14) prove a version involving four of Arrow's criteria, together with Criterion U. A different sort of proof is given by Fishburn (1970c), who shows that the Criteria U, P, I, and D together imply the contradictory of Arrow's assumption that the set of individuals is nonempty and finite. (He also shows that the four Criteria are not inconsistent when the number of individuals is infinite.) Other versions of the theorem are given in Arrow (1950, 1963, pp. 96–103), Murakami (1961; 1968, Chapters 5 and 6), and Pattanaik (1971, Chapter 3 and Appendix). Perhaps the clearest proof of any version of the theorem is that given by Quirk and Saposnik (1968, pp. 108–114).

The critics of Criterion I, in the context of Arrow's theorem, have complained that it rules out the use of preference intensities in social choice. These critics believe either that intensities *should* be taken into account or that in practice they usually *are* taken into account. Thus, they argue, in the first case Criterion I is undesirable, and in the second case Arrow's theorem is simply irrelevant. But as we pointed out earlier, the use of intensities has already been prohibited in the *formulation* of the problem of social choice.

In Arrow's formulation of the problem, only individual preference orderings are to be taken into account, and the collective preferences must also be an ordering. Attempts at taking intensities into account and theorems similar to Arrow's which relax his assumption that individual preferences are orderings and require only that they be quasitransitive or acyclic will be introduced below. As for the social preferences, Kemp (1953–54), Buchanan (1954a, 1954b), and Buchanan and Tullock (1962, e.g., at p. 32) see no reason why 'collective rationality' should be required at all. Fishburn (1970a) has constructed some examples of sets of individual preferences for which the imposition of social transitivity seems to yield 'undesirable' outcomes. Schick (1969) objects to the transitivity of social indifference, which is implied by the transitivity of R. Pattanaik (1968a) and Sen (1969) argue that in most collective choice situations an *ordering* of the alternatives (a reflexive, complete, transitive R) is not required; all that is needed is a choice function specifying the best elements of each subset of S (see also Dummett and Farquharson, 1961). In other words, they suggest that it is the existence of SDF's rather than SWF's that is of interest. An SDF, it will be recalled, specifies a social preference relation that can generate a choice function $C(S, R)$. For this purpose, R need not be transitive; all that is necessary is that R be acyclic (so that I is not necessarily transitive).

The question now arises whether Arrow's theorem on SWF's holds also for SDF's. As Sen (1969) shows, it does not.

Theorem 2. If S is finite, there exists an SDF satisfying Criteria $U, P, I,$ and $D.$

Furthermore, an SDF still exists when P and D are strengthened to P^* and D^*, respectively.

Theorem 3. If S is finite, there exists an SDF satisfying Criteria $U, P^*, I,$ and $D^*.$

Thus there is a significant difference between SWF's and SDF's. Arrow's result holds for the former but not for the latter. However, if Criterion β is held to be desirable, then Theorems 2 and 3 are of little comfort, for it follows from Lemma 2(b) and Theorem 1 that:

Theorem 4. There is no SDF satisfying $U, P, I, D,$ and $\beta.$

Criteria A, N, S^*, and decisiveness were proposed by May (1952). Before introducing some possibility and impossibility theorems employing these Criteria, we note the following connections between them and some of those which appeared in the theorems above.

Lemma 3. (a) N implies $I.$ (b) A implies $D.$ (c) S^* implies S and S implies Arrow's "Positive Association." (d) Decisiveness, $N,$ and S^* together imply $P^*.$ (e) Decisiveness, $N,$ and S together imply either Criterion P or that all alternatives are socially indifferent.

Next we note an important theorem due to May (1952, 1953), adapted by Sen (1970d, p. 72) for any number of alternatives.

Theorem 5. Criteria $U, A, N,$ and S^* are together necessary and sufficient for a decisive Decision Rule to be the Method of Majority Decision.

Definition. A Decision Rule is the *Method of Majority Decision* (MMD) if and only if, for all x and y in $S,$

$$xRy \text{ if and only if } N(xPy) \geqslant N(yPx),$$

where $N(xPy)$ is the number of individuals who strictly prefer x to $y.$

The Method of Majority Decision, then, is the only Rule which satisfies $U, A, N,$ and S^*. But as we shall see later, the MMD is not an SWF because it does not yield transitive social preferences for every n-tuple of individual preferences. Hence, from Theorem 5 we have:

Theorem 6.   There exists no SWF satisfying Criteria U, A, N, and S^*.

As Sen (1970d, p. 73) points out, this also follows from Theorem 1 (Arrow's theorem) and Lemma 3 (b and d). The following result is stronger.

Theorem 7.   There exists no SDF satisfying U, A, N, and S^*.

Theorem 7 implies that we cannot have U, A, N, and S^* on the one hand and require the social decisions to be acyclic on the other. However, if S^* (Positive Responsiveness) is replaced by the weaker S (Nonnegative Responsiveness), then a Rule can be found which yields quasitransitive (and therefore acyclic) social preferences. In fact, we have:

Theorem 8.   For a Decision Rule that always yields a complete, quasitransitive social preference relation R, Criteria U, I, P^*, and A are together necessary and sufficient for the Decision Rule to be the Pareto-Extension Rule.

Definition.   A Decision Rule is the *Pareto-Extension Rule* if and only if, for all x and y in S,

$$xRy \longleftrightarrow \sim[(yR_ix \text{ for all } i) \ \& \ (yP_ix \text{ for at least one } i)].$$

In other words, xRy whenever y is not socially preferred to x according to the Strict Pareto Criterion (P^*). Thus, if xRy according to P^*, then xRy under the Pareto-Extension Rule also; but where the choice between two alternatives cannot be decided by P^* alone (as would be true if just one individual preferred x to y and another preferred y to x), the Pareto-Extension Rule declares x and y to be socially indifferent.

Theorem 8, proved by Sen (1970c; 1970d, pp. 74–77), is rather disturbing: a set of apparently reasonable Criteria together imply that all Pareto-optimal alternatives are socially indifferent; under these Criteria, the Strict Pareto Criterion must be the *only* basis of collective choice, and distributional considerations must be ignored.

Our final impossibility theorem, also proved by Sen (1970a; 1970d, Chapter 6), throws more light on the Pareto Criterion, this time in its weak form.

Theorem 9. (a) There exists no SDF satisfying Criteria U, P, and L. (b) There exists no SDF satisfying Criteria U, P, and L^*.

That is, if individual preferences are unrestricted, the Weak Pareto Criterion is incompatible with "Liberalism" and with "Minimal Liberalism." This is not so if we are concerned with choice between only two alternatives, but it holds as soon as we try to generate an acyclic collective preference relation (and hence an SDF) over more than two alternatives. The Criteria of Liberalism require, in effect, that there be issues with respect to which all individuals but one should 'mind their own business'; no matter how much their subjective utilities are affected, their preferences should not be taken into account. Theorem 9 says that, if such issues are present and "nosiness" (as Sen calls it) is ignored, then the Weak Pareto Criterion will not be satisfied by any SDF.

This completes the review of *general* possibility and impossibility theorems on the compatibilities of various Criteria when preferences are ordinal. In some of the following sections, the review is extended by an examination of the following three problems.

1. How must the admissible individual preferences be restricted so that the impossibility theorems above (with Criterion U modified) are no longer true?

2. Which of the theorems hold—and can any stronger impossibility results be established—when the assumption of the transitivity of individual preferences is relaxed?

3. Are the 'dilemmas' posed by these impossibility theorems alleviated by taking individual preference intensities into account?

MAJORITY RULE AND REPRESENTATIVE DEMOCRACY WITH ORDINAL PREFERENCES

Arbitrary Alternatives

Majority Rule

In various forms, majority rule is perhaps the most widely used Decision Rule in politics. Some of its properties are examined here; more will be discussed later, in the section on constitutional choice.

One version of majority rule, the Method of Majority Decision, has already been defined. The MMD, as we saw in Theorem 5, is the only decisive Decision Rule satisfying Criteria U, A, N, and S^*. Thus, by Lemma 3, it also satisfies both Pareto Criteria (P and P^*), Non-dictatorship (D), the Independence of Irrelevant Alternatives (I) and Nonnegative Responsiveness (S). However, the MMD may yield collective decisions which are intransitive or even acyclic. This follows, of course, from Arrow's theorem (Theorem 1 above), given that the MMD satisfies Arrow's Criteria (U, P, I, and D). But this property of the MMD has been known for some time. Condorcet examined it (and several other problems in the theory of collective choice) in an essay in 1785, and it was treated by Laplace in 1814, C. L. Dodgson (Lewis Carroll) in 1876, and Nanson in 1882. These early contributions are reviewed in some detail by Black (1958, Part II) and more briefly by Guilbaud (1952).

That majority rule may lead to intransitive social choices is often referred to as the "paradox of voting." The following set of three individual preference orderings of three alternatives provides a simple illustration.

1	2	3
x	z	y
y	x	z
z	y	x

Under the MMD, xPy, yPz, and zPx; that is, the social choices violate acyclicity. Black (1958, Part I) gives a detailed discussion of cyclical majorities. Necessary and sufficient conditions for their occurrence have been established by Nicholson (1965).

Some possible objections to the requirement that collective decisions be transitive were mentioned earlier; they apply here, of course, to the special case of cycles under majority rule. Some recent studies of a different kind have also examined the 'importance' of the paradox. They ask: Given a distribution of preference rankings over the population of individuals, what is the probability that a majority cycle will occur, for various values of n, the number of alternatives, and m, the number of individuals? It has been found that, if the distribution of preference rankings over the individuals is uniform, i.e., if all possible rankings are equally likely to occur, then the probability that there is no majority winner is small if the number of alternatives is small (with three alternatives, it varies from 0.0556 at $m = 3$ through 0.0811 at $m = 13$ and approaches 0.0877 in the limit as m becomes large); but for a very large number of individuals this probability rises rapidly with the number of alternatives (from 0.0877 at $n = 3$ through 0.4887 at $n = 10$ and 0.8123 at $n = 40$). (Guilbaud, 1952; Campbell and Tullock, 1965, 1966; Klahr, 1966; Garman and Kamien, 1968; Niemi and Weisberg, 1968). However, Williamson and Sargent (1967) claim that small departures from a uniform preference distribution—as, for example, when one of the rankings occurs with slightly greater frequency than any of the others—are sufficient to obtain transitivity with high probability. Niemi (1969) has also shown that the probability that the paradox will occur declines rapidly as the proportion of individuals whose preference ranking satisfies Black's single-peakedness criterion (see next subsection) increases—becoming, for example, as small as 0.05 when the proportion is about 75 percent with 45 individuals and three alternatives.

In the most recent study of this kind, DeMeyer and Plott (1970) have obtained analytic expressions for the probability (P) that the entire social ordering is transitive as well as the probability (Q) that one alternative is preferred by a simple majority to all the others. (The probability that there is such a 'Condorcet winner' *and* that the social ordering contains a cycle is then simply $Q - P$). Probabilities P and Q are found as functions of m and n for *any* distribution of preference orderings over the individuals.

Majority Decision and Restricted Preferences

One of the Criteria imposed in Arrow's theorem (and all the other impossibility theorems mentioned above) is that the domain of the Decision Rule should be unrestricted; i.e., all logically possible individual preference orderings are admissible. Clearly, if every individual had the same preference ordering, these theorems (without Criterion *U*) would no longer hold. For example, the MMD, which satisfies the Criteria, would now always yield transitive social choices. This prompts us to enquire whether a less severe restriction on admissible individual preferences will ensure transitivity. The problem has been exhaustively studied in the case of the MMD.

The first study of this kind is that of Black (1948a, 1948b)—although it was not, of course, presented as a modification of Arrow's work, which it preceded. Black proposed a condition of 'similarity' among the individual preferences, which he called "single-peakedness." Arrow's (1963, p. 7) more precise definition is given here. First, an ordering of the alternatives is said to be *strong* if there are no ties. It is assumed here that the individual preferences are orderings.

Definition. A set of individual preferences is said to be *single-peaked* over S if there exists a strong ordering *Q* over *S* such that, for all *x*, *y*, *z* in *S*, if $xQyQz$ or $zQyQx$ (that is, *y* is 'in between' *x* and *z* with respect to the strong ordering *Q*), then for each individual *i*,

$$xR_iz \to yR_iz \text{ and } zR_ix \to yR_ix.$$

Stated informally, a set of preferences is single-peaked if it is possible to arrange the individuals and the alternatives along some common axis such that the further away along this axis an alternative is from any individual's first preference, the lower it is in his preference ordering. In terms of Coombsian scaling theory, this amounts to saying that the individuals' preferences can be 'unfolded' into a single dimension (Coombs, 1950, 1954). The set of voters' preferences among political parties is sometimes offered as an example of this kind of similarity; but the limited evidence available suggests the contrary: voters do not perceive the parties as being located in only one dimension.

Black (1948a, 1948b) and Arrow (1951, pp. 78–79) show that if the condition of single-peakedness (SP) is met, then there exists an alternative against which no other alternative can obtain a simple majority (i.e., there is a nonempty choice set under the MMD), and that, if in addition the number of individuals is odd, the MDD yields transitive social choices (and hence is an SWF satisfying all of Arrow's Criteria except, of course, *U*).

Actually, it is not necessary that the individual preferences be SP over *all* alternatives, but only that they be SP over each *triple* of alternatives, with the strong ordering *Q* possibly varying from triple to triple. This weaker condition has been called "Weak Single-Peakedness" (WSP) and is defined below.

Several other conditions, representing even weaker restrictions on the admissible preferences and all defined over triples of alternatives, have been proposed. The most important ones, which subsume virtually all others, are the VR, ER, and LA conditions defined below.

Definitions (in each case, for any triple of alternatives x, y, z in S):

A triple is *Weakly Single-Peaked* (WSP) if it contains an alternative w such that each individual either strictly prefers w to one or both of the other two, or is indifferent between all three alternatives.

A triple is *Single-Caved* (SC) if it contains an alternative w such that each voter either strictly prefers at least one of the other two alternatives to w, or is indifferent to all three.

A triple is *Separable* (Sep) if it contains an alternative w such that each individual strictly prefers w to both others, or strictly prefers both others to w, or is indifferent to all three.

A triple is *Value-Restricted* (VR) if it is WSP or SC or Sep.

A triple (x, y, z) satisfies *Extremal Restriction* (ER) if, whenever some individual strictly prefers x to y to z, there is no other individual who strictly prefers z to x to y.

A triple satisfies *Limited Agreement* (LA) if it contains two alternatives x and y such that every individual weakly prefers x to y.

Definition.   A set of individual preference orderings over S is said to be VR, ER, etc., if every triple in S satisfies VR, ER, etc.

The SC condition first appeared in Vickrey (1960). Since WSP, SC, and Sep are subsumed under VR, they can now be discarded. Weaker forms of WSP, SC, and Sep were proposed by Dummett and Farquharson (1961). VR is due to Sen (1966), though it is equivalent to Ward's (1965) condition of "Latin-squarelessness" when preferences are strong. ER first appeared in Sen and Pattanaik (1969) and is equivalent to the union of three conditions (Dichotomous Preferences, Echoic Preferences and Antagonistic Preferences) previously given by Inada (1964, 1969). LA is also due to Sen and Pattanaik (1969) and is a weaker version of Inada's (1969) Taboo Preferences. We note that VR, ER, and LA are independent of one another.

Beginning with Black's proof that SP is a sufficient condition for the existence of an SWF under the Method of Majority Decision, there has been a steady stream of papers attempting to establish progressively more general conditions which are sufficient for the existence of a nonempty choice set in S, or a Social Decision Function or Social Welfare Function on S. Recently, however, conditions for each of these three things have been established which are both *necessary and sufficient*. Thus more general conditions (i.e., weaker restrictions on admissible individual preferences) are not likely to be found. "Necessity" is used here in the following special sense, suggested by Inada (1969).

Definition. A condition on the set of individual preferences is *necessary* if for every violation of the condition there is some way of assigning the resulting preference orderings to the individuals which is not in the domain of the Decision Rule (e.g., the social preferences under the MMD do not lead to an SWF).

We can now summarize this work by citing what appear to be the most general results so far proved in the case of the MMD.

Theorem 10

a) The necessary and sufficient condition for the MMD to be an SWF on S is that every triple of alternatives in S satisfies ER.

b) The necessary and sufficient condition for the MMD to be an SDF on a finite set S is that every triple of alternatives in S satisfies VR or ER or LA.

c) The necessary and sufficient condition for a finite set A of alternatives to have a nonempty choice set under the MMD is that every triple in the set A^* of Pareto-optimal alternatives in A satisfies ER or VR.

The third result gives the conditions for a specific set of alternatives to have a nonempty choice set; of course, the existence of a choice set for the set S does not imply that there is an SDF on S. Thus more demanding conditions are required for an SDF; these are given in part (b) of the theorem. Finally, an SDF requires only acyclic social preferences (Lemma 1 above); for the social preferences to be fully transitive (and hence for an SWF to exist) the conditions of (b) must be further strengthened, as indicated in part (a) of the theorem. It should be recalled (Lemma 2) that Criterion β (Arrow's condition of "rationality") is satisfied if and only if R is an ordering, i.e., if and only if an SWF exists.

Part (a) was first proved by Inada (1969), part (b) by Sen and Pattanaik (1969). Part (c) was proved by Pattanaik (1971, pp. 150ff); it is a generalization of earlier results of Pattanaik (1968a) and Sen and Pattanaik (1969). Proofs of (a) and (b) are also to be found in Sen (1970d, pp. 184–85), and proofs of all three results are in Pattanaik (1971).

When the individual preferences are *strong* orderings (or *chains*)—i.e., no individual is indifferent between any pair of alternatives—then the results above are simplified, because, in this case, ER $\rightarrow$ VR and LA $\rightarrow$ VR. The resulting theorems are proved in Sen (1970d, pp. 185–186) and Pattanaik (1971, pp. 85–86).

That the conditions in Theorem 10 for the existence of choice sets, SDF's and SWF's are necessary as well as sufficient suggests that more general conditions are not likely to be discovered. But it is difficult to appreciate just how weak these conditions in fact are, because they cannot be readily interpreted. The only restriction on individual preferences which has been given an interpretation is Black's Single-Peakedness. Later, however, in the section on 'spatial' alternatives, we shall see that, if the alternatives are points in a multidimensional space (a 'policy space' or 'commodity space') and if certain conventional assumptions are made about the individual utility functions, then all of these conditions, even the weakest of them (VR, ER, and LA), represent severe restrictions on the admissible preferences which are not likely to be satisfied.

Further results on the Method of Majority Decision will be presented in later sections.

Other Forms of Majority Rule

The MMD is only one of various forms of majority rule. It is, in effect, the binary version of what is usually called plurality voting. Alternative x is socially preferred to y if there are more people preferring x to y than there are preferring y to x. A stricter version of majority rule stipulates that x is socially preferred to y if and only if more than half the people prefer x to y. Following Sen and Pattanaik (1969) and Sen (1970d, p. 181), we call this the Strict Majority Rule.

Definition.   A decision rule is the *Strict Majority Rule* if and only if, for all x and y in S, $xPy \longleftrightarrow N(xPy)/N > \frac{1}{2}$, and $xRy \longleftrightarrow \sim yPx$, where N is the total number of individuals.

Leibenstein (1965) and Pattanaik (1968a; 1971, p. 96) call this Rule "the method of non-minority decision."

The Strict Majority Rule satisfies Decisiveness, U, A, N, S (but not S^*), and D. But like the MMD, it may violate acyclicity and hence fail to generate a choice function. The following example of Pattanaik (1968a) suggests another undesirable property. Suppose that there are 100 individuals and S consists of three alternatives x, y, and z. Thirty individuals have preferences zP_ixI_iy, 45 have yP_ixP_iz, and 25 have xP_izP_iy. Then under the Strict Majority Rule, we find that xPz, zPy, and xIy. Hence the choice set from S consists of x. Yet more individuals strictly prefer y to x than prefer x to y.

Pattanaik (1968a) also gives an example showing that the Strict Majority Rule may violate the Strict Pareto Criterion (P^*). In a choice between x and y, suppose that 51 individuals are indifferent between the two, while the other 49 strictly prefer x to y. Then according to P^*, x is socially preferred to y; but under the Strict Majority Rule they are tied.

The Strict Majority Rule can be adapted so that it no longer violates P^*, simply by 'incorporating' P^*. The result is called the *Pareto-Inclusive Strict Majority Rule* (Sen and Pattanaik, 1969).

Definition. A Decision Rule is the *Pareto-Inclusive Strict Majority Rule* if and only if, for all x, y in S, $xPy \longleftrightarrow N(xPy)/N > \frac{1}{2}$ or xR_iy for all i and xP_iy for at least one i, and $xRy \longleftrightarrow \sim yPx$.

In other words, if more than half the people strictly prefer x to y, then so does the society, but when less than half the people prefer x to y and less than half prefer y to x, yet x is preferred to y according to the Strict Pareto Criterion, then x is again socially preferred to y.

The properties of the three versions of majority rule and of the Pareto-Extension Rule defined earlier are collected together as Theorem 11 to facilitate comparison. Theorems 5 and 8 are incorporated, Lemma 3 is used, and it should be remembered that P^* implies P and S^* implies S.

Theorem 11

a) The Method of Majority Decision satisfies S^* and P^*.

b) The Strict Majority Rule satisfies S and P.

c) The Pareto-Inclusive Strict Majority Rule satisfies S and P^*.

d) The Pareto-Extension Rule satisfies S and P^*.

e) All four Rules satisfy U, A, N, I, D, and Decisiveness.

f) Of these four Rules, only the Pareto-Extension Rule guarantees acyclic social preferences and hence the existence of a choice function for all sets of individual preferences.

When the MMD and the Pareto-Extension Rule are compared with respect to these Criteria, the difference between them may appear at first to be slight. But the two respects in which they differ are important. First, the MMD satisfies S^* but the Pareto-Extension Rule does not. Positive Responsiveness (S^*) gives to each individual more 'power' than does Nonnegative Responsiveness (S), for under S^*, but not under S, each individual has the power to break a tie. But this 'democratic' property of the MMD is achieved at a cost: the social choices may not be transitive or even acyclic, whereas acyclicity (and in fact quasitransitivity) is always achieved with the Pareto-Extension Rule. Some sufficient conditions, in the form of restrictions on the admissible individual preferences, for the existence of a Social Decision Function are given by Pattanaik (1971, pp. 107–114) for both the Strict Majority Rule and the Pareto-Inclusive Strict Majority Rule.

Multi-Stage Decision Rules and Representative Democracy

So far, we have studied majority rule as it operates in isolation. In political decision-making, however, it is very often embedded in a *hierarchy* of majority votes. Pattanaik (1968c; 1971, p. 102) calls these hierarchies *Multi-Stage Ma-*

jority Rules. Thus a representative assembly's decision-making could perhaps be analyzed in terms of the Method of Majority Decision (if the relation between its decisions and the representatives' preferences is of interest), or it could be analyzed in terms of a Multi-Stage Majority Decision Rule, the two stages in the hierarchy being the election of the representatives (each by MMD) and the majority voting in the assembly itself.

Murakami (1966, 1968) and Fishburn (1971) have given a general analysis of Multi-Stage Decision Rules, not necessarily composed of majority votes. Most of their results are for the case in which there are two alternatives, though of course they will be valid for any number of alternatives if the Decision Rule satisfies Criterion *I* (the Independence of Irrelevant Alternatives).

Let the two alternatives be x and y. The ith individual's preference is denoted by D_i, which can take one of three values, as follows:

$$D_i = 1 \text{ when } xP_iy \text{ (pro)}$$
$$= 0 \text{ when } xI_iy \text{ (abstention)}$$
$$= -1 \text{ when } yP_ix \text{ (con).}$$

Similarly for the social decision D. The Decision Rule is written as $D = F(D_1, \ldots, D_n)$. Since D and the D_is are three-valued variables, the Decision Rule can be viewed as a three-valued *logical function.*

The function $F(X_1, \ldots, X_m)$, where $X_1, \ldots, X_m$ are the preferences of any subset of m individuals, is called a *voting operator* if it takes values 1, 0, -1 according to whether $X_1 + X_2 + \ldots + X_m$ is positive, zero, or negative. A voting operator, which is just a simple majority vote, is denoted by $((X_1, \ldots, X_m))$.

By making use of a theorem in three-valued logic, Murakami shows (1968, pp. 16–21) that *any* three-valued Decision Rule can be expressed in terms of votings, negations, and constants (1, 0, -1). Two examples, involving only votings are $((D_1, \ldots, D_n))$, which is a *direct democracy* (a simple majority vote among all the individuals), and

$$((((D_1, D_2, D_3)), ((D_4, D_5, D_6)), ((D_7, D_8, D_9)))),$$

which is a *representative democracy* of nine persons, where the majority decisions of the three 'subcommittees' are represented in a higher 'committee' of three. An example involving votings and constants is

$$((((D_1, D_2, D_3, D_4, D_5, D_6, -1, -1)), ((D_1, D_2, D_3, D_4, D_5, D_6, -1, -1)), 1)),$$

which represents the version of *two-thirds majority rule,* whereby x is preferred to y only if at least two-thirds of the nonabstainers prefer x to y.

Negations represent *reversals* of individual decisions ($-D_i$ 'negates' or 'reverses' D_i). Constants represent, in effect, 'fixed', outside votes.

Murakami introduces the Criteria of *Non-dictatorship, Monotonicity* and

Strong Monotonicity, which are the analogues for the two-alternative case of the Non-dictatorship (D), Nonnegative Responsiveness (S) and Positive Responsiveness (S^*) Criteria defined above. In addition, he uses the following Criteria.

Definitions

1) F is *Autonomous* if it can be expressed by voting operators and negations, without resort to constants.
2) F is *Self-Dual* if $F(-D_1, \ldots, -D_n) = -F(D_1, \ldots, D_n)$.
3) F satisfies the Criterion of *Nonreversal* (or "Faithful Representation") if no individual decisions are reversed (negated), i.e., if F can be expressed by voting operators and constants, without resort to negations.

Self-Duality implies that the Decision Rule treats every pair of alternatives similarly. The Neutrality Criterion (N) defined earlier is one possible generalization of Self-Duality.

The following theorem collects together some of the important relations between these criteria. Proofs can be found in Murakami (1968, Chapter 3).

Theorem 12

a) F is Autonomous if and only if it is Self-Dual.
b) If F is Strongly Monotonic, then it satisfies Nonreversal.
c) F is Monotonic if it satisfies Nonreversal.
d) If each individual variable D_i can enter only one voting operator, then F is Monotonic if and only if it satisfies Nonreversal.

A *Representative Democracy* (Murakami calls it simply a "democracy") is defined to be a Nondictatorial Decision Rule F consisting only of voting operators; that is, F is Nondictatorial and can be expressed without negations and constants. Murakami establishes *necessary* conditions for F to be a Representative Democracy.

Theorem 13. If F is a Representative Democracy, then it is Self-Dual, Monotonic, and Nondictatorial.

The following conjecture of Murakami's (1968, p. 45) was subsequently proved by Fishburn (1971).

Theorem 14. F is a Representative Democracy if it is Self-Dual, Strongly Monotonic, and Nondictatorial.

These two results should be compared with May's theorem (Theorem 5 above), which can be expressed in Murakami's terms, for the two-alternative case, as follows: F is the MMD (or a Direct Democracy) if and only if it is Self-Dual, Strongly Monotonic, and Anonymous.

Theorem 13 gives necessary conditions for a Representative Democracy, and Theorem 14 gives sufficient conditions. Conditions which are both necessary and sufficient are provided by Fishburn (1971). They are Self-Duality, Monotonicity, Unanimity [$F(1, 1, \ldots, 1) = 1$], and a new criterion given by Fishburn which, as he notes, does not appear to have any simple interpretation.

A Decision Rule F composed only of (simple majority) voting operators (but not necessarily Nondictatorial) is called a *Multi-Stage Majority Decision Rule* (MSMD Rule). Pattanaik (1968c; 1971, pp. 57–61, 102–106, and 130–132) gives a detailed discussion of such Rules for any number of alternatives. He shows that every MSMD Rule is Binary, Decisive, Neutral (N), and Nonnegatively Responsive (S), and it satisfies the Strict Pareto Criterion (P^*). Since P^* implies P and N implies I (Lemma 3), it follows from Theorem I (Arrow's theorem) that if the MSMD Rule is Nondictatorial (i.e., if it is a Representative Democracy), then it cannot satisfy Criterion U; i.e., it cannot yield transitive social choices for every set of individual preferences.

Thus, with the Method of Majority Decision, it is of interest to know the extent to which the admissible individual preferences must be restricted in order to guarantee the transitivity of social choices (or merely the existence of an SDF or of a nonempty choice set) under the Multi-Stage Majority Decision Rule. This problem has been solved by Pattanaik (1968c; 1971, Chapters 6 and 7), who has established the following results.

Theorem 15

a) Given that, in each voting operator, the number of individuals who are not indifferent between any triple of alternatives is odd, the necessary and sufficient condition for the MSMD Rule to be an SWF is that every triple of alternatives in S satisfies VR or LA.

b) The necessary and sufficient condition for the MSMD Rule to be an SDF on a finite set S is that every triple of alternatives in S satisfies VR or LA.

c) The necessary and sufficient condition for a finite set A to have a nonempty choice set under the MSMD Rule is that every triple in the set A^* of Pareto-optimal alternatives in A satisfies VR or La.

These results should be compared with the corresponding three parts of Theorem 10. Note that only in part (a) is there any restriction on the number of individuals.

Multi-Stage Majority Decision Rules form a subclass of the class of Binary (i.e., satisfying Criterion I), Decisive, Neutral (N), and Nonnegatively Responsive (S) Decision Rules. The MMD, the Strict Majority Rule, and the Pareto-Inclusive Strict Majority Rule also belong to this class (cf. Theorem 11).

Some sufficient conditions for the existence of an SDF for this wider class of Decision Rules are given by Pattanaik (1971, Section 6.2).

Intransitive Individual Preferences

Although we have permitted the social preference relation R to be, variously, transitive or quasitransitive or even acyclic, up to this point we have not relaxed the assumption that the *individual* weak preferences are transitive. But this assumption can be criticized on a number of grounds, and recently attempts have been made to establish some of the theorems of collective choice on the basis of a less demanding assumption.

It will be recalled that if R_i is reflexive, complete, and transitive, then P_i and I_i are transitive also. May (1954) has ingeniously adapted Arrow's theorem (Theorem 1 above) to argue that even the strict preference relation P_i may not be transitive, if the alternatives vary in several respects. An individual is assumed to choose as if he ranked the alternatives with respect to each of their attributes. Of course, these rankings, one for each attribute, may not be the same. The individual then 'aggregates' the rankings by some method which is assumed to satisfy Criteria $U, P, I,$ and D. Thus Arrow's theorem implies that the resulting individual preferences will not always be transitive. Criteria P and D are quite reasonable in this context, and possibly I is, too. But, as Pattanaik (1971, Chapter 7) points out, Arrow's formulation of the problem does not permit social choice to be based on preference intensities, and although this may be reasonable (or a practical necessity) in collective decision-making, its analogue in May's formulation is perhaps not so appealing: an individual may be able to take account of the 'intensity' (or 'relative importance' to him) of the various attributes in making an overall assessment.

Some (rather inconclusive) experimental evidence for this kind of intransitivity is presented in Papandreou (1963), May (1954), and Davis (1958) and is discussed by Edwards (1954, 1961). Rose (1957) concludes from his experiments that 'true' intransitivity is rare, observed intransitivity being the result of 'carelessness' or 'random choice' among indifferent alternatives.

Most of the critics of the assumption of transitive individual preferences take exception to the transitivity of *indifference*, rather than that of strict preference. Most of these criticisms are founded on the supposed inability of the individual to discriminate finely. Luce (1956) gives an example: A person likes his coffee without sugar; he is likely to be indifferent between a cup of coffee with no sugar and a cup with one grain of sugar, and between the latter and a cup with two grains, and so on; but he will prefer a cup with no sugar to a cup with 1000 grains of sugar. Thus indifference is intransitive in this case. This kind of argument was made by Armstrong (1951). The problem has since been studied in detail by psychologists, economists, and others interested in utility theory and the theory of measurement. A comprehensive survey and bibliography is given by Fishburn (1970d). One of the consequences of this interest in discrimination and intransitive indifference has been the development of theories of *probabilistic individual choice*. These theories are reviewed in Luce and Suppes (1965).

Other reasons for intransitive individual indifference are suggested by Buchanan (1954b), Weinstein (1968) and Schick (1969).

One assumption often used in probabilistic choice theories is *weak stochastic transitivity* (WST). This requires that

$$p(x, y) \geqslant \tfrac{1}{2} \ \& \ p(y, z) \geqslant \tfrac{1}{2} \rightarrow p(x, z) \geqslant \tfrac{1}{2},$$

where $p(x, y)$ is the probability that the individual chooses x out of x and y. Tversky (1969) has experimentally found "consistent, systematic and predictable" violations of this axiom. The alternatives used in his experiments were constructed by means of a *lexicographic semiorder*, which was a just-noticeable-difference structure (see section below on cardinal preferences) combined with a lexicographic ordering (see following section). Two criteria are used lexicographically to evaluate the alternatives, except where two alternatives are within a just-noticeable difference on the first criterion; they are then considered to be indifferent according to that criterion, and the second criterion is used to choose between them. Tversky presents a model of probabilistic choice to explain this type of intransitivity.

Only recently, however, have these criticisms made any impact on the theory of collective choice. Some of the theorems given above have been extended to the case in which individual indifference is not required to be transitive. The transitivity assumption can be weakened in various ways: quasitransitivity or merely acyclicity can be required of some or all of the individual preference relations. Pattanaik (1971, Chapter 7) shows that Theorem 2 ('there exists an SDF satisfying U, P, I, and D') is still valid even if just *one* individual strict preference relation (P_i) is acyclic (assuming still that all the R_i's are reflexive and connected). Unfortunately, the stronger Theorem 3 does not still hold. In fact, even if all the individual weak preference relations (R_i) are quasitransitive, there is no SDF with unrestricted domain which satisfies the Strict Pareto Criterion (P^*). Finally, we note that some of the theorems stated which give sufficient conditions, or necessary and sufficient conditions (in the form of restrictions on the admissible individual preferences) for the Method of Majority Decision and the Strict Majority Rule to yield transitive or quasitransitive social choices, have been extended to the case of quasitransitive individual weak preferences by Inada (1970), Fishburn (1970b, 1970f) and Pattanaik (1970b; 1971, Chapter 7).

Spatial Alternatives

Equilibrium Under Majority Rule

Thus far, no topological assumptions have been made about the alternatives between which the society is choosing. Now, however, we assume that the alternatives are points in a multi-dimensional *policy space;* they are described by the *m* variables $(x_1, x_2, \ldots, x_m)$. The society might be deciding between alternatives which possess several attributes, or it might be deciding several distinct issues at once.

It is assumed that each individual has an *optimum* or most preferred point in the space and that his (weak) preferences among all pairs of points in the space are complete and transitive. In most models it is also assumed that these preferences can be represented by an ordinal utility function. (A weak preference relation R is said to be represented by an *ordinal utility function* u if, for all pairs of alternatives x and y, $u(x) \geqslant u(y) \longleftrightarrow xRy$).

As in the previous sections, we are again interested in the existence of 'best' alternatives when the Decision Rule is Strict Majority Rule (although in some models other simple Decision Rules have also been studied). Whereas before the set of best alternatives was called the 'choice set,' it is usually called the *equilibrium set* when the alternatives are spatial. An *equilibrium point* (a point in the equilibrium set) is thus a point x such that no other point is strictly preferred to x by a simple majority of the individuals.

The existence of equilibrium points depends on the assumptions made about the form of the individuals' preferences. Economists (dealing with consumers and commodity spaces rather than voters and policy spaces) usually assume that each individual's preferences are convex and may be represented by continuous ordinal utility functions with continuous first-order partial derivatives. Black and Newing (1951) studied the equilibrium problem under Majority Rule using this assumption. Some of their results are generalized by Plott (1967), who established the following necessary and sufficient conditions for the existence of an equilibrium point in the case in which the number of voters (n) is odd.

1) An equilibrium point must coincide with one of the individual optima (O), and

2) the remaining optima can be paired so that all the contract curves (one for each pair) intersect at O.

Clearly, these conditions are extremely restrictive and will rarely be met in practice: equilibrium points are highly unlikely.

Parenthetically, we note here that under these assumptions (the alternatives are points in a multidimensional space and individual utilities are convex and differentiable), all the restrictions on admissible individual preferences which were presented earlier as sufficient conditions for the existence of SWF's or SDF's under the Method of Majority Decision are unlikely to be satisfied. This is the implication of a theorem due to Kramer (1973), who has shown that if at some point in the space there are three voters whose marginal rates of substitution between any two policy dimensions (or commodities) differ, then none of these conditions of the individual preference orderings will be met. Furthermore, he shows that, under these assumptions, less restrictive conditions do not exist.

Other assumptions about individual preferences have been used in spatial models of collective choice. Rae and Taylor (1971) assume that the individual utility functions are of the 'city-block' form. With the ith voter's optimum denoted by $(x_1^i, x_2^i, \ldots, x_m^i)$, the utility for him of the point $x = (x_1, x_2, \ldots, x_m)$ is

$$u^i(x) = \sum_{j=1}^m c_j^i \mid x_j^i - x_j \mid,$$

where $c_1^i, c_2^i, \ldots, c_m^i$ are positive constants (the 'weights' he attaches to the various dimensions). In other words, each individual simplifies the problem of choosing between complex multidimensional alternatives by comparing their distances from his optimum *in each dimension separately,* then combining these differences in a simple linear way. In the special case in which the weight for each dimension is the same for each voter (though the weights may differ between dimensions), Rae and Taylor prove that there always exists at least one equilibrium point for any simple Decision Rule from simple majority through unanimity, for any number of voters and any number of policy dimensions. However, as soon as the weights differ between individuals, the equilibrium sets may be empty.

The existence of equilibrium points under majority rule has also been established in the case in which the individual pairwise comparisons are based on the *lexicographic principle.* Suppose that each individual ranks the *dimensions* of the policy space (in order of their 'salience' or importance to him) in such a way that, of any two alternatives he prefers the one which is closest to his optimum on the first-ranked dimension; only if they are tied on this first dimension does he use the second dimension to choose between them; and so on. Then his preferences are said to be *lexicographic.* It has been proved that, if all individuals have the same salience ranking of the dimensions, then the equilibrium set is nonempty for every simple Decision Rule from simple majority through unanimity. But if the salience ranking differs between individuals, the equilibrium sets may be empty (Taylor, 1970). The first result has been generalized, in some respects, by Pattanaik (1973), who establishes a sufficient condition for the existence of a nonempty choice set under all binary, decisive, neutral and nonnegatively responsive Decision Rules, given that all individuals have lexicographic preferences based on the same ranking of the dimensions.

The city-block and lexicographic assumptions are unfortunately rather strong. They are both, of course, exceptions to the broad class of utility functions assumed by Plott and Kramer (and most economists). The city-block functions are convex (though not strictly so), but they are not differentiable. The lexicographic principle yields a complete and transitive weak preference ordering of all the points in the policy space, but these preferences cannot be represented by a continuous ordinal utility function, unless the policy space contains only a *finite* number of points (cf. Fishburn, 1970e, Chapter 4). The lexicographic assumption represents a very strong form of independence between the policy dimensions: there is absolutely no 'trade-off' between any of them. Nevertheless, lexicography seems to be a plausible basis of individual choice in the case in which the policy space is bounded and 'discrete' in such a way that no two points in the space are either 'very far' from each other or 'very close.'

A distressing implication of this section is that equilibrium policies exist only under very restrictive conditions. Thus equilibrium theory may be of little help in explaining policy outcomes or in evaluating institutions. Where equilibrium points do not exist, we might search instead for those points, P, such that the largest number of individuals wishing to move away from P in any direction is smallest. Clearly, such points always exist. This appealing 'equilibrium' criterion was suggested by Simpson (1969).

Two-Party Electoral Competition

The equilibrium theory of collective decision-making described above can be applied to certain aspects of political party competition. The multidimensional policy space is now defined by the set of criteria with reference to which the voters evaluate the parties. (We continue to speak of a 'policy space,' even though its dimensions may include criteria of evaluation which are not related to policy issues.) As before, each voter is characterized by an optimum point in this space, corresponding to his most-preferred position on the various dimensions. Since there are now a large number of voters, we do not specify each optimum as we did before, but we make assumptions about a frequency *distribution* of optima over the policy space. Each point in the space is a possible *program* or *platform* for one or more of the parties, and it is assumed that each party can adopt *any* program. In the two-party case, each party is assumed to choose a program in order to maximize its vote plurality over the other party. (An alternative assumption, examined by Hinich and Ordeshook, 1970, is that parties maximize votes per se.) Each voter is assumed to possess a utility function over the points of the policy space and to choose between the parties so as to maximize his utility.

As before, a point P is an *equilibrium* if there is no other point which a majority of the voters prefer to P. Thus, in the two-party case, a party can assure itself of winning (or at least of not losing) if it adopts a program corresponding to an equilibrium point. Furthermore, under certain conditions (and with additional assumptions governing *changes* in party programs), it might be predicted that the two parties would move over time to equilibrium points (converging to a single position if there is a unique equilibrium point).[1]

This spatial, rational-choice approach to party competition was first suggested by Hotelling (1929), whose work was later developed by Smithies (1941) and Downs (1957). In these works, the space was assumed to be one-dimensional, the single dimension corresponding to the conventional 'left-right' ideological spectrum. (Downs later replaces a party ideology by a set of positions on several issues, but he proceeds immediately to collapse them by taking a weighted average into a 'net position' on the same left-right scale. See Downs, 1957, p. 132.) We have seen that in the one-dimensional case a quite weak assumption (that each voter's utility decreases monotonically with distance from his optimum) is sufficient to guarantee the existence of an equilibrium point (which will be at the median optimum). But we have also seen that, if the policy space has two or more dimensions, equilibrium points exist only under very restrictive conditions.

As before, several assumptions are possible concerning the voters' preferences. One model uses *quadratic* utility functions, which belong to the class of convex, continuous functions with continuous first-order partial derivatives (Davis and Hinich, 1966, 1967, 1968; Hinich and Ordeshook, 1969, 1970; Davis, Hinich, and Ordeshook, 1970). Under this assumption, it can be shown that, if the distribution of voters' optima is symmetric and unimodel, then the (multivariate) *mean* is the only equilibrium point and hence should be adopted by either party if it wishes to avoid defeat. (Note that the mean of a symmetric distribution coincides with the median.) The *existence* of an equilibrium point for symmetric distributions is guaranteed by Plott's theorem, introduced in the previous section; the same theorem, establishing conditions which are both sufficient and *necessary* for equilibrium, gives little hope for finding equilibrium points when the distribution is nonsymmetric.

The lexicographic model described earlier may also be interpreted as a theory of party competition. If the policy space is bounded and discrete, the lexicographic principle appears to be a plausible basis of electoral choice: the voter, typically not well informed and not very interested, will use the lexicographic principle to help him simplify his problem of choosing between candidates. One issue area (say, welfare policy) will be salient for him, and he will disregard the other dimensions (such as foreign policy) unless the candidates appear to be indistinguishable on the first. But even under this strong assumption, equilibrium points may not always exist when the voters differ in their 'salience rankings' of the dimensions.

Subrata Sen (1969) has suggested the use, in the party competition context, of a three-stage individual decision criterion, proposed by MacCrimmon (1968), which consists of the successive application of the principles of (1) *satisficing:* exclude candidates beyond some tolerance limit from consideration (a version, of course, of the satisficing principle associated with Simon, 1955); (2) *dominance:* if one candidate is best on *every* dimension, vote for him; and (3) *lexicography* (as above).

The multidimensional formulations of the theory of party competition meet most of the criticisms of the spatial aspect of Downs's work made by Stokes (1963; see also Converse, 1966): there is no limitation on the number of dimensions of the 'policy space,' no requirement (in principle) that these dimensions represent only policy issues or that they be continuous, and no requirement that all voters attach the same set of weights to the various dimensions.

Nevertheless, the basic Downsian assumption of a voter's choosing rationally between parties on the basis of policy platforms may not be met in practice, in part because the voter typically lacks information and finds the costs of acquiring it to be too great. A more restricted notion of rationality might be more appropriate. Kramer (1971) has suggested that the voter might use a 'satisficing' rule, voting for the incumbent party if it has performed satisfactorily and otherwise voting against it, and that his 'satisfaction' will be based on certain standard-of-living indicators—specifically, real personal income, price inflation, and the level of unemployment. A regression analysis of the two-party vote for the U.S. House of Representatives from 1896–1964 as a function of these variables showed that two of them—inflation and the rate of change of real personal income—were indeed important. A similar analysis by Goodhart and Bhansali (1970) showed that inflation and unemployment may be fairly good predictors of the monthly party popularity opinion series in Britain, although the presence of serially correlated disturbances in the regression equations which did not contain a lagged endogenous variable leaves room for doubt.

Recently, a game-theoretic approach has been made to party competition. Shubik (1968, 1970), for example, assumes that two-party competition is a zero-sum game, the payoffs being the vote pluralities, and the players' pure strategies being alternative party platforms or policies. He shows that the outcome of the election will be Pareto-optimal; that if there is a policy uniquely preferred by a simple majority of the electorate to all others, then both parties should offer it; that if there is a set of policies which are preferred to all others but are indifferent among themselves, then any one of them is an equilibrium policy which either party should offer; and that, if there are cyclical majorities among a set of policies, each of which is preferred to all others, then each party should offer a *mixed* strategy over the set of intransitive policies.

This approach is further developed by Hinich, Ledyard, and Ordeshook (1973). There is unfortunately some difficulty in interpreting a mixed strategy in this context.

In all the formulations of party competition outlined above, it is usually assumed that whenever a voter prefers one party to the other, he will vote for it. But a voter may abstain even if he has a definite preference for one of the parties—because, for example, he believes that his vote will 'make no difference' to the outcome of the election. We return to this possibility in the last section, where it can be viewed as a special case of a general problem of individual rationality in politics. The effects of abstentions on party competition have been considered by Hinich and Ordeshook (1970).

Some general comments on the theory of electoral competition will be found in the concluding remarks at the end of the chapter.

CARDINAL PREFERENCES AND 'UTILITARIANISM'

So far, only the *ordinal* properties of preferences have been used. Individual preferences have been represented either by binary relations (usually assumed to be orderings) or, as in the discussion of spatial alternatives, by ordinal utility functions. An individual's preferences are represented by an ordinal utility function u if, in effect, u can be replaced by any positive monotonic transformation of itself, i.e., by any transformation which preserves the individual's preference ordering. Clearly, ordinal utility functions do not in any way represent or take account of the *intensity* with which an individual prefers one alternative to another. For this purpose, a *cardinal* utility function is required. A cardinal utility function is one which, in effect, can be replaced by any positive *linear* transformation of itself, i.e., by any transformation which not only preserves the preference orderings of the alternatives but preserves also the order of the *differences* in utility. A cardinal utility indicator still has an arbitrary zero and an arbitrary unit. Thus utility differences cannot be compared between individuals unless some correspondence can be established between the zeros and units of the different utility indicators. If this can be done, the utilities are said to be *interpersonally comparable*.

The problem of whether preference intensities should be taken into account in making collective decisions has been prominent throughout the history of democratic theory. The ethical problem has been discussed particularly in connection with simple majority rule (although it is not, of course, peculiar to that Rule): Should an apathetic majority be allowed to have its way over an intense minority? Intensities have also been discussed in political theory in connection with regime stability: Should public policy take account of preference intensities in order to ensure the stability of the regime? Both problems are treated by Dahl (1956, especially pp. 48–50 and Chapter 4).

It has often been argued that there is no need of any provision for preference intensities in formal political Decision Rules, because intensities are taken into account informally. Buchanan and Tullock (1962, especially Chapter 10) and Coleman (1966a, 1966b) have argued that *logrolling* provides such an informal mechanism. Through the trading of votes across issues, voters are able to express "relative intensities" of preference, and hence, it is argued, *cardinal* utilities may be inferred from their voting. Buchanan and Tullock (1962, for example, at p. 126) go even further and claim that these cardinal utility indicators are interpersonally comparable.

On these grounds (among others, for Buchanan and Tullock) they argue that Arrow's theorem (Theorem 1 above) is in practice unimportant. It is "relevant only to those social mechanisms in which it is not possible to express relative intensities of preference" (Coleman, 1966b, p. 1106), whereas, they believe, most Decision Rules permit the expression of preference intensities and take them into account, for example, through logrolling (which need not take the form of explicit vote-trading). Arrow's theorem is then indicted because the Criterion of the Independence of Irrelevant Alternatives rules out any dependence of social decisions on intensities.

Criterion *I* certainly excludes intensities; but as we pointed out earlier, intensities are in any case ruled out by the very formulation of the problem of social choice in terms of a function of individual preference *orderings* (or more generally, binary relations). But there are more serious problems with the criticisms of Buchanan, Tullock, and Coleman. The first is that, even if intensities *are* taken into account through logrolling, this fact has no bearing on Arrow's theorem. The reason is that the 'alternatives' in Arrow's formulation are not simply the possible outcomes of voting on a single bill but are 'social states,' each of which, in the case of voting in a legislature, would specify a *combination* of outcomes, one for each issue (cf. Arrow, 1963, p. 109). Second, although logrolling may permit *some* individuals to express their intensities, it may not permit *all* individuals to do so. Vote-trading among a group of voters on some set of bills occurs only under special configurations of preferences and intensities. (In the simplest case, two voters trade across two bills because one of them cares very much about Bill I but is indifferent about Bill II, and the other cares about II but is indifferent about I.) There is no reason to expect that every voter will always be able to arrange a trade (or set of trades), even if he feels very intensely about some of the issues. Third, a voter's decision to trade votes depends not only on his preference intensities but also on his subjective probabilities for the outcomes of the various bills (and hence on his estimation of how all the other individuals will vote on each bill). If he is certain that a bill will pass anyway, why should he 'buy' a vote in support of it, whatever his preference intensities? [2]

Finally, we note that, when each bill itself consists of a sequence of votes (on amendments, amendments to amendments, and substitute amendments, for example), an individual's actual voting cannot necessarily be taken as an indication of his real preferences. In view of the possibility of strategic voting (on a single bill), it may be extremely difficult to infer preferences from voting behavior. The theory of strategic voting is the subject of a later section.

Nevertheless, in view of these arguments, it is interesting to enquire whether there is an analogue of Arrow's theorem for cardinal individual preferences. The Social Welfare Function must now be replaced by a Social Welfare Functional, the individual binary preference relations replaced by cardinal utility indicators, and the Criteria used by Arrow adapted accordingly. This reformulation is made by Sen (1970d, pp. 123–25 and 128–30), who proves a conjecture of Samuelson's (1967) that, if these cardinal utility indicators are not interpersonally comparable, then the analogue of Arrow's theorem is still valid.

This result does not imply, of course, that 'full' comparability (entailing a precise, one-to-one correspondence between the utility scales of all pairs of individuals) is a necessity for every kind of social choice based on cardinal utilities. However, several methods of aggregating fully comparable cardinal utilities have been attempted. They are of two kinds: those based on the notion of a 'bare preference' or 'discrimination level' and those based on the cardinal utility construction of von Neumann and Morgenstern.

The first approach was proposed by Armstrong (1951) and Goodman and Markowitz (1952). It is based on the supposed inability of the individual to discriminate finely, and it rejects the assumption that individual indifference is transitive (cf. the earlier discussion of Intransitive Indifference). Each individual has a finite number of 'discrimination levels'; two adjacent levels are separated by what the psychologists would call a *just-noticeable difference* (or 'jnd'). If two alternatives are within a single jnd of each other, then the individual is indifferent between them. Otherwise, the number of discrimination levels or jnd's which separate two alternatives is taken to be a cardinal measure of the difference in utility between them. Before these cardinal utilities can be aggregated, some further assumption must be made which will render them interpersonally comparable. Goodman and Markowitz simply *assume* that every individual's jnd should count equally in making social choices; Armstrong derives this assumption (incorrectly) from more fundamental assumptions.

Quite apart from the obvious difficulty of empirically determining discrimination levels, this procedure appears unattractive on ethical grounds, for it clearly makes an individual's influence on collective decisions a function of his 'sensitivity' or power of discrimination (cf. Arrow, 1963, pp. 115–118). A detailed critique of this approach is given by Rothenberg (1961, Chapters 7 and 8).

The second group of approaches to the aggregation of cardinal utilities is based on the use of the von Neumann and Morgenstern utility indicator. Von Neumann and Morgenstern (1947) showed that, if an individual's choices among *risky* alternatives satisfied certain postulates, then they could be used to construct for him a cardinal utility function, such that his choices could be construed as those which maximize his expected utility. Several sets of postulates have been given, in addition to the von Neumann-Morgenstern formulation. A review of them is given by Rothenberg (1961, Chapters 9 and 10). Luce and Raiffa (1957, Chapter 2) provide an excellent introduction to the subject. The set of postulates given by Marschak (1950) can be summarized in the following way.

Let the basic alternatives or 'outcomes' be $x_1, \ldots, x_n$. A *prospect, f,* is a probability distribution (or 'mixture') over the x_is: $f = (f_1, \ldots, f_n)$ with $\sum_{i=1}^{n} f_i = 1$. Let $f, g, h, \ldots$ be prospects. A prospect $(0, \ldots, 0, 1, 0, \ldots, 0)$ which promises one outcome with certainty is called a *sure prospect;* all other prospects, of course, are *uncertain.*

Postulate I. The individual weak preference relation (R_i) establishes a complete ordering of all prospects.

Postulate II. (*'Continuity'*). If prospect f is preferred to g and g is preferred to h (that is, fP_igP_ih), then there exists a mixture of f and h which is indifferent to g; that is, there exists a probability r, with $0 < r < 1$, such that $g\ I_i\ [rf + (1 - r)\ h]$.

Postulate III. There are at least four mutually nonindifferent prospects.

Postulate IV. (Often called 'the strong independence axiom'). If prospects f and f' are indifferent, then for any prospect g, a given probability mixture of g and f is indifferent to a similar mixture of g and f'.

These postulates have met with considerable criticism. Much of it amounts to the objection that the utility indicator, which these postulates guarantee, measures not merely preference intensities but also, in various ways, the individual's attitudes toward risk. Rothenberg (1961, Chapter 10) gives a full discussion of these criticisms.

The first attempt to base collective choice on individual von Neumann-Morgenstern utilities was made by Hildreth (1953). He requires the social preferences to yield a complete ordering of all the alternatives. Since the von Neumann-Morgenstern utilities are merely cardinal, with arbitrary origins and units, an additional assumption is necessary to render them interpersonally comparable. Hildreth achieves this by singling out two alternatives which are used as reference points, having the same utilities for every individual. No justification is given for this procedure, and there is no indication of how the two alternatives would be identified. The method of aggregation itself (a Social Welfare Functional) is required to satisfy the Strict Pareto Criterion (P^*), the Criterion of Anonymity (A), and another symmetry condition stipulating "similar treatment for similar people, similar treatment being realized when the individuals would be indifferent to an exchange of prospects" (Hildreth, 1953, pp. 85–86). Denote the individual cardinal utilities by $u_i(x)$, $i = 1, \ldots, n$; let $g(u_i)$ be any continuous, monotonically increasing and strictly concave function of u_i; and let

$$v = \sum_{i=1}^{n} g(u_i) = \sum g\ [u_i(x)] = h(x).$$

Then Hildreth shows that any procedure yielding social preferences R, such that

$$xRy \longleftrightarrow h(x) \geqslant h(y),$$

satisfies his assumptions.

Harsanyi (1955) has also considered Decision Rules based on von Neumann and Morgenstern utilities. Strictly speaking, he was interested not in a Decision Rule as this term has been used above but in the construction of a "social welfare function" *for each individual,* the social preference relation R being interpreted as the individual's "ethical preferences," which are based on his "subjective preferences" (the R_i's). This interpretation will be discussed in the next section; here we deviate from Harsanyi's intentions and treat his "social welfare function" as a Social Welfare Function, i.e., as an aggregation of individual preferences.

Harsanyi's postulates are as follows.

1. The social preference relation R is an ordering. (This summarizes his postulates A, B, and C.)

2. R satisfies the Strict Pareto Criterion (P^*). (This summarizes his postulates D and C.)

3. There are at least three individuals. Suppose that individual i is indifferent between x and x' and between y and y' but prefers x and x' to y and y'. Suppose individual j is also indifferent between x and x' and between y and y' but, unlike i, prefers y and y' to x and x'. And suppose all other individuals are indifferent between x and y and between x' and y'. Then $xRy \longleftrightarrow x'Ry'$.

4. The social preferences and every individual's preferences satisfy the von Neumann-Morgenstern postulates (or those of Marschak, given above).

Postulate 3 in effect makes collective choice "dependent solely on the *individual* interests directly affected." But as Harsanyi goes on to stress, this does not mean that externalities are ignored: the postulate "requires that the distribution of *utility* between two individuals (once the utility levels of the two individuals are given) should always be judged independently of how utility and income are distributed among other members of the society" (p. 312), and of course, in the presence of externalities, the two individuals' *utilities* may be affected by the distribution of income (for example) among the *other* individuals.

The requirement, in postulate 4, that the *social* preferences satisfy the von Neumann and Morgenstern axioms is a rather strong one. Assuming that individual preferences satisfy the axioms and that risk is shared by the individuals Pareto-optimally, Wilson (1968) has shown that only under very restrictive conditions will the social preferences also be consistent with those axioms.

Harsanyi's central result is as follows:

Theorem 16.   Let W be an SWF satisfying postulates 1–4. Let U_i denote individual i's utility function, whose existence is guaranteed by postulate 4. Let W be chosen so that $W = 0$ when, for all i, $U_i = 0$. Then W is a weighted sum of the individual utilities, of the form $W = \Sigma a_i U_i$, where a_i is the value of W when $U_i = 1$ and $U_j = 0$ for all $j \neq i$.

Essentially the same result is derived by Strotz (1958, 1961) from a different set of postulates.

A similar approach to the aggregation of cardinal utilities is taken by van den Bogaard and Versluis (1962) and Theil (1963; 1964, pp. 333–56). They assume that the individual preferences are represented by von Neumann-Morgenstern cardinal utility functions, $u_i(x)$, $i = 1,2, \ldots , n$. Let x^i denote the most preferred alternative (or optimum) of the ith individual. Then i's *loss function* is

$$l_i(x) = u_i(x^i) - u_i(x).$$

Van den Bogaard and Versluis *define* the *social loss function* as a weighted sum of the individual loss functions:

$$l_s(x) = \sum_{i=1}^{n} d_i l_i(x),$$

where the d_i's are positive weights.

Note that each loss function has a natural zero, which occurs at the optimum, x^i. The units are of course arbitrary. Theil derives the same social loss function from Harsanyi's assumptions. In both formulations, however, the weights are to be found.

Van den Bogaard and Versluis show that, in the special case in which all the individual loss functions are quadratic and all have the same coefficient matrix, the *socially optimal decision* (the x which maximizes $l_s(x)$) is simply the *mean* of the individual optima:

$$x^s = \frac{1}{n} \sum_{i=1}^{n} x^i$$

(cf. Davis and Hinich, 1966). In general, they suggest that the weights d_i (or more precisely, their ratios) should be determined by imposing the symmetry condition that the loss inflicted on an individual i by another individual j, in the event that j's optimum becomes the social decision, should equal the analogous loss inflicted on j by i, for every i and j. But this condition can be met only if there are just two individuals. For $n > 2$, they suggest that the d_i's be found by imposing the conditions that for each individual, the total loss he inflicts on all others (if his optimum becomes the social decision) should equal the total losses they inflict on him.

Theil (1963, 1964) has 'justified' this approach by establishing a set of necessary and sufficient conditions for the symmetry condition to be met and by showing that the more general method satisfies certain desirable properties.

This completes our review of Decision Rules which attempt to take account of individual preference intensities. Some general comments on these attempts are in order. First, the only generally acceptable method of constructing cardinal measures of intensity is that proposed by von Neumann and Morgenstern. But this construction is based on individual choices among risky alternatives and, as we noted earlier, makes an individual's utilities dependent on his attitudes toward risk. For this reason, it is at least questionable whether collective choices among certain alternatives should be founded on utility functions of this type—whether, as Arrow puts it, social choice should be "governed by the tastes of individuals for gambling" (1963, p. 10). However, there is one area of collective choice where utility functions based on risky choices may be especially appropriate, namely, the choice of Decision Rules in "the original position," where people are uncertain about how they will be affected by future decisions. (In fairness to Harsanyi, it should be said that this is how he interprets his theory.) This area is the subject of the next section. Second, the 'utilitarian' Decision Rules reviewed above require strong assumptions to guarantee interpersonal comparability. "In general, there seems to be no method intrinsic to utility measurement which will make the choices compatible. It requires a definite value judgment not derivable from individual sensations to make the utilities of different individuals dimensionally compatible and still a further value judgment to aggregate them according to any particular mathematical formula" (Arrow, 1963, p. 11). It should be noted, however, that full comparability (placing all the individual utility functions in a one-to-one correspondence) may not be needed for certain kinds of Decision Rules. Sen (1970d, p. 99) gives an example:

> Suppose we are debating the consequences on the aggregate welfare of Romans of the act of Rome being burnt while Nero played his fiddle. We recognise that Nero was delighted while the other Romans suffered, but suppose we still say that the sum total of welfare went down as a consequence. What type of interpersonal comparability are we assuming? If there is no comparability at all, we can change the utility units of different individuals differently, and by multiplying Nero's utility measures by a suitably large number, it should be possible to make Nero's gain larger in size than the loss of others. Hence we are not assuming noncomparability. But are we assuming that every Roman's welfare units can be put into one-to-one correspondence with the welfare units of every other Roman? Not necessarily. We might not be sure what precise correspondence to take, and we might admit some possible variety, but we could still be able to assert that no matter which of the various possible combinations we take,

the sum total went down in any case. This is a case intermediate between noncomparability and full comparability of units.

Sen (1970b; 1970d, pp. 99–104 and Chapter 7*) develops a continuum of assumptions ranging from noncomparability to full comparability, and shows that certain kinds of rational social choice may be made in the intermediate cases.

CONSTITUTIONAL CHOICE IN "THE ORIGINAL POSITION"

Our evaluation of Decision Rules has thus far been 'objective,' having been mainly concerned with establishing whether certain Rules (or any Rules) satisfy various Criteria. But it is also of interest to view Decision Rules from the point of view of a specific or of a 'typical' individual. Of course, if the Criterion of Anonymity is met, i.e., the Rule treats all individuals impartially, then an evaluation of the Rule according to any set of Criteria will be the same from the point of view of every individual.

Of special interest are the choices among Decision Rules which would be made by an individual when he is in "the original position" (as Rawls calls it)—when, before the Rule has come into operation, he is uncertain about how the Rule will affect him, because he is uncertain about what 'social position' he will occupy.

In the previous section, Harsanyi's result was treated as a theorem about Social Welfare Functions, defined in the usual way. But the preference relation, R, which we viewed as the social preference relation, was intended by Harsanyi to represent an individual's "ethical preferences." These are distinct from his "subjective" preferences. The 'utilitarian' Decision Rule of Theorem 16 specifies the way in which an individual must aggregate the set of subjective preferences to obtain his ethical preferences if the various preferences and the Decision Rule are to meet Harsanyi's postulates.

Harsanyi (1955, p. 316) regards his postulates 2 and 3 (see above) as "an implicit definition of what sort of 'impartial' or 'impersonal' attitude is required to underlie 'ethical' preferences," and earlier (Harsanyi, 1953) he had argued that an individual's preferences satisfy this requirement of impersonality if they are the preferences he would have in the original position on the assumption that he had an equal chance of occupying any of the social positions, i.e., "of being 'put in the place' of any individual member of the society, with regard not only to his objective social (and economic) conditions, but also to his subjective attitudes and tastes." Thus, in deriving his "ethical preferences" (or, in the SWF interpretation, in choosing between Rules), an individual is faced with choices among uncertain prospects.

As we have seen, Harsanyi assumes that both subjective and ethical preferences satisfy the von Neumann and Morgenstern postulates. Thus his ethical choices are those which maximize expected utility. If the individual assumes that he has an equal chance of being in any 'position,' this is equivalent to maximizing aggregate utility (Theorem 16). (Cf. also Vickrey, 1960, pp. 523–525).

Two kinds of possible objections to this view of "ethical" preferences (or of SWF's) are made by Sen (1970d, pp. 142–43). First:

> Consider a slave society with 99 free men and 1 slave. The latter serves the former to their convenience and to his great discomfort. Given an equal chance of being in anyone's position it is possible that someone might be ready to take a 1% chance of being a slave, since the 99% of being a free man served by a slave might tickle his fancy. Would a slave society be then morally supportable? Many people will not accept this test.

Second, the expected utility criterion ignores distributive considerations: two social states may have equal expected utility, but one may distribute welfare much more equally among the individuals than the other.

In the theories of collective choice examined earlier, social preferences are derived from "subjective preferences"; whereas Harsanyi considers *ethical* preferences as a function of subjective preferences. A third possibility of interest—the derivation of social preferences from ethical preferences—is considered by Pattanaik (1968b), who notes that ethical preferences will not necessarily be the same for every individual, because their attitudes toward risk may differ.

Rawls's analysis of "justice as fairness" is similar to Harsanyi's in its approach. For Rawls (1958, 1963, 1967, 1971), institutions and principles are "fair" if they are the ones which would be chosen by individuals in "the original position." He argues, in particular, for two principles of *justice* which would be fair in this sense (Rawls, 1958). The second of these principles, he claims, implies that those institutions should be chosen which maximize the "expectations" or long-term "prospects" of the least advantaged individual (Rawls, 1967).

The same procedure, used by Rawls to choose between institutions, can be used to choose between social states: state A is socially preferred to state B if the utility of the worst-off individual in A is greater than the utility of the worst-off individual in B. Considering Rawls's procedure as a Decision Rule in this way, Sen (1970d, pp. 137–39) notes that (1) it is not a Social Welfare Function, (2) it may not satisfy the Strict Pareto Criterion, P^* (although it always satisfies the Weak Pareto Criterion, P), and (3) it "is not sensitive to magnitudes of gains and losses": if the worst-off individual in State A is only slightly better off than the worst-off individual in state B, while all other individuals are much better off in B than in A, state A is chosen nevertheless.

A more specific problem of 'constitutional choice' is the choice by an individual between all possible *simple* Decision Rules. A simple Decision Rule specifies a number k such that if k individuals prefer x to y, then x is socially preferred to y. In principle, k may take any value from 1 through n, where n is the total number of individuals; in practice (and presumably to rule out such theoretical possibilities as the simultaneous existence of two or more disjoint winning coalitions), k usually lies between the simple majority value and the unanimity value. Buchanan and Tullock (1962, especially Chapter 6) have given a detailed analysis of this constitutional choice problem. They argue that the choice between Rules should be made on the basis of the results produced by the Rules, not on a single issue, but on the whole set of issues extending into the future. (Cf. also the discussion of "long-run welfare criteria" by Leibenstein, 1965.) The individual should judge the various Rules according to two costs incurred under them: first, *external costs,* which (according to Buchanan and Tullock's definition) represent his losses when a policy he opposes becomes the collective choice; and second, *decision-making* (or *bargaining*) *costs,* which represent the value to him of the resources he expends in participating in the collective choice. They conclude that, in the absence of bargaining costs, an individual would most prefer the unanimity rule. Their reasoning is fallacious in several respects (see, for example, Barry, 1965, Chapters 14 and 15); perhaps the most important is their argument (amounting almost to an assumption) that external costs decrease monotonically as the Decision Rule becomes more inclusive (approaches unanimity) (Buchanan and Tullock, 1962, p. 64).

This argument rests on a number of unstated assumptions: that there is a distinguished social state, the status quo; that an individual suffers external costs when a policy to which he is opposed becomes the collective choice, but not when a policy he favors is rejected; and that the individual, far from being in Rawls's "original position," expects generally to favor the status quo under the future operation of the Rule. Commenting on this aspect of Buchanan and Tullock's analysis, Baumol (1965, p. 44) writes that

> ... every voting rule not only specifies those whose approval will suffice to institute change but it also designates residually what groups can prevent change. Moreover, in the set of all possible legislative decisions any given legislative proposal has what may be called its negative equivalent. ... Considering the range of possibilities between majority rule and the rule of unanimity we can say that the more closely the arrangements approximate the latter, the smaller the group which we empower to perpetuate the follies of previous actions or failures to act. Majority rule, therefore, is certainly not entirely arbitrary, for it is the rule which may be said to minimize the tyranny of a conservative minority while not at the same time offering any minority the unilateral power to institute change. In sum, there is very little distinction between imposing costs on others and preventing costs on others from being removed. Power resides both in the

group which can impose and the one which can prevent. Majority rule is the one arrangement which makes the smaller of these groups as large as possible.

Robert Paul Wolff, in espousing unanimous decision-making as an (unattainable) ideal in his *Defense of Anarchism,* commits the same sort of mistake as Buchanan and Tullock—although elsewhere his views contrast sharply with theirs (Wolff, 1970, pp. 22–27). Under the operation of the unanimity rule, nobody's 'moral autonomy' is infringed *only if everybody finds the status quo acceptable.*

The assumptions which are implicit in Buchanan and Tullock are brought out explicitly in an analysis by Rae (1969) of a more specific problem of constitutional choice. Suppose that a committee (any body which makes collective choices) is to vote on a succession of policy proposals, imposing or rejecting each of them in turn. Each member may support or oppose each proposal. Consider a 'typical' individual ("Ego"). He faces four possibilities:

A. He may support a proposal, which the committee rejects.

B. He may oppose a proposal, which the committee imposes.

C. He may support a proposal, which the committee imposes.

D. He may oppose a proposal, which the committee rejects.

It is assumed that Ego wishes to 'have his way' as often as possible; i.e., he wishes to minimize the frequency ('in the long run') with which events A and B occur. Suppose that Ego is "in the original position"; more specifically here, he is ignorant of the proposals which will come before the committee and, a fortiori, of the preferences of the members on each proposal. If, therefore, Ego assumes that every member (including himself) is equally likely to support or reject each proposal, then of all the simple Decision Rules, simple majority rule is the one which minimizes the frequency of A and B (Rae, 1969). Simple majority rule is still optimal even if the probability of a member supporting a proposal is not equal to one half, as long as this probability is the same for every individual (Taylor, 1969).

Under these assumptions, it is possible to speak of a "typical" member of the whole committee: all the members have identical preferences among Decision Rules. But if the probabilities of supporting each proposal are not all the same, or if the individuals differ in their assessments of these probabilities, there will no longer be a single typical individual. The Decision Rules must now be evaluated from the point of view of a *specified* individual, and his optimal Decision Rule may no longer be simple majority rule (Badger, 1972; Curtis, 1972; Schofield, 1972). The most general formulation of this problem is that of Plott (1972), who places the models above in the general context of decision-making under uncertainty (as in Harsanyi's treatment).

These more general models are of interest perhaps only as *explanatory* theories of an individual's choices between Decision Rules (which in turn can be used as a basis for explaining the *group's* choice among the Rules, as in Badger, 1972). But the model originally proposed by Rae seems to be the appropriate one for an 'ethical' analysis of Decision Rules: every individual is assumed to be ignorant of everyone's future preferences and accordingly assumes that everyone is just as likely to support as to oppose a proposal. In other words, the individuals are in Rawls's "original position," so that the Decision Rule which they choose is 'fair' (in Rawls's sense).

ARBITRATION AND BARGAINING

We turn now to a special kind of collective decision-making which is of considerable importance in politics, namely, two-person bargaining. A bargaining situation occurs when two 'players' are competing for some resources, but it is in their mutual interests to cooperate in reaching a settlement, and they are free to communicate in order to do so.

Most of the relevant theories have been developed by economists interested in bilateral monopoly and collective bargaining; but in principle the models should be applicable to a wide variety of political bargaining situations in addition to labor-management negotiations (although the difficulties of specifying the parameters of the models and of testing them are formidable in some of these situations).[3] Harsanyi (1962b, 1966) has suggested, too, that certain social institutions and social practices (such as the ascription of social status) can be explained in terms of a 'balance of bargaining power' or a 'bargaining equilibrium' among the interested social groups or individuals.

Formally, we represent a bargaining situation by (1) two variables, x and y, which represent the demands of the two players at any point of time, and (2) two utility functions, $u(x)$ and $v(y)$, representing the preferences of the two bargainers. Thus, to every feasible 'trade' (x, y) there corresponds a pair of utilities (u, v). Let R (see Figure 1) be the region of the (u, v) plane containing all such feasible points (u, v). Denote by (u^*, v^*) the point of disagreement—the payoffs to the two individuals which result if they cannot agree.

Arbitration Schemes

Our first approach to the bargaining problem is 'normative.' We ask, 'What would be a *fair* outcome of the bargaining situation?' or 'What settlement would be made by an impartial arbiter?' Nash (1950) has posed this problem in an axiomatic manner analogous to Arrow's formulation, in his Impossibility theorem, of the problem of a 'fair' aggregation of individual preferences. The Decision Rule in this context is called an *Arbitration Scheme*—a functional relation which associates with each bargaining situation (defined by u and v, the point (u^*, v^*), and the region R) a unique payoff to the two individuals.

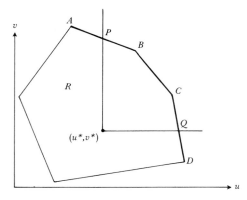

Figure 1

Individual preferences are described by *cardinal* utility functions (u and v); in view of the remarks made in an earlier section, it will be of interest to discover that Nash's Arbitration Scheme involves no interpersonal comparisons of these utilities.

Nash (1950) stated a number of axioms which he believed should be satisfied by any Arbitration Scheme and looked for Schemes satisfying them. Following Luce and Raiffa (1957, pp. 126–27), we can state the axioms informally as follows:

N1. The outcome is independent of utility transformations, i.e., of the origins and units of the two utility functions.

N2. The outcome (u^o, v^o) is

1) at least as good as the status quo for each individual; that is, $u^o \geqslant u^*$ and $v^o \geqslant v^*$;

2) feasible; that is, (u^o, v^o) lies in R;

3) Pareto-optimal; that is, there is no point (u, v) in R, other than (u^o, v^o), such that $u \geqslant u^o$ and $v \geqslant v^o$.

N3. The outcome is independent of irrelevant alternatives; i.e., if two different bargaining situations (B_1 and B_2) have the same point of disagreement (u^*, v^*) but the set R of B_1 is a subset of that of B_2, and if the outcome of B_2 is a feasible point in B_1, then it is also the outcome of B_1.

N4. If the formalization of the bargaining situation is such that the two individuals are placed in symmetric roles, then in the arbitrated outcome they must receive equal payoffs. More formally, if $u^* = v^*$ and (v, u) is in R whenever (u, v) is in R, then $u_o = v_o$.

Nash has proved that there is *only one* Arbitration Scheme which satisfies these four axioms. This is the Scheme which defines as the outcome the point (u, v) which maximizes the product $(u - u^*)(v - v^*)$. In Nash's treatment, this point exists and is unique because R is assumed to be convex and compact. (For more general conditions on the shape of R which guarantee uniqueness, see Coddington, 1968, pp. 31–34).

Since an excellent critique of Nash's axioms is given by Luce and Raiffa (1957, pp. 128–34), we confine our comments to what seems to be the most serious *ethical* failing of Nash's Scheme. In our earlier discussion of Decision Rules based on individual cardinal utilities, we noted the difficulties of comparing these utilities interpersonally; and in the 'Utilitarian' Rules discussed there, it was necessary to introduce an assumption facilitating such comparisons. In Nash's Scheme, however, no interpersonal comparisons need be made; the origins of the individual utility functions are placed at the disagreement point, and the units are irrelevant because the individual utilities are *multiplied* (in contrast to the additive form of the Utilitarian Decision Rules) so that, in conformity with N1, the social ordering of the points in R is invariant with respect to transformations of the two utility functions. One consequence of this is that the arbitrated outcome depends to some extent on the disagreement point (u, v), that is, on the 'bargaining power' or 'threat advantages' of the two bargainers. For example, "In a labor market with unemployment, workers may be agreeable to accept subhuman wages and poor terms of employment, since in the absence of a contract they may starve $[u^*]$, but this does not make that solution a desirable outcome in any sense. Indeed, compared with $[(u^*, v^*)]$, while a particular solution may be symmetric in distributing utility gains from the bargain between workers and capitalists, we could still maintain that the workers were exploited because their bargaining power was poor" (Sen, 1970d, p. 121).

This criticism can also be made of Nash's (1953) extension of his Arbitration Scheme (yielding in effect a two-stage noncooperative game, in the first stage of which each player must choose *threat* strategies which determine the disagreement point in the bargaining game) and of Schemes proposed by Raiffa (1953) and Braithwaite (1955). (Both are summarized and criticized by Luce and Raiffa, 1957, pp. 143–50.) Braithwaite explicitly claims that his treatment is "ethically neutral between the collaborating parties" (p. 5) but later explains that the arbitrated outcome he recommends is based on the "balance of power" between the two bargainers (p. 32) and is *"sensible, prudent and fair"* (p. 52). We might say that all of these Schemes are 'fair' only *relative* to the two utility functions, the region R and the point (u^*, v^*).

A generalization of Nash's Arbitration Scheme to the n-person case is considered by Harsanyi (1959). Another possible generalization is the *Shapley value*. This was put forward as a solution of the n-person cooperative game

(Shapley, 1953), but it has been interpreted by Luce and Raiffa (1957, pp. 250–252) as an Arbitration Scheme for the n-person case.[4] When $n = 2$, it is equivalent to Nash's scheme (Rapoport, 1970, Chapter 10). An alternative treatment of the 'value' of an n-person game is given by Selten (1964).

Bargaining Theory

The Arbitration Schemes considered above are *normative* models, "whose aim is to apply moral or political value judgments to bargaining situations," and although, as we have seen, they are 'normative' in only a very limited sense, they should be distinguished, as Harsanyi (1962b, p. 446; 1966, p. 615) urges, from models which try to *explain* the outcome of the bargaining process on the assumption that the players "are interested only in maximizing their own payoffs." Explanatory theories of bargaining are the subject of this section.

The earliest such theory is that of Edgeworth (1881, pp. 20–30). He argues that no point in R is an acceptable bargain if there is some other point which increases the utility of *both* players. Thus the outcome will lie on the 'welfare frontier', the line $ABCD$ in Figure 1. Furthermore, neither player can be expected to accept less than he can guarantee himself by not cooperating at all, i.e., less than the payoff when there is no agreement (u^* or v^*). Thus the bargain must lie in the 'negotiation set', the line $PBCQ$ in Figure 1. This is as far as Edgeworth goes; his solution is indeterminate, in the sense that it does not isolate a single point in R as *the* outcome. The same solution was obtained by von Neumann and Morgenstern (1947), treating the bargaining situation as a two-person nonzero-sum game.

More recently, a number of dynamic theories of bargaining have been proposed, which, unlike the 'classical' theory of Edgeworth, are concerned with the *process* of reaching a bargain and are generally completely determinate. The forerunner is Zeuthen's theory (Zeuthen, 1930). Harsanyi (1956) has shown that Zeuthen's solution is equivalent to the one given by Nash, described above. Suppose that bargainer i ($i = 1, 2$) is demanding an outcome with utilities (u_i, v_i) to the two bargainers. Then it is rational for bargainer 1 to take any risk of disagreement r_1, where

$$(1 - r_1)u_1 + r_1 u^* \geqslant u_2,$$

and bargainer 2 can take any risk of disagreement r_2, such that

$$(1 - r_2)v_2 + r_2 v^* \geqslant v_1.$$

If we assume that the bargainer who can afford the least risk will make a concession first, then it follows from the two inequalities that bargainer 1 will make a concession whenever

$$(u_1 - u^*)(v_1 - v^*) < (u_2 - u^*)(v_2 - v^*),$$

and bargainer 2 will make a concession whenever this inequality is reversed.

According to Harsanyi, it follows that, if the players make concessions according to this rule, they will arrive at an outcome at the maximum of the product $(u - u^*)(v - v^*)$, which is the same as the outcome defined by Nash's Arbitration Scheme.

But this appears to be incorrect, insofar as there is no reason for the required convergence to occur. For it is rational, on Zeuthen's assumptions, for bargainer 1 to concede only so much as to cause the inequality above to become an equality, and this may occur at a point other than the maximum of $(u - u^*)$ $(v - v^*)$. It is not rational for him to concede enough to reverse the inequality; and thus bargainer 2 will make no concession. Conceding enough to reverse the inequality ('overshooting') will be accidental. And if one bargainer overshoots accidentally, the other bargainer will concede, but again only so much as to produce the equality. Convergence in fact requires a whole series of irrationally large concessions, and it seems unlikely to occur. The concession process of Zeuthen's model is only a sort of 'pseudo-dynamics'; the detailed mechanism of concession-making is not specified.

A similar model has been proposed by Pen (1952), though his is less determinate.

Time does not appear explicitly in any of the theories mentioned so far. Yet, clearly, the (present) utility of an expected outcome to a bargainer depends not only on the outcome itself but on the *future time* at which it is expected to occur. Future time was first introduced as a variable in theories of the bargaining process by Foldes (1964) and Bishop (1964). It is emphasized by Harsanyi (1962a), Nicholson (1967), and Contini (1968). It plays an even more crucial role in the theories of Cross (1965, 1969) and Coddington (1968).

The framework common to both their efforts is presented and discussed at length in Coddington (1968). Like most of the theories above, their approach is still via individual decision-making, but they go on to develop a theory of two *interacting self-steering systems*. At the outset of bargaining, each of the bargainers has certain expectations, which may turn out to be mistaken, concerning the other bargainer's responses to his possible outcomes (where an outcome is considered as a bargain made *at a point in time*). On these two bases each bargainer chooses a plan and makes his initial demand. But as soon as one of them (bargainer 1, say) has made an initial demand, and the other has responded with his first demand, bargainer 1 can see whether bargainer 2's response is in accord with his (1's) initial expectations. If not, then he *adjusts* them accordingly. He then makes his second demand. Bargainer 2 views this as a response to his own first demand, and he may then adjust *his* expectations. And so on, in a repetition of cycles, as shown in Figure 2.

Cross's (1965) model is based on the following simplifying assumptions. (1) Each bargainer expects the other bargainer's future sequence of demands to be independent of his own current demand. (2) Each bargainer expects the other to make concessions at a constant rate. (3) Each bargainer is intran-

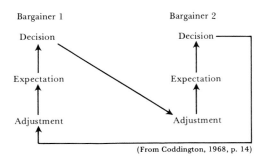

(From Coddington, 1968, p. 14)

Figure 2

sigent: he plans to maintain his current demand until agreement is reached. (4) The utility functions express utilities at the time of agreement, *adjusted back to the present* on the assumptions (a) that there is an exponential discounting function, and (b) that, until agreement is reached, there is a constant cost per period of time. (5) Each bargainer chooses each current demand so as to maximize utility.

The first two of these assumptions are clearly rather drastic. Coddington (1968, Chapter 6; see also Cross, 1969) develops this model by relaxing them, in order to allow for a greater degree of interdependence between the two bargainers and to deal with the problem of adjustment of expectations in the manner suggested earlier. The resulting model gives rise to a system of differential equations, which cannot be solved analytically, so Coddington (pp. 95–96) gives illustrative numerical solutions for several sets of parameters.

Unfortunately, there appear to be fundamental problems with the non-game-theoretical approach of Cross and Coddington. In particular, in Cross's theory, in the case when utility functions are linear in the demands, it can be shown (Carling, 1973) that (1) when the bargaining process is unstable (according to Cross's equations), no outcome is possible; (2) when the process is stable, some initial demands yield no outcome; (3) there are two convergence solutions of the type investigated by Cross, of which one is unstable and the other corresponds to an impossible outcome; (4) in view of the above, the choice of initial demands is much more crucial than Cross and Coddington realize *and must be reformulated as a game-theoretical problem.*

A related dynamic theory, proposed by Contini and Zionts (1968), deals with so-called *restricted bargaining schemes.* These are designed to avoid the possibility of no agreement being reached or of 'unfair' agreements, by providing "an incentive for all the (bargainers) to engage in a bargaining process until agreement is reached. The incentive consists of the *threat* of a preannounced 'imposed' solution (or 'threat solution') that will be enforced if no settlement is reached." The theory appears to lead (in general) to a uniquely defined, Pareto-optimal outcome. Contini (1967) examines this type of bargaining in organizations, where the constraints are provided by the organizational structure.

An attempt to incorporate learning and adjustment processes into a *game-theoretic* treatment of bargaining has been made by Harsanyi, Aumann and Maschler, Stearns, and Mayberry in their contributions to *Models of Gradual Reduction of Arms* (listed under *Mathematica* in the references), and by Harsanyi and Selten (1972), who build upon the earlier work of Harsanyi (1967–68) on games with incomplete information.

STRATEGIC VOTING

Our discussion of collective choice has so far ignored any differences that may exist between *preference* and *choice*. We have tacitly assumed that individuals always choose in accordance with their preferences. For some writers, this presents no problems, for they would argue that preference does not exist prior to (or in any way independently of) choice: preference is *revealed* through choice. It may indeed be possible to specify the set of alternatives (as 'social states') in so much detail that, with an extended definition of 'choice,' it would always be true to say that choices reflected preferences. But such an approach would be (at least) cumbersome. There are many situations in which common sense and analytical convenience suggest a distinction between preference and choice and where it may then be said that an individual's choices are not in accordance with his preferences. An important instance occurs where the Decision Rule specifies a *sequence* of votes and an individual may be able to achieve a more favorable outcome by voting 'insincerely' (i.e., not in accordance with his preference ranking) in some of the early stages of the sequence. Such *strategic voting* is the subject of this section.

Apart from earlier scattered remarks (for example, in Arrow, 1951, pp. 80–81, and Majumdar, 1956), the first published treatment of strategic voting was by Farquharson (1969), whose work has recently been extended by Kramer (1972) in his study of strategic voting over multidimensional choice spaces.

We introduce the problem with one of Farquharson's delightful examples, taken from the letters of Pliny the Younger:

> The consul Afranius Dexter had been found slain, and it was uncertain whether he had died by his own hand or at those of his freedmen. When the matter came before the Senate, Pliny wished to acquit them; another senator moved that they should be banished to an island; and a third that they should be put to death. (Farquharson, 1969, pp. 6–7)

So there are three possible outcomes: to acquit (A), to banish (B), and to condemn to death (C). There were three blocs of voters in the Senate: the Acquitters, whose preference ranking was (A, B, C); the Banishers, whose ranking was (B, A, C); and the Condemners, with (C, B, A). The voting procedure used was as follows: A division is first taken on the issue of guilt (the subset (A) versus the subset (B, C)); then if the freedmen are convicted, there is a division between B and C to decide the punishment. This can be depicted as in Figure 3.

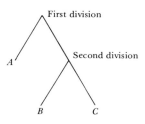

Figure 3

The voting procedure shown in Figure 3 is an example of a *binary* procedure, since each division is into two subsets. Another binary procedure—perhaps the one most commonly used in politics—is shown in Figure 4. This is the procedure normally used in voting in parliaments. In this case, A would represent the status quo, B a bill, and C an amended version of the bill. Parliamentary procedure may of course be more complicated than this, but it is still of the same type. For example, in the U.S. House of Representatives, a substitute amendment (SA) may be offered against the amendment (A), and each of these may be amended (ASA and AA). In this case, there is first a vote on the amendment to the amendment, i.e., between A and AA. Next there is a similar vote between SA and ASA. Then the winners of these two votes meet (for example, A versus ASA). There is next a vote on whether to incorporate the resulting amendment into the original motion (M), and the result of this vote determines the final form of the bill, which is then placed against the status quo (Q). This five-division binary voting procedure is represented by the tree shown in part in Figure 5.

Following Farquharson, we define a *voting strategy* as a specification of how an individual will vote at each division. For binary procedures, a strategy can be described by a sequence of binary digits, 0 denoting a choice of the 'left-hand' subset, and 1 a choice of the 'right-hand' subset. Thus, in the example of

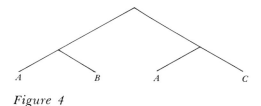

Figure 4

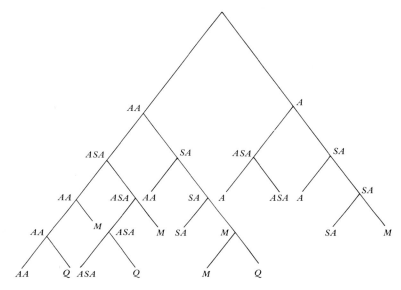

Fig. 5. Part of Voting Procedure in the United States House of Representatives

Figure 3, 01 denotes a vote for A at the first division and a vote for C at the second division (although, of course, a second division may not take place). A *contingency* is a list of strategies for all the voters but one. An individual's strategy is *sincere* if, at every division, he chooses the subset containing the alternative which is the most preferred of all those in the two subsets.

Consider again the procedure shown in Figure 3. Suppose now that the preferences of three individuals (1, 2, and 3) among three alternatives are 1 (A, B, C), 2 (B, C, A) and 3 (C, A, B). Their sincere strategies are 00, 10, and 11, respectively. If all three use their sincere strategies, the outcome is B. This is individual 3's least-preferred alternative. But if 3 had voted insincerely at the first division (i.e., for A), while individuals 1 and 2 used their sincere strategies, the outcome would have been A, which 3 prefers to B. How should 3 choose between these strategies? A rational basis for such choices is proposed by Farquharson, as follows.

He first defines a strategy to be *admissible* if there is no other strategy which leads to an outcome at least as good in every contingency and to a better outcome in at least one contingency. Clearly, it will never pay a voter to use an inadmissible strategy. It can be shown that a sincere strategy is always admissible. If a voter has only one admissible strategy (which must be his sincere one), then it is said to be *straightforward* (Farquharson, 1956). In the example above, individuals 1 and 2 have straightforward strategies; putting it informally, there is no dilemma for either of them, for whatever either believes the other voters will do, his sincere strategy is his best one. Individual 3, however, has two admissible strategies, 11 and 01. In order to choose between them, he will have to attempt to predict how the other individuals will vote.

Farquharson suggests that, when an individual has more than one admissible strategy and when he knows the preferences of the other voters, he will proceed by assuming that each of the others will use one of his admissible strategies. This defines a smaller game for him, where he need plan for fewer contingencies than originally. Strategies which are admissible in this reduced game are called *secondarily admissible* (and the previously admissible strategies are now called *primarily admissible*).

More generally, a strategy is said to be *m-arily admissible* if it is admissible on the assumption that all other individuals use only $(m - 1)$-arily admissible strategies.

In the case of binary procedures when all individual preferences are strong (contain no indifferences), Farquharson shows (p. 42) that, in adopting successively higher orders of admissibility, an individual must eventually arrive at a single strategy or a set of strategies which yield the same outcome. The strategies thus found are said to be *sophisticated,* and the procedure is in this case said to be *determinate.*

In the simple example considered above, individual 3's only secondarily admissible strategy is 01, and this is therefore his sophisticated strategy. The outcome of sophisticated voting is thus A (whereas the sincere outcome was B).

Farquharson also introduces a notion of *individual equilibrium.* This is a situation (a set of strategies, one for each individual) such that no single individual can achieve a better outcome using a different strategy, on the assumption that the other individuals' strategies remain unaltered. (Such an equilibrium corresponds to a Nash equilibrium in the theory of noncooperative games. See Nash, 1951, or Luce and Raiffa, 1957, pp. 170–73.) He extends this concept to allow for explicit cooperation between the voters—agreements to coordinate voting strategies—and defines an *equilibrium of order r* to be a situation such that no set of r individuals can obtain a situation which each of them prefers. (This corresponds to Shubik's notion of k-stability. See Shubik, 1959.) If a situation is an equilibrium of all orders from 1 through n (where n is the number of voters), it is called a *collective equilibrium.* (The set of collective equilibria corresponds to the *core* in the theory of n-person cooperative games.) Farquharson notes that a set of sophisticated strategies is always an individual equilibrium but is not necessarily a collective equilibrium.

INDIVIDUAL RATIONALITY AND COLLECTIVE ACTION

There is a tradition of political thought which holds that collective decisions—or at least public policies at the national level—can be viewed as the resultant of the pressures of all the interested groups and that policies determined in this way are 'just'. This view has flourished chiefly in the United States. Its modern exponents, notably Bentley, Latham, and Truman, are discussed in another chapter of this volume. Their confidence in the outcomes of this 'free competition' between interest groups is based on their assumptions that whenever a number of individuals share a common interest, they will act collectively to further it, and that the influence of such a group on public policy will be proportional to its size.

Inasmuch as the common interest of a group of individuals is in securing a *public good* (i.e., a good which, if it is consumed by any member of the group, can be freely consumed by all other members of that group), these assumptions may be highly implausible. As Olson (1965) has argued in *The Logic of Collective Action*, the larger the number of people with a common interest, the smaller the incentive for each of its members to act in that common interest:

> In a small group in which a member gets such a large fraction of the total benefit that he would be better off if he paid the entire cost himself, rather than go without the good, there is some presumption that the collective good will be provided. In a group in which no one member got such a large benefit from the collective good that he had an interest in providing it even if he had to pay all of the cost, but in which the individual was still so important in terms of the whole group that his contribution or lack of contribution to the group objective had a noticeable effect on the costs or benefits of others in the group, the result is indeterminate. By contrast, in a large group in which no single individual's contribution makes a perceptible difference to the group as a whole, or the burden or benefit of any single member of the group, it is certain that a collective good will *not* be provided unless there is coercion or some outside inducements that will lead the members of the large group to act in their common interest. (Olson, 1965, p. 44)

The implications of this argument for the 'group theory' of collective decision-making are clear:

> Since relatively small groups will frequently be able voluntarily to organize and act in support of their common interests, and since large groups normally will not be able to do so, the outcome of the political struggle among the various groups in society will not be symmetrical. (Olson, 1965, p. 127)

An instance of this general problem of participation, which has been examined independently of Olson's analysis, is the choice between voting and abstaining in an election. Downs (1957, Chapter 14) notes that, in the case of a two-party race, a rational individual should vote only if the expected differential benefit from the success of his more preferred party rather than his less preferred party, discounted by the subjective probability that his vote will decide the election, is greater than the costs of voting. This will not generally be the case, so the rational voter should abstain. In Olson's terms, the outcome of the election is a public good, which the voter believes he will enjoy (or not) whether he votes or not. In the absence of coercion (which is present in some countries in the form of compulsory voting), the individual will vote only if there are 'selective incentives.' These might include the satisfactions derived from such things as asserting a definite preference, carrying out one's social duty, and so on. Riker and Ordeshook (1968), in their attempt at a formal treatment of the problem, include these kinds of satisfaction in the voter's original cost-benefit calculations rather than treating them as Olson would. The result is a tautologous explanation of voting (as they seem to admit) according to which, as Barry (1970, Chapter 2) puts it, "people vote because they derive satisfaction from voting for reasons entirely divorced from the hope that it will bring about desired results."

Several writers have remarked that the situation facing the individual member of the large group (or potential group) in Olson's analysis is a non-zero-sum game known as the Prisoner's Dilemma. The following well-known example, from which the name of the game derives, will serve to introduce the two-person form of the game.

> Two prisoners, held incommunicado, are charged with the same crime. They can be convicted only if either confesses. . . . Further, if only one confesses, he is set free for having turned state's evidence and is given a reward to boot. . . . The prisoner who has held out is convicted on the strength of the other's testimony and is given a more severe sentence than if he also confessed. (Rapoport and Chammah, 1965, pp. 24–25)

Designating the players as I and II and the two choices ('strategies') open to them as C (Confess) and D (Do not confess), a plausible payoff matrix for this example would be

		II	
		C	D
I	C	1,1	−2,2
	D	2,−2	−1,−1

The numbers in each cell are the payoffs to I and II in that order.

The 'dilemma' arises because each player's 'rational' strategy is D (in the sense that his payoff is higher than if he chooses C, whatever the other does), but if both players pursue their rational strategy, the outcome is worse for both of them than the outcome they could have obtained if they had both chosen C. And communication will not improve the situation (unless agreements can be enforced), because it is in each player's interest to break any agreement to choose the cooperative strategy, C. The pair of strategies (D, D) is the game's only equilibrium.

Hardin (1971) has shown how Olson's analysis can be formulated as an n-person version of the Prisoner's Dilemma. He makes the following simplifying assumptions: (1) r units of the public good are provided for every unit 'paid' (not necessarily in money, of course) by any individual, the good being 'public' for a group (or potential group) of n individuals; (2) each individual can either pay (one unit, say) or not; (3) if one member of the group declines to pay his share, then the total benefit is proportionately reduced. (The other possibility is that the cost to the members is proportionately increased, but either assumption results in the same analysis). The (n-dimensional) payoff matrix need not be constructed, for it can be seen that the payoff to any individual will be $mr/n - 1$ if he and $m - 1$ other individuals pay, whereas his payoff will be $(m - 1)r/n$ if $m - 1$ other individuals pay and he does not. Thus, no matter how many others pay, his payoff is $1 - r/n$ units higher if he does not pay, so that this is his 'rational' choice so long as n exceeds r. As with the two-person game, the only equilibrium outcome corresponds to all individuals not paying; in this case each of their payoffs is zero, and there is another outcome (all individuals pay) which each prefers.

CONCLUDING REMARKS

The theory of collective choice (and the theory of politics viewed as collective choice) is probably still in its nonage. Although this approach to political theory has important precursors (chiefly among the Utilitarians), the beginning of the very rapid growth of the sort of work we have been studying here occurred in the early 1950's. It is perhaps too early to make an overall evaluation of the contribution of the theory of collective choice to the study of politics. Nevertheless, a few brief comments on some of the deficiencies and limitations of what has been done so far should not be amiss.

1. In nearly all of those studies of collective choice in which the Decision Rule is taken as given (and this includes the material in the large section above on 'Majority Rule and Representative Democracy' and the section on 'Strategic Voting'), the only Rules which have been studied in detail are the various versions of majority rule, and these usually in their 'one-stage' forms. Recently, the analysis has been extended (especially by Murakami, Fishburn, and Pattanaik) to a consideration of hierarchies of 'committees', each using majority rule—the resulting Decision Rule being called Multi-Stage Majority Rule. This work should be taken still further, for in practice the institutional structure within which political decision-making takes place is often much more complex: there is a hierarchy of committees and assemblies, but they may not all use the same Decision Rule; some of them (including 'degenerate' committees with only one

member) have veto powers, some may be concerned with only part of the set of alternatives or with changing this set, and so on.

In the explanatory theories of collective choice (for example, those mentioned in the section on 'Equilibrium under Majority Rule'), not even Multi-Stage Majority Rule has been considered. The need for considering a more realistic institutional structure is even greater here.

2. A large proportion of the writing on collective choice has been concerned with finding sufficient (and, in some cases, also necessary) conditions, in the form of restrictions on the admissible sets of individual preferences, for majoritarian Decision Rules to be Social Decision Functions or Social Welfare Functions. (See the sections on 'Majority Decision and Restricted Preferences' and 'Multi-Stage Decision Rules and Representative Democracy' above.) But very little effort has been made to try to discover whether any of these conditions are or are likely to be satisfied in any actual collective decision-making situations. (And in view of the theorem of Kramer mentioned above in the section on 'Equilibrium Under Majority Rule,' there seems little cause for optimism.)

3. Since the publication in 1957 of Downs's *An Economic Theory of Democracy,* a considerable volume of writing on the theory of electoral competition has accumulated. (See the relevant section above.) Some of the (extremely heroic) assumptions of the earliest models have been progressively relaxed, but we still do not have a theory which can be expected to explain electoral competition on a national scale even in a strictly two-party system. Most of the models treat only competition between two parties (or candidates) in a single 'constituency' for a single office. The following are some obvious omissions. First, multi-stage features are usually not considered; and it is clearly difficult to explain the positions taken by candidates in, for example, the U.S. presidential election, without also considering the earlier contests (possibly including primaries and conventions) for the parties' nominations. (A start is made in this direction by Aranson and Ordeshook, 1972, and Coleman, 1972.) Second, the positions which candidates for a national office adopt (or should rationally adopt) must also take account of geographical factors, especially where the final outcome depends on separate elections in a number of districts. These factors, too, have been omitted from the models. Third, the models assume only two parties and do not admit the possibility of the formation of new parties. But only a very few party systems in the world even approximate the pure two-party case. A theory of multi-party competition remains to be developed. It will be much more complicated (and interesting) than the two-party theory: the number of parties is not fixed, for new parties enter and others die (this being partly accounted for by the electoral laws, which in turn determine the minimum number of votes, or threshold, required by a party to secure the election of a

first representative); the electors generally do not vote for and against a government party, as in the two-party case, since government coalitions may be necessary, and rational voting (which is for parties, not coalitions) may thus be more complex; and so on.

4. All the theories discussed here take the set of alternatives as given. But the determination of the alternatives is itself often an important political activity. Part of an individual's (or group's) efforts to secure a particular alternative as the collective choice may consist of expanding or respecifying or restricting the set from which the collective choice must be made. Of course, this set may itself be determined by a process of collective decision-making—involving voting or bargaining or both—to which these theories could in principle be applied (although such applications have not yet been made). But often this will not be so, except in a tautological or trivial sense.

5. It was pointed out in the introduction that individual preferences, on which all the theories of collective choice are founded, may be extremely difficult to ascertain empirically. We are in a position now to see that the problem is important, because, though many theories can be tested (or are falsifiable in principle) without a direct test's being made of their assumptions, this is not true of some of the explanatory theories of collective choice. This is especially clear where strategic voting is (or is suspected of being) present. An illustration of the difficulty is to be found in Riker (1958), who has inferred preferences directly from voting (in the U.S. House of Representatives) in a case in which it is fairly certain that some of the voting was strategic; quite different and more plausible preferences (for the strategists) could have been inferred under an assumption of strategic behavior. Again, as Sen (1964) suggests, a voter who is indifferent between the two candidates in an election but derives positive utility from the act of voting, might rationally vote at random. Clearly, his choice does not reveal his preference. Choices, then, even a whole series of them, may be a poor guide to preferences. And the pitfalls of trying to elicit preferences directly from individuals—before or after collective decisions have been made—are obvious (and probably are more dangerous, the more important the decision).

6. Finally, we note that all the theories discussed above (with the important exception of some of the bargaining theories, especially those of Cross and Coddington) are 'static'. There is no explicit reference to *time*. During the process of collective decision-making there are no changes in preferences, in perceptions of the alternatives, in voting strategies, or in expectations about other individuals' preferences and behavior: no changes take place as a result of persuasion; there is no accumulation and reinterpretation of experience, no learning, no adaptation.

NOTES

1.   Buchanan (1968) has remarked that this convergence may not occur if voters are not "hypersensitive to distance differentials," i.e., if they are indifferent between two parties separated by less than a "threshold" (analogous to a 'just-noticeable difference'). Buchanan's remarks on party competition are derived from the work of Devletoglou and others, who have introduced the threshold concept into spatial duopoly theory. Devletoglou (1968) is the most recent contribution and gives references to earlier studies.

2.   Buchanan and Tullock go on to argue that, because logrolling gives scope to an individual's preference intensities, it thereby lowers the external costs to him of collective decision-making, and that, this being true for each individual, aggregate utility is therefore increased. This argument depends on their assumption that votes are private goods for the legislators. But as Rothenberg (1969, p. 251) says, "a vote outcome on any issue is a public good, not a private one. Each vote trade simply alters the expected shape of such a public good. It is inescapably saturated with significant externalities." Vote-trading cannot be treated simply as a market exchange economy possessing the usual optimality properties. A more careful treatment of logrolling is begun by Wilson (1969a, 1969b, 1971a, 1971b). His work will not be described here, because doing so would require a considerable digression into n-person game theory.

3.   There has been very little empirical work in connection with the bargaining theories which follow. Siegel and Fouraker (1960) experimentally test the classical theory's prediction that the bargaining outcome is Pareto-optimal, and they report further experimental work on bilateral monopoly in Fouraker and Siegel (1963). Bartos (1965, 1967, pp. 272–87) experimentally tests the Zeuthen-Nash theory (described below) and his own model of international negotiation, which involves more than two players. Direct testing of these bargaining theories against observations of labor-management negotiations or international negotiations presents enormous problems. But it may be possible to reformulate or augment a theory so that more readily observable predictions can be made from it. For example, Ashenfelter and Johnson (1969) build an econometric model of labor-management bargaining which predicts the duration of industrial strikes, and they test it on U.S. data for the period 1952–1967. Some of the problems of applying bargaining theories to arms control and other international negotiations are raised by some of the contributors to the Mathematica studies [(a) and (b)] for the U.S. Arms Control and Disarmament Agency (listed under *Mathematica* in the references).

4.   A careful definition of the Shapley value would require a considerable digression into n-person game theory. An excellent introduction to this subject is given by Rapoport (1970); his Chapter 5 is devoted to the Shapley value and Chapter 11 to Harsanyi's generalization of Nash's Scheme. The Shapley value has also been proposed as an index of 'a priori power' in voting bodies (Shapley and Shubik, 1954) and as such has been used to evaluate 'power' distributions in the U.S. Congress (Luce and Rogow, 1956), the U.S. Electoral College (Mann and Shapley, 1960, 1962), the U.S. House of Representatives (Riker and Niemi, 1962), the French Assembly (Riker, 1959) and the United Nations (Schwödiauer, 1968). The papers by Shapley and Shubik, Luce and Rogow, and Mann and Shapley are reprinted in Shubik (1964) and discussed by Luce and Raiffa (1957, pp. 252–59). An alternative index of 'a priori power' has been proposed by Coleman (1971) and Rae (1971).

REFERENCES

Aranson, Peter H., and Peter C. Ordeshook (1972). "Spatial strategies for sequential elections." In R. Niemi and H. Weisberg (eds.), *Probability Models of Collective Decision Making*. Columbus, Ohio: Merrill.

Armstrong, W. E. (1951). "Utility and the theory of welfare." *Oxford Economic Papers*, New Series 3:259–71.

Arrow, Kenneth J. (1950). "A difficulty in the concept of social welfare." *The Journal of Political Economy* 58:328–46.

——————— (1951, 1963). *Social Choice and Individual Values*. New York: Wiley. First edition, 1951. Second edition, 1963.

——————— (1959). "Rational choice functions and orderings." *Economica*, New Series 26:121–7.

——————— (1967). "Values and collective decision-making." In P. Laslett and W. G. Runciman (eds.), *Philosophy, Politics and Society, Third Series*. Oxford: Blackwell.

Ashenfelter, Orley, and George E. Johnson (1969). "Bargaining theory, trade unions, and industrial strike activity." *American Economic Review* 59:35–49.

Aumann, Robert J. (1962). "Utility theory without the completeness axiom." *Econometrica* 30:445–62.

——————— (1964a). "Utility theory without the completeness axiom: a correction." *Econometrica* 32:210–2.

——————— (1964b). "Subjective programming." In M. W. Shelly and G. L. Bryan (eds.), *Human Judgments and Optimality*. New York: Wiley.

Badger, Wade W. (1972). "Political individualism, positional preferences, and optimal decision rules." In R. Niemi and H. Weisberg (eds.), *Probability Models of Collective Decision Making*. Columbus, Ohio: Merrill.

Barry, Brian (1965). *Political Argument*. London: Routledge and Kegan Paul.

——————— (1970). *Sociologists, Economists and Democracy*. London: Collier-Macmillan.

Bartos, Otomar J. (1965). "A model of negotiation and some experimental evidence." In F. Massarik and P. Ratoosh (eds.), *Mathematical Explorations in the Behavioral Sciences*. Homewood, Ill.: Richard D. Irwin and the Dorsey Press.

——————— (1967). *Simple Models of Group Behavior*. New York: Columbia University Press.

Baumol, William J. (1952, 1965). *Welfare Economics and the Theory of the State*. London: Bell. First edition, 1952. Second edition, 1965. Reprinted by permission.

Bishop, R. L. (1964). "A Zeuthen-Hicks theory of bargaining." *Econometrica* 32:410–17.

Black, Duncan (1948a). "On the rationale of group decision making." *Journal of Political Economy* 56:23–34.

——————— (1948b). "The decisions of a committee using a special majority." *Econometrica* 16:245–61.

Black, Duncan (1958). *The Theory of Committees and Elections.* Cambridge: Cambridge University Press.

Black, Duncan, and R. A. Newing (1951). *Committee Decisions with Complementary Valuation.* London: Hodge.

Blau, Julian H. (1957). "The existence of social welfare functions." *Econometrica* 25: 302–13.

Braithwaite, R. B. (1955). *Theory of Games as a Tool for the Moral Philosopher.* Cambridge: Cambridge University Press.

Buchanan, James M. (1954a). "Social choice, democracy and free markets." *Journal of Political Economy* 62:114–23.

——————— (1954b). "Individual choice in voting and the market." *Journal of Political Economy* 62:334–43.

——————— (1968). "Democracy and duopoly: a comparison of analytical models." *American Economic Review* 58 *(Papers and Proceedings)*:322–31.

Buchanan, James M., and Gordon Tullock (1962). *The Calculus of Consent.* Ann Arbor: University of Michigan Press.

Campbell, Colin D., and Gordon Tullock (1965). "A measure of the importance of cyclical majorities." *The Economic Journal* 75:853–7.

——————— (1966). "The paradox of voting—A possible method of calculation." *American Political Science Review* 60:684–5.

Carling, Alan (1973). "Cross's theory of the bargaining process." Unpublished manuscript, University of Essex.

Coddington, Alan (1968). *Theories of the Bargaining Process.* London: Allen and Unwin.

Coleman, James S. (1966a). "Foundations for a theory of collective decisions." *American Journal of Sociology* 71:615–27.

——————— (1966b). "The possibility of a social welfare function." *American Economic Review* 61:1105–22.

——————— (1971). "Control of collectivities and the power of a collectivity to act." In B. Liebermann (ed.), *Social Choice* (Proceedings of a Conference at the University of Pittsburgh, September 1968). New York: Gordon and Breach.

——————— (1972). "The positions of political parties in elections." In R. Niemi and H. Weisberg (eds.), *Probability Models of Collective Decision Making.* Columbus, Ohio: Merrill.

Contini, Bruno (1967). "Threats and Organizational Design." *Behavioral Science* 12: 453–62.

——————— (1968). "The value of time in bargaining negotiations: some experimental evidence." *American Economic Review* 58:374–93.

Contini, Bruno, and Stanley Zionts (1968). "Restricted bargaining with multiple objectives." *Econometrica* 36:397–414.

Converse, Philip E. (1966). "The problem of party distances in models of voting choice." In M. K. Jennings and H. Zeigler (eds.), *The Electoral Process*. Englewood Cliffs, N.J.: Prentice-Hall.

Coombs, C. H. (1950). "Psychological scaling without a unit of measurement." *Psychological Review* 57:145–58.

——————— (1954). "Social choice and strength of preference." In R. M. Thrall, C. H. Coombs, and R. L. Davis (eds.), *Decision Processes*. New York: Wiley.

Cross, J. G. (1965). "A theory of the bargaining process." *American Economic Review* 56:522–30.

——————— (1969). *The Economics of Bargaining*. New York: Basic Books.

Curtis, Richard B. (1972). "Decision rules and collective values in constitutional choice." In R. Niemi and H. Weisberg (eds.), *Probability Models of Collective Decision Making*. Columbus, Ohio: Merrill.

Dahl, Robert A. (1956). *A Preface to Democratic Theory*. Chicago: University of Chicago Press.

Davis, John M. (1958). "The transitivity of preferences." *Behavioral Science* 3:26–33.

Davis, Otto M., and Melvin Hinich (1966). "A mathematical model of policy formation in a democratic society." In J. L. Bernd (ed.), *Mathematical Applications in Political Science, II*. Dallas: Southern Methodist University Press.

——————— (1967). "Some results related to a mathematical model of policy formation in a democratic society." In J. L. Bernd (ed.), *Mathematical Applications in Political Science, III*. Charlottesville: University Press of Virginia.

——————— (1968). "On the power and importance of the mean preference in a mathematical model of democratic choice." *Public Choice* 5:59–72.

Davis, Otto M., Melvin Hinich, and Peter C. Ordeshook (1970). "An expository development of a mathematical model of the electoral process." *American Political Science Review* 64:426–48.

DeMeyer, Frank, and Charles R. Plott (1970). "The probability of a cyclical majority." *Econometrica* 38:345–54.

Devletoglou, Nicos E. (1968). "Threshold and rationality." *Kyklos* 21:623–36.

Downs, Anthony (1957). *An Economic Theory of Democracy*. New York: Harper.

Dummett, Michael, and Robin Farquharson (1961). "Stability in voting." *Econometrica* 29:33–43.

Edgeworth, F. T. (1881). *Mathematical Psychics*. London: Kegan Paul.

Edwards, Ward (1954). "The theory of decision making." *Psychological Bulletin* 51:380–417. Reprinted in W. Edwards and A. Tversky (eds.), *Decision Making*. Harmondsworth, Middlesex: Penguin, 1967.

——————— (1961). "Behavioral decision theory." *Annual Review of Psychology* 12:473–98. Reprinted in W. Edwards and A. Tversky, eds. (1967). *Decision Making*. Harmondsworth, Middlesex: Penguin.

Farquharson, Robin (1956). "Straightforwardness in voting procedures." *Oxford Economic Papers,* New Series 8:80–9.

——————— (1969). *Theory of Voting.* New Haven: Yale University Press; Oxford: Blackwell.

Fishburn, Peter C. (1970a). "The irrationality of intransitivity." *Behavioral Science* 15:119–23.

——————— (1970b). "Intransitive individual indifference and transitive majorities." *Econometrica* 38:482–9.

——————— (1970c). "Arrow's impossibility theorem: concise proof and infinite voters." *Journal of Economic Theory* 2:103–6.

——————— (1970d). "Intransitive indifference in preference theory: a survey." *Operations Research* 18:207–28.

——————— (1970e). *Utility Theory for Decision Making.* New York: Wiley.

——————— (1970f). "Conditions for simple majority decision functions with intransitive individual indifference." *Journal of Economic Theory* 2:354–67.

——————— (1970g). "Comments on Hansson's 'Group Preferences'," *Econometrica* 38:933–5.

——————— (1971). "The theory of representative majority decision." *Econometrica* 39:273–84.

——————— (1973). *The Theory of Social Choice.* Princeton: Princeton University Press.

Foldes, L. (1964). "A determinate model of bilateral monopoly." *Economica* 122:117–31.

Fouraker, Lawrence E., and Sidney Siegel (1963). *Bargaining Behavior.* New York: McGraw-Hill.

Garman, M., and M. Kamien (1968). "The paradox of voting: probability calculations." *Behavioral Science* 13:306–16.

Goodhart, C. A. E., and R. J. Bhansali (1970). "Political economy." *Political Studies* 18:43–106.

Goodman, L A., and Harry Markowitz (1952). "Social welfare functions based on individual rankings." *American Journal of Sociology* 58:257–62.

Guilbaud, G. Th. (1952). "Les théories de l'intérêt général et le problème logique de l'aggrégation." *Economique Apliquée* 5:501–84. An English translation of parts of this article appears in P. F. Lazarsfeld and N.W. Henry (eds.), *Readings in Mathematical Social Science.* Cambridge, Mass.: M.I.T. Press, 1966.

Hansson, Bengt (1969). "Group Preferences." *Econometrica* 37:50–4.

Hardin, Russell (1971). "Collective action as an agreeable *n*-prisoners' dilemma." *Behavioral Science* 16:472–81.

Harsanyi, John C. (1953). "Cardinal utility in welfare economics and in the theory of risk taking." *Journal of Political Economy* 61:434–5.

——————— (1955). "Cardinal welfare, individualistic ethics, and interpersonal comparisons of utility." *Journal of Political Economy* 63:309–21.

_____ (1956). "Approaches to the bargaining problem before and after the theory of games: a critical discussion of Zeuthen's, Hicks's, and Nash's theories." *Econometrica* 24:144–57.

_____ (1959). "A bargaining model for the cooperative *n*-person game." In R. D. Luce and A. W. Tucker (eds.), *Contributions to the Theory of Game: IV (Annals of Mathematic Studies,* No. 40). Princeton: Princeton University Press.

_____ (1962a). "Bargaining in ignorance of the opponent's utility function." *Journal of Conflict Resolution* 6:29–38.

_____ (1962b). "Models for the analysis of balance of power in society." In E. Nagel, P. Suppes, and A. Tarski (eds.), *Logic, Methodology, and the Philosophy of Science.* Stanford, Cal.: Stanford University Press.

_____ (1966). "A Bargaining model for social status in informal groups and formal organizations." *Behavioral Science* 11:357–69.

_____ (1967–68). "Games with incomplete information, Parts I, II and III." *Management Science* 14:159–82, 320–34, and 486–502.

Harsanyi, John C., and Reinhard Selten (1972). "A generalized Nash solution for two-person bargaining games with incomplete information." *Management Science* 18:80–106.

Hildreth, Clifford (1953). "Alternative conditions for social orderings." *Econometrica* 21:81–94.

Hinich, Melvin, and Peter C. Ordeshook (1969). "Abstentions and equilibrium in the electoral process." *Public Choice* 7:81–106.

_____ (1970). "Plurality maximization vs. vote maximization: a spatial analysis with variable participation." *American Political Science Review* 64:772–91.

Hinich, Melvin, John O. Ledyard, and Peter C. Ordeshook (1973). "A theory of electoral equilibrium: a spatial analysis based on the theory of games." *Journal of Politics* 35:154–93.

Hotelling, Harold (1929). "Stability in competition." *The Economic Journal* 39:41–57.

Inada, Ken-Ichi (1955). "Alternative incompatible conditions for a social welfare function." *Econometrica* 23:396–9.

_____ (1964). "A note on the simple majority decision rule." *Econometrica* 32:525–31.

_____ (1969). "The simple majority decision rule." *Econometrica* 37:490–506.

_____ (1970). "Majority rule and rationality." *Journal of Economic Theory* 2:27–40.

Kemp, M. C. (1953–54). "Arrow's general possibility theorem." *Review of Economic Studies* 21:240–3.

Klahr, David (1966). "A computer simulation of the paradox of voting." *American Political Science Review* 60:384–90.

Kramer, Gerald H. (1971). "Short-term fluctuations in U.S. voting behavior, 1896–1966." *American Political Science Review* 65:131–43.

Kramer, Gerald H. (1972). "Sophisticated voting over multidimensional choice spaces." *Journal of Mathematical Sociology* 2:165–80.

Kramer, Gerald H. (1973). "On a class of equilibrium conditions for majority rule." *Econometrica* 41:285–97.

Leibenstein, Harvey (1965). "Long-run welfare criteria." In J. Margolis (ed.), *The Public Economy of Urban Communities*. Baltimore: Johns Hopkins Press.

Luce, R. Duncan (1956). "Semiorders and a theory of utility discrimination." *Econometrica* 24:178–91.

Luce, R. Duncan, and Howard Raiffa (1957). *Games and Decisions*. New York: Wiley.

Luce, R. Duncan, and Arnold A. Rogow (1956). "A game theoretic analysis of congressional power distributions for a stable two-party system." *Behavioral Science* 1:83–95.

Luce, R. Duncan, and Patrick Suppes (1965). "Preference, utility, and subjective probability." In R. D. Luce, R. R. Bush, and E. Galanter (eds.), *Handbook of Mathematical Psychology*, Vol. III. New York: Wiley.

MacCrimmon, K. R. (1968). *Decision Making Among Multi-Attribute Alternatives*, Santa Monica, Cal.: The Rand Corporation, RM 4823.

Majumdar, Tapas (1956). "Choice and revealed preference." *Econometrica* 24:71–3.

Mann, Irwin, and L. S. Shapley (1960, 1962). "Values of large games IV: evaluating the Electoral College by Monte Carlo techniques." Santa Monica, Cal.: The Rand Corporation, RM 2651 (1960) and RM 3158 (1962). Excerpts reprinted as "The a priori voting strength of the Electoral College." In M. Shubik (ed.), *Game Theory and Related Approaches to Social Behavior*. New York: Wiley, 1964.

Marschak, Jacob (1950). "Rational behaviour, uncertain prospects, and measurable utility." *Econometrica* 18:111–41.

Mathematica studies for the U.S. Arms Control and Disarmament Agency:
  a) *Applications of Statistical Methodology to Arms Control*. Contract No. ACDA/ST-3 (1963).
  b) *Development of Utility Theory for Arms Control and Disarmament*. Contract No. ACDA/ST-80 (1966).
  c) *Models of Gradual Reduction of Arms*. Contract No. ACDA/ST-116 (1967). Princeton, N.J.

May, Kenneth O. (1952). "A set of independent, necessary and sufficient conditions for simple majority decisions." *Econometrica* 20:680–4.

——————— (1953). "A note on the complete independence of the conditions for simple majority decision." *Econometrica* 21:172–3.

——————— (1954). "Intransitivity, utility, and the aggregation of preference patterns." *Econometrica* 22:1–13.

Murakami, Yasusuke (1961). "A note on the general possibility theorem of the social welfare function." *Econometrica* 29:244–6.

——————— (1966). "Formal structure of majority decision." *Econometrica* 34:709–18.

——————— (1968). *Logic and Social Choice*. London: Routledge and Kegan Paul; New York: Dover.

Nash, John F. (1950). "The bargaining problem." *Econometrica* 18:155–62.

—————— (1951). "Non-cooperative games." *Annals of Mathematics* 54:286–95.

—————— (1953). "Two-person cooperative games." *Econometrica* 21:128–40.

Nicholson, Michael (1965). "Conditions for the 'voting paradox' in committee decision." *Metroeconomica* 42:29–44.

—————— (1967). "The resolution of conflict." *Journal of the Royal Statistical Society* (Series A) 130:529–40.

Niemi, Richard G. (1969). "Majority decision-making with partial unidimensionality." *American Political Science Review* 63:488–97.

Niemi, Richard G., and Herbert Weisberg (1968). "A mathematical solution for the probability of the paradox of voting." *Behavioral Science* 13:317–23.

Olson, Mancur (1965). *The Logic of Collective Action.* Cambridge, Mass.: Harvard University Press. Copyright 1965 by the President and Fellows of Harvard College. Reprinted by permission.

Papandreou, A. G. (1953). "An experimental test of an axiom in the theory of choice." (Abstract) *Econometrica* 21:477.

Pattanaik, Prasanta K. (1968a). "A note on democratic decision and the existence of choice sets." *Review of Economic Studies* 35:1–9.

—————— (1968b). "Risk, impersonality, and the social welfare function." *Journal of Political Economy* 76:1152–69.

—————— (1968c). "Transivity and choice under multi-stage majority decisions." Discussion Paper 52, Harvard Institute of Economic Research. Cambridge, Mass.: Harvard University.

—————— (1970a). "Sufficient conditions for the existence of a choice set under majority rule." *Econometrica* 38:165–70.

—————— (1970b). "On social choice with quasitransitive individual preferences." *Journal of Economic Theory* 2:267–75.

—————— (1971). *Voting and Collective Choice.* Cambridge: Cambridge University Press.

—————— (1973). "Group choice with lexicographic individual orderings." *Behavioral Science* 18:118–23.

Pen, Jan (1952). "A general theory of bargaining." *American Economic Review* 42:24–42.

Plott, Charles R. (1967). "A notion of equilibrium and its possibility under majority rule." *American Economic Review* 57:788–806.

—————— (1972). "Individual choice of a political-economic process." In R. Niemi and H. Weisberg (eds.), *Probability Models of Collective Decision Making.* Columbus, Ohio: Merrill.

Quirk, James, and Rubin Saposnik (1968). *Introduction to General Equilibrium Theory and Welfare Economics.* New York: McGraw-Hill.

Rae, Douglas W. (1969). "Decision-rules and individual values in collective choice." *American Political Science Review* 63:40–56.

Rae, Douglas W. (1971). "Decisiveness in election outcomes." In B. Liebermann (ed.), *Social Choice* (Proceedings of a Conference at the University of Pittsburgh, September 1968). New York: Gordon and Breach.

Rae, Douglas W., and Michael Taylor (1971). "Decision rules and policy outcomes." *British Journal of Political Science* 1:71–90.

Raiffa, Howard (1953). "Arbitration schemes for generalized two-person games." In H. W. Kuhn and A. W Tucker (eds.), *Contributions to the Theory of Games, II (Annals of Mathematics Studies* No. 28). Princeton: Princeton University Press.

Rapoport, Anatol (1970). *N-Person Game Theory: Concepts and Applications.* Ann Arbor: University of Michigan Press.

Rapoport, Anatol, and Albert M. Chammah (1965). *Prisoner's Dilemma: A Study in Conflict and Cooperation.* Ann Arbor: University of Michigan Press. Reprinted by permission.

Rawls, John (1958). 'Justice as fairness." *Philosophical Review* 67:164–94. Reprinted in P. Laslett and W. G. Runciman (eds.), *Philosophy, Politics and Society, Second Series.* Oxford: Blackwell, 1967.

_____ (1963). "The Sense of Justice." *Philosophical Review* 72:281–305.

_____ (1967). "Distributive Justice." In P. Laslett and W. G. Runciman (eds.), *Philosophy, Politics, and Society, Third Series.* Oxford: Blackwell.

_____ (1971). *A Theory of Justice.* Cambridge, Mass.: Harvard University Press.

Riker, William H. (1958). "The paradox of voting and congressional rules for voting on amendments." *American Political Science Review* 52:349–66.

_____ (1959). "A test of the adequacy of the power index." *Behavioral Science* 4:120–31.

Riker, William H., and Richard G. Niemi (1962). "The stability of coalitions on roll calls in the House of Representatives." *American Political Science Review* 56:58–65.

Riker, William H., and Peter C. Ordeshook (1968). "A theory of the calculus of voting." *American Political Science Review* 62:25–42.

Rose, A. M. (1957). "A study of irrational judgments." *Journal of Political Economy* 65:394–402.

Rothenberg, Jerome (1961). *The Measurement of Social Welfare.* Englewood Cliffs, N.J.: Prentice-Hall.

_____ (1969). "The process of group choice in a legislative context." In G. T. Guilbaud (ed.), *La Décision: Aggrégation et Dynamique des Ordres de Préférence.* Paris: Editions du Centre National de la Recherche Scientifique.

Samuelson, Paul (1967). "Arrow's mathematical politics." In S. Hook (ed.), *Human Values and Economic Policy.* New York: New York University Press.

Schick, Frederick (1969). "Arrow's proof and the logic of preference." *Philosophy of Science* 36:127–44.

Schofield, Norman (1972). "Ethical decision rules for uncertain voters." *British Journal of Political Science* 2:193–207.

Schwödiauer, Gerhard (1968). "Berechnung eines Shapley-Wertes für die Vereinten Nationen." In *Gesammelte Beiträge zur Konferenz, "Mathematical Theory of Committees and Elections,"* Vol. III. Vienna: Institute for Advanced Studies.

Selten, Reinhard (1964). "Valuation of *n*-person games." In M. Dresher *et al.* (eds.), *Advances in Game Theory (Annals of Mathematics Studies,* No. 52.). Princeton: Princeton University Press.

Sen, Amartya K. (1964) "Preferences, votes and the transitivity of majority decisions." *Review of Economic Studies* 31:163–65.

_____ (1966). "A possibility theorem on majority decisions." *Econometrica* 34: 491–9.

_____ (1969). "Quasi-transitivity, rational choice and collective decisions." *Review of Economic Studies* 36:381–93.

_____ (1970a). "The impossibility of a Paretian liberal." *Journal of Political Economy* 78:152–7.

_____ (1970b). "Interpersonal aggregation and partial comparability." *Econometrica* 38:393–409.

_____ (1970c). "On Pareto optimality." (Abstract) *Econometrica* 38:6.

_____ (1970d). *Collective Choice and Social Welfare.* Edinburgh: Oliver and Boyd; New York: Holden-Day. Reprinted by permission.

Sen, Amartya K., and Prasanta K. Pattanaik (1969). "Necessary and sufficient conditions for rational choice under majority decision." *Journal of Economic Theory* 1:178–202.

Sen, Subrata (1969). "Models of political campaign strategies." Paper read at the 65th Annual Meeting of the American Political Science Association, New York.

Shapley, L. S. (1953). "A value for *n*-person games." In H. W. Kuhn and A. W. Tucker (eds), *Contributions to the Theory of Games, II (Annals of Mathematics Studies,* No. 28). Princeton: Princeton University Press.

Shapley, L. S., and Martin Shubik (1954). "A method for evaluating the distribution of power in a committee system." *American Political Science Review* 48:787–92.

Shubik, Martin (1959). *Strategy and Market Structure: Competition, Oligopoly, and the Theory of Games.* New York: Wiley.

_____ ed. (1964). *Game Theory and Related Approaches to Social Behavior.* New York: Wiley.

_____ (1968). "A two-party system, general equilibrium, and the voters' paradox." Santa Monica, Cal.: the Rand Corporation, RM-5770.

_____ (1970). "Voting, or a price system in a competitive market." *American Political Science Review* 64:179–81.

Siegel, Sidney, and Lawrence E. Fouraker (1960). *Bargaining and Group Decision Making: Experiments in Bilateral Monopoly.* New York: McGraw-Hill.

Simon, Herbert A. (1955). "A Behavioral model of rational choice." *Quarterly Journal of Economics* 69:99–118. Reprinted in H. A. Simon, *Models of Man.* New York: Wiley.

Simpson, Paul B. (1969). "On defining areas of voter choice." *Quarterly Journal of Economics* 83:478–90.

Smithies, Arthur (1941). "Optimum location in spatial competitions." *Journal of Political Economy* 49:423–39.

Stokes, Donald E. (1963). "Spatial models of party competition." *American Political Science Review* 57:368–77.

Strotz, Robert H. (1958). "How income ought to be distributed: a paradox in distributive ethics." *Journal of Political Economy* 66: 189–205.

——————— (1961). "How income ought to be distributed: paradox regained." *Journal of Political Economy* 69:271–8.

Taylor, Michael (1969). "Proof of a theorem on majority rule." *Behavioral Science* 14:228–31.

——————— (1970). "The problem of salience in the theory of collective decision-making." *Behavioral Science* 16:415–30.

Theil, Henri (1963). "On the symmetry approach to the committee decision problem." *Management Science* 9:380–93.

——————— (1964). *Optimal Decision Rules for Government and Industry.* Amsterdam: North Holland.

Tversky, Amos (1969). "Intransitivity of preferences." *Psychological Review* 76:31–48.

Van den Bogaard, P. J., and J. Versluis (1962). "The design of optimal committee decisions." *Statistica Neerlandica* 16:271–89.

Vickrey, William (1960). "Utility, strategy, and social decision rules." *Quarterly Journal of Economics* 74:507–35.

von Neumann, John, and Oskar Morgenstern (1947). *Theory of Games and Economic Behavior,* 2nd edition. Princeton: Princeton University Press.

Ward, Benjamin (1965). "Majority voting and alternative forms of public enterprise." In J. Margolis (ed.), *The Public Economy of Urban Communities.* Baltimore: Johns Hopkins Press.

Weinstein, A. A. (1968). "Individual preference intransitivity." *Southern Economic Journal* 34:335–43.

Williamson, Oliver E., and Thomas J. Sargent (1967). "Social choice: a probabilistic approach." *Economic Journal* 77:797–813.

Wilson, Robert (1968). "The theory of syndicates." *Econometrica* 36:119–32.

——————— (1969a). "An axiomatic model of logrolling." *American Economic Review* 59:331–41.

——————— (1969b). "The role of uncertainty and the value of logrolling in collective choice processes." In G. Guilbaud (ed.), *La Décision: Aggrégation et Dynamique des Ordres de Préférence.* Paris: Editions du Centre National de la Recherche Scientifique.

——————— (1971a). "A game-theoretic analysis of social choice." In B. Liebermann (ed.), *Social Choice* (Proceedings of a Conference at the University of Pittsburgh, September 1968). New York: Gordon and Breach.

_____ (1971b). "Stable coalition proposals in majority rule voting." *Journal of Economic Theory* 3:254–71.

Wolff, Robert Paul (1970). *In Defense of Anarchism*. New York: Harper and Row.

Zeuthen, Frederik (1930). *Problems of Monopoly and Economic Warfare*. London: Routledge.

5
REVOLUTIONS AND COLLECTIVE VIOLENCE

CHARLES TILLY

THE TASK

Suppose we were looking ahead to yet another uncertain year in the political life of our country—whichever country it is—and we wanted to reduce our uncertainty. For that year and that country, how could we go about estimating the probability of two conditions: (a) that a revolution would occur; (b) that more than some minimum proportion (say ten percent) of the country's population would take direct part in collective violence?

These are more or less meteorological questions: What will the political weather be like? Should I get ready for a storm? We might also complicate the problem by turning the two into engineering questions. Suppose we want to *produce* a revolution, or more than a minimum involvement in collective violence, or both, within that country-year. What would it take?

The turbulent twentieth century has brought plenty of attention to bear on both the meteorological and the engineering versions of these questions. Yet the reliability of our answers to them has not improved notably over that of the answers offered by Aristotle at the very dawn of systematic thinking about revolution and political violence. (With no particular embarrassment, indeed, a respectable political science journal once published an article treating the

The Canada Council and the National Science Foundation supported the research into political conflict in Europe which lies behind this paper, and the Institute for Advanced Study gave me the time to write it. At several points in the paper I have drawn freely on an unpublished paper, "The Historical Study of Political Conflict," presented to the conference on new trends in history sponsored by *Daedalus* and the Ford Foundation, Rome, June 1970. David Bayley, Henry Bienen, Harry Eckstein, Daniel Headrick, and Edward Shorter have all given me valuable criticism of earlier drafts; I must confess, however, that I have been unwilling and/or unable to make all the changes that any one of them proposed.

quantification of Aristotle's theory of revolution; see Kort, 1952.) I don't mean to belittle Aristotle. He was a master political analyst. His formulations have lasted 24 centuries. Some formulations in this essay will be thoroughly Aristotelian. Still, one might think that in 24 centuries men could have improved on his politics, as they have on his physics. No doubt Aristotle would be baffled by the enormous, powerful national states which populate today's political world; his theories tend to lose their shape when stretched over twentieth-century politics. But the same thing happens when current theories of revolution are applied to the city-states with which Aristotle was familiar. In this strict sense of predictability, the systematic formulations of political scientists improve little on the haphazard formulations of common sense. And the formulations of common sense improve little on casting dice or reading omens.

I am talking about systematic knowledge; the acid test is whether it helps us anticipate what will turn up in some as-yet unexplored corner of experience with less error than other ways of thought. That sort of knowledge overlaps with several other kinds which have a lot to do with revolution and collective violence. Political philosophy, in examining the principles according to which men attempt to organize their public life and comparing them with the alternative principles men might employ, has much to say about conflict. Statements of political programs and credos usually include strong ideas concerning the justification—or lack of it—for violence and revolution. Theoreticians and practitioners have created a vast tactical literature: how to make revolutions, how to foil them, principles of guerrilla warfare, principles of "counterinsurgency." Systematic knowledge obviously sets constraints on all these other ways of knowing, but it does not exhaust or replace them. Systematic knowledge concerns us here.

It is possible that the pursuit of systematic knowledge about collective violence and revolution destines the pursuer to failure and irrelevance in all but the longest of long runs. A scheme which will predict elections with no more than five percent error embodies quite an intellectual achievement, but it does little good to anyone in a political system in which most elections hang on a margin of less than five percent. With every reason to believe that revolutions and collective violence are at least as complicated and contingent as elections, we have to beware of the "quick fix" and resign ourselves to the prospect of repeated blunders. Any careful examination of the constantly accumulating writings on revolution and collective violence will convince the reader that the blundering has been going on for a long time and shows no signs of ceasing. Nor do I hope for an instant that this essay will end the trend—or even avoid it.

AVAILABLE IDEAS

Like the old-time doctors who gravely sniffed the chamber pots of their patients, we could seek to diagnose the ills of political science by close examination of the large variety of available theories of revolution and collective violence. That unpleasant task will not occupy us much here, as it has been done thoroughly and well elsewhere (see Bienen, 1968; Converse, 1968; Stone, 1966; Gurr, 1969; Alberoni, 1968, Chapter 1; Eckstein, 1965; Fink, 1968). This review will catalog or criticize established theories only where they will clarify the argument. It will follow the riskier course of concentrating on a single approach to political conflict, one which is promising, which takes into account a good deal of previous thinking and research, but which is also far from accepted or proved.

The task itself needs defining. Whether we are trying to anticipate or to manipulate the political weather, it is quite easy to confuse two different procedures. The first is the explanation of a particular conflict or class of conflicts by moving backward from the effect of the complex of causes which lies behind it: Why the Whisky Rebellion? Why the recurrent military coups of Latin America? The question is *retrospective*, moving from outcome to origin. The second procedure is the assessment of the probable consequences of a given set of circumstances: What effect does rapid industrialization have on the nature or frequency of protest? What sorts of power struggles tend to follow losses in war? What is this year's likelihood of a rebellion in South Africa, under suppositions A, B, or C about her relations with the rest of the world? These questions have a *prospective* character, moving from origin to outcome—or more likely, to a set of outcomes varying in probability.

The prospective procedure and the retrospective one converge under some special conditions: (1) if a particular outcome follows uniquely and with high probability from a particular antecedent circumstance, and (2) if the only question that matters is the likelihood of that one outcome, or (3) if all the relevant variables are known. In political analysis, these conditions are (to put it gently) rare. Yet in the analysis of revolution, the standard procedure is to draw prospective conclusions from retrospective analyses, going from the fact of revolution in particular to the conditions under which revolutions occur in general.

Although collective violence occurs every day, revolutions are rare events. They don't lend themselves to the sorts of statistical procedures which help us make sense of births or traffic patterns or shifts in everyday speech. Their occurrence almost certainly depends on the convergence of different conditions, rather than one sure-fire cause. It is even possible that the phenomenon we label "revolution" is simply the most visible resultant of several relatively independent processes, in the same sense that the change in a city's population is a sum of the effects of in-migration, out-migration, births, and deaths. The movement from growth to decline may well have devastating effects on the life of the city; yet it is quite likely that nothing whatsoever happened at the point of transition from growth to decline but the continuation of long-established trends in migration, fertility, and mortality.

Tradition and common sense argue against the application of that sort of model to revolution—but then tradition and common sense also treat urban growth and urban decline as products of drastically different situations. The probability that revolution is a much more complex process, or bundle of processes, than urban growth should encourage us to break it up into its parts before reconstructing a single model of the revolutionary process.

Deeply ingrained prejudices struggle against this sort of analytical disaggregation of revolutionary processes. Nineteenth-century sociology bequeathed to us a view of large-scale social structure and social change which remains marvelously compelling despite the mounting evidence against it. The correspondence of the formulations of a Durkheim or a Tönnies to the folk sociology of our era makes them persuasive. So we find ourselves dealing with variations on the theme of a coherent society (conveniently matched to a national state, with the problem of whether Italian society existed before 1860, or Canadian society exists today, left conveniently vague) precariously integrated by commitment to common values (conveniently described as those of the dominant elites) responding to every structural change by a temporary disintegration which leads to new efforts at integration.

The adoption of this world view leads almost without effort to the sharp separation of "orderly" and "disorderly" responses to structural change, and hence to the argument that the likelihood of orderly responses to change is a function of (a) the strength of commitment of all members of the society to its common values, and (b) the gradualness and evenness of the change. Those who adopt this vision of the way the world works will find it natural to assume that mobility is more disruptive for individual and society than immobility, that crime is performed by people who are "poorly integrated" into routine social life, that a rising suicide rate, a rising illegitimacy rate, and a rising divorce rate are reliable signs of social disintegration, and that movements of protest draw their clientele from marginal members of society but—fortunately!—tend to become more moderate, reasonable, and realistic, as well as to shed their wildest members, in the course of political experience. All of these assumptions can, of course, be made true by definition. If we leave that trap aside, however, every one of them remains unproved and, at best, dubious (see Cornelius, 1970; Nelson, 1969, 1970; Bienen, 1968; Gurr, 1969, Chapter 4; Kantor, 1965).

Dozens of observers of our times, lulled by the retroactive pacification of the past and then shaken by the violence of the present, have supposed that a fixed, instinctive drive to aggression underlies the readiness of men to attack one another. Remove the restraints or flash the signals, goes the argument, and the fateful urge will rise. One popular account relying heavily on animal studies observes:

> We already know that if our populations go on increasing at their present terrifying rate, uncontrollable aggressiveness will become dramatically increased. This has been proved conclusively with laboratory experiments. Gross overcrowding will produce social stresses and tensions that will shatter our community organizations long before it starves us to death. It will work

directly against improvements in the intellectual control and will savagely heighten the likelihood of emotional explosion.*

If we adopted this reasoning in detail, we would have to expect that American cities, especially automobile cities like Dallas and Los Angeles, would be among the least "aggressive" in the world, for they are settled at far lower densities than their European or Asian counterparts and have been getting less dense for decades. They are not so peaceful as all that. If we take the argument as simply identifying one of the factors behind violence, on the other hand, its capacity to account for the large, genuine variations in violence from time to time, place to place, group to group dwindles. We have as yet no good means of distinguishing the effects of crowding from that of a great many other characteristics of cities. For the present, then, attempts to apply to human aggregates the alleged lessons of animal-aggression studies lead us into a dead end.

A more powerful version of the argument has "aggression" resulting mainly from the amount of frustration endured by men, tempered by existing constraints on the release of that aggression. A wonderful variety of conditions win nomination as frustrations capable of producing aggression—not only high densities but also sexual repression, sexual freedom, wealth, poverty. If these analyses of aggressive impulses were correct, aggression would rise and fall regularly with the alteration of the signals, the frustration, and/or the restraints. So far as I can tell, they do not. But even if such theories of impulse were valid, the necessity of establishing exactly which conditions were frustrating, or restraining, or stimulating, would involve us again in analyzing the social relations which actually turn to violent encounters.

Our nineteenth-century sociology also favors a particular interpretation of political conflict, especially revolution. Revolutions and other major conflicts arise, in this view, because structural change builds up unresolved tensions which burst into disorder when and where restraints are weak. Those tensions build up in several ways: through expectations which rise faster than achievement and thus produce frustration; through the disorientation suffered by those who cut traditional social ties; through the inherent psychic costs of mobility, complexity, variety, and impersonality; through the difficulty of performing contradictory roles. The tensions build up in individuals, but eventually they achieve collective expression.

Embedded in this foundation for the study of political conflict are a whole series of related fallacies:

1. that rebellion is an individual act intimately dependent on a certain attitude—a rebellious attitude—toward some or all authorities;

---

* From *The Naked Ape* by Desmond Morris, p. 145. Copyright 1967 by Desmond Morris. Used with permission of McGraw-Hill Book Company.

2. that the likelihood of mass rebellion is a linear function of the sum of individual hostilities to the regime, which is in turn a linear function of the sum of deprivations experienced by the individuals;

3. that there is a close correspondence between the sum of individual intentions of participants in revolutionary actions and the changes produced by those actions;

4. that revolution is simply the extreme position on a scale running from fleeting individual protests to durable anger on the part of the entire population, which implies that the extent of discontent and the likelihood of a transfer of power are closely related to one another;

5. that revolution and revolutionary propensity are conditions of a "society" or a "social system" rather than of a particular government or a particular population.

This variety of reasoning permits theorists like Chalmers Johnson, James Davies, Ted Gurr, and Neil Smelser to erect schemes in which some inefficiency in "the system" expands the fund of discontent, which in turn leads to assaults on those who hold power. These social scientists concentrate their theorizing and their research on individual attitudes or on the condition of the social system as a whole. They neglect the struggles among classes and power blocs, which constitute the bulk of political conflict.

In the standard social-psychological treatment, the implicit crude model of the whole process therefore looks something like Figure 1. Hence the recipe for avoiding major conflicts goes: slow down the pace of change; dampen unrealistic expectations; expand the opportunities for gradual release of tension;

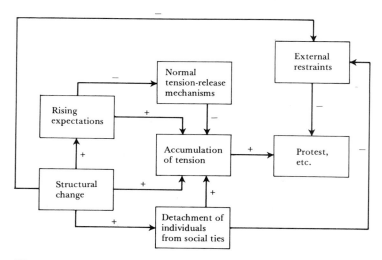

Figure 1

reinforce existing social ties and speed the acquisition of new ones; strengthen external restraints, especially by reinforcing commitments to common values.

This is, to be sure, a caricature. I hope it is recognizable in the same way that Daumier's nineteenth-century caricatures were; it represents a reality. In any case, my plan is not to summon the caricature to life and do battle with him, but to sketch another contrasting figure and see how much vitality he has.

We have to face some serious problems of definition. Yield to the temptation to single out a small set of "true" revolutions in which a whole class gained power, or an even smaller set in which deep, long-run structural changes resulted from the transfer of power. The danger is then not only that the number of cases you are working with will be too tiny to permit effective comparison (a distinguished student of political change, commenting on a student's proposal to undertake the study of revolutions, asked, "Which of the four are you studying?") but also that you will be making the wrong comparisons. If, for example, attempts to make revolutions differed fundamentally from all other sorts of political conflicts, but successful and unsuccessful attempts differed only through the intervention of chance, then a lifelong study of successful revolutions alone would probably yield nothing but shaky hypotheses about the causes of revolution. This is an argument not for abandoning the analysis of the so-called Great Revolutions, but for trying to link their study with that of the larger set of events to which they belong. Then we can preserve the distinctness of the Great Revolutions by treating revolutionary character—the extent to which the particular series of events at hand produced class realignments, transformations of governments, further structural change, etc.—as a variable.

Social scientists, I must admit, have been giving—and even trying to follow —this brand of advice for some time without resounding success. For example, we have passed through numerous twists and turns in simply trying to decide what phenomenon is under examination: "rebellion," "violence," "collective violence," "internal war," "conflict," "instability," "protest," "disorder." Each of these is plausible. Each carries with it a somewhat different agenda and implicit theory. The failure of any of them to stick and the ease with which writers on revolution and political conflict switch from one to another bespeak both confusion and discord about the nature of the problem at hand.

There are exceptions to the general feebleness of social-scientific work on the subject; only the repeated application of the weight of quantitative evidence assembled by psychologists and sociologists is getting across the fact that the participants in the American ghetto rebellions of the 1960s tended to be young men well integrated in their local communities, well convinced that they were battling injustice, and well supported by many of their kinsmen and neighbors. Again, the general models developed by Lewis Richardson and Kenneth Boulding offer a good deal of analytic power to those who will use them. But they have had little influence on the way students of political conflict actually do their work.

In short, the promise is there in principle. In practice, it has been little realized.

Chalmers Johnson on Revolutionary Change

A glance at Chalmers Johnson's *Revolutionary Change* and Ted Gurr's *Why Men Rebel* will give a clearer idea what the model builders have—and don't have—to offer. The books by Johnson and Gurr resemble each other in bringing to bear on a single model a whole broad tradition of thought. Johnson's *Revolutionary Change* braids together many fibers of social-system theorizing, which assumes a functioning system and then follows a sequence of the sort: challenge → dysfunction → inadequate control → revolution. Gurr's book, on the other hand, follows a much more psychological reasoning, which finds the cause of rebellion in a widening discrepancy between what men expect of life and what they get from it. Between the two, they employ almost all the well-defined ideas concerning the origins of violent conflict which are in common use among American social scientists.

Before writing his general analysis of the revolutionary process, Chalmers Johnson wrote a valuable and well-informed study of the Chinese Revolution, emphasizing the importance of anti-Japanese nationalism as a source of support for the Communists. Whatever weaknesses his theorizing may display, then, do not come from ignorance of the world outside North America. Rather, it seems to me, they come from heavy reliance on the systemic metaphor and from confusion of state with social system.

Johnson identifies three clusters of causes of revolution:

First, there are the pressures created by a disequilibrated social system—a society which is changing and which is in need of further change if it is to continue to exist. Of all the characteristics of the disequilibrated system, the one that contributed most directly to a revolution is *power deflation*—the fact that during a period of change the integration of a system depends increasingly upon the maintenance and deployment of force by the occupants of the formal authority statuses.

The second cluster of necessary causes revolves around the quality of the purposeful change being undertaken while a system is disequilibrated. This quality depends upon the abilities of the legitimate leaders. If they are unable to develop policies which will maintain the confidence of non-deviant actors in the system and its capacity to move toward resynchronization, a *loss of authority* will ensue. Such a loss means that the use of force by the elite is no longer considered legitimate, although it does not necessarily mean that a revolution will occur at once. So long as the leaders can still use the army successfully to coerce social interaction, the system will continue to persist. However, the power deflation will approach maximum proportions, producing a "police state" (e.g. South Africa today).

The final, or sufficient, cause of a revolution is some ingredient, usually contributed by fortune, which deprives the elite of its chief weapon for enforcing social behavior (e.g. an army mutiny), or which leads a group of revolutionaries to *believe* that they have the means to deprive the elite of its weapons of coercion. In this study, such final, or immediate, causes of revolution are referred to as "accelerators." They are the pressures, often easily sustained in functional societies, which when they impinge on a society experiencing power deflation and a loss of authority immediately catalyze it into insurrection. They are also the factors which determine, when an insurrection does occur, whether or not the revolutionaries will succeed in establishing and occupying new statuses of authority. (Johnson, 1966, pp. 90–91)

Johnson then attempts to link these very general phenomena to individual behavior through the sequence: rapid change————————➔ systemic disequilibrium————————➔ overtaxing of existing means of homeostatic and purposive response to change————————➔ individual disorientation————————➔ panic-anxiety-shame-guilt-depression, etc.————————➔ formation of movements of protest. True to his predecessors, he proposes the suicide rate as a prime index of disequilibrium.

Johnson peppers his work with bright ideas and good critiques of previous analyses of revolution. His scheme, however, has little value for the systematic analysis of political conflict. One major reason is that the scheme is *retrospective;* there appears to be no way to know whether "homeostatic" and "purposive" responses to change were adequate except by observing whether a revolution actually occurred. Whether the questions we are asking are meteorological or engineering in style, that is a disappointing outcome. Again, the treatment of a government as an emanation of a "social system," or vice versa, leads to proposals for the detection of disequilibrium which are both logically and practically hopeless. "Ideally," as Johnson says, "this index would portray the magnitude of dissynchronization between the structure of values and the social division of labor, thereby indicating the potentiality for termination of a system due to its failure to fulfill its functional prerequisites" (p. 120).

The concrete proposals for predictors which follow from this general principle, according to Johnson, are rising suicide rates, heightened ideological activity, rising military participation ratio, and increases in rates of crime, especially political crime. These items have the advantage of being measurable, at least crudely; we therefore can investigate whether they predict revolution with better than chance accuracy. Even if they do, however, no test of the theory has occurred. Acceptance of crime, suicide, ideological activity, and military participation as indicators of the badness of fit between "values" and "division of labor" requires acceptance of the very theory which is supposedly up for test.

Finally, the argument provides almost no means whatsoever of inferring which people take what parts, when, and why. The main implicit proposition is that those segments of the population most disoriented by structural change will take the most active part in revolutionary movements:

> As the disequilibrium of a social system becomes more acute, personal tensions are generated in all statuses. These tensions may be controlled by some people through internal psychological defense mechanisms, and the alienative sentiments of others may be dissipated through deviant behavior (e.g. fantasies, crime, mental disease, and psychosomatic illnesses). However, with the passage of time, these mechanisms tend to lose their efficacy, and persons subject to highly diverse status protests will begin to combine with each other and with deviants generally to form a deviant subcultural group or movement. (p. 81)

Again, we are dealing with a proposition which runs a great risk of becoming true by definition; all it takes is to give a high weight as "deviant" to those sorts of behavior which happen to be associated with the adoption of a revolutionary position. Leaving aside that tendentious way of setting up the problem, however, we simply have no reliable evidence of a general tendency for revolutionaries, protestors, rioters, or participants in mass movements to come disproportionately from the marginal, criminal, and/or disorganized parts of the population. In short, Johnson's scheme assumes that nineteenth-century folk sociology is correct.

Even within the framework of classic sociology, Johnson takes a step which is open to serious challenge: he essentially equates state and society. The equation shows up most clearly in the identification of the societal elite with those who run the state, but it recurs in general statements throughout.

> The true mark of society, therefore, will be institutions charged with the exercise of physical force both to insure the perpetuation of the division of labor and to regulate the use of violence in conflicts of political interest. The most typical form of such institutions is the state. (p. 18)

> The most important function of the value system in a society is to authorize, or legitimatize, the use of force. (p. 26)

> Despite numerous efforts over the past century to bring about some form of world government, either through purposive organization along political lines or through the indirect linking of national representatives in task-oriented associations (postal unions, health organizations, bodies for establishing common standards, and so forth), the national state has remained the largest form of self-contained social system. (p. 169)

The consequence of this particular equation is to brush aside the problematic character of the state's very existence and of its particular boundaries at many moments of rebellion, war, revolution, and counterrevolution. States are organizations which rise, fall, experience changes of management, and even cease to exist. Only an extreme view of that mysterious entity called "a society" grants it those same properties. Only a muddled view equates the experience of the one entity with the experience of the other.*

Ted Gurr on Why Men Rebel

Ted Gurr shows more awareness that these problems *are* problems. His side comments and subhypotheses amount to an extensive attempt to take the organizational characteristics of governments into account. Yet his basic theory does not permit him to deal with the phenomena of political conflict much better than Johnson does.

In his book *Why Men Rebel,* Gurr seeks to provide a general explanation of "political violence." Political violence includes all collective attacks on major political actors—especially agents of the state—within a particular political community. Instead of elaborating a theory of how political communities operate, however, he concentrates on experiences which happen to individuals and then cumulate into mass action.

The key ideas have been around a long time. Individuals anger when they sense a large gap between what they get and what they deserve. That can happen through a decline in what they get or a rise in what they feel they deserve. Given the chance, angry people rebel. When many people go through that same experience of increasing relative deprivation plus widening opportunity for rebellion at the same time, political violence generalizes. Similar ideas have often emerged in the analysis of American ghetto rebellions, of Latin American palace coups, and of the French Revolution. Gurr has explicated the logic of such analyses and developed means of measuring a number of the variables involved. Compared with the argument of Johnson's *Revolutionary Change,* the Gurr scheme has the advantage of avoiding both the assumption of a self-regulating society and the equation of government with social system.

Seen as a *retrospective* analysis, Gurr's argument hangs together very well. It is, indeed, virtually true by definition. Political violence requires some shared dissatisfaction, granted. Shared dissatisfaction requires individual dissatisfaction, true. Individual dissatisfaction results from an unfavorable comparison between things as they are and things as they ought to be, no doubt. What, then, have we excluded? The two extremes: (1) purely instrumental accounts of rebellion, in which violence is simply the most efficient means available for accomplishing some collective end; (2) treatments of rebellions as emanations of instinct, madness, random impulse, or occult force. Gurr's theory stands well within Western political philosophy since it rejects the ideas that the most efficient means may be hurtful to many and that the irrational plays a signifi-

---

* From Chalmers Johnson, *Revolutionary Change,* pp. 18, 26, 81, 90–91, 169. Copyright © 1966 by Little, Brown and Company (Inc.). Reprinted by permission.

cant part in large political movements. But the sealing off of those two extremes still leaves a great deal of room between them.

A *prospective* version of the argument, on the other hand, becomes more determinate and more dubious. Now the argument says that deprivation produces anger and lack of deprivation prevents it; that under specified conditions individual anger coalesces, with high regularity, into collective discontent; that under further specified conditions collective discontent has a high probability of producing violent action. It is not enough to show that these things happen sometimes. At the very least, they must happen more often than they would by chance.

Gurr himself approaches the problem through the analysis of 1100 "strife events" which occurred in 114 states or colonies from 1961 through 1965. The analysis produces some striking statistical results (including multiple correlation coefficients on the order of .80), which Gurr takes as confirming the influence of the variables he calls Persisting Deprivation, Short-Term Deprivation, Regime Legitimacy, and especially, Social and Structural Facilitation.

The last variable, Social and Structural Facilitation, illustrates some of the difficulties in interpreting Gurr's results. After considerable experimentation, Gurr combined three different indexes:

1. a measure of geographic inaccessibility, which gave high scores to countries with rough terrains and poor transport nets;

2. a measure of the extent to which the Communist party was both active and illegal;

3. a measure of foreign support for domestic "initiators of strife."

All of these are plausibly related to the level of conflict—the Communist party and foreign support items so much so that one must wonder whether Gurr has measured the same thing twice. (The same worry about contamination dogs the interpretation of the finding that "legitimate" regimes have lower levels of strife.) The considerable explanatory strength of these variables, however, provides no evidence whatsoever for the central relative-deprivation argument.

The two measures of deprivation are more crucial to the theory and more clearly independent of the phenomena Gurr is seeking to explain, but their interpretation also raises serious problems. First, the quality of data is low. Second, the 114 polities form a cross-section at the same point of time; therefore one must judge the effects of long-run changes in deprivation, for example, through the comparison of regimes which vary in "economic discrimination," "political discrimination," "potential separatism," "dependence on private foreign capital," "religious cleavage," and "educational opportunity" (for those are the essential criteria of long-run deprivation) at a given moment. Third, the basic variables went through so much selection and remeasurement in the course of Gurr's research (the two deprivation measures, for example, combining in a particular way the 13 sturdiest survivors of the 48 separate measures of deprivation with which Gurr began) that the data may well have become a glove shaped well to one hand and to no other.* The crucial tests will come when Gurr's model is checked against good data for appropriately lagged time series, with independently measured variables covering new time periods and new sets of political units.

The further research is definitely worth undertaking. For one thing, Gurr has reduced to a manageable model the essentials of a shapeless but pervasive set of ideas encountered in branch after branch of political analysis. For another, he has worked out an ingenious series of procedures for measuring the major variables within the model. For once we have a genuine opportunity to confront theory with data.

If the arguments of this essay are correct, that confrontation will deliver a smashing blow to the very social-psychological theory Gurr espouses. To make sure that so crucial a contest proceeds to a fair and full conclusion will require some reworking of the theory. For example, Gurr's definitions eliminate one major category of collective violence: collective violence carried out by agents of the state. Actually, a good deal of action of this variety slips into Gurr's analysis disguised as the work of "dissidents." For—contrary to the image of Dissidents lashing out at Regimes—the great bulk of the killing and wounding in the course of modern collective violence is done by troops, police, and other specialized repressive forces. More important, the regime normally has the greater discretion in this regard. Many demonstrations, for instance, pass peacefully. But a few bring death, usually when some representative of the government decides the demonstrators have gone too far. Nothing in Gurr's scheme permits us to infer when repressive violence will occur and to whom.

Likewise, an important portion of collective violence pits contenders for power against one another, rather than rebels against regimes. Gurr's scheme eliminates such conflicts in principle, although his data include them in practice. No category in the scheme, furthermore, deals with the probability or the effect of agitation, organization, mobilization, leadership, pooling of resources, development of internal communications among potential rebels. We have only the gross differences combined in Social and Structural Facilitation.

One might be able to meet these objections by refocusing the frustration-aggression analysis on groups *within* a state and relations among them. Gurr makes some valuable, if fleeting, suggestions as to how one might do that: separate discontent scores for each major segment of the population, and so on. To

---

* With my own data on collective violence and industrial conflict in Western Europe, a judicious selection of cases, variable lags, and models makes it easy to produce multiple correlations above .80.

496   *Revolutions and Collective Violence*

do that work seriously, however, would amount to taking up the very sorts of structural analysis the central argument dismisses.

Alternative Sources of Theory

At this moment, better guidance for those who wish to sort out the historical experience of political conflict is coming from social scientists who have elected to work less abstractly, close to historical fact, with greater attention to divisions and variations within the countries under study, and in a comparative framework. (This might seem inevitable; it is, in fact, exceptional; the strongest influences of social scientific procedures on historical practice, as in the cases of demography, linguistics, and economic theory, normally involve complex, abstract theories.)

Barrington Moore's *Social Origins of Dictatorship and Democracy*, for example, commands the interest and respect of a wide range of historians. Its concentration on the class divisions and alliances which create revolutionary situations, and the coalitions which make the revolutions themselves, strongly counters the sociological tendency to consider revolution as the expression of a critical level of tension, aggression, or malfunction in the system as a whole.

The complex web of the book's argument hangs on two pegs: (1) the idea that the class coalitions involved in the great modernizing revolutions, and hence the character of those revolutions, have depended especially on the fates of the agrarian classes in the course of the commercialization of agriculture and the growth of the state, with the liquidation of the peasantry and the co-optation of the aristocracy and gentry, for example, being crucial in England; (2) the further idea that the class coalition making the revolution has strongly influenced the subsequent political organization of that country, with a coalition of bureaucrats and landlords, for instance, tending to produce fascism. Thus parliamentary democracy becomes the historically specific consequence of the early emergence of agrarian capitalism in certain countries, a circumstance perhaps never to be repeated. Moore provides evidence for his twin theses via extended comparisons of the history of England, France, the United States, China, Japan, and India, plus numerous allusions to Germany and Russia.

Revolution takes on an interesting role in Moore's scheme. The major revolution—the English Civil War, the French Revolution, and so on—acts as a crucial switch in the track along which a particular country moves. Yet revolution dissolves as a phenomenon sui generis, for it becomes simply the maximum moment of conflicts which endure long before and long after the transfer of power itself; indeed, the case of Germany shows that the fundamental transfers of power which occupy the center of Moore's analysis can occur without any revolution at all in the conventional sense of the word.

The notion that a violent popular revolution is somehow necessary in order to sweep away "feudal" obstacles to industrialization is pure nonsense, as the course of German and Japanese history demonstrates. On the other hand, the political consequences from dismounting the old order from above are decidedly different. As they proceeded with conservative modernization, these semiparliamentary governments tried to preserve as much of the original social structure as they could, fitting large sections into the new building wherever possible. The results had some resemblance to present-day Victorian houses with modern electrical kitchens but insufficient bathrooms and leaky pipes hidden decorously behind newly plastered walls. Ultimately the makeshifts collapsed. (Moore, 1966, p. 438)

We find ourselves at the opposite position from Chalmers Johnson's "disequilibration" and "dysfunction." In Moore's analysis, the major conflicts which occur—including the revolutions themselves—are part of the very logic of the political systems they shake apart.

To take one more case in point, Eric Wolf's *Peasant Wars of the Twentieth Century* bears a number of resemblances to Moore's daring synthesis. Wolf, an anthropologist, takes on the revolutions of Mexico, Russia, China, Vietnam, Algeria, and Cuba. He extracts from them important lessons about the response of peasants the world over to being drawn into the capitalist world economy. Even less concerned than Moore to lay out an explicit theoretical structure, Wolf nevertheless builds an extraordinarily powerful analysis of the structural foundations of peasant life, the precise ways in which the expansion of national and international markets shakes those foundations, the conditions under which peasants resist the threat with force, and the circumstances under which that resistance (however reactionary its inception) serves revolutionary ends. The most general argument is simple and telling.

The major aim of the peasant is subsistence and social status gained within a narrow range of social relationships. Peasants are thus unlike cultivators, who participate fully in the market and who commit themselves to a status game set within a wide social network. To ensure continuity upon the land and sustenance for his household, the peasant most often keeps the market at arm's length, for unlimited involvement in the market threatens his hold on his source of livelihood. He thus cleaves to traditional arrangements which guarantee his access to land and to the labor of kin and neighbors. Moreover, he favors production for sale only within the context of an assured production for subsistence. Put in another way, it may be said that the peasant operates in a restricted factor and product market. The factors of production—land, labor, equipment—are rendered relatively immobile by prior liens and expectations; products are sold in the market to produce the extra margin of returns with which to buy goods one does not produce on the homestead. In contrast, the farmer enters the market fully, subjects his land and labor to open competition, explores alternative uses for the factors of production in the search for maximum returns, and favors the more profitable product over the one entailing the smaller risk. The change-over from peasant to farmer, however, is not merely a change in psychological orientation; it involves a major shift in the institutional context within which men make their choices. Perhaps it is precisely when the peasant can no longer rely on his accustomed institutional context to reduce his risks, but when alternative institutions are either too chaotic or too restrictive to guarantee a viable commitment to new ways, that the psychological, economic, social and political tensions all mount toward peasant rebellion and involvement in revolution. (Wolf, 1969, pp. xiv–xv)

From that springboard, Wolf leaps to a close examination of the experience of the peasantry in each of his countries, to scrutiny of the conditions under which each of the revolutions in question broke out, and to comparative analysis of the determinants of the considerably different forms of involvement of these various peasant populations in their national movements.

Some common features emerge: the crucial role of the middle peasants, rather than the rural proletarians or the kulaks; the influence of alliances with disaffected intellectuals: the initially defensive and inward-looking character of all the present rebellions: the frequent occurrence of a deadlock of weak contenders for power, ultimately favorable to well-organized central groups allied with military power; the final inability of peasants to accomplish their political ends, however successful their rebellions in the short run, in the absence of strong alliances with determined and organized nonpeasants.

In the long run, Wolf's sense of the variables involved will probably contribute more to our understanding of political conflict than his enumeration of the constants. He shows very effectively (in a line of argument similar to Moore's) that the coalitions formed by rebellious peasants strongly affect whether their actions go beyond the immediate redress of grievances; that where commercialization has proceeded so far as to dissolve the traditional organization of the peasant community, rebellion does not occur (contrary to the mass-society notion that atomized and anguished men make ideal rebels); that a center-outward pattern of rebellion, as in Russia, China, and Vietnam, favors the expanded power of a single party as opposed to an army and/or a national bourgeoisie.

At present, extensions of simple but powerful analyses like Wolf's are likely to aid the systematic study of political conflict more than the borrowing of more elaborate and abstract schemes like those of Johnson and Gurr. It would help to explicate and formalize Wolf's argument, to find quantitative representations of the argument and quantitative evidence to test it out where possible, and to computerize portions of the analysis where the data are rich enough. The choice is not between handwork and apparatus but between strong theory and weak. The junction of the powerful ideas of a Wolf or a Moore with the new methods emerging in historical research will produce exciting results.

Collective History

I have in mind especially the increasing richness of the work now being done in *collective history*—history from the bottom up. Collective history is the systematic accumulation of comparable information on numerous social units (most often individuals but sometimes families, firms, communities, or other units) in order to detect some structure or some change which is not readily visible to the participants or the observers. The sharpest examples come from demography, where changes in the average age at marriage or in the death rate have none of the dramatic visibility of the death of a king or the outbreak of a war, but they often have more profound effects on the living conditions of large populations than the dramatic events do. Historical demographers like E. A. Wrigley and Louis Henry have been transforming our knowledge of European society with their ingenious exploitation of everyday sources like parish registers and genealogies. The logic of many studies of elites and of social mobility resembles that of historical demography: assemble small, uniform, and ostensibly trivial fragments of information about individuals into evidence of major changes in structure. Essentially similar procedures should make it possible to renew psychological history, the history of consumption and production, intellectual history, and the history of political power; so far they have been little tried.

In studies of political conflict, they *have* been tried with resounding success. The French and the francophiles have led. Georges Lefebvre, the great, long-lived historian of the Revolution, provided much of the inspiration, if not much of the technique. He forwarded the idea of multiple, semiautonomous revolutions converging into a single Revolution. More important methodologically, he demonstrated that the semiautonomous revolutions—especially the peasant revolution—were accessible to study from the bottom up. But he did not systematize the study of the populations involved. Albert Soboul did. Soboul has no doubt been Lefebvre's most influential heir in both regards. His 1958 thesis, *Les sans-culottes parisiens en l'an II,* shone a spotlight on faces previously deep in shadow—the faces of the day-to-day activists of the Parisian sections. (The "sections" were essentially neighborhood governments and political associations.) It did so mainly through the straightforward but extremely demanding analysis of the papers of the sections themselves and the painstaking reconstitution of their membership.

At about the same time, Richard Cobb was carrying out a close study of the composition and characteristics of the volunteer Revolutionary Armies which played such a crucial role in the early years of the Revolution; Kåre Tønnesson was following the Parisian sans-culottes through the Year III; George Rudé was analyzing the actual composition of the revolutionary crowds of the great *Journées;* Adeline Daumard, Louis Chevalier, and François Furet were closely scrutinizing the changing composition and wealth of the Parisian population from the late eighteenth century to 1848; and Rémi Gossez was applying many of the same microscopic procedures to the Revolution of 1848. These historians vary greatly in preconceptions, techniques, and subject matter. What brings them together, with dozens of their compatriots, as exponents of a new brand of history is the deliberate accumulation of uniform dossiers on numerous ordinary individuals in order to produce solid information on collective characteristics not readily visible in the experiences of any one of them. The solid information was often quantitative, although the quantification involved was ordinarily elementary.

The adoption of collective history did not, of course, guarantee success. It could have been a terrible waste of time. Indeed, it *would* have been, if old theories about the blind spontaneity of the masses had been correct. As it turned out, however, collective history yielded great returns when applied to French political conflicts. Historians now understand how wide and deep the political mobilization of ordinary Frenchmen was in 1789 and 1848, how coherent the action of the so-called mob was, how sharp the rifts within the coalition which made the Revolution had become by 1793. The Marxist approach to the study of French political conflicts gained new strength, both because Marxists were more inclined than others to take up the close study of the "little people" which this sort of collective history involved, and because the Marxist tradition provided more powerful means of analyzing major divisions within the population than its rivals did.

Although much more has been accomplished along these lines in French history than elsewhere, the cosmopolitan George Rudé brought the procedures he perfected in dealing with French crowds back across the channel to Britain, and students of the Puritan Revolution, of the American Revolution, and of modern Germany have been devising versions of collective history which also promise to renew their areas of study. In some of these enterprises the unit under examination is not the individual but the event, the declaration, the movement, or something else. But the logic is still the same: comparable information about numerous units summed into patterns and changes which are otherwise difficult to detect.

These developments in historical research make it possible, as never before, to join together the richness of the historical record, the strength of the kinds of historically based theory elaborated by Moore and Wolf, and the searching analytic procedures of contemporary social science. Not that we should abandon the study of the present. On the contrary, the point is to integrate the examination of today with the investigation of yesterday.

That integration will be easier if we stop treating the past as a repository of

Great Revolutions and the present as a container of other kinds of conflicts. In particular, the attempt to place the great struggles for power in the context of the whole range of political conflict will itself bring out many of the continuities between past and present.

AN APPROACH AND SOME CONCEPTS

Such an expansion of the field of vision presents its own problems. If revolution is indeed a multidimensional phenomenon, along which dimensions should we expand? For example, one easy but inadequate formulation treats revolution as an extreme case of a more general phenomenon called "violence." If we were to manufacture a violence detector which would clang louder and louder as it passed greater and greater degrees of damage to persons or property, however, it would raise a hullabaloo around wars, hockey games, barroom brawls, or everyday life in prisons, mental hospitals, and housing projects, but it would only chime gently in the vicinity of a great many coups d'etat, demonstrations, general strikes, and so-called rebellions. If violence and revolution go together to some extent, it is not because violence is the essence of revolution, but because men turn to unlimited means of coercion in the fluidity of a revolutionary situation, as in a number of other fluid situations.

Let us return to the exact relationship between violence and political conflict later on. For now, the important point is that violence by itself does not define a continuum of "revolutionness," at one end of which we find the full-fledged Great Revolution. The same applies to all the other obvious possibilities: (a) transfer of power as a continuum, with the largest transfer (however "large" is defined) the most revolutionary; (b) "social change" as a continuum, with the most rapid and/or most far-reaching the most revolutionary; (c) illegitimacy of political action, with the most illegitimate the most revolutionary; (d) scale of collective action, with large-scale more revolutionary; (e) locus of action, with action by underdogs more revolutionary. Each of these concepts identifies some significant link between revolutions and other events. None of them singly defines the range of phenomena including revolution.

For the moment, then, let us assume that we are exploring the area of convergence of *all* these roads. We can call the entire region "political conflict" and leave its outer limits indefinite. The more violent, power-transferring, illegitimate, etc., the event, the closer we are coming to home. As we work, we can decide which roads are actually dead ends and which are main highways.

A preliminary map of the region should include several important landmarks: a government, a polity, contenders for power. For any specified population, let us identify the organizations which control the principal concentrated means of coercion; such organizations are *governments*. In any particular population there may be several governments operating—or none at all. To the

extent that such an organization is formally coordinated, centralized, differentiated from other organizations, and territorially exclusive, it is a *state*, but many
governments are not states. Let us now single out every group within the population which during some specified span of time collectively applies resources to
the influence of a particular government; all such groups are *contenders for
power* with respect to that government. That does not mean they are equally
powerful or equally successful. To the extent that a contender exercises a
routine claim to response on the part of agents of the government, the contender is a member of the *polity;* the polity consists of all contenders routinely
and successfully laying claims on the government. The nonmembers that are
contending for power we may call *challengers*. Most groups within any particular population are not contenders, many contenders are not members, and
some members are able to exercise far greater control over the activity of the
government than other members. Obviously, a group may contend for power in
more than one polity (and even be a member of more than one) if more than
one government is operating within a population. These are simply matters of
definition.

I lay out these ungainly definitions (and others, alas, still to come) with
trembling hands. Albert Hirschman (1970b)—no mean wielder of paradigms
himself—has warned eloquently against "the search for paradigms as a hindrance to understanding" revolutions and political conflict. Sociologists and
political scientists are exceedingly vulnerable to the old magical misconception
that naming a phenomenon has the effect of taming it. Most conceptual schemes,
as Hirschman claims, are more trouble than they are worth: blinders, not tele-
scopes. The tests of a scheme's value come from the understanding, the further
explorations, the new hypotheses, the verifiable propositions which spring from
its use. The scheme at hand is little tested in any of these regards.

Yet the definitions make it possible to map out a set of relations among contenders, polities, and governments. (The mapping is of course hypothetical, in
the same way that one might envision a straight road between London and
Paris, only to discover the inconvenient fact of the English Channel.) Every
polity, let us say, establishes tests of membership. The tests may include proof
of sanctity or wealth or any number of other characteristics, but they always
include the ability to mobilize or coerce significant numbers of people. Members of a polity repeatedly test one another's qualifications. When a member
fails a partial test, more serious challenges to that membership follow; repeated
failure leads to exclusion from the polity. New members enter by passing the
tests of membership; old members exit by failing them. Each entry and each
exit change the criteria of membership in a direction favorable to the resulting
set of members, and the members of the polity come to treat the prevailing
criteria as matters of right, justice, and principle.

Within the polity, according to this hypothetical construction, several different kinds of interactions are constantly going on.

1. Members of the polity are routinely applying resources to the influence of the government.

2. Nonmembers are also attempting to influence the government and to acquire membership in the polity, and members (acting mostly through agencies of the government) are resisting those attempts.

3. Members are testing one another through a wide range of interactions which could include contested elections, parliamentary debates, ceremonial displays, gang wars, or advantageous marriages.

The testing process by which contenders acquire or lose membership tends to increase the extent of collective violence when the membership of the polity is changing fast. Prospective members ordinarily treat admission to the polity as due them on general grounds, and they therefore fight in the name of large principles. Existing members on the way out ordinarily treat their privileged position as guaranteed by particular agreements and customs, and they therefore fight in the name of the defense of hallowed rights. Either of these orientations increases the willingness of the individuals in the group to risk damage or injury, thus to participate in violence. (Note, however, that over the long run contenders entering and leaving the polity tend to *receive* more damage and injury than they inflict, since the concentrated and effective means of coercion are under the control of the members via their influence over the government. We shall return to this problem later on.) If this general line of reasoning is correct, most collective violence will oppose members of the polity to nonmembers, members to members, and agents of the government to nonmembers. Violent conflicts of agents of government against each other, agents against members, and nonmembers against nonmembers will be correspondingly rare.

MOBILIZATION AND CONTENTION FOR POWER

How do contenders for power come and go? Here the idea of mobilization is helpful (see Deutsch, 1953; Etzioni, 1968; Nettl, 1967). People get their work done by accumulating and employing a great variety of resources to influence one another and to transform the world around them. The resources include loyalties, knowledge, wealth, machines, communication lines, and any number of other things. We can conveniently group them into three categories: normative, coercive, and utilitarian (the terminology comes from Etzioni, 1968, but the general idea is commonplace). Normative resources include the commitments of men to ideals, groups, and other people; coercive resources include means of punishing other men and limiting the alternatives open to them; utilitarian resources include all the rest, especially those things men find it rewarding to acquire.

When a group increases its collective control over any of these three varieties of resources, we say the group is *mobilizing;* when its collective control over such resources decreases, we say it is demobilizing. The group in question may range from a family to a tribe to a state to an international federation of states; the important thing is that the group as a whole acquires or loses collective control of resources. No group can take any sort of collective action without some degree of mobilization; demobilization ultimately destroys a group's capacity for collective action.

Although the terminology may be ponderous, the core meaning comes close to a standard notion of active revolutionaries. In one of his most influential statements of strategy during the resistance to Japan, Mao Tse-tung wrote as follows:

> What does political mobilization mean? First, it means telling the army and the people about the political aim of the war. It is necessary for every soldier and civilian to see why the war must be fought and how it concerns him. . . . Secondly, it is not enough merely to explain the aim to them; the steps and policies for its attainment must also be given, that is, there must be a political programme. . . . Thirdly, how should we mobilize them? By word of mouth, by leaflets and bulletins, by newspapers, books and pamphlets, through plays and films, through schools, through the mass organizations and through our cadres. What has been done so far in the Kuomintang areas is only a drop in the ocean, and moreover it has been done in a manner ill-suited to the people's tastes and in a spirit uncongenial to them; this must be drastically changed. Fourthly, to mobilize once is not enough; political mobilization for the War of Resistance must be continuous. Our job is not to recite our political programme to the people, for nobody will listen to such recitations; we must link the political mobilization for the war with developments in the war and with the life of the soldiers and the people, and make it a continuous movement. (Mao, 1965b, p. 155)

All the current idea of mobilization does, then, is to broaden Mao's central notion to explicitly include controls over objects and organizations as well as commitments of individuals.

We are now piling definitions on definitions. Nevertheless, these ideas of mobilization make it easier to see the properties that a wide range of group activities have in common: accumulating a strike fund, building an ethnic identity, storing weapons, sending members off to school, working out a secret ritual, laying a claim to a certain part of every member's time, building a headquarters, and so on. Some of these activities do not increase the total resources members of the group possess; they simply transfer resources from individual to group. All of them, on the other hand, increase the resources of which the group as a whole can dispose.

The structure, the environment, and the already-accumulated resources of a group greatly limit the avenues toward mobilization open to it at any point in its history. Resources effectively spent bring in new resources of a different kind, as when an ethnic leader uses his group's funds to bribe a politician disposing of jobs for his people, or a revolutionary committee activates the loyalties it commands to bring in cash contributions from its following. Whether the net effect of such exchanges is additional mobilization depends on the terms of trade between jobs and bribes on the one hand and between depletion of reserve loyalties and augmentation of the treasury on the other. Again, the environment may be abundant, yielding resources readily with little effort, or it may be harsh, full of competitors, and barren of resources. All other things being equal, an abundant environment obviously facilitates mobilization.

Finally, the group's organizational structure limits the means of mobilization. Perhaps the most important dimension in this regard is the one which runs from communal to associational organization. (The basic idea is one of the oldest in sociology; it has frequently been abused through the assumption that it describes the basic path of human evolution, the disguising of the fact that it lumps together several variables which do not always change in the same direction, and the implicit assertion that the one end is good, the other bad. Here I offer it only as a preliminary sorting device.) Communal structures are small, local, and relatively undifferentiated in structure. They recruit largely through inheritance. Among frequent contenders for power at one level or another in the world of the last few centuries, corporate kin groups, peasant villages, craft brotherhoods, and religious congregations tend toward this extreme type. Associational structures are large, extensive, and complex. They recruit largely through open tests of intention and performance. In the modern world, parties, firms, trade unions, and voluntary organizations are frequent contenders of this type.

To the extent that a contender is communal in structure, it is unlikely to be able to expand its manpower rapidly, but it is quite likely to be able to generate strong loyalties on the part of the members it does possess. To the extent that a contender is associational in structure, the accumulation of intense commitments is likely to be very costly, whereas the acquisition of a range of specialized skills will be relatively easy. Whether the possession of intense commitments will be more or less advantageous than the possession of specialized skills, of course, depends entirely on the nature of the collective tasks at hand and the character of the surrounding world.

The organizational structure of the contenders for power within a particular polity also has a strong impact on the typical forms of collective violence within the polity. To be more exact, it affects the kinds of collective actions which ordinarily produce violence. With communal contenders, collective action tends to be uncoordinated, localized, raggedly bounded in time and space, responsive to routines of congregation such as those of religious observance, festivals, planting, marketing, and so on. Violence engaging communal contenders therefore tends to spring from such settings. The free-for-all between guilds and the rural tax rebellion illustrate what I have in mind.

With associational contenders, the collective action (and hence the setting of collective violence) tends to be planned, scheduled, bounded, disciplined, and large in scale. The violent strike and the turbulent demonstration are typical cases. This does not necessarily mean that they are more serious or more destructive than the violence involving communal contenders. In fact, peasant revolts are legendary for their bloodletting; associational participants in violence often have the advantage of being able to call off their forces as soon as they have won—or lost. Nevertheless, collective violence on a large scale rarely occurs without the significant involvement of associations.

In the Western experience, on which this analysis is based, there is a tight connection between a contender's organizational structure and the locus of its power. The tightness of the connection may have led me to misstate the relationship between organizational structure and collective action. For the most part, communal groups wield power on a small scale, in local polities. To an important degree, associational groups wield power on a large scale, especially in national polities. If the correspondence were perfect, we would have no problems; localism and communal organization would simply be two features of the same phenomenon. But organizations such as guilds and sworn brotherhoods have complex formal structures, and yet they often operate on a purely local scale; likewise, ethnic and religious groups sometimes band together, without any single association to unify them, on a national scale. One could make a plausible case that local guilds and sworn brotherhoods behave the same as other local groups which lack their complex formal structures, that national ethnic and religious groups behave the same as national associations. Or scale and formality of structure could have distinct effects. As I use it here, then, the communal-associational scheme contains two hypotheses which should be treated as hypothetical: (1) in general, the larger, the more extensive, the more complex the organization, the larger is the scale at which it wields power; (2) the scale at which a group wields power, *as such,* does not significantly affect its predominant forms of collective action. At least the hypotheses are plausible and open to empirical examination.

TYPES OF COLLECTIVE ACTION

These statements deal with collective action, not with violence itself. Violence is an interaction among people or between people and objects. Let's save the discussion of definitions and shades of meaning for later. For now, a simple observation. In the Western experience, three fundamental forms of collective action (each with many variants) have led to violence.

Form 1, *competitive* action: members of a group which defines another particular group as a rival or as an enemy attack the resources of that rival or enemy. Thus two armies fight it out; members of a cabinetmakers' guild vandalize the headquarters of a rival guild; armed peasants lay waste the castles of the local nobility. Groups which are members of some particular polity are likely to employ competitive actions with respect to other members of the same polity. If we maintain the distinction between communal and associational groups, then it will be convenient to call the communal group's version of competitive collective action *primitive,* and the associational group's version *interest-group.*

Form 2, *reactive* collective action: some group or its agent lays claim to a resource currently under the control of another particular group, and the members of the second resist the exercise of that claim. The action of the second group is reactive. Thus the government's tax collector arrives to enforce a new levy, and the villagers drive him out of town; a group of bandits abduct a young woman, and her kinsmen arm to hunt down the bandits; Socialists burst into a Communist meeting and seize the podium, only to be beaten up by the Communists. I suggest that contenders which are losing membership in a polity are especially prone to reactive collective action. For communal contenders, the subtitle *reactionary* seems appropriate; for associational contenders, *defensive.*

Form 3, *proactive* collective action: some group carries out an action which, under the prevailing rules, lays claim to a resource not previously accorded to that group; at least one other group intervenes in the action and resists the claim. The action of the first group is *proactive;* obviously, proactive motions by one group often lead to reactive motions by another. Thus an unauthorized association holds a public meeting, and police break it up; organized squatters move onto vacant land, and the landlords try to drive them away; demonstrators seize the city hall, and counterdemonstrators attack them. I suggest that contenders which are gaining membership in polities have an especial propensity to proactive collective action. Here, I suggest the name "revitalization" for the communal version, on the basis of work by Anthony F. C. Wallace. Revitalization movements, in Wallace's analysis, form around a whole new way of understanding the world. My speculation is twofold: (a) A communal group is not likely to mobilize extensively, bid for membership in a polity, and therefore become newly involved in collective violence unless its members are undergoing a major collective transformation of their perception of the world; a millennarian movement would be an example. (b) No rapid change in the membership of a polity composed mainly of communal contenders is likely to occur except through the creation of an entirely new group identity via a drastic revitalization process. The associational form of proactive collective action we may simply call "offensive."

In all three basic forms, the "resources" involved cover quite a range; they include people, land, private spaces, rights to act in certain ways. Reactive and proactive forms resemble each other in centering on the sequence assertion of claim → challenge to claim → damage to one party by another. Although they have a gray area between them, they differ. In the reactive form, the resources in question are already under the control of some particular group. In the competitive form, the disagreement between groups may very well center on claim and counterclaim, but the immediate action does not consist of the exercising of claims.

The three forms are so broad that they might seem to exhaust the logical possibilities. Not so. All three forms relate specific groups to each other and thereby exclude action by chance crowds, by the general population, and by the disorganized dregs of social life. By the same token, they exclude random, expressive, purely destructive actions. The typology rests on the argument that the excluded forms of collective action—spontaneous, disorganized, random, etc.—are rare or nonexistent.

The observations made so far on mobilization, contention, and collective action crystallize into a useful classification of the forms of collective action leading to violence in which different kinds of contenders are likely to be involved. We distinguish first among groups which are not contending/challenging/maintaining membership/losing membership. Then we array the organizational structures of contenders from communal to associational, as shown in Figure 2.

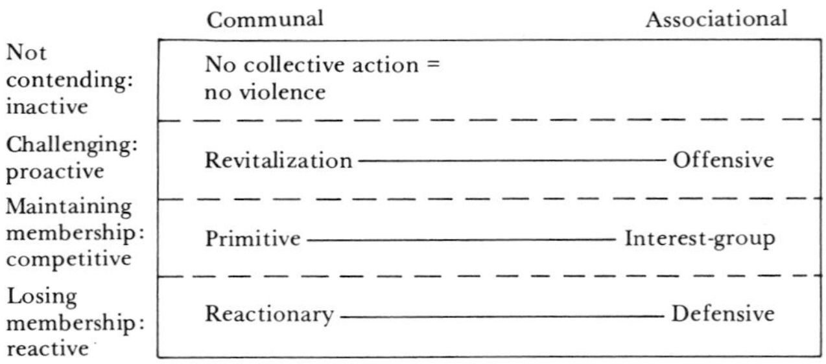

	Communal		Associational
Not contending: inactive	No collective action = no violence		
Challenging: proactive	Revitalization ——————————— Offensive		
Maintaining membership: competitive	Primitive ——————————— Interest-group		
Losing membership: reactive	Reactionary ——————————— Defensive		

Figure 2

Figure 2 incorporates several hypotheses, some of them quite speculative. The first hypothesis represents one of the chief arguments of this essay: segments of the population which are unmobilized and not contending for power are rarely involved in collective violence. On the communal side of the continuum, the diagram indicates that communal contenders maintaining membership in a polity will ordinarily test each other via "primitive" actions of the type of ceremonials, games, drinking bouts, or contacts in routine assemblies, and that these occasions will constitute their opportunities for collective violence. Those *losing* membership, on the other hand, will find themselves banding together to defend prerogatives or to resist encroachments, and will therefore form the nucleus of classic older forms of collective violence like the food riot, machine-breaking, the tax rebellion, or true guerrilla.

On the associational side of the continuum, the diagram tells us that the collective action likely to involve an associational challenger in violence— "offensive" action—will center on displays of the facts that the contender meets the tests of membership in the polity, attempts to coerce existing members and agents of the government, concerted efforts to acquire some lasting control over the actions of the government. Interest-group actions (especially orderly shows of strength, like parades) will be the main occasions on which associational members of the polity are involved in collective violence. And the word "defensive," applied to associationally organized contenders losing their membership, calls to mind the extensively organized movement to resist change, secure old privileges, reactivate old symbols, bolster faltering strength.

The propositions embedded in the scheme are imprecise where they are not speculative or tautological; the main use of the scheme is as a classification. Nevertheless, the taxonomy as a whole emphasizes two ideas: (1) unmobilized segments of the population are little involved in collective violence, whereas certain kinds of mobilized groups are heavily involved in it; (2) the form of collective violence depends closely on the relationship of the participants to the existing structure of power.

Another assertion likewise lurks in the typology: governments and their agents are not simply onlookers, arbiters, or cleaners-up in collective violence; they are often major participants in the action. Governments often lay new claims, which other parties challenge. Governments often resist the exercise of new claims. In war and elsewhere, governments often play a major part in violence among rivals and enemies—at the extreme, arrogating to themselves the sole right to employ force in such encounters. The extent to which governments act autonomously in such circumstances and the extent to which they act on behalf of particular members of the polity undoubtedly vary considerably from one kind of government to another. What those variations are and how much autonomy the average government has in this regard make up two of the most important political questions of our time.

APPLYING THE MODEL TO WESTERN POLITICAL EXPERIENCE

The scheme provides a convenient means of summing up the largest trends in the evolution of collective violence in Western countries over the last four or five centuries. Two main processes have dominated all the rest: (1) the rise of national states to preeminent positions in a wide variety of political activities; (2) the increasingly associational character of the principal contenders for power at the local as well as the national level. In 1500, no full-fledged national state with unquestioned priority over the other governments within its territory existed anywhere in the West. England was probably the closest approximation. Most statelike organizations faced serious challenges to their hegemony from both inside and outside the territory; in fact, only a small minority of the hundreds of more or less autonomous governments survived the next two centuries of state-making. Most power was concentrated in polities of smaller than national scale: communities, city-states, principalities, semiautonomous provinces. Most contenders for power in those polities were essentially communal in structure: craft brotherhoods, families, peasant communities. The predominant forms of collective violence registered these circumstances: wars between rival governments, brawls between groups of artisans, battles among the youth of neighboring communes, attacks by one religious group on another.

The rise of the state, however, threatened the power (and often the very survival) of all these small-scale polities. They resisted; the state-makers won their struggle for predominance only over the furious resistance of princes, communes, provinces, and peasant communities. For several centuries the principal forms of collective violence followed what I have called the "reactionary" pattern: communally based contenders fighting against loss of membership in polities—in fact, against the very destruction of the polities in which their power was invested. Collective resistance to conscription, to taxation, to billeting, to a whole variety of other exactions of the state exemplify this reactionary variety of collective action that characteristically produced violence.

Two things eventually put an end to the predominance of the reactionary forms, though at times and tempos which varied markedly from one part of the West to another. First, the state won almost everywhere. One may ask how complete the victory of the state was in the remote sections of vast territories like Canada, Australia, or Brazil, and speculate whether recent surges of sectionalism in Belgium, Great Britain, and even France presage the end of state control. But on the whole the two centuries after 1700 produced an enormous concentration of resources and means of coercion under the control of national states, to the virtual exclusion of other levels of government. Second, a whole series of organizational changes, closely linked to urbanization and industrialization, greatly reduced the role of the communal group as a setting for mobilization and repository for power, while the association of one kind or another came to be the characteristic vehicle for collective action. The rise of the joint-stock company, the political party, the labor union, the club all belong to the same general trend.

Working together, the victory of the state and the rise of the association transformed the collective actions which most commonly produced violence. In country after country, politics nationalized; the polity that mattered was the one that controlled the national state; the crucial struggles for power continued on a national scale. And the participants in those struggles were most often associational in organization. Revitalization, primitive, and reactionary collective actions declined in prevalence and importance, while offensive, interest-group, and defensive collective actions took over. The strike, the demonstration, the party conspiracy, the organized march on the capital, the parliamentary session, the mass meeting became the usual settings for collective violence. And the state became an interested participant in almost all collective violence—as policeman, as party to the conflict, and as *tertius gaudens*.

That brings us back to contention for power. Contenders for power with respect to any particular government are groups which collectively apply resources to the influence of that government. In theory, a group can mobilize without contending for power, if it applies its collective resources entirely to recreation, the search for enlightenment, or some other nonpolitical end. A commune or religious community retiring from the world moves in that direction. Within the modern world, however, governments are so likely to claim the power to regulate and to extract resources from any mobilizing group that (above some low minimum) mobilization usually propels a group into contention for power over one government or another. Eric Wolf's analysis of the involvement of peasant communities in revolutions, for example, shows how regularly they mobilize and then contend for power in self-defense.

Wolf's analysis also tells us how crucial to the success of that contention for power are the coalitions peasant communities make with other groups outside. No coalition = lost revolution. In a great many situations, a single contender does not have enough resources—enough committed men, enough guns, enough trained lawyers, enough cash—to influence the government by itself. A coalition with another contender which has overlapping or complementary designs on the government will then increase the joint power of the contenders to accomplish those designs.

Although coalitions most commonly occur between members of the polity (that is, between groups which can already routinely lay claims to response and to delivery of resources by agents of the government) or between nonmembers of the polity (between groups which have no routine claims to response and delivery of resources), coalitions between members and nonmembers frequently occur when the members are seeking ends for which there are not enough coalition partners within the polity, and for which the resources being mobilized by the nonmembers would be useful. This happens when a party wins an election by buying off the support of a tribe through promises of jobs and influence, or when a dissident but established group of intellectuals forms an alliance with a new workers' movement. These coalitions take on special importance because they often open the way to the new contender's acquisition of membership in the polity, or the way to a revolutionary alliance.

Member-nonmember coalitions matter also because they appear to strongly affect the amount of violence which grows out of contention for power. Under most conditions a coalition with a member reduces the violence which attends the acquisition of power by a nonmember. The coalitions of the woman's suffrage and temperance movements in England and the United States with other established segments of the middle classes, for example, almost certainly restrained the use of force against them. Where the effect of the coalition is to split the polity into factions making exclusive and incompatible claims on the government, however, a high degree of collective violence is likely to follow.

VIOLENCE

In order to understand why this should be so, we ought to look more closely at the nature of "violence." The term often serves as a catchall containing all the varieties of protest, militancy, coercion, destruction, or muscle-flexing which a given observer happens to fear or condemn. Violence, as Henry Bienen (1968, p. 4) comments, "carries overtones of 'violating,' and we often use violence to refer to illegitimate force" (cf. Converse, 1968, pp. 481–485). With that usage, we shall never be able to make systematic statements about the conditions of violence. If we restrict our attention to human actions which damage persons or property, however, we have at least a chance to sort out the regularities in their appearance. Even that restriction calls immediately for further distinctions; violence so defined still includes the following.

—cut thumbs
—murders
—hockey games
—rebellions
—normal wear of automobiles or the roads they drive on
—disposal of noxious wastes
—cigarette smoking

The obvious temptation is to add some qualifications concerning the intentions of the actors: they want to destroy, they are angry, they seek power or something else. The trouble with letting a lot depend on intentions is that intentions are mixed and hard to discern. The judgments outsiders make concerning the intentions of participants in conflicts usually include implicit theories of causation and responsibility. Even with full knowledge, intentions often turn out to be mixed and divergent, often change or misfire in the course of the action. We must ask *whose* intentions *when*. Violence is rarely a solo performance; it usually grows out of an interaction of opponents. Whose intentions should count? The small group of demonstrators who gather on the steps of the capitol? The larger group of spectators who eventually get drawn into the action? The police who first stand guard and then struggle to disperse the crowd? Both in theory and in practice, then, intentions provide very shaky criteria for the distinction of violence from nonviolence.

In her brilliant essay on violence, Hannah Arendt (1970) urges a fundamental distinction between *power* and *violence*. Power, in her view, is "the human ability not just to act but to act in concert." But the difficulties with which we are now wrestling come out in one fact: Arendt never quite defines violence. This is the closest approach:

> *Violence,* finally, as I have said, is distinguished by its instrumental charac-
> ter. Phenomenologically, it is close to strength, since the implements of
> violence, like all other tools, are designed and used for the purpose of
> multiplying natural strength until, in the last stage of their development,
> they can substitute for it. (Arendt, 1970, p. 46)

As a distinction in political philosophy—that is, in the principles on which we can reasonably found a system of government and by which we can justify or condemn public actions—I find Arendt's treatment of power and violence illuminating. As a guide to observation of acting men, however, it has the fatal flaw of resting exactly on the features of collective action which observers and participants dispute most passionately, precisely because they are the features of action which will bring on it justification from some and condemnation from others. The justification and condemnation are important business, but they are not our business here.

Nor do any easy alternatives lie close at hand. We may try to define "normal" or "expected" or "legitimate" uses of force in social life and define deviations from them as violent; that approach not only requires the (rather difficult) assessment of the normal expected state of affairs but also tends to define away violence exerted by professional specialists in coercion. If, on the other hand, we turn to the amount of damage sustained by the individuals involved, we face the difficulty of determining how direct and material the damage must be: Does a firm's dumping of garbage which promotes disease count? Does the psychic burden of enslavement count?

I recite these tedious complications in order to emphasize that in the present state of knowledge and theory concerning violence *any* definition will be arbitrary in some regards and debatable in many others. Men do not agree on what they will call violent; what is more, their disagreement springs to an important extent from differences in political perspective. My own inclination is toward what Terry Nardin calls a "brute harm" conception of violence: any *observable interaction in the course of which persons or objects are seized or physically damaged over resistance.* (Direct or indirect resistance, in the form of attacks on persons, erection of barriers, standing in the way, holding on to the persons or objects at issue, and so on, enters the definition in order to exclude self-destruction, potlatches, ceremonial mutilation, urban renewal, and other collective damage in which all parties have more or less agreed to the action.)

Further distinctions start from there: collective versus individual, depending on the number of parties to the interaction; games versus nongames, depending on the extent to which all participants begin with an agreement to work toward a determinate set of alternative outcomes by following some standard rules; continuous versus discontinuous, depending on how great a time span we observe and how large an interval we permit to elapse before we call the action at an end; and so forth.

A Way of Defining and Studying Collective Violence

Within this broad field, let us concentrate on collective violence within a population under the control of a single government. Let us agree to pay little attention to war, to full-fledged games, to individual violence, or to highly discontinuous interactions. We are then still free to examine events in which agents of the government do all the damaging, and other events in which the damage was only incidental to the aims of most of those involved. In a series of investigations of collective violence in modern Europe, my own research group has discovered that we can, without enormous uncertainty, single out events occurring within a particular national state in which at least one group of 50 or more persons seizes or damages someone or something from another group. Below that scale, collective violence begins to fade into banditry, brawling, vandalism, terrorism, and a wide variety of threatening nonviolent events, so far as our ability to distinguish them on the basis of the historical record is concerned.

We use the community-population-day as an elementary unit. On a particular day, did this segment of the population of this community engage in collective violence, as just defined? If so, we have the elementary unit of a violent incident. Did an overlapping set of people carry on the action in an adjacent community? If so, both communities were involved in the same incident. Did an overlapping set of people continue the action the following day? If so, the incident lasted at least two days. Introduce a break in time, space, or personnel, and we are dealing with two or more distinct incidents. The result of this modular reasoning is both to greatly simplify the problem of bounding the "same" incident and to fragment into many separate incidents series of interactions (like the Spanish Civil War as a whole) which many analysts have been willing to treat as a single unit.

For some purposes, like the comparative study of revolutions, a broader criterion may serve better. Still other investigations will require more stringent standards: more participants, a certain duration, someone killed, a particular minimum of property damage. But the general reasoning of such choices would be the same: identify *all* the events above a certain magnitude, or at least a representative sample of them, before trying to sort them out in terms of legitimacy or in terms of the aims of the participants.

Once collective violence is defined in these terms, interesting conclusions begin to emerge from the close examination of the actual record of violent incidents. Our study of thousands of violent incidents occurring in western Europe since 1800 reveals several strong tendencies which affect our understanding of the roots of violence.

First, most collective violence—in the sense of interactions which actually produce direct damage to persons and property—grows out of actions which are not intrinsically violent and which are basically similar to a much larger number of collective actions occurring without violence in the same periods and settings. The clearest example is the demonstration, in which some group displays its strength and determination in the presence of the public, of the agents of the state, and perhaps of its enemies as well. The overwhelming majority of demonstrations pass without direct damage to persons or property. But a small proportion do turn to violent encounters between police and demonstrators or to attacks on property by the demonstrators. The demonstration is such a common way of doing political business in modern Europe that even that small proportion of violent outcomes is enough to make the demonstration the most common setting for collective violence. The strike, the parliamentary session, the public meeting, the fiesta follow something like the same pattern: the great majority of them go off without violence, the violent ones not differing in any fundamental way from the nonviolent ones.

A second important feature of collective violence which stands out in the modern European record is the heavy involvement of agents of the state, especially such repressive agents as police and soldiers. This is, unsurprisingly, a matter of scale: the fewer the people involved, the less likely it is that repressive agents will be there. But it does not mean simply that the larger the scale of *violence,* the more likely the police are to step in. For in the modern European experience, repressive forces are themselves the most consistent initiators and performers of collective violence. There is a sort of division of labor: repressive forces do the largest part of the killing and wounding, whereas the groups they are seeking to control do most of the damage to property. The division of labor follows from the usual advantage repressive forces have with respect to arms and military discipline; from the common tactics of demonstrators, strikers, and other frequent participants in collective violence, which are to violate symbolically charged rules and prohibitions whose enforcement is the business of agents of government; from the typical sequence of events, in which demonstrators are carrying on an action which is illegal yet nonviolent, and repressive forces receive the order to stop them.

Since no one has done detailed studies of contemporary Latin America, North America, Africa, or Asia, it is hard to say how generally these generalizations apply. The fragments of evidence now available indicate that they apply very widely in contemporary countries with strong governments. Jerome Skolnick (1969, p. 258) says in summary of one part of his analysis of contemporary American protests, "It is misleading to ignore the part played by social control agencies in aggravating and sometimes creating a riot. It is not unusual, as the Kerner Commission observed, for a riot to begin *and* end with police violence." A chronological review of violence in American labor-management disputes makes it clear both that over the long run police, troops, and plant guards have done the bulk of the killing and wounding, and that the typical starting point has been some sort of illegal but nonviolent collective action by the workers—a walkout, a sitdown, a demonstration, picketing, sending of delegations. In their sketch of the usual circumstances in which the total of at least 700 persons died in American "labor violence" during the nineteenth and twentieth centuries, Taft and Ross (1969, pp. 289–90) report:

> Facing inflexible opposition, union leaders and their members frequently found that nothing, neither peaceful persuasion nor the intervention of heads of government, could move the employer towards recognition. Frustration and desperation impelled pickets to react to strikebreakers with anger. Many violent outbreaks followed efforts of strikers to restrain the entry of strikebreakers and raw materials into the struck plant. Such conduct, obviously illegal, opened the opportunity for forceful police measures. In the long run, the employer's side was better equipped for success. The use of force by pickets was illegal on its face, but the action of the police and company guards were in vindication of the employers' rights.

The same general pattern recurs in the bulk of contemporary American collective violence: a group undertakes an illegal and/or politically unacceptable action, forces of order seek to check the group, a violent encounter ensues, the "rioters"—for that is the label the group acquires at the moment of violent contact with police or troops—sustain most of the casualties.

Reflecting on the long succession of violent encounters between contenders for power and power-holders in America, Richard Rubenstein (1970, pp. 15–16) makes an important observation.

> At the outset, one thing seems clear: those groups which achieved success without participating in sustained rioting, guerrilla terrorism or outright insurrection were not necessarily more talented, hardworking or "American" than those that resorted to higher levels of violence. The resistance of more powerful groups to change is one key struggle; another is the match between out-group characteristics and the needs of a changing political-economic system.

Then he goes on to contrast the fluidity of the economic and political arrangements open to the immigrants of 1880–1920 with the formation, in the 1930s and 1940s, of a new ruling coalition quite resistant to displacement: "Ironically, since these are the groups most wedded to the myth of peaceful progress and the culpability of the violent—it is the existence of this coalition, exercising power through a highly centralized federal bureaucracy, which helps keep emerging groups powerless and dependent" (p. 17). The consequence, in Rubenstein's view, is that recent bids for power have met determined resistance and brought forth the pious recommendation that the members of the groups involved attempt to enter the system as individuals, on their own merits, rather than destroying the system through collective efforts to wrest benefits from it.

Rubenstein's analysis includes both an idea of how the American system usually works and a notion of the changes it has undergone since the 1930s. The general picture corresponds to William Gamson's portrayal of "stable unrepresentation" in American politics: "... the American political system normally operates to prevent incipient competitors from achieving full entry into the political arena" (Gamson, 1968b, p. 18). That description applies to all political systems; the real questions are: How great are the obstacles? How do they vary from system to system and time to time?

That brings up the second part. Has the American system closed down since the 1930s? To try that question out seriously, we shall need much more precise information than we now have concerning the fates of successive challengers. Gamson's investigation, indeed, is one of several current efforts to attack that very problem. In the meantime, it is not obvious that recent challengers—antiwar students, organized blacks, gay activists, and aircraft manufacturers are likely candidates for the post-1940 list—have met more resistance than craft unions, Prohibitionists, or Abolitionists had in the nineteenth century. There is probably variation over time, and there may well be a long-run trend. But both are no doubt too subtle to show up in a few offhand comparisons.

P. M. G. Harris has taken a close look at the elite figures of the eighteenth and nineteenth centuries described in the *Dictionary of American Biography*. He finds both that there was some decline over the nineteenth century in the proportion of elite men coming from working-class and lower-middle-class origins, and that there were cyclical variations in the recruitment of elites; he suggests a connection with Kuznets cycles of economic activity. *If* (a) Harris's conclusions are correct and *if* (b) fluctuations in individual mobility into the national elite correspond to group movements into the national polity, *then* it is plausible that American entries and exits change over time in response to the rhythms of economic life. If that were true, I would be surprised to see Rubenstein's treatment of the period since the New Deal onward as a single block hold up to close scrutiny. The discovery that he was wrong in that regard would not challenge his basic analysis of the difficulties of acquiring power, however.

Political Action and Involvement in Violence

In the terms we were using earlier, Rubenstein is saying that members of the polity, acting mainly through agents of the state, have banded together to resist the claims of newly mobilized contenders for membership. His most prominent case is organized blacks, but the analysis applies more generally to the past and present contention of wheat farmers, women, believers in temperance, students, and organized labor. In these cases and many others, the acceptance of the group's collective claims would significantly reallocate the resources under the control of the polity, redefine the rules of membership for further contenders, change the likely coalitions inside and outside the polity. In such cases, the main link between violence and contention for power consists of the repeated sequence in which members of the challenging group publicly lay claim to some space, object, privilege, protection, or other resource which they consider due them on general grounds, and the agents of the government (backed by the members of the polity) forcibly resist their claims. Proactive collective action on the one side, reactive collective action on the other.

A complete picture of the process linking contention and violence, however, requires a distinction between nonmembers bidding for power and members on their way out of the polity. Members losing their position are more likely to find themselves trying to maintain exclusive claims to some particular resource—a school, a distinctive costume, a source of income, a tax exemption—and unable to enlist the support of other members or of agents of the government in maintaining those claims. Under those circumstances, they commonly attempt to exert those claims on their own, and to keep others from claiming the same resources. We have *reactive* collective action.

Then two different sequences are likely to produce collective violence involving declining members of a polity. The first is like the one involving new claimants for membership in the polity, in that agents of the government directly resist the claims of the parting member to keep exerting its former rights to certain resources. The second pits the parting member directly against others seeking to acquire the disputed resources; vigilante movements, private armies, and gangs of thugs are especially likely to enter the action at this point, as the old member seeks to substitute its own force for that of the now-unreliable government. The regional movement of resistance against a centralizing state commonly takes this form. So does the classic European food riot, in which the members of a community collectively dispute the right of anyone to store grain in times of hunger or ship grain out of the community when local people still need food, and they reinforce their dispute by acting in the traditional role of the authorities: inventorying the grain on hand, accumulating it in a public place, and selling it off at a price locally determined to be just and reasonable. And finally, so do various fascist movements formed in opposition to the threatening claims of a mobilized working class.

The sequence involving new contenders and declining members means that collective violence tends to cluster around entries into the polity and exits from it. When membership is stable, collective violence is less prevalent. And the most important single reason for that clustering is the propensity of the government's repressive forces to act against new contenders and declining members.

I do not mean that the sequences I have described are the *only* ones which produce collective violence; they are just the most regular and reliable. Routine testing among established members of a polity produces a certain amount of violent conflict, but it tends to be limited and to be treated as a regrettable error. Conventional combats among teams, communities, youth groups, or schools sometimes fit the pattern of "testing violence" but more often escape it; they, too, operate on a small scale, within large restrictions. Drunken brawls, private vengeance, festival madness, impulsive vandalism, all reach a dangerous magnitude now and then. What is more, the frequency of conventional combats, brawls, vendetta, and so on undoubtedly varies with the basic conceptions of honor, obligation, and solidarity which prevail within a population. Nevertheless, I would say that in populations under the control of states, all these forms account for only a small proportion of the collective violence which occurs, and they change far too gradually to account for the abrupt surges and recessions of collective violence which appear in such populations. The chief source of variation in collective violence is the operation of the polity.

Nor do I mean that most collective violence goes on in calculating calm. Far from it. Both those who are arguing for the acquisition of rights on the basis of general principles and those who are fighting for the defense of privilege on the basis of custom and precedent are usually indignant and often enraged. Moments of dangerous confrontation (as Louis Girard says of the French revolutions of 1830 and 1848, and as almost everyone says of the French events of May 1968) frequently bring an air of festival, of exhilaration, of release from ordinary restrictions. Plenty of individual venting of resentments and settling of old scores takes place under the cover of collective action in the name of high principle. The argument up to this point simply denies the conclusion that the rage, the exhilaration, or the resentment *causes* the collective violence.

REVOLUTION

A fortiori, the argument denies that accumulated rage, exhilaration, or resentment causes revolutions. It leads instead to a conception of revolution as an extreme condition of the normal political process. The distinguishing characteristic of a revolutionary situation, as Leon Trotsky said long ago, is the presence of more than one bloc effectively exercising control over a significant part of the state apparatus. Trotsky built into this idea of "dual sovereignty" two restrictions which appear unnecessary: (1) that each of the blocs consist of a single social class; (2) that there be only two such blocs at any point in time. Either of these restrictions would eliminate most of the standard cases of revolution, including the French, Chinese, and Mexican classics.

Trotsky's idea retains its analytic strength if expanded to include blocs consisting of coalitions of classes and/or other groups and to allow for the possibility of three or more simultaneous blocs. *Multiple sovereignty* is then the identifying feature of revolutions. A revolution begins when a government previously under the control of a single sovereign polity becomes the object of effective, competing, mutually exclusive claims on the part of two or more distinct polities; it ends when a single sovereign polity regains control over the government.

Such a multiplication of polities can occur under four different conditions.

1. The members of one polity attempt to subordinate another previously distinct polity. Where the two polities are clearly sovereign and independent at the outset, we are more likely to consider this conflict a special variety of war. Circumstances like the annexation of Texas to the United States or the transfers of power to various communist regimes in eastern Europe at the end of the Second World War fall, in fact, into an uncertain area between war and revolution.

2. The members of a previously subordinate polity, such as the group of contenders holding power over a regional government, assert sovereignty. Here the words "rebellion" and "revolt" spring readily to mind. Yet in recent years it has become quite usual to call one version of such events a *colonial* or *national* revolution.

3. Contenders not holding membership in the existing polity mobilize into a bloc successfully exerting control over some portion of the government apparatus. Despite the attractiveness of this version to leaders of the dispossessed, it rarely, if ever, occurs in a pure form.

4. The more usual circumstance is the fragmentation of an existing polity into two or more blocs, each exercising control over some part of the government. That fragmentation frequently involves the emergence of coalitions between established members of the polity and mobilizing nonmembers.

How would we recognize the onset of multiple sovereignty? The question is stickier than it seems at first glance. Neither the presence nor the expansion of areas of autonomy or of resistance on the part of the subject population is a reliable sign; all governments excite some sorts of resistance, and all governments exert incomplete control over their subjects. Most states face continuing marginal challenges to their sovereignty: from within, bandits, vigilantes, religious communities, national minorities, or uncompromising separatists hold them off; from without, powerful states infiltrate the challengers and encroach on their prerogatives. All these circumstances have some distant kinship to revolution, but they do not constitute revolution. Even rival claims to the claims of the existing polity by the adherents of displaced regimes, revolutionary movements, or outside states are quite common. The claims themselves do not amount to revolution.

The question is whether some significant part of the subject population honors the claim. The revolutionary moment arrives when previously acquiescent members of that population find themselves confronted with strictly incompatible demands from the government and from an alternative body claiming control over the government—and obey the alternative body. They pay taxes to it, provide men for its armies, feed its functionaries, honor its symbols, give time to its service, or yield other resources, despite the prohibitions of a still-existing government they formerly obeyed. Multiple sovereignty has begun. When only one polity exerting exclusive control over the government remains, and no rivals are successfully pressing their claims—however that happens—the revolution has ended.

PROXIMATE CONDITIONS OF REVOLUTION

If the conditions just described constituted revolution, a revolutionary meteorologist would keep his eyes peeled for the following conditions, and a revolutionary engineer would try to create them.

1. The appearance of contenders, or coalitions of contenders, advancing exclusive alternative claims to the control over the government currently exerted by the members of the polity.

2. Commitment to those claims by a significant segment of the subject population (especially when those commitments are not simply acknowledged in principle, but activated in the face of prohibitions or contrary directives from the government).

3. Formation of coalitions between members of the polity and the contenders advancing the alternative claims.

4. Incapacity or unwillingness of the agents of the government to suppress the alternative coalition or the commitment to its claims.

Conditions 1, 2, and 4 are necessary for revolution. The third condition, the formation of coalitions, is not logically necessary. It may not even be practically necessary, but it greatly facilitates condition 4. Coalitions between members and challengers, that is, make it less likely that suppression of the challengers will work. That is one reason for the importance of a "symptom" to which Crane Brinton and many other analysts of revolution have devoted considerable attention: the transfer of intellectuals and elites to the revolutionary opposition. Historically, the incapacity or neutralization of the armed forces has often followed this sort of division of the polity and has usually been essential to the success of the revolutionary coalition.

The explanation, prediction, or production of revolution therefore comes down to the specification, detection, or creation of the circumstances under which conditions 1 to 4 occur. The four proximate conditions leave out a number of things which have often been considered defining features of revolution: permanent transfer of power, displacement of one ruling class by another, extensive structural change, high levels of violence, widespread participation, action by the oppressed, activation in the name of a vision of a transformed world.

Of course, anyone has the right to restrict his category of True Revolutions to those displaying any or all of these additional features. All of them are related as likely cause or probable effect to the particular form of multiple sovereignty which characterizes the revolution. Yet each of them has occurred historically in the absence of multiple sovereignty. Moreover, multiple sovereignty has occurred in the absence of each of them; none is a necessary condition. (I doubt, however, whether multiple sovereignty has ever occurred in the absence of all four conditions.) Hence the desirability of distinguishing the conditions for transfers of power, extensive structural change, high levels of violence, etc., from the conditions for revolution.

Most analysts of revolution have taken a different tack. They have restricted the meaning of revolution in two ways: (1) by insisting that the actors and the action meet some demanding standards—that they be drawn from an oppressed class, that they have a comprehensive program of social transformation in view, or that they exhibit some other gauge of seriousness; (2) by dealing only with cases in which power actually changed hands. Peter Calvert (1970, p. 4), to take a recent example, builds the following elements into his conception of revolution.

(a) A process in which the political direction of a state becomes increasingly discredited in the eyes of either the population as a whole or certain key sections of it. . . .

(b) A change of government (transition) at a clearly defined point in time by the use of armed force, or the credible threat of its use; namely, an *event*.

(c) A more-or-less coherent programme of change in either the political or the social institutions of a state, or both, induced by the political leadership after a revolutionary event, the transition of power, has occurred.

(d) A political myth that gives to the political leadership resulting from a revolutionary transition short-term status as the legitimate government of the state.

Thus, he goes on, "in order to investigate fully the concept of revolution it would be necessary to study in detail process, event, programme, and myth as distinct phenomena" (Calvert, 1970, p. 4). He confines his own study to revolutionary events: changes of government accomplished by force. As compared with standard definitions of Great Revolutions, that greatly increases the number of cases he has to examine. Yet the insistance on armed force and on an actual transfer of power eliminates a number of cases in which multiple sovereignty appeared without the use of armed force or, especially, a change of government. His general definition is quite narrow, and even his working definition of revolutionary *events* is somewhat narrower than the definition of revolution I have proposed.

My reasons for preferring a broad definition are at once theoretical and practical. Theoretically, I am not convinced that revolutions in the narrow sense of violent, extensive transfers of power are phenomena sui generis. On the contrary, I am impressed with the carry-over of routine forms of political action into revolutionary situations, the apparently small initial differences separating "successful" from "unsuccessful" revolutions, and the apparent contingency of the degree of violence itself. Yet multiple sovereignty does seem to mark out a domain of situations which have a good deal of homogeneity by comparison with all cases of single sovereignty. Practically, the usual criteria of revolution—the extent and durability of the transfer of power, the amount of social change called for by the revolutionary program, the prominence of the powerless in the revolutionary action, for instance—single out as defining conditions features of the event which are likely to be mixed, controversial, and ambiguous. That is, to say the least, inconvenient. Multiple sovereignty has its own difficulties. But it is rather easier to identify than is, say, "fundamental social change."

We might hold on to the classic questions by adopting a taxonomic strategy. We could classify revolutions initially identified by the presence of multiple sovereignty as

   violent/nonviolent,

as involving

   no transfer/little transfer/much transfer,

and so on. The taxonomies of revolution which follow most directly from the argument unfolding here, however, differentiate among (a) processes leading to multiple sovereignty, (b) processes leading to the termination of multiple sovereignty, (c) patterns of mobilization, coalition, and opposition among the contenders involved. A *coup d'état,* then, would turn out to be a revolution in which one member of a polity attempted to displace another via a temporary seizure of a major instrument of government, with only a brief interval of multiple sovereignty. A *civil war* would be a revolution in which the blocs of contenders had distinct territorial bases. And so on.

If we proceeded in this way, it would not be hard to work out a comprehensive classification scheme. There is no point in doing that here. In such a scheme, whether the revolution was "successful" or "unsuccessful," whether one group of participants hoped to transform the entire structure of power, whether fundamental social change went on before the revolution, whether important transformations occurred as a result of it, whether many people died during the conflict would remain important questions, but questions that would not enter into the classification of revolutions.

The critical signs of revolution, in this perspective, are signs of the emergence of an alternative polity. These signs may possibly be related to rising discontent, value conflict, frustration, or relative deprivation. The relationship must be proved, however, not assumed. Even if it is proved that discontent, value conflict, frustration, and relative deprivation do fluctuate in close correspondence to the emergence and disappearance of alternative polities—a result that would surprise me—the development to watch for would still be the commitment of a significant part of the population, regardless of their motives, to exclusive alternative claims to the control over the government currently exerted by the members of the polity.

We have narrowed the focus of explanation and prediction considerably. It now comes down to specifying and detecting the conditions under which four related outcomes occur: (1) the appearance of contenders making exclusive alternative claims; (2) significant commitment to those claims; (3) formation of coalitions with the contenders; (4) repressive incapacity of the government. The short-run conditions for these outcomes may of course be quite different from the long-run changes which make them possible. Let us concentrate for the moment on the short-run conditions.

Alternatives to the Existing Polity

What I mean by "exclusive alternative claims to control of the government" comes out dramatically in an article written about a year after the October Revolution, as the other parties which had joined the revolutionary coalition were being squeezed out of power.

> Now, however, the course of world events and the bitter lessons derived from the alliance of all the Russian monarchists with Anglo-French and American imperialism are proving *in practice* that a democratic republic is a bourgeois-democratic republic, which is already out of date from the point of view of the problems which imperialism has placed before history. They show that there is no *other* alternative: *either* Soviet government triumphs in every advanced country in the world, *or* the most reactionary imperialism triumphs, the most savage imperialism, which is throttling the small and weak nations and reinstating reaction all over the world—Anglo-American imperialism, which has perfectly mastered the art of using the form of a democratic republic.
>
> One or the other.
>
> There is no middle course; until quite recently this view was regarded as the blind fanaticism of the Bolsheviks.
>
> *But it turned out to be true.* (Lenin, 1967a, p. 35)

These claims came from a party already in power, but they were addressed to revolutionary strategists in other countries who wished to continue a collaborative approach within Russia itself.

When can we expect the appearance of contenders (or coalitions of contenders) advancing exclusive alternative claims to the control of the government currently exerted by the members of the polity? The question is a trifle misleading, for such contenders are almost always with us in the form of millenial cults, radical cells, or rejects from positions of power. The real question is when such contenders proliferate and/or mobilize.

Two paths lead to that proliferation and/or mobilization. The first is the flourishing of groups which from their inception hold to transforming aims which are incompatible with the continued power of the members of the polity. Truly other-worldly and retreatist groups seeking total withdrawal from contemporary life do not fully qualify, since in principle they can prosper so long as the rest of the world lets them alone. True radicals, true reactionaries, anarchists, preachers of theocracy, monists of almost every persuasion come closer to the mark. The second path is the turning of contenders from objectives which are compatible with the survival of the polity to objectives which spell its doom: a claim to all power, a demand for criteria of membership which would exhaust all the available resources or exclude all its present members.

Why and how the first sort of group forms—the group committed from the start to fundamental transformation of the structure of power—remains one of the mysteries of our time. Max Weber taught that such groups formed around charismatic individuals who offered alternative visions of the world, visions that made sense of the contemporary chaos. Marx suggested that from time to time a few individuals would swing so free of their assigned places in the existing class structure that they could view the structure as a whole and the historical process producing it; they could then teach their view to others who were still caught in the structure. Since Marx and Weber we have had some heroic conceptualizing and cataloging of the varieties of intrinsically revolutionary groups (see Smelser, 1963; Lipset and Raab, 1970; Gamson, 1968a). But the rise and fall of diverse movements of protest since World War II have shown us that we still have almost no power to anticipate where and when such committed groups will appear.

The turning of contenders from compatible objectives is rather less of a mystery, because we can witness its occurrence as old members lose their position in the polity and as challengers are refused access to power. The former is the recurrent history of right-wing activism, the latter the standard condition for left-wing activism. Marx gave the classic analysis of the process of radicalization away from some sort of accommodation with the existing system toward an exclusive, revolutionary position. His argument was precisely that through repeated victimization under bourgeois democracy (a victimization, to be sure, dictated by the logic of capitalism) workers would gradually turn away from its illusions toward class-conscious militancy. That he should have overestimated the absorptive capacity of the polities it supported does not reduce the accuracy of his perception of the relationships. So far as Marx was concerned, a newly forming and growing class was the only candidate for such a transformation. In fact, the general principle appears to apply as well to national minorities, age-sex groups, regional populations, or any other mobilizing group which makes repeated unsuccessful bids for power.

The elaboration of new ideologies, new theories of how the world works, new creeds is part and parcel of both paths to a revolutionary position: the emergence of brand-new challengers and the turning of existing contenders. Most likely the articulation of ideologies which capture and formulate the problems of such contenders in itself accelerates their mobilization and change of direction; how great an independent weight to attribute to ideological innovation is another recurrent puzzle in the analysis of revolution. The need for elaboration of ideologies is one of the chief reasons for the exceptional importance of intellectuals in revolutionary movements. The reflections of a leading French Marxist intellectual on current political strategy are revealing.

> The revolutionary party's capacity for hegemony is directly linked to the extent of its influence in the professions and in intellectual circles. It can counter bourgeois ideology to the degree that it inspires their inquiries and draws their vanguard into reflection on an "alternative model," while respecting the independence of these inquiries. The mediation of the intellectual vanguard is indispensable in combatting and destroying the grip of the dominant ideology. It is also necessary in order to give the dominated classes a language and a means of expression which will make them conscious of the reality of their subordination and exploitation. (Gorz, 1969, pp. 241–42)

This is a congenial doctrine for an intellectual to hold. Yet it corresponds to a vigorous reality: an outpouring of new thought articulating objectives incompatible with the continuation of the existing polity is probably our single most reliable sign that the first condition of a revolutionary situation is being fulfilled.

Acceptance of Alternative Claims

The second condition is commitment to the claims by a significant segment of the subject population. The first and second conditions overlap, since the veering of an already-mobilized contender toward exclusive alternative claims to control of the government simultaneously establishes the claims and produces commitment to them. Yet expansion of commitment can occur without the establishment of any new exclusive claims through (a) the further mobilization of the contenders involved and (b) the acceptance of those claims by other individuals and groups. It is in accounting for the expansion and contracting of this sort of commitment that attitudinal analyses of the type conducted by Ted Gurr, James Davies, and Neil Smelser should have their greatest power.

Two classes of action by governments have a strong tendency to expand commitment to revolutionary claims. The first is the sudden failure of the government to meet specific obligations which members of the subject population regard as well established and crucial to their own welfare. I have in mind obligations to provide employment, welfare services, protection, access to justice, and the other major services of government.

Italy, for example, experienced a series of crises of this sort at the end of World War I, despite the fact that she had ended up on the "winning" side. The demobilization of the army threw more than two million men on a soft labor market, the fluctuation and relaxation of controls over food supplies and prices aggrieved millions of consumers, and peasants (including demobilized soldiers) began to take into their own hands the redistribution of land they argued the government had promised during the war. The consequent withdrawal of commitment from the government opened the way to fascism. Both Right and Left mobilized in response to the government's inability to deliver on its promises. In the event, the regime chose to tolerate or support the Fascist strong-arm *squadri* in their effort to destroy the most effective working-class organizations. For that reason (rather than any fundamental similarity in their social bases) the initial geographic distribution of Italian Fascism resembled the distribution of socialist strength: the Po Valley, the northern industrial cities, and so forth. The Right + Far Right coalition worked, more or less, in crushing the organized segments of the Left. But it left the Fascists in nearly autonomous control of large parts of Italy: multiple sovereignty.

The case of postwar Italy has a threefold importance, for it illustrates a process which was widespread (although generally less acute) elsewhere in Europe at the same time, falls into a very general pattern in which the end of war (victorious or not) produces a crisis of governmental incapacity, and demonstrates the way in which movements of protest that are themselves not clearly "right" or "left" in orientation sometimes open the way to a right-wing (or for that matter, left-wing) seizure of power.

The *second* class of governmental action which commonly expands the commitment of important segments of the population to revolutionary claims is a rapid or unexpected increase in the government's demand for surrender of resources by its subject population. An increase in taxes is the clearest example, but military conscription, the commandeering of land, crops, or farm animals, and the imposition of corvees have all played a historical role in the incitement of opposition. Gabriel Ardant (1965) argues, with widespread evidence, that increased taxation has been the single most important stimulus to popular rebellion throughout Western history. Furthermore, he points out that the characteristic circumstances of tax rebellions in Europe since 1500 are not what most historians have thought. Instead of being either the last resort of those who are in such misery that any more taxation will destroy them or the first resort of privileged parties who refuse to let anything slip away from them, the rebellion against new taxes most commonly arises where communities find themselves incapable of marketing enough of their goods to acquire the funds demanded by the government.

Ardant considers "incapable of marketing" to mean either that the local economy is insufficiently commercialized or that the market for the particular products of the community in question has contracted. Eric Wolf's analysis of the relationship between peasants and the market, however, suggests that "incapability" refers more generally to any demands which would make it impossible for people to fulfill the obligations which bind them to the local community, and whose fulfillment makes them honorable men. It follows directly from Wolf's argument that increased taxation in the face of little commercialization or the contraction of demand for the products already being marketed by a peasant community tends to have devastating effects on the structure of the community.

Other types of communities face different versions of the same problems. The consequence is that rapidly increased extraction of resources by the government—which in Western countries has most frequently occurred in preparations for war—regularly persuades some segment of the population that the government is no longer legitimate and that those who oppose it are.

Such a shift in position sometimes occurs rapidly, with little advance warning. This appears to be especially likely when a contender or set of contenders mobilizes quickly in response to a general threat to its position—an invasion, an economic crisis, a major attempt by landlords, the state, or someone else to deprive it of crucial resources. We find the villagers of northern England rising in a Pilgrimage of Grace to oppose Henry VIII's dispossession of the monasteries, Mexican peasants banding together to resist the threat of takeover of their common lands, Japanese countrymen recurrently joining bloody uprisings against the imposition of new taxes.

This defensive mobilization is not simply a cumulation of individual dissatisfactions with hardship or a mechanical group response to deprivation. Whether it occurs at all depends very much, as Eric Wolf and others have shown, on the preexisting structure of power and solidarity within the population experiencing the threat. Furthermore, its character is not intrinsically either "revolutionary" or "counterrevolutionary"; that depends mainly on the coalitions the potential rebels make. Defensive mobilization is the most volatile feature of a revolutionary situation, both because it often occurs fast and because new coalitions between a rapidly mobilized group and established contenders for power can suddenly create a significant commitment to an alternative polity.

If that is the case, there may be something to the common notion that revolutions are most likely to occur when a sharp contraction in well-being follows a long period of improvement. James Davies has recently propounded the idea under the label of "J-curve hypothesis," and Ted Gurr has treated it as one of the chief variants of his general condition for rebellion: a widening of the expectation-achievement gap. All the attempts to test these attitudinal versions of the theory have been dogged by the difficulty of measuring changes in expectations and achievements for large populations over substantial blocks of time and by the tendency of most analysts to work from the fact of revolution back to the search for evidence of short-run deprivation and then further back to the search for evidence of long-run improvement, not necessarily with respect to the same presumed wants, needs, or expectations. The latter procedure has the advantage of almost always producing a fit between the data and the theory, and the disadvantage of not being a reliable test of the theory. The question remains open.

If we assume that sharp contractions following long expansions *do* produce revolutions with exceptional frequency, however, the line of argument pursued here leads to an interesting alternative explanation of the J-curve phenomenon. It is that during a long run of expanding resources, the government tends to take on commitments to redistribute resources to new contenders, and the polity tends to admit challengers more easily because the relative cost to existing members is lower when resources are expanding. In the event of quick contraction, the government has greater commitments, new matters of right, to members of the polity, and it has acquired partial commitments to new contenders, perhaps not members of the polity but very likely forming coalitions with members. The government faces a choice between (1) greatly increasing the coercion applied to the more vulnerable segments of the population in order to bring up the yield of resources for reallocation or (2) breaking commitments where that will incite the least dangerous opposition. Either step is likely to lead to a defensive mobilization and thence to a threat of revolution. Such a situation does, to be sure, promote the disappointment of rising expectations. But the principal link between the J-curve and the revolution, in this hypothesis, lies in the changing relations between contenders and government likely to occur in a period of expanding resources.

This is speculation bolstered by hypothesis. In the present state of the evidence, both the existence of the J-curve phenomenon and any proposed explanation of it remain little more than informed guesswork. A proper verification that the phenomenon exists will require comparisons of periods of J-curve, U-curve, M-curve, and no curve, as well as between revolutions and nonrevolutions, in order to see whether there is in fact an affinity of one for the other.

In a longer historical view, the changes which have most often produced the rapid shifts in commitment away from existing governments and established polities are processes which directly affect the autonomy of smaller units within the span of the government: the rise and fall of centralized states, the expansion and contraction of national markets, the concentration and dispersion of control over property. Prosperity and depression, urbanization and ruralization, industrialization and deindustrialization, sanctification and secularization occur in a dispersed and incremental fashion. Although state-making, the expansion and contraction of markets, and property shifts also develop incrementally most of the time, they are especially susceptible of producing dramatic confrontations of rights, privileges, and principles; this tax collector wants the family cow, this merchant proposes to buy the village commons, this prince fails to protect his subjects from bandits. S. N. Eisenstadt (1963) has brought out the extreme vulnerability of vast bureaucratic empires to overexpansion and to damage at the center; both, in his analysis, tend to produce rebellions in which peripheral agents of the empire seek to establish autonomous control over the lands, men, organizations, and wealth first mobilized by the empire. Fernand Braudel (1966) has stressed the frequency with which banditry and related struggles for local power proliferated as the ephemeral states of seventeenth-century Europe contracted. In all these cases, spokesmen for large-scale organization and centripetal processes find themselves locked in struggle with advocates of small-scale autonomy.

In order for a situation to produce multiple sovereignty and thus become revolutionary, commitments to some alternative claimant must be activated in the face of prohibitions or contrary directives from the government. The moment at which some men belonging to members of the alternative coalition seize control over some portion of the government and other men not previously attached to the coalition honor their directives marks the beginning of a revolution. That acceptance of directives may, to be sure, occur as a result of duress of deception, as well as of conversion to the cause. A mixture of duress, deception, and conversion will often do the job.

The presence of a coherent revolutionary organization makes a great difference at exactly this point. An organization facilitates the initial seizure of control, spreads the news, activates the commitments already made by specific men. If so, Lenin provides a more reliable guide to revolutionary strategy than Sorel; his closely directed conspiratorial party contrasts sharply with the spontaneous and purifying rebellion in which Sorel placed his hopes. But the existence of such an organization also makes the start of revolution more closely dependent on the decisions of a small number of people—and thus, paradoxically, subject to chance and idiosyncrasy.

In the last analysis, activation of revolutionary commitments occurs through an extension of the same processes which create the commitments. Conspiratorial organization simply happens to be the one which maximizes the opportunity of the committed to calculate the right moment to strike against the government. The government's sudden inability to meet its own responsibilities (as in the German insurrections during the disintegration of the imperial war effort in 1918) or its violation of the established rights of its subject population (as in the 1640 rebellions of Portugal and Catalonia against Castile, which followed Olivares's attempt to squeeze exceptional resources from those reluctant provinces for the conduct of his war with France) can simultaneously spread and activate the commitment to its revolutionary opposition.

In a case like that of the Taiping rebellion, the rapid mobilization of a contender advancing exclusive alternative claims to control over the government itself leads quickly and inevitably to a break and to an armed struggle.

The dramatic weakening of a government's repressive capacity through war, defection, or catastrophe can simultaneously create the possibility of revolution and encourage the revolutionaries to make their bid; the quick succession of the French revolution of 1870 to the defeat of the Emperor by Prussia falls into this category.

Coalitions between Members and Challengers

The *third* revolutionary condition is the formation of coalitions between members of the polity and the contenders advancing exclusive alternative claims to control over the government. Obviously, this condition and the first one (the appearance of alternative claims, etc.) overlap, both because by definition no such coalition can occur until the alternative exists and because a coalition sometimes turns into a commitment to the alternative claims. Yet this is a separate condition, as some reflection on the coalition between industrialists and the Nazis before 1933 will suggest. In such a coalition a member of the polity typically trades resources with a challenger; for example, there is an exchange of jobs for electoral support. Such a coalition is always risky, since the challenger will always be on the losing end of the exchange as compared with the value of the resources when traded among members of the polity, and therefore disposed to move its extensive mobilized resources elsewhere. Nevertheless, the challenger is likely to accept a coalition where it offers a defense against repression or devaluation of its resources, and the member is likely to accept it when the polity is closely divided, or when no coalition partners are available within the polity, or when its own membership is in jeopardy for want of resources. Standard coalition theory applies here (see especially Gamson, 1968a).

A classic revolutionary tactic also falls under the heading of challenger-member coalition: the penetration of an organization which already has an established place in the structure of power. As early as 1901, Lenin was clearly enunciating such an approach to trade unions.

> Every Social-Democratic worker should as far as possible assist and actively work in these organizations. But, while this is true, it is certainly not in our interest to demand that only Social-Democrats should be eligible for membership in the "trade" unions, since that would only narrow the scope of our influence upon the masses. Let every worker who understands the need to unite for the struggle against the employers and the governments join the trade unions. The very aim of the trade unions would be impossible of achievement, if they did not unite all who have attained at least this elementary degree of understanding, if they were not very *broad* organizations. The broader these organizations, the broader will be our influence over them—an influence due, not only to the "spontaneous" development of the economic struggle, but to the direct and conscious effort of the socialist trade union members to influence their comrades. (Lenin, 1967b, p. 191)

In these cases, the trade unions were normally established members of their respective polities, and the Social Democrats in question were challengers still outside the polity. In this same message, Lenin concludes by recommending the
control of the large, open, legal union by the secret, closed, disciplined revolutionary party.

Splinter groups of intellectuals appear to have a special propensity to form
coalitions outside the party. They trade off ideological work, publicity for the
demands of the challenger, leadership skills, and access to persons in high places
for various forms of support: personnel for demonstrations, electoral strength,
defense against other threatening challengers, and so on. Analysts of revolution
as diverse as Crane Brinton (1938) and Barrington Moore (1969) have considered the "desertion of the intellectuals" to be a crucial early omen of a revolutionary situation. The "desertion" may consist of individual acceptance
of exclusive alternative claims to control of the government. It may also
take the form of rejecting *all* claims, in good anarchist fashion. But the shifts
in commitment by intellectuals which contribute most to hasten a revolutionary situation, in my view, consist of coalitions between revolutionary challengers and groups of intellectuals having membership in the polity. The propensity of French left-wing intellectuals to form such coalitions—without quite
relinquishing their own claims to power and privilege—is legendary.

Governmental Inaction

Condition *four* is the incapacity or unwillingness of the agents of the government to suppress the alternative coalition or the commitment to its claims.
Three paths are possible: (a) sheer insufficiency of the available means of coercion; (b) inefficiency in applying the means; (c) inhibitions to their application. The starkest cases of insufficiency occur when the balance of coercive
resources between the government and the alternative coalition swings suddenly toward the latter, because the government has suffered a sudden depletion
of its resources (as in a lost war), because the alternative coalition has managed
a sudden mobilization of resources (as in the pooling of private arms), or because a new contender with abundant coercive resources has joined the coalition
(as in the defection of troops or foreign intervention). However, the massing
of rebels in locations remote from the centers of coercive strength, the implan-
tation of the alternative coalition in a rough and unknown terrain, and the
adoption of tactics unfamiliar to the professional forces of the government all
raise the costs of suppression as well.

Ted Gurr (1969, pp. 235–36) develops an interesting argument about the
balance of coercive resources between a government and its opponents. In his
phrasing, "The likelihood of internal war increases as the ratio of dissident to
regime coercive control approaches equality." He is referring directly to the
probable magnitude of collective violence. Where the balance strongly favors
the government, goes the argument, only dispersed acts of rebellion occur;

where the balance strongly favors its opponents, the government tends to be a pawn in their hands. The analysis applies even more plausibly to the likelihood of revolution, for an alternative coalition with large coercive resources is likely to seize control with at most an instant of multiple sovereignty, whereas an alternative coalition with small coercive resources will never get multiple sovereignty started.

Inefficiency in applying means which are, in principle, sufficient is harder to pin down and explain; the inefficient almost always plead insufficient means. William Langer (1969, especially pp. 321–22) contends that, had the authorities not bungled their repression of various popular movements, the European revolutions of 1848 would not have occurred. To have confidence in his conclusion we have to assess the balance of coercive means between popular movements and governments, as well as the political inhibitions to repression. In prerevolutionary 1848 the governments clearly had the edge in men, weapons, supplies, and coercive technique. Two factors stayed the government's hand, however: (1) the strong commitment of the new bourgeois, who had been acquiring significant roles in European governments, to certain kinds of civil liberties, and (2) various working-class movements. From a strictly instrumental perspective, all such inhibitions are "inefficient." Yet not to distinguish them from the apparent incompetence of the Egyptian regime toppled in 1952 or the Turkish sultanate displaced in 1919 blurs the essential explanation of these events.

Inhibitions to the application of available coercive means are more interesting than shortages or inefficiency, because they are so likely to flow from the political process itself. The great importance of coalitions between established members of the polity and revolutionary challengers exemplifies the point very well. The United States of the 1960s witnessed the constant formation and reformation of coalitions between groups of intellectuals, opposition politicians, black liberation movements, students, and peace activists, some within the American polity and some outside it. The total effect of these coalitions fell considerably short of revolution, but while operating, the coalitions shielded those whose principles offered the greatest challenge to the existing distribution of power from the treatment they received from police, troops, and other repressors when acting on their own.

Despite the implications of this example, however, the most crucial coalitions over the whole range of revolutions surely link challengers directly with military forces. The Egyptian and Turkish revolutions stand near the extreme, at which the chief claims to alternative control of the government come from within the military itself; in both revolutions soldiers dominated a coalition linking dissident politicians and local movements of resistance. In the middle of the range we find events like the Russian revolution, in which the military were far from paramount, but important segments of the military defected, disintegrated, or refused to repress their brethren. The more extensive the prerevolutionary coalitions between challengers and military units, the more likely such results are to occur.

In this respect and others, war bears a crucial relationship to revolution. Walter Laqueur (1968, p. 501) puts it this way:

> War appears to have been the decisive factor in the emergence of revolutionary situations in modern times; most modern revolutions, both successful and abortive, have followed in the wake of war (the Paris Commune of 1871, the Russian revolution of 1905, the various revolutions after the two World Wars, including the Chinese revolutions). These have occurred not only in the countries that suffered defeat. The general dislocation caused by war, the material losses and human sacrifices, create a climate conducive to radical change. A large section of the population has been armed; human life seems considerably less valuable than in peacetime. In a defeated country authority tends to disintegrate, and acute social dissatisfaction receives additional impetus from a sense of wounded national prestige (the Young Turks in 1908, Naguib and Nasser in 1952). The old leadership is discredited by defeat, and the appeal for radical social change and national reassertion thus falls on fertile ground.

No doubt the statement suffers from a superabundance of explanations. Still, it points out the essential relationship between war and the repressive capacity of the government. Although war temporarily places large coercive resources under the control of a government, it does not guarantee that they will be adequate to the demands placed on them, that they will be used efficiently, or that they will even remain under the government's firm control. Defeat and demobilization provide especially favorable circumstances for revolution because they combine the presence of substantial coercive resources with uncertain control over their use.

War also matters in quite a different way. By and large, wars have always provided the principal occasions on which states have rapidly increased their levies of resources from their subject populations. Conscription is only the self-evident case. Demands for taxes, forced loans, food, nonmilitary labor, manufactured goods, and raw materials follow the same pattern. The increased exactions almost always meet widespread resistance, which the agents of states counter with persuasion and force. Despite the advantage of having extensive estates to squeeze and a wealthy church to dispossess, the Tudors pressed their England hard to support the military forces they committed to sixteenth-century warfare. They faced serious rebellion in 1489, 1497, 1536, 1547, 1549, 1553, and 1569. The last three—Kett's, Wyatt's, and the Northern Rebellion—centered on dynastic issues and consisted largely of risings engineered by regional magnates. The first four, on the other hand, were popular rebellions; every one of them began when the crown suddenly laid hand on resources previously outside its control. The general pattern is the same as the one I have already described for tax rebellions: the rapid mobilization of an entire population, which then challenges the very justice of the royal demand for men, money, or goods.

On the other hand, the contention model makes it appear likely that once multiple sovereignty begins, collective violence will continue at high levels long after the basic issue is decided and will taper off gradually. Schematically, the contrast is as shown in Figure 3.

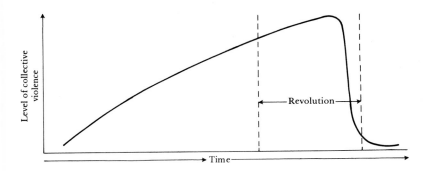

Fig. 3 (a). Tension-Release Model

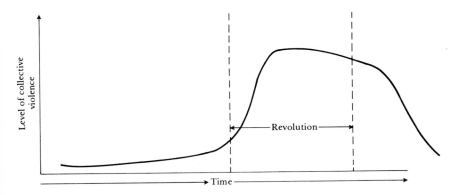

Fig. 3 (b). Contention Model

There are several reasons for this general prediction. First, the appearance of multiple sovereignty puts into question the achieved position of every single contender, whether a member of the polity or not, and therefore tends to initiate a general round of mutual testing among contenders. That testing in itself produces collective violence.

Second, the struggle of one polity against its rival amounts to war: a battle fought with unlimited means. Since control of the entire government is at stake, high costs and high risks are justified. High costs and high risks include destruction of persons and property.

Third, the revolutionary coalition is likely to fragment once the initial seizure of control over the central governmental apparatus occurs, and that fragmentation itself tends to produce further struggles involving violence. The revolutionary coalition fragments for several reasons: it takes a larger mobilized mass to seize power than to maintain it; the inevitable divergence of some major objectives of the contenders within the coalition will come to the fore once the common objective of seizure of power has been accomplished; those contenders which have mobilized rapidly up to the point of revolution are also likely to demobilize rapidly because of the underdevelopment of their organization for the management of the mobilized resources, and thus they will tend to lose position in the next rounds of testing.

Fourth, the victorious polity still faces the problem of reimposing routine governmental control over the subject population, even after multiple sovereignty has ended. As the government returns to its work of extracting and redistributing resources, it finds people reluctant to pay taxes, give up their land, send their sons to war, devote their time to local administration. And so a new round of violent imposition and violent resistance begins. Where the initial locus of the revolution is constricted, the new round is likely to produce a spread of collective violence to other parts of the population. In a centralized governmental system, therefore, the most common sequence is likely to be a large and decisive struggle at the center followed by a more widespread but less critical series of battles through the rest of the territory.

To sum up, we might put together an ideal sequence for revolutions.

1. Gradual mobilization of contenders who make exclusive claims to governmental control and/or whose sheer existence is unacceptable to the members of the polity.

2. Rapid increase in the number of people accepting those claims and/or rapid expansion of the coalition including the unacceptable or exclusive contenders.

3. Unsuccessful efforts by the government (at the behest of members of the polity) to suppress the alternative coalition and/or the acceptance of its claims. May well include attempts at forced demobilization—seizure, devaluation, or dispersion of the resources at the disposal of contenders.

4. Establishment by the alternative coalition of effective control over some portion of the government—a territorial branch, a functional subdivision, a portion of its personnel.

5. Struggles of the alternative coalition to maintain or expand that control.

6. Reconstruction of a single polity through the victory of the alternative coalition, through its defeat, or through the establishment of a modus vivendi between the alternative coalition and some or all of the old members. Fragmentation of the revolutionary coalition.

7. Reimposition of routine governmental control throughout the subject population.

This series of stages suffers from the same defects as all "natural histories" of revolution. It consists mainly of an explication of a definition, and yet it has an unjustified air of inevitability. I lay it out merely to summarize and clarify the previous argument.

Some Related Generalizations

Within this framework, several conditions appear likely to affect the overall level of violence produced by a revolution. In general, the larger the number of contenders involved in the struggle for power (holding constant the number of *people* involved), the higher the level of violence, because the number of mutual tests of position between contenders is likely to rise exponentially with the number of contenders. The greater the fluctuation in control of various segments of the government by different coalitions of contenders, the higher the level of violence, both because the seizure of control itself brings violent resistance and because each change of control sets off further testing of position. Finally, the character of the repressive means under government control strongly affects the degree of violence. The connections are obvious, yet complicated: the use of lethal weapons for crowd control increases deaths through collective violence; the division of labor between specialists in domestic order (police) and war (armies) probably decreases it; the relationship to overall repressive capacity of the government is probably curvilinear (little damage to persons or property where the government has great repressive capacity, little damage where its repressive capacity is slight); the level of violence probably rises as the armament of the government and of its opponents approaches equality. All these relationships and others are plausible, but no more than slivers of systematic evidence for their actual validity exist.

If these generalizations have something to them, the extent of collective violence produced by a revolution should be only weakly and indirectly related to the extent to which the distribution of power changes. A zero redistribution of power (which most of us would call a failure of the revolution) can occur as an outcome of any of the ideal stages presented before, although it becomes less probable as the stages proceed. A glance back at that scheme will make clear how complicated any tracing of general conditions for "success" or "failure" must be.

A single best-established relationship is an obvious and fundamental one: the pivotal influence of control over the major organized means of coercion within the population. Within all contemporary states, that means control of the military forces. No transfer of power at all is likely in a revolution if the government retains control of the military past the revolution's beginning, although defection of the military is by no means a sufficient condition for a takeover by the rebels (Chorley, 1943; Andreski, 1968; Russell Ekman, 1970).

It follows more or less directly that the greater the coercive resources—including private armies, weapons, and segments of the national armed forces—initially controlled by the revolutionary coalition, the more likely a transfer of power. Similarly, the earlier the transfer of coercive resources to the alternative coalition, the more likely a transfer. The mobilization of other resources, normative and utilitarian, probably affects the chances of acquiring power significantly as well, but much less lower than the mobilization of coercive resources. It also follows that the presence of existing members of the polity in the revolutionary coalition will increase the chances for some transfer of power (although it reduces the chances for a *complete* wresting of power from members of the polity), both because of the additional resources it brings to the coalition and because of the greater likelihood that the armed forces will defect, waver, or remain neutral when confronted with established members of the polity.

Beyond these rather banal conclusions, I find myself rummaging around in vintage clichés about tactics, terrain, leadership, chance, and information. That is surprising when one considers the huge amount that has been written about success and failure in revolution. Perhaps the poverty of systematic conclusions comes from the essential unpredictability of transfers of power. I am more inclined to think it comes from our failure to bring keen analytic intelligence to bear.

I fear the same is true of the next question which springs to mind: Under what conditions does extensive structural change accompany or result from a revolution? To the degree that structural change *means* transfer of power from class to class, party to party, contender to contender, of course, we have just examined the question. But if it means further redistribution of resources, changes in the quality of life, urbanization, industrialization, moral reconstruction, then everything depends on the time scale one adopts.

Relatively few permanent changes of this sort actually occur in the course of revolutions. Engels, Sorel, and Fanon all held out the hope of a vast moral regeneration within the act of revolution itself, but the historical experience is sadly lacking in examples thereof. The other structural rearrangements which occur in the course of revolutions are typically temporary: the mobilization of men, loyalties, organizational talents, and weapons at a national level, which recedes as the new structure of power crystallizes; the disruption of daily routines for festivals, deliberations, emergencies; the provisional appearance of commissars, governing committees, task forces. Michael Walzer has brilliantly portrayed a revolutionary outlook for seventeenth-century England, Richard Cobb a revolutionary mentality for eighteenth-century France; nevertheless, for the outlooks and mentalities of most people, revolutions are but passing moments.

A few great revolutions provide exceptions to this absence of short-run transformation; that is perhaps what permits us to call them great revolutions. Although the nobles and the clergy regained some of their position in France with and after Napoleon, the confiscation and sale of aristocratic and ecclesiastical property from 1790 to 1793 permanently shifted the weight away from those two powerful classes. The soviets survived the Bolshevik Revolution. The Chinese communists began reorganizing village structure almost as soon as they were on the scene. Contrary to the world-weary view of Crane Brinton, who argued that a revolution took a country through tremendous turmoil to a position approximately the same as it would have occupied anyway after an equivalent lapse of time, it may be that the extent of structural alteration occurring while multiple sovereignty persists is our best sign of the depth of the permanent change to be produced by the revolution.

Over the long run, revolutions appear to change the direction of structural transformation to the extent that they produce a transfer of power. Where there is a large transfer of power among classes, the particular coalition that gains power profoundly shapes the subsequent political development of the country. Barrington Moore's comparison of India, Japan, China, the United States, France, England, Germany, and Russia makes precisely that point. Military coups almost never produce any significant structural change—despite the declarations of national renovation which ritually accompany them these days—because they involve minor rearrangements among extremely limited sets of contenders. The apparent exceptions to this rule—revolutions from above, like those of Japan and Turkey—ordinarily have a reforming segment of the ruling elite effectively cutting off their fellows from further access to power and forming coalitions with classes previously excluded from power.

However, the organizational means available to those who emerge from the revolution with power affect the degree of structural transformation deliberately promoted by the government in postrevolutionary years. In a discussion of the effect of the "confining conditions" under which a revolutionary coalition seized power on its subsequent capacity to transform social organization, Otto Kirchheimer comes to the conclusion that the emergency powers accruing to states during twentieth-century crises, e.g., World War I, drastically reduced the confinement of power-holders.

> The revolution of the 20th Century obliterates the distinction between emergency and normalcy. Movement plus state can organize the masses because: (a) the technical and intellectual equipment is now at hand to direct them toward major societal programs rather than simply liberating their energies from the bonds of tradition; (b) they have the means at hand to control people's livelihood by means of job assignments and graduated

rewards unavailable under the largely agricultural and artisanal structure of the 1790s and still unavailable to the small enterprise and commission-merchant-type economy of the 1850s and 1860s; (c) they have fallen heir to endlessly and technically refined propaganda devices substituting for the uncertain leader-mass relations of the previous periods; and (d) they faced state organizations shaken up by war dislocation and economic crisis. Under these conditions Soviet Russia could carry through simultaneously the job of an economic and a political, a bourgeois and a post-bourgeois revolution in spite of the exceedingly narrow basis of its political elite. On the other hand, the premature revolutionary combination of 1793–94 not only dissolved quickly, but left its most advanced sector, the *sans-culottes,* with only the melancholy choice between desperate rioting—Germinal 1795—or falling back into a pre-organized stage of utter helplessness and agony. (Kirchheimer, 1965, p. 973)

This analysis can be generalized. Despite the "confining conditions" faced by the French revolutionary coalitions of 1789–94, they seized a state apparatus which was already exceptionally centralized and powerful by comparison with those which had grown up elsewhere in the world. They were able to use that great power, in fact, to destroy the juridical structure of feudalism, effect large transfers of wealth, subjugate the Church, build a mass army. The nineteenth-century revolutionaries who repeatedly seized control of the Spanish state grabbed an apparatus whose extractive and repressive capacities were insufficient to any task of national transformation. It is true that the mobilization of contenders which occurs before and during a revolution may itself facilitate a further national mobilization, putting resources at the disposal of the state which were simply unavailable before the revolution: property, energy, information, loyalties. That is, indeed, a characteristic strategy of contemporary national revolutions. Yet I am inclined to think that in general the already-accrued power of the state much more strongly affects the probability that fundamental structural change will issue from the revolution than does the extent of mobilization during the revolution itself.

   These facile generalizations, I confess, do not do justice to a critical question. For on our estimate of the long-run effects of different kinds of revolution must rest our judgment as to whether any particular revolution, or revolutionary opportunity, is worth its cost. I estimate some revolutions as worth it, but at present no one has enough systematic knowledge about the probable structural consequences of one variety of revolution or another to make such estimates with confidence.

   Except, perhaps, in retrospect. Historians continue to debate what the English, French, and Russian revolutions cost and what they accomplished, but in those cases (at least in principle) the historians are dealing with actualities rather than probabilities. That potential certainty, however, has a self-destructive side; when it comes to an event as sweeping as the English Revolution, al-most every previous event which left some trace in seventeenth-century England is in some sense a "cause," and almost every subsequent event in the country and its ambit constitute in some sense an "effect." Making cause-and-effect analysis manageable in this context means reducing the revolution to certain essentials, identifying the sufficient conditions for those essentials, and then specifying subsequent events which would have been unlikely without the revolutionary essentials. In fact, therefore, the causal analyses of real, historic revolutions and of revolutions in general converge on statements of probability.

HISTORICAL APPLICATION OF THE SCHEME

How, then, might we set concrete historical experience into the frame devel-oped in this essay? If the point was to account for the revolutions and the vari-ous forms of collective violence occurring within that experience—and that would have to be the point of employing this particular scheme—the historical work would consist of grouping political actions within that experience into governments, contenders, polities, coalitions, processes of mobilization, and so on. Other fundamental phenomena, like changes in beliefs, demographic change, or economic crisis, would enter the account only insofar as they af-fected the pattern of contention for power.

In the case of France since 1500, for example, the largest frame for analysis would be set by the interplay of a gradually industrializing and urbanizing population with a national state which was first emerging, then establishing priority, then consolidating its hold on the population. The two sets of processes did of course depend on each other to some degree—for example, in the way that expanding taxation drove peasants to market goods they would otherwise have kept at home, on the one hand, and the way that the degree of commer-cialization of land, labor, and agricultural production set stringent limits on the return from land taxes, income taxes, or excise taxes, on the other. But their timing differed. The epic periods of French state-making were the times of Louis XIII and Louis XIV. Those periods had their share of economic tur-moil; furthermore, they saw both a significant increase in the importance of Paris and a few other major cities for the life of France as a whole and the spread of trade and small-scale manufacturing through the towns and villages of the entire country. Yet in terms of productivity, organization, and sheer numbers of persons involved, the urbanization and industrialization of the nineteenth and twentieth centuries produced incomparably greater changes. To oversim-plify outrageously, the drama consists of two acts: first a fast-growing state act-ing on a slow-moving population and economy; then a fast-changing popula-tion and economy dealing with a consolidating state.

In analyzing this interplay, we need to ask over and over, for different places and points in time, what contenders for power (potential and actual) the existing social structure made available, and what governments the existing stage of state-making left them to contend over. For example, the most strenuous current debates over the history of the turbulent French seventeenth century pivot, first, on the extent to which the national government squeezed out its provincial rivals and acquired firm control over French social life; second, and even more strenuously, on the extent to which the operative divisions of the population were social classes in something like a Marxian sense (see Mousnier, 1970; Lebrun, 1967; Porchnev, 1963; Lublinskaya, 1968). The analytic scheme I have laid out provides no pat answers to those serious questions; if it did, one would have to suspect that its principal assertions were true by definition. It does suggest that the tracing of the actual issues, locations, and personnel of violent encounters in seventeenth-century France will provide crucial evidence on the pace and extent of political centralization, as well as on the nature of the groups which were then engaged in struggles for power. The basic research remains to be done. Yet the recurrent importance of new taxation in seventeenth-century rebellions, the apparent subsidence of those rebellions toward the end of the century, and the frequent involvement of whole peasant communities in resistance to the demands of the crown all point toward a decisive seventeenth-century battle among local and national polities.

Not that all struggle ended then. As Tocqueville declared long ago, the Revolution of 1789 pitted centralizers against guardians of provincial autonomies. The contest between crown and provincial parlements (which led quite directly to the calling of the Estates General, which in turn became the locus of multiple sovereignty in 1789) continued the struggle of the seventeenth century. Throughout the Revolution, in fact, the issue of predominance of Paris and the national government remained open, with tax rebellions, movements against conscription, and resistance to the calls of the nation for food recurring when the center weakened and when its demands increased sharply. Most of the events of the so-called peasant revolt of 1789 took the form of food riots and other classic eighteenth-century local conflicts.

Yet they did not just represent "more of the same," because they came in extraordinary clusters, because they occurred in the presence of multiple sovereignty, and because the participants began to form coalitions with other contenders for power. Now, the exact contours of the major contenders and the precise nature of their shifting alliances are the central issues of the big debates about the history of the Revolution (for example, see Cobban, 1964; Mazauric, 1970). However, it is at least roughly true to say that a loose coalition among peasants, officials, urban commercial classes, and small but crucial groups of urban craftsmen and shopkeepers carried the revolution through its first few years, but that coalition began to fall apart irrevocably in 1792 and 1793. Looked at from the point of view of coalition formation and multiple sovereignty, the Revolution breaks into a whole series of revolutions, from the first declaration of sovereignty by the Third Estate in 1789 to the final defeat of Napoleon in 1815.

Again, in this perspective we begin to grasp the significance of materially trivial events, like the taking of the Bastille. The attack by Parisians on the old fortress finally set a crowd unambiguously against the regime, revealed the uncertain commitment of part of the armed forces to the government, brought the king to his first accessions to the popular movement (his trip to the National Assembly on the fifteenth of July and his trip to Paris on the seventeenth), and stimulated a series of minor coups in the provinces.

> Until July 14th the handful of revolutionary institutions set up in the provinces were disparate and isolated. Henceforward most of the towns and many of the villages of France were to imitate Paris with extraordinary swiftness. During the weeks that followed the fall of the Bastille there arose everywhere revolutionary Town Councils of permanent committees, and citizen militias which soon assumed the name of national guards. (Godechot, 1970, p. 273)

So if we date the start of multiple sovereignty from the Third Estate's Tennis Court Oath to remain assembled despite the prohibitions of the king, we still have to treat July fourteenth and its immediate aftermath as a great expansion of the revolutionary coalition.

Obviously the four proximate conditions for revolution enumerated earlier—coalitions of contenders advancing exclusive alternative claims, commitment to those claims, coalitions between members of the polity and the revolutionary contenders, failure of the government to suppress them—appeared in the France of 1789. What cannot be obvious from a mere chronicle of the events is how long each of the conditions existed, what caused them, and whether they were sufficient to cause the collapse of the old regime. At least these are researchable questions, as contrasted with attempts to ask directly whether the rise of the bourgeoisie, the increase in relative deprivation, or the decay of the old elite "caused" the Revolution. What is more, they call attention to the probable importance of shifting coalitions among lawyers, officials, provincial magnates, peasants, and workers in the nationwide political maneuvering of 1787 to 1789, as well as to the effect of "defensive" mobilization of peasants and workers in response to the multiple pressures impinging on them in 1789.

The Revolution produced a great transfer of power. It stamped out a new and distinctive political system. Despite the Restoration of 1815, the nobility and the clergy never recovered their prerevolutionary position, some segments of the bourgeoisie greatly enhanced their power over the national government, and the priority of that national government over all others increased permanently. In Barrington Moore's analysis, whose main lines appear correct to me, the predominance of the coalition of officials, bourgeois, and peasant in the decisive early phases of the Revolution promoted the emergence of the attenuated parliamentary democracy which characterizes postrevolutionary France (Moore, 1966, Ch. 2; for explication and critique, see Rokkan, 1969; Rothman, 1970a; Stone, 1967). On that scale and in the details of public administration, education, ideology, and life style, the Revolution left a durable heritage.

None of the old conflicts, nevertheless, disappeared completely with the Revolution. The counterrevolutionary Vendée, despite having come close to destruction in 1793, again rose in rebellion in 1794, 1795, 1799, 1815, and 1832. Further revolutions overcame France as a whole in 1830, 1848, and 1870. Most of the characteristic forms of resistance to demands from the center—food riots, tax rebellions, movements against conscription, and so on—continued well into the nineteenth century. Indeed, these "reactionary" forms of collective action reached their climax around the Revolution of 1848 before fading rapidly to insignificance.

From that mid-century crisis we can date the definitive reduction of the smaller polities in which Frenchmen had once done most of their political business, the virtual disappearance of communal contenders for power, the shift of all contenders toward associational organization and action at a national level. The massive urbanization and industrialization of France, which gained momentum after 1830, transformed the available contenders for power, especially by creating a large, new urban working class based in factories and other large organizations. From that point on, the demonstration, the meeting, the strike were the usual matrices of collective violence, as well as the settings in which an enormous proportion of all struggles for power went on. Collective violence evolved with the organization of public life and the structure of political action.

QUALIFICATIONS AND CONCLUSIONS

This all-too-quick sketch of the evolution of political conflict in France lacks two elements which belong to the conventional wisdom: the explanation of popular protests before the Revolution as angry or impulsive responses to economic crisis, and the explanation of popular protests after the Revolution as angry or impulsive responses to the strains of rapid industrialization and urbanization. Before the Revolution, the characteristic forms of "protest" were much more closely tied to the major political transformations of the time than any such account makes plausible. After the Revolution, such detailed studies of conflicts and collective violence as we have reveal no particular tendency for "protest" to come in the wake of rapid and unsettling structural change. Indeed, the evidence runs in the other direction, with rapid urbanization and industrialization appearing to *reduce* the capacity for collective action of the populations most directly affected, and thereby to reduce their involvement in collective violence.

The general implications of our analytic scheme also run in that direction. We have good reason to expect large structural transformations to change the character of collective violence and the probability of revolution through their effects on the emergence and decline of different contenders for power. So far the most coherent general theory of those linkages we have comes from the Marxist tradition. We have no reason, on the other hand, to expect a close relationship between the pace of structural transformation (or even the amount of displacement and personal disruption it causes) and the extent of protest, conflict, and collective violence. The mediating variables are political ones: the nature of repression, the established means for acquisition and loss of power, the predominant modes of mobilization, the possibilities for coalition-making, the concentration or dispersion of government.

I have to admit that the method employed in this essay to build up to that conclusion has some unfair facets to it. The discussion often takes on the air of confident demonstration, when at best it actually contains a series of illustrations of an incompletely articulated theoretical scheme. Worse still, the discussion often proceeds as though "polity," "contender," and other entities were acting realities rather than hypothetical constructs. The truly responsible alternative would be, first, to present the full scheme as a wholly theoretical statement and, only then, to review the evidence pro and con. I fear, however, that under those conditions all readers would fall exhausted before the end. The high level of abstraction of the first part would leave them gasping and groggy; the second part would drown them in the sea of diverse details needed to make a reasonable case in the present scattered evidence. So I have fashioned a life-saving compromise.

The systematic evidence required to put the scheme to the test would fall into three parts. First would come the examination of individual polities working out from governments to the persons interacting with them, to see whether the behavior of men with respect to those governments falls into sufficiently coherent patterns of mobilization and contention for power to justify the use of those concepts, and to determine whether the patterns are measurable in some reliable way. Second would come the tracing of the operation of those polities over considerable spans of time, in order to determine whether frequent changes of membership do accelerate the rate of collective violence, whether challenger-member coalitions do characteristically precede revolutions, and so on. Third—if the process got that far—would come systematic comparisons among similar and dissimilar polities in order both to make sure that the negative cases behave as predicted and to detect the major variables producing differences in the experience of revolution and collective violence between one kind of political organization and another. We stand a long, long way from that third test.

Even if the scheme does encompass the materials reviewed here, it may well have a much more limited application than my discussion has implied. I have worked out the scheme with the experience of western Europe over the last few hundred years very much in view. That is an important experience but only a small portion of man's total political life. The arguments embedded in the scheme tend to assume two conditions which are generally characteristic of modern western Europe and rather uncommon in world-historical perspective: (1) the presence of relatively exclusive, strong, centralized instruments of government, especially in the form of states; (2) the unimportance of corporate solidarities, like large kin groups, which crosscut and penetrate the governmental structure. The first limitation makes the scheme fit Prussia a little more comfortably than Spain. The second limitation causes less uncertainty in northern Europe than around the Mediterranean. Outside Europe and its immediate offshoots, the difficulties multiply.

No doubt one could attempt to generalize the analysis by converting the importance of the states and the power of corporate solidarities into variables to be accounted for in their own right. For my part, I have too little confidence in the strength of the argument on its home ground and too little certainty that the word "revolution" retains any common meaning when extended beyond the world of relatively strong states and weak corporate solidarities to propose that extension now. The first problem is to examine systematically the fit between the model and the range of modern Western experience. My excuse for imposing the argument on readers whose primary interests may lie with Africa or Oceania is the sense that most areas of the world are now moving willy-nilly toward a condition of strong states and weak corporate solidarities. To the extent that such a view of the world is mistaken, most theories of collective violence and revolution based on modern Western experience—including the one unfolded in this essay—will prove irrelevant to the future of political conflict.

All qualifications and apologies understood, what sorts of answers does this argumentation yield for the meteorological and engineering questions with which we began? The likelihood of collective violence within a given country in a given period depends especially on the number of mobilized challengers bidding for membership in the polities of that country without effective coalitions with members of the respective polities, the number of established members losing position within those polities, and the extent to which the agents of the governments involved routinely employ violence in the repression of collective action. If that is true, the ways to raise the level of collective violence are to mobilize new contenders, break existing coalitions between challengers and members, accelerate the loss of position by established members, and increase the routine use of violence in repression.

The analysis of revolutions identified four proximate conditions: (1) the emergence of coalitions of contenders making exclusive alternative claims to control of the government; (2) the expansion of commitment to those claims by members of the population under control of that government; (3) the formation of coalitions between members of the polity and members of the revolutionary bloc; (4) repressive incapacity of the government's agents. A revolutionary strategy is therefore to mobilize new contenders with exclusive claims to control of the government, encourage acceptance of those claims by people outside the contenders, form coalitions with established members of the polity, and neutralize the government's repressive capacity. That, come to think of it, is more or less what effective revolutionaries have been doing all along.

REFERENCES

This list contains (1) every work mentioned in the text, (2) a few of the main sources relied on for points of fact which were not cited in the text, (3) a few more general reviews of topics taken up in the essay which are especially valuable as synthetic statements or as sources of bibliography.

Adams, Graham, Jr. (1966). *The Age of Industrial Violence.* New York: Columbia University Press.

Alberoni, Francesco (1968). *Statu nascenti.* Bologna: Il Mulino.

Amann, Peter (1962). "Revolution: a redefinition." *Political Science Quarterly* 77:36–53.

Amiot, Michel, *et al.* (1968). *La violence dans le monde actuel.* Paris: Desclée de Brouwer for Centre d'Etudes de la Civilisation contemporaine.

Anderson, Bo (1968). "Revitalization movements: an essay on structure and ideology in a class of exclusive underdog systems." *Acta Universitatis Upsaliensis* 17:347–75.

Anderson, Eugene N., and Pauline R. Anderson (1967). *Political Institutions and Social Change in Continental Europe in the Nineteenth Century.* Berkeley and Los Angeles: University of California Press.

Andreski, Stanislav (1968). *Military Organization and Society.* Berkeley: University of California Press.

Ardant, Gabriel (1965). *Théorie sociologique de l'impôt.* Paris: SEVPEN, 2 vols.

Arendt, Hannah (1970). *On Violence.* New York: Harcourt, Brace and World.

Aston, Trevor, ed. (1965). *Crisis in Europe, 1560–1660.* London: Routledge and Kegan Paul.

Baechler, Jean (1970). *Les phénomènes révolutionnaires.* Paris: Presses Universitaires de France, series SUP.

Bendix, Reinhard (1967). "Tradition and modernity reconsidered." *Comparative Studies in Society and History* 9:292–346.

Bernoux, Philippe *et al.* (1969). *Violences et société.* Paris: Editions Economie et Humanisme/Editions Ouvrières.

Bienen, Henry (1968). *Violence and Social Change: A Review of Current Literature.* Chicago: University of Chicago Press.

Birnbaum, Norman (1969). *The Crisis of Industrial Society*. London: Oxford University Press.

Blok, Anton (1974). *The Mafia of a Sicilian Village*. New York: Harper and Row.

Boulding, Kenneth E. (1962). *Conflict and Defense: A General Theory*. New York: Harper.

Braudel, Fernand (1966). *La Méditerranée et le monde méditerranéen à l'époque de Philippe II,* 2nd edition. Paris: Colin, 2 vols.

Brinton, Crane (1938). *The Anatomy of Revolution*. New York: Norton.

Brode, John (1969). *The Process of Modernization: An Annotated Bibliography on the Sociocultural Aspects of Development*. Cambridge: Harvard University Press.

Calhoun, Daniel (1970). "Studying American violence." *Journal of Interdisciplinary History* 1:163–85.

Calvert, Peter (1970). *A Study of Revolution*. Oxford: Clarendon Press. Copyright © 1970 by Oxford University Press. Reprinted by permission.

Chapman, Brian (1970). *Police State*. London: Pall Mall.

Chevalier, Louis (1958). *Classes laborieuses et classes dangéreuses à Paris pendant la première moitié due XIXe siècle*. Paris: Plon.

Chorley, Katherine (1943). *Armies and the Art of Revolution*. London: Faber and Faber.

Cobb, Richard (1961–63). *Les armées revolutionnaires, instrument de la Terreur dans les départements*. Paris: Mouton, 2 vols.

——————— (1970) *The Police and the People*. Oxford: Clarendon Press.

Cobban, Alfred (1964). *The Social Interpretation of the French Revolution*. Cambridge: Cambridge University Press.

Conant, Ralph W., and Molly Apple Levin, eds. (1969). *Problems in Research on Community Violence*. New York: Praeger.

Connery, Donald, ed. (1968). "Urban riots: violence and social change." *Proceedings of the Academy of Political Science,* 29: entire issue. Also published separately.

Conot, Robert (1968). *Rivers of Blood, Years of Darkness*. New York: Bantam.

Converse, Elizabeth (1968). "The war of all against all: a review of *The Journal of Conflict Resolution,* 1957–1968." *Journal of Conflict Resolution* 12:471–532.

Cornelius, Wayne A., Jr. (1970). "The political sociology of cityward migration in Latin America." In Francine F. Rabinowitz and Felicity M. Trueblood (eds.), *Latin American Urban Annual*. Beverly Hills, Cal.: Sage Publications.

Crozier, Brian (1960). *The Rebels: A Study of Post-War Insurrections*. London: Chatto and Windus.

Daumard, Adeline (1963). *La bourgeoisie parisienne de 1815 à 1848*. Paris: SEVPEN.

Davies, C. S. L. (1969). "Révoltes populaires en Angleterre (1500–1700)." *Annales: Economies, Sociétés, Civilisations* 24:24–60.

Davies, Ioan (1970). *Social Mobility and Political Change*. London: Pall Mall.

Deutsch, Karl (1953). *Nationalism and Social Communication*. Cambridge: MIT Press.

Eckstein, Harry, ed. (1964). *Internal War: Basic Problems and Approaches*. New York: Free Press.

_____ (1965). "On the etiology of internal wars." *History and Theory* 4:133–63.

Eisenstadt, S. N. (1963). *The Political Systems of Empires*. New York: Free Press.

_____ (1966). *Modernization: Protest and Change*. Englewood Cliffs, N.J.: Prentice-Hall.

Eisinger, Peter K. (1973). "The conditions of protest behavior in American cities." *American Political Science Review* 67:11–28.

Ellul, Jacques (1969a). *Autopsie de la revolution*. Paris: Calmann-Levy.

_____ (1969b). *Violence*. London: SCM Press.

Engels, Friedrich (1886). *Herrn Eugen Dühring's Umwälzung der Wissenschaft*. Zürich: Volksbuchhandlung.

Etzioni, Amitai (1968). *The Active Society*. New York: Free Press.

Fanon, Frantz (1964). *The Wretched of the Earth*. New York: Grove.

Feierabend, Ivo K., and Rosalind L. Feierabend (1966). "Aggressive behaviors within polities, 1948–1962: A cross-national study." *Journal of Conflict Resolution* 10:249–71.

Feuer, Lewis S. (1969). *The Conflict of Generations: The Character and Significance of Student Movements*. New York: Basic Books.

Fink, Clinton F. (1968). "Some conceptual difficulties in the theory of social conflict." *Journal of Conflict Resolution* 12:412–60.

Fischer, Wolfram (1966). "Social tensions at early stages of industrialization." *Comparative Studies in Society and History* 9:64–83.

Fletcher, Anthony (1968). *Tudor Rebellions*. London: Longmans.

Fogelson, Robert M., and Robert B. Hill (1968). "Who riots? A study of participation in the 1967 riots." *Supplemental Studies for the National Advisory Commission on Civil Disorders*. Washington: Government Printing Office.

Fried, Morton H. (1967). *The Evolution of Political Society: An Essay in Political Anthropology*. New York: Random House.

Friedrich, Carl J., ed. (1966). *Revolution*. New York: Atherton.

Furet, Francois (1963). "Pour une définition des classes inférieures à l'époque moderne." *Annales: Economies, Sociétiés, Civilisations* 18:459–74.

Gamson, William A. (1968a). *Power and Discontent*. Homewood, Ill.: Dorsey.

_____ (1968b). "Stable unrepresentation in American society." *American Behavioral Scientist* 12:15–21.

Geertz, Clifford (1968). "Is America by nature a violent society?" *New York Times Magazine*, April 28.

Gillis, John (1970). "Political decay and the European revolutions, 1789–1848." *World Politics* 22:344–70.

Girard, Louis (1961). *Etude comparée des mouvements révolutionnaires en France en 1830, 1848, et 1870–71*. Paris: Centre de Documentation Universitaire, 3 parts.

Gluckman, Max (1963). *Order and Rebellion in Tribal Africa.* New York: Free Press.

Godechot, Jacques (1970). *The Taking of the Bastille.* New York: Scribner.

Gorz, Andre (1969). *Réforme et révolution.* Paris: Seuil.

Gossez, Rémi (1967). *Les ouvriers de Paris. I. L'Organisation, 1848–1851.* La Roche-sur-Yon: Imprimerie Centrale de l'Ouest.

Graham, Hugh Davis, and Ted Robert Gurr, eds. (1969). *Violence in America; Historical and Comparative Perspectives.* Washington: Government Printing Office.

Gurr, Ted (1968). "A causal model of civil strife: a comparative analysis using new indices." *American Political Science Review* 62:1104–24.

——————— (1969). *Why Men Rebel.* Princeton: Princeton University Press.

Guzmán, German, *et al.* (1962). *La Violencia en Colombia.* Bogota: Universidad Nacional.

Harris, P. M. G. (1972). "Occupational change, historical variations in mobility, and the origins of American leadership in the 18th, 19th, and early 20th centuries." Unpublished paper presented to the Conference on International Comparisons of Social Mobility in Past Societies, Institute for Advanced Study, Princeton, N.J.

Henry, Louis (1956). *Anciennes familles génévoises.* Paris: Institut National d'Etudes Demographiques: Cahiers Travaux et Recherches, 26.

Hibbs, Douglas A., Jr. (1973). *Mass Political Violence: A Cross-National Causal Analysis.* New York: Wiley.

Hirschman, Albert O. (1970a). *Exit, Voice, and Loyalty: Responses to Decline in Firms, Organizations, and States.* Cambridge: Harvard University Press.

——————— (1970b). "The search for paradigms as a hindrance to understanding." *World Politics* 22:329–43.

Hobsbawm, E. J. (1959). *Primitive Rebels.* Manchester: Manchester University Press.

——————— (1969). *Bandits.* New York: Delacorte Press.

Hobsbawm, E. J., and George Rudé (1968). *Captain Swing: A Social History of the Great Agrarian Uprising of 1830.* New York: Pantheon.

Hofstadter, Richard (1970). "Reflections on violence in the United States." In Richard Hofstadter and Michael Wallace (eds.), *American Violence: A Documentary History.* New York: Knopf.

Huntington, Samuel P. (1968). *Political Order in Changing Societies.* New Haven: Yale University Press.

Janos, Andrew (1966). *Revolutionary Change.* Boston: Little, Brown.

Johnson, Chalmers (1966). *Revolutionary Change.* Boston: Little, Brown. Reprinted by permission.

Kantor, Mildred B., ed. (1965). *Mobility and Mental Health.* Springfield, Ill.: Thomas.

Kaplan, Morton A., ed. (1962). *The Revolution in World Politics.* New York: Wiley.

Kiernan, V. G. (1965). "State and nation in western Europe." *Past and Present* 31:20–38.

Kirchheimer, Otto (1965). "Confining conditions and revolutionary breakthroughs." *American Political Science Review* 59:964–74.

Kirkham, James F., Sheldon G. Levy, and William J. Crotty (1970). *Assassination and Political Violence.* Washington: Government Printing Office.

Kornhauser, William (1959). *The Politics of Mass Society.* New York: Free Press.

Kort, Fred (1952). "The quantification of Aristotle's theory of revolution." *American Political Science Review* 46:486–93.

Krader, Lawrence (1968). *Formation of the State.* Englewood Cliffs, N.J.: Prentice-Hall.

Kuczynski, Jürgen (1967). *Darstellung der Lage de Arbeiter in Frankreich von 1789 bis 1848.* Berlin: Akademie Verlag.

Kuhn, Thomas S. (1962). *The Structure of Scientific Revolutions.* Chicago: University of Chicago Press.

Langer, William L. (1969). *Political and Social Upheaval, 1832–1852.* New York: Harper and Row.

Laqueur, Walter (1968). "Revolution." *International Encyclopedia of the Social Sciences* 13:501–7. New York: Macmillan. Copyright © Crowell Collier and Macmillan. Reprinted by permission.

Larson, Reidar (1970). *Theories of Revolution, from Marx to the First Russian Revolution.* Stockholm: Almquist and Wiksell.

Lebrun, Francois (1967). *Le XVIIe siècle.* Paris: Colin; Collection "U."

Lefebvre, Georges (1924). *Les paysans du Nord pendant la Révolution française.* Lille: Robbe.

Leiden, Carl, and Karl M. Schmitt (1968). *The Politics of Violence: Revolution in the Modern World.* New York: Spectrum.

Leites, Nathan, and Charles Wolf, Jr. (1970). *Rebellion and Authority. An Analytic Essay on Insurgence Conflicts.* Chicago: Markham.

Lenin, V. I. (1967a). "The valuable admissions of Pitirim Sorokin." In *Selected Works.* New York: International Publishers, 3:31–38. First published 1918.

——————— (1967b). "What is to be done? Burning questions of our movement." In *Selected Works,* 1:97–256. Written in 1901–1902.

Lipset, Seymour Martin, and Earl Raab (1970). *The Politics of Unreason: Right-Wing Extremism in America, 1790–1970.* New York: Harper and Row.

Lorwin, Val (1958). "Working class politics and economic development in western Europe." *American Historical Review* 63:338–51.

Lowi, Theodore (1971). *The Politics of Disorder.* New York: Basic Books.

Lublinskaya, A. D. (1968). *French Absolutism: The Crucial Phase, 1620–1629.* Cambridge: Cambridge University Press.

Lupsha, Peter (1969). "On theories of urban violence." *Urban Affairs Quarterly* 4:273–96.

Mao Tse-tung (1965a). "The Chinese Revolution and the Chinese Communist Party." In *Selected Works of Mao Tse-Tung*. Peking: Foreign Languages Publishing House, 2:305–34. First published in 1939.

——————— (1965b). "On protracted war." In *Selected Works*, 2:113–94. Written in 1938.

Marx, Karl (1958). "The eighteenth Brumaire of Louis Bonaparte." In Karl Marx and Frederick Engels, *Selected Works*. Moscow: Foreign Languages Publishing House, 1:243–344. First published in 1852.

——————— (1964) *Pre-Capitalist Economic Formations*, E. J. Hobsbawm, ed. London: Lawrence and Wishart.

Masotti, Louis H., and Don R. Bowen, eds. (1968). *Civil Violence in the Urban Community*. Beverly Hills, Cal.: Sage Publications.

Mazauric, Claude (1970). *Sur la Révolution française*. Paris: Editions Sociales.

Monnerot, Jules (1969). *Sociologie de la révolution*. Paris: Fayard.

Meier, Richard L. (1966). "Some thoughts on conflict and violence in an urban setting." *American Behavioral Scientist* 10:11–21.

Melotti, Umberto (1965). *Rivoluzione et società*. Milan: La Culturale.

Milliband, Ralph (1969). *The State in Capitalist Society*. London: Weidenfeld and Nicholson.

Mehden, Fred von der (1973). *Comparative Political Violence*. Englewood Cliffs, N.J.: Prentice-Hall.

Moore, Barrington, Jr. (1966). *Social Origins of Dictatorship and Democracy: Lord and Peasant in the Making of the Modern World*. Boston: Beacon Press. Reprinted by permission.

——————— (1969). "Revolution in America?" *New York Review of Books*, January 30, pp. 6–12.

Morris, Desmond (1967). *The Naked Ape*. New York: Dell.

Mousnier, Roland (1967). *Fureurs paysannes: Les paysans dans les révoltes du XVIIe siècle (France, Russie, Chine)*. Paris: Calmann-Levy.

——————— (1970). *La plume, la faucille et le marteau*. Paris: Presses Universitaires de France.

Mühlmann, Wilhelm E. (1961). *Chiliasmus und Nativismus*. Berlin: Dietrich Reimer.

Nardin, Terry (1971a). "Theories of conflict management." *Peace Research Reviews*, Vol. IV, No. 2:1–93.

——————— (1971b). *Violence and the State: A Critique of Empirical Political Theory*. Beverly Hills, Cal.: Sage Publications. Professional Papers, Comparative Politics Series, Series 01–020, Vol. 2.

——————— (1972). "Conflicting conceptions of political violence." In Cornelius P. Cotter (ed.), *Political Science Annual*. Vol. 4. Indianapolis: Bobbs-Merrill.

Nelson, Joan (1969). "Migrants, urban poverty and instability in new nations." Cambridge: Harvard Center for International Affairs, Occasional Paper No. 22.

_____ (1970). "The urban poor: disruption or political integration in third world cities?" *World Politics* 22:393–414.

Nettl, J. P. (1967). *Political Mobilization*. London: Faber and Faber.

Nieburg, H. L. (1969). *Political Violence*. New York: St. Martin's.

Oberschall, Anthony (1969). "Rising expectations and political turmoil." *The Journal of Development Studies* 6:5–22.

_____ (1972). *Social Conflict and Social Movements*. Englewood Cliffs, N.J.: Prentice-Hall.

Olson, Mancur, Jr. (1963). "Rapid economic growth as a destabilizing force." *Journal of Economic History* 23:529–62.

_____ (1965). *The Logic of Collective Action*. Cambridge: Harvard University Press.

Paret, Peter, and John W. Shy (1964). *Guerrillas in the 1960s*. New York: Praeger.

Payne, James L. (1965). *Politics and the Military in Modern Spain*. Stanford: Stanford University Press.

Penrose, L. S. (1952). *The Objective Study of Crowd Behaviour*. London: Lewis.

Pinkney, David (1964). "The crowd in the French Revolution of 1830." *American Historical Review* 70:1–17.

Plumb, J. H. (1967). *The Origins of Political Stability: England 1675–1725*. Boston: Houghton Mifflin.

Porchnev, Boris (1963). *Les soulèvements populaires en France de 1623 à 1648*. Paris: Mouton.

Richardson, Lewis F. (1960). *Statistics of Deadly Quarrels*. Pittsburgh: Boxwood Press.

Ridker, Ronald (1962). "Discontent and economic growth." *Economic Development and Cultural Change* 10:1–15.

Rimlinger, Gaston V. (1960). "The legitimation of protest: a comparative study in labor history." *Comparative Studies in Society and History* 2:329–43.

Rokkan, Stein (1968). "The structuring of mass politics in the smaller European democracies." *Comparative Studies in Society and History* 10:173–210.

_____ (1969). "Models and methods in the comparative study of nation building." *Acta Sociologica* 12:52–73.

Rosenau, James N., ed. (1964). *International Aspects of Civil Strife*. Princeton: Princeton University Press.

Rothman, Stanley (1970a). "Barrington Moore and the dialectics of revolution: an essay review." *American Political Science Review* 64:61–82.

_____ (1970b). *European Society and Politics*. Indianapolis: Bobbs-Merrill.

Rubenstein, Richard E. (1970). *Rebels in Eden: Mass Political Violence in the United States*. Boston: Little, Brown. Reprinted by permission.

Rudé, George (1959), *The Crowd in the French Revolution*. Oxford: Oxford University Press.

Rudé, George (1970). *Paris and London in the 18th Century*. London: Collins.

Rule, James, and Charles Tilly (1971). "1830 and the unnatural history of revolution." *Journal of Social Issues* 28:49–72.

Rummel, Rudolf J. (1966). "Dimensions of conflict behavior within nations." *Journal of Conflict Resolution* 10:65–74.

Russell, Diana (1974). *Rebellion, Revolution, and Armed Force*. New York: Academic.

Russett, Bruce M. (1964). "Inequality and instability: the relation of land tenure to politics." *World Politics* 16:442–454.

Schattschneider, E. E. (1960). *The Semi-Sovereign People*. New York: Holt, Rinehart and Winston.

Sharp, Gene (1973). *The Politics of Nonviolent Action*. Boston: Porter Sargent.

Short, James F., Jr., and Marvin E. Wolfgang, eds. (1972). *Collective Violence*. Chicago: Aldine-Atherton.

Shorter, Edward, and Charles Tilly (1971). "The shape of strikes in France, 1830–1960." *Comparative Studies in Society and History* 13:60–86.

Silver, Allan (1967). "The demand for order in civil society: a review of some themes in the history of urban crime, police and riots." In David J. Bordua (ed.), *The Police*. New York: Wiley.

Skolnick, Jerome (1969). *The Politics of Protest: Violent Aspects of Protest and Confrontation*. Washington: Government Printing Office.

Smelser, Neil J. (1963). *Theory of Collective Behavior*. New York: Free Press.

Snyder, David, and Charles Tilly (1972). "Hardship and collective violence in France." *American Sociological Review* 37:520-32.

Soboul, Albert (1958). *Les sans-culottes parisiens en l'an II*. La Roche-sur-Yon: Potier.

Sorel, Georges (1961). *Reflections on Violence*. New York: Macmillan. First published in 1906.

Sorokin, Pitirim A. (1962). *Social and Cultural Dynamics*. New York: Bedminster. III. Fluctuation of Social Relationships, War and Revolution.

Spilerman, Seymour (1970). "The causes of racial disturbances: a comparison of alternative explanations." *American Sociological Review* 35:627–49.

Stinchcombe, Arthur (1965). "Social structure and organizations." In James March (ed.), *Handbook of Organizations*. Chicago: Rand McNally.

Stone, Lawrence, ed. (1965). *Social Change and Revolution in England, 1540–1640*. London: Longmans.

——————— (1966). "Theories of revolution." *World Politics* 18:160–76.

——————— (1967). "News from everywhere." Review of Barrington Moore, Jr., *Social Origins of Dictatorship and Democracy*. *New York Review of Books*, August 24.

Taft, Philip, and Philip Ross (1969). "American labor violence: its causes, character and outcome." In Graham and Gurr, 1969.

Tanter, Raymond, and Manus Midlarsky (1967). "A theory of revolution." *Journal of Conflict Resolution* 11:264–80.

Thompson, E. P. (1963). *The Making of the English Working Class.* London: Gollancz.

Tilly, Charles (1969). "Collective violence in European perspective." In Graham and Gurr, 1969.

_____ (1975). "European statemaking and theories of political transformation." In Charles Tilly (ed.), *The Formation of National States in Western Europe.* Princeton: Princeton University Press.

Tilly, Louise (1971). "The food riot as a form of political conflict in France." *Journal of Interdisciplinary History* 2:23–57.

Tilly, Richard (1971). "Popular disorders in nineteenth century Germany: a preliminary survey." *Journal of Social History* 4:1–40.

Toch, Hans (1969). *Violent Men: An Inquiry into the Psychology of Violence.* Chicago: Aldine.

Tocqueville, Alexis de (1955). *The Old Regime and the French Revolution.* New York: Doubleday Anchor. Originally published in 1856.

Tønnesson, Kåre (1959). *La défaite des sans-culottes.* Oslo: Presses Universitaires/ Paris: Clavreuil.

Touraine, Alain (1968). *La société post-industrielle.* Paris: Seuil.

Trotsky, Leon (1965). *History of the Russian Revolution.* London: Gollancz, 2 vols. Originally published in 1919.

Wakeman, Frederic, Jr. (1966). *Strangers at the Gate; Social Disorders in South China, 1839–1861.* Berkeley: University of California Press.

Wallace, Anthony F. C. (1956). "Revitalization movements." *American Anthropologist* 58:264–81.

Walter, E. V. (1969). *Terror and Resistance: A Study of Political Violence.* New York: Oxford University Press.

Walzer, Michael (1970). "The revolutionary uses of repression." In Melvin Richter (ed.) *Essays in Theory and History: An Approach to the Social Sciences.* Cambridge: Harvard University Press.

Wilkinson, Paul (1971). *Social Movement.* London: Pall Mall.

Wolf, Eric (1969). *Peasant Wars of the Twentieth Century.* New York: Harper and Row. Reprinted by permission.

Wolfgang, Marvin E., and Franco Ferracuti (1967). *The Subculture of Violence.* London: Tavistock.

Womack, John, Jr. (1969). *Zapata and the Mexican Revolution.* Cambridge: Harvard University Press.

Wrigley, E. A. (1969). *Population and History.* New York: McGraw-Hill.

Zolberg, Aristide R. (1968). "The structure of political conflict in the new states of tropical Africa." *American Political Science Review* 62:70–87.

SOCIAL STRUCTURE AND POLITICS

ARTHUR L. STINCHCOMBE

INTRODUCTION

When we judge a political act we usually ask three fundamental questions: (1) Which side are we on if we support (or oppose) this action? (2) Is the action intelligent in the sense that it really will achieve the objectives it is meant to achieve? (3) Is it responsible, in the sense that it will not, in the process of achieving what it sets out to do, destroy social structures we would like to preserve because they serve other values we hold dear? We can be on the right side but act stupidly and disloyally. We can act with the greatest competence to serve alien interests and to destroy what is a permanent achievement of modern civilization. We can be loyal to permanent values embedded in a social system in a way that defies reason and aids our enemies.

Ideologies must always answer the three basic political questions of partisanship, or the road to power; of intelligence, or what to do with power; and of loyalty, or the limitation of power in the light of higher values. Ideologies may answer these questions by denying them, but critics will demand that the questions be denied specifically. An intelligent partisan may deny that there are any perma-

Nelson W. Polsby as an editor of this *Handbook* evidently took the attitude that every sentence of this essay should be worthy of being associated with his name as well as satisfying the much weaker criterion of being worthy of being associated with mine. As a result there are many fewer sentences here than in the first draft. I have benefited also from critical comments by Susan Eckstein, Gudmund Hernes, Maurice Pinard, a faculty seminar on society and politics at the University of Essex, and a number of seminar audiences to which I presented parts of this material in England. I consent to the general academic norm that I am responsible for any defects that remain, but whatever merits the essay may have are a collective product. My consent to this norm is grudging.

nent values independent of his or her party's political success (for instance, Trotsky in *Their Morals and Ours*); an intelligent loyalist may discreetly ignore the problem of who inside a country benefits from "national" success (a good example is Admiral Mahan's *The Influence of Sea Power on History*); a loyal partisan may naively identify patriotism and service of his or her own interest in a way that is ultimately unintelligent and self-destructive, as the South African government does today.

A sociology of politics, to have relevance to the central ideological questions of the time, must address itself to the questions of partisanship, intelligence, and loyalty. We want to know why people take the side they do in political conflicts, why they act so ineffectively (or competently), and why they limit their conflicts (if they do) by considerations of collective welfare and permanent values. Unfortunately political sociology has grown rather than developed, so that topics are not treated in relation to their importance but in relation to the convenience of investigation and of popular interest. The topics we will treat in this essay therefore stand in different relations to the historical tradition.

An individual's choice of a party and a party's choice of a social base, which together make up the sociology of partisanship, have had the great good fortune to have been linked in the West to the earliest form of public opinion poll, the election. Further, who is going to win the election, and why, are most easily studied by the same method as the election decision is made, by a "scientific" opinion poll.[1] Consequently, from earliest modern history we have had quantitative measures of partisanship. We know a good deal about it. Even in this field we know more about the loyalty of members of the public than we know about the other half of the partisan relationship, the active attempt by parties to win adherents. But generally the problem in this area is to present a theory or scheme that reduces an immense variety of material to some understandable order. The sins we commit are likely to be sins of omission of well-known connections between social structure and partisan attachments, missed because we have put on the blinders involved in an oversimplified theory.

With political intelligence the problem is the opposite. There are about as many ideas about what policy is intelligent and what policy is stupid as there are analysts. Since there are no clear measures of what we want to explain—the dependent variable—explanations tend to reduce questions of the intelligence of policy either to questions of partisanship (the "sociology of knowledge" approach) or to the problem of the individual talent of leaders. If the first section of this chapter is abstract and schematic in an attempt to deal with the quantity of data, the second section is abstract and schematic in response to the lack of data.

The section on loyalty has all the difficulties of the section on political intelligence, with the added difficulty of an almost hopeless theoretical confusion in the literature about what is to be explained. In general what we want to know is what determines the degree of commitment to a larger normative order, which limits today's partisan conflicts by referring them to a deposit of past conflicts in a normative constitution of a society. This constitution defines what other values, such as legality or civil liberty, must be taken into account in the intelligent solution of a particular problem, and it mobilizes people's sense of identity in the defense of the normative order under which they live.

But commitment to a normative order is given its vigor by people's *interests* in the rights defended by that order. Conservatism can be defined and is typically defined by conservatives as loyalty to the normative order. But one can be loyal to the creative principles of a normative order as well as to its current content; one may, for instance, favor democracy because it gives a chance for reform as well as because one happens to be doing pretty well under a democracy that does not go too far. Thus questions of loyalty are in fact intimately intertwined with questions of partisanship, and it is always an interesting question theoretically whether one would be as loyal to norms as one claims to be now if the loyalty cost him or her more. This problem makes it very difficult to disentangle the definition of loyalty from the definition of conservative partisanship.

Commitment to a normative order can be a way of extending the rights given by that order to more people, or it can be a way of maintaining a monopoly over those rights for people now defined as inside the normative boundary. The relation of a normative order to people outside it can be conceived as a chance to extend justice or a chance to stamp out competing normative systems. Loyalty can be a way of organizing faith, hope, and charity on a large scale, transcending narrow personal interests in the larger interest. But loyalty can also organize distrust, despair, and hostility on a large scale, transcending personal inclinations to be a Good Samaritan. Finally loyalty to a normative order can be a demand that the norms expand in content and increase in complexity so as to regulate more human activity in the light of all its human effects. Or it can be a demand for simplification of the normative order, for its reduction to mindless principles of "my country right or wrong," for the suppression of alternative interpretations as heresy.

It seems that in fact conservatism, restriction of normative boundaries to create monopolies, organized distrust and hostility, and oversimplification of normative questions all go together and have common causes. It also seems that seeing the normative system as a set of opportunities for extending justice, averting ingroup monopoly of the rights of the system, organizing charity under the normative system, and expanding the complexity of normative opinions also tend to go together and to have common causes. This dilemma will occupy us further before we get near to the causes of loyalty to a normative order and to a social system in which this normative order is embedded.

As far as possible we will state the theory of this essay in a form so that it might apply to tribal politics, office politics in business corporations, totalitarian politics, and so forth. But in order to get some empirical content of a familiar kind into the abstract schemata, we will hold modern Western experience in the forefront. Concretely the parties in the section on partisan attachment will mostly be ordinary Western political parties, and attachments will mean votes; we will make side glances at proxy fights in corporations or political representation in totalitarian systems. Concretely the agencies that add intelligence to policy preferences in our analysis will be bureaucratic planning agencies or congressional committees, and we will make only passing reference to discussions among tribal elders. And concretely the normative systems to which general loyalty is attached which we will analyze will be nations and ethnic groups. Since we must of necessity be excessively abstract, it is better to suggest the empirical criticism to which the abstraction is subject by reference to as specific a body of empirical material as possible. What we have then is a theory of modern Western democratic politics, with a penumbra of suggestions about primitive, authoritarian, bureaucratic, or other political orders.

SOCIAL STRUCTURE AND THE UTILITY OF POWER: EXPLAINING PARTISAN ATTACHMENTS

The most important social relation in the internal politics of a government or other corporate group is the attachment of individuals and small groups to organizations that actively try to gain power and make policy in the system. Groups that actively try to gain power in any kind of system will be called "parties" (Weber, 1953). These include, then, ordinary political parties in national, state, or local governments, factions in one-party states, challengers and defenders of boards of directors in proxy fights, contending factions or parties in trade unions, conspiratorial groups that try to mount coups d'etat, totalitarian parties that actively suppress potential contenders for power, and so forth. Usually in well-organized groups legitimate powers are attached more or less permanently to specific offices, so the usual object of contention for parties is incumbency in an office. However, revolutionary parties often try to create dual governments (Trotsky, 1932, pp. 206–15)—soviets or works councils, for example—which concentrate power in a new set of roles. Attachment to parties, involving any kind of contribution to their achievement of power, will be called a "partisan attachment." The activity done for the party may range from contributing a vote to guerrilla warfare.

The usual unit that has an effective partisan attachment is a small group, a group constituted on a basis different from politics. Families, friendship groups, associations such as trade unions, communal groups such as ethnic groups or local communities all tend to be much more politically homogeneous than would be expected if one analyzed the variety of nongroup causal forces bearing on the individual. In stable political systems such as that in the United States there is a high degree of continuity of the partisan color of families, friendship groups, trade unions, ethnic groups, local communities, states, etc. People interpret the relation of distant power conflicts to their own interests and values mainly by listening to people they trust, people with whom they have multiple contacts in many areas of life, people who, they are convinced, are on their side and have their interests at heart. The main determinants of party success are the partisan attachments of small nonpolitical groups.

Parties are generally divided into an active core of people who make plans for taking power and who actively seek to stimulate partisan attachments, and a relatively inactive group of followers whose partisan attachments are stimulated by the active core and who do activities of a relatively simple kind. In corporations there are people who vote proxies and people who give proxies; in national politics there are people who nominate and campaign for candidates and people who vote for them; in revolutions there are cadres and the masses. A theory of the creation of the social relation of partisan attachment must therefore explain two things: (1) how much vigor the active core puts into stimulating partisan attachments and (2) the willingness of the electorate or the masses to contribute to the active core's power aims.

The Utility of a Partisan Attachment to the Party

The net utility to a party of another partisan attachment besides those it already has, for instance a new group of voters, depends on how much this new attachment increases the chances of winning power for the party and how much the party has to sacrifice to get the attachment. In general the active core of a party is interested both in getting into office and also in having office on its own terms. Politically active people are generally more ideological than the general population—they have definite ideas about how power should be used. Adding a new partisan attachment generally involves promising something to the last group that comes in; this dilutes the utility of winning. On the other hand it increases the probability of winning or the amount of power won (e.g., the number of offices won). The balance between these contrasting forces determines the amount of effort and the amount of adaptation of the party program which the active core is willing to put into creating new partisan attachments.

For simplicity we will treat the party as if it has a single set of utilities, a single definition of what winning is, and a single ideology about what to do with power. This single utility function is worked out in the internal politics of the party—in party conventions, in the exercise of the party whip in the legislative chambers, in deals in smoke-filled rooms, and so forth. It very often happens in fact that what we usually call a party has little ideological unity. The American national parties are essentially coalitions of state parties for the purpose of electing presidents. These coalitions are not idea free, by any means. But quite often, for example, southern Democrats advocated the election of a Democratic president for reasons opposite from the reasons offered in Harlem. It is not so much that presidents lie to people in Harlem (or in the South), though that is certainly involved to some extent, as that a vote for a Democratic president in New York means that, if elected, that president will use his federal powers to support the Democratic party of New York in state matters, which favors black people. He will use his federal powers to support the Democratic party of Alabama as well (or at least he used to), which in Alabama matters used to be more anti-black than the Republicans. This is inconsistent only *to the degree that* there exists a national moral and legal system that guarantees the rights of blacks, whose support or emasculation is in question. There used to be no such national structures. When they developed to a significant degree, the alliance of northern blacks and southern racists to elect a president broke down very rapidly. The northern members of the coalition more and more insisted on national policies that alienated southern racist voters, who then moved toward third parties and toward the Republicans.

The utility of an added partisan attachment to the party appears to depend on three main factors: (1) the arrangements of the power system (e.g., the electoral laws) and the number of attachments of opposing parties, which determines how much an added partisan attachment affects the probability of winning, (2) the social, ideological, and policy distance between the potential added attachment (e.g., the marginal voter) and the present constituency of the party, and (3) the relative power within the party of people who are primarily interested in power (office seekers) as compared with those who are primarily interested in ideological objectives (militants).

Party Competition and Utility of Attachments

Let us consider the ideal case, in which each partisan attachment has approximately equal weight—a one-man, one-vote electoral system. No system of course ever fits exactly this ideal, for richer or more prestigious people are more valuable to a party than are people with less money and status. Election polls and parliamentary votes often approximate the one-man, one-vote ideal.

There are two main ways of organizing such systems in Western democracies: (1) single ballot plurality elections, as is typical in the United States and England and (2) some version of proportional representation or multiple ballot elections, as is typical on the European continent. The central distinction between these two types of system, from our point of view, is that the value of additional partisan attachments in a plurality system depends on the differences between the parties: if both parties have close to half of the electorate as their expected vote if they do nothing, then an additional attachment of a group can greatly change the probability of winning. If the opposition is very small or splintered, then the first few votes that put a party ahead of its largest opponent are very valuable, but after that an additional vote does not add much to the chances of winning. If the opposition is large and one's own party is small, then the first few extra votes still do not give one much chance.[2] In a system of proportional representation, each additional vote increases the power of the party equally. Multiple ballot systems have much the same effect.[3]

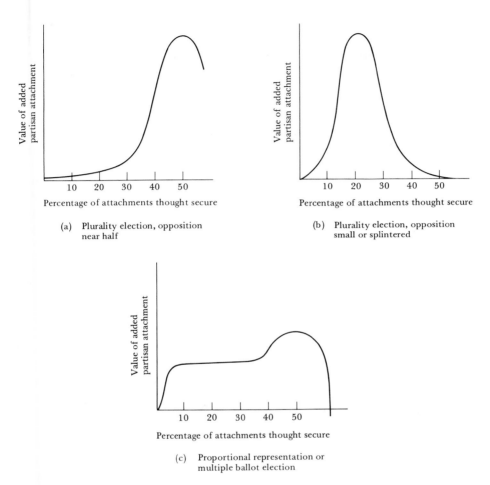

Fig. 1. The Increment of Probability of Winning ("Value of Added Partisan Attachment") Brought by a Marginal Vote, for Different Electoral Situations and Different Sizes of Parties

Thus we have the situation as graphed in Fig. 1. In plurality elections in competitive districts (Fig. 1a) we would expect the major contenders to be intensively seeking additional adherents. We would expect small parties or candidates of minor interest and small popularity to generate little enthusiasm by activists. Such a situation encourages two strongly organized parties to be highly active in seeking partisan attachments. As one party grows beyond 50 percent of the firm attachments, the value of additional attachments to the minority party is cut down, and its organization tends to weaken. Thus one-party constituencies are a frequent outcome of such situations, if the two-party balance is upset for a considerable period.

When the opposition in a plurality election is splintered or small, as it is for example in the primary contests in many southern states in the United States (Key, 1949, pp. 36–57), intense activity tends to be generated by small factions in their local areas as a candidate tries to get a little ahead of the pack. But there is little motivation to continue to build a stable faction with half or more of the voters. Thus if shifting small factions characterize a plurality electoral system, there are few forces tending to create large stable parties (see Fig. 1b).

In a proportional representation or multiple-ballot system, each additional partisan attachment brings an approximately equal increment of power. We would expect that in such systems the level of activity of a party would depend very little on its size. Both large and small parties would actively seek partisan attachments. One-party constituencies with weak and inactive oppositions should be rare.

The proportional representation graph (Fig. 1c) has a hump around 50 percent, just as the graph of plurality with strong opposition (1a) has, though the hump of the former is not as high. Once a party's vote gets beyond 50 percent of firm attachments, it can rule by itself in most parliamentary systems without coalitions and so need make no more compromises beyond those that got it elected. The reason the hump is not as high is that in a coalition a party can win part of the time with smaller votes than if it weren't in a coalition, so the increment in the probability of winning is not as high at the 50 percent mark. That is, the nearer a party gets to 50 percent, the more nearly it already rules in its own right, because the compromises it has to make to form a government become less onerous. Nevertheless when, for example, the Gaullists in France became the first party with a real chance at a majority, they, like any Anglo-Saxon party, compromised away intransigent demands of some of their extreme right wing militants to get the loyalty of center voters. The summed graph below (3c), after going negative, goes back positive to indicate the Gaullist pattern of resurgent interest in marginal voters around 50 percent.

There may be special circumstances in which an individual party that is a member of a coalition, by being in a pivotal position, may reap most of the benefit of the hump in the middle. If, for example, neither the Conservative nor the Labour party in Britain had a majority, then what looks like the first few percent the Liberal party picks up is *also* the last few percent of (say) the Liberal-Labour coalition party. Thus in a few circumstances the hump of the last few votes that make a majority coalition might fall to a party anywhere along the axis. We will ignore these unusual circumstances in what follows. As a practical matter they are sufficiently unusual so as to be mainly a part of the ideology of minor parties rather than a political reality.

Compromise of Ideology and Utility of Attachments

The greater the social and ideological distance of a voter or a group of voters from the militants of a party, the more of the ideas and values of the militants will have to be given up in order to add the new partisan attachment. The relevant distance is not the true distance, but rather the distance perceived by the militants. When a party is still small, it is likely that it has not exhausted the constituency it potentially has without compromising its ideas, programs, and camaraderie. As it grows beyond this point, it tends to exhaust its natural constituency and has to dilute its ideological and social purity in order to recruit new voters.

By the ideology of the party I mean the set of policies and ideas the presently active core party members would be prepared to advocate. It includes such things as the ethnic balance of the slate they would put forward, the local machines whose support they will welcome and reward with control over federal agencies and patronage within their jurisdiction, the proposed agenda of action for the next government, what class interests are considered especially sacred, and so on. The ideology is, of course, a deposit of past resolutions of the dilemma of choosing between ideology and power. Once a party has incorporated, for example, the Catholic ethnic groups, it can no longer use an anti-Catholic ideology. Once a large number of civilized people have become active in a party, it is hard for the party to take up the cruder forms of racism. There may be latent ideological factions in a party, such as latent racists, returned from the colonies, in the English Conservative party, who will enthusiastically urge the incorporation of their potential allies outside the party (e.g., working-class racists) on the grounds that it wins elections while in fact being mainly concerned with changing the ideology of the party. Thus the analysis here is "piecewise historical." A historically given party makes compromises and alliances in this election, and these compromises involve co-optation of a new group of active people into the party and perhaps losing some others. This structure and history then become the ideological stock with which the party enters the following election.

Parties vary in the extent of the natural constituency implied by their ideology and their practices of solidarity. The extreme is Bill Bailey of the song that parodies the splitting in radical American political sects. By the time Bill Bailey dies, he has split with so many comrades that he is the only member of the Marxist League. He finally refuses to enter Red Heaven because Karl Marx "ain't no comrade of mine."

The cost then of each new partisan attachment in terms of ideological, programmatic, and social purity tends to increase with the size of the party. This is represented in Fig. 2. The top of the graph of Fig. 2 represents zero value (i.e., zero cost). As the cost increases, the value that we will want to *sub-*

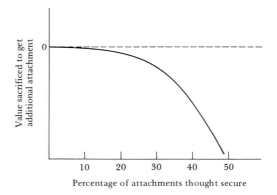

Fig. 2. The Cost of Added Partisan Attachments in Terms of Principles Sacrificed, as a Function of Proportion of the Electorate in the Party

tract from the total value of the added partisan attachment increases. Hence we have drawn the value of each additional vote, considered now in terms of party principles that have to be sacrificed, as a negative value. The greater the cost of the additional vote, the farther toward the bottom of the graph the line goes. In Fig. 2, I have made the arbitrary assumption that the Bill Bailey effect starts to set in around 20 percent of the electorate already in the party. Beyond 20 percent something has to be sacrificed to get new voters.

Clearly the net value to a party of an added partisan attachment will be the difference between its positive value in increasing the chances of winning and its cost in terms of principles sacrificed. We can get an idea of the shapes of this net value in different political circumstances by adding the appropriate graph in Fig. 1 to the graph in Fig. 2. This is done in Fig. 3.

As long as the net value of an additional partisan attachment is positive, we will expect the active core of a party to devote itself to creating the partisan social relations. In plurality elections with strong oppositions (see Fig. 3a) we will expect the active core of small parties to keep the parties small and sectarian, not seriously seeking additional attachments. For larger minorities the value of a vote for winning becomes serious just when the sacrifice of taking in impure members becomes serious. That is, as we go from small parties at the left of the graph to larger parties near the 50 percent mark, the contrasting growth of the value of a vote for winning and the growth of the cost of a vote in terms of principles just about balance. We would expect that, with a great deal of ambivalence and internal battles, the larger minority party would pursue the main chance at the cost of its principles. We would expect such large parties in

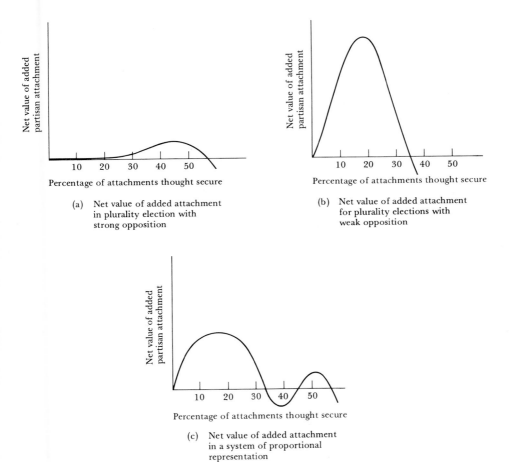

(a) Net value of added attachment
     in plurality election with
     strong opposition

(b) Net value of added attachment
     for plurality elections with
     weak opposition

(c) Net value of added attachment
     in a system of proportional
     representation

Fig. 3. Party Size Related to Net Value of Added Partisan Attachment for Different Electoral Situations (sums of figs. 1 and 2)

competitive plurality systems to do well at the social function of "aggregating interests," that is, working out compromises before the election.

When the party is confronted with weak or splintered opposition or when it is in a proportional representation system, the equilibrium size—the point at which it stops actively seeking partisan attachments—should generally be less than half of the vote. We have, however, guessed that there should be a "Gaullist hump," a new disposition to compromise ideology for the sake of power, when the party nears half of the vote in proportional representation systems.[4]

The argument above implies that the ideological unity of the party is most problematic just before elections, when the party has to give up what it believes in to get more voters. Yet what we observe in reality is that the raw wounds of the party convention are papered over for the electorate by a spate of traditional party ideology in election speeches. That is, it looks as if the party gets *more* rather than *less* traditionally ideological as an election approaches, slipping back into its unidealistic, twisted positions again when it gets back into power. It looks as if the compromises are for the purpose of governing, while the ideology is to get elected with, the reverse of the argument above.

But the purpose of election rhetoric is mainly to activate partisan attachments—to bring the leaders of communities, ethnic groups, trade unions, chambers of commerce, and so on into activity so that the traditional allegiances will show up at the polls. The recruitment of new groups takes place at conventions; but new groups do not actually yield their votes until the election. Between the convention and the election the new group leaders are supposed to prepare to deliver the votes they have promised in return for their places on the ticket or the concessions in policy that they have demanded. Thus there are two forms of ideology: the form that enters into the actual compromises that bring together people in the party who have half their interests in common and half their interests opposed, and the form that activates and excites attachments and pretends that the result of shifting and uneasy compromise is a simple soul, issued from the hand of God, who will be our next president.[5]

Internal Party Politics and Utility of Attachments

Different people put different weights on the value of winning and of ideological or social homogeneity. We could define the pure office seeker (or opportunist) as a person whose utility function for an added partisan is that of the appropriate graph of Fig. 1 (depending on the electoral system). That is, he or she sees no cost whatever in adapting the party program and the party's composition to win the election. To him or her personally, the cost of added partisan attachments in terms of principles sacrificed (his or her personal figure 2) runs along the zero line all the way across, even if Satan himself stands on the 49 percent point. The pure militant (or ideologue) would be a person who sees no virtue in winning. He or she would sympathize with the attitude Trotsky is supposed to have had when a former comrade entered the Kerensky cabinet in Russia: "Such petty ambition; to give up his place in world history for a portfolio!" His or her value for an added partisan would be given entirely by the shape of Fig. 2. He or she is likely to see the party more as a vehicle for educating a misled public into the ideology of the party than as a vehicle for winning power in the political system. Pure militants write leaflets rather than run for office and have contempt for a person who actually would like to be president. Generally speaking, elected officials tend to be office seekers, to value winning highly and programmatic unity less; activists in the party who do not hold or aspire to office for themselves tend to be militants, to value the ideology and social compatibility of the party highly. As the aphorism of French politics has it, there is more in common between two deputies, one of whom is a socialist, than between two socialists, one of whom is a deputy.

The balance of power within the party of the office seekers and the militants therefore determines which one of the utility functions for added partisan attachments generally determines party policy. Parties largely created and run by office holders and candidates, such as the French Radicals or parties of the United States, tend to be opportunistic, as do many of the military conspiracies that carry out coups d'etat in South America or the Middle East. People in coups as well as in elections quite often would like to be president, and the assumption that they usually have some ideological objection to the government and represent right wing forces is probably wrong. The CIA, for example, may give the leaders of a coup enough support to knock down a government, but it is because the leaders are opportunists rather than because they agree with the CIA pro–United States ideology that they are corrupted from outside. Contrariwise those parties in which elected officials are subordinated to militants, such as the Communist parties of France and Italy, tend to exhaust their natural constituencies and then rely on "education" rather than compromise to bring them to power. Parties created as offshoots of other movements with active, aware, and powerful leaders, such as the socialist parties (offshoots of a much wider labor movement) and religious parties (offshoots of church organization) of western Europe, tend to have severe recurrent internal conflicts about how much opportunism they ought to show. All parties tend to show these conflicts, to be sure (Polsby and Wildavsky, 1968), but when the militants have a power base separate from the party, the conflicts are more acute. In general, by examining what would happen if the appropriate graphs in figs. 1 and 2 were reduced or amplified before adding them to get Fig. 3, we would expect that the more powerful the militants, the smaller the parties would be and the more ideologically homogeneous their constituencies would be.

The Formation of Partisan Attachments in the Population

There is a good deal of talk by various students of political development about a crisis of mobilization of traditional populations, that is, a crisis of the formation of the partisan attachments we have been discussing in this section. For instance, Eisenstadt (1966) talks about the mobilization of the periphery without appropriate "flexibility" of the center, which creates irrational protest movements during development. Germani (1962) has suggested that the explanation for Argentina's special political problems might be the extraordinarily rapid modernization and urbanization that took place from about 1890 to 1930. Kornhauser (1959) has noted the correlation of rapidity of industrialization in Scandinavia (Denmark slow, Sweden intermediate, Norway fast) with the radicalism of their labor movements. Trotsky's theory (1932) of "combined and uneven development" suggests essentially that underdeveloped countries grow faster toward modern capitalism than England did, so that the contradiction between new political demands and older political forms is more intense and revolution is more likely than it was in England. A theory of the formation of partisan attachments in a population ought therefore to take into account the creation of revolutionary populations during capitalist development.

Apathy, Revolution, and Incorporation

Let us define three states for small groups, interest groups, or individuals with respect to their relation to the political system: (1) apathetic or unmobilized, (2) revolutionary, or (3) politically incorporated. By apathetic, I mean that the group and its members do not consider themselves appreciably affected by the fates of parties, coups d'etat, or presidents. The contest for power does not, to their minds, affect them. Perhaps their support has no value for the parties, so the elite does not try to stir them up; perhaps they believe that all parties will follow the same obnoxious policy; perhaps they do not know anything about politics; perhaps their friends who used to be politically active have been shot.

By revolutionary ("utopian" or "anomic" are in some cases synonymous, and not all revolutionary movements are made up primarily of "revolutionaries" as I define them), I mean that a group or the individuals in it have become aware of the relation between their fate and the party that holds power; but they have no mechanism inside their own group for making a decision, in negotiation with other interests in the society, which is regarded as binding on the group and which will make the group decide to sacrifice its minor interests in order to get its major interests. If a group wants to win everything and not to allow opposing interests any representation in the political system, then it will be called revolutionary. The International Workers of the World (the Wobblies) were revolutionary when they would sign no collective contracts, because a collective contract admitted that some rights of the employer were legitimate and hence supported the system of wage-slavery. Ethnic movements that want to deny all political power to racists are likewise revolutionary.

If, on the other hand, a trade union has decision-making mechanisms whereby the union can and does sign contracts giving capitalists some rights of great importance to capital (sacrificing less important worker interests) in order to get concessions on questions of great immediate importance to workers, then the union is politically incorporated. The concession of legitimacy to capitalist interests may be symbolically temporary, "until the revolution," but as long as it is effectively binding on the workers as a group, we will call the workers incorporated. By incorporation then we mean that a group has agreed to pursue its own interests in the light of a quasi-constitutional system that recognizes that other people will be pursuing other interests, sometimes conflicting with those of the group. Political incorporation means that a group enters into a system of exchange in which, in order to secure its central interests, it sacrifices peripheral interests (or "long-run" interests, understanding by this that if a group could in the long run destroy the opposing interests, it could pursue its own interests more effectively); it sacrifices these peripheral, or long run, interests so that other groups get some of their central interests and thereby also become incorporated.

Of course, it takes at least two parties to enter into an exchange. If, for instance, the whites in Rhodesia or Mississippi refuse to give Blacks their central interests, no matter what Blacks offer to give up, then there is no way for Blacks to be politically incorporated. Likewise during the period of War Communism after the Russian Revolution, the Bolsheviks were unwilling to compromise with any capitalist interests; the New Economic Policy set up the conditions for the incorporation of some capitalist interests in the Soviet political system.

We distinguish then (1) groups and individuals that want nothing from the political system, (2) groups that want everything from the system, and (3) groups that are willing to sacrifice some things they want in order to get other things from the system. The counterpart of these attitudes about what groups want is attitudes toward opposing interests. Groups can believe (1) that the opposition has already won and will keep winning, (2) the opposition interests are illegitimate and will not be recognized at all when things are set to rights, or (3) the opposition has to be forced to give them what they most want, in return for which they will give the opposition its legitimate interests. Workers' movements for instance can (1) cave in before they start, (2) be revolutionary-socialist, wanting to root out the bourgeoisie, or (3) be democratic-socialist, urging the cause of workers with the power at their disposal but not destroying bourgeois parties.

I suggest that the small groups and interest organizations of a particular segment of the population rarely go directly from apathy to political incorporation. After they become aware of the impact of the political system on their lives, they first want "Freedom Now" as a potential means for redressing their grievances and bettering their lot. The rate at which they become aware and activated is determined by factors such as their urbanization, education, the formation of organizational communications channels, and the like (Deutsch, 1953). Then the rate at which they become politically incorporated depends on how fast organizations develop within the group which can bind the group to bargains for part of their freedom, and the willingness of other groups (especially political parties with a chance of gaining power) to grant them part of their freedom.[6]

A Picture of the Evolution of Revolutionaries

We can think of the evolution of a particular population group, for instance the peasants of a society who come of age at a particular time (a "cohort" of peasants), as having the structure of Fig. 4.

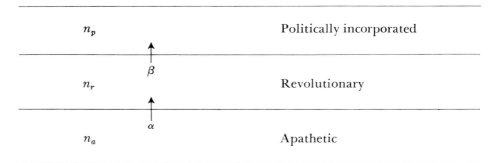

Fig. 4. The Evolution of a Population Governed by Its Rate of Activation (α) and Its Rate of Political Incorporation (β)

People in Fig. 4 start in the apathetic category. The rate per year at which they move into the revolutionary category, in which they want everything from the system, is α (alpha). The rate at which they are incorporated, once mobilized into politics, is β (beta). This rate will depend, as we have discussed above, on the utility their support has for different parties. This utility in turn depends on the parties' need for their support in order to win, on the group's social and ideological distance from the parties' old constituencies, and on the degree to which office seekers rather than militants control the parties.

If we supposed (which of course we do not—we are trying to outline the structure of the problem) that the rates of activation and of incorporation were constants, then the pattern of development over time would be exactly that of a system of radioactive decay with an intermediate isotope, where apathetic atoms decay into revolutionary atoms at a rate of α and the intermediate isotope revolutionary atoms decay into incorporated atoms at a rate β.[7]

Clearly if the transition into the revolutionary state goes on at a reasonably high rate and the political system is not "flexible" enough to incorporate this new surge, there can be a long period in which there are a lot of revolutionaries. For instance, if the population group is mobilized at the rate of .05 per year, while it is incorporated, once it has mobilized, at the rate of .03 per year, there will be a maximum number of revolutionaries in the group after about 25 years, at which time 45 percent of the population would be revolutionary. If, in contrast, people are being mobilized at the rate of .05 per year but incorporated (once mobilized) into political parties at a rate of .50 per year, then the maximum number of revolutionaries comes after about 5 years, at which time about 7 percent of the population will be revolutionaries. If the rate of activation, α, and the rate of incorporation, β, are constant, the number of revolutionaries will eventually decline. In the meantime, of course, a large number of revolutionaries may cause a revolution.

The purpose of this fictional model is to suggest how the static analysis can be related to the historical developments of partisan attachments. By making the coefficient β depend on the structural arrangements of parties and interest groups and the coefficient α depend on urbanization, literacy, and other forces of economic development, we can construct a theory of political instability during modernization. An appropriately constructed theory might have been able to predict, for example, that England during the nineteenth century, having a competitive two-party system and being confronted by a relatively slow rate of change in the education and urbanization of the poor, would have only a few near-revolutions by a Chartist movement split between compromisers and revolutionaries. Higher rates of growth combined with dictatorial government, for example in eighteenth-century France or early-twentieth-century Mexico and Argentina, would tend to produce more intransigent revolutionary movements and more governmental instability.

In particular, if in a one-party state there are a number of poorly incorporated groups or one of the poorly incorporated groups is very large, then the growth of activism can create a latent opposition. A political entrepreneur may be able to bring this latent set of revolutionary groups into a coalition in a very short period of time. If the minority party could not see its way to a majority, it may have failed to mobilize the revolutionary groups. If the majority party thought it was secure, it may have failed to be interested. But a new party that doesn't know of political impossibilities may bring a flash flood of opposition in one-party states. If there is a legitimate electoral system, this opposition can lead to the sudden formation of powerful "third" parties. The sudden conviction of a new party that it can win, glued together perhaps with apocalyptic visions of doing away with the whole old regime, can create radical (right or left) surges.[8] If the one-party state has suppressed electoral devices for the incorporation of surge movements, the result of a weakening of these controls is often the creation of revolutionary dual governments (Trotsky, 1932).

Both types of surge movements tend to create parties in which ideology dominates over internal bargaining, militants dominate over opportunists, latent internal conflicts of interest are papered over with rhetoric, and opposition interests outside the new party are denied legitimacy and are denied representation if the movement takes power. Such a party may then create another one-party regime, in which new oppositions have nowhere to go, or it may gradually "degenerate" into a bargaining system, often accompanied by military repression of objections by militants who still remember the revolutionary vision. Many nationalist revolutions with a dose of social vision, as for instance in Mexico or India, produce in the long run quite complex and effective internal bargaining structures within the single state party. The bargains the newly mobilized poor accept in these bargaining systems may not, of course, be very beneficial to the poor.

The Structure of Political Coalitions

We can imagine then a "state of nature" in a developing polity whose latent interest groups—nationalities and ethnic groups, regions, industries, social classes, etc.—are becoming mobilized. Each group has a latent wish for society to be restructured so that all of its grievances will be solved, all of its aspirations fulfilled. The question that faces the polity is to impose "realistic" goals on these groups. This involves getting the groups to arrange their grievances and aspirations in an order of priority, to impose on their disorganized, utopian aspirations a utility function that will say how much of which aspirations they would give up in order to get how much of alternative aspirations. This order of priorities, or utility function, is what makes possible the bargaining among interest groups to form political coalitions (parties or coalitions of parties); for each coalition is a more or less explicit agreement among the component interests that the benefits they will get from the coalition are sufficiently valuable to motivate partisan attachment to it (Coleman, 1966b).

Thus the formation of a political coalition consisting of a party and a developing mobilized group involves two interdependent processes. The political system produces a series of *offers* to the group, or rather to the potential leaders of the group. The offers specify which goals of the group (and of its leaders) the offering party will try to satisfy, without sacrificing the present social base of the party. These offers then make up the *resources* with which these potential leaders—the ones who are interested in the coalition—attempt to obtain leadership of their group, that is, to construct a decision-making apparatus within the group that will enable it to make demands on the coalition and to accept bargains in the name of the group. These potential leaders are usually in competition with other potential leaders, both those backed by alternative parties and the radicals who want "Freedom Now."

Thus there are three main sources of variation among political systems in the policy objectives (or parties) that a given group such as the proletarians or the clergy or the landlords follow. The first source of variation is that given groups may have, for historical and situational reasons, different compositions of interests or patterns of mobilization of interests. For instance, in the United States and Argentina much of the new proletariat were immigrants; in England, France, and Germany they were mostly natives. This gives cultural questions (e.g., attitudes toward prohibition in the United States or toward World War II in Argentina) as opposed to class interests different weights in the American and Argentine proletariats than in the English, French, and German proletariats.

A second source of variation is the structure of offers by the dominant contending parties in the political system. For instance, the Democratic party in the United States offered federal and state jobs and political influence to ethnic city machines,[9] while the dominant elites in Argentina excluded the immigrants as far as possible from the political system, leaving to Perón the construction of a political coalition in which ethnic interests (urban interests) could be represented.

A third source of variation is the internal competition among potential leaders of the group. Samuel Gompers, by happening onto the right organizational devices and rhetorical presentation of union aims so that the governmental support to unions in World War I went to him, won out over much more talented socialist leaders and came to be recognized as the leader of working men. Thus the businesslike character of American unions is to some considerable degree (there is a lot of debate of course about how far any other kind of unions could have grown up in the American environment) the product of a particular "unfortunate" relation of socialist ideology to the war effort at the time when the war administration of Wilson was ready to support union organization.[10] Or to take another example, the development of organizational technology by the Bolshevik party during the Russian Revolution gave an advantage to a type of potential leader of workers different from the type of leadership that developed before, so that labor movements that have grown up in many countries since 1917 have had distinctive international ties. The presence of communist union leaders in France or Italy provided competition between Russian-oriented leaders and locally oriented leaders but gave an organizational advantage to the Russian-oriented ones because of their mastery of communist organizational technique. The preference of French workers for pro-Soviet foreign policy is therefore due not to their own love for Russia but to communists' winning organizational leadership in their unions. Different social conditions in France and England (e.g., different degrees of concentration of the workers in Paris as opposed to London) may facilitate a different kind of organization among French workers than among English ones (e.g., possibly more political unions).

It seems more convenient to treat the policy of the party to which a given social group gives attachment on the aggregate level as a part of the sociology of different coalitions, rather than as a part of the sociology of alliances (i.e., from the point of view of the group). The reason for this is that it takes at least two sets of people to make an alliance, and such relational behavior is generally simpler to analyze when viewed from the point of view of the system as a whole than when viewed from the viewpoint of the group. Even if the major demands of a social group were identical in different political systems, there would be many possible structures of coalitions. If, for instance, the major demand of workers is high wages and the right to organize and strike and the major demand of the Catholic Church is support for parochial church schools, coalitions both of the church with workers (Christian socialism) and of the church with capitalism (clerical conservatism) are viable. Insofar as the public policies that dominate the utility function of a group are not directly contradictory to those of another group, the group can compromise on different of its minor utilities so as to make a deal with different alternative interests. Thus the number of viable coalitions in a political system is usually much larger than the number of actually existing coalitions. From the point of view of an individual group, e.g., the workers, this means that the party it supports in one system may have an ideology different from the party it supports in another system because the parties include different "noncompeting" interests. Thus, because the loyalty of, say, workers to Christian parties depends not only on what the workers want but also on what the church wants, it is more convenient to study the evolution of workers' loyalties from the point of view of the causes of a church-worker coalition than from the point of view of the causes of workers' religious loyalties. We can then ask whether coalitions are stable, such that the ideology that a given group supports this year is a very good predictor of the complex of interests it will be embedded in next year, or whether such coalitions are shifting and unstable. Some political systems are in fact marked by shifting and unstable coalitions and a corresponding tenuousness of the partisan attachment of social groups. This is particularly true when there are frequent coups d'etat, since coups involve a shift in the power resources relevant to the system. This in turn results in rapid shifts of the relative power position of different groups and consequently a shift in which coalitions will seem strategic to each. But Key (1949) has shown that some southern states have highly variable and shifting coalition structures in the primaries, while other states have solidly institutionalized factions, even under reasonably stable electoral laws.

In most political systems in which public office depends on elections, however, the coalitions are remarkably stable. That is, if we rank social groups of any kind (ethnic groups, local communities, classes, etc.) by the degree of support they give to a party in one election, they will be ranked almost the same way in the following election.[11] This means that coalitions formed early in the development of a political system tend to determine the lines of division among coalitions for long periods of time.

Therefore, in the following argument we will address two questions. First we will deal with the historical determinants of the structure of coalitions in different Western European countries, following work by Lipset and Rokkan (1967, pp. 1–64). Then we will attempt to develop a theory of the conditions under which coalitions among social groups in a party are likely to be stable. The problem is as follows: the classical theory of, say, the alliances of the working class postulated that there were certain "natural" alliances of the working class, so the continuity of the coalitions found in fact was not theoretically problematic. But if we succeed in showing that the structure of coalitions in political systems is problematic and historically determined, then the fact that whatever coalition gets established tends (in some political systems) to be very stable has no explanation in terms of natural alliances.

The Lipset-Rokkan Theory of the Structure of Coalitions

Lipset and Rokkan's theory is that the overall pattern of modern party systems in Europe was determined by the pattern of coalitions and oppositions in the upper classes before the introduction of the industrial workers into politics. These conflicts and alliances within the oligarchy both (1) produced permanent deposits in the political organization of the "right" and (2) determined the potential alliances and strategy of the working class when it emerged. The central coalition-forming group in the old upper classes was the "nation-building elite"—the higher civil servants, members of parliament, the notables of the old regime. Constrained by its circumstances, interests, and ideological complexion, this group of "ins" made a "choice" of alliance partners, which forced the "outs" to choose the opposite side of the cleavage.

The first "choice" was a choice of the religious orientation of the government, and in Europe the choice was constrained by the results of the Reformation. In England and Scandinavia, the elite was faced with a dominant Protestant church *under its own control.* It naturally chose to be allied with its own creature, pushing the opposition in the direction of alliance with Nonconformism, secularism, and Pietism. The line cut by the Reformation divided the next tier of countries, including the Low Countries, Germany, and Switzerland, into a state Protestant church majority with a strong Catholic minority or vice versa. Where the state Protestant church was a majority and was dominated by the nation-building elite, as in Germany and the Netherlands, the elite chose this alliance. Otherwise the results were variable. In the south of Europe and in France, the Roman Church was not under the control of the nation-building elite, so the elite was forced to choose between a secular, competitive attitude (e.g., choosing to support state schools rather than religious schools, as in France after the Revolution or in the northern Italian movement of unification) or an alliance with the Roman Church (as in Austria and Belgium).

These alliances by the governing elite forced the opposition into contrasting alliances. Thus in England and Scandinavia, the Liberals and the "left" were allied with the Dissenters and Fundamentalists. In the Prussian Reich there was both Catholic (Zentrum) and secular (Liberal) opposition to the Wilhemenian elite. In France, Italy, and Spain a Catholic right-wing opposition developed to the secular, centralizing state. In Austria and Belgium secular and Protestant forces supported the opposition.

The second decisive cleavage in the upper classes was the urban bourgeoisie versus the landowners, a cleavage that was aggravated by the industrial revolution but already prominent in commercial and trading countries (especially the Low Countries and some Italian city-states) in the Middle Ages. The landowners might be very rich, cosmopolitan gentlemen used to governing, as in England and in Germany east of the Elbe, or small peasants in mountain hamlets, as in Norway. Generally the governing elite chose the alliance with the richest and most powerful class: the landowners in Great Britain, Prussia, and Austria; the urban patriciate in commercial Netherlands, Belgium, Scandinavia (with its domination of rural areas by peasant landowners), and Paris-dominated France.

This choice more or less forced the group not chosen as an ally into opposition. The Liberals recruited much of the urban bourgeoisie in England and Germany. The agrarian radicalism of Scandinavian peasants mixed with fundamentalism on the left, opposed to the state-church urban patriciate. See Fig. 5.

Overall then this produces eight types of political organization of the upper classes, which confronted workers as they became organized in Western Europe. An elite could be split into a conservative state-Protestant-landowner group with a liberal urban-Dissenter-secular opposition, as in England. Or it could consist of a "left" secular government allied to the Parisian and provincial bourgeoisies, opposed by a Catholic landowning "right" opposition, as in France. These two types of opposition are likely to treat the developing workers' movement quite differently. In France the workers were not even allowed into the conservative hierarchical opposition, let alone into the government, and so formed a separated, alienated mass. Because French workers could not join the French opposition, they joined the opposition that grew up in Russia at the time of the Russian Revolution.

Lipset and Rokkan do not provide a very complete comparative theory of labor movements to correspond to their theory of the organization of the upper classes. This work remains to be done. But I think they have greatly clarified the structure of the problem and what it is that we need to know about workers' movements in Western Europe. We also need a theory of the structure of coalitions that form when various structures of majority and minority ethnic divisions exist: when the minority is richer than the majority (e.g., the Chinese in Southeast Asia, the Indians in East Africa, or the Jews in Eastern Europe) and when the minority is poorer than the majority (as the Black people in the United States); when the minority controls the government (e.g., the whites in South Africa) and when it is excluded from the government (e.g., the Jews in most of Eastern Europe), when the group is both rich and poor; and so forth. The Lipset-Rokkan approach is, as it happens, mainly applied to countries in which ethnic problems either are not serious or have been assuaged by secession (as with Ireland in Great Britain).

The Continuity of Coalitions

If, then, there are different structures of the coalition of interests in different political systems, determined by the early history of modernization, we must have a theory of why such coalitions tend to be stable once the process is under way. A continuing coalition is a continuing bargain about which of a subgroup's aims and grievances will be supported by a party. The aims and grievances of a group will tend to change over time; the relative power of different

Governing elite choices

Main determinants of choice	Catholic				Protestant			
Majority outcome in Reformation	Catholic				Protestant			
Control by elite of church	State Church		Dissenting and secular		State Church		Dissenting and secular	
Focus of wealth	Urban bourgeoisie	Rural landowners	Urban	Rural	Urban	Rural	Urban	Rural
Outcome								
Dominant coalition	Clerical conservatism (urban)	Clerical conservatism (rural)	"Enlightenment" government, urban and secular	Rare	Dutch and Scandanavian conservatism	Conservative "gentry" parties	American federalist-style parties	Rare
Opposition coalition	Rural anticlerical and Protestant parties	Urban anticlericalism	Rural clerical conservatism		Catholic and rural fundamentalism	Urban bourgeois dissent	Rural populism	
Lipset-Rokkan example (applies to nineteenth century)	Belgium	Austria	France		Netherlands, Scandanavia	England, Prussia	United States	
Workers' main pattern of opposition (applies to twentieth century)	Rural radical opposition	Urban secular class-conscious socialism with Enlightenment overtones	Split between Enlightenment center and alienated (communist) opposition		Socialist with fundamentalist overtones	Split between liberals and autonomous class action (socialist)	Populist coalition with farmers	

Fig. 5. Schematic Historical Development of Coalition Structures in Western Democracies

members of the coalition will change. Both of these changes require renegotiation of the terms of the coalition.

This suggests as the first major hypothesis that coalitions will tend to be more continuous if the creation of the coalition also involves the creation of institutions for continuous rebargaining of the terms of trade. If it were no easier to get what you want from your present partners than from other people, we would expect more shifting coalition structures. Thus the more flexible and representative the policy-making structure of the coalition or party, the more continuous we would expect the coalition or party to be. In particular, if positions of power to make policy within the coalition or party depend on the degree of support a group brings to the party (i.e., if the parties are internally democratic, in the sense that a person's weight in policymaking depends primarily on his or her enthusiasm and the resources he or she represents), then coalitions will tend to be continuous. If a central, nonrepresentative elite bargains for support (e.g., in a typical South American military regime), the coalitions should tend to be more ephemeral, because the elite does not typically establish structures for rebargaining the coalition and a new military entrepreneur can rebargain in a new situation and sap the support of the old nonrepresentative elite.

Second, the more the coalition itself forms an organization that can render services to its constituent groups, the more sanctions it has at its command to keep groups inside the party (Olson, 1965). The most important determinant of the services a party can render is whether or not it wins and how much power winning gives it. Thus winning coalitions should be more stable than losing coalitions; coalitions that gain command of extensive patronage should be more stable than coalitions that gain power in a civil service system; coalitions that raise money centrally and distribute it to local groups for their activities or that command from the center famous people for fund-raising dinners should be more stable than coalitions with dispersed money and fame; coalitions with large central staffs should be more stable than those with small staffs; and so on.

Third, the longer a coalition has been in existence, the more likely is it to have infused the values and ideology of the coalition as a whole into the subgroups. When such an infusion has taken place, the subgroups socialize their members into partisan attachments directly, rather than indirectly by teaching them subgroup priorities. Furthermore, the pattern of interest-group priorities worked out in the bargaining process is also, on the other side of the coin, the policy of the subgroup. Thus subgroup resources, organizations, leadership rhetoric, and other influences tend to socialize members into the order of priorities that is compatible with the coalition they are now in. Especially if future leaders of the group are trained and selected by the old leaders, the utility function most compatible with the present coalition structure is likely to be continually institutionalized in the group.

Fourth, the more dependent the coalition is on the support of its marginal members, the more effort and the more rewards we would expect it to spend in keeping their support. Rather than some central power group within the party taking a cavalier attitude toward growing potential dissent, the core of the coalition in a competitive situation should tend to be open to rebargaining the terms of the coalition. Thus, in a one-party situation we would expect both the majority and minority parties to have shifting bases of support. This follows from a combination of the previous analysis of electoral situations and the propositions given here about rebargaining.

Finally, we can generalize the above analysis of office seekers and militants to interest groups as well as parties. The greater the degree to which the articulation and organization of an interest group's aspirations is in the hands of people whose career prospects depend on the *coalition* winning, the more stable the coalition should be. This should be especially important when the interest group itself has few organizational resources; for instance, it should be more true of farmers than of workers, because farmers have more difficulty building solid interest groups to negotiate with parties and therefore depend more on elected officials to build party coalitions. Thus we would expect farmers' organizations to move more rapidly toward the political persuasion of the minister of agriculture than trade unions move toward the political persuasion of the minister of labor. The strength of the Radical party in France among farmers may be related to the fact that the Radical party has controlled the ministry of agriculture in many shifting circumstances. We expect coalitions of interests like the Radical party to be more stable because they themselves are the principal focus of organization for farmers, which makes farmers themselves have more difficulty renegotiating and makes farmers' leaders depend for their career prospects on the party itself. When the leaders of interest groups are careerists in the larger (party) coalition, for instance when trades union leaders look toward becoming Labour members of parliament, they may, of course, lose leadership of the trades unions to a new militant group without political prospects. The more that militant leaders form a separate structure, the more likely they might be to put demands on the coalition which other members of the coalition will not bear, and hence the more unstable coalitions are likely to be. We would expect, for example, that the French Socialists, the Gaullists, and to a lesser extent the MRP (*Mouvement Republicaine Populaire,* the Catholic center-left party) would have given the most difficulty to the center-right coalition that governed France during the Fourth Republic. The Radicals and the Moderates should have given less difficulty, since their parties have less strong militants to challenge the ideological purity of the coalition.[12]

Thus to summarize, we expect the partisan attachments of groups to be historically continuous to the degree that:

1. there are effective structures for rebargaining the terms of the coalition (inside the parties that organize the coalitions),
2. the centers of the coalitions are organized and command useful resources

that serve functions for their subgroups or gain power in the state, hence winning lucrative power for the coalitions,

3. the coalitions have socialized the members of subgroups into partisan attachment,
4. the situation of the coalitions is competitive, that is, they are in two- or multi-party systems as opposed to one-party dominant systems, and
5. the interest group or subgroup leaders have political ambitions.[13]

Revolutions and National Unity Coalition Structures

When a governing elite either does not see the challenge or is internally too rigid to do anything about it and incorporates developing forces too late, all the developing grievances and aspirations are forced into a single opposition movement, very often of a revolutionary character. Colonial regimes, absolutist monarchies, and military dictatorships are often inflexible in this way. If and when an opposition takes power, it is very often a broad coalition of many new forces and tends to create a dominant one-party state. Such a broad nationalist or revolutionary movement tends itself to create the interest groups that organize subgroups within it and consequently to imbue the subgroups from the beginning with ideologies, priorities, and career patterns of leadership that tie the interest groups to itself. For instance, trade unions tend to be created by the revolutionary coalition, to have their leaders chosen for party loyalty, to have the national revolutionary party's name in their titles and its ideology in the preamble to their constitutions, and so forth. Such one-party dominant systems are found today in many former colonial areas (e.g., India, Israel, Tanzania, Algeria, Tunisia, Egypt). Such a system was also created in Japan in the Meiji Restoration. A narrow military dictatorship produced a corresponding broad revolutionary movement in Mexico (what is now *Partido Revolucionario Institucional*), and a relatively narrow, inflexible, traditional elite unified many new social forces behind Perón in Argentina.

A very similar corporatist structure, with almost all interest groups attached to a governing party, is produced by the opposite extreme reaction by the old governing elite, one of great flexibility rather than great rigidity. If an elite attempts to sponsor the organization of all the major groups in the society, providing an arbitration function when their interests conflict and keeping control of the internal political processes in the interest groups created, then new forces are forced into a straightjacket of a utility function that is compatible with the interests of the old regime. This tends to create a conservative corporatism with aspirations to mobilize the entire society. The Vargas regime in Brazil is a fairly clear example, and the Meiji regime is probably more conservative-corporatist than national-revolutionary. Sometimes it takes a revolutionary action to institute such a flexible policy by the old elite, as in the institution of the Mussolini regime in Italy. The unsuccessful attempts to promote such a policy in the Tsarist government in Russia before the Revolution were sometimes called "police socialism," which captures the mood of such movements quite well.

Thus a corporatist style of coalition structure, in which all the interests of the society are presumed to be incorporated into the same party and governing apparatus (the party and the government are hardly distinguishable under these conditions) and all the interest groups are organized to pursue those of their purposes deemed appropriate by the government (by arbitration structures), can result from rather opposite historical circumstances. The first is one in which virtually all decent people are forced into a unified opposition by the narrowness of a colonial or military regime, which yields a revolutionary populist corporatism in the case of a successful revolution. The second is one in which virtually all decent people are bought off by the government and, if they refuse to be bought off, sent to prison or exile, creating a conservative corporatism of the old elite.[14]

Summary

We have tried here to deal with three main questions: (1) When will parties be disposed to actively seek members? (2) When will social groups be disposed to form partisan attachments and what will happen if social groups become politically active without forming such attachments? (3) What parties will social groups support? (We reconceptualized this as the problem of the structure of political coalitions.)

The first problem we answered with a theory of balanced forces, differentiating those that tend to make a party want to grow (the wish to win) and those that tend to make it want to stay the same size (the wish to be socially or ideologically pure). Then we discussed the circumstances under which there might be variation in the relative sizes of these forces when parties are of different sizes. The argument can be summarized in three generalizations: (1) the electoral situation determines the value of an added partisan attachment; the electoral situation in turn depends on the electoral law, the size of the opposition, and the size of the party; (2) the further a group of potential partisans is, in interest, ideology, or social standing, from the main social base of the militants of a party, the lower the value of their attachment will be because it will entail programmatic and ideological costs; (3) the more powerful the militants are in the internal structure of the party, the more the electoral value of added partisans will be ignored and the resulting cost to the party in terms of ideological, social, and programmatic sacrifices will determine the party reaction. Conversely the more powerful the office seekers are, the more the electoral value of added partisans will be the determining factor in the party's outlook.

We treated the second problem, the transition from apathy to incorporation by way of revolution, as a primarily historical problem. If the rate of mobilization of the population is high, due to urbanization and the extension of literacy, and the rate of the population's incorporation into the governing structure is low, we will expect the number of the people available for revolution to increase. If mobilization rates are high but incorporation rates are also high, then the result should be reasonably peaceful development. If the rates of mobilization and incorporation are both low, then an incorporated elite rules over an apathetic mass, though since the French Revolution they can hardly do so with confidence.

The third problem, who votes with whom, we subdivided into two problems to explain (1) the structure of coalitions historically and (2) the conditions under which those historically given coalitions would be continuous. We borrowed Lipset and Rokkan's theory of the structure of coalitions in Western Europe, which essentially reduces the problem to one of the political sociology of the fourteenth to eighteenth centuries. To this we added some hypotheses about when a coalition would continue to be rewarding to its members.

SOCIAL STRUCTURE AND POLITICAL INTELLIGENCE

The theory of partisan attachment given above assumes that everyone knows what can be done—what combination of interests and values will be achieved by any given policy. We have implicitly assumed that people have uniform and correct ideas about what will happen if their party wins and follows its announced policy. Hence all we had to study was what people preferred and how much power they had. In the language of economics, we assumed that the production function of public policy had already been determined and that the only problem left was to choose among the production possibilities according to the utility function of a party or coalition.

We know that in fact the manipulation of a complex interdependent social system by governmental intervention is highly problematic. The problem of political intelligence is to attach to a set of preferences for outcomes an accurate theory of the causes of those outcomes. The average person's theory of how to remedy his or her grievances and achieve his or her aspirations, by persuading the government to intervene and to change the causes of the grievances, is hopelessly primitive. All effective political systems must have a set of social arrangements that attach moderately accurate causal theories to the policy preferences of groups and individuals. Our problem in this section is to develop theories of the social determinants of the intellectual adequacy of policies.[15] We want to know: Under what conditions is it most likely that an intervention of government in the social or economic system will have the effects the dominant coalition wants?

Our problem is different from that of specifying the technical procedures of rational decision-making in the public arena. That is the problem of public administration, dealt with elsewhere. Instead we need only a brief introduction to the forms of rational decision-making so as to see where social factors interfere to turn aside rational decisions. The following treatment therefore slights the technology of planning or of incremental rationality. This is because the social sources of ignorance and error in technical decisions are relatively obvious and sociologically trivial, though of great practical importance. But once a technically rational decision or decision process is specified, the further stages, committing resources to solution (the politics of planning) and changing the systems of action so that the resources are actually used to realize the solution, have large social components.

Our purpose in the first section below is therefore merely to remind the reader of the general form of the two main solutions to the problem of rationality, "planning" and "incrementalism." Both of these result, under specified conditions, in rational solutions to policy problems. Both are affected by the social factors influencing intelligence, such as the education of crucial people, the social organization of information flows to those people, the social organization of censorship and criticism, especially by bureaucratic hierarchies in which superiors censor information from inferiors so as to make their decisions look good, and so forth.[16]

Two Models of Political Rationality

We can imagine two people who want to get to the top of a mountain: let us call them the aerial photographer and the nearsighted explorer. The aerial photographer gets in a plane, photographs the terrain, and lays out on the photograph the best path from where he or she is to the top of the mountain. Then he or she follows, as accurately as possible, the real path that corresponds to the mapped path. The nearsighted explorer looks around the immediate environment, decides which way looks like up, and heads off in that direction. After having gone a little way, he or she again looks for which direction is upward, and adjusts the path again.

The nearsighted explorer may end on a little hill sticking up out of a bog, though the larger the circle the explorer surveys before deciding which way is up, the less likely that is. The aerial photographer may have mistaken a chasm for a shadow when interpreting his photographic map. But theoretically both strategies lead, in appropriate circumstances, to the top of the mountain. Which strategy one would use would depend a good deal on whether one had a plane, whether one could read aerial photographs accurately, how much better the view was from the ground than from the plane, how important such detail was, and so on. The aerial photographer is following a strategy of rationality that we will call "planning." The nearsighted explorer is following a strategy we will call "incrementalism." We will first discuss how social factors affect the rationality of planning and then turn briefly to the sociology of incremental rationality.[17]

Elements of the Planning Process

Planned intervention in a complex interdependent system involves four stages, or elements: (1) constructing an abstract map or model of the system with the important causal connections in it, such that symbolic manipulation of the map or model produces the same effects (or rather, the symbolic analogue of the same effects) as the corresponding real manipulation the system would produce (as in the above example, the photograph); (2) choosing a policy by such manipulation of abstractions which will best achieve the ends in view (laying out the path above)—we will call these two elements the technology of planning, and we will ignore them here; (3) mobilizing resources (authority, money, commitment) and devoting them to the intervention chosen (packing up to go to the top of the mountain)—we will call this the politics of planning; and (4) supervising the application of these resources to carry out the planned intervention, monitoring the process to find bugs and imperfections of the plan, and preventing interference by those whose interests are negatively affected (actually following the path and climbing to the top above) —we will call this the administration of the plan.

For example, planners developed the TVA by first constructing a model of the Tennessee River system and analyzing how the river system would be affected by various dams, how it was related to the surrounding economic life, how the prices of electricity in the area were determined by monopolies of private companies, and the like. To this model of the system the leadership applied a set of purposes, or objectives, which included such values as free enterprise competition (antimonopolism), conservation of natural resources, equalization of income, raising farm income, and so on. This technology of planning then gave rise to the choice of a policy, for example to buy shore property as well as the property that would be flooded, for the introduction of conservation and planned utilization. The politics of the TVA required getting sufficient support in the local area to fight off the attacks in Congress backed by the main people whose interests were damaged—the private power companies. This involved co-opting local farm leaders into the policy-making structure, which in turn meant sacrificing some original policy objectives. For instance, the TVA did little toward ensuring that tenants, as opposed to landlords, got some of the benefits of the public investment; the TVA stopped buying much shore land to make way for farmers to develop their shore land privately; and so on. The administration of the plan involved actually constructing dams and building power plants that could undersell the private companies (Selznik, 1949).

The Politics of Planning

In order to be used in a planned intervention on a large scale, resources have to be liquid. That is, they must be in fact subject to the free decision of the planning authority. In the extreme, if all resources are bound, in the sense of being required to be used in specific ways, then there is only one possible policy—the one implied by the preexisting commitments of resources. In that case, it is of no practical use to specify an optimum allocation of resources by manipulating a model of the system. Unless the planning apparatus has sufficient credit, political or financial, so that its choice of policies can mobilize resources to carry out the intervention, the plan is of no import. We have to ask, then, What are the conditions under which a political authority that develops plans will have sufficient liquidity of resources to follow them?

To answer this question we have to understand how resources become illiquid—how they become committed to the servicing of previous obligations, created by previous decisions and commitments of the planning authority or by the history of the political system. When resources are illiquid, the people or organizations to whose purposes they are committed have vested interests in those resources. These vested interests are created by promises (with an appropriate enforcement apparatus to see that the promises are kept) by the holder of the resource to the vested interest. The vested interest is a promise to use the resources in a certain way. For instance, in the process described above for the TVA, the agricultural extension services and the wealthier farmers whom they served had a vested interest in the new TVA policy of private development of shore resources. We can therefore say that instead of wanting to know the social determinants of the liquidity of resources, we want to know the social structures that encourage the vesting of interests. The lower the degree of vesting of interests in resources, the more a plan can affect the use of those resources, i.e., the more liquid they are. By this very general definition of vested interest we find that many of the vested interests of greatest importance are executive agencies, ministers, presidents, legislators, and other members of the government.

But this illiquidity due to vested interests is modified by the possibility of convincing the holders of vested interests that the plan will serve them. This in turn depends first on how far the plan will in fact serve them (i.e., on the degree to which the interests represented in the objective function of the plan are the same as the interests that are vested in the old regime) and second on how far the interests are persuaded by the arguments of the technology of planning. Thus the persuasive capacity of the channels for the communications between the planning authority and the holders of vested interests is likely to increase liquidity in two ways: first by persuading planners to use a politically realistic set of criteria for evaluating effects and second by persuading holders of vested interests that they will be well served by the planned activity.

What we need then is a model of the social structure which combines a description of the distribution of power (i.e., the distribution of vesting of interests) over the relevant resources with a description of the persuasive capacity of the two-way communications channel between the planning authority and the holders of power. Further the relations among powerholders, especially their capacity to bargain with each other about what concrete objectives the planning authority should pursue, will increase the liquidity of resources available for planned intervention. But it will do so only if the communications capacity of the coalition of vested interests constructed to influence the planning authority is great; that is, only if the interests have high connectivity with the planning authority.

The elements of this structure are represented in Fig. 6. The powers of vested interests are represented by the numbers P_i. The capacity for authoritative influence between these powers and the planning authority are represented by the coefficients b_i. The capacity of interests to bargain among themselves about the objectives of planning are represented by the c_{ij}. There would be as many coefficients of such coalition-forming capacities as there were permutations of interests.

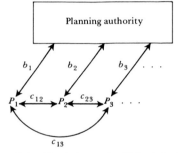

*P_i is the power of interest i; c_{ij} is the capacity of interests i and j to form coalitions; b_i is the capacity of the channel of mutual influence between interest i and the planning authority.

Fig. 6. The Structure of Relations between Vested Interests and a Planning Authority

For example, in the case of the TVA, P_1 might represent the power of the private electricity companies. This was very large for all kinds of reasons, which need not detain us here. If b_1 were large, that is, if the power companies had high influence on the policy of the TVA and the TVA planners could communicate the possibilities of the valley system accurately, then the TVA would have had more liquid resources. What this means concretely is that the TVA would have developed the river system and sold the power cheaply to the private companies, which then would have sold it at the going rate to the farmers and industries of the region. The kind of socialism characteristic of capitalist countries would have developed, in which taxpayers pay the losses and private companies take the profits. The power of the extension services of the local colleges, representing the interests of the richer farmers, might be P_2. By cooptation and "grass roots administration," b_2 was raised. This meant that the objectives of richer farmers became more important in the plans, as evidenced for instance by the TVA cutting back conservation buying of shore property. It also meant that the farmers were convinced that public development of hydro-electric power would benefit them.

Thus the capacity of the TVA plans to mobilize resources in their support depended on increasing the aggregate sum of interests with which the TVA was in close, policy-influencing communication. Concretely then b_i means the amount of co-optation and the availability of devices for the political modification of plans which Selznick described for the TVA.[18] The power of the electricity companies consisted mainly of money and of the general credibility of free enterprise ideology in the United States. The companies had, of course, been more powerful in the 1920s than in the 1930s, so the alliance between the TVA and the farmers could defeat them in the 1930s.

The extension services themselves were a device that increased the capacity of the richer farmers from different areas to come to agreement among themselves about what they wanted from the TVA. Farmers not owning new shore property might have benefited from the conservation programs. Farmers owning new shore property could make a good deal of money from private recreational development of the reservoirs or could continue to farm the remaining land. Through the common organizational framework of the extension services and associated organizations, the farmers could resolve those conflicting interests (in the event, against conservation and park development of the shores) and impose this resolution on the TVA through the co-optation mechanisms described above. Thus concretely the c_{ij} in the graph are devices like the extension services which organize interests like the dispersed farmers into a common front (Selznick, 1949).

The diagram implies that there are two distinct sources of planning effectiveness. The first is the capacity of the planning authority itself to serve as an aggregator of interests and a broker for bargaining out a common policy. The sociology of this process is essentially the same as the sociology of political parties as coalitions of interest, as outlined in the first section above. That is, our problem here is really one of how far the planning authority functions as a political party, as described above. The b's in the diagram correspond to the links between parties and interest groups. The P's correspond to the possible contribution of those interest groups to the party (planning authority) winning. The political context in which the planning authority operates is not, however, an electoral system. Instead it is a system in which opposing interests in coalition can cut the budget and authority of the planning body by operating in the rest of the political system. Nevertheless, most of the sociology of the authority of planning bodies can be written by direct analogy to the sociology of parties as coalitions of interest groups, and so it need not detain us here.

The diagram however suggests an alternative process of mobilization of interests to support plans. If the various interests concerned have a high degree of connectivity among themselves, they can get together, work out a compromise among themselves, and impose it on the planning authority. This is probably much more common for planning authorities than for political parties, for two reasons. First, the affected interests are likely to be in communication already because they are interdependent naturally, as well as interdependent in the planned intervention. For example, a regional development program like the TVA affects a group of interests that already have a common dependence on the region. Second, the normal structures for aggregating interests, such as political parties, legislatures, state and local governments, usually function autonomously from the planning authority. Consequently, if the interests with great powers have high connectivity (high c_i) and also high access to the planning body (high b_i), then they can make the planning body follow their preferences from the beginning. This is essentially equivalent to saying that the more the affected interests already form an effective political party, the more the plans of the planning authority are likely to be of such a character as to mobilize their support. Again the sociology of political coalitions outlined above could be suitably rewritten to apply to this case.

Therefore structures for bargaining among interest groups will tend to increase the effectiveness of plans but decrease the independent effects of planners' values. Effective parliaments, effective political party conventions, extensive representation of interest group organizations in political parties, elite clubs that include leaders of different interest groups, and similar structures will tend to increase the capacity of interest groups to bargain out their differences. These forces, by definition, will tend to increase the c_{ij} of the model and therefore increase the second kind of liquidity—that derived from a prior agreement among interests that the plan should be executed. The greater the effectiveness of communication between parliament or parties and the planning authority, the more difference the presence of such bargaining structures should make.

In particular, first, the greater the degree to which the planning authority is responsible to a legislature or to a ruling party (e.g., the Communist party in the USSR), the more liquid its resources are likely to be (provided that the legislature or ruling party actually is an effective bargaining structure). Some executive departments have functions that are basically bargaining functions. In general the budget or finance department and the apparatus most directly responsible to the chief executive (e.g., the *presidencia* in Mexico) have bargaining functions. The closer the ties of a planning authority to such bargaining bureaucracies, the more likely it is that the planning authority will use the utility function that is politically effective and will convince the interests that it knows what it is doing.

Second, the more isolated the planners are, by recruitment and socialization, from the political process, the less liquid their resources are likely to be. Foreign experts, people whose career lines depend on professional recognition rather than on political success, people technically trained rather than trained in politically sensitive fields, people trained in a profession like architecture with a distinctive value orientation, will tend to make a planning authority less responsive. Linguistic difficulties, created by either ethnic differences or specialized technical vocabularies, tend to decrease communication. The more the language of planners departs from political discourse, the less liquid the resources of the planners are likely to be.

Finally, the less organized the interests are that control the relevant resources, the less liquid a planning authority's resources are likely to be. If interest groups are weak and poorly organized, then communicating successfully with them does not do much good. Countries with dispersed political resources —for instance countries in which the government and interest groups do not penetrate autonomous villages or autonomous foreign firms—are not likely to have effective plans.

The Administration of Plans

The successful administration of a plan requires that the staff that is supposed to carry out the proposed intervention (or in a few cases, the mass of people who are supposed to carry it out—e.g., in the case of community development plans) actually carries it out. This seems to depend on three main factors: (1) whether the staff becomes committed to the plan, (2) whether the authority of the plan can be delegated successfully to local officials so that the concrete interests affected by actions of those officials can be overcome, and (3) whether the staff is competent to add the necessary details to the general course of action described by the plan.

For instance Granick's study of *Soviet Metal Fabricating* (1967) shows that there was no question that the plan for industrialization emphasizing the building of machines (automobiles, tractors, machine tools, tanks, etc.) had adequate political support and massive liquid resources. Yet, well-known efficiencies in metal fabrication, such as subcontracting for specialized processes, were not used. Instead factories tried to integrate backward vertically into the processes that supplied them, even when the factories could use only part of the capacity of the supplying process, and forward into the processes that used their output, even when this meant undersupplying other factories. Granick suggests that this is because both types of integration gave favorable outcomes for the measures of success used to evaluate the staff of the plan (i.e., to evaluate the factory executives—mainly gross physical product), even though the integration undermined the plan. That is, the lack of commitment to the plan was due to difficulties in the reward system.

Further, one of the reasons that backward integration into sources of supply paid off was that allocations of supplies made by the planning authority could not effectively be enforced by a factory executive who depended on them. The executive could not enforce the allocations because getting all the allocations for the factory made it more difficult for the *supplier* to maximize his or her own physical output. The suppliers could increase their gross output if they personally did the additional work on the goods before selling them. When the plan in its allocational aspect ran up against the supplier's concrete interests in opposition to it, the executive with an interest in seeing the factory's supply allocation plan fulfilled did not have enough authority to enforce deliveries.

Finally, many of the new plants were designed to function in a more advanced technology, having been modeled on similar plants in advanced countries. For instance, a continuous production line requires parts to be standardized within narrow tolerances and delivered according to a predictable schedule. Unless the other plants in the system provide such tolerances and schedules, the particular plant cannot function properly. Thus the technical designs for advanced plants created technical systems that the plants were not competent to run. The general theory that what works in America ought to work in Russia failed because the staffs were not competent to add the details of required tolerances and schedules. We need to specify the social sources of these three determinants of administrative effectiveness.

1. The degree to which the staff members become committed to the plan probably depends mainly on the degree to which the criteria of performance which determine their individual reward levels are related to plan fulfillment. That is, we want an individual's reward to be proportional to the values achieved for all the output variables under the control of the individual, evaluated by the same utility function used to develop the plan. Theoretically all one has to do is to identify accurately the variables under an individual's control, disaggregate the plan into those variables, and make rewards depend on this disaggregated plan. If this is done correctly, then when the individual optimizes his or her own level of reward, the variables of the plan under his or her control are optimized. If all the staff optimize the variables under their control, then in the aggregate the system optimizes its achievement of the plan.

There are two general difficulties with this strategy. The first is illustrated by the Soviet example. Most performances by an individual affect measures both of his or her own output *and* of other people's output. The value of physical production, used as the main reward criterion for the Soviet industrial staff, is affected by the behavior of suppliers as well as by the plant's own behavior. These "external effects" make it hard to segregate the "variables under the control of" one individual from those "under the control of" another. The second difficulty is that the politics of determining civil servants' reward levels are often just as complicated as the politics of originating a plan. Insofar as civil servants' careers can be influenced as much by political favor as by job performance, they will pay as much attention to their own political fences as to their execution of the plan. That is, we have been talking as if the politics of purposes which will be pursued by the civil service were the only kind of politics. But in most countries, especially poorer countries, one of the main privileged classes consists of the civil service, the university staff, the planning staff, and the administrative staff of the state. The guarantee of their reward levels is one of the main "public purposes" to which politics is directed.

If the civil servants' reward levels also depend on bribery, the authority given them to execute the plan may be used in unpredictable ways. The better the performance measurement (that is, the more nearly that "authority"—the things over which one has control—is commensurate with "responsibility"— the things by which one is measured) and the more completely such measurement, instead of bribery, determines reward levels, the more the plan is likely to be exactly executed.

The concrete factors that are probably most important in relating individual performance accurately to aggregate performance are sophisticated and honest accounting procedures, apolitical careers for civil servants, and a low level of bribery.[19]

2.　If the staff is committed to the plan by virtue of an appropriately organized reward system, it must still have power to carry out the plan. The problem of appropriate delegation of authority is one of bringing administrative action into congruence with the causal system, so that it will successfully carry out the planned intervention. That is, we want to arrange the units of an administrative structure so that (a) as far as possible, they have within their jurisdiction the variables that cause the outcomes for which they are responsible and (b) they have adequate resources to manipulate the variables in their jurisdiction. To a large extent this is a technical problem of organizational design, and it need not detain us here. But many plans involve people outside the organization who have substantial interests in how the organization conducts itself. People who have a highway coming through their houses may have small power compared with the highway planning authority but a large role in the political system compared with the person who serves the eviction notice or who runs the bulldozer. The capacity of a subordinate official to reward or punish citizens whose behavior influences the outcomes in his or her jurisdiction is partly determined by the social structure of politics.

The first social structural factor influencing the adequacy of the authority of an official is the *internal* liquidity of resources in the bureaucracy itself. In particular, if a person who has trouble with a major power outside his or her control can reliably count on being backed up to the extent of the political resources behind the plan, he or she can act. If, however, the planning authority is cowardly in backing up its agents, the plan will be modified in execution. One policy for minimizing the political costs of a plan is to regard elements of the plan as dispensable when it turns out that they run into more opposition than expected. The lower the extent to which the plan has been bargained out ahead of time, the greater the likelihood that it will be bargained out in execution. Thus the lower the liquidity of resources of the planning authority, the more cowardly the planning authority is likely to be in administration. One wants to rank executive agencies of the plan by the degree to which a person who gets into difficulties will be backed up by his or her superior.

A second determinant of adequacy of authority delegation is the degree to which competition for advancement or power within the bureaucracy is normatively controlled. If a higher civil servant is quite likely to lose his or her job to an inferior, he or she will be cautious about delegating authority to the inferior. As Crozier (1964) has suggested, the superior will try to retain control over sources of uncertainty and to restrict the discretion of subordinates. One of the best ways to restrict the discretion of a subordinate is to make that person handle all of the difficulties he or she gets into.

Finally, if another person's action within the bureaucracy determines the outcomes within one's own jurisdiction, yet one has no influence over the measurement of the other's performance, then one's own rewards are not under his or her control. Inadequate partitioning of the causal system in the system of measurement of performance results in inadequate authority, for the other fellow bureaucrat acts essentially like an "outside" interest affected by one's official action.

3.   The structural determinants of the competence of the administrative apparatus are similar to the determinants of the competence of planners. Inadequate information for decisions or inadequate education of the staff has the same sorts of effects in the middle as in the top of a planning authority. Though this is factually very important, it is sufficiently obvious that we need not elaborate here.

The Rationality of Incrementalism

The basic notion of incrementalism is that the potential causal variables are changed one by one in small amounts, and stock is taken of the results. If the results are good, the same variable is changed some more, again by a small amount, and stock is taken again. Unlike the situation in planning, a complete representation of the causal system is not theoretically required. All that is required is that an increase of utility due to a small change in a single variable be accurately identified as being due to that change. Thus what we have to outline are the social structural variables that influence the rapidity and accuracy of the mapping of the effects of small changes in utilities on small changes in policy variables.

Since we are working in this section from the assumption that the politically determined utility function of a society is set—by who wins in politics, as discussed in the first part—we take the distribution of powers among groups with different interests or utility functions as given. We are interested in studying the rationality of an incrementalist system—the accuracy with which the direction of movement of policies reflects the utilities of powerful groups for such movement. This may be substantively very irrational, as when the utilities of powerful military and industrial groups lead to a gradual escalation of a meaningless war.

What is required for such a system to work (that is, to give powerful interests what they want) is that *each* interest diagnose correctly the effect of the small change on itself. Then the next small change, instead of depending on a previously worked out plan or on the inertia of bureaucratic interests created by the change, depends on the exercise of power on a decision about the next small change. In place of the exercise of power once and for all on the plan, there is a continuous exercise of power by people who keep close and exact track of the impact of public policies on themselves.

The total quantity of information required for rational decision-making is the same in the two systems, but the form in which the information comes is very different. Instead of the relation between interventions and outcomes being presented in the form of equations worked out by theoreticians in the planning authority, the equations in incrementalism are traced out piece by piece by all the interests involved. Instead of the feedback from powerful groups coming in the form of commitment of large resources to the plan, it comes in the form of dribbles that tell the planners to move a little further. Philosophically, the information in incremental planning is empiricist—one fact about a small section of the curve coming in at a time; the information in planning is theoretical—a bold trace of the curve across the paper at the beginning. From the point of view of the technology of planning, the dangers of empiricism are the same as the dangers of empiricism in science, namely, confusion about what is going on. The dangers of planning are the same as the dangers of any social theory, namely, a clear but wrong idea about how the world works. But these contrasting kinds of errors are not especially social, and so they do not concern us here.

Another Look at the Utility of Power

A general distortion of the rationality of near-sighted explorer processes is that the expected utility of an interest group can be increased by changes either in the substantive effect variables or in the power distribution. Much of the activity of government is directed at writing the "social constitution" of the country. Policy variables such as electoral laws, union recognition laws, business and professional licensing laws, corporation charters, cartel agreements backed by governments, laws on local government charters, and laws on political freedoms all regulate the distribution of power rather than the substantive policy of the society.

The maximizing behavior of firms comes to have an indeterminate relation to consumer utilities when business investments have a simultaneous effect on monopolistic position and on costs and returns. That is, when a market structure presents opportunities both to gain monopoly power and to make competitive profits, the classical economic "iron hand" theorem, that each firm in maximizing its profits will equate utilities sacrificed to produce commodities with utilities gained by having produced them and hence will maximize consumer utilities (given the distribution of means of production and the distribution of income), no longer holds.[20]

The same difficulties that confuse the theory of the market also confuse the theory of incrementalism. In particular, insofar as the specifically *political* interests of powerful groups in preserving their rule dominate their other policy objectives, it does not follow from incremental logic that their *policy* utilities will be maximized. For instance, an army officer corps may have its prestige and power increased in time of war. The officers may therefore be happier in time of war and, by incrementalist logic, end up supporting those belligerent policies that bring them the good things of life. It would be cheaper for everyone to provide them with free vacations in Portugal rather than an air base there; cheaper for the army officers because they wouldn't run the risk of getting killed and cheaper for the rest of us because we wouldn't either. Just as markets with strong political or monopolistic opportunities give rise to "adventure capitalism," (Weber, 1958) so incrementalist systems with opportunities for rewriting the social constitution give rise to policy adventurism.

Clearly the utility of changing the distribution of power by political maneuvering relative to the utility of changing substantive policy depends on the rate of change of the power distribution compared with the rate of change of the effect-of-policy variables. The more unstable the legal situation of different sorts of power, the more power oriented (as opposed to policy oriented) the interest groups are likely to be. If friends of the president are not taxed, and presidents frequently change, one may be better rewarded for supporting presidential candidates than for investing in blast furnaces. What then are the sorts of social structural variables that affect the stability of power distributions? [21]

First, the distribution of power will tend to be unstable if the number, wealth, education, and organizational capacity of social groups are changing rapidly. Economic development, mass migration, conquest, and the decay and incapacity of old regimes all tend to change the distribution of political resources among social groups. This usually creates pressures for a redistribution of political power, a rewriting of the social constitution. For instance, we would expect that in time of revolution, which we have argued above is partly the result of changes in wealth, education, and organizational capacity, an incrementalist strategy of trying out land reform and then stopping if it does not work would fail, because the reforms would be evaluated according to whom they left in power in rural areas rather than their economic and other effects. This would be more the case in a very rapidly developing economy; for instance the "land reform" policy, inherent in the movement to abolish slavery in the United States, led to a civil war in the United States but passed reasonably peacefully in Great Britain, which was not developing as fast.

Second, if major political resources (such as military power and collective violence, the right to propaganda and assembly, the right to vote) are not distributed according to a solid normative system, then the effects of their distribution become much more volatile. For example, if the conditions under which military violence will be used are specified by norms that have a validity independent of the constellation of powers that now hold office, those specifications will change much more sluggishly in response to changes in that ruling constellation than if uses of violence were not specified by valid norms. If the feedback between changes of power in one area and changes of the distribution of resources is decreased, normative solidity will cause a decrease in the instability of the power distribution.[22]

Third, as noted above in the discussion of planning, groups may vary in the degree to which government policy is generally causally relevant to the variables for which they have high utilities. An interest group with low interest in politically controlled variables will be more apathetic than a group with high interest. The former will therefore tend to focus its existing power on influencing those few variables it *does* care about rather than on getting more power. For instance the government affects every aspect of the welfare of the military and of the defense industries from day to day; the main people who have an interest in pacifist policies are affected only when it comes time for them to get killed. Thus pacifist movements very often fail because those interested in peace are apathetic while those interested in war are always on the lookout for more power in order to control their own daily lives. An incrementalist policy favors interests that are always on the *qui vive* for minor changes in their own position.

Offhand it might seem that all the above reasoning would also apply to planning as well as incrementalist processes. However, it is relatively rare for a plan to have as an explicit objective the change of the distribution of power in society. When such objectives are incorporated in plans (as they were marginally in the poverty programs in the United States and usually are in land reform programs), other power interests can fight these objectives explicitly. When the sources of utilities to different groups are obscure, as they are in incremental processes, power positions can change gradually and obscurely without opponents seeing what is going on. Secret power interests tend to corrupt incrementalist rationality more than planning.

The Impact of Ideology

The approach toward the optimum in incremental processes depends on correct causal attribution. If a group thinks that an increase in a variable it has an interest in is due to an increase of x_1 when in fact it is due to a decrease in x_2, then it will put pressure on to increase x_1 as long as it feels a need of more for its presumed consequences. People's ideas about causation can therefore take them off the course that would maximize their own utilities.

For instance, trade unions opposed many governmental social security and social welfare proposals in the United States before the 1930s on the doctrine that workers could get more from business by their own direct efforts. Many businessmen opposed the same programs on the doctrine that the programs were an undue burden on business profits and hence on economic progress. Both of these doctrines cannot be right. Given the niggardly level of social service benefits, one would think that the trade union theory that social security programs do not do much good was right. But at any rate at least some of the cause of the slower growth of social welfare programs in the United States must be due to incorrect causal theories by one or the other side of the labor-capital conflict.

Of course ideological blinders may also deform the causal theories of planners. But there is much more systematic causal analysis by planners than by a mass public. The level of causal attribution by the electorate is measured by the common observation that whatever party is in power when economic conditions get worse loses votes, even if its policies constitute a much more sensible treatment of the problem than those of the opposition. All sorts of social and historical forces that shape the causal theories of the general public and of interest group leaders thus affect incrementalist rationality somewhat more than planning.

Summary

Our strategy in this section has been to lay out models of calculation processes and to discuss the conditions under which elements of those models would be affected by social forces. That is, rather than evaluating public policy intelligence, we have rated the intelligence of different degrees of approach to two models of rational problem-solving. This is almost a necessary device for studying rationality, because otherwise a social scientist would have to be smarter and better informed than a policy-maker.[23]

The model of planning presented above involved three main elements: (1) the technology of planning, consisting of a causal model of the system in which the intervention is to take place, an outline of the resources available for the intervention, and a system for evaluating possible outcomes; (2) the politics of planning, consisting of mechanisms for mobilizing resources and making them sufficiently liquid so that they can be used by the plan; and (3) the administration of planning, consisting of creating the human actions that will actually carry out the intervention chosen. We explained variations in the rationality of the technology with two main variables: the competence of the planners and the quality of information at their disposal. Various miscellaneous social forces are thought to influence these two main variables.

We explained variations in the liquidity of resources by the structure of communications between interest groups and the planning authority and the structure of bargaining processes outside the planning authority. In the administration of plans the primary problem is disaggregating the plan as a causal system into the activities that individuals are supposed to carry out which are causally effective and carrying out a corresponding disaggregation of the utilities created by the plan so that the utilities constitute a reward system that will motivate the appropriate individual actions.

We also outlined briefly two sorts of subversion to which incrementalist processes are especially prone. The first is that the good things that come from a little change in public policy may be due to the effects of that policy on who rules rather than its effects on the public welfare. The second is that people may, because of their ideological blinders, go out to change the world in order to cure a pain in their bowels.

In general the sociology of the intelligence of political action is much worse developed than the sociology of partisan attachment. Individual intelligence became an easily researchable topic when the developers of intelligence tests translated a complex mental entity into a simple series of criteria, like whether a person got question 56 right or wrong. The invention of voting and elections turned the question of which side are you on into such a "Democrat or Republican" type of question. We have no immediate prospect of turning the effectiveness of public policy into such an easily measured variable, so its sociology will continue to have to be studied by such indirect methods as we have used here.

THE SOCIOLOGY OF ETHNIC AND NATIONAL LOYALTIES

By national or ethnic loyalty we mean the identification by an individual of his or her interests with the interest of a nation or ethnic group. A person is loyal if he or she is willing to sacrifice some personal interests for the sake of group interests. This often is caused by a person's belief that the group interests are truly his or her personal interests rather than by any special altruism. Thus nationalism is in part a *belief system* which asserts that one's own interests are promoted by the promotion of the group and are damaged by damage to the group.

But often, perhaps usually, there is really no cognitive separation between individual and group interests, so "belief system" is too flattering a word. "Of course we have to resist invasion"—this leaves the "we" unanalyzed, a part of the natural order of things, a natural subject of the verb "have to." The analogies that naturally occur to people defending the national draft against pacifists are family analogies: "Wouldn't you kill a man to defend your mother from being raped?" The assumption that the "we" of a nation is like the "we" of a family is implicit in this argument. What we want to do here is to develop a theory of the social conditions under which such unanalyzed "we" concepts come to be the natural subject in sentences about political values and policies.

Likewise it seems perfectly natural to a nationalist that my income and your income should be added together to make up the National Income and that you and I should both praise the politician who increases the sum of our incomes. It is not that we *believe* that if you are better off and I am worse off this is a good thing; instead the sum itself has an unanalyzed magic as a measure of a good thing.

Further, many of the psychological phenomena of nationalism have very little cognitive content at all. They consist of direct sentimental ties to the nation or ethnic group and to its symbols, possessions, prestige, and history. A massacre of comembers of the group hurts more than a massacre of other strangers, even though one had no personal ties with those killed. Trampling the flag or writing an unflattering history of a national or ethnic hero makes a loyal person angry. That is, national or ethnic loyalty consists in large measure of an unreflective tendency to take joy in the successes of a group and sorrow in its failures and to devote oneself to the promotion and defense of the group as if one were promoting and defending one's own integrity and honor.

Clearly ethnic groups and nations vary in the degree to which they have such loyalty among their constituencies. And different potential constituents of an ethnic or national group will have different degrees of loyalty. Thus there are two separate problems for explanation: the variation among groups in the average level of national and ethnic loyalty and the variation among individuals or subgroups in their degree of loyalty. Below we will offer a theory of these variations in terms of the degree to which a person's social identity depends on the group.

But so far we have not touched on the use of national and ethnic hatreds in politics.[24] Under what conditions are governmental policies justified (or attacked) in terms of national or ethnic solidarity and loyalty? There surely is a sense in which the Nazi regime was more nationalistic than the socialist regime of the Weimar Republic that preceded it. The American Legion's patriotism is different from the loyalty of the American Civil Liberties Union to the Constitution and in some sense is more nationalistic. Black Power movements that involve distrust of any whites in positions of power over blacks are more nationalistic than Civil Rights movements that aim to make powerful whites behave decently. The people who want to win in Vietnam were more nationalistic in some sense than those who want to get out, though the question of what was "in the national interest" was open (in fact, it was what the debate was mainly about).

What all these various nationalistic movements have in common is a wish to suppress internal divisions within the nation and to define people outside the group as untrustworthy as allies and implacably evil as enemies.

The problem of creating a theory of nationalism, then, is that it is composed of diametrically opposed forces, which have opposite explanations. It is on the one hand a generous spirit of identification with the sufferings of a group, a love of compatriots. As such it has the causes of generosity and solidarity as its causes. But it is on the other hand a spirit of distrust of the potential treason of any opposition within the group and a hatred of strangers. As such it has the causes of hatred and suspicion as its causes. Thus an explanation of why a society *can* wage war, can call on its young men to sacrifice their lives and its workers to sacrifice real wages and consumption so that war material can be supplied, is somewhat the opposite of the explanation of why a society *wants* to wage war or why some people call so exquisitely loud for the suppression of trade unions and strikes so that we can unite against the enemy.

We need a theory with two parts: one of them an explanation of the solidarity of groups, the other an explanation of why solidarity goes sour. We need to understand how a person mixes his or her own identity with the fate of a group and why he or she chooses to defend that identity by hating outsiders and suspecting insiders. It is the great tragedy of social life that every extension of solidarity, from family to village, village to nation, presents also the opportunity of organizing hatred on a larger scale. The first half of this part will be directed to the explanation of variations in solidarity; the second half to variations in hatred.

The Normative System and Identity

By a person's "identity" we mean the set of social statuses in which one expects to pursue one's purposes, gratify one's lusts, solve one's problems, find fellowship and support.[25] An identity then is an organization of one's social life in the future, in the light of one's motives and future motives, in relation to one's social opportunities. An identity is solid when one has an expectation that he or she can marry, make a living, keep out of jail, make friends, have and educate children, by doing the sorts of things that he or she now knows how to do. A firm sense of identity then is an accrued confidence in the social validity of one's problem-solving capacities. It consists concretely in the expectation that one's competence will allow him or her to get a good job, find a spouse to love and be loved by, throw darts or cook or play poker well enough to be accepted as one of the crowd, and so on.

When one's identity is attacked, as it is by unemployment, retirement and loss of capacity with old age, exile, a crippling injury or brain damage, a person's fate passes psychologically out of his or her hands. The things he or she has learned how to do are no longer worth anything. Such a person can no longer rely on being loved and appreciated for being the kind of person he or she has learned how to be. The usual symptoms of severe identity crises are apathy, free-floating rage, and avaliability for new identities that would have been uncivilized by a person's old standards.[26]

In order to understand what social conditions might produce a solid identity, we have to analyze under what conditions the culture that a person learns will actually solve his or her life problems. A culture, in the famous definition, is a "design for living." But like architectural designs, cultural designs sometimes work and sometimes do not. From the point of view of identity formation, a culture is integrated if the design for solving life problems taught by a culture does in fact solve those problems. Broadly speaking our hypothesis is that if an ethnic group or nation teaches a person techniques for making a living, defending his or her rights, marrying and raising children, *and can make those techniques work for him or her,* then there will be a direct tie between a person's identity and the group. This direct tie is where the energy of ethnic and national loyalty comes from. An attack on such a group is an attack on a person's capacity to solve the problems of his or her life, and so it releases great patriotic energies. The promotion of such a group is, in a sense, an expansion of an individual.

Ecological Range and Citizenship

We can define a person's *ecological range* as the set of social relations within which most of his or her problems arise and have their solutions. In a subsistence farming village in the jungles of southern Mexico, in which the people speak an indigenous language, most problems arise and are settled (if at all) in the village itself. As the inhabitants go out for wage labor, their wages are settled in a national labor market, exploitation is controlled by national political movements and laws, education is provided by a national school authority, and so forth. The ecological range of a typical person in such a modernized village is the nation. The "brain drain" from poorer countries to the United States indicates that some professional people's ecological range is worldwide. A civil servant or a military officer almost invariably has a national ecological range. One of the main causes of maimed identities in developing countries is that the solutions to life problems learned for an ecological range of village level must be applied to cope with problems whose solution is only possible with national institutions.

A person's "citizenship" in the normative system of a group may be defined as the proportion of his or her life problems which is solved according to the normative system. The question we ask is, Of all the institutional services a person gets, how many are provided within the group?

From the point of view of the group, this is a question of "institutional completeness." [27] Groups that provide within themselves the institutions by which people make a living, defend their property, marry, school their children, and retire make members highly dependent on the group. If in addition people within the group have a good deal of influence through representative institutions on how the problem-solving organizations are set up, then their fate in life depends in great measure on their activity within the group. Thus groups that are highly institutionally complete will tend to have people solving the problems of their lives within the group.

The same variable appears for individual attachment as for group attachment. If a person's problems typically require that he or she go beyond a group to work them out, then the person is dependent on the larger setting for the normative regulation of his or her central life concerns. If a person's problems typically can be resolved in the village by influence on neighbors, then he or she need take no interest in larger national institutions. If a person is downtrodden and exploited in a group, he or she cannot solve any problems by means of influence on group institutions. That is, one's citizenship in a group is a product of how much one is *subject to* the group, multiplied by how much one is *influential in* the group. If one is highly subject to a group, then the more influential one is, the more one can control his or her fate by group activity. If one is influential in a group *but* has no interest in group arrangements because he or she acts on a larger stage, then one fails to be incorporated in the group.

Clearly the average ecological range of a national society will determine to what extent people are dependent on national institutions. In "traditional" societies only civil servants, merchants, military men, and a few others have an ecological range as large as the nation, and often many of them have an international range. For instance in colonial societies a large proportion of the production that is shipped out of any given local area is shipped abroad. In that case the merchants depend on international, "imperial" institutions rather than on national institutions. The higher the rate of interchange of people, goods, and communications among the subparts of a national society, the more an individual's problems will typically be solved only in national institutions (Kunkel, 1961; Deutsch, 1953).

Further an individual's identity will depend more on a group the more his or her individual ecological range corresponds to the range regulated by group institutions. Retail traders will tend to have more local identities than wholesalers, domestic wholesalers more national identities than cosmopolitan importers and exporters, importers and exporters more national identities than shipping lines flying flags of convenience; tankers registered in Liberia or Panama are not noted for Liberian or Panamanian nationalism. That is, a person's social role and the normatively regulated social solutions to a person's life problems will tend to be created by a set of institutions whose own range corresponds to his or her own. Hence a person's identity will tend, given reasonably benign social institutions, to correspond to his or her ecological range. An economy like that of the United States, which exports and imports about a fourteenth of its national income each year, will tend to give people more national economic identities than an economy like Scandinavia or the Low Countries, which have a much higher ratio of foreign trade to national income, because a person's daily economic life in the Low Countries depends on the world trade situation more than on national regulation of economic life.

In general we would expect that when citizens of imperial and international countries (e.g., England or the United States) emigrate, they will probably be incorporated into foreign societies *less* than immigrants whose national loyalties are not reinforced by international institutions. For instance, we would expect the English community in Argentina to have assimilated into Argentine society less than the Italian or Chilean immigrant streams, because an Englishman's economic and political role *in Argentina* depended on his relationships to metropolitan economic and political institutions.

If an ethnic group such as the French Canadians is large and geographically segregated, has its own local governmental institutions (especially schools) and a well-developed religious and social welfare organization, then it is likely to get the loyalty of most of its members. But if an individual French Canadian is isolated in Saskatchewan, is well served by local governmental and social welfare institutions, comfortable in a Catholic Church dominated by immigrants from Eastern Europe, and has children progressing well in an English-language school, then he or she as an individual may have very little French Canadian loyalty. If on the contrary he or she is a professional, French-speaking intellectual, for instance a broadcast announcer or a French-speaking Catholic theologian, then his or her ecological range in Canada will be exactly the French cultural group.

Now our problem is to formulate these complex interdependencies among the ecological structure, the institutional structure, and people's loyalties in a sufficiently clean form so that we can work with them. What we are trying to explain first is the embedding of people's political conflicts and the formulation of their planning problems in a set of general national or ethnic loyalties. That is, the significance of loyalty for the political process is that it brings to bear on particular political conflicts and particular governmental administrative problems those considerations of other values and of the general health of the social system which limit the conflict. Conversely, if a conflict of interest occurs between different national or ethnic groups and those groups have high degrees of internal loyalty, then each of the conflicting parties can call on the loyalties of the nation or ethnic group as a whole to support its particular interests. Roughly speaking, then, loyalty explains why there is social peace within groups and great risks of war among groups. The empirical proposition here is that generalized or diffuse loyalty of a group depends on that group being in fact the locus of normative solutions to life problems, resulting in the group being a central point in the organization of people's personal identities, in their confidence that their competencies and social rights will in fact solve those life problems.

This proposition can be elaborated by defining a set of related concepts: "ecological range," "institutional completeness," and "citizenship." The definitions of these concepts rather go around in circles, because each specifies an aspect of the relation between the problems a person has in his or her life and the problems solved by the institutions of a group. (1) The degree to which a person is subject to a group depends on (a) the degree to which the group has institutions for solving the problems of a given kind (the degree of institutional completeness of the group), times (b) the degree to which the person has those problems. (2) A group's institutional completeness for a given set of people (a above) will depend on (c) the aggregate ecological range of the set of people, times (d) the ecological range of the institutions of the group itself, times (e) the number of areas of life for which the group has institutions. (3) The degree to which a person can control his or her own fate through action within the group (a person's citizenship in the group) depends on (f) the degree to which the person is subject to the group (1 above), times (g) the degree of influence or representation he or she has in the group's government. The central hypothesis restated is that a person's loyalty to a group depends on the degree to which the person can control his or her own fate through action in the group, that is, his or her citizenship in the group (3 above).

Propositions on National Loyalty

From this general line of argument we can derive the following propositions about the degree to which a person's identity will be invested in an ethnic or national group, the degree to which a person is likely to sacrifice his or her individual interests (e.g., interest in staying alive) for group interests (e.g., national defense), the degree to which a person conceives of his or her own and the group's interest to be identical so that when pursuing the national defense he or she is pursuing the defense of an unanalyzed "we," the degree to which a person's particular conflicts within the group will be limited by considerations of the general value of the institutional life of the group as a whole.

1.   For an ethnic or national group, the *average* level of loyalty will rise as the group becomes more institutionally complete. More specifically: (a) the more functions that are performed by group organizations, the more loyal its members; (b) the greater the coverage or content of the rights of citizenship in a group and the more a person has a *right* to the institutional services provided by the group, the more loyal the group's members (this may be roughly estimated by the proportion of a country's gross national product spent by the government on social and educational services); (c) the more representative a group's government, the more loyal its members, because then the institutions of the group are likely in fact to solve the members' problems; (d) the more segregated territorially a group is, the more loyal its members, because many

institutions that solve people's problems are, more or less necessarily, geographically organized.

2.   The greater the proportion of members of an ethnic or national group who have an ecological range identical to the boundaries of the group, the greater will be the average level of loyalty of the group, and hence: (a) the greater the internal development of markets for labor and goods and the less the dependence on local subsistence economy, the greater the national loyalty; (b) the less the international market for labor and goods, the greater the national loyalty; (c) the larger the employment by institutions that themselves have a national ecological range (e.g., the civil service or national army), the greater the national loyalty.

3.   The more an *individual's* life problems have their solutions within an ethnic or national group, by use of group institutions, the greater the individual level of loyalty, and hence: (a) the more the defense of an individual's property, job rights, or livelihood depends on a national legal or trade union system, the greater his or her loyalty; (b) the more that the success or failure of an individual's employing organization is defined in national terms (e.g., this is very high for military men), the greater his or her loyalty; (c) the more the individual's developed needs (e.g., religious preferences) are the same as the needs developed by his or her conationals (and served by national institutions), the greater his or her loyalty; (d) the more the individual's ecological range is extended above the local community and kin relations to dependence on ethnic or national institutions (e.g., the more the individual migrates to find work), the greater his or her national loyalty; (e) the more solid an individual's enfranchisement in the group, that is, the greater the individual's rights and the less exploitation there is of that individual, the greater his or her loyalty.

"Racism" and Ethnic Loyalty

In many societies some large group of families and their descendants are given a distinct social and legal status because they are thought to belong to a distinct "people." Such a "people" is most often created by forced migration (e.g., Negroes in the United States), by conquest (e.g., Catholic Irishmen in Ireland), or by voluntary migration of a group with a distinctive set of institutions (e.g., Jews or Gipsies in Eastern Europe). Very often the distinctive social position of these families is explained ideologically by a theory of genetic differences among the peoples involved, that is, by a "racist" ideology. For the sake of convenience and evocativeness, we will call the general phenomenon of differential status that is determined by communal attachment by the name of one of its most common ideological defenses, "racism," but the analysis is supposed to apply to all communally organized status systems.

Racist systems may be classified by the proportion of the areas of life of the people of subordinate status which is administered by ethnic criteria. In the extreme of *apartheid* systems, the economy, the civil courts, rights of travel, political citizenship, as well as residence, schooling, marriage, and sociability are all administered with ethnic criteria dominant. In the American North, the civil courts, the voting booths, and large parts of the economy are administered on formally nonracial grounds, while residence, schooling, marriage, religion, and large parts of recreational life are highly racist for blacks. Jews in most American cities have moved from the present position of blacks (Jews seem to me to have been about at the same state as black people now around 1920) to a position of exclusion only from marriage and religious institutions of the gentiles (and those exclusions are not perfectly tight).

The point of this definition of racism is that in addition to depending on his or her group's internal institutions, a person may be more or less dependent on the jural status of his or her group in a societywide normative system. That is, regardless of the institutional development of the individual's own group, if a dominant group has developed special ethnic institutions and imposed them on him or her, so that the individual's life problems must be solved in relation to institutions informed by ethnic criteria, then the jural status of the ethnic group penetrates his or her identity. A person cannot solve the problems of his or her life without reference to his or her ethnic identity unless other people treat the person (with respect to those problems) without reference to ethnic identity. The greater the degree of racism in a society, the greater the extent to which we will expect the minority groups to have intense ethnic loyalties. For example, to a considerable extent putting Japanese in concentration camps during World War II created the Japanese ethnic group in the United States (Grodzins, 1956).

There should be a greater effect of racism on the ethnic loyalty of minorities than of majorities, and this should apply whether the minority is subordinate, as the Negroes and Jews in the United States, or superordinate, as the whites in Rhodesia or South Africa. The reason is that a minority member will be distinguished by race from the person he or she is dealing in many more relations in daily life than will a majority member. If there are, say, a hundred thousand interracial contacts per day in an area, that hundred thousand will be a much larger proportion of the contacts of a minority of a hundred thousand (one per person per day) than of a majority of a million (one contact per person every ten days).

The Cognitive Construction of Citizenship

The analysis above has been almost entirely an "objective" analysis, in the sense that it assumes that if people depend on a nation they will see that they do depend on it and direct their attention to the national scene. Or we assume that if the true reason people are poor is racial discrimination, they will see it. I believe that in fact groups of people are, in the long run, statistically right about such questions. But at any given time there will be differences in the degree of correspondence between the objective and the ideological situations.

For the average person, institutional problems take the form of difficulties in his or her interaction with particular other people in particular settings. A worker's problem is not, in the first instance, that the wage rate in his or her occupation is too low—it is that the employer will not pay a fair wage. To manipulate the employer by changing the structure and government of the national labor market is not the most obvious way to get more money. As Lenin taught us to formulate the problem, the masses can only by themselves reach the level of trade union consciousness.

Changes in the ecological range of people's problems tend to be perceived in the first instance by intellectuals and publicists, secondly by the leadership of concrete groups, and lastly by the membership of those groups themselves. Thus we find broadly speaking that early in the course of national development, intellectuals are more nationalistic than the population.[28] Later on in national development, intellectuals tend to be more internationalist than others. The same generalizations apply, though in lesser degree, to group leaders as compared with members.

The Social Causes of Group Hatred

By outgroup hatred I mean the infusion in a group on which one's identity depends (as analyzed above) of an ideology that says (a) that the only acceptable relation of the ingroup to the outgroup is unconditional surrender or extinction and (b) that those in the ingroup who have attachments to or tolerance of the outgroup are traitors and should be treated as enemies. This is a caricature (commonly called an "ideal type") of aggressive nationalism but identifies the core of the concept. Any sort of solidarity can have such outgroup hatred attached to it. It produces the "liquidation of the *kulaks* as a class" in the Soviet Union in the 1930s as well as "the final solution of the Jewish question" in German-ruled Europe in the 1940s. Class, ethnic, religious, or familial solidarities as well as more implicit solidarities of "normal" people against "deviants" (witches, lunatics, juvenile delinquents) can produce patterns of group hatred. Our problem is to outline the social sources of such hatreds.

The classic case of nationalism as outgroup hatred is Nazism. What we need then is a sociology of Nazism. The combination in the Nazi movement of outgroup aggression and internal suppression of dissent as treason is characteristically authoritarian. But the same pattern can be seen in, for example, some police-oriented movements to stomp out juvenile delinquency; the delinquents are seen as embodiments of the satanic principle rather than as human beings, and judges or criminologists who want to "mollycoddle" them (treat them as people) are seen as subversive of the normative order. This similarity suggests that a common orientation to the nature of the normative order is involved. The orientation is that (1) the privileges of those now advantaged by the normative order are especially valuable or sacred—the *conservative* principle, (2) the advantages of that normative order should be reserved for those now protected by it—the *exclusiveness* principle, (3) the normative order is under attack by evil forces outside and also within the group—the principle of *satanism,* (4) normative judgments are easy to make and involve simple and fundamental values—the *fundamentalism* principle.

We argue then that any normative order is subject to movements showing conservatism, exclusiveness, satanism, and fundamentalism. When the normative order that primarily organizes the institutional life of groups is embedded in a nation-state, the form that such fundamentalist movements takes is nationalism. That is, part of the explanation of extremist nationalism is the same as the explanation of the extension of citizenship discussed above. It is exactly because the principles of solidarity, justice, and the good life are now embedded in nation-states that fundamentalism now so often takes a Nazi style rather than, as formerly, a witch-burning style.

The Embedding of Fundamentalism in Other Ideologies

The conservatism of the psychology of fundamentalist movements of all kinds can be revolutionary. This is of course true of all conservative ideologies; there have probably been more conservative revolutions than radical ones. But it is peculiarly true of fundamentalist movements that all sorts of sophisticated established systems of administration and privilege can come under attack. There were strong fundamentalist elements in the Reformation, which was certainly revolutionary toward established church organization. Fundamentalist patriotism often attacks such sophisticated systems of privilege as universities or supreme courts. There is in fact a certain inherent affinity between fundamentalism and populism. If all the complexities of the normative order are merely veils to hide the simple truth, the "people," with the simple truth, are more to be trusted than the elite with their pettifoggery. One of the complexities of the Roman Church, for example, was to treat sin realistically, to forgive heresy on renunciation of heresy, to consider infidels as creatures created in the image of God. That is, a simpleminded statement that Christians were more worthy than agents of the devil, a common theme in fundamentalist parts of the Reformation, is simultaneously a conservative defense of the privileged position of Christians and a radical critique of the "corrupt" elite of the Church.

But the problem of isolating national and ethnic hatred for a unified explanation is more complex still. For fundamentalist ideals and movements can be identified with the most various conceptions of the nature of the normative order. Consider for example the following varieties of racist ideology. By racist ideology I mean a fundamentalist ideology in which the privileges to be preserved are the privileges of an ethnic group, the principle of exclusion from the normative order has racial content, the satanic principle is applied to mean corruption by another race, and the simpleminded solution to normative questions is to apply hostility to racial groups. This ideology is not to be confused with institutional racism described above, though of course they are generally linked in practice.

Racism in an Attack on the Lumpenproletariat

All modern societies have a subpopulation that has failed to make a satisfactory connection with the world of work. Some people in the subpopulation have spoiled identities because they have prison records. Some cannot perform the required activities of work roles because of illness, alcoholism, drug addiction, or mental incapacity. Some cannot form the will to perform work roles because they lack faith that the system will reward them, because they do not want those rewards, or because they lack faith in their own capacities. Some have a run of bad luck—getting jobs for which they were not qualified, getting laid off because they were hired last in a declining industry. Some leave spouses with whom they have quarrelled for years. These people form the lumpenproletariat, the ragged casual laborers, petty criminals, drunks, and cast-offs of urban society.

Such people offend the principles of bourgeois society. They are the kind of people that respectable workers fear their sons-in-law will turn out to be. Respectable middle-class people use them as a symbol to explain why the poor must always remain poor—they obviously lack the bourgeois virtues of thrift, hard work, and keeping out of prison. By serving as a counterexample, they reinforce the self-satisfied complacency of respectable people. (Conversely, of course, they are also a symbol of romantic rebellion; serving for a period as a member of the lumpenproletariat is almost a qualification for the career of a radical writer). The point is not that the lumpenproletariat is not really what respectable people think it is, although many careful studies by novelists and a few careful studies by social scientists show that it is mostly not—that in fact the value of the lumpenproletariat are similar to the values of the respectable middle class.[29] Rather we want to identify the rejection of the lumpenproletariat as a general ideology held by the hard-working proletariat and the bourgeoisie.

This rejection of the lumpenproletariat often takes a racist form in which, without much reflection or evidence, the characteristics of the lumpenproletariat are attributed to a low-status ethnic group, such as Negroes in the United States. All the attributes of fundamentalism can be associated with racism of an antilumpenproletarian variety. For example a typical ideology would hold that (1) the respectability of neighborhoods where whites now live ought to be preserved against black-lumpenproletarian contamination (conservatism); (2) the rights of respectable people should not be extended to respectable black people (exclusivism); (3) various satanic forces (communists, "blockbusters" and real estate speculators, outside agitators), including both misled whites and blacks, are trying to undermine the integrity of neighborhoods by integration (satanism); and (4) one need not answer the question of where a growing population of blacks *should* live—it is enough to follow the simple principle that they should not invade white neighborhoods (fundamentalism). Such fundamentalist racism, with the basic function of praising respectability in a fundamentalist way, can also have international political repercussions, as when it informs the American immigration laws (Higham, 1965).

Populist Racism

Often the group that relates a traditional feudal land tenure system to the institutions of internal capitalism is an urban commercial ethnic group. Such a group seems, to residents of the societies, to have the functions both of shoring up the worst features of the old regime by bringing money to landlords, collecting their rents, and so on and introducing the worst features of the new capitalist regime: usury, unsteady prices, the use of the law rather than the local norms of justice in commercial dealings, treatment of customers and laborers as strangers, the principle of *caveat emptor,* and so on. The Jews in Eastern Europe, the Chinese in Southeast Asia, the Indians in Kenya and Uganda are examples of urban commercial groups that function to create these combined conservatizing and subversive effects.

The response to this structural situation by the peasantry subject to it and often by the landlords and bureaucrats (colonial or native) disturbed by capitalistic invasions into the old regime is "anti-Semitism." The anti-Semitism of Eastern Europe was often associated with populist ideas. The "social racism" of the Nazis, in which the evils of credit and money and cosmopolitan contamination of the nation were identified with Jews, had a great appeal in Poland. Similar populist racism is characteristic of the response to the Chinese in Southeast Asia or to the Indians in Kenya and Uganda.[30]

Populist racism therefore claims to restore the normative order, reclaim virtues of the old regime, and take from the ethnically alien exploiters their illgotten gains. Its fundamentalist forms lead to pograms, concentration camps, and the creation of "displaced persons" deprived by popular national revolutions of their status in the societies in which they were born, with no place else to go. Such displaced persons can sometimes be recognized by their British passports, which once allowed people to come to Britain.

Racism as a Justification of Exploitation

In situations in which plantation labor is imported, in colonial or semicolonial circumstances, or the native population of a conquered territory is put to work, the workers are usually deprived of all political rights, all access to coercive power. This means on the one hand that they cannot defend themselves against exploitation and on the other that they cannot tax themselves to build communal institutions or to sue runaway fathers for child support. The reason they are denied political rights is that they would use these rights to temper the rate of exploitation. In this circumstance a racial ideology alleging communal incompetence of the proletarian race, lack of integrity and good faith, incapacity for the higher forms of civilization, justifies continued governance by the plantation elite.

That is, a racial ideology may serve the function of giving a lesser value to the grievances and aspirations of one social class as compared with another, when the social classes belong to different "peoples" with different conditions of immigration and citizenship. This is the "gentlemanly racism" of the plantation counties of the American South, where, typically, innocent men were not lynched; only rebels were.

The fundamentalist form of exploitative racism is characteristic of South Africa, where fundamentalist racism seems to be mixed with a good dose of religious Boer fundamentalism as well. It (1) preserves the monopoly of political and economic rights to the whites (conservatism); (2) excludes black people, who are set apart by racial norms, and lately also civilized white people who oppose apartheid, from the benefits of citizenship (exclusivism); (3) sees the possibility of subversion of the system of stratification in every white-black contact, even playing tennis (satanism); and (4) upsets delicate and complex institutions (e.g., the exploitive labor market itself) by applying simple norms of apartheid (fundamentalism).

Thus even though there is some inherent tendency for fundamentalist movements to be populist, fundamentalism can be embedded in ideologies having quite different social and historical functions. The same is true of the opposite, of course: the main artistic, scientific, and legal achievements of human civilization have been embedded in ideologies justifying all sorts of exploitation and all sorts of revolution. The reason is, of course, that what people think the normative order is and ought to be is determined by their positions in it. For their positions create the grievances and aspirations and interests that a just order would remedy, satisfy, and serve. The grievances of a Malaysian peasant against a Chinese moneylender give the peasant a notion of what a just order should do that is different from the notion held by a white South African who has grievances against the belated constitutionalism of the British Colonial Office. Responding to the normative order in one's own interest gives rise to an appropriate form of racist fundamentalism. Because each of us internalizes a different part of the normative order, a part in keeping with our own interests and grievances, our fundamentalism takes different substantive forms.

Alternative Explanations of Aggressive Fundamentalism

If fundamentalism can be embedded in different substantive ideologies, then it can be explained neither by the content of those ideologies nor by the causes appropriate for explaining that content. The populist (and reactionary) character of anti-Semitism in Eastern Europe must be explained in terms of the role of Jews in Eastern Europe and the grievances of peasants (and landlords or bureaucrats) against that role, by the role of Jews in Christian popular theology, and the like. This explains why, *when pograms and concentration camps come,* they are directed against the Jews. But what we want to know is whether, given the content of a loyalty to a normative order, we can locate conditions that will make the level of hostility embedded in that loyalty increase and the cognitive and normative complexity decrease, so as to produce a fundamentalist variant of that loyalty.

1.   Reality.   In social scientific explanations of people's beliefs, the first hypothesis should be that the people are right. If for example the leaders of Arab states proclaim that they want to destroy Israel, shoot artillery at Israel, expel Jews from their countries, refuse to negotiate with or to recognize Israel, it is not terribly surprising if Israelis think Arabs are out to get them. Conversely of course, Israeli bombers flying over Cairo seem hostile, and the fundamentalist solution of shooting them down seems simple in normative theory, if technically somewhat difficult.

War causes fundamentalism. When someone really is out to destroy a person's normative order and to kill that person and his or her conationals, it tends to produce in that person a feeling of simpleminded patriotism.

2.   Fundamentalism as a mental disease.   The thesis of the *Authoritarian Personality* (Adorno *et al.*, 1950) can briefly be summarized in two propositions: (1) conservatism, exclusivism, satanism, and fundamentalism form a unified psychological entity, roughly measured by the famous *F*-scale and (2) certain disturbances in people's biographies which produce other sorts of psychological disorders also produce the *F*-scale complex. The first of these propositions seems to me very well established for Western democracies by repeated demonstrations of correlations among the items of the scale. (Note however that conservatism as defined above does not necessarily imply support for conservative parties, though in the United States at high levels of political activity it generally seems to do so in fact.) The second proposition really has two components, that the *F*-scale complex is *associated in fact* with other symptoms of mental disease and imperfect social functioning and that both *are produced by* disordered biographies. The first seems to have been thoroughly demonstrated by McClosky (1963). The second component has been repeatedly demonstrated for one aspect of biography: education discourages fundamentalism (except of the realistic variety mentioned above: educated Arabs are just as hostile to Israel as Arab peasants are).[31] No other biographical inferences seem to me to have been solidly established.

3.   Fundamentalism as a movement of desperation.   None of the above explanations could account for the rapid growth of fascist movements in most advanced capitalist countries during the depression of the 1930s. People's social identities had been deeply attacked: capitalists who thought their skills would always make them money were going bankrupt, and profits were cut drastically in the most powerful companies, especially in heavy industry; workers were thrown out of work; students faced careers without prospects, if they could find jobs at all; shopkeepers extended credit to respectable people who then couldn't pay. It did not seem to matter which government was in power, for they were all (save perhaps the Soviet Union) impotent to reconstruct satisfactory lives for people. Since the sophisticated answers, ranging from Hoover's stalwart capitalism in the United States to social democracy in Germany, did not work, their advantage over the simple answers of fascism were not obvious. (In fact, if one is willing to ignore the ultimate consequences of war and extermination camps, one can conclude that the simple fascist answer worked somewhat better than the others.)

When people who do not ordinarily much analyze public questions have deep and persistent grievances because of a historical crisis, fundamentalist answers to those questions have a disproportionate appeal. The fundamentalist elements of much of the Black Power movement in the United States can perhaps be explained in this way. An elaborate theory maintaining essentially this proposition is argued by Smelser (1962).

4. Fundamentalist cultural traditions.   Fundamentalist Christianity is associated with anti-Semitism in the United States (Glock and Stark, 1970). The traditional "isolationist" vote in the American Congress, which I think can be called fundamentalist, is disproportionately concentrated in the midwestern rural home of northern religious fundamentalism. Education, which decreases fundamentalism in religion, also decreases commitment to racism and to oversimplified punitive treatment of deviants. The more fundamentalist religion of the Boers in South Africa coincides with their more fundamentalist racial policies.

From such bits and pieces of evidence one can suggest that socialization into one sort of fundamentalism predisposes people to other forms. One may first learn to explain one's troubles in satanic terms, for example, by learning about a literally fallen angel. But Jewish conspiracies may easily substitute for fallen angels psychologically, once the efficacy of satanic agents is firmly implanted in the mind.

5. Fundamentalism as an ideology of policies which will not bear examination. Systematic hysteria and rejection of critical reason may be a tool in the hands of people who know perfectly well that the policies they are following would not be acceptable to the public if the public knew what was going on. Politicians who promise all things to all people, give rich-rolling oratory that we associate with southern demagogy in the United States, or constantly change the number of communists in the State Department, may allow the government to follow no policy at all but rather respond to particular pressures or to follow a policy that serves secret devious interests. The lack of correspondence between promise and delivery is covered with a rhetoric of national unity of a fundamentalist kind.

It is hard to think of the evidence that would support or refute this view. It is true that much nationalist rhetoric is strangely silent on who gets what, but that may be because to a fundamentalist it is obvious that everyone should get what he ought to get. It seems to me that our sociology of conflict and solidarity and of the functions of wrong-headed ideologies is too primitive to deal productively with the role of conspiracy and deliberate obfuscation in nationalist movements.

Summary

Our problem in this section has been to describe the social sources of system loyalty. That loyalty can take a generous form of willingness to sacrifice one's own interest for perceived group welfare. It can take a selfish form of willingness to sacrifice outsiders or opponents within the system for perceived group welfare. The pervasiveness of loyalty in political affairs is illustrated by the large majority of group decisions, especially decisions about group defense against outsiders, which are not the focus of political divisions. Bipartisan foreign policies or socialist parties' "betrayals" of their pacifist positions in times of war are examples to be explained. Ethnic groups and nations are much more unified than one would predict from the sociology of partisan clashes.

But not all nations and ethnic groups have the same level of consent, the same confinement of loyalties within the group. We have been trying to suggest why nationalism is more of a political resource of some governments and elites than of others. We have also tried to specify why that resource is sometimes used in primitive and obnoxious ways.

The core idea of our theory of when a nation will be able to call on its citizens and diverse interest groups to sacrifice for the group is the institutional grounding of people's identities. The more a person's life problems have their solution in the institutional order created by the political system, the more that system becomes identified in that person's mind with his or her own life. The capacity of individuals to solve the problems of constructing a satisfactory life in a group's institutional order depends on a complex interrelation between his or her particular social location and the character of the group's institutional order. Thus that interrelation will tend to predict the frequency of "statesmanship" in that group, if we understand by statesmanship the special priority of conceptions of collective welfare over partisan interests.

The variables we have suggested to use in analyzing this problem are the institutional completeness of the group, the group's ecological range, the ecological range of various types of individuals within the group, and the particular relation of each person's needs in constructing his or her type of life to the needs satisfied by the institutional order. Propositions relating these variables to loyalty are outlined.

Then we turned to ethnic relations, to the fact that institutional solutions to the problems of the lives of some ethnic groups are imposed on them from outside. In particular, a ruling ethnic group with high internal loyalty often imposes a "racist" institutional order on another group, so that the others are repetitively in all institutional areas treated as outsiders, as rightless. The more pervasive that jural exclusion, the more ethnic loyalty will be imposed from outside. Thus the extreme of ethnic loyalty would come when people are involved in a rich institutional order *within* their own groups and are systematically treated as rightless outsiders in a normative order imposed from outside. Some colonized peoples have approximately confronted those extreme conditions.

In the last sections above, we have tried to outline some alternative explanations for why ethnic and national loyalties are sometimes infused with fundamentalist group hatred. That is, the statesmanship produced by group loyalty mentioned above can consist of sacrificing partisan interest to wage holy wars against outsiders or to establish concentration camps for minorities. The alternative theories of fundamentalist nationalism offered were: that outsiders and minorities really are conspiring to destroy the group; that fundamentalists are mentally diseased; that the identities dependent on group institutions are maimed by extensive malfunction of problem-solving techniques, as in economic depressions; that fundamentalism in one area of life (e.g., religion) tends to produce fundamentalism in other areas; and that fundamentalist loyalties are a resource of leaders of nations to distract people from the leaders' incapacity or unwillingness to solve the actual problems of people's lives in the group.

Because of the superposition of group loyalty and fundamentalist ideologies, the sociology of nationalism is filled with theoretically intractable ironies. One symptom of a high level of group loyalty, for example, is a large number of issues in a political system which are resolved without partisan conflict. But another symptom of a high level of group loyalty in its fundamentalist variant is partisanship carried to the extreme of genocide, treason trials, and intergroup hatred. The sociology of nationalism depends for its future development on an adequate theoretical composition of the variable to be explained.

NOTES

1.   The reason for putting "scientific" in quotation marks is that there are good reasons to think that people take their votes more seriously than they do their answers to an interviewer. They think about their votes more, talk to their friends more, read the news more, to vote than to give an opinion. Hence probably election choices are better measures of a people's considered beliefs than are answers to interviewers, because of the *consequential* nature of an election poll.

2.   This observation and most of the theoretical basis for this section were given by Coleman (1967). Note that the "chances of winning" by growing depend on an indi-

vidual's or party's time perspective; they may have no chance at all in the next election but a good chance within the next 20 years.

3.   The reason the multiple ballots system is similar to proportional representation is that a vote in the first election adds to the bargaining power of the party between the first and second elections, during which it trades its support in the second election for policy concessions, offices for its people, symbolic homage to its principles, etc.

4.   Perhaps the best study of the effects of different power situations on party (in this case, factional) structure is Key (1949). See also Duverger (1959, pp. 206–280).

5.   Occasionally of course he is really a simple soul and believes that a political system can be run with election-time rhetoric.

6.   The formulation used here of the difference between revolutionary and incorporated is based on Coleman (1966a, pp. 615–27).

7.   The equations for constant transition rates are:
for the number of apathetic atoms, $n_{at} = Ne^{-\alpha t}$;

for the number of revolutionary atoms, $n_{rt} = N \dfrac{\alpha}{\beta - \alpha} (e^{-\alpha t} - e^{-\beta t})$,

which has a maximum point where $\dfrac{ln \dfrac{\alpha}{\beta}}{\alpha - \beta} = t$;

and for the number of incorporated atoms, $n_{pt} = N \dfrac{1}{\beta - \alpha} [\alpha(e^{-\beta t} - 1) - \beta(e^{-\alpha t} - 1)]$.

The first of these tails off, decreasing toward zero by a constant proportion of how far it got during each period. The second has a hump and then a long tail, which eventually approaches zero. The third has a kind of ogive shape, as it grows slowly at first (because there are so few revolutionaries), then grows quickly as it soaks up the hump of revolutionaries, then slows down as it approaches 100 percent of the population and has no more people to incorporate.

8.   See especially the rise of the Social Credit party in Quebec (Pinard, 1971, Chapter 2). See also Key (1949, pp. 27–34, 70–75). MacRae (1967) has analyzed a similar relation between *"immobilisme"* in the Fourth Republic in France and the surge movements of Gaullism, Mendesism, and Poujadism. What *immobilisme* is all about is secure dominance of a "one-party" type of system, where the one "party" that permanently controls the government is a coalition of legal parties, a coalition that is guaranteed by sharp lines dividing it from the Communists on the left and Gaulists (much of the time) on the right.

9.   This is an oversimplification for emphasis. See Wolfinger (1965, pp. 896–908) on incorporation of New Haven Italians by the Republican party.

10.   Most of the conventional interpretations among sociologists of the victory of business unionism in the United States seem to me not to take account of the crucial importance of World War I. Immediately before the war the socialist vote in the United States was of the same order of magnitude as the membership of "business unions." Neither was very big, of course, and the question was which would grow faster.

11.   For the United States, see various works by Key (especially 1955, pp. 3–18). For France, see Siegfried (especially 1913).

12.   Cf. MacRae (1967) on the defections that brought down various governments. One has to dig rather hard in the various records of votes and in various scales to get the

information out about the character of the defections, but all the necessary data seem to be there.

13. Perhaps the best information on the variations in the continuity of factions is (again) Key (1949). One excellent theoretical treatment of the conditions for the continuity of partisan attachments to a minority party is by Lipset, Trow, and Coleman (1956).

14. The best study of conservative corporatism is by Schmitter (1968). There are a great many studies of the relations between interest groups and revolutionary national unity regimes, but probably the relation that has attracted the most talent is the one between the Bolshevik party in the Soviet Union and the trade unions. See, for instance, Carr (1950).

15. The following owes a great deal in devious ways to Wilensky (1967).

16. For a summary of these factors, see Wilensky (1967). For studies of social organization of bureaucracies and their effects, see Granick (1967) and Stinchcombe (1974).

17. "Planning" corresponds closely to the neoclassical economic model of firm decision-making, in which the production functions (and the prices of factors and of commodities) are known, and the entrepreneur makes a decision that maximizes a return. "Incrementalism" corresponds to the "method of steepest ascent" for solving maximizing problems and has been treated in economics and in Lindblom (1965).

18. Actually we are interested in "actualized power" rather than "inherent power." That is, an interest group's utility function may have no value set, one way or the other, on any of the variables involved in the plan, either as resources or as outcomes. If the vested interest does not care what policies are followed in a given area, then its power is irrelevant. Thus the P_i in the text is a multiplicative function of the absolute power or resources of group i, say R_i, and the degree of activation of these resources, say D_i. D_i in turn would depend on an inner product of the vector of utilities of group i and a vector of variations on various social and economic variables likely to be influenced by the plan. If the utility of group i for variable j is u_{ij} and the potential variation in that variable that might be caused by the plan is dx_j, then $D_i = f(u_{ij}dx_j)$, where f is an increasing function.

$$P_i = R_iD_i = R_if(u_{ij}dx_j)$$

19. Note however that *if* the plan does not correspond to political realities, a politicized civil service may adapt it so as to increase the liquidity of its resources. An unpolitical paper plan may become politically viable only by being modified by bribery.

20. That is, the theory of imperfect competition tends to regard monopoly power as given, as a cost-free resource of the firm, rather than (as it obviously usually is) a result of deliberate policy and investment. The proof that investments in monopoly power combined with substantive investments do not yield "iron hand" equilibria is usually known as "the oligopoly problem." If monopoly power is given, then it can be treated like any other resource supplied in the factor market, I think, and it will be used in the most productive way by its owners just as money and other forms of power are used. But if one's production at the same time affects consumers and also one's market position with respect to a few competitors, then the equilibrium is indeterminate under classical economic assumptions.

21. The following outline of an answer to this question is a précis of Stinchcombe (1965).

22. The same point for monopolistic powers and market structures is analyzed by Weber (1968) in the section on law in various places. Weber talks of the degree of formality or the degree of calculability of law to refer to this phenomenon. The proposition in Weber then is that the greater the certainty of legal powers, the more that firms will decide what to do in the light of the market chances and consequently the more they will produce useful things, organize themselves efficiently, etc. By the solidity of a normative order then we mean that the principles by which a decision will be taken under various future circumstances can be known and relied on in advance.

23. This strategy is common to several of the best studies of the sociology of rationality. For Max Weber, see Stinchcombe (1969). See the excellent outline of different models of calculation (bureaucratic, market, bargaining, etc.) of welfare problems in Dahl and Lindblom (1953). For a model of scientific rationality, see Hagstrom (1965, pp. 9–69). The Pareto approach to studying rationality was for Pareto to derive the correct answer, compare it with reality, and then explain the difference as due to social causes of the irrationality of the man he was studying. There are obviously two possible hypotheses about who is more intelligent than whom under that procedure. Pareto's studies of the sociology of rationality have therefore not led anywhere. See the summary of Pareto's approach in Parsons (1968, pp. 178–218).

24. The inadequacy of the reasoning of the first sections below for explaining hysterical nationalism was brought home to me especially by a seminar audience at Manchester University.

25. The ideas here are derived from some combination of Erikson (1959) and Grodzins (1956).

26. The analysis of the apathy of Sioux Indians by Erikson (1950, pp. 114–65) is the classic source. For unemployment see Jahoda *et al.* (1933); for the effects of total institutions with total unpredictability of life and more or less complete identity destruction, see Bettelheim (1943). For various kinds of imperfect or maimed identities, see Goffman (1963).

27. This concept is used by Breton (1964). A very similar conception, in completely different language, is developed by Marshall (1950) in talking about different types of citizenship. If a government provides civil legal institutions and "equality before the law" it is less institutionally complete than one that also provides political and group representation institutions but more complete than one that provides no access to the king's courts. When governments provide for various life crises (old age, sickness, child support, and schooling) they are still more institutionally complete. Marshall calls these different institutional services types of citizenship rights.

28. For two monographs using extremely divergent methods but coming to the same conclusion on this point, cf. Kohn (1951) and Lerner (1958, pp. 221–32).

29. I especially like Orwell (1933) and Hamsun (1920). Studies by Lewis are perhaps more prolix than realistic. See for example 1964 and 1965. Whyte (1961) does one of the best portrayals of the variety of people and conditions. A very careful statistical study that shows that the values of the young potential lumpenproletariat are not very different from those of other people is by Gordon *et al.* (1963).

30. Much of the anti-Semitism of Eastern Europe was thoroughly reactionary, characterized by feudal romanticism, clericalism, and bureaucratic conservatism. The anti-Indian sentiment in Kenya and Uganda was undoubtedly shared by colonial English administrators and commercial agents. Populist movements often call upon the same themes of a golden age corrupted by evil modern forces as do reactionary movements, and hence reject the same bearers of modern commercial impersonality. Commercial

impersonality invades personal dignity. Personal dignity means, to a colonial administrator or a feudal lord, the personal subjection of others to him—servility. Personal dignity means to a peasant a proper respect for the economic value of his work, a defense of his ancient tenure, and help in time of need. The reasons Jews are the image of unpleasant servility in, for example, Elizabethan drama is because their servility was not personal subjection, and hence honest, but rather it was impersonally given to anyone with money, and hence dishonest.

31. The argument that lack of education causes fundamentalism in personal ideology is the brunt of Lipset's controversial article (1959).

REFERENCES

Adorno, T. W., *et al.* (1950). *The Authoritarian Personality.* New York: Harper.

Bettelheim, Bruno (1943). "Individual and mass behavior in extreme situations." *Journal of Abnormal Psychology* 38:417–52.

Breton, Raymond (1964). "Institutional completeness of ethnic communities and the personal relations of immigrants." *American Journal of Sociology* 70:193–205.

Carr, E. H. (1950). *A History of Soviet Russia,* Vols. 1–3. New York: St. Martin's Press.

Coleman, James S. (1966a). "Foundations for a theory of collective decisions." *American Journal of Sociology* 71:615–27.

―――――― (1966b). "The possibility of a social welfare function." *American Economic Review* 56:1105–22.

―――――― (1967). "The marginal utility of a vote commitment." Johns Hopkins University, unpublished.

Crozier, Michael (1964). *The Bureaucratic Phenomenon.* Chicago: University of Chicago Press.

Dahl, Robert A., and Charles Lindblom (1953). *Politics, Economics and Welfare.* New York: Harper.

Deutsch, Karl (1953). *Nationalism and Social Communication.* New York: Wiley: Cambridge, Mass.: Technology Press of M.I.T.

Duverger, Maurice (1959). *Political Parties,* 2nd English edition. New York: Wiley.

Eisenstadt, S. N. (1966). *Modernization, Protest, and Change.* Englewood Cliffs, N.J.: Prentice-Hall.

Erikson, Erik (1950). *Childhood and Society.* New York: Norton.

―――――― (1959). "The problem of ego identity." *American Psychoanalytic Journal* 4:56–121.

Germani, Gino (1962). *Politica y Sociedad en un Epoca de Transition.* Buenos Aires: Editorial Paidos.

Glock, Charles Y., and Rodney Stark (1970). *Christian Beliefs and Antisemitism.* New York: Harper & Row.

Goffman, Erving (1963). *Stigma: Notes on the Management of Spoiled Identity*. Englewood Cliffs, N.J.: Prentice-Hall.

Gordon, Robert A. *et al.* (1963). "Values and gang delinquency: a study of street corner groups." *American Journal of Sociology* 69:109–28.

Granick, David (1967). *Soviet Metal Fabricating*. Madison: University of Wisconsin Press.

Grodzins, Martin (1956). *The Loyal and the Disloyal, Social Boundaries of Patriotism and Treason*. Chicago: University of Chicago Press.

Hagstrom, Warren O. (1965). *The Scientific Community*. New York: Basic Books.

Hamsun, Knut (1920). *Hunger*. New York: Knopf.

Higham, John (1965). *Strangers in the Land*. New Brunswick, N.J.: Rutgers University Press.

Jahoda, Marie, *et al.* (1933). *Die Arbeitslosen von Marienthal*. Leipzig: S. Hirzel.

Key, V. O. (1949). *Southern Politics in State and Nation*. New York: Knopf.

——————— (1955). "The theory of critical elections." *Journal of Politics* 17:3–18.

Kohn, Hans (1951). *The Idea of Nationalism*. New York: Macmillan.

Kornhauser, William (1959). *The Politics of Mass Society*. New York: Free Press.

Kunkel, John (1961). "Economic autonomy and social change in Mexican villages." *Economic Development and Cultural Change* 10:51–63.

Lerner, Daniel (1958). *The Passing of Traditional Society*. New York: Free Press.

Lewis, Oscar (1964). *Pedro Martinez*. New York: Random House.

——————— (1965). *La Vida*. New York: Random House.

Lindblom, Charles (1965). *The Intelligence of Democracy*. New York: Free Press.

Lipset, Seymour Martin (1959). *Political Man*. Garden City, N.Y.: Doubleday.

Lipset, Seymour Martin, Martin Trow, and James S. Coleman (1956). *Union Democracy: The Internal Politics of the International Typographical Union*. New York: Free Press.

Lipset, Seymour Martin, and Stein Rokkan (1967). "Cleavage structures, party systems and voter alignments." In Lipset and Rokkan (eds.), *Party Systems and Voter Alignments*. New York: Free Press.

MacRae, Duncan (1967). *Parliament, Parties and Society in France 1946–1958*. New York: St. Martin's Press.

McCloskey, Herbert (1963). "Conservatism and personality." In Nelson Polsby, R. A. Dentler, and P. A. Smith (eds.), *Politics and Social Life*. Boston: Houghton Mifflin.

Marshall, T. H. (1950). *Citizenship and Social Class*. London: Cambridge University Press.

Olson, Mancur (1965). *The Logic of Collective Action*. Cambridge, Mass.: Harvard University Press.

Orwell, George (1933). *Down and Out in Paris and London.* New York and London: Harper and Brothers.

Parsons, Talcott (1968). *The Structure of Social Action.* New York: Free Press.

Pinard, Maurice (1971). *The Rise of a Third Party.* Englewood Cliffs, N.J.: Prentice-Hall.

Polsby, Nelson, and Aaron Wildavsky (1968). *Presidential Elections,* 3rd edition. New York: Scribner's.

Schmitter, Phillipe C. (1968). "Development and interest politics in Brazil: 1930–1965." Unpublished Ph.D. dissertation, Department of Political Science, University of California at Berkeley.

Selznick, Philip (1949). *TVA and the Grass Roots.* Berkeley: University of California Press.

Siegfried, André (1913). *Tableau politique de la France de l'Oest sous la troisieme republique.* Paris: A. Colin.

Smelser, Neil J. (1962). *Theory of Collective Behavior.* New York: Free Press.

Stinchcombe, Arthur L. (1965). "Stratification among organizations and the sociology of revolution." In James G. Marsh (ed.), *Handbook of Organizations.* Chicago: Rand McNally, pp. 169–80.

——————— (1969). "Review of *Economy and Society.*" *American Journal of Sociology* 75:282–87.

——————— (1974). *Creating Efficient Industrial Administrations.* New York: Academic Press.

Trotsky, Leon (1932). *The History of the Russian Revolution,* Vol. 1. New York: Simon & Schuster.

Weber, Max (1953). "Class, status and party." In Reinhard Bendix and S. M. Lipset (eds.), *Class, Status and Power.* New York: Free Press.

——————— (1958). *The Protestant Ethic and the Spirit of Capitalism.* New York: Scribner's.

——————— (1968). *Economy and Society.* New York: Bedminster Press.

Whyte, William Foote (1961). *Street Corner Society.* Chicago: University of Chicago Press.

Wilensky, Harold L. (1967). *Organizational Intelligence.* New York: Basic Books.

Wolfinger, Ray (1965). "The development and persistence of ethnic voting." *American Political Science Review* 59:896–908.

INDEX

INDEX